REFLECTING ON OUR PAST AND EMBRACING OUR FUTURE

# Reflecting on Our Past and Embracing Our Future

## A Senate Initiative for Canada

Edited by Serge Joyal and Judith Seidman

*Published for the Senate of Canada by*
McGill-Queen's University Press
Montreal & Kingston • London • Chicago

© The Senate of Canada 2018

ISBN 978-0-7735-5539-6 (cloth)
ISBN 978-0-7735-5611-9 (ePDF)

Legal deposit first quarter 2019
Bibliothèque nationale du Québec

Printed in Canada on acid-free paper

We acknowledge the support of the Canada Council for the Arts, which last year invested $153 million to bring the arts to Canadians throughout the country.

Nous remercions le Conseil des arts du Canada de son soutien. L'an dernier, le Conseil a investi 153 millions de dollars pour mettre de l'art dans la vie des Canadiennes et des Canadiens de tout le pays.

Library and Archives Canada Cataloguing in Publication

Reflecting on our past and embracing our future:
a Senate initiative for Canada / edited by Serge Joyal and Judith Seidman.
Issued also in French under title: Réfléchir sur notre passé pour aborder notre avenir.
Published for the Senate of Canada.

Issued in print and electronic formats.
ISBN 978-0-7735-5539-6 (hardcover). –
ISBN 978-0-7735-5611-9 (ePDF)

1. Canada–Social conditions. 2. Civil rights–Canada. 3. Canada–Politics and government.
4. Canada–Relations. 5. Canada. Parliament.  I. Joyal, Serge, 1945–, editor  II. Seidman, Judith, editor
III. Canada. Parliament. Senate, issuing body

HN103.5.R435 2018          306.0971          C2018-904194-3
                                              C2018-904195-1

# Contents

# Contents

# Contents

# Contents

# Acknowledgments

The co-editors are very grateful to the individuals who helped bring this work to fruition, particularly the authors of chapters, who agreed to share their thoughts on the book's various topics. The co-editors would also like to thank the following people and organizations:

*McGill-Queen's University Press:*
Philip Cercone, Executive Director
Natalie Blachere, Project Lead
Neil Erickson, Book Designer, Sayre Street Books

*Office of the Clerk of the Senate and Chief Legislative Services Officer:*
Richard Denis, Clerk of the Senate
Jodi Turner, Chief of Staff

*Parliamentary Translation Directorate, Translation Bureau:*
Josée Cardinal, Director, and her team for the translation of the entire text into both official languages

*Library and Archives Canada:*
Guy Berthiaume, Librarian and Archivist of Canada

*Canadian Museum of History:*
Xavier Gélinas, Curator, Political History
Vincent Lafond, Collection Information Specialist – Photo Archives
Erin Gurski, Copyright Officer, Business Partnerships and Information Management

# Acknowledgments

*The following employees of the Senate assisted in obtaining illustrations and copyright permissions:*

Marianne Sincennes, Chief, Creative Services, Communications Directorate

Indrani Laroche, Parliamentary Counsel, Office of the Law Clerk and Parliamentary Counsel

Ginette Fortuné, Parliamentary Counsel, Office of the Law Clerk and Parliamentary Counsel

Rachel Boersma, Purchasing Clerk, Finance and Procurement Directorate

Peter Thornton, Digital Content Producer, Communications Directorate

Manon Champagne, Coordinator, Ceremonial and Protocol, Office of the Usher of the Black Rod

Julien Labrosse, former Administrative Officer, Office of the Usher of the Black Rod

Victoria Deng, Press Secretary, Speaker of the Senate

This work was published in the wake of the Senate of Canada's symposium to mark the 150th anniversary of Confederation, which took place on 25 and 26 May 2017. Thanks to the cooperation and support of the following people and organizations:

The Right Hon. David Johnston, former Governor General of Canada

The Hon. George J. Furey, QC, Speaker of the Senate, and his parliamentary office

The Hon. René Cormier, Senator, Session Chair

Claudette Tardif, retired Senator, Session Chair

Charles Robert, former Clerk of the Senate, and his team

Greg Peters, Usher of the Black Rod, and his team

Michel Patrice, former Law Clerk and Parliamentary Counsel and Chief Parliamentary Precinct Services Officer

Protocol Office, International and Interparliamentary Affairs, Parliament of Canada

*Communications Directorate:*
Mélissa Leclerc, Director, and her team

*Library of Parliament:*
Sonia L'Heureux, former Parliamentary Librarian, and her team

# Acknowledgments

Corporate Security Directorate
Property and Services Directorate
Information Services Directorate
Finance and Procurement Directorate
Food Services for Parliament

*The broadcast of the entire symposium on the CPAC television network was made possible by the following individuals:*
Catherine Cano, President
Peter Van Dusen, Executive Producer

The company Innovaxiom for producing the video used by speaker Hubert Reeves

The Hon. Serge Joyal would like to extend special thanks to the members of his Senate parliamentary office for their unfailing generosity and steadfast support: Sébastien Payet (Director of Issues Management), Aram Adjemian (Parliamentary Affairs Advisor), and Momar Diagne (former Director of Parliamentary Affairs). He would also like to specifically recognize the contributions of Paul Maréchal and Vincent Dugas in Montreal, and the assistance of Alain Bouchard, Jay Gagne, and Jack Delmond.

Finally, this project could not have been completed without the interest and financial support of the Senate, as authorized by the Standing Committee on Internal Economy, Budgets and Administration; its former chair, the Hon. Leo Housakos; and its former deputy chair, the Hon. Jane Cordy.

The Hon. Serge Joyal, P.C.
The Hon. Judith Seidman

# Preface

The 150th anniversary of Canadian Confederation offers a unique opportunity to celebrate a society that has evolved without civil conflict thanks to a climate of social peace in which the country could develop freely. But this event also offers an opportunity to reflect on the values that have influenced democratic debate and continue to shape the country's future.

As an independent chamber of sober second thought responsible for reviewing legislation, the Senate decided to add its own perspective to this process, by inviting twenty-one distinguished Canadians to participate in a symposium on 25 and 26 May 2017 entitled *Reflecting Our Past, Embracing Our Future / Réfléchir à notre passé, accueillir l'avenir.*

It was decided to narrow the focus of the symposium to the fifty years since Canada's centennial in 1967. In addition to still being fresh in the minds of the generation that lived through it, this period was also a time of great change in Canadian society – change that is ongoing and likely to influence the future.

The purpose of the symposium is essentially to explore a number of ideas so that the next generation can learn from the difficulties and obstacles that previous generations overcame, and build a world of its own design and shape it in turn. If this generation is to be the architect of its own future, it needs to understand how Canada has evolved, the challenges it has met, and the destination it is pursuing. By understanding the past, the next generation can avoid the pitfalls of ignorance.

With 150 years of history behind it, Canada is not starting with a blank slate: its identity is composed of parts of its collective memory. Certain historical facts are sometimes painful to remember and some realizations upset the image Canadians like to have of themselves. It would be wrong to think that Canada's advanced state

A TEEPEE ON PARLIAMENT HILL, 1 JULY 2017, DURING THE CELEBRATIONS MARKING CANADA'S 150TH BIRTHDAY

On 1 July 2017, Indigenous people from Sault Ste. Marie (the Bawating Water Protectors) raised their teepee on Parliament Hill, which is unceded Algonquin territory, to remind Canadians about what Indigenous peoples had suffered since the Canadian federation was created in 1867. They were in no mood for celebration, but were thinking about what the country's colonial past had meant for them and what the future might hold. Credit: Postmedia, Tony Caldwell

of development was achieved without conflict or clashes or the intervention of the highest courts in the land. Whether in the streets or in the media, democracy has constantly made its voice heard.

The values that have emerged out of public debate lend Canada an enviable maturity. We must examine the past to understand the present and be better able to envisage the Canada of the future.

This publication takes its title directly from this duty to remember the past. Ignoring the past could lead to a society that, although called on to evolve, lacks the foundation it needs to validate emerging concepts of freedom. Canadians share in creating a common fabric. Each individual is responsible for weaving a thread, adding to the colours, and creating a varied pattern of complex values in order to better understand an increasingly diverse world that must accommodate these differences.

That was the objective of the Senate symposium: to listen attentively and receptively in order to encourage understanding without moral judgement but rather with a constant sense of empathy for the human condition over time in this great country.

Canada is unlike any other nation: it did not grow out of an ideology or an imperialist desire to impose a certain order. It grew out of an ideal to bring together, for the common purposes of prosperity, peace, and respect for regional aspirations and identities, people who were united by values that foster a humanist vision, in which individual freedom is balanced with the shared responsibility of maintaining a safety net to prevent marginalization and eliminate the degradation of inequality.

Canada's success does not lie in a fervent nationalism or a "melting pot" approach to society. Its current strength and its future promise lie in the way that Canadians view their relationships and in their respect for each other.

Canada's ability to bring together people from different cultural and linguistic backgrounds to live in an equal and harmonious society shows that our approach is sound.

This philosophy dictated the ten symposium themes presented to the twenty-one people invited to share their thoughts and experiences at this point in Canada's development. To stimulate debate, each theme was prefaced by a brief synopsis of key events since 1967 and the major challenge for the future.

It was clearly important for the symposium to begin with the Indigenous peoples. Since 1967 they have been emerging from marginalization to start building a new nation-to-nation relationship with Canada. What degree of sovereignty will these self-directed governments exercise? Phil Fontaine, former National Chief of the Assembly of First Nations (1997–2000), and Ellen Gabriel, former President of the Quebec Native Women's Association (2004–10) and official spokesperson of the People of the Longhouse during the Oka Crisis (1990), spoke with authority on the expectations of Indigenous peoples at this point in the country's history.

Over the past fifty years, Canada has emerged onto the international stage and taken positions that distinguish it from American interests and from its British and French roots. In the future, will Canada be able to meet the expectations that it has helped to create and the role that is expected of it? Paul Heinbecker, former Ambassador and Permanent Representative to the United Nations (2000–04), and Huguette Labelle, former President of the Canadian International Development Agency (1993–99), addressed these issues by sharing their complementary experiences with symposium participants.

Linguistic duality has long been a challenge for Canada, one that was at the root of the decision to form a federal union in 1867. The nationwide coexistence of two

CANADA'S PAVILION AT THE 1967 INTERNATIONAL AND UNIVERSAL EXPOSITION
Postcard, Plastichrome of Canada, Benjamin News Co., Montreal, EX201, © 1963 Expo 67
The Canadian Pavilion was named Katimavik ("gathering place" in Inuktitut). It was the largest of the forty-eight national pavilions at Expo 67, whose central theme was "Man and His World." The pavilion took the form of an inverted pyramid, symbolizing man's conquest of time, space, nature, and mankind; on the right is the People Tree, a stylized maple tree. The enthusiasm generated by the centennial celebrations, the festive atmosphere all across the country, the younger generation's optimism, and Canada's openness to the world greatly contributed to the emergence of a national identity of Canada as a country with confidence in the future. Credit: Collection of the Hon. Serge Joyal (hereinafter: CHSJ)

languages, spoken by communities large and small, is often a real test of determination. The political dimension of this issue is a key concern for Canada's francophone community and it calls for the perspectives of two people who have been and continue to be committed to this subject: the Right Honourable Michaëlle Jean, Secretary-General of the Organisation Internationale de la Francophonie and former Governor General of Canada (2005–10), and the Honourable Michel Bastarache, former Justice of the Supreme Court of Canada (1997–2008).

The Canada of 2017 is much different from the Canada of 1967. The Canadian Charter of Rights and Freedoms, passed in 1982, redefined the foundation of our society. It recognized citizens' rights, and citizens wasted no time in having the courts enforce those rights, thereby regaining control of the freedom to make their own decisions. The Right

Honourable Beverly McLachlin, Chief Justice of Canada (2000–17), and Professor Mark D. Walters, F.R. Scott Chair in Public and Constitutional Law at McGill University, drew on their invaluable experience to examine the Canada of today.

During the Quebec referendums of 1980 and 1995, Canada had to fight to stay together. It has also dealt with ongoing political demands from the West that splintered the country. What lessons have we learned for the future, and how have these tensions helped us to advance? Three former provincial premiers were the obvious choices to address these questions: Bob Rae from Ontario (1990–95), Jean Charest from Quebec (2003–12), and Gary Doer from Manitoba (1999–2009).

During this period, Canada changed from a patriarchal society to one that fully supports gender equality. This is now a guiding principle, politically and economically, in the country's widespread decision-making centres. The Right Honourable Kim Campbell, former Prime Minister of Canada (1993), and Monique F. Leroux, President of the International Co-operative Alliance and former CEO of the Fédération des caisses Desjardins du Québec (2008–16), drew on their experiences to offer an accurate picture of the challenges and issues involved in gender equality.

A country of wide-open spaces and breathtaking scenery, Canada claims to make the environment its number-one priority. Yet it has no qualms about plundering resources and trying to limit the damage afterward, often in the face of public pressure. Canada has a poor environmental record. Even the mythic Arctic is grappling with the harmful effects of climate change, and the Inuit living there experience all the social ills of the "South" but more intensely. David Suzuki, the geneticist and co-founder of the David Suzuki Foundation, and Natan Obed, national Inuit leader and President of the Inuit Tapiriit Kanatami, were the ideal choices to speak on this issue.

Canada boasts about being one of the most advanced countries in the world. Yet its support for science, research, and innovation is inconsistent with this self-image, and public discourse shows only minimal interest in funding engineering and creative intelligence. Astrophysicist Hubert Reeves, who has spent his life probing the universe, could attest to this situation, and Professor Yves Gingras, Scientific Director at the Observatoire des sciences et des technologies, offered a historical perspective.

Over the past fifty years, Canadian performers have seen spectacular international success and been ranked among the best in the world, thanks in part to government support. However, Canada risks being sidelined by the digital giants – all or most of them American – if it does not ally itself with other cultures facing the same fate. Pierre Lassonde, philanthropist and Chair of the Board of Directors of the Canada Council for the Arts, has tackled the challenge of cultural support in Canada and spoke with authority on the subject.

# Preface

\* \* \*

Canada is a prosperous country with a seemingly enviable standard of living. How have repeated energy crises, digital globalization, and the 2008 financial crisis impacted the country, and how will it now deal with artificial intelligence and robotics – the fourth industrial revolution? Has our standard of living really increased since 1967 and what can Canadians look forward to in the future? David A. Dodge, former Governor of the Bank of Canada (2001–08), and Hassan Yussuf, President of the Canadian Labour Congress, offered complementary perspectives: that of the institutions which support the economy and that of the people who work in it every day.

Lastly, the purpose behind this entire process is to enrich democratic debate in Parliament because that is where choices and decisions that affect all Canadians are made and where the course for the future is charted. What should we expect of the Senate and House of Commons, where different viewpoints and alternatives should be expressed freely and openly so that Canadians can judge for themselves and elect a government they believe can steer the country? In the age of social media, what is the role of political parties and how relevant is parliamentary debate? Social media is so important that it has become a new form of citizen-based engagement. It is an alternative forum for public debate and as likely to be a channel for protest as manipulative "fake news" or foreign intervention in Canada. In their presentations, Professor David E. Smith, Distinguished Visiting Scholar at Ryerson University, and David Docherty, President of Mount Royal University, took a critical and insightful look at both houses of Parliament.

Democracy is a fragile thing and can be derailed even in countries that were among the first to embrace it. Brexit and the election of President Trump are two examples of a populist movement fed by social inequities, unbridled views on social media, and the perception that immigration is threatening identity. Canada can avoid these pitfalls by continuing along the path of reflection begun in the Senate during this 150th celebration of Confederation.

We would like to thank the Speaker of the Senate, the Honourable George J. Furey, Q.C., for assisting future generations by making this event possible, and the Right Honourable David Johnston, former Governor General, for inspiring Canadians to continue with the incredible experience of nation building.

The Hon. Serge Joyal, P.C.        The Hon. Judith Seidman

# Prologue

# Welcoming Address by the Speaker of the Senate[1]

It is my great pleasure to welcome you to the Senate of Canada for this symposium marking the 150th anniversary of Canadian Confederation.

Although these proceedings are the product of much work by a great number of people, I would like to give special recognition to the hard work, dedication, and vision of Senator Serge Joyal and Senator Judith Seidman. The Senate wanted a special initiative to mark Canada's sesquicentennial. Senators Joyal and Seidman took up the challenge, and this symposium is the result.

To call it a "symposium" does not do justice to this event. For, as you can see just by looking around the chamber and at the program, Senators Joyal and Seidman have assembled a truly extraordinary group of Canadians, each of whom has made a remarkable contribution to Canada in ways that have significantly shaped our great nation.

The idea of this symposium is deceptively simple to articulate: it is to look back over the past fifty years since Canada celebrated its centennial in 1967 and to reflect upon the critical changes that have taken place, how they have influenced the lives of Canadians today, and where we might go as a nation in the years ahead.

These discussions will be led by some of the very individuals who were and are an integral part of those pivotal changes.

These questions are particularly appropriate for discussion here, in the Senate. The Senate is, of course, Canada's chamber of sober second thought. And it was the Senate

---

1 This is Speaker George J. Furey's welcome speech for the 25–6 May 2017 symposium "Reflecting Our Past, Embracing Our Future" ("*Réfléchir à notre passé, accueillir l'avenir*"). It was preceded by a moment of silence marking the Manchester Arena bombing three days earlier, on 22 May 2017.

that became the fundamental dealmaker for Confederation. Almost 153 years ago, at the Quebec Conference, our Fathers of Confederation gathered to discuss their vision for Canada – not unlike the purpose of our gathering here today and tomorrow.

Madeleine Thien, one of Canada's great contemporary writers, included a fascinating insight in her award-winning book *Do Not Say We Have Nothing* – which seems particularly appropriate to reference in this company, as it won, among many other awards, the Governor General's Literary Award for English fiction last year. She described how here in the West, we speak of facing the future, with the past lying behind us. But in China, she wrote, the language is quite different. The day before yesterday is the day "in front," while the day after tomorrow is the day "behind." Future generations are not the generations ahead, but the ones behind. So to look into the future, she wrote, one must turn around. That makes so much sense on so many levels, for no one can see the future; we actually face our past, individually in our lives and collectively as a nation. We know what has happened, and we use our knowledge and experience from the past to guide us into a future we cannot see. We look behind to then move forward. Our hope is that we have the wisdom to learn the right lessons from the past, so that we can then turn around to look into the future, informed by the past and not merely formed by it.

I look forward to the discussions over the next two days, for these are very challenging times in the world. Values and ideas that have perhaps been taken for granted are being questioned. Buzzwords and phrases such as "alternative facts" are giving rise to a reality that is no longer recognizable to many. And there is a genuine need to bring together the collective wisdom of both knowledge and experience to face these challenges, to do our part so that future generations can build an even greater Canada and greater world.[2]

The Hon. George J. Furey, Q.C.

---

2  The Speaker's welcome address continued with an introduction of the Right Honourable David Johnston, twenty-eighth governor general of Canada.

# Opening Speech by the Governor General

This is a year to celebrate, and a year to further realize the promise of Canada, the potential of this great experiment! Even after 150 years, Canada is still a constantly evolving social experiment. And this experiment is continually being tested and challenged, both within our communities and by world events. But I believe there is nothing more practical than a good working theory continually tested and refined against reality.

In that vein, we, as Canadians, must learn from our experience, adjust our approach, and always strive to do better. We define our country by how we respond to tests, how we learn from the evidence, and how we act accordingly. This is why I'm so pleased to see all of you here, taking the time to think about where we have been and where we want to go.

What could be a better setting for asking the big questions about Canada? This is our Parliament, a sacred public space for dialogue, debate, and dreaming. Let this location remind us of our responsibilities as citizens and as leaders who wish to serve our country.

Over the next two days you will consider ten subjects of national significance. Among them are common threads that will tie these issues together and show you a path forward. Inclusiveness, for one. Inclusion is not simply making people feel welcome. It means allowing everyone a shared stake in society, drawing on and rewarding their talents, and recognizing their efforts.

Canada is home to a population that has more than two hundred ethnic origins and speaks more than two hundred languages. This includes some sixty-five individual Indigenous languages. It also has the highest proportion of foreign-born population (20.6 per cent) of any G7 country.

This diversity is something to be proud of. I've met refugees as they landed in Canada for the first time, hesitant, yet hopeful. And on the other side, I could see the outpouring of support from Canadians. But that isn't the whole story. Our diversity does not guarantee inclusiveness. Not for refugees, not for our Indigenous peoples, not for women or families or young people. In this, we cannot be complacent.

At this symposium, you will hear from those who continue to be excluded from participating fully in our society. Social inclusion, solving matters of housing, water, education, mental health, can go a long way towards building a better Canada. It can lead to renewed hope. It can lead to change.

How do we do this?

By listening to diverse voices – not only established experts, but new voices as well. Young people, in particular, will inherit our country and are even now contributing in so many exciting ways. I've learned time and again not to discount their ideas, energy, and enthusiasm for change. They deserve a voice, as do the scientists, academics, public servants, economists, entrepreneurs, and others you will hear from. And we want to hear from you, every one of you, because in our democratic society, everyone has something to give.

We're living through an extraordinary moment in time: one of profound globalization, technological changes, demographic shifts, and changing expectations. And if change can be said to be the new constant, then innovation is the new imperative.

What we must do to thrive is embrace new and better ways of doing things, and new ideas that will allow us to build a better country. We must consider creative solutions. Think innovatively. Dream big.

And let's get to work making the next 150 years even better.

His Excellency the Rt. Hon. David Johnston

REFLECTING ON OUR PAST AND EMBRACING OUR FUTURE

# 1

# What Does a Nation-to-Nation Relationship with Indigenous Peoples Really Mean?[1]

The Hon. Serge Joyal, Senator

Over the past fifty years, Indigenous peoples have been emerging from a context of hostile paternalism. Under the authority of the Indian Act, *the federal policy on Indigenous peoples was intended to assimilate them, either subtly, by trying to eliminate reserve lands and abolish Indigenous title to them (1969),[2] or overtly, by moving Indigenous children to residential schools willingly or unwillingly and eradicating their culture and language – to the point of making children ashamed of being Indigenous[3] – or having Indigenous children adopted by non-Indigenous families, a forced assimilation that had all the hallmarks of "cultural genocide." This was the continuation of a policy of "gradual civilization of the Indians" introduced in United Canada in 1857 and perpetuated after Confederation by each successive government and by many different means.*

*This policy was derived from an imperialist concept of British culture and civilization, and a sense of moral, religious, and linguistic superiority that justified taking over the resources and lands possessed or occupied by Indigenous peoples.[4] This notion was rooted in the theory of racial superiority over Indigenous peoples that persisted in Canada well after it was deemed inhumane and abandoned, in particular after the 1948 Universal Declaration of Human Rights, which Canada signed. Canada is also a signatory to all of the related international agreements and protocols, including* the United Nations Convention on the elimination of discrimination, *which requires Canada to report to Geneva every two years. As long as there is an* Indian Act, *which entrenches assimilation, and a department responsible for implementing it,[5] there will be systemic discrimination in Canada, to this country's shame.*

*For far too long, Canadian policy on Indigenous peoples was racist, regressive, discriminatory, and lacking in respect for the fundamental equality of all peoples.*

"ORIGINAL OWNERS OF OUR COUNTRY"

Postcard, "Custom House, Quebec," Young Bros., Toronto, end of the nineteenth century. The ancestral land of these two Indigenous men is now occupied by the Custom House in Quebec City, at the foot of Cap Diamant, with its proudly neoclassical architecture, a symbol of the superiority of European civilization. The Indigenous people, left aside, are forced into a marginal existence on their own land.
Credit: Young Bros., Toronto – CHSJ

*A major turning point arrived in 1982 during the repatriation of the Constitution, when Indigenous representatives formally participated in the constitutional debate, a first in the country's history since the signing of the* Great Peace of Montreal *in 1701. Section 35(2) of the* Constitution Act, 1982, *officially recognizes the existence of three main Indigenous groups – the Indian, Inuit, and Métis peoples – and section 35(1) in particular recognizes the existing "aboriginal and treaty rights of the aboriginal peoples of Canada". Everything changed following this historical recognition and the broader scope that lower courts and the Supreme Court have given to it over the years in order to rectify past colonial abuses.*[6]

*In its 1973 decision in* Calder, *the Supreme Court had already recognized the validity of Indigenous title and ruled that it had not been extinguished by conquest or military occupation of the country. This was a key finding, as the Court opened the door to claims to traditional territories and the historic rights of Indigenous peoples. It also contributed to the creation of an Indigenous title resolution process, with the ultimate goal of introducing Indigenous self-government. Along the way, Indigenous associations have been established to represent various groups, among them the Inuit (1971), the Indians living off reserve, Indians living on reserve (1972), Indigenous women (1974), and Métis (1983).*

*A number of court cases have since been launched by individuals and Indigenous groups, mainly to improve their living conditions and, in particular, to recover their Indian status, which the* Indian Act *defined in a restrictive and discriminatory manner in an obvious attempt to progressively limit the number of Status Indians[7] and essentially deprive them of their rights. The process bordered on the diabolical: first, their identity and land rights were taken away and then they were forced to prove these rights in court.[8] The Department of Indian Affairs enlisted a battery of experts and lawyers, and protracted and gruelling negotiations ensued until the government took the court-ordered*

« MISSIONS D'EXTRÊME NORD CANADIEN – UNE CLASSE À L'ORPHELINAT SAINT-JOSEPH DU GRAND LAC DES ESCLAVES » [MISSIONS IN CANADA'S FAR NORTH – A CLASS AT ST JOSEPH'S ORPHANAGE IN GREAT SLAVE LAKE]

Postcard, Missionnaires oblats de Marie-Immaculée, Œuvre des Missions O.M.I., Paris (XVIe arrondissement). For 150 years, Indigenous children were torn from their families, taken hundreds of kilometres away from their villages, stripped of their traditional clothing, forced to dress and wear their hair like Europeans, and punished for using their mother tongue. The government's policy was designed to kill the Indian in them. In addition to being often abused physically and mistreated, they returned as adults to a life that was foreign to them. After Prime Minister Harper made an official apology on behalf of Canada in 2008, fifty-eight thousand of these survivors would be compensated. Credit: CHSJ *corrective measures. In more than 250 cases involving Indigenous title, the courts had to intervene and order remedial legislation to be passed, frequently after epic legal battles that led all the way to the Supreme Court and left the applicants exhausted. It was never assumed the government would act in good faith! The recent ruling in* Descheneaux[9] *(August 2015), which found that provisions of the* Indian Act *regarding a group of women infringe the* Canadian Charter of Rights and Freedoms, *and the government's response via Bill S-3[10] showed that the government was not prepared to repeal other provisions of this colonial act that discriminate against Indigenous women.*

*When the Senate insisted, the government eventually gave in but refused to set a deadline for eliminating the discriminatory provisions.[11] The courts will have to intervene again to force the government to respect Indigenous women's right to equality.*

*In early 2018, the Supreme Court finally recognized the right of the Williams Lake Indian Band to be compensated for land it lost in 1860 during the Gold Rush.[12] The federal government pleaded that it should not be held responsible, because this event occurred before Confederation in 1867 and before British Columbia joined Canada in 1871. In its majority decision, the Court found that the Crown is the Crown and that it has a responsibility in principle to Indigenous peoples, no matter what form the government subsequently takes. It took ten years of costly court proceedings to arrive at a definitive ruling in favour of the Williams Lake Indian Band.*

*Three specific events related to natural resource development or the occupation of land claimed by Indigenous peoples would force the government to make a major shift: the James Bay hydroelectric development (Quebec, 1975); the construction of the Mackenzie Valley pipeline (Northwest Territories, Yukon, Northern Alberta, 1977); and the Oka Crisis (Kanesatake, Quebec, 1990), a conflict involving the expansion of a municipal golf course into disputed traditional territory that received wide media attention and continues to this day.*

*In 1981, Mi'kmaq fishermen were prohibited from catching salmon because the stocks were depleted. That event led the Mi'kmaq to occupy a bridge on Quebec's Restigouche River and lodge numerous claims to their ancestral hunting and fishing rights, guaranteed by peace and friendship treaties signed in 1760 and 1761 and by the Royal Proclamation of 1763. The Donald Marshall case in 1992 was a milestone: Mi'kmaq and Maliseet fishing rights were at last recognized in 1999 based on their protection under the 1760* Treaty of Peace and Friendship *and section 25 of the* Constitution Act, 1982. *Protests of this nature snowballed, and Indigenous groups began to mobilize and make the headlines. For example, in Clayoquot Sound, British Columbia, territory of the Nuu-Chah-Nulth, there were protests in 1993 against clear-cutting on the west coast of Vancouver Island, where a number of First Nations hold rights. Elsewhere in the country, First Nations fighting for their rights were forced into civil disobedience as they became exasperated with the government's evasiveness or refusals.*

*Indigenous peoples have consistently had to assert their claim to title and take on the government and public opinion in court to highlight the injustice and exploitation they have continually faced since the mid-nineteenthth century.*

*Living conditions are deplorable on some reserves, and one-third of First Nations still do not have access to clean drinking water,[13] wastewater treatment facilities, or reliable electricity. In many cases, several families live crowded together in inadequate housing, where they are at risk of psychological distress and mental health problems, and where sanitary and physical conditions are substandard.[14] Indigenous peoples also have a much higher youth suicide rate, often the legacy of residential schools and other colonial policies. Every day, the public learns more about the third-world conditions facing Indigenous peoples. As a case in point, tuberculosis, which has been eradicated in the South, has been diagnosed in Inuit communities in Nunavik.*

"CAUGHNAWAGA, QUE."

Postcard. For a long time, to earn a little money, the Mohawks of the village of Caughnawaga (the Kahnawake reserve on the outskirts of Montreal) would entertain visitors from Montreal on Sunday afternoons with dances and songs in their ancestral language while wearing headdresses and costumes of western tribes. To "white" tourists, they embodied the conventional image people had of "Indians." In his youth, the author remembers attending such performances with his parents. The "Indians" were reduced to quaint, inoffensive, cartoonish characters. Credit: CHSJ

*Governments can no longer plead ignorance; they have gradually been identified as the perpetrators of a policy of assimilation that has led to marginalization – a shameful state of affairs in a highly developed country like Canada, which has one of the highest standards of living in the world.*

*Indigenous peoples make up only 4.9 per cent of Canada's adult population,[15] but represent 26 per cent of male inmates and 36 per cent of female inmates.[16] Indigenous women represent 50 per cent of the incarcerated women in maximum security prisons.[17] Their sentences are often longer, their conditions of confinement more severe, and their rehabilitation almost non-existent. And what about the thousands of missing and murdered Indigenous women and girls whose disappearances were not fully investigated because of systemic discrimination that continues to this day? Since 2016,[18] an independent national commission of inquiry has painstakingly been trying to identify and eliminate the many causes and origins of this tragedy that is a disgrace in a civilized country. According to one report, Indigenous women are five times more likely to die by violence than other Canadian women the same age. Between 1997 and 2000, the homicide rate for Indigenous women was nearly seven times higher than for non-Indigenous women.[19]*

*The average lifespan of Indigenous men is nine years shorter than that of other Canadian men; there is a six-year difference among women. It was recently revealed that Indigenous women underwent forced sterilization after giving birth in Saskatoon hospitals.[20]*

*Indigenous peoples are also virtually invisible on Canadian television, aside from negative stereotypes.[21]*

*In a long series of extremely detailed decisions,[22] the Supreme Court provided the right standpoint by defining government obligations and ordering the restorative measures that Canada must now implement. The Court has continued to reiterate the basic principles to follow in the numerous court cases between Indigenous peoples and government.*

*The Court has consistently pointed out that the federal government must uphold the honour of the Crown in fulfilling its fiduciary responsibility toward Indigenous peoples. It has found that the federal government failed to meet its constitutional responsibilities, and that the Indigenous peoples of Canada have never been conquered or had their rights taken away. It emphasized that Indigenous titles are entrenched in the Constitution and recognized in the Royal Proclamation of 1763. This confirmation has significant consequences that the federal and provincial governments must address without delay. These are the same governments that Indigenous groups have constantly had to fight to obtain recognition of their status and constitutional rights.*

*The Supreme Court has rendered a number of landmark decisions on the status and rights of Indigenous peoples and Métis:* Sparrow *(1990),* Van Der Peet *(1996),* Delgamuukw *(1997),* Marshall *(1999),* Powley *(2003),* Haida Nation *(2004),* Tsilhqot'in Nation *(2014), and* Daniels *(2016). Added to this list is the recent decision by the Canadian Human Rights Tribunal in* Blackstock/First Nations Child and Family Caring Society *(2016). The Tribunal found that First Nations children living on reserve were being discriminated against. All of these decisions have gradually restored the rights of Indigenous peoples and helped to position the courts as a key arbiter in the ongoing struggle between governments and Indigenous peoples.*

*In 2012–13, Indigenous peoples had to take to the streets once again to demand justice through the national Idle No More movement. This movement has drawn attention to a wide range of Indigenous issues and called for greater consultation by government on legislative amendments and decisions affecting Indigenous peoples. Far too often, Indigenous peoples have had to resort to civil disobedience to shake governments out of their lethargy and get them to take action. In August 2017, a United Nations committee on the elimination of racial discrimination reported that it was "alarmed" by the government's delay in acting on the recommendations of the Canadian Human Rights Tribunal to help children and families.[23]*

*The federal and provincial governments are fully obligated to recognize and reintroduce the use of Indigenous languages. According to the latest Statistics Canada figures, more than seventy Indigenous languages were reported in the 2016 Census, thirty-six of which have at least five hundred speakers.[24] However, no concrete steps have been taken so far. The colonialist policy and its avatars have tried to wipe out these languages as a means of destroying Indigenous peoples' identity. Many of these languages will disappear completely if immediate action is not taken. A private bill was tabled in the Senate in 2009 and two subsequent bills in 2015 and 2016,[25] but the federal government is engaging in endless interdepartmental consultations. The government committed itself to introducing a bill in the fall of 2018.[26] Without language, there is no identity.[27]*

*However, the government has taken certain positive and sometimes significant steps: the Royal Commission on Aboriginal Peoples (Erasmus/Dussault, 1996); the creation of Canada's third territory, Nunavut, in 1999, where the majority of the population is Inuit; the creation of an Indigenous tribunal in Toronto in 2001 and in Ottawa in August 2017, following the Supreme Court's 1999 ruling in* Gladue;[28] *the Kelowna Accord on access to education, improved health care, housing, and economic development, signed by the Martin government in 2005 following lengthy negotiations (and then cancelled in 2006 by the Harper government); the United Nations Declaration on the Rights of Indigenous Peoples, which attracted international attention to the living*

INDIANS OF CANADA PAVILION

Designed by J.W. Francis, an architect with the Department of Indian Affairs, the Indians of Canada Pavilion at Expo 67 took the form of a teepee with a totem pole in front of it, even though the teepee and the totem pole are two completely different symbols of Indigenous identity: one Plains, the other West Coast. This juxtaposition was meant to be picturesque and reassure visitors. However, inside the pavilion were exhibits about the impact of the colonial policies under which Indigenous people had suffered for over one hundred years. Credit: Wikimedia Commons, Laurent Bélanger

*conditions of Indigenous peoples and in which Canada participated in 2007 but did not fully endorse until 2016; Prime Minister Harper's historic apology in 2008 to residential school survivors following the settlement of their class action suit in 2007, and the subsequent creation of the Truth and Reconciliation Commission; Prime Minister Trudeau's 2015 promise to implement the Commission's ninety-four recommendations even though, three years later, only three recommendations have been implemented;[29] the $4.7 billion that has been paid to date against the 116,309 claims by residential school survivors; the 2017 agreement to pay $800 million to settle the class action suit filed by sixteen thousand First Nations and Inuit children taken from their families between 1951 and 1991 and placed in non-Indigenous foster homes; the agreement signed in August 2017 with twenty-three Anishinabek First Nations in Ontario to transfer full responsibility for education from kindergarten to grade 12, in collaboration with the provincial government, which represents an important step in Indigenous self-government; the formal apology made in November 2017 by Prime Minister Trudeau to the residential school survivors of Newfoundland and Labrador – although the* *government still refuses to compensate Métis who were victims of forced adoptions and the same school system, and who must seek justice in the Saskatchewan courts;[30] the federal government's public promise in the 2015 Speech from the Throne to work with Indigenous peoples in a renewed "nation-to-nation [relationship] based on recognition of rights, respect, co-operation and partnership"[31] and its commitment in 2018 to introduce legislation (Bill C-262) bringing Canadian laws into harmony with the United Nations Declaration on the Rights of Indigenous Peoples; and, lastly, Prime Minister Trudeau's announcement on 14 February 2018 concerning national consultations with Indigenous peoples on the legislative arrangement that will replace the hated Indian Act,[32] its goal to define "a new recognition and implementation of indigenous rights framework that will include new ways to recognize and implement indigenous rights."[33] All of these initiatives should pave the way to restoring self-determination and self-government for the Indigenous peoples.*

*But what does this commitment to a "nation-to-nation, government-to-government" relationship mean? What is really behind this solemn pledge? Is this statement of honourable intentions hiding something?*

*Does this nation-to-nation relationship mean a commitment by Canada to explicitly recognize Indigenous nations in the exercise of reciprocal sovereignty represented by a distinct self-directed government? If this is the case – independent nations politically expressing their autonomous and distinct sovereignty – then we need to clear up a number of ambiguities to avoid becoming tangled up in words and misunderstandings that could lead to conflict.*

*The existence of an independent government with sovereignty over its own areas of jurisdiction implies that it has the political authority to enact laws applicable to its "citizens." In the present case, this entails a requirement to recognize a national territory where the Indigenous residents can govern themselves as they did before European colonization.*

*Is there truly a nation-to-nation relationship if one of the supposedly self-determining governments is in fact subject to the other for decisions on its economic development and access to its own revenues?*

*There is also a looming grey area concerning the federal government's duty to consult and accommodate Indigenous peoples on major resource development and extraction projects – forestry, mining, oil and gas, and other strategic resources – in regions where Indigenous peoples hold title. Will they or will they not exercise full sovereignty over the use of their recognized lands? That question remains unanswered.*

*The Supreme Court has repeatedly upheld the duty to consult and accommodate to a reasonable extent and, in some cases, has quashed federal approvals of development projects. The most recent case, Clyde River (Hameau) v. Petroleum GeoServices Inc., involved Inuit opposition to a project and was decided in July 2017.*

*But shouldn't the duty to consult beforehand also apply to the drafting of bills that could affect treaty rights, in order to respect the sovereignty of Indigenous peoples in a nation-to-nation and government-to-government relationship, to prevent negative impacts, and to respect the principles of consultation?[34] When reconciling the exercise of two sovereignties within the same territory, we must be consistent in the way that we deal with all the underlying implications.*

*The Supreme Court ruled on this issue in 2018[35] and it is directly related to defining the scope of Indigenous sovereignty over traditional and treaty lands.*

*But if Canada and the Indigenous nations have true and equal sovereignty over their territory, how can Canada impose development projects and laws on Indigenous lands without their consent? That is the issue to resolve and we must not try to avoid it by pretending we do not see it.*

*Determining the sovereignty of Indigenous self-governments is at the heart of an ongoing debate. This debate entails a change in the power dynamic with First Nations that will force reconciliation.[36]*

*We can no longer claim that the Crown possesses the inherent title to Indigenous lands when, in fact, Indigenous peoples themselves hold this constitutional title. And when this same government, which upholds the honour of the Crown in its fiduciary obligation regarding Indigenous rights and title, is also a stakeholder and direct beneficiary in the development of these lands, then there is a glaring and inherent conflict of interest that brings this equal nation-to-nation relationship to an impasse that must eventually be tackled head-on. The federal and provincial governments have so far avoided addressing this matter directly. But it is now emerging as a critical issue and must finally be resolved through true nation-to-nation negotiations where there is no room for equivocation or platitudes.*

*The Indigenous peoples have a direct historical relationship with the Crown. The Crown must remain impartial and objective in issues involving Indigenous title. It must be objective in order to be credible when assuming its fiduciary obligations regarding Indigenous title.*

*Moreover, the United Nations Declaration on the Rights of Indigenous Peoples, which Canada formally endorsed in 2016, clearly recognizes the right of Indigenous peoples to give their consent to any project or activity affecting their lands. That is an unequivocal recognition of their sovereignty. In other words, Indigenous peoples must have full sovereignty in their territory in the manner of the old common law adage "A man's house is his castle."*

*Canadian sovereignty flows from the traditional right of the British Crown regarding discovery, occupation, the establishment of governments able to enforce borders, the adoption of laws governing the subjects or persons within those borders, and the recognition by other sovereign states of the existence of a separate state. This sovereignty implies the title to land and the ability to grant or dispose of part of it, or to develop it according to one's own interest and benefit. In other words, this retroactive interpretation of international law implies that the British Crown became the rights-holder to Indigenous lands[37] without the consent or knowledge of the Indigenous peoples even though, as the Supreme Court has stated repeatedly, they were never conquered or subjugated militarily when England took over Canada at the end of the Seven Years War.*

*As the Supreme Court noted in* Van Der Peet *in 1996, the Crown has a fiduciary obligation toward Indigenous peoples, and this obligation applies to any decision or statute that affects their rights. This interpretation allows for "reconciliation of the pre-existence of aboriginal societies with the sovereignty of the Crown."[38]*

*In other words, Canada would have been a kind of "terra nullius"[39] that belonged to no one and was free from any sovereignty, even Indigenous, and could therefore be taken over by any country that managed to establish itself. This legal theory has been denounced and is now internationally repudiated.[40]*

*When Indigenous title to territory is recognized, it should be accompanied by all of the rights related to legal ownership,[41] especially the right to develop the territory or not, and to give or refuse consent to extract resources. "If it is truly a nation-to-nation relationship, then we can't have projects on the land of another nation without that nation's consent," said* NDP *leader Jagmeet Singh.[42]*

*In a number of its decisions, the Supreme Court has recognized the federal government's duty to consult and accommodate Indigenous peoples who are affected by resource development projects. More recently, however, it has not recognized Indigenous people's right to consent to a development project on their territory, and by extension to withhold their consent.[43]*

*This is a subtle difference, and the federal government was well aware of it when it released its ten* Principles Respecting the Government of Canada's Relationship With Indigenous Peoples *in July 2017. In this document, the government did not actually recognize the duty to obtain the consent of Indigenous peoples affected by development projects on their traditional lands, but it took a tentative step toward doing so.*

*Principle 6 specifically states that consultation and cooperation with Indigenous peoples must be carried out "with the aim of securing their free, prior and informed consent," but it does not mention a specific duty to obtain this consent before approving development projects.[44]*

"MOMENTS DE FIERTÉ" [PROUD MOMENTS] – CLOSING CEREMONY OF THE GAMES OF THE XXI OLYMPIAD – MONTREAL, 1976

Postcard: Gordon F. Callaghan, Montreal. The Olympic Stadium in Montreal is filled to capacity for the closing ceremony of the 1976 Summer Olympics. Canada appropriated the architecture of five teepees painted in bright colours, and a group of performers that did not include any Indigenous representatives mimed traditional rites that the Canadian government had been trying to eliminate since the Indian Act was passed one hundred years earlier in 1876. Credit: Paul Charles Howell, *The Montreal Olympics: An Insider's View of Organizing a Self-Financing Games* (Montreal and Kingston: McGill-Queen's University Press, 2009)

*In other words, the Canadian government must make an honest effort to obtain the consent of Indigenous peoples, but if it fails to do so for any reason owing to the will or decisions of the Indigenous peoples, can this "setback" be considered a blank cheque for the government to proceed with the required legal authorizations even though the Indigenous peoples have formally refused to give consent? The United Nations Declaration on the Rights of Indigenous Peoples says that it cannot,[45] while the federal government says that it can, provided that it has made an honest and reasonable effort to obtain consent. Therefore, the government remains the sole judge and arbiter of its good intentions while maintaining the duty to protect the honour of the Crown, the fiduciary of the rights of Indigenous peoples.*

*However, speaking before the United Nations General Assembly on 21 September 2017, Prime Minister Trudeau stated, "We are now without qualification a full supporter of the Declaration."[46]*

*The federal government says that it wants to "have a renewed nation-to-nation relationship with Indigenous Peoples, based on recognition, rights, respect, co-operation, and partnership," and it tells the world that it endorses the United Nations Declaration on the Rights of Indigenous Peoples "without qualification," in other words, without reserve. The ambiguity and contradictions in the government's approach have become apparent. Indigenous leaders are fully aware of them and understand that when claiming and exercising their sovereignty, there is still a strategic area that must be defined and, in particular, an ambiguity that must be examined and resolved.*

*Moreover, the interests of the federal government, in which staggering economic benefits are at stake, conflict with the Crown's fiduciary obligation toward Indigenous peoples and their right as a nation to self-determination over their recognized traditional lands.*

*The matter will soon be before the courts, as British Columbia's new government under John Horgan has decided to intervene in legal proceedings and champion Indigenous groups in the conflict over the Trans Mountain pipeline project, a project that will cross Indigenous land and that the previous provincial government and the federal government approved but Indigenous groups oppose. In May 2018, the federal government purchased the pipeline for $4.5 billion, and its construction cost is now estimated at $9.3 billion.[47] Simply put, if an Indigenous people has traditional title to land and is the most directly affected by the project, do they have the protected and inherent right to make decisions about the development of this land?[48] Indigenous peoples and British Columbia's new provincial government say that they do. Once again, the courts will be an important step in defining what a nation-to-nation and government-to-government relationship really is.*

*That is the greatest challenge facing the parties: defining Indigenous sovereignty in the initial context recognized by the Supreme Court – that of a people who have never been conquered and therefore are not required to submit to the law of a conqueror or occupier that would be free to impose its will. The Indigenous community knows very well that it means "reasserting our jurisdiction and sovereignty over our own lands, titles and rights," as the National Chief of the Assembly of First Nations stated.[49]*

*Will we have to go to international arbitration under the United Nations Declaration on the Rights of Indigenous Peoples to untangle this now obvious issue? Can negotiations alone lead to a definition of what a nation-to-nation relationship really means?[50]*

STANDOFF IN OKA — "FACE TO FACE"

Oka, Quebec, 1 September 1990. One of Canada's most famous photos. The face to face match is between Private Patrick Cloutier of the *Van Doos* (22nd Canadian Army Infantry Regiment based in Quebec) and the Ojibway Brad Laroque of Saskatchewan during the summer 1990 conflict between the Mohawks and the political and military authorities of the country, involving the territory that the town of Oka intended to expropriate. The symbolism of the image, a young white soldier directly facing a strong Aboriginal warrior, and its expressive strength – which of the two would give in – dramatically illustrates the challenge Canada faces regarding Aboriginal land claim resolution and the exercise of their sovereignty. This still-open question can not be resolved by the force of arms, but rather in the respect of the honour of the Crown, but as it has dragged on for far too long, exasperation may occasionally lead to violent confrontations. Credit: The Canadian Press/Shaney Komulainen

*There is also the issue of Indigenous governments' fiscal autonomy: regular revenues are needed to administer a territory. A number of First Nations do not collect taxes, even though they have the authority to do so.[51] Where will they get the funds needed to grow and develop, and emerge from four centuries of colonialism?[52] The Royal Commission on Aboriginal Peoples in its 1996 report well identified the fundamental issue: "a critical element of fiscal autonomy is a fair and just redistribution of lands and resources for aboriginal peoples. Without such redistribution, aboriginal governments, and the communities they govern, will continue to lack a viable and sustaining economic base".*

*Now that we are redefining a mature, responsible, and peaceful relationship between Canada and Indigenous nations, we can see the consequences of this unavoidable impasse.*

*The provinces will also have to deal with outcomes related to their areas of jurisdiction, such as recognizing Indigenous customary laws, teaching Indigenous languages, or recognizing cultural, social, or religious practices that have been significantly marginalized by two hundred years of colonialism.*

*Over the past fifty years, Canada has been gradually experiencing a radical transformation in its relationship with Indigenous peoples. However, we must still fight to stamp out deep-seated prejudices[53] and smouldering racism. We must make systemic changes, instil them in the minds of Canadians, and entrench them in various social, economic and professional structures and throughout the education system, which has been rid of its prevailing colonial mentality. These changes should eventually help Canada become a country that takes pride in the status of the Indigenous peoples, whose identity, culture, and self-determination will have been fully restored.*

*The road to reconciliation with Indigenous peoples extends far beyond the next generation. As of October 2017, negotiations were still underway concerning twenty-nine claims to Indigenous lands not covered by previous treaties or other legal title. More than four hundred and five specific claims are pending concerning Canada's obligations under historic treaties or the way in which it has managed First Nations funds or assets. In addition, seventy-three claims are before the Specific Claims Tribunal. All in all, there are more than five hundred active claims, and this number is expected to rise.*

*Before Indigenous peoples can establish responsible self-directed government, before federal and provincial legislation and practices are decolonized, and before the rule of law based on the United Nations Declaration on the Rights of Indigenous Peoples and its principles can prevail, a great deal must be done to ensure old attitudes and practices stay in the past and the demoralizing status quo that is unworthy of Canadian society does not become our future.*

### NOTES

1 The author would like to thank the Library of Parliament for checking the figures and historical facts in this document.

2 *Statement of the Government of Canada on Indian Policy, 1969* (The White Paper, 1969), published under the authority of the Hon. Jean Chrétien, p.c., m.p., Minister of Indian Affairs and Northern Development, 1969, Queen's Printer Cat. No. R32-2469.

3  Eric Andrew-Gee, "The secret legacy of the man who caught Louis Riel," *The Globe and Mail*, 21 July 2017, p. A8.

4  Winfried Baumgart, *Imperialism – The Idea and Reality of British and French colonial expansion 1880–1914* (New York: Oxford University Press, 1982), 1-9. The French colonial empire embraced a similar ideology during the same period.

5  On 27 August 2017, Prime Minister Trudeau announced the decision to split Indigenous and Northern Affairs into two separate departments, the Department of Crown-Indigenous Relations and Northern Affairs, and the Department of Indigenous Services, in order to better serve the government's objective of dismantling "existing colonial structures."

6  René Morin, *La construction du droit des Autochtones par la Cour suprême du Canada* (Quebec, Septentrion, 2017).

7  *The Indian Act* establishes three categories of "Indian": Status or Registered Indians, Non-Status Indians, and Treaty Indians.

8  Jody Wilson-Raybould, "Indigenous reconciliation requires recognition," *The Globe and Mail*, 19 July 2017, p. A11.

9  *Descheneaux v. Canada (Procureur général)*, 2015 QCCS 3555.

10  In June 2017, the House of Commons returned *An Act to amend the Indian Act* (elimination of sex-based inequities in registration) to the Senate without the corrective amendments that the Senate had made.

11  An amendment to this effect was defeated in the Senate; Dan Levin, "Canada Moves Closer to Gender Equity for Indigenous Women," *The New York Times*, 14 November 2017, p. 6.

12  *Williams Lake Indian Band v. Canada*, 2018 SCC 4.

13  Dominique Degré, "Des problèmes d'eau potable perdurent dans les communautés," *Le Devoir*, 26 July 2017, p. A5. As of April 2018, there were 152 boil water advisories in effect in 104 communities across the country. The government plans to remedy the situation by 2021.

14  Tom Spears, "Can we inherit fear?," *The Ottawa Citizen*, 9 September 2017, p. D1.

15  According to the latest Statistics Canada figures, published 25 October 2017, the Indigenous population totalled 1,673,785 persons.

16  They represent 28 per cent of male and female inmates in federal prisons.

17  Senate of Canada, Open Caucus – Quick Facts, 18 April 2018.

18  The mandate of the Commission of Inquiry is scheduled to expire by 31 December 2018.

19  Luc Boulanger, "Femmes autochtones: encore loin de la guérison," *La Presse.ca*, 25 July 2017.

20  Kristy Kirkup, "National review needed following report on coerced tubal ligations: researchers," *The Globe and Mail*, 31 July 2017, p. A2.

21  Terry Pedwell, The Canadian Press, "Not enough diversity on Canadian television, report says," *TheStar.com*, 16 July 2017.

22  René Morin, *La construction du droit des Autochtones par la Cour suprême du Canada*.

23  Tim Harper, "The long Liberal road to Indigenous reconciliation," *Toronto Star*, 30 August 2017, p. A6.

24  Mélanie Marquis, "La population autochtone, déjà en constante croissance, progressera 'rapidement,'" *La Presse.ca*, 25 October 2017.

25  The author introduced bills S-237 (2009), S-229 (2015), and S-212 (2016).

26  Statement by Prime Minister Justin Trudeau, 42nd Parliament, 1st Session, Revised Hansard, No 264, 14 February 2018, pp. 17217–17219.

27  Caroline Montpetit, "Perspective – Langues autochtones: la survie à contre-courant," *Le Devoir*, 16 September 2017, p. B1. Budget 2016 allocated $55 million per year for instruction in Indigenous languages, but the promised legislation has not been introduced.

28  *R. v. Gladue*, [1999] 1 SCR 688.

29  Gloria Galloway, "Most calls to action in reconciliation commission report remain unmet," *The Globe and Mail*, 13 August 2018, p. A4.

30  Ibid., "Sixties Scoop survivor suing over Métis exclusion," *The Globe and Mail*, 27 January 2018, p. A11.

31  "Making Real Change Happen," Speech from the Throne to Open the First Session of the Forty-second Parliament of Canada, 2015.

32  Marie Vastel, "Une loi pour forcer Ottawa à respecter les droits des autochtones," *Le Devoir*, 15 February 2018.

33  Statement by Prime Minister Justin Trudeau, 42nd Parliament, 1st Session, Revised Hansard, No 264, 14 February 2018, pp. 17217–17219.

34  Bob Weber, "First Nations seek role in drafting laws," *Ottawa Citizen*, 15 January 2018, p. N4.

35  *Mikisew Cree First Nation v. Canada* (Governor General in Council), 2018 SCC 40.

36  François Cardinal, "Autochtones: de quoi Trudeau a-t-il peur?," *LaPresse.ca*, 13 September 2017.

37  *Tsilhqot'in Nation v. British Columbia*, 2014 SCC 44, [2014] 2 SCR 256, para. 69: "At the time of assertion of European sovereignty, the Crown acquired radical or underlying title to all the land in the province [British Columbia]."

38  *R. v. Van der Peet*, [1996] 2 SCR 507, para. 31.

39  The Supreme Court's decision in *Tsilhqot'in Nation v. British Columbia*, 2014 SCC 44, [2014] 2 SCR 256, clearly established that the "doctrine of terra nullius (that no one owned the land prior to European assertion of sovereignty) never applied in Canada."

40  Azeezah Kanji, "Supreme Court's colonial roots are showing," *Toronto Star*, 10 August 2017, p. A17.

41  Henry Myeengun, "First Nation questioning relationship with Canada," *Toronto Star*, 13 August 2017, p. A17; Sunny Dhillon, "Indigenous rights advocate to guide B.C. in Trans Mountain pipeline challenge," *The Globe and Mail*, 11 August 2017, p. S1.

42  Miriam Katawazi, "Energy projects on Indigenous land should be subject to veto, Singh says," *Toronto Star*, 16 September 2017, p. A16.

43  *Chippewas of the Thames First Nation v. Enbridge Pipelines Inc.*, 2017 SCC 41, para. 59.

44  Dwight Newman, "Ottawa's sly change on consent may damage Indigenous relationships," *The Globe and Mail*, 3 August 2017, p. A11.

45  United Nations Declaration on the Rights of Indigenous Peoples, articles 18, 19, and 32.

46  Live address by the Right Hon. Justin Trudeau before the United Nations General Assembly in New York, *Primetime Politics* – CPAC, 21 September 2017.

47  "Le coût d'acquisition de Trans Mountain grimpe," *Le Devoir*, 8 August 2018, p. B4.

48  James Munson, "B.C.'s new approach to Trans Mountain a threat to Trudeau's indigenous agenda," *Ipolitics*, 13 August 2017; Sunny Dhillon, "Indigenous rights advocate to guide B.C. in Trans Mountain pipeline challenge," *The Globe and Mail*, 11 August 2017, p. S1.

49  Alex Ballingall, "Ottawa sets out to scrap 'colonial' ways: Trudeau's proposal to strengthen Indigenous nationhood could signify a new frontier, but critics say it's not enough," *Toronto Star*, 4 September 2017, p. A3.

50  Conrad Black, "Aboriginals deserve a fair deal, but enough with us hating ourselves," *NationalPost.com*, 4 August 2017.

51  See the *Indian Act, First Nations Fiscal Management Act, and First Nations Goods and Services Tax Act*.

52  Paul Journet, "Est-on prêt pour cette révolution?," *La Presse+*, 13 September 2017.

53  Frank Iacobucci, "The path to reconciliation starts with consent," *The Globe and Mail*, 31 July 2016, p. A11.

# Setting the Record Straight on the Origin Story of Canada

Phil Fontaine, former national chief of the Assembly of First Nations[1]

I join all of you in respectful recognition of the traditional lands of the Algonquin peoples. I'm deeply honoured to be here this morning to share with you some perspectives on matters of great importance, not just to Indigenous peoples but to all Canadians.

We Indigenous peoples are living in a time of great promise. For the first time in our history, the Government of Canada has described the relationship with the First Peoples as one of nation to nation. At the same time, very important Supreme Court decisions have clearly articulated our unique rights and interests and established our special rights with respect to our land. We have become better educated and more politically engaged. We are in the process of revitalizing our economies to deal with the crushing poverty many of our people still experience. We have no desire to be dependent peoples. We wish to exercise our rights to give full expression to our cultures, languages, and legal traditions, and most importantly, since the Truth and Reconciliation Commission of Canada's final report, the country like never before appears ready to embark on a process of reconciliation and healing with us. I believe that recognition of who we are and where we have come from is the first step toward meaningful reconciliation and permanent change.

There could be no better time than the 150th anniversary of Confederation to reflect on the role of Indigenous peoples in the founding of Canada, how the country developed, and what our rightful place is in this, our country. Confederation is the starting point.

---

1  This speech is co-authored by Mr Phil Fontaine and Professor Kathleen Mahoney. An earlier version was first presented at a Royal Society of Canada "Big Thinking" lecture in Victoria in 2016 by Professor Mahoney.

As the story goes, Canada was founded by two races, the British and the French. In 1867, they created the Constitution that formed the bedrock of our Canadian identity, the basis for what most Canadians like to believe is a caring, sharing, and peaceable nation, a nation that practises equality as a supreme value. But this story is incomplete and misleading. In 1996, the Royal Commission on Aboriginal Peoples wrote in its report that a country cannot be built on a living lie.

The lie is a lie of omission. It fails to recognize the critical role Indigenous peoples played in the formation of Canada and, as a result, it tainted the Confederation story from its very beginning, causing profound harm to our peoples and to the country. Unless we mend this broken tale, the celebration of 150 years of Confederation will be a celebration of the mistakes of the past, not a celebration of reconciliation and renewal.

My proposal to you here may be considered bold, but it is straightforward. We should celebrate 150 years of Confederation by finally and officially setting the record straight, through an act of Parliament, about Canada's founding by three peoples, the British, the French, and indigenous peoples. This would build the necessary context and foundation for discussion and action on our nation-to-nation relationship and build momentum for the implementation of the Truth and Reconciliation Commission's ninety-four calls to action.

My presentation to you will have four themes: first, the importance of origin stories and how Canada's is historically inaccurate; second, the legal and philosophical justifications for denying recognition and why they must be rejected; third, the deep and lasting harms caused by Canada's flawed origin story; and, fourth, the importance of getting the origin story right.

The importance of origin stories cannot be underestimated. An origin story explains how a culture or, in this case, a nation came into being. Every country, every community, every family has a story of its beginning to express who it is and where it has come from. Connecting our past to the present and explaining its relevance to everyday life helps us to navigate our world and to consider deep ethical questions about how we should conduct ourselves. A society with no stories or stories that exclude some of its members creates alienation and disaffection, like denying a person a name or a family its roots. When origin stories describe the beginnings of politics and power, they serve as scripts for citizenship, a form of consent to a political vision.

For the past several years, the country has gone through a painful existential crisis with respect to its relationship with us and how we have been denied and alienated from citizenship compared to everyone else. The Indian Residential Schools

Settlement Agreement, the apology in Parliament, and the report of the Truth and Reconciliation Commission have all revealed shocking facts contradicting many commonly held beliefs about Canada, its values and origins as a nation, and what it means to be a Canadian. The disconnect between the comfortable story of Canada and the lived reality of our peoples must be confronted. The great African-American writer James Baldwin's insight that people are trapped in history and history is trapped in them captures the Canadian identity crisis and shows the need for a sincere re-examination of what Canada is and what we should truly be.

The commonly understood story of Canada's creation asserts that our country came into being on 1 July 1867, founded by thirty-six Fathers of Confederation who represented two races or peoples, the British and the French. British and French colonial leaders drafted a Constitution, known as the British North America Act, that was passed by the Parliament of the United Kingdom. This act, the first of several, set out the governance structure for Canada, including the division of powers between the new provinces and the new federal government. In addition, and most importantly, the Fathers of Confederation embedded in the Act protection of the languages, cultures, and civil rights of the British and the French.

Over time, Canada has welcomed millions of immigrants with backgrounds other than British or French. Multiculturalism was added to the definition of what it means to be Canadian.

Parliament passed legislation recognizing multiculturalism for its historic contributions to Canadian society and characterized it as fundamental to our Canadian heritage.

The legislation, in its preamble, briefly mentions that the rights of Aboriginal peoples in Canada are recognized. The fundamental character of the country, however, was and still is defined as bicultural, with the acknowledgment that ethnic groups, which include Indigenous peoples according to the Multiculturalism Act, add value. The unique Indigenous contribution to the character of the country is erased by this legislation, which simply includes Indigenous peoples with immigrants who are neither French nor British.

We can see this origin story repeatedly reinforced over the years. In 1963, for example, Prime Minister Lester B. Pearson convened the Royal Commission on Bilingualism and Biculturalism. In its introduction, the report of the commission asserts that the commission will not examine the question of the Indians and the Eskimos. The report states, "Our terms of reference contain no allusions to Canada's native populations. They speak of two founding nations, namely Canadians of British and French origin." In other words, understanding Canada as a product of anything other than British or French origins was unthinkable in 1963.

From our perspective, Canada's origin story is quite different. The British-French story fails to acknowledge the constant presence of our nations for thousands of years all over the land we now call Canada. There were hundreds of our nations, as different from one another as the European nations are, with distinct cultures, languages, laws, and unique knowledge and understanding of our part of the world. Before colonization, we were self-determining, sovereign nations. We negotiated with one another and enforced our own laws and forms of governance and spiritual traditions.

When the settlers landed, our ancestors welcomed the newcomers and provided land for them, entered into trade and peace and friendship treaties, and fought alongside them as allies in colonial wars. Our knowledge systems, languages, and forms of social organization influenced the way the settlers survived and prospered.

Our ancestors were instrumental as well in the development of the fur trade, which was the mainstay of colonial economies for more than 250 years. The fur trade opened the continent to exploration and settlement, missionary work, and social and other economic development.

But, by far, the most significant contribution of our nations to the building of the Canadian nation were the land treaties that the Crown negotiated in just about every part of the country. These vast tracts of land made the country what it is today and have produced immense riches, leading Canada to become one of the wealthiest nations in the world.

Our land was the subject of legal agreements, starting with the Royal Proclamation of 1763, also known as the Indian Magna Carta and Canada's first constitutional document. It set the legal foundation for the Canada-Indigenous relationship, especially with respect to land rights, treaties, and the right to self-determination. Although the royal proclamation gave ownership over North America to the British Crown, it explicitly stated that Aboriginal title existed and continues to exist, and that all land would be considered Indigenous land until ceded by treaty.

Professor John Borrows, a leading Indigenous legal scholar, makes the point that the proclamation was a vigorously negotiated document subsequently ratified by two thousand chiefs, and it has never been repealed. We know this because it was incorporated in the 1982 Constitution Act.

Once Britain gained effective control over North America, it ignored its legal obligations under the proclamation. Large tracts of Indigenous lands were appropriated to accommodate the settlers' ever-increasing demands, and the imposition of the reserve system, and attempted assimilation of the First Peoples, replaced the nation-to-nation relationship.

IDLE NO MORE

Joining together as part of the IDLE NO MORE movement, members of Indigenous communities from various parts of the country protest against being dispossessed of their ancestral lands, marginalized politically, and forced to live under the discriminatory government guardianship still imposed on them by the Indian Act. Sometimes driven to engage in civil disobedience in order to be heard, they frequently have no power other than the judgments they succeed in winning from the country's highest courts. Credit: The Canadian Press/Sean Kilpatrick

It should therefore come as no surprise that we were not welcomed at the Confederation table in 1867. No one asked us if we wanted to be British subjects or Canadian citizens, yet the decisions taken by the Fathers of Confederation would have profound implications for our future from that day forward. Instead of incorporating our sovereign rights guaranteed in the proclamation into the new Constitution, the Fathers of Confederation mandated that the federal government would have total control over "Indians and lands reserved for the Indians." No protection for our languages, education, laws, or cultures were in the BNA Act. Those guarantees only applied to the French and the British, allowing their cultures to flourish ever since.

After relegating us to virtual non-citizen status, it became easy for the Fathers of Confederation and subsequent governments to promote the myth that only the British and the French were responsible for the foundation of Canada.

After Confederation, things got even worse. Our ancestors were herded onto smaller and smaller tracts of land to make way for more and more settlers and resource development. Today, we occupy less than 2 per cent of the land mass of Canada. Sealing the deal on our structural inequality was the passage of the first Indian Act in 1876, when just about every aspect of the life of the Indigenous population came under the control of the federal government and its bureaucracy. The Indian Act, *inter alia,* prohibited Indians from hiring lawyers to fight for our land rights – I reference "Indians" because that's how we were known until very recently – forbade the raising of funds to organize politically, mandated attendance at Indian residential schools, confined us to reserves, enforced the pass system, criminalized cultural activities, took our Indian status away from those who attended university, imposed alien forms of governance, redefined gender roles, and denied us the right to vote. Apparently, it struck no one as improper to hand the control of an entire race to a branch of the federal bureaucracy.

The land and resources taken from our nations, without compensation or consent, formed the foundation for the high quality of life enjoyed by other Canadians from then on. Only a small portion of resource income has ever come back to us, usually in the form of transfer payments that have never been sufficient to sustain our communities or our citizens. How did this happen? None of it was done without some legal and philosophical justification. The two most important justifications were the Doctrine of Discovery and the formal equality principle.

The Doctrine of Discovery, with its origins in 1493 in a papal bull of Pope Alexander VI, was the legal fiction through which Europeans claimed rights of sovereignty and ownership of property in regions they claimed to discover. The doctrine held that Indigenous peoples could not claim ownership of their lands but only rights of occupation and use.

The formal equality principle, on the other hand, derives from the teachings of Plato and Aristotle, who understood that to achieve equality, people who are the same must be treated the same. However, the standard of comparison was set by those in power, so it allowed distinctions to be made between those who should rule – namely, elite male landowners – and those who should not – namely, common men, slaves, and women.

The Fathers of Confederation adopted both the formal equality principle and the Doctrine of Discovery. Positions of power were open only to those who met the normative standard of an elite, landowning male class. This, combined with the Doctrine of Discovery, ensured the perpetual domination of the British and French founders and the permanent subordination of the Indigenous peoples.

The formal equality philosophy rationalized imposition of the Indian Act. It was justified because Indians and non-Indians were not the same, and so long as all Indians were treated the same, the laws met the standards the formal equality principle required. The flip side of formal equality is assimilation, a process whereby a person or group acquires the social and psychological characteristics of another group. Assimilation is seen as the solution to the problem of difference. In the Canadian context, as the colonial settlements grew, Indians were regarded as a problem that needed fixing through forced assimilation.

The most egregious example of assimilation was the Indian residential school policy. We now know that the government policy of assimilation through residential school education amounted to cultural genocide. The fact that government policy treated Indian children differently, as compared to non-native children, by destroying our family bonds, our languages and cultures, and ultimately our identities did not raise eyebrows or alarm bells. Our difference made it okay. As long as all Indian children were treated the same and the problem of difference was addressed through assimilation, that was seen as good and right.

Nicholas Flood Davin, MP, wrote the Davin report in 1879, shortly after Confederation. In it, he explicitly dictated the assimilation policy, saying the government must carry out the Indian residential school policy "until there is not a single Indian in Canada that has not been absorbed into the body politic."

Duncan Campbell Scott, deputy minister of Indian Affairs, was in charge of implementing the policy. He went so far as to refuse to close down schools where up to 43 per cent of the children in them were dying from tuberculosis. He said this death rate "does not justify a change in the policy of this Department, which is geared towards a final solution of our Indian Problem." He is also credited with saying, "We can't kill the Indian, but we can kill the Indian in the child."

Campbell Scott came very close to setting a policy to actually kill Indian children, which was the accusation made by Dr P.H. Bryce, a physician whose responsibility was to investigate the health of Indian children in the tuberculosis-infested schools. Bryce tried to expose it in a book, titled *The Story of a National Crime*, after the federal government refused to make his report public.

Interestingly enough, Campbell Scott was named a Confederation poet. The Government of Canada's official biography of him is quite ironic, actually. It says that Campbell Scott's "widely recognized and valued 'Indian poems' cemented his literary reputation."

Finally, in 1989, the formal equality theory was firmly rejected as a foundational legal concept by the Supreme Court of Canada. The court said the concept, more often than not, perpetuates inequality.

The Doctrine of Discovery, too, has been discredited by all major human rights organizations and the United Nations as a socially unjust, racist concept in violation of basic and fundamental Indigenous human rights.

Had the French and British Fathers of Confederation recognized and appreciated the importance and centrality of the contributions of Indigenous peoples to Canada instead of being guided by assimilationist values, formal inequality, and the Doctrine of Discovery, we would not now be trapped in the narrow framework of an origin story that has left us Indigenous Canadians marginalized, dispossessed, and unrecognized and the rest of the country intellectually debilitated, morally disempowered, and personally depressed, wondering who they really are as a nation.

So where does this leave us? Well, we've had the Oka Crisis, the Royal Commission on Aboriginal Peoples, the United Nations report of James Anaya, years of acrimonious litigation, roadblocks, unresolved land claims – so many in every part of the country – hundreds and hundreds of missing and murdered Aboriginal women, and the Truth and Reconciliation Commission. All of these say the same thing: division between Indigenous and nonindigenous peoples in Canada has grown deeper and more hostile since Confederation. The paradox here is that as this divide grows deeper, our common destiny binds us ever more tightly together. Put differently, the consequences of non-recognition have been harmful and costly, both to First Peoples and to all Canadians. Lower life expectancy, poor health, and disproportionately high rates of incarceration, suicide, poverty, high school drop out, unemployment, and addiction are too big a price to pay to maintain a status quo that cannot be morally, ethically, or legally justified.

In many parts of Canada, our peoples are the fastest-growing demographic. For example, in 2016 the percentage of Indigenous students entering grade one in Manitoba was over 30 per cent. In Saskatchewan next year, 45 per cent of all students entering kindergarten will be Indigenous. Two thirds of these children live in poverty, which is more than quadruple the national average. These children deserve better. Indeed, Canada deserves better.

Whether future conversations are about self-determination, the nation-to-nation relationship, the realization of Indigenous culture, or the sharing of land and resources, the depth of these issues and the acrimony they engender will never be fully understood unless all Canadians embrace the true origin story of this country, understand where we went wrong, and then determine together to fix it.

The federal government's promises are encouraging. The minister of Indigenous and Northern Affairs' goal, for example, is to renew the relationship between Canada and Indigenous peoples. This renewal is meant to form a nation-to-nation relationship based on recognition and to support the work of reconciliation. For the Parliament of Canada to recognize Indigenous peoples as equal partners in the founding of the nation would be an incredibly good and important start and a powerful catalyst for reconciliation. This would mean being truthful about what divides us. It should mean talking about power and understanding how power was exercised

AANISCHAAUKAMIKW CREE CULTURAL INSTITUTE
The work of Algonquin architect Douglas Cardinal, the Cree Cultural Institute is a remarkable success that marries the lines of traditional Indigenous buildings with a modernism that is perfectly suited to the building's surroundings. The Institute clearly illustrates a newfound harmony that honours and respects the restored Indigenous identity. Credit: Aanischaaukamikw Cree Cultural Institute, Mitch Lenet

over the past so as to determine who should have power over the present. It may mean giving the pen to the First Peoples to write the master narrative. If that were the case, it would mean honouring treaties and self-determination rights, preserving dying Indigenous languages, strengthening Indigenous cultures and traditions, sharing economic opportunities, and appointing Indigenous Canadians to high positions of power. In other words, it would lead to all of the things that should have been part of the history of our peoples, had they taken their rightful place at the Confederation table in 1867 as one of the three founding peoples.

So here I have presented what some would consider a bold proposal, but it's a simple and straightforward one, as I suggested in my opening remarks. I believe the 150th anniversary of Confederation offers an opportunity for Canadians to reflect upon our origin story and to set the record straight.

However, setting the record straight by officially recognizing that Canada is a country of three founding peoples will not end the suffering. It will not heal all wounds or eradicate all poverty. What it will do is create a powerful narrative that will become part of the shared story of every Canadian for generations to come. It will create a compelling platform for Indigenous peoples and for every level of government to achieve the real progress promised on issues most important to First Nations, Inuit, and Métis nations and communities.

What is clear is that reconciliation will not be achieved unless a climate conducive to its realization is fostered. Recognizing the true role of Indigenous peoples in Canada's story of origin will be the important first step toward creating and nurturing that climate.

# Moving Forward: Addressing Indigenous Rights Honourably, Respectfully, and Courageously

Katsi'tsakwas Ellen Gabriel, is an Indigenous Human Rights and Environmental Activist. She is a former president of the Quebec Native Women's Association and official spokesperson of the People of the Longhouse during the 1990 Oka Crisis/Kanehsatà:ke Siege

*Wa'kwanonweràton, Katsi'tsakwas ne ióntiats, wakeniénton tánon Kanehsatà:ke akenà:keron*
*Teiotohontsonhon ne ohenton aketahsewen, tsi tatsitenonwerá:ton ne Shonkwaia'tíson tsi awén:ton ó:ia awenhnísera ionkwanakera ne ken'en Iethinisténha Ohóntsa*
*Tánon teithinonweráton ne Iethinistén Ohóntsa ne akwén:kon nahóten ionkhiiáwis*
*Tánon teithinonwerá:ton ne Ka'shentsténshera Shaoiéra*

I wanted to start off in Kanien'kéha, a language that is my first language. It is a language I heard as a child growing up. Both my parents were speakers. As a child, I grew up hearing three languages. Kanien'kéha at home, then I went to school in English. My father had a business with horses, renting them for riding, and his clients were predominantly Québécois, so I heard French.

I'm very pleased to have this opportunity on this day to greet the Creator and Mother Earth for all they bring and give us – the food, the water, the strength to carry on each day.

I'm very humbled by Mr Fontaine's previous words. He has covered those issues so well that I don't need to revisit them and I can talk about the kinds of things, as an Indigenous woman and as an Indigenous person, that Canada needs to remember as it celebrates 150 years.

Many of you here understand the impacts of colonization. As Mr Fontaine talked about origin stories, I thought about Iroquois culture. The creation stories talk about the first two human beings on this earth, who were women. Those women were the basis of and the foundation for Iroquois culture. My culture is matrilineal, and in our customary laws it is the women who hold title to the land. It is the women who declare war, and the war chief works for them.

I see today as an opportunity to perhaps begin a discussion about real reconciliation. Real reconciliation must be human-rights based, not economically based. It must include the rights of all our relations – those we mention during Ohén:ton Kariwatékhwa (the words said before all else) and the environment that we rely so heavily upon. Indigenous peoples' cultures and their languages are land based. We are nothing without our land. For Indigenous people, many of the treaties that were signed in Canada were peace and friendship treaties. For the colonizer, they were a way of land dispossession. We must keep in mind the context in which those treaties were signed.

I want to quote today the Right Honourable Beverley McLachlin from 2002 at the Order of Canada luncheon. She was chief justice of Ontario. She said:

> Aboriginal rights from the beginning have been shaped by international concepts. More recently, emerging international norms have guided governments and courts grappling with Aboriginal issues. Canada, as a respected member of the international community, cannot ignore these new international norms. . . . Whether we like it or not, Aboriginal rights are an international matter.

Human rights are universal; they're indivisible, interdependent, and interrelated. Canada should be trying to promote the highest attainable standards of human rights when it comes to Indigenous peoples, not the lowest, which is what we are experiencing today.

Human rights must be enjoyed as a whole. They must not be categorized into little boxes. If we don't enjoy one right, then we cannot enjoy our human rights; and if we cannot enjoy all our human rights, we cannot enjoy our rights to self-determination.

It is difficult for me to say that I am celebrating Canada 150. I say this with the utmost respect to all Canadians. I am celebrating Indigenous peoples' resiliency and the richness of our cultures that still remain today.

Our languages are threatened today. UNESCO (United Nations Educational, Scientific, and Cultural Organisation) has stated that Indigenous languages are most threatened in Canada. Canada's linguistic duality threatens Indigenous languages because French and English dominate the education system, laws and popular culture. Therefore in order to succeed an Indigenous person must be fluent in one or both these colonial languages. As the former Auditor General, Sheila Fraser, stated in her 2006 report: There is less money put into place for Indigenous children to have access to their languages. In fact, Ms Fraser stated that it would take twenty-eight years for on-reserve schools to catch up with the quality of education received in the rest of Canada. And the Indian residential school system did a very good job of shaming people for speaking their languages and shaming them for being proud of their culture.

As I look today at the youth who are leaders in the Idle No More movement and at the leaders who are passionate about preventing more damage to our climate, I am inspired. I have been doing this for twenty-seven years (this is up to 2017). I have seen many things. I have seen incremental changes. I have seen a lot of dialogue. But I do not see human rights being part of the education of your children and youth. I do not see human rights being part of the policies that control Indigenous peoples' lives. I do not see human rights being implemented or even being taught to the policing authorities or to politicians. It seems to go out the door. They are just words on paper. So I implore Canada today, as it celebrates 150 years, to begin to teach your citizens about human rights and environmental rights. Those two are not separate; they are part of each other.

We, as Indigenous peoples, helped your ancestors survive on this land. As more immigrants come to Canada, they need to know the story of Canada. They need to know the stories of the Indigenous people. They need to know that Indigenous women have been the most influential in changing the laws that impact Indigenous peoples.

Indigenous women have fought against the discriminatory laws embedded in the Indian Act, which is one of the most racist pieces of legislation in the world, which still exists. It is important to note that the reservation system established in Canada under the Indian Act was the foundation for the apartheid system in South Africa.

Indigenous women were integral to the decision-making processes in our nations. I come from a community that existed before European contact, but Canada's version of my community's history is that we are seventeenth-century immigrants from the Mohawk Valley. The minister of Indian Affairs in 1990, Tom Siddon, stated that we had no rights to the land on which thousands of generations left their footprints on that sand, in Kanehsatà:ke, the place where the crusty sand dunes lie. The British in the seventeenth century called it a castle because from the river you could see the glimmering sand. You could see the glorious earth of Kanehsatà:ke. Kanehsatà:ke was the first community to accept the Kaianera'kó:wa – the great shining peace, the laws and constitution of the Iroquois Confederacy. So I am proud to come from the community of Kanehsatà:ke.

In 1990, your government lied to you when it said it resolved the long standing historical land problem. In fact, we have the oldest land dispute in Canada, three hundred years old. I have talked to bureaucrats and the minister of Indian Affairs to ask for some kind of settlement or resolution to this long-standing land dispute. I have been stalled by the bureaucracy; I have been ignored but the disrespect extends to the Haudenosaunee of Kanehsatà:ke which I am part of.

THE NEGOTIATORS OF OKA CRISIS (QUEBEC), SUMMER 1990

The Oka crisis that began in the summer of 1990 was not resolved peacefully, force was used by Canada and Quebec using both the provincial police force, the Sûreté du Québec and the Canadian army sent in to both Mohawk communities of Kanehsatà:ke and Kahnawà:ke at the request of the Quebec government; this was because the Sûreté du Québec could not ensure public safety since they themselves were taking the law onto themselves, committing numerous human rights abuses. The SQ did not obey any orders by the two levels of government – Federal and Provincial – to respect the free passage of food, medicine and people. The negotiators who resolved the standoff appear in this photo: in the center, Ellen Gabriel, spokesperson for the Mohawks; and to her right, John Ciaccia, the provincial minister responsible for Native Affairs. Behind Ellen Gabriel is Mohawk Percy Gabriel, and to her left, Mohawk Elizabeth Beauvais. To the right of Minister Ciaccia, his chief of staff Laurier Thibault. The conflict over the extent of the Mohawk territory and its urban limits persists to this day.  Credit: Robert Galbraith

So we are still experiencing land dispossession. And while we may have stopped the expansion of the nine-hole golf course – which still exists today, by the way – we are losing more land than ever because of an act of Parliament in 2001 called the Kanehsatà:ke Interim Land Base Governance Act.

I was born in 1959, which is the same year that the golf course in Oka was created, so I'm as old as that golf course. It was a place where people put their cattle, a place where people picked berries. My mother talked about going skiing there. It is a beautiful place.

My grandmother on my father's side went to Shingwauk Indian Industrial school in the early 1900s. When I started Day School – my first two years of education were in Day School – when I was five years old, my grandmother Gladys told me, "You're lucky you're going to come home. Because when I went to school, I could not see my mother. I didn't see my mother until I was eighteen."

Afterwards I attended St Eustache elementary school. The children there had no idea who we were. They just thought we were dirty Indians, and we were told that. My parents thought it was very important for us to have an education, so my mother helped us study. Both my parents went up to grade seven because there was no high school in Kanehsatà:ke and their parents did not want to send them to an Indian residential school, not that the Day Schools were much better.

When I think about those times, those stories that I missed because my grandmother had passed away when I was five, I am sad that I didn't get to learn her stories. She didn't get to hear that apology. I hear stories about her experiences from my uncle, the youngest in his family. My father had fifteen siblings; ten of them lived. My mother had seven sisters. Large families were typical during those times. My Uncle Harvey Gabriel told me that my Grandmother talked about going to the end of the fence where they were out of earshot of their teachers so they could speak the language. That's why I'm able to know my language, but as well, my mother was Mohawk and also spoke Kanien'kéha, so that was the language in our home.

Language is really precious, because the fluent speakers understand the traditional knowledge that's embedded in our language. They understand what words mean when you break them down starting with links from the creation story to now, how it is about relationships. It is about honouring those medicines. It is honouring the water, the fish, and the trees and all our relations.

I remember reading this article a while back about scientists who had discovered that the same DNA that is in trees is also in us. The same DNA that is in the stars is also in us. When we say, "We acknowledge all of life's creation," we acknowledge the stars as our ancestors. It's really important for our children to continue to hear those stories, to know those things in which our moral values and cosmology are embedded with.

I'm glad to know that in my sister communities the language is still being worked on. But Indigenous languages will not make you a rich person and some who are assimilated do not see the potential economic impacts of restoring our languages to use them in our daily lives. Indigenous women were the first to start immersion schools. They cut out papers from magazines to make the curriculum for children. They did it all without any funding because they were passionate about passing on the language to a new generation; because language connects us to who we are, to our ancestors, to the land. It reminds us to be humble. It reminds us of the origins of our people and to be proud of them.

Indian residential school took that away from us. When the apology came out, I remember my director at the Kanehsatà:ke Language and Cultural Centre where I work saying, "It took over a hundred years to get us to this point. It's going to take another hundred years for us to heal from that, from that genocide".

I disagree with Justice Beverly MacLaughlin that the Indian Residential School was cultural genocide. I think it is just genocide. If you look at the definition of genocide at the United Nations, you will see that when states/governments target an identifiable group of people, when they forcibly removed the children of a people who had a land base, a culture, a language, a government, and they killed those children, this constitutes Genocide. The most current records researched by the Truth and Reconciliation Commission estimate that there are over three thousand children who did not go home. So we are nations of grieving people.

I admire so much Cindy Blackstock, who created a formal complaint against Canada for the treatment of Aboriginal children in the child welfare system. She said, "Why do we have to take the Government of Canada to court for them to treat Indigenous children fairly and with respect?" Today she is still fighting. We are still fighting to bring our children the kinds of care they need, to bring the needed support to those families affected, in order to understand that what they are feeling is that impact of colonization, those assimilation policies, that box that we are supposed to be happy to be put into.

During the 1990 crisis, it was the first time other Canadians heard that we are not Canadian citizens but that we are proud to be part of the Iroquois Confederacy – a confederacy of nations that fought as allies on both sides in the War of 1812 and who over a century later declared war against Germany before Canada did. My maternal grandfather fought in Vimy Ridge during World War I. He was a proud old soldier, and he died when I was very young, but I hear stories from my cousins who knew him better about the songs that he sang from World War I, and I am proud to know that he was there at Vimy Ridge fighting for freedom for all.

As an Indigenous woman, in 2004, I was proud to be part of that group of women who stood by the Native Women's Association of Canada and Amnesty International when they released the report *Stolen Sisters*. I'm not sure if "epidemic" is the right word to use for the level of violence that Indigenous women face because of colonization. But the issue of Murdered and Missing Indigenous women is rooted in colonization where Indigenous women suffer double discrimination: being a woman and being Indigenous. If you have not read the Stolen Sisters report, you need to read

"ARE YOU AWARE THAT THIS IS MOHAWK TERRITORY?"
Engaged in a land dispute with the Government of Quebec and Canada to protect a piece of Kanehsatà:ke's Common land that the Municipality of Oka wanted to appropriate for a golf course, on 9 March 1990 Kanehsatà:ke Mohawks erected a barricade on a secondary dirt road. Their protest was supported by Indigenous people from across Canada. The "Crisis" began on 11 July 1990 and lasted seventy-eight days. On top of the thousands of Sûreté du Quebec police officers surrounding both Kanehsatà:ke and Kahnawà:ke, the Canadian Army was deployed by Canada and Quebec to pressure the communities to dismantle the barricades. The Mohawks of Kahnawà:ke blocked the Mercier Bridge on the south shore of Montreal. Credit: Ellen Gabriel Collection

it, because Indigenous women have been the backbone of our nations. Indigenous women have been the ones behind immersion schools. They changed the Indian Act in 1985 because of the tenacity of Senator Sandra Lovelace Nicholas, who addressed the United Nations Human Rights Committee in 1981 and helped bring about a badly needed change for our people that resulted in Bill-C-31.

The Royal Commission on Aboriginal Peoples stated:

It is a denial of the principles of peace, harmony and justice for which this country stands – and it has failed. Aboriginal peoples remain proudly different.
    Assimilation policies failed because Aboriginal people have the secret of cultural survival. They have an enduring sense of themselves as peoples with a unique heritage and the right to cultural continuity.

This is what drives them when they blockade roads, protest at military bases and occupy sacred grounds. This is why they resist pressure to merge into Euro-Canadian society – a form of cultural suicide urged upon them in the name of "equality" and "modernization."

Mr Fontaine talked about the rupture to the family unit. When an Indigenous woman married a non-Indigenous man, they were forced to leave the communities they were born and raised in. Mary Two-Axe Early, a Mohawk woman from Kahnawà:ke and one of the pioneers of the Indigenous women's movement, formed Indian Rights for Indian Women and helped form both the Quebec Native Women's Association and the Native Women's Association of Canada. She said, "A dog can be buried in Kahnawà:ke, but I can't be."

I say these things to you so that you know your history. I don't want you to feel sorry for me. I don't want you to feel guilty. I want you to act. I want you to be that change that Canada claims it wants to be. There is no nation-to-nation relationship right now. It's just talk. It's just discussion. And I ask, "Where are the women at these tables? There are some forty-three-odd tables, discussing decolonization? Because if the women are not there and part of the discussion, then we are just repeating the same patterns that the patriarchy of Canada has perpetuated all these 150 years.

I want to reference the UN Permanent Forum on Indigenous Issues that talked about climate change. Climate change is one of the most pressing issues for Indigenous peoples as our culture, our ceremonies and language are based upon the land. Climate change is affecting our human rights and our ability to enjoy our rights to self-determination. If predictions from our elders and even scientists are right, its impacts will be irreversible, and they severely affect present generations and, more so, future generations. Climate change affects the food sovereignty of Indigenous people, from hunting and fishing to traditional agricultural forms of survival. Corn, beans, and squash – these are the three sisters of the Iroquois people and are known as Tiohnhékwa – Tiohnhékwen – the sustainers of life. Nutritionists only recently, in the last couple of decades, figured out that corn, beans, and squash together make a complete protein. So the science behind traditional knowledge, the science behind Indigenous peoples' survival, should be respected.

When I participated in the negotiations for the Convention on Biodiversity's, Nagoya Protocol, I learned that 76 per cent of all pharmaceuticals come from Indigenous peoples' traditional knowledge throughout the world. Indigenous peoples have enriched the world globally. They have enhanced the prosperity of countries like Canada to continue, and yet we still remain the most marginalized group in this country.

I'm glad that Mr Fontaine talked about us being categorized among minorities, with immigrants. We do not have the same history to tell as immigrants. We do not have the same experience as immigrants, and we are peoples, with an "S," who have the right to self-determination, to decide for ourselves what our destiny will be.

As human beings, we are imperfect. We are imperfect in every way, shape, and form. But I think we try hard not to be, and it's that trying that I want you to get inspired by. I want you to remember the stories of the Indigenous women who have been lost. Remember the Manitoba justice inquiry, one of the first stories that I had heard about was that of Helen Betty Osborne, a nineteen-year-old Anishinabe woman who went to school in Winnipeg because there were no schools in her community, who was brutally raped and murdered by four men. The RCMP knew who her killers were. In fact, the community around that area knew who the culprits were, and nobody did anything until six years later. The Manitoba justice inquiry said Helen Betty Osborne would be alive today had she not been an Indigenous woman.

If this country is going to celebrate, if it is indeed going to be a champion of human rights, it must begin in its own backyard. It must stop the kind of development that threatens the prosperity and the very survival of Indigenous peoples, because we have human rights. People look at our rights as special rights, or privileges, and perhaps we will never be able to convince people that being an Indigenous person is not accompanied by any special privileges.

Our rights are legislated to the very last period. It's now time that we take control of our rights and destiny. It's time that Indigenous women stand side by side and shoulder to shoulder with our men. It's time that the men take responsibility to protect the people of their nations and to participate proactively to stop the level of violence that Indigenous women face and that Indigenous children face, and it is time for Canada to pull up its socks and honour its human rights obligations that it has signed on to at the United Nations. The United Nations Declaration on the Rights of Indigenous Peoples is something to behold and to be honoured. It is not to be taken lightly. It is time for justice for Indignenous peoples to restore the traditional institutions and teachings of our ancestors that helped them survive on Mother Earth for centuries.

As all our peoples share the issue of climate change, an issue that is affecting all human beings, and as we look at the floods that just happened in our regions, we need to see each other as the human beings that we are. We need to see all our relations and respect their habitats that allow them to survive, for their survival will be our survival. in order for their survival. Canadians, you need to learn your history. You need to help us preserve, perpetuate, and revitalize our languages. The Canadian government allots annually something like $4,000, approximately, per child, for instruction of minority languages, in French or English. I think it goes down to maybe $200 for Aboriginal children.

So I want you to take a look at the UN Declaration on the Rights of Indigenous Peoples because it is a framework for reconciliation. In my community, Kanehsatà:ke, there are some very brilliant fluent speakers who translated the UN Declaration on the Rights of Indigenous Peoples into Kanien'kéha, so our people can understand the concepts and spirit of the Declaration. Among the beliefs of the Iroquois people is that in order to achieve peace, you must love, you must have courage, and you must have respect for each other. It is important that we all remember that as we move forward.

I am not a Canadian citizen. I am your ally. Our nation has always been your ally. The Longhouse, the Iroquois Confederacy, needs to be respected and recognized as it is a legitimate government that has survived colonization. But Canadian laws during the 1920s outlawed it and so Canada, and of course INAC does not respect our right to participate in discussions affecting our homelands/country.

In fact, as I think about the history of this land and first contact with Europeans who were weak and sickly, who were also sending people escaping tyranny in Europe, then I think it is us who should have been assimilating you, not the other way around. Perhaps we would have had more of a peaceful coexistence with each other.

When I thought about what I was going to be doing for this coming year, for a long time I was very angry and, I guess, very opposed to anything that had to do with celebrating Canada because we never received any kind of acknowledgment for the harms done to us during the 1990 crisis. But then I looked at the allies that we have garnered over the years, the people who have been our allies and who have supported us, from non-governmental organizations to ordinary people in grassroots organizations. What that took was relationship building. It took education. It took awareness, patience, and understanding.

So when you blow out those candles on your birthday cake, let it be the first breath that will bring positive change of reconciliation and restitution for the First Peoples of this land, because we are still here. We are not going anywhere. So you must deal with us in a very honourable, respectful, and courageous way.

*Niá:wen tsi tahskwatahónhsatat*
*Thó nikawén:nake*
*Thank you for listening to me*
*These are all the words I have to say*

2

# Canada's International Identity: Between Image and Reality[1]

The Hon. Serge Joyal, Senator

*F*or the past fifty years, Canada has followed an international policy that has enabled it to pursue two objectives. The first is to solidify its status as a middle power independent from the major powers, entirely distinct from both the United Kingdom, its traditional Commonwealth ally, and the United States, its indispensable neighbour, in order to pursue its own political goals that reflect the humane values of tolerance, peace, and human rights. The second is to strengthen the influence it chooses to have depending on its own global interests.

Yet between the image that Canada presents to other countries, the perception that Canadians themselves have of it, and the reality of the initiatives and actions it undertakes, whether it is humanitarian aid or an armed presence, there is a gap that reveals the depth of its real convictions. In other words, Canada promises sometimes more than it in fact does, and skilfully holds its own among the great powers.

Starting in 1965, the United States made a major commitment to the Vietnam War (1955–75). This was one of the first conflicts that Canada kept its distance from, even going so far as to welcome into the country American recruits who were fleeing mandatory military service.[2] However, Canada – along with Poland, Hungary, and Indonesia – has been part of the international commission tasked with monitoring the withdrawal of American forces after the Paris Peace Accords were signed on 27 January 1973.[3]

Canada stays away from the Americans' multiple foreign interventions, but remains available to offer assistance in other ways and to support an ally with which it shares North America. There was the memorable episode of the six American diplomats who hid in the Canadian Embassy in Tehran, Iran, and made their escape on 28 January 1980, and the taking in of 224 aircraft and their thirty-three thousand passengers that were diverted to Canada when every American airport was closed following the attack on the

AMERICAN HOSTAGE CRISIS IN IRAN, 1979–81

Following the assault by Iranian protesters on the American embassy in Tehran on 4 November 1979, six staff members managed to escape and find refuge at the Canadian embassy. Ken Taylor, the Canadian ambassador, obtained Canadian passports for them and closed the embassy, claiming a national holiday. The Americans were smuggled out of the country among the Canadian staff. Canada has had no diplomatic representation in Iran since 2012, when Canada designated Iran as a state sponsor of terrorism. Credit: The Canadian Press Images/Peter Bregg

*twin towers in New York on 11 September 2001. Obviously, Canada has worked hand in glove with the United States on continental defence since the creation of the DEW Line in 1954 and NORAD in 1957.[4] It has also benefitted from a secure border that binds it to American defence. Still, Canada's refusal to take part in the Strategic Defense Initiative, or "Star Wars," advanced by President Reagan in 1983 and George W. Bush's proposed missile shield in 2005 shows that it has always enough room to manoeuvre to make its own strategic decisions on security.[5]*

*In 1990, Canada stood with President George Bush during Operation Desert Storm, which was a response to Iraq's invasion of Kuwait (the first Gulf War). However, in 2003 it refused to fight alongside the United States and the United Kingdom in the Iraq War (the second Gulf War), despite enormous pressure from Tony Blair, George W. Bush, and the powerful American financial lobby. Resisting Canada's traditional allies, with whom it had fought since World War 1 "against barbarism and for civilization," was almost an act of bravery on the part of the Jean Chrétien government. The rest of the history speaks for itself. These refusals to "co-operate" did not prevent Canada from contributing to the stabilization forces in Iraq starting in 2014,[6] following the American withdrawal in 2011.*

*Moving beyond military operations, Canada's political positions at international bodies and organizations have also differed from those of its two traditional allies. The years-long debate in the Commonwealth on the apartheid in South Africa pitted Prime Minister Mulroney against the Thatcher government in 1986.[7] Canada's influence was decisive in the events that followed and in the liberation of South Africa from the shameful and dishonourable vestiges of slavery, inherited from the former colonial regime, in the late twentieth century. Indeed, Nelson Mandela publicly acknowledged South Africa's debt to Canada. It was this type of powerful anti-colonial action that helped establish Canada's credibility with developing nations. Canada had already broken with the United Kingdom on Zimbabwe and Ian Smith's Rhodesia in 1980 by calling for recognition of the rights of the black majority.*

*Over time, Canada has built a reputation as a country that can make its own decisions, as it has repeatedly shown in times of tremendous international tensions. The positions it has taken have allowed it to gradually develop indisputable credibility and earned it recognition as an independent and trustworthy actor on the international stage. Canada's talks with Mao's China starting in 1968 and the formal diplomatic relations established by the Pierre E. Trudeau government in 1969 did not go unnoticed. The same can be said of Canada's relations with Fidel Castro's Cuba since 1959, to the great dismay of American administrations.*

*After all, there is a reason that Canada, despite its small population, became a member of the G7 in 1976 with the support of the American president Gerald Ford. Canada's participation in the G7, and the valuable role it has played over the years, led Finance Minister Paul Martin to propose in 1999 the creation of a G20 bringing together finance ministers from the north and south countries, on five continents. The goals pursued by the G20 are to support international financial stability, maintain dialogue between leaders of the world's major economies to prevent financial crises. The G20 quickly proved its usefulness, so much so that in 2008 the heads of state and government gathered at the initiative of France and the United Kingdom to promote economic dialogue at the highest level. Canada chaired the summit in 2010 in Toronto.*

*Over the years, Canada has served as a go-between for the largest countries in those two groups, never claiming to have power it did not possess. Canada's legendary modesty protects it from any whiff of pretention or double dealing. All of the country's prime min-isters have kept their international actions within this blueprint for influence.*

*Canada's independence and its ability to take action in its own interest and show leadership, as it did in signing the Kyoto Protocol on climate change in 1997, when the United States refused to sign, or at the Montreal Climate Change Conference in 2005, plainly demonstrate that Canada takes its own positions and advocates for its own interests, despite American opposition. Canada's international personality emerged not only through making different decisions from those of the British or the Americans, which it has made for decades, but also through positive initiatives that it has taken to improve standards, international institutions, and support for peace. This was true of the Canadian initiative to create the Anti-Personnel Mine Ban Convention in 1997, which the United States refused to endorse, and the 1998 International Criminal Court (ICC) Statute, of which Canada was one of the prime movers, but which the United States rejected as a limit on its national sovereignty.[8] It was a Canadian, Philippe Kirsch, who was the first elected president of the ICC. The United States' recent withdrawal from the Paris Agreement on climate change (COP21) is another illustration of this principle: this decision had the effect of reaffirming the independence of Canada in the promotion on the international stage of a more dynamic environmental policy. The recent conclusion of the Comprehensive Economic and Trade Agreement (CETA) between Canada and the European Union (EU), which came into force on 21 September 2017, is another example of a distinct initiative. The United States is still in the early stages of negotiations with the EU, which the current American govern-ment views with real suspicion, and a great many obstacles will need to be overcome before such an agreement can be signed. The American trade dispute with Germany is virtually insurmountable. Likewise, the United Kingdom is mired in the Brexit negoti-ations, which are almost entirely contrary to the free trade positions that Canada has promoted, leading Canada's minister of Foreign Affairs, Chrystia Freeland, to say last June about the Americans (and this applies equally to the British) that they are "shrug-ging off the burden of world leadership."[9]*

*Canadian, American, and British interests very often converge, but they are not identical. Granted, the three countries uphold the principles of a free-market econ-omy, recognition of human rights, the rule of law, and democracy, but the content of each of these principles and the interpretation of the circumstances that condi-tion their meaning as events unfold vary from one to the next – often substantially. Experience has shown over and over again that Canadian actions, if they are not defined in opposition to those of the United States, are often taken in a different manner. They often represent an expanded and dynamic view of human rights and a stricter definition of democratic rules, certainly less influenced by the power of money that weighs heavily on the United States.*

*Over the years, Canada has developed self-confidence; it has established the foundation of its independence, and it is recognized for promoting a humanist conception of the roles and responsibilities of the state in the dialogue between sovereign nations. Of course, its reputation is not beyond reproach: the historical condition of Indigenous peoples seriously tarnishes that reputation, but Canada's endorsement without reserve of the* United Nations Declaration on the Rights of Indigenous Peoples *in May 2016 put it on the path to correcting that wrong.*

*Canada's relations with France have clearly evolved since 24 July 1967, when they teetered on collapse. For years, France's deliberately ambiguous position on the Quebec sovereignty debate kept relations civil but not without tensions. The passage of time, two failed referenda, and diplomacy finally improved the tone of the relationship. It must also be admitted that the political paradigms surrounding the national question have changed significantly since 1967 and that the Parti Québécois's decision to postpone the referendum debate has changed the outlook dramatically.*

*The former president of the French Republic, François Hollande, described what is hoped of Canada as a free country in the most eloquent terms on 9 April 2017, at Vimy Ridge (Somme), no less: "Yes, the soldiers of Vimy tell us that nationalism leads only to war and fundamentalism to destruction. They tell us that the future of our countries is to be united, to stand together in fraternity in the resolute fight for freedom. They tell us that history is not about celebrating the past, but about preparing for the future. That is the lesson of Vimy."*[10]

*Fifty years after General de Gaulle made his famous declaration from the balcony of Montreal's city hall, and after the strain that long marked France-Canada-Quebec relations, the president of France recemented the bond of friendship between France and Canada "to advance the cause of humanity," the very goal of much of Canada's international policy. President Sarkozy had already taken the first steps toward this reconciliation in the common defence of freedom at the cemetery in Bény-sur-Mer in Normandy in 2008 when, with his characteristic aplomb, he stated, "And those who died here were never asked where [in Canada] they came from. People knew what country they came from. They were not even asked what language they spoke. Those who lie buried here saved us and helped us, even though they didn't speak our language."*[11]

*France – twice occupied and twice liberated – and Canada cannot forget the one hundred and eleven thousand Canadians who gave their lives for her, forty-seven thousand of whom lie beneath French soil.*[12] *The sacrifice of all those lives for her freedom remains the foundation of an unbreakable bond. Canadians were on the ground*

"A CEUX QUI L'ONT SECOURUE — LA FRANCE ENVAHIE — 1914–1918"
[TO THOSE WHO CAME TO HER AID — FRANCE INVADED — 1914–1918]

Medal, Bronze, 1919. Victor Prouvé (1858–1943). This medal, designed by French painter and sculptor Victor Prouvé, was struck to thank the individuals and organizations that came to the aid of France when it was invaded in World War I. The medal depicts an old man sitting prostrate above the destruction and a mother protecting her child; they are being assisted by a tall woman with a starry cloak, symbolizing the spirit of compassion and humanity of countries such as Canada, which sent soldiers to fight in France from the outset of that war, and then again between 1940 and 1945. Credit: CHSJ

*in France in December 1914, after France was invaded by the enemy; years later, on 12 June 1940, Canadians arrived in France a few days before the country surrendered to the Nazis, and they remained there, steadfast, despite a national debate that twice pitted Quebec against the rest of the country. Yet thousands of soldiers from Quebec fought on the front lines each time as members of the Royal 22ᵉ Régiment, which was founded on 15 October 1914 as a regiment for francophone soldiers.*

*This humanism in the defence of freedom and French sovereignty would cement this now-harmonious relationship. Canada's influence at COP21 in December 2015 broadens the scope of Franco-Canadian alignment.*

*The question deserves to be stated clearly: Do the geopolitical interests pursued by Canada and France internationally convey enough points of convergence to make them reliable and stable partners, equally respectful of their sovereignty during the time of President Trump?*

*This is how the strength and authenticity of the relationship between France and Canada are to be measured. Canada's international credibility and capacity are certainly important assets that France can rely on and does call on when necessary. The situation in Mali since 2012 and Canada's immediate support for France are a recent example. The relationship took on another dimension in this regard because it became complementary, especially since the current president of the United States sees Europe as an enemy ("foe"), the decision of Great Britain to leave the EU, and the election in Italy of a government that turns its back to Europe. The visit of French president Emmanuel Macron to Ottawa, 6 and 7 June 2018, was an opportunity to confirm the commitment of the two countries to jointly stand for the need of a shared policy that favours multilateralism, support for international institutions that promote free trade (WTO) and contribute to stability and peace through the respect of the rule of law (NATO). Canada and France have, in fact, decided to hold joint ministerial meetings every two years to monitor their shared political objectives.*

*One of the bases of Canadian policy and one of the country's defining personality traits is the value it places on the recognition of human rights and the resulting initiatives to recognize new, emerging rights. But Canada does not always make available the necessary budgets to support needed interventions.[13]*

*Canada supports international institutions whose mandate is to enforce rights and freedoms, impose sanctions, and support private organizations working to denounce human rights abuses and whose initiatives put an end to human rights violations or bring about reparations.*

*To that end, Canada remains committed in all the international organizations of which it is a member. It has held a seat on the UN Security Council four times, and with its seniority among the fifty-two Commonwealth nations, it has been able to provide effective leadership, particularly in decolonization efforts and initiatives to promote democracy.[14] At the various bodies of the Organisation Internationale de la Francophonie (OIF – of which the Right Honourable Michaëlle Jean was elected secretary general in 2014),[15] Canada was one of the first members at the 1986 summit of the francophone countries, and it was particularly active in the summit in Mali in 2000, where it supported the Bamako Declaration to promote democracy and human rights and freedoms among the fifty-eight member states and twenty-six observers of OIF and establish related sanctions.[16] Canada was one of the key founders of the Organization*

**THE FALL OF THE BERLIN WALL**

The fall of the Berlin Wall on 9 November 1989 is one of the pivotal events of the past fifty years of world history. It signalled the end of Communism, which had appeared in 1917 and had led to millions of deaths in the name of a totalitarian ideology. It also marked the end of the Cold War, which was still going on in the sixties and seventies and had prompted Canada to take what are now considered discriminatory measures against its own people, out of fear of a nuclear attack. The 1962 Cuban missile crisis, which posed a threat to North America, was still fresh in people's memories. Credit: AP Photo/File

*for Security and Co-operation in Europe in 1973 and took an active role in standing up for human rights in Eastern bloc countries until the fall of the Berlin Wall in 1989. Lastly, as a member of the Organization of American States (OEA) since 1990, Canada has promoted the goals of democracy to Western nations.*

*In each of these forums and at several other levels where it is engaged multilaterally, Canada strives to spark debate on protecting and expanding human rights and respecting the rule of law through resolutions, action programs, themed conferences, and a wide variety of initiatives. Canada and Chile currently co-chair the Equal Rights Coalition, a new international organization with over thirty member countries founded in July 2016 to protect and promote the basic rights of sexual minorities around the world.[17] Canadians see their country as having a "universal ethical responsibility" and expect it to stand up abroad for the values of freedom they benefit from at home.*

*In 2000, with the goal of protecting human safety, without regard for national interests, Canada took the initiative of creating the International Commission on Intervention and State Sovereignty (ICISS) in response to a call from Kofi Annan, then secretary-general of the UN, and released the report entitled* The Responsibility to Protect *(R2P), in December 2001. The R2P principle applies in countries where people are victims of government abuses, natural disasters, or pandemics. This essentially humanitarian approach raises a number of questions: What is the scope and what are the limitations of this commitment in today's world, where numerous regional conflicts affecting disadvantaged populations are breaking out? What should Canada and its allies do today to make this humanitarian goal a reality? Should it be more clearly defined and narrowly targeted? Ultimately, how is it possible to balance the need for limited military intervention with the necessary humanitarian assistance? What sort of responsibility for supervision should UN agencies have? Is this principle, which was initially quite broad, not being eroded today, with pressure from the Americans to increase NATO military budgets for arms and defence equipment, which would benefit the United States, the world's largest arms dealer?*

*The US president denounced the NATO countries, among them Canada, which do not devote 2 per cent of their GDP to their defence budget as agreed in 2014. Prime Minister Trudeau went at length to explain that while Canada will spend only 1.23 per cent in its 2018 budget, Canada's overall expenses for peacekeeping missions and NATO-mandated interventions are more than the intended target.[18]*

*Canada also seeks to promote the appointment of Canadians to various international tribunals, commissions, and councils in order to enhance Canada's credibility and support and defend these bodies. Canada's commitment to protect human rights gains momentum when Canadians are appointed as judges on international bodies, commissioners, special envoys, arbitrators, observers, or heads of mission to resolve a conflict that threatens human rights. Louise Arbour, Louise Fréchette, Robert Fowler, and Roméo A. Dallaire are all fine examples. Lieutenant-General Roméo A. Dallaire remains a model of this type of individual: initially sent to head a mission to buy time in Rwanda in 1993, with no real ability to do anything to put an end to the massacre that was underway, he returned a broken man and took up the cause of child soldiers, for whom he became a respected international advocate.[19] Through the years, Lieutenant-General Dallaire, Louise Arbour, and others have embodied Canada's altruism and humanitarian values. Earlier, it was Father Georges-Henri Lévesque, who founded the National University of Rwanda in 1963 and served as its rector until*

*1971. The education-focused Fondation Paul Gérin-Lajoie, which served more than 270 schools in 2000 in Senegal, Mali, Niger, Benin, and Burkina Faso, and Cardinal Paul-Émile Léger, who worked with lepers in Africa from 1967 to 1973, added to the long line of Canadian missionaries who served throughout the continent and in Asia from the late nineteenth century onward. The humanitarian work of Dr Lucille Teasdale-Corti, who for nearly thirty-five years treated thousands of Ugandans free of charge, also left an important mark. All these figures convey a certain image of Canada, reinforcing its reputation as a country that cares about alleviating the suffering of disadvantaged people and improving their health and living conditions. These figures are the most credible Canadian ambassadors for the country's ideals, and Canadians spontaneously recognize themselves in that kind of humanitarian engagement.*

*Among the world's most influential countries when it comes to soft power, which is defined as the ability to wield international influence without military means, Canada ranks fifth, after France, which holds the top spot, the United Kingdom, the United States (which fell to third place), and Germany.[20] The annual study on soft power by the University of Southern California Center on Public Diplomacy and Portland Communications clearly illustrates the success of Canadian diplomacy in defending the values with which the country is identified internationally and also the very real responsibilities that result for Canada. However, this real success also comes with the obligation to remain true to oneself as one enters the big leagues. That is what underpins Canada's international credibility.*

*This image that Canada projects reflects on Canadians, who identify with these values. They also have a significant impact abroad. Canadians realize this when they travel to other countries with the maple leaf flag on their luggage. Canada's 2017 initiative to secretly evacuate gay Chechens suffering government persecution from Russia to Canada is a strong humanitarian gesture and compelling proof of its convictions,[21] shared by a large segment of the Canadian population.*

*Canada's initiatives to protect human dignity and its actions to demonstrate the wealth of its cultural achievements work in synergy. There is no better window on the humanistic society that Canada claims to be than its culture, which finds expression in a stunning variety of films, concerts, performances, and exhibits of art in all media that are second to none in their originality. Canada certainly benefits from facilitating cultural exports. Not only do the creators themselves derive an immediate benefit, but Canada gains by being identified in the world's finest venues as a society that values the potential and the creative resources of human expression.*

*The incalculable benefits of such recognition far outweigh the money Canada invests to facilitate artistic expression abroad. Canada's initiatives to protect human dignity and its actions to demonstrate the wealth of creative diversity work in symbiosis. A reasonable level of ongoing funding should be allocated to these efforts. It is fitting that the Trudeau government has recently reinstated financial support for international cultural initiatives.[22]*

*The second major feature of Canada's international identity is co-operation and development assistance. Created in 1950 with a modest budget of $11 million, the External Aid Office rapidly proved that there was a need for such assistance; by 1967, its budget increased to $279 million. Following the Chevrier mission report, the Office formally became the Canadian International Development Agency (CIDA) in 1968.[23] It was made part of a departmental portfolio, which gave CIDA the visibility and prominence required to embed within government the values of altruism, development assistance, and aid to people in developing countries.*

PRIME MINISTER STEPHEN HARPER (2006–15) VISITS A TEMPORARY HOSPITAL IN JACMEL, HAITI, AFTER THE EARTHQUAKE ON 12 JANUARY 2010 THAT KILLED TWO HUNDRED THOUSAND PEOPLE Aware of the extent of the humanitarian catastrophe in Haiti following the January 2010 earthquake, Prime Minister Harper immediately sent in the Canadian Forces and travelled to the country himself so that Canada's aid would spur other humanitarian initiatives. Since 1968, CIDA has deployed many resources to assist populations faced with the natural catastrophes, civil wars, and pandemics that strike poor countries. These aid programs have become more targeted over the years, causing the agency to redefine its humanitarian priorities. Credit: The Canadian Press/Fred Chartrand

*The fact that Canada does not have a colonial past certainly helped create an image of generosity and altruism that gave its assistance and co-operation initiatives an immediate credibility and set Canada apart from former colonial powers, especially in Africa. Canada's forgiveness of $740 million in debt built up by a number of African countries in 1987 remains a compelling example of the genuineness of its commitment.[24]*

*This image of a country that comes to the aid of the disadvantaged and those whom fate has dealt with cruelly is coupled with a deep sense of humanism among Canadians, which helps them feel good about themselves, despite having one of the highest standards of living in the world. But there is a gap between the perception entertained by public opinion and the reality that analysts have well described.[25]*

*Nevertheless, funding for CIDA has never reached 0.7 per cent of GDP, the target level that a UN panel of experts led by former prime minister Lester B. Pearson set in 1969. In fact, CIDA's budget has never exceeded 0.53 per cent, the level it reached in 1975–76, and at times it has dropped to a mere 0.3 per cent.[26] In the 2016 federal budget, CIDA accounted for 1.7 per cent of federal spending, compared with 2 per cent the previous year. CIDA's funding was reduced in spite of high public praise for its actions. The Canadian Council for International Co-operation and many other organizations in the field have consistently called on the government to come up with a stable plan to increase CIDA's budget to the international target set by the UN.[27]*

*Canadians are generous and will join together to raise money when a humanitarian disaster occurs abroad. In 2017, more than $21 million was raised in just three and a half months to help fifty agencies fighting famine in Africa, and the government matched that amount.[28] In 1956, when Soviet tanks invaded Hungary, Canada welcomed 37,000 refugees, an unprecedented number. In 1985, after the Vietnamese boat people crisis of the mid-seventies, Canada took in more than 110,000 refugees. Others would not be so lucky, however. In the summer of 1999, four ships smuggling Chinese nationals dropped 596 boat people who had survived a horrific crossing on the shores of Vancouver Island. All of them were arrested by the RCMP. Public opinion in Canada was divided as to whether they should be allowed to stay, and the government felt it had to send a message. One hundred people were returned to China in May 2000.*

*According to the UN, Canada was among the top ten destinations for refugees in 2011, receiving more than 25,000 asylum claims annually. Canadians showed spontaneous generosity on 29 January 2017, when with open arms they welcomed 40,081 refugees fleeing Syria, which was being ravaged by the civil war under Bashar al-Assad and the Islamic State. Prime Minister Trudeau himself clearly illustrated the sentiment when he twice tweeted "To those fleeing persecution, terror & war, Canadians will welcome you, regardless of your faith," followed by the hashtag "#WelcomeToCanada." Six months later,*

*Canada was opening its doors more guardedly to the thousand Haitians, Salvadorans, and other migrants whom the Trump government is threatening to deport in 2018,[29] and enter Canada without visa. Public opinion is becoming distant and rather skeptical because of the significant resources required by the government to deal with the influx.[30]*

*Over the years, CIDA financial aid was tied to various conditions, such as giving precedence to Canadian suppliers; helping to develop local technologies; focusing aid in areas of priority for Canada's trade or geopolitical relations; supporting populations already heavily represented in the country; and aligning assistance goals with the positions or values of the government of the day. For example, in 2015, aid excluded family planning and supported breastfeeding, and in June 2017, the international development minister announced support for "feminist" objectives and initiatives that promote female empowerment and the work women do.[31] The image Canada wants to convey seems to prevail over the altruistic assistance impoverished people need. Of course, other countries to the same thing, but could Canada raise the bar without being candid?*

*This development assistance policy – which Canada has emphasized – remains an almost indispensable complement to the country's major international policy objectives. To some degree, it has become inseparable from the humanitarian image Canada enjoys abroad. It is worth noting that, for the past fifteen years, Canada's interest in Africa and the fifty-four African countries has focused more on trade relations and less on development priorities. This is not a wise course of action. In 2040–50, one person in four on the planet will be African. Canada is not leveraging all the credibility it built up in the seventies and eighties that led it to have the ear of most of those countries. In a sense, it has squandered that credit and must now rebuild it.[32]*

*In the public's mind, these initiatives are inseparable from the missions of Canadian peacekeepers and the role they played in bloody conflicts that have remained etched in memory since the Suez crisis in 1956 and Lester B. Pearson's suggestion that the UN dispatch a task force to separate the combatants and maintain a ceasefire zone.[33] This memory has remained vivid. Lester B. Pearson was awarded the Nobel Peace Prize in 1957, and Canadian peacekeeping missions were looked on almost as a national duty. The peacekeeping monument, which was designed by Jack K. Harman and built in Ottawa in 1992 at the corner of Sussex Drive and Murray Street on the initiative of the Department of National Defence and the National Capital Commission, honours these international peacekeepers. This monument, the only one of its kind in the world, stands as a permanent tribute to these individuals: in a way, it celebrates national heroes just as other war memorials do.*

*Since 1960, Canada has taken part in more than thirty-four UN peacekeeping and observation missions: in Africa, in Angola, Mozambique, the Western Sahara, Ethiopia,*

PEACEKEEPING MONUMENT, OTTAWA

A busy street corner in Ottawa (the intersection of Sussex Drive and Murray Street) was an inspired choice for the location of a monument to Canadians who have given their lives and have served or are still serving on peacekeeping missions around the world. The only monument in the world dedicated to these nameless heroes, the work by sculptor Jack K. Harman is inscribed with the words "Reconciliation" and "In the Service of Peace" on its base. Peacekeepers, who enjoy widespread public support, have embodied Canadians' concept of one of the international roles of their country since Lester B. Pearson made such a proposal to the United Nations in 1956. Credit: Aram Adjemian, photographer *and Sudan; in South America, in Haiti and Guatemala; in Asia, in Cambodia and East Timor; and in Europe, in the former Yugoslavia and Bosnia-Herzegovina. There is a long list of conflicts in which the Canadian Forces have served in parts of the world that Canadians previously knew little about. Not all of these missions were unalloyed successes. The Somalia mission, the abuses, and the subsequent inquiries were seen almost as a national shame and a dark stain on Canada's reputation.*

*Canada subsequently pulled out of peacekeeping missions. As of June 2016, its contribution to peacekeeping put it in sixty-seventh place, with 103 personnel among the 101,280 international soldiers who were serving on missions; 80 per cent of these Canadians were police officers deployed in Haiti, meaning that there were only about twenty soldiers. Pressed by its allies and the UN to recommit to peacekeeping missions, Canada dragged its feet. The federal government called for missions that would reduce violence against women and the use of child soldiers.[34]*

*Canada had hinted in 2016 that it would devote a budget up to $450 million, as well as a contingent of 600 soldiers and 150 police officers, to these missions.[35] Ultimately, though, Canada's contribution would be limited to 200 soldiers, a few aircraft and $21 million to increase the number of women in the peacekeeping force.[36]*

*Certainly, the conditions in which these conflicts take place today are vastly different from the conditions on the ground during past peacekeeping missions: there is a much greater risk of loss of human life now, and terrorism is a constant threat.*

*But if Canada sees itself as an independent middle power that can play a useful role in peacekeeping and as a response force, then it must also take on responsibilities that come with real risks and that it cannot always put off, or else it will damage its credibility and erode the trust of the international community.*

*Canada's unwavering support for a number of values through various crises and confrontations has gradually earned it the attention and the trust of the vast majority of the world's nations.*

*This is vital to the credibility of Canada's international actions and also to the economic interests it pursues in negotiating trade deals and free trade agreements, which it still seeks to conclude to support its economy. Since the eighties, Canada has signed no fewer than fifty-eight free trade agreements, and another twenty-four are under negotiation. Canada actively supported the proposed Trans-Pacific Partnership, which is designed to integrate the Asia-Pacific and North and South American economies. Although Donald Trump pulled the United States out of the agreement early in 2017, Canada signed the* Comprehensive and Progressive Agreement for Trans-Pacific Partnership *on 8 March 2018. Too many countries have an interest in this agreement for one lone nation, powerful though it may be, to block it.[37]*

*The question remains: How is it possible to reconcile the promotion of rights and freedoms with the country's economic interests while entering into free trade agreements with powers such as China, which is quite capable of being independent, given the size of its market, and is of huge geopolitical importance to Canada?[38] China remains extremely protectionist. Now an economic powerhouse, it is transitioning from a manufacturing economy to an innovation-driven economy. It is investing in research and development and buying Western industrial firms so that it can improve its products directly. Some see this as a form of "pillage investment." Canada has no choice but to set clear limits on investments and keep for itself the control of its strategic natural resources.[39]*

*Moreover, how should Canada, the second-largest exporter of arms to the Middle East,[40] set effective limits to ensure that civilians are genuinely protected in contracts to sell arms to countries that do not recognize the obligation to respect rights and freedoms, as seen in 2014 with the sale of $15 billion worth of armoured vehicles to Saudi Arabia?[41] The legality of the permit issued by the minister responsible to authorize the export of these vehicles is currently being challenged in court.[42] After photographs surfaced showing the vehicles being used against civilians in Yemen and an inquiry by the department, the export permit was temporarily suspended,[43] later re-established. Leave to appeal is now pending before the Supreme Court.[44] In January 2018, Germany announced that it was suspending all arms exports to the countries involved in the conflict in Yemen.*

*Following public Canada's criticisms of Saudi Arabia in August 2018 for the imprisonment of human rights activists, the Kingdom immediately expelled the Canadian ambassador, suspended all economic and financial relations and called back from Canada seven thousand Saudi students and their families. Saudi Arabia denounced the "blatant and unacceptable interference" in the internal affairs of the Kingdom. Will Canada have the "courage to maintain its position and pay the price for standing up to its principles?"[45] as did Sweden in 2015, accepting the financial costs of cancelled defence contract,[46] or will Canada bend shamefully "to pick up the money"? The prime minister responded: "Canadians have always expected our government to speak strongly, firmly, clearly and politely about the need to respect human rights at home and around the world. We will continue to do that, we will continue to stand up for Canadian values and indeed for universal values and human rights at any occasion."[47] The time may have come for Canada to pay the price for holding to its principles[48] even though Saudi Arabia purchased half the arms exported by Canada and is one of its best trading partners.[49]*

*The government should certainly ensure that its legislation complies with the UN* Arms Trade Treaty *and contains effective controls for countries with disastrous human*

11 SEPTEMBER 2001, NEW YORK

When the twin towers of the World Trade Center collapsed on 11 September 2001, the world was turned upside down early in the twenty-first century. The fight against terrorism became governments' top priority, and security concerns now dominate the news, creating a permanent climate of instability. Large countries that preached the benefits of the global free market are now retreating behind their borders, and foreigners are once again looked on with suspicion. The religious divide has reappeared. These dramatic changes had lasting impacts on movements of capital, investment decisions, and protectionist policies. Credit: Wikimedia Commons, Robert J. Fisch

*rights records.[50] Bill C47, which gives effect to this treaty, does not include any specific assessment criteria and allows too much ministerial discretion to be effective.[51] In addition, it does not cover arms exports to the United States.[52]*

*Canada has no control over Canadian firm Streit Group's sale of 173 armoured vehicles to Libya and South Sudan, which is engaged in a genocidal civil war, when the supplier is operating out of the United Arab Emirates. The situation in Nigeria is similar: two Canadian suppliers are exporting parts and armoured vehicles that will*

MIKHAIL S. GORBACHEV (1931–   )

Oil on canvas, artist unidentified, circa 1989. One of the most significant figures of the second half of the twentieth century and the last leader of the Soviet Union, Mikhail Gorbachev put an end to the Communist regime and its empire, comprising the Eastern bloc countries, and to its influence in the world. Today admired in the West and ostracized in Russia, Gorbachev sought to reform a corrupt and dysfunctional regime, but was swept away by reactionary forces that he had not seen coming. Now Russia is once again under an authoritarian government. Credit: Paul Maréchal Collection

*be used by a repressive government that the previous US administration had excluded from arms export permits.[53] Although perfectly legal, the export is ethically indefensible:[54] Canadians know this and are overwhelmingly opposed to it.[55]*

*Recently, courts in British Columbia and Ontario have heard lawsuits seeking damages for human rights abuses from Canadian mining companies operating in South*

*America.[56] Because Canada has a "duty of humanity," it should recognize the extension of the rule of law beyond its borders, as the United Kingdom, the Netherlands, and France have done in their laws, requiring companies to map hazards and conduct regular assessments. The UN Human Rights Council has issued guidelines, but Canada is lagging behind in implementing them at home.[57]*

*In January 2018, the government announced that it had created an ombudsperson to receive complaints of human rights violations by Canadian companies operating abroad, conduct investigations, and recommend sanctions. This is a positive step toward creating a legal framework that better reflects the reality of international business, particularly in countries with weak human rights protections.[58]*

*Can the government plead ignorance and complacently look away? According to L'actualité, Canada has sold $850 million worth of arms to repressive regimes. Simply put, we need to ask ourselves these questions: What price or monetary value does Canada put on defending its values and its principles based on the rule of law in international business transactions or foreign transactions by Canadian nationals? Should geopolitical or commercial considerations be more important than respecting and promoting rights and freedoms? The time has come for Canada to walk the talk, or else it could see its credibility and its international commitment to defend human rights eroded.*

*At a time when populism is growing in Western societies, when fundamentalism is becoming deeply rooted and culture wars are breaking out, and when countries – even its most traditional partners – are increasingly turning inward, Canada needs to use the various tools of its international policy to uphold the values of political, financial, social, and economic stability and promote its openness as conditions for peace in the world, emphasizing respect for the ethnic and cultural diversity of its people, in order to combat these detrimental and toxic trends, which are increasingly visible and strong. As Professor Er Che of Beijing University wrote: "If the United States do not have a coherent (international) policy, small countries will follow and it will be disorder"[59] [our translation].*

*The nuclear threat is ever-present. The current US administration's attitude toward the New START treaty, which expires in 2021, is creating harmful tension that is threatening the planet's peaceful future. The International Campaign to Abolish Nuclear Weapons aims to keep the public aware of this issue, which every country must face. No one would be safe if a nuclear war broke out.[60]*

*Over fifty years, Canada has gained an enviable international reputation and established its credibility in the eyes of the world. Now it must take on the resulting responsibility for world affairs at a time when American leadership seems more and more problematic. Is Canada willing to play its part with its trusted partners and stay true to its convictions? Will it undertake its share of global leadership in promoting peace, nuclear disarmament, the respect of the rule of law, security, and human dignity?*[61]

## NOTES

1 The author is indebted to the Library of Parliament for its careful work in verifying the accuracy of the historical facts and figures in the text.

2 Note that the John Diefenbaker government had serious misgivings about the United States and President Kennedy's actions during the Cuban Missile Crisis of 1962 (source: Diefenbaker Canada Centre).

3 On 29 March 1973, American troops withdrew from Vietnam (Paris Peace Accords).

4 DEW: Distant Early Warning.

5 The government of Stephen Harper refused to reopen this debate, even though he supported the initiative while the Conservatives were in opposition. Hugo De Grandpré, "La politique américaine est de ne pas défendre le Canada," *La Presse+*, 15 September 2017.

6 David Pugliese, "PM commits up to 250 troops to train Iraqis – Canadian officer to head NATO initiative," *National Post*, 12 July 2018, A7.

7 The first (limited) economic sanctions were imposed in 1977 by Canada and were followed by further sanctions in 1986. Canada tried to convince the other members of the Commonwealth to follow its lead. The British, under Margaret Thatcher, were opposed, calling Brian Mulroney's policy counterproductive.

8 *Convention on the Prohibition of the Use, Stockpiling, Production and Transfer of Anti-Personnel Mines and on Their Destruction.*

9 "Shrugging off the burden of world leadership," speech by the Minister of Foreign Affairs, House of Commons, 6 June 2017.

10 Speech by President François Hollande at the centennial ceremony for the Battle of Vimy Ridge, 9 April 2017, at https://www.youtube.com/watch?v=2pQgvb-RJa4, consulted 31 January 2018.

11 Jacques Palard, "Les relations France-Canada-Québec depuis 1960 : intérêts complémentaires et défis contemporains," in Serge Joyal and Paul André Linteau (eds.), *France-Canada-Québec – 400 ans de relations d'exceptions* (Montreal: Les Presses de l'Université de Montréal, 2008), 251.

12 According to the Commonwealth War Graves Commission.

13 "On 20th anniversary of International Criminal Court treaty, Canada is missing in action," *Hill Times*, editorial, 25 July 2018.

14 1967–68; 1977–78; 1989–90, and 1999–2000. Canada campaigned for a seat in 2010 and then withdrew its bid in the face of certain defeat. It plans to make another bid in 2020.

15 The Right Honourable Michaëlle Jean, p.c., c.c., c.m.m., c.o.m., c.d.

16 Canada was previously a member of the Agence de coopération culturelle et technique, founded in 1970, which preceded the OIF.

17 Lesbian, gay, bisexual, transgender, and intersex people.

18 Marie Vastel, "OTAN en emporte le président – Donald Trump multiplie les remontrances aux alliés à quelques jours de sa rencontre avec Vladimir Poutine," *Le Devoir*, 12 July 2018, A1; Manon Cornellier, "Sommet de l'OTAN : semonce américaine," *Le Devoir*, 5 July 2018, A6.

19 Roméo Dallaire, *Shake Hands With the Devil – The Failure of Humanity in Rwanda* (Montreal: Libre Expression, 2003). He arrived in Rwanda "supported by only one Canadian officer, Major Brent Beardsley, and 81 unarmed military observers."

20 Agence France-Presse, "La France en tête du classement *soft power*," *Le Devoir*, 19 July 2017, B5.

21 John Ibbitson, "A Clandestine Chechen Exodus," *The Globe and Mail*, 2 September 2017, A10.

22 Pierre Saint-Arnaud, "Financement – Ottawa tend la main aux créateurs canadiens – Quelques 25 millions par an seront injectés pour soutenir l'exportation de la créativité," *Le Devoir*, Culture, 27 June 2018, B8

23 Report of the Canadian Mission to French-speaking Africa, Hon. Lionel Chevrier, p.c., Head, 1968.

24 The *Forgiveness of Certain Official Development Assistance Debts Act* applied to Togo, the Islamic Republic of Mauritania, and the countries in the former East African Community (Tanzania, Uganda, and Kenya).

25 Shachi Kurl, "Time to stop boasting about our global role," *Ottawa Citizen*, 14 July 2018, A12; John Ivison, "Time for liberal boost to prove out – Can Canada become 'essential'?," *National Post*, 12 July 2018, A1; Gérard Bouchard, "La grande illusion canadienne," *La Presse+*, Débats5.

26 Canadian International Development Agency report, consulted online by the Library of Parliament of Canada in October 2017.

27 Julia Sanchez, "Canada must not lecture, but show progressive global leadership on human rights and inclusive societies," *The Hill Times*, 2 February 2017.

28 Lisa-Marie Gervais, "Les Canadiens ont donné 21 millions pour soulager la faim en Afrique," *Le Devoir*, 17 August 2017, A3.

29 Lisa-Marie Gervais, "Les frontières de la compassion – un Québécois sur deux veut qu'on refoule les réfugiés, tandis qu'Ottawa tente de mieux faire comprendre les règles du jeu," *Le Devoir*, 15 August 2017, A1; Amanda Connolly, "Majority (57 per cent) disagree

with Trudeau's handling of illegal border crossings: Angus Reid," *IPolitics*, 1 September 2017; Michelle Zilio, "Country split on asylum seekers: poll," *The Globe and Mail*, 15 September 2017, A14.

30  Bruce Campion-Smith, "Trouble looming over refugee issue", *Toronto Star*, 4 August 2018, A8; Béatrice Paez, "Border-crossings debate could be liberal vulnerability if Tories can swoop in: pollsters," *Hill Times*, 27 August 2018.

31  Michelle Zilio, "Ottawa unveils 'feminist' foreign aid policy," *The Globe and Mail*, 10 June 2017, A12.

32  Jean-Louis Roy, "Le Canada, le G7 et l'Afrique, l'occasion de resserrer un lien distendu," *Le Devoir*, 15 September 2017, A9.

33  United Nations Peacekeeping Force.

34  Mélanie Marquis, "Ottawa veut accroître le rôle des femmes chez les Casques bleus," *Le Devoir*, 2 November 2017, A4.

35  Tonda McCharles, "Canada still hasn't decided on peace mission," *Toronto Star*, 13 September 2017, A2.

36  Lee Berthiaume, "Casques bleus : le Canada offre à l'ONU 200 militaires et des aéronefs," *La Presse canadienne*, 15 November 2017.

37  John Ivison, "Pacific trade deal may still get done," *National Post*, 21 September 2017, NP4.

38  Janet McFarland, "Gender equality is a trade priority: PM," *The Globe and Mail*, 12 September 2017, A4.

39  JeanMichel Bezat, "Moissons de promesse pour les Français en Chine," *Le Monde*, Economics and Business section, 11 January 2018, 3.

40  *Report on Exports of Military Goods from Canada, 2012–2013*. Sales of military goods to ninety-eight countries totalled $1.72 billion for those two years. Saudi Arabia and the United Arab Emirates accounted for half of these purchases. According to a 2016 report, Saudi Arabia imported approximately $142.2 million worth of Canadian military goods, which amounts to 19.81 per cent of the total value of Canadian exports of military goods, making Saudi Arabia the largest market after the United States. Tim Naumetz, "Canadian military efforts to Saudi Arabia exploded in 2016," *IPolitics*, 9 November 2017.

41  Tim Naumetz, "Canada rifle exports to Saudi Arabia spiked this year," *IPolitics*, 1 November 2017.

42  Hélène Buzzetti, "Vente de blindés : Daniel Turp remporte une première manche," *Le Devoir*, 11 January 2018, A2.

43  Hélène Buzzetti, "Ottawa a suspendu l'exportation de blindés vers Riyad," *Le Devoir*, 24 January 2018, A2.

44  Patriquin, Martin, "Saudi Arabia and Daniel Turp's heroic crusade – Despite setbacks, war against weapons rages on," *The Gazette*, 12 July 2018, A7.

45 Paul Journet, "Armez maintenant, dénoncez plus tard – le Canada et l'Arabie saoudite," *La Presse+*, Débats, 7 August 2018.

46 Taillefer, Guy, "Arabie saoudite: armes, mensonges et intimidation," *Le Devoir*, 7 August 2018, A6.

47 Bruce Campion-Smith, "Trudeau refuses to blink in scuffle with Saudi Arabia," *Toronto Star*, 9 August 2018, 91.

48 "Saudi Arabia's ugly spat with Canada," *The New York Times*, editorial, 8 August 2018, A22.

49 Samantha Wright Allen, "Arms exports top $1 billion, as Saudi sales spike," *Hill Times*, 27 June 2018.

50 Mike Blanchfield, "Liberals consider amending Arms Trade Treaty bill in face of criticism", *IPolitics*, 10 November 2017.

51 Bill C47, An Act to amend the Export and Import Permits Act and the Criminal Code (amendments permitting the accession to the Arms Trade Treaty and other amendments), 1st Session, 42nd Parliament.

52 Manon Cornellier, "Effort canadien insuffisant," *Le Devoir*, 2–3 December 2017, B8.

53 Geoffrey York, "Canadian firms part of Nigeria arms deals," *The Globe and Mail*, 14 September 2017, A4.

54 Geoffrey York, "Diplomat questioned Canadian company's arms sale to South Sudan," *The Globe and Mail*, 5 September 2017, A1.

55 Steven Chase, "Most Canadians oppose weapons sales to Saudi: poll," *The Globe and Mail*, 14 September 2017, A4.

56 Douglas Quan, "Mining firms accountable in Canadian court", *Ottawa Citizen*, 28 November 2017, NP3.

57 Sarah R. Champagne, "Le Canada peut faire mieux, disent deux autorités en matière de responsabilité des entreprises," *Le Devoir*, 10 October 2017, A9.

58 Bill Curry, "Ottawa takes aim at human rights for overseas firms," *The Globe and Mail*, 17 January 2018, B1.

59 Gaidz Minassiny, "Un monde de moins en moins occidental?," *Le Monde*, 15 May 2018, Débats et Analyse, 19.

60 Stéphane Baillargeon, "Regain de tension nucléaire," *Le Devoir*, 5 February 2018, 1.

61 Canada did not attend the vote on the proposed treaty banning nuclear weapons that was adopted on 9 July 2017 by the United Nations. The nine nuclear-armed countries voted against the proposal, as did some NATO members. However, 122 countries voted in favour of the treaty. The opponents called for phased disarmament.

# On the World Stage – Projecting Our Values and Advancing Peace

Paul Heinbecker, distinguished fellow at the Centre for International Governance Innovation, and former ambassador and permanent representative to the United Nations (2000–04)

*"[Canada's] multicultural character and bilingual tradition give it special qualifications as an exemplary UN member."* – Kofi Annan[1]

## PRELUDE AND INTRODUCTION

My career in diplomacy, spanning from 1967 to 2017, coincided with much of the time period covered by this book. In the early days, I was a hard-working young officer, raising a family and managing to stay just this side of dismissal. Over time I learned the trade and progressed to writing some of the last policy speeches of Prime Minister Pierre Trudeau and subsequently to writing three years of policy speeches for Prime Minister Brian Mulroney. I accompanied Prime Minister Mulroney to the G7 meetings at which presidents Mikael Gorbachev and Boris Yeltsin ended the Cold War. I attended bilateral meetings between Mulroney and Nelson Mandela of South Africa, George Bush of the United States, Helmut Kohl of Germany, John Major of the United Kingdom, François Mitterrand of France, Toshiki Kaifu of Japan, Robert Mugabe of Zimbabwe, Omar Bongo of Gabon, Bob Hawke of Australia, Carlos Salinas of Mexico, and many other leaders. During my career, I have lived in Turkey, Scandinavia, France, and the United States. I have served at the Organisation for Economic Co-operation and Development (OECD) in Paris and represented Canada as ambassador to Germany, and as Permanent Representative of Canada on the United Nations Security Council. I participated in the G8 talks that ended the Kosovo War. I was lead negotiator for Canada in the negotiations that produced the Kyoto Protocol on Climate Change, and I headed the delegation in the 2001 Durban Review Conference on human rights.

I cite all these experiences to demonstrate that I have had a pretty good seat in the years since 1967 to observe the passing world, and to add thereby to the credibility of my central judgment that Canada was and remains the country that most effectively makes diversity a strength, integrating new arrivals into our body politic. This diversity is integral to our international identity, as is our disposition toward constructive engagement in world affairs.

In the councils of diplomacy, my counterparts invariably gave me a respectful hearing because I was representing Canada, the country that, then, as now, was more welcoming of "others" than probably any other country on earth. Colleagues could see that pluralism actually works here, as the former foreign minister of Jordan Marwan Muasher remarked in the spring of 2017 at the opening of the Global Centre for Pluralism in Ottawa. They could see themselves in Canada's mosaic. In our own way, we reflect the world.

### THE PAST IS PROLOGUE

Canada's contemporary international identity as a diverse society open to "others" traces back to Canada's earliest days, when our First Nations welcomed French and subsequently British explorers and settlers into their midst. Eventually, competition in Europe between these and other European powers led to war, culminating in North America in the British victory on the Plains of Abraham. The Treaty of Paris of 1763 together with the Quebec Act of 1774 and the Constitutional Act of 1791 nevertheless endorsed the presence in what would become Canada of English-speaking and French-speaking peoples and protected their different languages, cultures, legal systems, and religious beliefs. Each found it necessary to live and comport with the other, albeit not always without friction. Waves of immigrants, first from Europe and then progressively from the four corners of the world, joined the Canadian experiment, creating the bilingual, multicultural mosaic that Canada is. Thus progressively emerged today's multi-ethnic country.

Formal, full independence from Britain was earned in Passchendaele and Vimy and the carnage of World War I, but diplomatic ambition lagged. In World War II, the occasional Mackenzie King photo-op with Churchill and Roosevelt notwithstanding, the Canadian government was largely content to leave the big decisions to its "betters," or at least to those with bigger battalions. The Canadian military effort was too outsized, however, to be disregarded after the war, and the national interest in the emerging new international liberal order was too compelling to be ignored.

## THE GRAY LECTURE'S ONGOING INFLUENCE
## ON CANADIAN FOREIGN POLICY

The Gray Lecture delivered by Prime Minister Louis St Laurent at the University of Toronto in 1947 marked the advent of a Canadian diplomacy ready and willing to participate in the management of global affairs. St Laurent enunciated five principles that have guided Canadian foreign policy from 1947 through the centennial in 1967 to the sesquicentennial celebrations in 2017 and, in all probability, will continue to do so far into an unforeseeable future. In June 2017, Foreign Minister Chrystia Freeland said on the CBC program *The House* that in drafting her own statement of foreign policy principles she took inspiration from the tenets of the Gray Lecture. Those tenets were the preservation of national unity ("a disunited Canada [would] be a powerless one"); political liberty ("stability is lacking where consent is absent"); the importance of the rule of law ("the freedom of nations depends upon the rule of law among states"); the centrality of human values ("the importance of the individual … the place of moral principles in the conduct of human relations, [and] standards … which transcend mere material well-being"); and the obligations inherent in international citizenship ("security for this country lies in the development of a firm structure of international organization").

It struck St Laurent as axiomatic that "we should give our support to every international organization which contributes to the economic and political stability of the world." In his memoirs, Prime Minister Lester B. Pearson commented favourably on the Gray Lecture, saying that "Canada could not escape the effects of international storms by burying [its] head in the sand" and that Canada "should play a part in trying to prevent the storms by accepting international commitments for that purpose."

This ambition to contribute to international order to protect Canada's interests was in stark contrast to Prime Minister William Lyon Mackenzie King's cautious instincts, which had managed Canadian policy for a generation. King considered the building of the UN structure, for example, to be none of Canada's business. Pearson for his part maintained that "to sit in a back seat at the UN, acquiescent or critical but in either case silent, was certainly not a policy." St Laurent's principles and Pearson's judgments guided Canadian foreign policy-making in what has come to be called Canada's Golden Age, and, with occasional exceptions, these principles and judgments have largely inspired Canadian foreign policy ever since, contributing strongly to the development of Canada's international, and indeed national, identity. To quote Pearson, "We had come of age. The voice of Canada was now being heard and it was listened to seriously and with respect during those years."

PRIME MINISTER PIERRE E. TRUDEAU (1968–79, 1980–84)

Campaign sign, 1979. Pierre E. Trudeau had a clear idea of the sort of independence he wanted Canada to demonstrate on the world stage. He wanted to distance himself from Great Britain, which had previously inspired Canada's foreign policy. He saw the Commonwealth as a forum to support decolonization in countries such as Zimbabwe, Rhodesia, and South Africa. Moreover, he could not express complete confidence in France, because of its ambiguous position on Canadian unity. Trudeau made a point of showing that the United States could not take Canada for granted in its initiatives elsewhere in the world. At the end of his mandate, he toured the world promoting peace. Credit: Canadian Museum of History (CHSJ), IMG2016-0220-0001-DM

The St Laurent principles lay at the heart of the efforts of Canada's first diplomatic Golden Age, in Canadian officials' contributions to the drafting of the UN Charter and the Universal Declaration of Human Rights, in the Refugee Convention of 1951, and in the core human rights treaties, as well as in the creation of the International Court of Justice. The national interest in seeing these principles realized motivated Canadian efforts in the creation of the International Monetary Fund (IMF) and the OECD; in the negotiations of the General Agreement on Tariffs and Trade and the World Trade Organization (WTO); and in participation in the Colombo Plan. The principles were a factor, as well, in Pearson's conception of peacekeeping and in the midwifery of Foreign Minister Paul Martin Sr in bringing former British and French colonies into the UN in 1955. Further, those principles influenced Canadian policy-making with respect to the creation of the North Atlantic Treaty Organization (NATO) and the North American Aerospace Defense Command (NORAD).

In the years following our centennial, the Gray Lecture principles were evident in the support of the Pierre Trudeau government of the Outer Space Treaty, the Nuclear Non-Proliferation Treaty, the Biological Weapons Convention, the Organization for Security and Co-operation in Europe, the Convention on the Law of the Sea, and the North South Summit on economic co-operation. Decisions by the Mulroney government respecting Canadian participation in the International Organisation of La Francophonie and the Organisation of American States were consistent with the St Laurent principles, as was Canadian support for the Convention on the Elimination of All Forms of Discrimination against Women, an international bill of rights for women, for the Convention on the Rights of the Child, which he co-chaired, for the Comprehensive Nuclear-Test-Ban Treaty, for the Montreal Protocol on Substances that Deplete the Ozone Layer, for the Rio Earth Summit, with its Framework Convention on Climate Change and Convention on Biological Diversity, and for the Canada–United States Free Trade Agreement and the North American Free Trade Agreement (NAFTA).

The Gray Lecture principles were also motivating factors in the development of the Foreign Minister Lloyd Axworthy's Human Security Agenda. His leadership brought about the Responsibility to Protect and the Protection of Civilians in Armed Conflict, two norms that have transformed UN approaches to peacekeeping by putting people at the heart of policy. It also produced the Ottawa Treaty on Anti-Personnel Landmines, thanks to which forty-nine million landmines have been destroyed and countless lives and limbs saved, as well as the creation of the International Criminal Court. They also motivated Canadian thinking respecting the creation of the G20, the funding and promotion of maternal and child health programs and rights in the developing world, and the reception of refugees.

## THE SIGNIFICANCE OF POLICY DECISIONS

Canada's contemporary international reputation is not just some happy happenstance but the consequence of sound public policy decisions down through our history. Canada's capacity to integrate others and to harness their talents has been no mere accident. We are not some kind of magical kingdom in this regard, as Europeans sometimes suggest as they cope raggedly with refugee influxes and the integration of foreigners, but something both more prosaic and more consequential.

US PRESIDENT RICHARD NIXON (1969–74) – "NIXON'S THE ONE!"
Plasticized button, 1969. President Nixon had no love for Canadian Prime Minister Pierre E. Trudeau, who was too independent of the Americans. He disapproved of the fact that Canada had maintained diplomatic relations with the Cuban government of Fidel Castro since Castro rose to power in 1959 and especially the fact that Canada had entered into diplomatic relations with Mao's China in 1969, before the United States. In the infamous secret Oval Office tapes, Nixon called Trudeau an "SOB." Credit: CHSJ

Canada embodies public policy choices that governments have made through the decades, most good, but some bad, too. On the negative side of the leger, in 1939 we denied landing to the 907 Jews aboard the *St Louis*, a transatlantic liner, who were seeking sanctuary from Nazi Germany, effectively condemning them to their fates and thereby indelibly staining our history. We discriminated against Japanese-origin Canadians and Chinese migrants, against southern Europeans, Ukrainians, and Caribbean blacks, and against Muslims. Our checkered struggle to right the wrongs of discrimination against the Indigenous population of Canada and tolerance of their third-world living standards cast an enormous shadow over our current self-image and international reputation. The Harper government's eloquent apology on behalf of Canadians for the Indian residential school system represents only one necessary step along a long, difficult road of redress. Prime Minister Mulroney had promised during his second term that all disputed land claims by First Nations would be resolved by the turn of the century. Despite considerable effort, few were.

Still, despite the difficulty of finding an effective and fair relationship with First Nations in Canada, Canadian governments have learned from some of our past mistakes and are continuing to learn from them, fitful though that process can be. As a consequence, we have also made *good* public policy decisions. In 1967, we promulgated regulations that enshrined the principle of non-discrimination in our immigration policy and mitigated the influence of latent cultural bias in the selection of immigrants. In 1969, we passed the Official Languages Act. In 1971, Canada became the first country in the world to adopt multiculturalism as an official policy, affirming the value and dignity of all Canadian citizens. In 1982, we entrenched the Charter of Rights and Freedoms into our constitution. More recently, we have recognized LGBTQ rights and also funded programs abroad in policy areas that traditionally were kept in the shadows.

These public policy decisions literally and figuratively have changed the face of Canada, and the way the world sees Canada. Our diverse attributes, together with our successful economy, vibrant cities, rich culture, excellent education systems, extraordinary natural environment, and effective bilateral and multilateral diplomacy underwrite our soft power, our capacity to achieve international goals not by force and coercion but by example and suasion.

At the same time, Canadian diplomacy and development sometimes require the backing of hard power, as Foreign Minister Freeland observed in her speech setting out Canada's foreign policy priorities in June 2017. Military strength remains important, but, regrettably, Canada's defence spending in the years since 1967 has consistently trailed that of almost all our NATO partners, to the point that our expenditures as a proportion of our gross domestic product (GDP) are at the lowest level since the beginning of World War II. We cannot argue that we are compensating for our shortfalls on defence with expenditures on foreign aid. Spending on official development assistance declined under Prime Minister Stephen Harper's time in office to 0.24 per cent of Canada's gross national income in 2014, falling for the first time since 1969 below the average of members of the OECD. Canada now has an aid budget of about $5 billion, but Canada's development spending as a percentage of gross domestic product (GDP), still just 0.26, ranks eighteenth in the world, according to the OECD.[2] Our expenditures as a percentage of GDP are at one of the lowest ebbs. Not ever have we come close to meeting the generally accepted aid target of 0.7 per cent of GDP established by the then former prime minister of Canada Lester Pearson in his commissioned report entitled "Partners in Development" that he submitted to the World Bank in 1969. During Mulroney's tenure, Canada's development assistance budget was proportionately nearly double, at 0.46 per cent of GNI. Growth in military and aid budgets, however, should not come at the expense of our diplomacy budget, which like defence and aid needs adequate funding if it is to serve the government and Canadians well.

Budget shortfalls notwithstanding, our major participation in two world wars and Korea, our contributions to the first Gulf War and Afghanistan, our current engagement in Eastern Europe through NATO, and our contribution to the coalition against the Islamic State (ISIS), as well as our now-faded reputation on peacekeeping, are evidence that we can make an effective military contribution when the chips are down and the cause is just. Our decisions on the 2003 Iraq War and on the decade-long Vietnam War demonstrated that we could also be relied on *not* to participate when the cause was *not* just or lawful. The Security Council's denial of authorization for the United States to invade Iraq stands as one of its key decisions in the new century, and Prime Minister Jean Chrétien's rejection of the offer to participate in the American-led coalition was one of the best and most important foreign policy decisions made by a Canadian government in the modern era.

## CANADA AND THE UN AND GLOBAL GOVERNANCE

A basic principle of foreign policy is that everything is connected to everything else. There is no security without development, no development without security, and no security or development without human rights. (It is surprising how many international leaders lose sight of this simple truth, or never learn it.) The corollary is that multilateral cooperation is essential to the achievement of all three. The UN, along with NATO, the WTO, the IMF, the World Bank, Asia-Pacific Economic Cooperation (APEC), the G7, and the G20 are crucial to the preservation of peace and of the liberal international order built following World War II. The G20, elevated to the heads of government by the financial crisis of 2008, was conceived by then prime minister Paul Martin and adopted by world leaders when they realized that the G7 was too small to deal with the financial crisis and the UN was too big.

The UN remains central to global governance. To put the UN in its proper perspective, it is important neither to demonize the organization nor to romanticize it. The UN is not the incompetent, indolent obstacle to the effective conduct of international relations that its more conservative critics portray it as being. Nor is it the high-minded, all-powerful agency some of its liberal proponents imagine it to be. As the legendary Swedish secretary general Dag Hammarskjöld once said, "[T]he UN is not intended to take you to heaven, just to save you from hell."

The UN effectively is a club of 193 nation states that pool some of their sovereignty and resources to address international problems that are beyond the capacity of individual states to handle. The UN is not an independent, executive actor; it is the instrument of its members. The UN works when its members agree on what should be done. When they disagree, stasis follows. The problems the UN faces are usually intractable and the member countries often intransigent. Most UN problems originate in the member countries, not with its professional secretariat or in the iconic building on First Avenue in New York. Criticism of the latter two is especially misguided and pointless.

To keep things in some perspective, it is worth recalling what has been achieved under the UN banner, to remind ourselves what is of value and what is worth preserving. Otherwise, as Joni Mitchell once sang in another context, we won't know what we've got till it's gone. Despite its shortcomings, the UN remains indispensable to preserving and promoting peace and progress. The UN's unique legitimacy is derived from its universal membership and from the adherence of all 193 members to the UN Charter as the basis of international law. The UN Charter constitutes the international "rules of the road" that most countries see as being in their interest to respect, most of the time. Those that flout the rules can find themselves sanctioned, as North Korea now is.

Over the seventy years of the UN's existence, member states have progressively brought the resort to war under the discipline of the UN Charter. They have also brought the conduct of war in line with the rules of international humanitarian law, in order to restrict the means and methods of warfare and mitigate the effects of combat. As a consequence, in part, of the universal endorsement of the UN Charter, aggression has been stigmatized, e.g., Russia's intervention in Ukraine. The members of UN Security Council, especially the permanent five members, communicate on a 24-7 basis. The result is that the world's most powerful countries are intimately familiar with each other's "redlines," which means that the risks of war by inadvertence or miscalculation are greatly reduced. In fact, partly because of the non-stop diplomacy of the council – a kind of permanent Concert of Nations – there has not been a war between major powers since Korea.

PRIME MINISTER BRIAN MULRONEY (1984–93)

Plasticized button, 1984. Brian Mulroney was a skilled diplomat. During his term of office, Canada signed a free trade agreement (FTA) with the United States in 1989, which was later expanded in 1994 to include Mexico (NAFTA). On 13 March 1991, he also signed an air quality treaty with the United States to limit acid rain. He sought closer relations with President François Mitterrand's France in order to organize the first summit of francophone nations in 1986. Like his predecessors, he stood up to Prime Minister Margaret Thatcher and supported abolishing the apartheid regime in South Africa. Credit: Canadian Museum of History (CHSJ), IMG2017-0068-0195-DM

All told, 560 multilateral treaties have been concluded under UN auspices. The member countries of the UN have, thus, spawned an extensive body of international laws, treaties, norms, practices, and institutions that govern most facets of interstate relations and contribute directly and indirectly to global security and stability. With these "apps," the UN Charter has become the world's central operating system, making it possible for ideas such as the 2015 Millennium Development Goals and the follow-on Sustainable Development Goals to become policy drivers. In the process, they make it possible also for other, less representative organizations, notably NATO and the G8 and G20, as well as non-governmental organizations and civil society, to function with less friction from non-members. The UN also provides a platform for the products of other smaller entities, notably of the G7 and G20, to be considered by the larger membership of the world body.

Often overlooked in the many criticisms of the UN is the fact that the organization has undergone extensive innovation and renovation and, in the process, substantial reinvention. From peacekeeping to peace-enforcement and peacebuilding, international criminal justice systems, sustainable development, refugee protection, humanitarian coordination and food relief, democracy and electoral support, human rights conventions, and health protection, the organization has been adapting to its increasingly demanding responsibilities. As a consequence, the UN has a broader political presence in the world than any other organization and much substantive expertise in dealing with contemporary challenges, such as instability and fragile states.

All of this brings greater order, predictability, and progress to global relations, and greater modernity, security, and dignity to people's lives, as St Laurent and Pearson, Mulroney and Joe Clark, and Chrétien and Axworthy believed it would. Not every prime minister saw the UN in the same positive light. Prime Minister Pierre Trudeau tended to look outside the UN in his efforts to bring about a new deal for the world's poorer countries, and Prime Minister Harper overtly condemned Canada's UN policy as excessively focused on fixing others' problems, not our own. But the object never was merely to be nice; it was always to be effective. Mulroney believed that Canada's vast, difficult-to-defend territory, comparatively modest-sized population, and dependence on international trade and investment meant that cooperation in creating and upholding international rules of the road, from the UN to the IMF to NATO, were in Canada's hard national interests. In Mulroney's day, Canada participated in every peacekeeping mission and paid its UN dues in full and on time on 1 January every year.

## CANADA AND THE BENEFITS OF GLOBALIZATION
### With apologies to Charles Dickens!

Ours is the best of times and the worst of times;
It is the age of information and the age of ignorance;
An era of global integration and national xenophobia
A time of economic progress and political regression
It is a season of peace and light and a time of violence
    and darkness …

Canadians in particular have never been more prosperous, more educated, healthier, longer lived, better connected, or even safer than they are now. For many, this perception is counter-intuitive, even out of touch with the times. World news coverage is dominated by fear and violence. "If it bleeds, it leads" is a TV news aphorism I learned in my years in Washington. One plane crashing at Ottawa Airport will always be bigger news than one million planes landing safely there. Further, beyond journalism's attraction to bad news, thanks to digital media we are more aware of more bad news than ever before. No mountain valley on the other side of the earth is too remote to escape our fleeting attention and empathy. And the twenty-four-hour news cycle and the endless repetition of the same "breaking" news by cable news networks bathes us in doom and gloom. Further, "falsehood flies," as Jonathan Swift once observed, "and truth comes limping after it."

Social media exacerbate the problem. Twitter's 140 characters are enough to frighten and provoke, but rarely enough to hearten and construct. Appeals to xenophobia, tribalism, racism, religiosity, and extremism are rampant. It is not surprising that the world seems an increasingly troubled, dangerous place.

In reality, the reverse is true. We have come a very long way from Hobbes' depiction of the natural state of humanity as one of "continuall fear, and danger of violent death; And the life of man [was] solitary, poore, nasty, brutish, and short." In fact, most people around the world and here in Canada are living vastly better and fuller lives than their forebears did, including their grandparents and parents.

In the year 1900, about eighty per cent of the world's population lived in poverty, many in extreme poverty. One hundred years later or so, only about ten to fifteen per cent do.[3] It is a remarkable evolution, a major change in the world's history. That's still a lot of poor people – more than seven hundred million people – but huge progress has been made. Adjusted for inflation, the world economy has grown fifty-four out of the past fifty-five years. Only the Great Recession of 2008–09 saw a slight dip in real global GDP, measured in purchasing power parity (PPP).

Since 1990, extreme poverty rates worldwide have been cut by more than half. According to the UN, "Never in history have the living conditions and prospects of so many people changed so dramatically [for the better] and so fast." China alone has pulled more than five hundred million of its citizens out of extreme poverty.[4] Thanks to the phenomenal progress in China, the world reached the UN Millennium Development Goal of cutting extreme poverty in half five years ahead of schedule.

Here in Canada, since 1960 the economy has grown nearly fourfold to $1.8 trillion in current dollars, while the population has just doubled. In the last twenty-five

US PRESIDENT RONALD REAGAN (1981–89) AND VICE-PRESIDENT GEORGE H.W. BUSH
Plasticized button, 1984. Ronald Reagan's election as president coincided with Brian Mulroney's election as prime minister of Canada. It was a time of détente between the two neighbours. Of the same political stripe and compatible characters, the two men were made to agree and arranged numerous social occasions to cement their relationship. Vice-President George H.W. Bush became president in 1989, thereby ensuring that the good relations between the two countries would continue. The emphasis was on all the issues that could bring the neighbours closer together. Credit: Ronald Reagan Presidential Library, John T. Hay Collection

years, Canadian GDP per capita (PPP) has increased by 70 per cent.[5] GDP statistics do not translate directly into the well-being of individual citizens, but they are an indicator. Further, they are consistent with the anecdotal evidence of increased wealth all around us – our homes are bigger, our cars are better, our civic infrastructure is newer, at least in those jurisdictions that choose to pay taxes to finance it, and Canadians travel more often, and farther.

It is true that there are disparities between countries and within them, and that many people feel disadvantaged as they see the wealthiest 1 per cent prosper disproportionately. It is also true that technology and trade really have disadvantaged some groups even while benefiting other people, probably the great majority of other people. In international trade, the benefits are generally incremental, and are seen mostly in lower prices dispersed across society while the losses are concentrated and the losers much easier to identify than the winners. But these disparities can be attenuated by policy responses, including social policy measures, to cushion the losses. The presence of governmental social safety nets in Canada is one reason why NAFTA is not seen as darkly in Canada as it is in the United States. A job loss in Canada does not mean a loss of health insurance. But, at the same time, if disparities between rich and poor here as elsewhere are allowed to widen, and if wealth is not shared more equitably, one day the disadvantaged populace might take pitchforks to the privileged. In any case, today most people really are better off in absolute terms whatever the relative state of their prosperity and dissatisfaction.

Canadians and people generally are also better off in matters of education. In 1900, almost eight of every ten people worldwide could not read or write. Global adult literacy was an estimated 21 per cent. Today, global adult literacy is about 85 per cent.[6] The mean number of years children go to school has also increased. In Canada in 1950, the mean number of years of schooling was 7.6. In 2005, the mean number was 12, almost a 70 per cent increase, for a population that had effectively doubled. So there are far more Canadians attending school far longer. Nearly 53 per cent of Canadian adults have a tertiary level of education, the highest figure among OECD member countries.

Levels of physical well-being are also better. People everywhere are living longer and healthier, according to the *World Health Statistics 2014* report published by WHO.[7] Based on global averages, a girl who was born in 2012 can expect to live to around seventy-three years, and a boy to the age of sixty-eight, an improvement of six years over similar children born in 1990. Reduced mortality rates in children are a product of higher levels of immunization coverage for childhood diseases. Globally, over the last twenty-five years, the number of children who died before their fifth birthday has declined by 49 per cent. Over the last fifteen years, measles deaths have decreased by almost 75 per cent. The incidence of polio has been reduced by 99 per cent world-wide in a generation.[8] HIV/AIDS has seen a major decline in mortality levels. Malaria deaths worldwide have declined by 42 per cent, according to the Bill and Melinda Gates Foundation.[9] Overall, despite SARS, Ebola, and the Zika virus, people around the world are healthier than they have ever been and living longer.

Canadians and people around the world are also incomparably better connected. Ninety percent of Canadians used the Internet in the past year.[10] Half of the world's population now has a mobile phone subscription – up from just one in five 10 years ago.[11] There are more mobile phones in the world now than there are people,[12] and more people have access today to a cell phone than to a flush toilet.[13]

We are also safer and more secure. Conflicts these days are fewer and smaller than they used to be. According to the Human Security Research Project of Simon Fraser University, from the early nineties to the present day, the overall number of conflicts has dropped by some 40 per cent.[14] The number of deadliest conflicts, those that kill at least a thousand people a year, has declined by more than half. The decline in the fatality rate in combat has been even more dramatic. According to the Human Security Report, in 1950, the annual rate of battle-related deaths was approximately 240 per million of the world's population; in 2007, it was less than 10 per million, a twenty-four-fold decrease. Whether the deadly conflict in Syria will change this calculus or instead constitute a one-off departure from the new norm remains to be seen.

In the early sixties, President John F. Kennedy predicted that "10, 15, or 20 nations will have a nuclear capacity, including Red China." Thanks to a combination of diplomacy, deterrence, and common sense, Kennedy's worst-case scenario never materialized. North Korean programs notwithstanding, more countries have given up nuclear weapons programs in the past thirty years – including Ukraine, Belarus, Kazakhstan, Libya, Iraq, and South Africa – than have acquired them. Today, twenty-five years after the end of the Cold War, the world's combined stockpiles of nuclear weapons remain hugely, unimaginably destructive, but, since their peak in the mid-eighties, global arsenals have actually shrunk by over two-thirds.

That direction is positive, albeit not fully reassuring, as the modernization of stockpiles continues. The countries permitted by the Non-Proliferation Treaty to have nuclear weapons (i.e., the five permanent members of the UN Security Council), as well as the states whose possession of such weapons has not been sanctioned under international law but which have them anyway (Israel, India, Pakistan, and North Korea), boycotted the recently concluded negotiation of the 2017 Treaty on the Prohibition of Nuclear Weapons. One hundred and twenty-two countries, not including Canada, adopted the treaty.

PRIME MINISTER JEAN CHRÉTIEN (1993–2003) AND US PRESIDENT GEORGE W. BUSH (2001–09)
Unquestionably, the most important international policy decision made by Prime Minister Jean Chrétien was to refuse, on Canada's behalf, to take part in the war in Iraq in 2003, despite pressure from president George W. Bush, British prime minister Tony Blair and a powerful business lobby. The argument that Iraqi president Saddam Hussein had weapons of mass destruction would turn out to be false and a manipulative tactic. The war destabilized that entire region of the Middle East for many years, and the after-effects are still very much in evidence. Credit: AP Photo/Doug Mills

What is new is that terrorism has "democratized" violence, with ordinary citizens now vulnerable to violence as never before. Although terrorist savagery is horrific and unnerving to a population that senses itself personally at risk, it is not an existential threat to Canada or most other countries. Attacks by ISIS and its ilk, including home-grown, self-radicalized acolytes, have caused perceptible damage and instilled widespread fear – from Orlando to Istanbul, Ankara, Paris, Nice, Baghdad, Berlin, Brussels, Kabul and Bamako, Dhaka and Delhi, and beyond.

Appalling as they are, however, terrorist murders amount to a small fraction of deaths by other causes. According to START, a US organization studying terrorism impacts in the United States, in 2014, thirty-two Americans lost their lives at the hands of terrorists. According to the White House, in 2015 more than thirty thousand Americans lost their lives to guns (including suicide deaths). Americans are almost one thousand times more likely to kill other Americans than terrorists are. Since 2001, 3,380 Americans died at the hands of terrorists, the great majority on 9/11. In the same period, 406,500 Americans died of gun violence. Terrorist killings did not make the list of the top ten causes of death in the United States.

Canada happily does not make the top twenty countries suffering from terrorism. Statistically, Canadians are vastly more likely to die from medication mistakes, or at the hands of their spouses, than by attacks from terrorists. Bees and wasps probably represent a much greater danger than terrorist bullets.

## THE INTERNATIONAL ORDER AT RISK

Despite this irrefutable progress, the international order is being buffeted both by nihilist terrorist gangs and by nativist authoritarian leaders. As Madame Justice Rosalie Abella observed in a speech at Brandeis University in Waltham, Massachusetts recently, under the pressures of "narcissistic populism, an <u>un</u>healthy tolerance for <u>in</u>tolerance, a cavalier indifference to equality, a deliberate amnesia about the instruments and values of democracy that are no less crucial than elections, and a shocking disrespect for the borders between power and its independent adjudicators like the press and the courts, our global democratic consensus is fragmenting."

It is time for those who can act to restore faith in global governance to do so, and that emphatically includes Canada. The liberal international order needs investment, and global institutions need innovation and renovation. Making these organizations work better – to serve Canadian interests better – is in our national DNA. It is also in our interests and entirely appropriate for us to devote major efforts to doing so.

Canada is widely admired. In February 2017, the Gallup organization reported that 92 per cent of Americans have a very favourable view of Canada, ranking this country first. In June, Reputation Institute ranked Canada first in its annual assessment of most reputable countries, the world's largest annual international survey of country reputations for effective government, advanced economy, and appealing environment. Canada ranked seventh of 155 countries in the 2017 World Happiness Report and tenth of 188 countries in the UN's Human Development Index. We can offer diplomatic leadership without fear of derision or accusations of arrogance on a range of issues.

## CANADA AND THE INTERNATIONAL REFUGEE CRISIS

The international refugee system is dysfunctional. Sixty percent of the world's refugees are hosted by ten states, nine of which are in the global south, including Pakistan,

US PRESIDENT BARACK OBAMA (2008–16)

The first person of colour to be elected president of the United States, Barack Obama represented such a break with the past that people allowed themselves to hope. However the hawkish foreign policy of the governement of Stephen Harper in relation to the Iran nuclear treaty, Isreali-Palestinian relations, and Syrian refugees did not help to nurture a closer relationship. Moreover President Obama was delaying the approval of the construction of the Keystone XL pipeline from Canada, which was strongly supported by the Harper government. Nonetheless, the American president remained rather popular with Canadians. Credit: The Senate of Canada

Lebanon, Iran, Ethiopia, Jordan, Kenya, Uganda, Chad, and Sudan, as well as Turkey. Three countries – the United States, Canada, and Australia – account for 83 per cent of global refugee resettlement efforts. Ten donors, including Canada, account for 79 per cent of all financial contributions to the UN Refugee Agency.

The issue is exacerbated by a core deficiency of the global refugee regime: while countries of first asylum have an obligation to receive refugees and not to forcibly return them to a country where they legitimately fear for their lives, other states have no comparable obligation to share the responsibilities, costs, and social burdens associated with the provision of asylum. When a crisis erupts, frontline countries find themselves coping with millions of unexpected refugees within their borders. These states host 90 per cent of the world's refugees, while only a limited number of other states regularly contribute resources to meet the needs of refugees, and a still smaller number resettle refugees out of harm's way. Absent change, responses to refugee flows will remain discretionary, ad hoc, piecemeal, and inadequate. The impact on regional and national stability will be potentially enormous.

Canada has a near unique standing to lead on the reform of the refugee system, one of the major problems roiling international stability. Over time, Canadians have unlocked this land to refugees, at first from Europe and subsequently from wherever they originated. In 1956, we opened the door to Hungarian refugees; in 1968, we did the same for Czechoslovaks; in 1972, we accepted Ugandan Ismailis; in 1973, we admitted Chilean refugees; and by 1985, we had resettled a hundred and ten thousand Vietnamese "boat people." Since 2015, we have resettled over forty thousand Syrian refugees.

Our Syrian resettlement and humanitarian funding programs are not large compared to Germany's, for example. But in the context of our large, ongoing immigration program, which has encouraged hundreds of thousands of people to settle in Canada year after year for decades and to take up Canadian citizenship, our refugee effort *is* exceptional and it *does* give us a voice in global councils. And the refugee system needs that voice to be heard. It is struggling to cope today with twenty-one million people, half of them children, who have fled their homelands in search of safety. These people face severe limitations on the number of sanctuary destinations available; their average time displaced is about twenty years. Further, the quality of asylum they receive is inadequate – for example, only 50 per cent of refugee children attend elementary school and only 22 per cent of them attend high school.

The world's refugee crisis is undoubtedly a tragedy. It is not, however, an insurmountable problem in a world of 7.4 billion people. Responsibility needs to be shared. Abroad, there is an appetite for Canadian leadership on this issue. There is an urgent need for bold, creative thinking and far-sighted leadership, a need that the newly announced World Refugee Council, chaired by Lloyd Axworthy and launched by the Centre for International Government Innovation in Waterloo with the support of the Government of Canada and other partners, hopes to help fill.

The liberal international order is under stress. Reforming the refugee system would address a problem that threatens only to worsen. Doing so would also demonstrate that the liberal international order can adapt, that it is not frozen in 1951, the year the refugee convention was concluded. Canada is strongly positioned to help lead that reform, as we did in the fifties and in the years following Canada's centennial. Doing so would be consistent with the tenets of Louis St Laurent and the principles enunciated by Chrystia Freeland. Leadership on the refugee file would serve our interests, respect our values, and honour our history.

NOTES

1 Kofi Annan, address to the Canadian Parliament, 9 March 2004, https://www.un.org/sg/en/content/sg/statement/2004-03-09/secretary-generals-address-canadian-parliament/.

2 "OECD DAC Aid at a Glance by Donor," Organisation for Economic Co-operation and Development, last modified 22 December 2017, http://www.oecd.org/dac/financing-sustainable-development/development-finance-data/aid-at-a-glance.htm.

3 See Max Roser chart of people in and out of poverty (1820–2011) globally in Dylan Thomas in Vox, August 13, 2015 data derived from Bourgignon and Morrison (2002) and World Bank.

4 "Poverty, Equity and Governance," United Nations Development Programme in China, http://www.cn.undp.org/content/china/en/home/democratic-governance-and-peace-building.html.

5 "Canada GDP Constant Prices 1961–2018," Trading Economics, last modified April 2018, https://tradingeconomics.com/canada/gdp-constant-prices/.

6 *The World Fact Book* (Washington, DC: Central Intelligence Agency, 2018), https://www.cia.gov/library/publications/the-world-factbook/index.html.

7 Margaret Chan, "Ten Years in Public Health 2007–2017" (Geneva: World Health Organization, 2017), http://www.who.int/publications/10-year-review/en/.

8 "Does Polio Still Exist? Is It Curable?" World Health Organization, accessed April 2018, http://www.who.int/features/qa/07/en/.

9 "Malaria Strategy Overview," Bill and Melinda Gates Foundation, accessed April 2018, https://www.gatesfoundation.org/What-We-Do/Global-Health/Malaria/.

10 "Individuals Using the Internet (% of Population)," World Bank, accessed April 2018, https://data.worldbank.org/indicator/IT.NET.USER.ZS?locations=BD-IN-CA/.

11 "Number of Mobile Subscribers Worldwide Hits 5 Billion," GSMA, press release, last modified 13 June 2017, https://www.gsma.com/newsroom/press-release/number-mobile-subscribers-worldwide-hits-5-billion/.

12 GSMA Intelligence, https://www.gsmaintelligence.com/.

13 "Deputy UN Chief Calls for Urgent Action to Tackle Global Sanitation Crisis," UN News, last modified 21 March 2018, https://news.un.org/en/story/2013/03/435102-deputy-un-chief-calls-urgent-action-tackle-global-sanitation-crisis/.

14 "Human Security Report 2013: The Decline in Global Violence – Evidence, Explanation, and Contestation" (Vancouver: Human Security Research Group, Simon Fraser University, 2014), https://www.files.ethz.ch/isn/178122/HSRP_Report_2013_140226_Web.pdf.

# Canadian Aid: Reflecting Humanist Values and Supporting Economic Development

Huguette Labelle, former chancellor of the University of Ottawa (1994–2012) and former president of the Canadian International Development Agency (1993–99)

Canada's role in the world has been varied and consistent over decades and has contributed to building our international identity. Through diplomacy, leadership on key world issues, development co-operation, peacekeeping, humanitarian assistance, military intervention, and representation on key international institutions, Canada has played a key role over the past several decades.

Some of our advantages have been our pluralistic society with its multiple cultural expressions, including those of Indigenous peoples; our two official languages; and the multiple additional languages spoken by Indigenous peoples and many other Canadians. Our approach to supporting new immigrants and refugees as they reach our country, as well as the fact that they can be granted Canadian citizenship within a reasonable time, is also an important feature of who we are and what we value. As well, our readiness to share our expertise and co-operate without dictating has been a hallmark of our international collaboration.

Some countries invite us to co-operate with them in particular areas specifically because of our French North American know-how. Some of the causes that we have championed, such as gender equality, human rights, and welcoming refugees, highlighted our reputation of respecting others and of putting into practice human values essential to the proper functioning of a society.

Romeo Dallaire sums this up very well: "With a stable economy and a culture that cares, Canada is well placed to intervene and help tackle larger issues such as resource sustainability, peace and humanitarian efforts around the world."[1]

My focus will be on Canada's international co-operation and humanitarian assistance, which has contributed significantly to our international identity; why this was important in the past; and why it remains important today and in the future.

Canada's international responsibility to assist remains vital in light of the major issues we face today, some of which have been with us for far too long. Major humanitarian crises, the high mortality rates of women and children, human rights abuses, and the destabilization of countries and regions have impacts worldwide, not just in those countries and regions.

Persistent world poverty continues in all countries, but especially in the developing world. The World Bank estimates that 767 million people still live on less than $1.90 per day.[2] The rise of inequality is clear; *Forbes* estimates that the net worth of the world's billionaires was $7.65 trillion in 2017, giving additional opportunity for state capture to a few and leaving the poor voiceless.[3] The number of fragile states and countries in ongoing conflict is another sign that development work must continue. And, of course, the increasing frequency and intensity of natural disasters such as floods and droughts, exacerbated by climate change, affects food supply and destroys essential infrastructure. In all these cases, people are the victims.

This combination of factors, in addition to lack of economic opportunities, has increased world migration and the flow of refugees to an estimated 244 million in 2015[4] with about 65.3 million refugees being forcibly displaced,[5] thus creating new pressures worldwide, including xenophobia. Populism and retrenchment in certain countries is a reminder of past world history. We watch these developments with grave concern. Similarly, global terrorism is sapping world energy and creating a new fear of the "other."

The rapid development of information technology has brought tremendous benefits while also making it easier for terrorists to connect and for illicit funds to be transferred and hidden. Illicit financial flows from developing and emerging countries are estimated by the illicit financing watchdog Global Financial Integrity to be one trillion USD, robbing these countries of essential resources while sowing the seeds of conflict.[6] These crimes undermine national economies at all levels, feeding illicit trade in drugs, arms, and people. Surrounded by rampant corruption, local and national treasuries are robbed of the funds required to deliver services to citizens, resulting in a devastating impact on development. Those who launder money or evade taxes often benefit from the co-operation of western institutions or their lack of due diligence. Facilitators such as lawyers, accountants, and real estate specialists make all this possible. The essential role of the Organisation for Economic Co-operation and Development (OECD), the World Bank, the International Monetary Fund (IMF), and other multilateral agencies, as well as G20 countries, remains key to tackling this global scourge. Many commitments have already been made; implementation is now what matters.

UNITED NATIONS FLAG

Postcard, Official United Nations Office of Public Information, P54014. Since Lester B. Pearson, Canada has enjoyed a reputation as a country that is concerned about preventing conflict through negotiation and open communication between belligerents, which has earned it support to occupy a seat on the Security Council four times. Appreciated for its openness and its ability to act as an independent agent, Canada has a strong interest in promoting a multilateral approach because it is generally seen as one of the countries with no preconceived interest, often ahead of those whose power lies in their military capacity. Credit: CHSJ

International co-operation and humanitarian assistance are critical in helping to lift people out of poverty; in supporting the development of social, physical, and governance infrastructure; and in helping countries move toward greater stability, sustainability, and peace. Considering the importance of achieving sustainable development for all countries, it is timely to look at Canada's role in the past and to determine what considerations should be part of its future contributions.

## I. CANADA'S EARLY INVOLVEMENT

The forties up through the sixties was an important period for building the institutions and instruments that remain today in our world development and humanitarian architecture. This was the response to the period of uncertainty after World War II. Canada was at the table and sometimes played a leading role in the development of these institutions, so they naturally became part of Canada's evolving international role, influencing our future approach to international co-operation.

The 1945 United Nations Charter was a foundation piece. Its preamble, "to promote better standards of life in larger freedom" and "to employ international machinery for the promotion of the economic and social advancement of all peoples," set the tone for what followed. The three points of article one provided more specific guidance: (1) to maintain peace and security, (2) to develop friendly relations among nations, and (3) to achieve international co-operation in solving international problems and encouraging respect for human rights and fundamental freedoms.[7] Today these remain fundamental to a peaceful, secure world. Canada was important in drafting the charter and was a signatory along with the other fifty-one member countries.

What followed was the creation of several institutions – the Food and Agriculture Organization (FAO) in 1945 in Quebec City; the United Nations International Children's Emergency Fund (UNICEF), the World Bank, and the IMF in 1946; and the World Health Organization (WHO) in 1948. With Canada as part of their development and as an ongoing partner, these institutions remain essential to supporting developing countries.

For its part, the United States launched the Marshall Plan, with a strategy of reconstruction and reconciliation, which provided the impetus for future development co-operation with a strong focus on infrastructure.

In 1950, Canada was one of the founders of the Colombo Plan, as countries gaining their independence around the world were in need of special support. Lester B. Pearson represented Canada as minister of foreign affairs. This assistance began in Commonwealth Asia, expanded to Commonwealth Caribbean, and reached Commonwealth Africa in 1960 and Francophone Africa in 1961. Canada was also a driving force for peace with the development of peacekeeping by Pearson and General E.L.M. Burns in 1956. Peacekeeping was rapidly recognized in 1957 by countries around the world.

This was also a period of financial crisis in various countries. In 1958, Canada was one of five founding nations when the World Bank created a consortium to assist India in meeting its balance-of-payment crisis. In 1960, a similar consortium provided support for Pakistan.

Given Canada's participation in establishing these international development institutions, it was to be expected that Canada establish its own external aid office in

1960, which in 1968 became the Canadian International Development Agency (CIDA) under Prime Minister Pierre Elliott Trudeau. With the strong leadership of Maurice Strong as its first president, CIDA rapidly became Canada's brand for international co-operation, working in over a hundred countries. Canadian assistance was delivered in co-operation with many Canadian organizations – voluntary, public, and private. Its central mandate has remained to reduce world poverty in developing countries. Our non-colonizing past and our reputation as an "honest broker" made it possible for Canada to be a constructive player on sensitive matters such as the rule of law and human rights. Canadians generally believed that helping those with less was the right thing to do for our country.

The 1968 to 1970 period was important because Pearson chaired the Commission on International Development.[8] In delivering its report – best known as the Pearson Report – the commission recommended that countries raise their international development assistance to 0.7 per cent of gross national product (GNP). The 1970 UN General Assembly then followed by mandating that "each economically advanced country will progressively increase its official development assistance to the developing countries and will exert its best efforts to reach a minimum net amount of 0.7 per cent of GNP by the middle of the decade." A number of European countries either reached this goal several years ago or are close to it. In this area, Canada has not fulfilled its pledge. It was in the higher group of donors for over two decades but is currently in the lower group of significant bilateral donors.

The turn of the century saw the adoption of the Millennium Development Goals by UN members, the result of several years of world summits, with specific targets to reduce poverty by 2015. Progress was achieved on several goals, including halving the number of people living in extreme poverty, providing an extra two billion people with improved sources of drinking water, reducing maternal and child mortality, and increasing life expectancy. However, progress has been very uneven in different regions of the world.[9] In light of the lessons learned, the UN launched its Sustainable Development Goals in 2015 after extensive consultation with countries and other groups around the world. The seventeen goals provide a more comprehensive plan, with significant follow-up on implementation. Canada again was a participant in formulating these two important sets of goals and has been supporting their implementation through CIDA.

In 1970, the International Development Research Centre (IDRC) was also established as a Crown corporation, giving Canada a special edge in development research. Its mandate has been "to initiate, encourage, support and conduct research into the problems of the developing regions of the world and into the means for applying and adapting scientific, technical and other knowledge to the economic and social development of these regions." This institution continues to discharge this mandate and has been an important part of Canada's international legacy.

## II. INTERNATIONAL CO-OPERATION AND HUMANITARIAN ASSISTANCE: THE CANADIAN APPROACH

Bilateral development co-operation has been one of Canada's main relationships with a large number of countries around the world, as our trade with some developing countries is not yet well developed, and in a limited number of countries is focused on the extractive sector. Although our aim has been to share what we have in the spirit of human solidarity and to contribute to a secure and peaceful world, strong bilateral relations with developing countries have several positive consequences, including support on major international issues. The relationships that develop through the planning and delivery of international co-operation also establish lasting bonds between Canadians and the people of the host countries, to our mutual benefit. At the same time, how we deliver this co-operation matters for its impact and sustainability, and for Canada's reputation.

Responding to the needs and priorities of developing countries and building sustainability in its interventions has long been Canada's general approach to bilateral co-operation, which is critical in achieving long-term success. In trying to help, it is easy to fall into the trap of identifying what we think requires our support and then offering it, but unless the recipient feels that this is what they really need, it is unlikely to be sustainable over time. Canada has generally been able to respond in a constructive way, but this requires constant diligence. One must also be careful of each new government that is tempted to start with a clean slate. Caution is required in ensuring that we do not make Canada an unstable provider by shifting our support or by changing our priorities too frequently. Having priorities that are fundamental to sustainable development should ensure less disruption.

Canada has gradually shifted its support from major infrastructure projects to essential human needs, including education, health, access to water, food, and sanitation, as well as gender equality and economic capacity. Various supports to strengthen governance in justice and financial institutions, as well as to help mitigate future natural disasters, have also been part of our co-operation. This is especially evident in the 1995 Canadian policy review of *Canada in the World* – another milestone whose purpose was "[t]o support sustainable development in developing countries in order to reduce poverty and to contribute to a more secure, equitable and prosperous world."[10] Its priorities were basic human needs, women in development, infrastructure services, human rights and democracy, and good governance. Strengthening partnerships with Canadian non-governmental organizations (NGOs), educational institutions, and the business sector was seen as an important part of the policy. As well, addressing social, economic, environmental, and political issues in an integrated way with a focus on impact and effectiveness were central to the policy. Other more targeted policy statements have also been made since 1995, with the eventual policy decision to merge CIDA with Foreign Affairs in 2013.

Humanitarian assistance has been an important part of Canada's role in responding to natural disasters such as droughts, floods, typhoons, and earthquakes and, increasingly, to conflict. Canada was present at such disasters as the Ethiopian famine, the Haitian earthquake, the Honduran floods, and various refugee crises. In such cases, a whole-of-Canada mobilization has been most successful with our major NGOs such as the Red Cross, CARE Canada, World Vision, Médecins Sans Frontières, and many other organizations supported by the exceptional generosity of Canadians. In a number of cases, CIDA matched the funds raised by these organizations, doubling our capacity to assist. This made it possible both to provide direct assistance and to support the work of the World Food Program, the United Nations High Commissioner for Refugees (UNHCR), and UNICEF. In several cases, the Canadian Armed Forces has been a strong partner, deploying their Disaster Assistance Response Team (DART). The origin of DART dates to 1994, following the Rwandan genocide, when it became obvious that such a resource would allow us to deliver directly on essential services, including water purification, medical care, and engineering. Canadian missions in affected countries were critical in providing strong leadership.

A whole-of-Canada approach has therefore been most evident in dealing with humanitarian crises, where diplomacy, development and humanitarian resources, the military, and the expert organizations that Canadians support come into unison in a timely way to save lives and create transitional support for shelter, food, and sanitation. In situations of prolonged conflict, even education for children must be provided. In humanitarian situations, women and especially children are most vulnerable. That approach is why the four principles of humanitarian assistance must always be respected: humanity, impartiality, neutrality, and independence.

Canada's development co-operation contribution has been vast, so I offer only a few examples to illustrate our impact, its sustainability, and how our country is perceived internationally.

Canada's contribution to education has varied over the years. In the early sixties, Rwanda asked the Dominican Order to establish a university in their country. With the support of the Canadian government, Father George Henri Lévesque founded the National University of Rwanda in Butari. Father Lévesque was dean of the Social Sciences faculty at Laval University, offering him the opportunity of attaining the support of this Canadian institution to rapidly complete his mission of establishing the National University, a comprehensive institution that prepared a large number of young Rwandans. Unfortunately, many of those graduates were killed during the genocide. The institution nevertheless remains significant for that country to this day.

The fact that girls did not reach graduation or even attend primary school was also a major issue. CIDA began to work with local communities in Africa with groups of mothers to better understand why this was happening and established the types of programs that these communities wished to see, with schools closer to their homes to provide greater safety for girls. The lesson learned was that parents had a real grasp of the problem and were keen to work on the accommodation with CIDA. Because CIDA listened carefully to these communities, many more girls began to attend school and graduate.

On the economic front, the world's poor do not have access to regular banking, so the arrival of microcredit brought major changes. Microcredit has been used extensively by women, giving them financial opportunity. In discussing microcredit, we automatically and rightly think of Bangladesh and the Grameen Bank, BRAC, and Proshika – all partners of CIDA at different times – which have provided microcredit and capacity support to thousands of Bangladeshi women.

Across the world, in Bolivia, microcredit has flourished over several years with some original support from Canada. Prodem was the first institution to build a sustainable microlending operation in both urban and rural areas of the country. After several years of success, it expanded its capacity, launching Latin America's first micro-enterprise bank, Banco Solidario S.A., which continues to be the largest microlending institution in Bolivia. Since more was also needed in rural areas, it created Prodem Oportunidad, the country's first rural-based private financial fund. Another first was their introduction of smart cards and ATMs. Calmeadow, a Canadian NGO, provided technical assistance for this project from the eighties to the late nineties. The growth of this project over time is remarkable, and the dedication and leadership of the staff has been vital. The impact on the poor and the sustainability of the program were both notable. In 2014, the Multilateral Investment Fund ranked BancoSol number one out of the one hundred top such institutions.[11]

Canada's support to the global non-profit financing organization Women's World Banking in the early eighties is another example. Microcredit treats women as economic actors, and women, in turn, start and grow their own enterprises while paying back each loan. Women spending the income from these small businesses consistently prioritize their children's health and education and the welfare of their families. In Senegal, a group of women who had received microcredit loans decided to pool some of their income to start a nursery. From this venture, they developed their own lending institution in their community.

Canada's support for microfinance is an important part of our legacy. Not every loan helped to move the financial situation of recipients beyond the micro-enterprise level, but even so, it provided additional resources to these families.

Canada's development support for fundamental governance can best be illustrated in the case of South Africa. As South Africa was developing its new constitution, including the type of federation it wished to become, Canada supplemented its first-hand experience with that of various countries having a federation (Germany, Australia, and so on).

The historic 1994 non-racial one-person-one-vote elections that brought the African National Congress (ANC) to power provided new opportunities for additional co-operation. Al Johnson, a former deputy minister and former president of the CBC, played a key role and stayed in South Africa during the early years of the new government. Canada's co-operation during this period intensified and included special training for the new deputy ministers and support in bringing housing, water, sanitation, and electricity to the townships. Through IDRC and CIDA, Canada was a strong partner to South Africa for several years.

Three situations were critical in creating a trusted relationship between Canada and the ANC. Most important was the fact that successive Canadian governments, both Progressive Conservative and Liberal, took a principled approach regarding the importance of dismantling apartheid in South Africa while some other Western nations were against sanctions. Prime Minister Brian Mulroney and minister of Foreign Affairs Joe Clark were key players in establishing the geopolitical climate throughout transition negotiations. Second was IDRC's presence prior to the nineties in bringing early contingent capacity to South Africa. This included scholarships, various symposiums, and round tables, as well as studies on such critical topics as science and technology and a macroeconomic framework review. Third, the establishment of an African regional office in South Africa by IDRC and Canada's mission in South Africa provided the opportunity for discussions and a better understanding of the local situation.

A successful approach generally has been to work closely with Canadian partners in providing expertise as requested, especially in improving the governance of key state institutions. This has been a tremendous way of strengthening institutions but also of building lasting relations between Canadian institutions and countries of co-operation. Efforts have included the twinning of various organizations between Canada and their counterparts in other countries, such as the Supreme Court, the Bank of Canada, the auditor general, the tax and agriculture departments, and provincial government departments. One lasting program has been the twinning of Canadian universities and municipalities with their counterparts in China. Not only do such approaches strengthen developing country institutions, but they also provide learning experiences for our own institutions and help create lasting relationships. NGOS, the private sector, the agricultural sector, and numerous other organizations such as universities have all benefitted from such programs.

Canada's support to international financial institutions and to UN agencies remains a hallmark of our work. International financial institutions are important providers of soft loans to help countries with infrastructure development, something that bilateral donors like Canada are less able to do currently. Our contributions to UN agencies, such as UNICEF for immunization, WHO for research and global health issues, the UN Development Programme for co-ordination, and UNHCR for humanitarian crises, are part of doing our share to support the agencies that can best deliver certain programs.

### III. LOOKING TO THE FUTURE

In assessing our future role, Canada should be cautious about some of the excuses being given in cutting the budget for development assistance. Some say that remittances will help to solve the poverty problem, as an estimated $511 billion is sent back home by people living outside of their respective countries. However, half of these funds go to only four countries – India, China, the Philippines, and Mexico – with only 6 per cent going to low-income countries.

Another excuse is that trade and foreign direct investment will solve the poverty of developing countries. However important, this will not happen in a comprehensive way without the necessary social, economic, and physical infrastructure. Or, it will be concentrated in the extractive sector, in a limited number of countries, without local processing of the product, and having little employment impact.

Still others promise that the business sector will take care of financing the infrastructure needs of developing countries. This can work for sectors where costs can be recouped by user fees, but for roads, water, and sanitation in poor countries, user fees are not an option. This approach would leave only a new wave of debt at a much higher price tag than soft loans provided by international financial institutions.

In looking to the future, therefore, I would like to identify some avenues of work to continue Canada's trajectory of being open to the world, contributing our support and expertise, and aiming to mitigate the impacts on humanity and world stability of the major issues of our time. This assumes that Canada's development co-operation will remain based on each developing country's needs and priorities and that the development co-operation programs will be based on an integrated approach. It also assumes that Canada will review its financial contribution to development in order to eventually fulfill its previous commitment.

1. Ensuring that Canadians have a strong sense of ownership of our contribution to development remains essential. This will happen if we redouble their engagement and foster public support. Working with NGOs, the private sector, and institutions has been and remains important. Involving our youth and helping them becoming world citizens with a direct understanding of other countries and peoples remains vital today. The number and impact of university and college exchanges around the world and the need to grow these should not be underestimated. Supporting young people's involvement with national and international organizations through scholarships has worked well and could be enhanced.

2. From the early days of Canada's development co-operation, gender has been recognized as central to successful development, and much has been accomplished so far. Yet it is the right time for Canada to provide new, additional support to achieve gender equality with a full recognition of the role of women as agents of change and peacebuilders. When women have access to education, land, finance, driver's licences, and leadership positions, then children, families, and communities are the direct beneficiaries. Canada is also well placed to work collectively at creating a new intolerance for violence against women and recognizing that gender equality is a human rights issue.

3. Special attention to youth in developing countries is becoming even more critical, especially with some countries having over 70 per cent of their

population below age thirty. If these young people do not have access to education or employment, their future is stolen from them, leaving them without hope. They may also become the victims of – or be lured into – human trafficking or other illicit activities as a means of survival. In other cases, children as young as eight or ten become heads of households after the death or disappearance of their parents. With the right support, young people can become a force for constructive change and innovation in their country's development.

4. Canada should be a strong player in achieving the recently adopted Sustainable Development Goals both at home and in the developing world. These comprehensive goals provide a needed new agenda. Fulfilling our commitment is a responsibility that we must not shirk. We have a unique opportunity to share in the tasks of bringing people out of poverty, achieving a more equitable and prosperous world, preventing the destabilizing effects of climate change, and helping to prevent fragile states from deteriorating into conflict. Ways should be found with national governments to build capacity in governing not only at the national level but also at the local government level, where delivery of services increasingly takes place. It is vital to assist countries in sustaining their own progress.

5. Over the years, categorizing priority countries and forming other such divisions has not reflected the reality of development and has been disruptive as nations are dropped from the priority list. The right balance is essential between significant assistance to the poorest countries and fragile states and continuing more modest support to middle-income countries that seek our co-operation in various aspects of strengthening their institutions. In addition, development is not a continuous and smooth process, so our flexibility should reflect this reality.

6. Canada must implement important commitments made at a number of UN and G20 meetings. The Paris Accord on climate change, for example, would be instrumental in helping countries to prevent and prepare for future natural disasters. As important would be taking the necessary measures to curb illicit financial flows in developing countries by freezing and returning stolen assets, fully implementing multilateral tax information exchange and rigorous financial regulatory regimes, and encouraging all countries to establish a public

register of the real beneficial owners of companies. Canada is well placed to exercise leadership in this regard.

7. A whole-of-government and whole-of-Canada approach has served us well in the past; we should revisit how best to expand it. Canada has been successful in using such an approach to deal with humanitarian crises and other development situations. Lessons from past experience could be useful in learning how to multiply our capacity to deliver bilateral co-operation while recognizing the vital importance of building local capacity and working with local stakeholders.

Finally, as we consider Canada's future development co-operation, let us ensure that we build on our strengths and base our assistance on the twin spirits of generosity and human solidarity, as well as on security, peace, and prosperity for all.

NOTES

1 Romeo Dallaire, "Canada's Role in the World," Liberal Senate Forum, http://liberalsenateforum.ca/issue/canada-in-the-world/.

2 World Bank, "Understanding Poverty," 2 October 2016, http://www.worldbank.org/en/understanding-poverty.

3 Luisa Kroll and Kerry A. Dolan, "Forbes 2017 Billionaires List: Meet the Richest People on the Planet," Forbes, 20 March 2017, https://www.forbes.com/sites/kerryadolan/2017/03/20/forbes-2017-billionaires-list-meet-the-richest-people-on-the-planet/#5746514d62ff.

4 UN DESA and OECD, "World Migration in Figures, 2013", https://www.oecd.org/els/mig/World-Migration-in-Figures.pdf.

5 UNHCR, "Figures at a Glance: Global Trends, Forced Displacement, 2016," http://www.unhcr.org/statistics/unhcrstats/5943e8a34/global-trends-forced-displacement-2016.html.

6 Global Financial Integrity, "Illicit Financial Flows from Developing Countries 2004–2013," 2015, http://www.gfintegrity.org/report/illicit-financial-flows-from-developing-countries-2004-2013/.

7 Charter of the United Nations, 1945.

8 World Bank, "Pearson Commission on International Development: Partners in Development," September 1969.

9 United Nations, "The Millennium Development Goals Report, 2015," http://www.un.org/millenniumgoals/2015_MDG_Report/pdf/MDG%202015%20rev%20(July%201).pdf.

10 Department of Foreign Affairs and International Trade, "Canada in the World: Canadian Policy Review 1995," http://.dfait-maeci.gc.ca/foreign policy/cad-world.

11 Multilateral Investment Fund, "2014 Microfinance Americas: The Top 100," October 2014, https://www.microfinancegateway.org/library/2014-microfinance-americas-top-100.

# 3

# Major Challenges Are on the Horizon for Francophone Communities and Their Political Dimension[1]

# The Hon. Serge Joyal, Senator

*O*ver the past fifty years, the francophone reality in Canada has undergone fundamental change. In 1982, the Canadian Charter of Rights and Freedoms guaranteed equal status and equal rights to the French language. Yet history has shown that a minority's status is constantly under threat. Nevertheless, we should still recognize that definite progress has been made, even if equally significant challenges loom ahead. It is idealistic to think or hope that equality will someday be a given rather something that must always be defended. Sociological realities shape the cultural power struggles that occur between the majority and the francophone minority and that are rooted in history, struggles, conflicts, and an idealism and inspiring sense of humanism. This constant tension demands vigilance and unwavering commitment. Canada deserves no less. To survive and prosper, a minority, whether linguistic or otherwise, cannot depend on or be at the mercy of the whims or goodwill of the majority, no matter how well intentioned that majority may be. The law is the minority's only true refuge, and the courts its most steadfast protector.*

*By 1967, Canada had inherited several years of neglect, inaction, and denial regarding the French fact in this country; for example, most of the francophones in the federal public service at that time were relegated to the sidelines.[2] Canada's full cultural identity and linguistic duality were largely ignored in favour of the dominant majority's identity.*

*In general, the federal government used English when communicating with Canadians. It was not obligated to foster the vitality of Acadian and francophone communities, particularly in areas of provincial jurisdiction such as education, and most provinces were non-committal if not hostile when it came to supporting French-language education or the development of francophone communities. As demonstrated by francophones' endless battles over education – in New Brunswick in 1871, the Northwest Territories in 1888, Manitoba in 1890, Ontario's Regulation 17 in 1912 – there was no climate of support for the country's French-language heritage. Aside from Quebec, Canada looked like a unilingual English country.*

*The Royal Commission on Bilingualism and Biculturalism (the Laurendeau-Dunton Commission) released its preliminary report[3] in 1965, and its conclusions were alarming: a gulf separated the country's two major linguistic communities, Quebec sought greater cultural recognition if not separation,[4] and most Canadians were not quick to embrace the idea of a bilingual and bicultural Canada. The country was headed straight for an impasse unless things could be turned around quickly. Recognition of the French fact and respect for francophone identity were at the heart of the issue facing the country. During the 1967 constitutional conference known as the "Confederation of Tomorrow Conference,"[5] a number of provinces recognized the need to act quickly and announced they were ready to take steps to support bilingualism.*

*Pierre E. Trudeau decided it was time for a more drastic approach. If new rules were not imposed on the linguistic dynamic that had prevailed until then, francophones would continue to be marginalized in their own country and would eventually turn their backs on it. When he became prime minister in June 1968, Trudeau made it a priority to pass legislation confirming the equal status of Canada's two official languages. National unity depended on it: francophones needed to be able to reclaim an equal role in managing and governing Canada.*

*Things have certainly changed in fifty years, and while we have seen noteworthy progress and concrete constitutional guarantees, we have also seen major setbacks. Opposition still exists and, in some locations, political will is weak if not downright hostile, as shown in the following examples.*

*In 1967, there were no federal or provincial laws governing the status or use of French. The only relevant provision was section 133 of the* Constitution Act, 1867, *which recognized the use of French in Parliament and in the Quebec legislature as well as in federal and Quebec courts. Section 93 of the Act protected pre-Confederation education rights, particularly for denominational schools.*

*In 2017, there were specific constitutional guarantees (sections 16 to 23 of the Charter, adopted in 1982) regarding all of the federal government's linguistic obligations (and those of the New Brunswick government) as well as the education rights of the French minority and Quebec's English minority.*

*These provisions were preceded in 1969 by the* Official Languages Act *(OLA),[6] which recognized the equal status and use of English and French as languages of work and service in the federal public service. This legislation reversed what was thought to be an immutable state of affairs and, when it was passed, it let the genie out of the bottle and fanned the sense of superiority of the old English-Protestant imperialism.[7]*

*The OLA challenged one hundred years of domination by the English language. It could not help but offend people's sensibilities and upset the dominance of English – a language that was expected to take precedence given that North America had 219 million[8] English speakers at the time. Some even thought that it would be helpful to make francophones speak English when dealing with the federal government because it would increase their mobility throughout North America.*

*The conflict simmered and eventually boiled over several years later in 1976 with the* Gens de l'air du Québec *crisis.[9] This group was a coalition of Quebec flight personnel and aeronautics employees. Otto Lang, then minister of Transport, was under pressure from CALPA and CATCA, two powerful Canadian unions[10] that maintained that English was the international language of aviation and that French should be banned from aircraft cabins in the interest of passenger safety. Lang responded with NOTAM 18, prohibiting the use of French in air traffic communications. That was the spark that lit the powder keg.*

*Emotions ran high during the conflict and the atmosphere bordered on explosive. Was passenger safety really at risk when communications between the pilot and the control tower were, in fact, partly in code? It seemed a reasonable question. The case bounced around the courts, starting with an application to eliminate the requirement making English the language of work[11] in the aeronautic industry, an industry with an important future, particularly at Air Canada, a Crown corporation, followed by a second application to nullify NOTAM 18[12] in air traffic control.*

*The central issue in the conflict was the legal significance of recognizing the equal status of English and French in federal institutions (section 2 of the OLA). In other words, was the* Official Languages Act *declaratory (not enforceable by the courts) or executory (subject to legal recourse)?*

*The attorney general of Canada and Keith Spicer, commissioner of Official Languages, intervened before the Court to stress the intentional and non-obligatory nature of the OLA. In other words, the OLA did not establish a right for francophones; it simply expressed a great sensitivity toward the French language. In cases of infringement, the commissioner could make recommendations but they would not be binding.*

*The country quickly found itself in the midst of a national crisis. Within days of the opening of the Montreal Olympics on 17 July 1976, and the arrival of close to one hundred delegations from as many countries, CALPA launched a general strike to put pressure on air safety authorities and rally public opinion against the use of French.[13]*

*Pierre E. Trudeau responded to the public panic by addressing the nation on television. He also decided to establish a commission of inquiry,[14] chaired by Justice Julien Chouinard, to determine whether the use of two languages for aviation communications affected safety. The Chouinard Commission tabled its interim report in 1977 and a final report in 1979, concluding that the use of national languages for air traffic control, whatever those languages may be, is safer when both people involved speak the same language. However, if this is not possible, then English should be used.*

*This was a significant test for the validity and usefulness of the OLA and, in particular, for determining the legal significance of the equal status and use of English and French in federal institutions.*

*The Court found that the principle of the equality of both languages bound the federal government and included a legal obligation.*

*The rulings found that, without legal protection, the principle of equality of both languages could always be circumvented and that if the courts played no role in ensuring compliance, this principle was soon nothing more than a good intention, constantly at risk of being put off and watered down under pressure from the majority.*

*This major turning point had a direct impact in 1980: section 16 of the draft Charter established the equal status of both languages, and section 24 recognized the role of the courts in interpreting and enforcing these language rights.[15]*

*From that point on, the courts were responsible for interpreting the recognition and protection of language rights and for ordering the appropriate remedies. This paradigm shift would have a significant impact in the coming years, as it made the legislative activities of Parliament and the provincial assemblies subject to compliance with Charter rights.*

*Language rights, like other Charter rights, were no longer at the mercy of the whims of the majority. The courts were now the arbiters and the means of recourse when governments did not respect the spirit or the letter of the law.*

*This new constitutional guarantee over language rights was clear and protected these rights from any "political" interpretation by the government of the day and from the vagaries of public opinion.*

*However, there was still one fundamental issue to resolve: it is all well and good to have rights enshrined in a document, but they are meaningless unless a plaintiff has the resources to go to court and have them enforced. In other words, did the expense of going to court constitute an obstacle to obtaining redress and compliance?*

*The Gens de l'air du Québec crisis discussed previously highlighted this difficulty. To bring this case to court, the coalition had to sell buttons and posters to the public, seek contributions from supporters[16] who were ready to do their part, and ask the lawyers involved to work pro bono[17] and charge only court costs. In other words, they had to pass the hat to obtain a landmark decision, which did not impose damages and interest but rather would protect the future language rights of thousands of other people who would not have shared in the expense.*

*There is usually no financial benefit for plaintiffs seeking a ruling on language issues. In every case, they are up against government institutions with deep pockets, represented by the attorney general. In the above-mentioned case against Air Canada in 1976, counsel for the Crown corporation[18] asked the judge to acknowledge the benefit of sending a rogatory commission to France and Belgium to see how French was being used in air traffic control at their airports. This request involved travel costs for the entire court, the plaintiff and defendant, and their counsel. It was an enormous expense and risk given that the losing party could end up paying all court costs, their own legal expenses, and those of the successful party! You had to think twice, especially*

"IL Y A DU FRANÇAIS DANS L'AIR," 1976 [THERE'S FRENCH IN THE AIR]
Button of Les Gens de l'air du Québec. To elicit public support for bilingualism in air communications and the aerospace industry, this button, produced in 1976 by Les Gens de l'air du Québec, was sold to supporters of the cause. The argument against language equality was based on the importance of air safety and rapidly escalated into emotional opposition to the equal use of both languages. A national crisis ensued, paralyzing all of the country's airports on the eve of the July 1976 Summer Olympics in Montreal. A national inquiry proved that it was completely safe to use both languages.
Credit: Canadian Museum of History (CHSJ), IMG2012-0249-0117-DM, artifact 2011.21.207

*since the Air Canada pilots, who had agreed to be the plaintiffs in the case, wanted to be absolved of all financial responsibility.*

*There were lessons to be learned from this case. Was it fair for one person to bear the financial burden of a court case on equal language rights when that person would derive no financial benefit? Without financial support, the right to use one's own language would likely be ignored most of the time.*

*The question arose again the following year, in 1977, when Quebec passed Bill 101. The bill did not respect the letter of section 133 of the* Constitution Act, 1867, *which states that the legislation passed by the Quebec legislature must be published simultaneously in both languages.*

*The plaintiff, Peter Blaikie, was a lawyer with the large Montreal law firm of Heenan-Blaikie.[19] He requested federal funding to uphold the rights of Quebec's anglophone minority. The federal government agreed and, in 1978, established a precedent by granting financial support for legal challenges related to sections 133 and 193 of the* Constitution Act, 1867.

*The issue arose again after the Charter was passed in 1982: since section 24 of the Charter allows citizens to apply to the courts to uphold their rights, couldn't financial support be extended to cases involving the language rights in sections 16 to 23? The Trudeau government accepted the proposal by the secretary of state at the time,[20] and the financial support program was extended to language rights in the Charter. It was a major step and would go a long way toward enhancing respect for language rights.*

*The first case to benefit from this expanded funding involved Georges Forest of Saint-Boniface, Manitoba, who claimed that an English-only parking ticket violated section 23 of the* Manitoba Act.[21] *This section dated back to the establishment of Manitoba in 1870 and stipulated that the legislature must pass legislation in both languages.*

*The immediate impact of invalidation was almost inconceivable: every statute passed by the Manitoba Legislative Assembly since 1890 (when it repealed section 23 of its constitution) would be null and void since it would have been passed in English only. The political task was enormous! However, there was a principle at issue, and the Supreme Court of Canada sided with Mr Forest.[22]*

*The case ignited public opinion, and the decision was criticized for being unrealistic and causing legal chaos. There was also the huge cost of translating all the laws passed since 1890 within two years, as ordered by the Court. The secretary of state sent translators to Winnipeg to tackle the project, and the federal government provided Manitoba premier Howard Pawley with funding. Key legislation was given priority and what had initially seeked like an insurmountable task became a reality thanks to the outstanding efforts of the translation team.*

*It was clear that the most effective way to advance recognition of language rights was to provide funding through a court challenges program.*

*The case involving a Manitoba traffic ticket carried significant symbolic weight. It clearly demonstrated that constitutional language rights were real and that their scope was broad enough to allow the courts to redress "100 years of injustice." No practical argument could prevent an infringement from being remedied. A segment of the population was in shock: Was this the objective when the Charter was passed in 1982 and language rights enshrined in the Constitution?*

*If the court's interpretation of guaranteed language rights could reverse one hundred years of legislation, could the same be true for other rights in the Charter, such as the right to equality under section 15?*

*The opportunity to ask the courts to recognize language rights led to both tangible and promising results. From 1984 to 1992, Canadian courts handed down ninety-seven decisions[23] on language rights through the federal Court Challenges Program.*

*A number of these were landmark decisions, such as the one recognizing linguistic minorities' right of governance over their own schools,[24] and to receive related public funding based on the same requirements and criteria for quality as those in effect for majority-language students.*

*These rulings shook up the established order, overcame inertia and often challenged a century of stubborn prejudices on the part of provincial governments, which were parsimonious, finicky and sometimes hostile toward francophone minority education rights.*

*The courts had become the key arbiters in the changing legal significance of language rights, and governments were gradually realizing that the Court Challenges Program was causing uncertainty for them. The program supported the Charter in the eyes of minority communities and it gave a push to governments that preferred to do nothing, allowing them to conveniently hide behind the claim that they did not want to take a certain action, but "the courts in Ottawa ordered them to."*

*Faced with mounting pressure, the government of Brian Mulroney decided to cancel the Court Challenges Program in 1993 to silence provincial criticism. It was claimed that the program had run its course and it was time to let people act according to their convictions!*

*Jean Chrétien's government saw things differently: he promised to restore the program during the 1993 election campaign.[25] It was reinstated in 1994, and in the next twelve years it led to fifty-one decisions on language rights, many of them significant – such as* Beaulac *(1999),* Arsenault-Cameron *(2000), and* Doucet-Boudreau *(2003) – and others that confirmed budget cuts were not a valid excuse for refusing to upgrade minority schools, given that a constitutionally guaranteed right was involved.*

*However, the case that had the greatest impact was the 2001 decision by the Ontario Court of Appeal in* Lalonde v. Ontario, *which ended efforts to close the Montfort Hospital in Ottawa, Ontario's only French-language hospital.*

*The same arguments were invoked against the Court Challenges Program in 2006, when Stephen Harper's government announced its cancellation. The parliamentary secretary to the minister of Canadian Heritage made this specious claim: "The Canadian court challenges program … encourages special interest groups to advance causes that do not reflect the view of the majority of Canadians … to promote a public policy agenda that is not always in line with the majority of Canadian voters."* [26]

*Based on this argument, most voters did not want to help minorities defend their constitutional right to their language before an impartial court, and they did not support minority rights, even though these minorities were taxpayers just like them! So the majority sided with the government, and the minorities had to defend themselves against unconstitutional laws or decisions that attacked their rights. In short, might is right!*

*The government's reasons for cancelling the Court Challenges Program in 2006 was obviously based on an ideology and set of values.*

*The Fédération des communautés francophones et acadienne du Canada challenged the government's decision in court, and the Harper government had to back down. It maintained the language rights component of the program but eliminated the component dealing with equality rights and other Charter rights.*

*Justin Trudeau's government reviewed the program and announced increased funding for it in February 2017.* [27] *Since 1984, the program's budget for language rights cases had not exceeded $1.5 million per year. That is very little when you consider the impact this funding had on increasing the recognition of and respect for minority language rights.*

*A number of observations can be made about the evolution of language rights over the past fifty years.*

*Firstly, the courts consistently had to be invoked to recognize rights that date back more than 240 years to the* Quebec Act, 1774, *and the establishment of the first legislative assembly in Quebec City in 1791! Do we learn nothing from the previous generation? The courts clearly did not always welcome cases brought by francophones.* [28] *In the territories and the West, for example, progress was often slow if not disappointing.*

*The second observation concerns governments' penny-pinching mentality, doling out concessions after repeated tugs on their sleeve. It is not an appealing characterization and it is far from Canadians' self-image as a generous people, proud of their country's identity.*

*The recent legal conflict between Rose-des-Vents elementary school and Vancouver's French school board is deplorable and unworthy of a provincial government in 2017. Citizens had to wage a ten-year battle until, in 2015, the Supreme Court of Canada recognized their constitutional right to a French-language school of equal quality to that of the majority. This case is reminiscent of the worst prejudices of an era that was a dark chapter in our history. And the worst example of bad faith was demonstrated by Christy Clark's provincial government: it opposed the case every step of the way, right up to the Supreme Court!*[29]

*On the other hand, we should acknowledge the spirit of openness that is emerging elsewhere in the country. In Ontario, for example, Kathleen Wynne's government showed leadership when it passed Bill 177 establishing the* Université de l'Ontario français. *The bill also deserves mention for recognizing the "bilingual character" of the nation's capital, after a century of struggles.*

*As for the federal government, for the past twenty-five years it has done nothing to recognize the French version of the* Constitution Act, 1867, *as official, in compliance with section 55 of the* Constitution Act, 1982. *It runs the risk of being taken to court on this issue. This omission is shameful and reprehensible.*[30]

*It is now recognized that the justices of the Supreme Court, the highest court in the land and the court of final appeal that rules on issues regarding the scope and equal status of both official languages, should be able to hear cases in both official languages.*

*The Supreme Court is clearly a symbolic and significant institution in the minds of Canadians. The Court's decision in 2015*[31] *may have raised doubts about Parliament's authority to require justices to be proficient in both official languages, and this uncertainty must now be addressed. The federal government should put the question directly to the Court. Why should the highest court avoid the provisions of an act that has made our system of government a constitutional democracy subject to the rule of law?*

*The third observation is that, intentionally or unintentionally, governments vary in their commitment to advance language rights, as demonstrated by the overall political climate, the positions of various political parties on advancing language rights, and the cancellation of the Court Challenges Program, once in 1993 and again in 2006. This commitment is not consistent among political parties and it is not absolute.*

*Lastly, without the ongoing activities of the Senate and House of Commons standing committees on official languages, established in 1983,*[32] *and the annual reports of the Commissioner of Official Languages, the visibility and significance of language rights would no longer receive public attention or be of daily concern to government.*

*To address this instability once and for all, access to justice in both official languages needs to be enhanced and, most importantly, the Court Challenges Program needs to be entrenched in the* Official Languages Act *and taken out of politicians' hands. The* OLA *must include provisions stating the program's objectives and criteria. Otherwise, we are*

### THE FOREST CASE IN MANITOBA: AN UNEXPECTED OUTCOME IN 1979

What had begun rather quietly in 1975 as a challenge of a unilingual municipal parking ticket ended with a Supreme Court ruling in 1979 that all the laws passed by the Legislative Assembly of Manitoba since 1890 were unconstitutional! It was a completely unexpected turn of events. The province had to translate the most important laws into French within two years, which it was able to do with the help of the translation services under the Department of the Secretary of State of Canada. The principle of equality of the two languages dated back to Manitoba's creation in 1870 and was entrenched in section 23 of its constitution, and the right to use French had remained valid. The Supreme Court ruled that constitutional language guarantees were intangible. Credit: *Winnipeg Free Press*, front page, 13 December 1979

*condemned to have the same discussions about its survival every time there is a change of government. As the Commissioner of Official Languages stated in Federal Court in 2008, the program "directly and significantly assisted in the advancement of language rights in Canada and, in so doing, contributed to the vitality and development of our official language minority communities."[33]*

*For the past thirty-five years, the program has repeatedly shown that it provides a vital service to official language minorities!*

*In addition, we need to better define the role of the Commissioner of Official Languages in defending the equal status of the official languages before the courts. The Commissioner cannot simply continue to be an intervenor, but must be given the responsibility to launch court proceedings to remedy a violation of the law and request financial compensation or other remedies.*

*However, another power struggle between majority-language speakers and linguistic minorities is emerging as Canada's demographics change. Our population will continue to become more diverse in the coming decades and this trend will profoundly change the demographic distribution of these groups.*

*Statistics Canada data from the last census shows that immigration and ethnocultural and linguistic diversity have caused the proportion of francophone minorities to decrease in relation to provincial populations as a whole.[34] It is quite clear that, in a number of Canadian cities, linguistic communities other than English and French will increase significantly in future. French is the third, fourth, or fifth language in most of the Western provinces. More people living in the West speak Punjabi, Cantonese, or Tagalog than French: close to one quarter of a million people speak German at home, compared with 144,000 French speakers.[35] Pressure to receive provincial services in other languages is already being felt in various locations across the country. Statistics Canada estimates that, in the coming years, 30 per cent of Canadians will speak a mother tongue other than English or French.[36] Where these linguistic groups form homogeneous communities, they will increasingly want students to be educated in their own language.*

*This pressure will not threaten the English language. English will always be useful in a global economy because it is the language of the US digital giants. It is the French language that will suffer.*

*As a result, there is an urgent need to review the federal government's obligation to provide services in French.[37] Part IV of the OLA stipulates that services must be provided where there is "significant demand." However, the method of calculating whether demand is significant is completely discriminatory. It seeks to minimize demand, likely to avoid having to provide service in French, rather than support the vitality of minority communities. The formula is set out in a Treasury Board regulation dating back to 1991 and is based on "first official language spoken," which excludes anyone who has a "knowledge of the official language."*

*Why invest in immersion schools and fund French-as-a-second-language instruction when the people who benefit from this education are excluded from the calculation, as are those who have a knowledge of the language?*

*In 2001, French services were reduced in more than one hundred federal offices based on the government's interpretation of its obligation to provide services in French.*

*The overall growth of the anglophone population in absolute numbers works against the francophone minority, which grows more slowly. In 2006, the francophone minority totalled 997,000 persons, or 4.2 per cent of the population. It is now more than one million, but accounts for only 4 per cent of the population.*

*Based on the formula, although there may be more francophones, they still receive fewer services in their language. This approach is flawed and damaging to communities. It would be grossly negligent to amend the OLA and not change this harmful criterion to "vitality of the official language community," which would take into account various factors related to the community's cultural, economic, and social life. This new criterion better reflects what it means to live in French,[38] especially since experts agree that the language spoken in the public sphere is the best indicator of its vitality.[39] This criterion is even more important when you consider that, by 2036, scarcely 1.8 per cent of francophones in minority communities will speak French at home.[40] French-speaking immigration is all the more important to support those communities.*

*The significant numerical imbalance between English speakers and French speakers is rising steadily.[41] The increase in linguistic diversity will lead to an increased demand for services in other languages and increased public pressure on the provincial and federal governments to provide multilingual services. There is a risk that French will become one among many languages spoken by homogeneous communities, or that it will be relegated to the sidelines.*

*There is an urgent need to stipulate in Part VII of the OLA what "positive measures" the federal institutions must take to support the development of official language communities.*

*This section of the Act was amended in 2005 to create an obligation on the federal government, following multiple attempts by former senator Jean Robert Gauthier.[42] It is now urgent to recognize the OLA's remedial purpose to repair the damage inflicted on francophone communities during the last hundred years through various interventions by governments to limit the use and expression of French language and ultimately the assimilation and disappearance of the French culture. This remedial objective should be entrenched in the Act to guide its interpretation.*

*In a judgment of 23 May 2018,[43] the Federal Court completely discharged the Canadian government from undertaking active measures to support the linguistic expansion of minority communities, that was entrenched in Part VII of the OLA, as amended in 2005. The Court determined that Part VII imposes no such obligation either to support or to encourage French language rights, but only to avoid deliberately undermining them. The Court reasoned that the government had not been explicit in imposing an obligation on itself having omitted to adopt regulations (article 41.2) and, as such, Part VII was of no force or effect. In fact, the judgment is even more pernicious: it allows the federal government to evade its obligation in respect to official languages by signing administrative agreements with provinces (in this case an agreement for the development of a labour market with British Columbia) that do not include this obligation. This legal interpretation creates a dangerous precedent that must be addressed. The Trudeau government commitment to modernize the OLA provides the opportunity to overturn the consequences of the judgment. How can it be right for the federal government to subcontract its responsibilities to a province and thereby enabling it to escape binding constitutional obligations to provide services in French or in English?*

*If the federal government allows the judgment to stand, it directly violates the OLA, a quasi-constitutional statute according to the Supreme Court, the spirit, and the letter of the law. It is totally unworthy of Canada in 2018.*

*In addition to the current demographic challenges, we can include the dominance of English in the global economy and corporate control over digital mass communications.*

*The pressure on the French language in Canada also stems from globalization and is no longer solely the result of coexisting with English. The dominance of the United States means that other countries must turn to international forums such as the United Nations Educational, Scientific and Cultural Organization (UNESCO) and the Organisation internationale de la Francophonie to restore some sort of balance and protect linguistic and cultural diversity. Every language except English – Spanish, Italian, German, etc., – experiences the pressures associated with a loss of status in its use, even in the country where it is spoken.*

*Canada cannot let down its guard in terms of threat to the official languages and minorities. Their vitality enabled the country to come into being by uniting two different linguistic communities that embraced tolerance and peaceful coexistence, and were protected by the rule of law. This is part of Canada's founding identity, its social cohesiveness, its national unity, and the sense of humanity it seeks to preserve to safeguard its future.*

## NOTES

1 The author would like to thank the Library of Parliament for checking the figures and historical facts in this document.

2 Marcel Chaput, *Pourquoi je suis séparatiste* (Éditions de l'Homme, 1961); a recent report ordered by the Clerk of the Privy Council found that "English is the dominant language for most daily activities and Francophone employees do not consistently feel that they can work in the language of their choice," in Buzetti, Hélène, "Les primes au bilinguisme dans la fonction publique fédérale," *Le Devoir*, 20 September 2017, p. A5.

3 *Preliminary Report of the Royal Commission on Bilingualism and Biculturalism* (Ottawa: Queen's Printer, 1965).

4 Daniel Johnson, Égalité ou Indépendance, Éditions de l'Homme, 1968.

5 The Confederation of Tomorrow Conference (Robarts), Toronto, 1967.

6 The Act underwent significant amendments in 1988 and was expanded in 2005 thanks to a private member's bill amending Part VII, introduced by Senator Jean-Robert Gauthier.

7 *Jones v. A.G. of New Brunswick* [1975] 2 SCR 182.

8 Total of the US population (202 million) and Canada's English-speaking population (close to 17 million) in 1969.

9 Sandford F. Borins, *The Language of the Skies: The Bilingual Air Traffic Control Conflict in Canada*, The Institute of Public Administration of Canada (Kingston and Montreal: McGill-Queen's University Press, 1983).

10 CALPA: Canadian Air Line Pilots Association; CATCA: Canadian Air Traffic Control Association.

11 *Joyal et al. v. Air Canada*, [1976] Québec SC 1211; Bastarache, Michel, "La valeur juridique du projet de loi reconnaissant l'égalité des deux communautés linguistiques officielles du Nouveau-Brunswick," *Les Cahiers de droit*, vol. 22, no. 2, 1981, pp. 455–71.

12 *Association des gens de l'air du Québec Inc. v. The Honourable Otto Lang*, 1977, 76 DLR (3d) 455.

13 Ninety-two countries and 6,084 athletes.

14 Commission of Inquiry into Bilingual Air Traffic Services in Quebec (Canada). Interim report tabled 23 June 1977, final report tabled 10 August 1979.

15 Section 24(1) of the *Canadian Charter of Rights and Freedoms* states as follows: "Anyone whose rights or freedoms, as guaranteed by this Charter, have been infringed or denied may apply to a court of competent jurisdiction to obtain such remedy as the court considers appropriate and just in the circumstances."

16 The author agreed to assume all the costs of the case against Air Canada, and released all the pilots involved from any financial obligations.

17 Michel Décary and Gino Castiglio in *Serge Joyal et al. v. Air Canada*. Clément Richard and Guy Bertrand in *Association des Gens de l'Air du Québec Inc. v. the Honourable Otto Lang*.

18 Air Canada was not privatized until 1988.

19 *Blaikie v. Attorney General of Quebec* [1978] SC 3.

20 The author was Secretary of State from 1982 to 1984.

21 S. 23 of the *Manitoba Act* replicates s. 133 of the *Constitution Act, 1867*.

22 *Forest v. Attorney-General of Manitoba* [1979] 2 SCR 1032; Attorney-General of Canada, Intervenor, 1978 CanLII 2093 (MB QB); *Forest v. Manitoba* (Attorney General), 1979 CanLII 2509 (MB CA); *Attorney General of Manitoba v. Forest*, [1979] 2 SCR 1032, 1979 CanLII 242 (SCC).

23 Figures provided by the Library of Parliament's research branch, 22 September 2017.

24 Michael D. Behiels, *Canada's Francophone Minority Communities: Constitutional Renewal and the Winning of School Governance* (Montreal: McGill-Queen's University Press, 2005), p. 325 et seq.

25 The author was then the Chair of the Policy Committee of the Liberal Party of Canada

(Quebec) and drafted himself the paragraphs of the *Red Book*, the electoral platform (1993) of the LPC on that very issue.

26  Jim Abbott, (Kootenay–Columbia), Parliamentary Secretary to the Minister of Canadian Heritage, House of Commons, *Edited Hansard*, No. 063, 1st Session, 39th Parliament, 17 October 2006, p. 3852.

27  Government of Canada, *Backgrounder – Court Challenges Program.*

28  *Yukon Francophone School Board, Education Area #23* v. *Yukon (Attorney General)*, 2015 SCC 25, [2015] 2 SCR 282; *Northwest Territories (Attorney General) v. Commission Scolaire Francophone, Territoires du Nord-Ouest*, 2015 (NWTCA 1); *Caron v. Alberta*, 2015 SCC 56, [2015] 3 SCR 511.

29  Maxime Laporte and Christian Gagnon, "Le Canada de 2017 toujours anti-francophone," *Le Devoir*, 4 August 2017.

30  Linda Cardinal and François Larocque (eds.), *La Constitution bilingue du Canada – un projet inachevé*, Presses de l'Université Laval, 2017. The author is considering bringing this constitutional issue before the courts as a declaratory action.

31  *Reference re Supreme Court Act, ss. 5 and 6*, 2014 SCC 21, [2014] 1 SCR 433.

32  In 1981, the author tabled the first motion in the House of Commons concerning the creation of a joint Senate-House of Commons committee on official languages. The motion was passed in 1982. The joint committee was split in 2007 following the election of the Harper government, and each House had has its own committee since then.

33  Memorandum of Fact and Law of the Intervener, *Commissioner of Official Languages, Fédération des communautés francophones et acadienne du Canada v. Canada* (Attorney General), Federal Court of Canada, 21 December 2007, para. 29.

34  Statistics Canada, *2016 Census of Population: Language*, August 2017.

35  *Blacklock's Reporter*, "French Now a 4th language," 3 August 2017.

36  Statistics Canada, *2016 Census of Population: Language*, August 2017.

37  See the testimony of the author at the Senate Standing Committee on Official Languages on 30 April 2018 in relation to the amendments to the OLA.

38  A bill on this subject (S-209), sponsored by former senator Maria Chaput is on the Senate *Order Paper*. This is the fourth time such a bill has been tabled since 2011.

39  Monelle Guertin, "Langue française: savoir lire les indicateurs avant de partir en peur," *Le Devoir*, 24 August 2017, p. A7.

40  Statistics Canada, *2016 Census of Population: Language*, August 2017.

41  Standing Senate Commitee on Official Languages, *Aiming Higher: Increasing bilingualism of our Canadian youth*, June 2015, pp. 4–5.

42 After the retirement of Senator Jean Robert Gauthier, on 22 October 2004, the then leader of the government (Senator Sharon Carstairs) thought that the proposed private member Bill by Senator Gauthier would die on the Order Paper. There were many attempts by other senators (among them the author) to finally have the vote being called on third reading of the Bill and have the amendment adopted in November 2005.

43 *Fédération des francophones de la Colombie-Britannique v. Canada (Employment and Social Development)*, 2018 FC 530.

# Living Your Language to its Fullest

Her Excellency the Right Honourable Michaëlle Jean, secretary general
of the Organisation internationale de la Francophonie and former
governor general of Canada (2005–10)

The strength and greatness of a country lies in its willingness to put itself to the test and its capacity for self-examination.

This morning, Phil Fontaine and Ellen Gabriel allowed us to rise above the temptation of overly glorious celebrations by reminding us, with great dignity, of facts that could too easily be relegated to the backdrop of a much too convenient version of history, where whole chapters are whited out. This is an opportunity for us, they said, to take into account those who were silenced and, without looking the other way, to recognize—and herein lies the hope—that we can be reborn together from the ashes of the disaster, as long as we have the willingness, and act together as we must. I also want to commend this initiative by Senator Joyal and Senator Judith Seidman, so rife with lessons on all these struggles, the acts of resistance that are foundational to Canada.

Canada's 150th anniversary is, first of all, an opportunity to reflect on the full extent of our progress to date, this vast country that is still developing and changing. This anniversary must also be an opportunity to consider the infinite possibilities before us. The Francophonie in Canada and around the world is a fundamental part of human history and of Canada's collective experience.

We saw this morning how quickly the language issue arises. All human experience begins with language. Every language brings together and is surrounded by the unique characteristics that give it life, make it distinctive, and enable it to spread. Language is the vital, visceral, organic connection through which we describe the world around us, recognize ourselves in others and others in ourselves. Language is a taproot, anchoring us deep in the soil of civilization.

Yet the first peoples of this land, our Indigenous brothers and sisters, have seen their languages strangled in the grip of colonialism. It is a tragic loss for these nations, for all of us, and for all humanity.

As the writer Amin Maalouf said unequivocally, "It is extremely dangerous to try to break the maternal cord connecting a man to his own language. When it is ruptured or seriously damaged his whole personality may suffer disastrous repercussions."[1] I would add that those repercussions can extend over whole generations.

In other words, we cannot feel good about ourselves and others unless our language is recognized and respected. That is why we are so attached to "our" language and defend it tooth and nail. Its survival demands that we show a spirit of resistance, always and everywhere.

When I say resistance, I mean the efforts of every community, people, and nation to assert their language, and to keep it alive and central to their identity. This is still a struggle for Canada's Francophone minority communities, even though the Constitution fully recognized Canada's two official languages and their coexistence in 1867. From that date forward, either English or French could be used in debates in Parliament and in any court in Canada.

It is a struggle even though language rights are clearly recognized in the Canadian Charter of Rights and Freedoms and entrenched in the Constitution Act, 1982.

Each of these languages is a window on the world. All Canadians should understand just how lucky we are! English and French are the only two languages that are spoken on all five continents. While English is the main language of the business world, French is the third most commonly used language for business after Mandarin. French is still the most popular second language taught around the world.

English and French give Canada significant weight and influence within two major multilateral intergovernmental organizations: the Commonwealth, which is composed of fifty-two countries; and the Organisation internationale de la Francophonie, which is composed of eighty-four states and governments and which I am proud to represent here.

I am so proud to be Canadian and to tell the world what my adoptive country has helped me accomplish. I am proud to be Haitian and part of a culture that draws its strength from its deep African roots entwined with those of the first nations of the Caribbean – the Taino and Arawak, who were decimated by colonization. I am proud to be a Quebecker; Quebec will always be my home and where my heart lies. I am also proud of my Acadian ancestry through my great-grandmother Célia Leblanc, grand-daughter of Cangé Leblanc, who was deported during the Expulsion of the Acadians on a boat that would drop anchor in Santo Domingo, the former French colony that became the Republic of Haiti in 1804, the first black republic in the world's history and an international leader in the abolition of slavery and the slave trade. I am proud that all of this history is part of who I am.

Thanks to these collective strengths and perspectives, I became the first woman elected secretary general of the Organisation internationale de la Francophonie in

November 2014, after having served as governor general of Canada, again thanks to these collective strengths and perspectives. If the French language has served as a bridge throughout Canada's history, it has also been a bridge throughout my own life.

Two years after Parliament passed the Official Languages Act in 1969, the Prime Minister of Canada, Pierre Elliott Trudeau, welcomed the Agency for Cultural and Technical Cooperation to Ottawa. This agency would give rise to the Organisation internationale de la Francophonie, which I now lead.

Mr Trudeau was quite right when he described this gathering in Canada's capital as the world's confirmation of the permanence of French Canada.[2]

In his eloquent speech to the delegates in Ottawa, he said that the Francophonie was not a memory of the past but a vision of the future.[3] Mr Trudeau's ideal was similar to the Canadian ideal, and focused on creating solidarity by nurturing diversity.[4] As Canadians, we can be proud to be defined by this broad perspective.

I would also like to highlight the words of Quebec Cabinet minister Camille Laurin, who saw French as a tool for self-development.[5] In his last speech, delivered in December 1998, Mr Laurin told a hometown audience in Charlemagne that he had wanted to give them a language that would help them not only rediscover their pride in an extraordinary culture and civilization, but also get any job for which they had the skills and aptitudes.[6]

Some people might think it daring or even foolhardy to evoke the father of the federal Official Languages Act and the father of the Quebec Charter of the French Language in the same breath but, aside from the ideology and differences separating these two men, they both possessed the same desire to celebrate and establish measures to protect the development of French in North America.

Internationally, it is likely this same steadfast determination that led my predecessor, the first secretary general of the Francophonie, Boutros Boutros-Ghali of Egypt, to state during the fiftieth anniversary of the United Nations, where he also served bravely as secretary general, that French is also a language of revolt against injustice, intolerance and oppression.[7]

The French language – from which sprang the Enlightenment and the values of liberty, equality, and fraternity that in turn inspired a new humanism – is also central to Canada's heritage.

The resistance I spoke of earlier is not new and it punctuates the saga of Francophones in Canada and our collective history. To ignore it is to be willfully blind.

As far back as 1902, at Laval University in Quebec City, the first French-language university in North America, the Societé du parler français was founded by priests and the laity to protect "our" language, as they said, from rampant anglomania.

Anglomania is the trend to imitate and adopt English words; it creates uniformity and standardization, while eroding other languages until they crumble.

Francophone nations around the world praise the Francophones of this country and their institutions for their ingenuity and determination to preserve and enhance the integrity and linguistic distinctiveness of the French language in this northern part of a predominantly anglophone continent.

Francophone communities that survive and flourish are one of Canada's distinctive features. Imagine a Canada without this heritage. It is part of our DNA.

A Canada that takes pride in itself is a Canada that treasures its two official languages and can step confidently onto the world stage, bolstered by pride in this dual heritage and double blessing. To maintain this heritage, we must take appropriate and responsible action, as Francophones have demonstrated through their determination and commitment across this vast country.

I can testify to this determination. Having served as the twenty-seventh governor general of Canada from 2005 to 2010, I had the great privilege of visiting our cities, our rural areas, and our regions. I crossed the country many times, from the St Lawrence to the Atlantic coast, from the Western plains to the Pacific shore, and up to the Arctic.

Everywhere I went, I met women, men, and young people who never stop looking for new ways to live in French. My journeys across the country were like a long, productive, and moving conversation with Canadians, Anglophones and Francophones alike. I can say with the deepest of emotion that I supported them wholeheartedly. I was aware of our differences, but more than anything, I was struck by how much we have in common. I saw that we draw our energy from the land and from the richness of our relationships.

What we have in common is a remarkable capacity to create, invent, innovate, work on a grand scale, flourish and achieve our potential, in English or in French, and for the more determined among us, in both languages.

I admired the Francophones in minority communities, who spoke confidently of positioning their culture as a "value-added" for all of society in their province or territory. I visited their schools, these places of learning created to foster success, and saw peoples' hope and confidence that their children will also live life to the fullest in French. I learned about the French immersion programs that they establish or run to increase the number of francophiles in the country. I saw their busy community centres that offer inclusive services tailored to neighbourhood needs. So much is being done to break down walls, build bridges, and combat prejudice. Everywhere I went, I was constantly moved by Francophones' aspirations and inspired by their desire to maintain their unique contribution to the personality of this country.

They do not see themselves as an endangered species. They resist with determination and imagination, and theirs is a constant struggle.

On the positive side, I am pleased that Manitoba recently passed the Francophone Community Enhancement and Support Act. And while I had seen the vitality of Franco-Ontarian culture, it has now enriched my family life, as my daughter attended French public school in Ottawa.

However, just over a hundred years ago in this city, mothers waged the "battle of the hatpins" not far from here at École Guigues on Murray Street. It may sound funny today, but these women were in no laughing mood when they armed themselves with hatpins to fight Ontario's Regulation 17, which restricted education in French to the first two years of elementary school.

And in 1997, an unprecedented grassroots movement sprang up to fight the closure of the Montfort Hospital, Ontario's only French hospital. Today, it is a university hospital working in partnership with the University of Ottawa, La Cité College, and other post-secondary programs to train future health-care providers in French.

These are two hard-fought victories by courageous Franco-Ontarians here in the nation's capital, which is such a lovely place year round. Ottawa should be proud of this Francophone identity and make it a powerful symbol of our commitment to Canada's two official languages.


Allow me to speak openly, as you have asked me to speak, as a friend with convictions, wholeheartedly and candidly. From the day Ottawa became home to me in 2005, I have found it passing strange that our capital city, the capital city of Canada, had yet to be the potent official emblem of bilingualism that we like to showcase as a long-standing, primordial value of our country.

As a capital city, Ottawa proudly welcomes chancelleries and embassies from around the world. It is the canvas on which the hopes and values that define Canada are depicted. Every year, hundreds of thousands of Canadians enjoy visiting Ottawa to discover the focal point of our federal history.

A capital city must set an example, be a model, and send a message to the rest of the country. Every gesture matters. Every action carries meaning. We can't rationalize purely from an accountant's calculation, assuming that the cost of a bilingual capital city is simply too high.

Such an investment pales in comparison to what we are building together through our outlook, our way of life and ability to live together, our full appreciation of what defines our identity, and our relationship with each other and with the world.

"PARLONS FRANÇAIS ET PARLONS BIEN" [LET'S SPEAK FRENCH AND LET'S SPEAK PROPERLY] Plaster with silver finish. Pride in speaking a minority language stems from a number of factors. One is that speaking a language allows people to express their attachment to their roots, their culture, their personal identity, and their community's identity. Many associations and initiatives have boosted that pride, including the Société du bon parler français, founded in 1902, which organized two major conferences around the importance of promoting spoken French and advocating for better quality of the spoken language. Credit: CHSJ

With this in mind, we should celebrate the decision at the Francophonie Summit in Madagascar last fall to approve Ontario's request for observer status within the Organisation internationale de La Francophonie. And we should salute the Ontario premier's commitment to "protecting and promoting French language and identity."

Ontario, which has more than half a million Francophones – the second-largest Francophone community in the country – joins the federal government and the governments of Quebec and New Brunswick, which are full and founding members in many regards of the Organisation internationale de la Francophonie.

I would like to take a moment to highlight other excellent examples and promising initiatives across Canada that have allowed me to take the pulse of Canadian Francophone communities and see just how strongly it beats.

In 2007, I travelled to Whitehorse and discovered that the Yukon was the only place in Canada, outside Quebec, where the Francophone population was on the rise. Why? Because of the enthusiastic efforts of French-speaking Yukoners, the many services available – from education, training, and job-search techniques to help for entrepreneurs, youth activities, and cultural events – and, of course, the dazzling beauty of the Yukon. The Francophone community also won a victory when the territory passed the French as a First Language Instruction Regulation, greatly increasing access to education in French for immigrants and francophiles.

Acadia, where language and pride go hand in hand, is an outstanding example of the spirit of resistance at work. History has shown us that nothing can discourage Acadians in their struggle for their rights and, thanks to their unwavering commitment, New Brunswick is the only officially bilingual province in Canada. French is deeply rooted in New Brunswick and helps to give that province its spark.

New Brunswick's growth and its appeal are based on this dual foundation and this convergence, which truly represents who we are as Canadians, as I was happy to note in Caraquet.

Those are just some of Canada's Francophone communities that I visited, discovered and embraced, and this quick overview brings me to Quebec, which, as I mentioned, I will always think of as the place where I put down roots in this land of opportunity. My own story on Canadian soil began in Quebec, on a February day in 1968 – my introduction to winter. Like thousands of others, my family was forced to flee Haiti and the greedy and repressive Duvalier dictatorship. We found asylum in Canada and settled in Quebec.

In 1968, scarcely a year after Canada celebrated the one hundredth anniversary of Confederation, an event that propelled Canada into the heady era of the second half of the twentieth century, a new global consciousness began to emerge for the first time and on a scale never seen before. It was the start of a new age, as the wonderful Quebec performer Renée Claude sang in "Le début d'un temps nouveau."

Montreal's Expo 67 inspired us to open our doors and invite the world in. It was a time of great hopes and dreams. That is the Quebec I love and the Canada I love. Montreal became my city and I will certainly be there for its 375th anniversary, as I was for the 400th anniversary of Quebec City in 2008, which also marks 400 years of the French presence in North America. What a long way we have come!

From the French settlers who became Canadians through their contact with the Indigenous peoples who taught them about the bounty of this generous land, from the French Canadians who spread throughout the country, to the Francophones of today who have welcomed other Francophones from around the world to start over again. My own journey, much like Canada's, tells stories of hither and thither, of encounters and propinquity.

However, the fate and future of French in Canada and America must not be the sole responsibility of Francophones: it must be everyone's business, for the sake of the common good. This is our language. It is a unique asset for each of us and a shared and collective responsibility. It is the expression of our individuality and a gateway to the world.

In this light, I believe that the unanimous decision by the provincial and territorial premiers in July 2016 to ask the federal government to increase Francophone immigration outside Quebec to 5 per cent is a positive step for the vitality of Canada's Francophonie and for the country as a whole.

Our Francophonie is an unbelievable treasure and an undeniable asset, both nationally and internationally, and Canadians across the country should leverage it with confidence.

Canada is the second-largest contributor and country of influence within the Organisation internationale de la Francophonie, after France. This organization works on a global scale, with eleven member countries from West Africa, sixteen from Central Africa and the Indian Ocean, seven from North Africa and the Middle East, thirty-one from Europe – seventeen of which are EU members – seven from Asia and the Pacific, four from the Caribbean, four from Latin and South America and, lastly, the North American members – the governments of Canada, Quebec, New Brunswick, and most recently, Ontario.

Imagine the sphere of influence and possibilities offered by the Francophonie. Imagine the forums for co-operation, sharing, and investment. Imagine the opportunities to be seized. Imagine the many bridges to build, the energy to harness, and the resources, expertise, and skills to share.

The French language is a bridge, a strategic vehicle, a powerful lever, and a tremendous opportunity. The Francophone nations on the five continents expect Canada, which is a model of openness, a symbol of hope, and an exemplary and trusted partner, to step up its efforts, its presence, and its focus within the Francophonie.

In addition, Canadian expertise in general, like that of Quebec, New Brunswick and now Ontario, is highly valued and solicited. This know-how is applied in many areas of activity of the Francophonie recognized by our close international partners, such as the United Nations and all of its agencies and institutions, the European Union, the African Union, the Organization of American States, and the African, Caribbean, and Pacific Group of States.

The Francophonie has become a valued partner in many fields. Whether building the capacity of rule-of-law institutions, preventing and resolving conflicts, fighting terrorism, participating in peacekeeping, and dealing with the huge threats that face the world, or contributing to learning, vocational training, higher education, and research, we are the champions of cultural and linguistic diversity.

We are also at the forefront of sustainable development and very active in the fight against climate change and its devastating impact on the world's most vulnerable people.

Population exodus and migration are also a priority for us. The Organisation internationale de la Francophonie can attest to the facts as its members include countries of origin, transit, destination, and asylum, and some members are all those things at once. We know what causes these often dramatic mass movements of people and therefore what must be done to prevent them.

The Francophonie is involved in every issue, and we promote a spirit of global humanism that calls on us to rethink some of our behaviours and patterns of production and consumption, in favour of a true principle of sharing and solidarity.

Canada and the Organisation internationale de la Francophonie embrace the same fundamental values, and this country must continue to play an ever-larger and more important role in the organization.

In times of great and sometimes unanticipated change, during periods of extreme tension and upheaval around the world, and when our desperate calls for solidarity fall on deaf ears, we must consider the words of Senegalese poet and president Léopold Sédar Senghor, one of the founding fathers of the Francophonie, who saw in it the hope for fraternity based on mutual respect and dialogue between cultures.[8]

Let's not miss any opportunity to "innervate"[9] all the international networks with our common perspectives, to use the phrase of Quebecker Jean-Louis Roy, one of my predecessors at the Francophonie, who points out that the Francophonie stands in solidarity with all people and all languages. Abdou Diouf, another great Senegalese leader and former secretary general of the Francophonie, stated that the strength of the Francophonie is that it instantly saw the battle for one language as the battle for all languages.[10] These are words of wisdom in a language that seeks to shelter all living beings, all beings capable of love and resistance in the name of an integral humanism.

One of the greatest promises of the future in Canada is our pride in speaking French, as Francophones or francophiles, no matter where we are, from East to West and North to South.

I would also like to give a tip of the hat to Le français pour l'avenir, a dedicated not-for-profit organization that encourages anglophone Canadian high school students to study and live in French, and to make this heritage an asset for today and an investment for the future. Young people are the key to bringing down barriers and bridging the distance between languages.

I could not imagine a better legacy at the end of my term as Canada's twenty-seventh governor general. This urgent need to invest in the words, energy, drive, and creativity of young people across the country inspired the creation of the Michaëlle Jean Foundation. The Foundation supports their highly innovative grassroots projects to address our most pressing social issues. I have seen how even the most marginalized young people still do not lose their imagination and their fighting spirit. The work supported by the Foundation plays a vital preventive role.

We must give young people the resources to help us develop who we are and everything that makes us a model for other countries. We are a land of harmony, a place of peaceful and productive coexistence, a country where all cultures meet and intermix. It is our responsibility – one we must fulfill – to make this a solid foundation for shared growth, and inclusive, responsible, and sustainable development.

I would like to conclude as I began, with a question that Pierre Elliott Trudeau posed to Francophone nations in Paris in 1982: Is it too great a dream to seek a formally established Francophonie with a strong international voice?[11]

Thirty-five years later, as we celebrate this 150th anniversary, I would like to say that no, Mr Trudeau, it is not too great a dream. We have achieved it. Let's make the most of it!

### NOTES

1 Amin Maalouf, *In the Name of Identity: Violence and the Need to Belong* (New York: Arcade Publishing, 2001), 133.

2 The Right Honourable Pierre Elliott Trudeau, Prime Minister of Canada, "La francophonie: porte ouverte sur l'avenir," speech, General Conference of the Agency for Cultural and Technical Cooperation, Ottawa, 11 October 1971.

3 Ibid.

4 Ibid.

5 Last speech delivered by Camille Laurin to friends and residents in his hometown of Charlemagne, on 11 December 1998, *Le Testament* (Montreal: Les Intouchables, 1999).

6 Ibid.

7 Statement by Boutros Boutros-Ghali during the fiftieth anniversary celebration of the United Nations.

8 Statement by Léopold Sédar Senghor on the occasion of the fiftieth anniversary of the launch of *Présence d'Afrique*, November 1997.

9 Jean-Louis Roy, *La francophonie: le projet communautaire* (Quebec: Hurtubise, 1993), 17.

10 Speech by Abdou Diouf to the National Assembly, Libreville, March 2003.

11 The Right Honourable Pierre Elliott Trudeau, Prime Minister of Canada, "Le Canada et la francophonie," speech, Agency for Cultural and Technical Cooperation, Paris, 10 November 1982.

# Language Equality: Between Aspirations and Day-to-Day Reality

The Honourable Michel Bastarache, former judge of the New Brunswick Court of Appeal (1995–97) and former justice of the Supreme Court of Canada (1997–2008)

I thought I would address this topic by examining the evolution of language rights and its importance to Canada's development as a country where official language communities can take part in public affairs without giving up their language and culture and can develop freely as members of Canada's francophone community and the French-speaking world.

The issue of language rights was controversial before Confederation and has continued to be since. It is not possible here to trace the complete history of language rights since 1760, but that is when governments began taking steps to preserve and promote the French fact.

After the conquest of 1760, the goal of the regime in place was the wholesale assimilation of the French-speaking population. A few necessary concessions would be made for Quebec. However, the Royal Proclamation of 1763 would quickly lead to the complete abolition of the use of French, including in the Custom of Paris. In his comprehensive analysis of the history of language rights, Michael D. Behiels (Behiels, 2008) says that it is surprising that the English learned nothing from the failure of this policy in Acadia, where they had ultimately decided to deport the Acadians in 1755, having failed to assimilate them and convert them to Protestantism.[1] Eventually, the English passed the Quebec Act in 1774.[2] This act unified Quebec, restored customary French law, and allowed Catholics to hold public offices.

The 1774 act was nonetheless vigorously challenged by a coalition that wanted to put in place a representative government. In 1791, this petition was rejected, but the colony was divided in two and Upper and Lower Canada were created. The two colonies were independent of each other, but both under the authority of an all-powerful representative of the Colonial Office. The act maintained customary French law, but introduced the English land tenure system in the Eastern Townships.[3] The English were counting on mass immigration, which did not occur until the 1840s.

Lower Canada became bilingual out of necessity. Later, the council and the assembly could veto each other; a crisis ensued. The decision was made to suspend the powers of the assembly. In 1837, following the rebellion by the Patriotes, martial law was imposed. In 1840, the Act of Union was proclaimed.[4] Lord Durham was tasked with analysing the situation and coming up with a solution. He proposed reunification and a representative assembly within a totally English system.[5] Upper and Lower Canada were united, but representative government was not put in place; English was adopted as the official language. This measure was ineffective, as many members of the assembly were unilingual francophones. Unilingualism was abolished in 1848.

The movement for representative government grew. John A. Macdonald and George-Étienne Cartier joined forces to promote a federation. In it Cartier saw partial sovereignty for Quebec; in section 133 of the Constitution Act, 1867, he agreed to limited bilingualism that would apply only at the federal level and in Quebec.[6] There was little discussion of this provision; it was meant simply to perpetuate the compromise that the previous regime had arrived at. The importance of the powers given to Quebec enabled this regime. In reality, it would not change much. In Quebec, the government functioned in French, and until 1970, the federal bureaucracy and federal courts functioned in English.[7]

What about the minorities outside Quebec, including the Acadians? Had they been forgotten? No, their demands had been rejected.[8] Three petitions presented by members of the Legislative Assembly of New Brunswick to obtain protections were rejected.[9] Manitobans were the only ones who obtained constitutional protection, in the law creating Manitoba, a few years later. Section 22 of the Manitoba Act guaranteed instruction in French, while section 23 repeated the guarantees in section 133 of the Constitution Act, 1867.[10] After the 1885 rebellion and the massive influx of anglophones, the government decided to abolish the language guarantees in 1890. Two legal decisions declared the measure unconstitutional; the government did not appeal the decisions and ignored them.[11] The fight to restore language rights was long and hard, culminating in the ruling in the *Reference re Manitoba Language Rights* in 1985.[12]

It is important to note that francophone minorities outside Quebec and anglophone minorities in Quebec were counting on section 93 of the Constitution Act, 1867, to guarantee instruction in the minority language. This section guaranteed publicly funded denominational schools for the Catholic and Protestant minorities; Catholic schools generally functioned in French outside Quebec, and Protestant schools in English in Quebec. The courts ruled that only schools established by law were protected and that the language of instruction was not part of the guarantee.[13] Linguistic minorities had two avenues of recourse: the federal government's power of disallowance and the remedial power set out in subsection 93(4) of the Constitution Act. The recourse was a complete failure.

In New Brunswick, the Common Schools Act of 1871 established a unilingual English public school system.[14] The system was challenged unsuccessfully up to the Privy Council. A member of Parliament then moved a motion demanding that Prime Minister Macdonald disallow the law. A second MP called for legislation under subsection 93(4) of the Constitution Act, 1867. The motion passed, but the prime minister refused to act on it.[15] The discrimination persisted until an Acadian premier was elected in 1960.

In Manitoba as well, people battled to have the Act Respecting Public Schools struck down.[16] The law was wrongly declared valid in Canada, but that decision was overturned by the Privy Council. There were calls for federal intervention. Laurier refused to intervene, claiming that provincial jurisdiction over education had to be honoured. He negotiated an administrative agreement with Premier Greenway that did nothing to restore Franco-Manitobans' education rights.

In 1905, Alberta and Saskatchewan were created, but no provisions were enacted to protect the francophone minority. The North-West Territories Act was also passed without protections, but it was amended two years later to include guarantees similar to those in section 133 of the Constitution Act, 1867.[17] The courts ruled on two major cases in this regard. In *Mercure*, the Supreme Court held that the guarantees in the North-West Territories Act had been violated, but that they were not constitutional in nature.[18] The guarantees were immediately eliminated by the two provincial assemblies.[19] A new court challenge was filed in 2015; the Supreme Court heard the *Caron* case, but francophones lost in an unconvincing majority decision.[20]

In Ontario, in 1916, a major conflict resulted from the adoption of Regulation 17, which did away with French-language instruction, except for the first two years of school, in order to enable unilingual children to transition from French to English.[21] This led to significant civil disobedience. The case made its way to the Privy Council, which ruled that the province could abolish French-language instruction.[22] The regulation was rescinded in 1944, but French-language instruction was not brought in until the sixties.[23]

The sixties marked the beginning of what was called the Quiet Revolution in Quebec and the Acadian Awakening in New Brunswick. In Quebec, nationalists called for a law making French the province's only official language. What is more, they wanted all immigrants to be educated in French and French to be the language of business and all public and quasi-public institutions. The Parti Québécois was founded in 1968 and won 24 per cent of the popular vote just two years later in 1970. In New Brunswick, Louis Robichaud became premier and began a major overhaul of provincial institutions; he brought in the Official Languages Act and oversaw the creation of the Université de Moncton.[24]

The Royal Commission on Bilingualism and Biculturalism had been created in 1963 to address the gap separating the country's two major language communities. In its preliminary report in 1965 and its final report in 1967, the commission found that Canada was in crisis and that institutional reform was needed to save the country. Commissioner Laurendeau, who died before the final report was released, recommended special status for Quebec and constitutional protection for francophone minorities outside Quebec. The final report recommended that New Brunswick and Ontario have bilingual status, that bilingual districts be created in the other provinces when the linguistic minority reached 10 per cent of the population, and that minority-language instruction be guaranteed in all the provinces and territories. The report also recommended sweeping changes to the federal public service.

The Trudeau government rejected the territorial conceptualization of the Canadian duality and passed the Official Languages Act.[25] Official bilingualism was established and largely affirmed in the Canadian Charter of Rights and Freedoms in 1982.[26] The federal government then put in place various programs to support the provincial and territorial linguistic minorities. The provinces received large subsidies to put in place French immersion programs, and those subsidies continue.

Minority-language instruction was heavily subsidized, but it still took twenty years of court challenges before a full network of French-language schools was put in place outside Quebec. Moreover, this fight is still not over in many places, including British Columbia, the Northwest Territories, and the Yukon.

In Quebec, the language debate was very intense and led to the passage of Bill 63, Bill 22, and Bill 1.[27] Bill 1, which set out to repeal section 133 of the Constitution Act, 1867, was declared unconstitutional and later replaced with Bill 101. Some parts of Bill 101 were declared unconstitutional, but the law remained in place.[28] It was a major factor in Quebec's development into a resolutely francophone society. The provincial protections for English are designed to prevent discrimination rather than promote bilingualism.

The Canadian Charter of Rights and Freedoms would strengthen the right to education in the minority official language. It is important to note here that the first draft of the charter did not include the section 23 guarantees, as Pierre E. Trudeau was opposed to intruding directly into an area of provincial jurisdiction. However, his trusted minister of justice, Jean Chrétien, was convinced that the right to minority-language instruction at the provincial and territorial level was essential. Some members of his own family had settled in Alberta and had not been able to keep their language, which they would have liked to pass on to their children. He persuaded Pierre E. Trudeau to include section 23, and sections 16 to 23 of the charter were exempted from the notwithstanding clause. This afforded much better education protection for provincial and territorial linguistic minorities.

The Government of Quebec opposed the passage of the Constitution Act, 1982, and the education protection the charter gave to linguistic minorities. Quebec's aim in opposing the legislation was to protect provincial jurisdiction over education. A myth was even circulated in Quebec that the federal government and the provinces had secretly negotiated this agreement at the 1981 constitutional conference. I myself was present when a federal representative invited two members of the Quebec delegation to join the other delegates in the discussions. They refused, promised to meet with the anglophone delegates the following morning, and did not attend the meeting. In no way did Quebec's political refusal result from its exclusion from the negotiations. Moreover, Quebec regularly went to court to support the provinces that opposed francophone minorities' right to manage their own schools, for fear that this would hurt its school system.[29] These actions also created serious tension with francophones elsewhere in the country. Over the years, however, Quebec has adopted a policy of co-operation with francophone associations in the other provinces to support the French fact in Canada, and it has also signed co-operation agreements with Ontario, Manitoba, New Brunswick, and the Yukon.

After these political battles, the provinces and territories took action to create schools for the linguistic minority and give the minority control over them. Quebec offered no freedom of choice when it came to education. Immigrants were required to adopt French. In Manitoba, section 23 of the Manitoba Act was reinstated as a result of the Supreme Court decision in the 1985 *Reference re Manitoba Language Rights*.[30] French-language services were subsequently extended as a result of a study by Justice Richard Chartier. The 1999 Supreme Court decision in *Beaulac* broadened the very concept of a language right, rejecting the idea that language rights must be interpreted restrictively because they are the product of a political compromise.[31]

In New Brunswick, the Acadians won recognition of French as an official language and the equal status of the two official language communities in a second law in 1981.[32] This law, known as Bill 88, which confirmed the equality of French and English and the government's obligation to respect the duality of educational and cultural institutions, was partially constitutionalized in 1993.[33] In 1981, the schools act was amended to guarantee that francophones would have a homogeneous system. French schools would no longer be open to anglophones, and competing immersion schools would no longer be open to francophones. This provision was challenged up to the Supreme Court, which ruled in favour of the Société des Acadiens du Nouveau-Brunswick in 1986.[34] Nova Scotia and Prince Edward Island eventually established the right to schools managed by the minority linguistic community.

Outside New Brunswick and, more recently, Prince Edward Island, few provincial services are offered in French in the Maritimes. Ontario, Nova Scotia, and Quebec have laws governing services for the linguistic minority, and the other provinces have an administrative structure to provide for the delivery of limited services in French. The federal government provides financial support for the provincial initiatives. In the criminal justice system, litigants are entitled to proceedings in the language of their choice at the trial level, except in Quebec, Manitoba, New Brunswick and Ontario, where the right extends to all courts. New Brunswick, has adopted a regulatory code to fulfil its constitutional obligation.

In Ontario, the French Language Services Act was passed in 1990.[35] It provides for the delivery of services in French in specific linguistic regions. The Ontario Court of Appeal has handed down several very liberal decisions concerning service delivery in French in the health[36] and education fields.[37] Nevertheless, following the Supreme Court of Canada decision in *Mahe*, Ontario had to revise its education law to give representatives of the linguistic minority broader management rights.

The issue of the right of management exercised by representatives of the linguistic minority was clarified by the Supreme Court in the 1992 *Reference re Manitoba Language Rights* and the 2000 *Arsenault-Cameron* case.[38] In Quebec, the policy of French predominance affected the services offered to the anglophone linguistic minority.

As this brief history shows, the progress that has been made is both remarkable and relatively recent. One hundred years after Confederation, there was no legislation on official languages, the application of constitutional guarantees by the federal government was restrictive, and language rights were denied in Manitoba and the federal territories. Twenty-five years later, language rights were recognized by the federal government and five provinces; numerous court decisions gradually defined the scope of these rights.

In fact, the lot of provincial and territorial francophone minorities did not change substantially until the Canadian Charter of Rights and Freedoms took effect in 1982. The charter not only established the right to instruction in the language of the provincial or territorial minority across Canada, but added to the bilingualism obligations of the federal and New Brunswick governments.

With the most important language rights now enshrined in the Constitution, does that mean that there has been a fundamental change in direction and that Canada recognizes the collective right to maintain the minority culture, a right based mainly in the right to education, and the right to homogeneous schools managed by representatives of the linguistic minority? Some continue to doubt that it does, partly because these provisions were enacted after a constitutional battle with Quebec and therefore smack of another political compromise and partly because the provinces did not agree to implement the new education rights until they were forced to do so by the courts.

In reality, it is the courts that, in their rulings, have laid down the moral foundation for rights and affirmed governments' duty to preserve official language minorities and promote their cultural diversity. However, the federal government amended its Official Languages Act in 1988 to include the obligation to promote the official languages, after Quebec adopted a language regime that was very protective of the rights and privileges of the linguistic majority in order to protect it against the forces of assimilation in the North American context.[39] New Brunswick also passed a law on the equality of the official language communities that severely restricts the government.

Modern democracy in Canada and elsewhere needs the judiciary to uphold the Constitution, including the Canadian Charter of Rights and Freedoms. Basically, the issue centres around the concept of constitutional review and, to some extent, judicial review. These concepts are the most important in characterizing our justice system. In Canada, constitutional review is well known and has long been accepted in light of the division of powers and, formerly, the compliance of national laws with imperial laws. The Canadian Charter of Rights and Freedoms changed everything in people's minds. Decisions about a vague document that gives a great deal of latitude to judges, who will consider the general principles of law, new sources of law, and also historical and cultural factors, institutional arrangements, and social values, have given rise to new debates. The recognition of new individual and collective rights and greater opportunities to challenge government actions have multiplied the number of decisions to be made. This accounts for the public's impression that all the important social issues are before the courts.

In fact, the issue of the scope of section 16 of the Constitution Act, which affirms the status of the two official languages, has to do with what standards and values are in play in the judicial process. It is true that in common law countries, judges have always had broad power to make law without causing too much of an uproar, or at least less than in countries where the role of high court judges has traditionally been limited to interpreting the law. Basically, it is a question of legitimacy, and we are still trying to determine how far judges can go in interpreting laws so as to establish new rights and what criteria will be used to create those new rights. While it is accepted

SUPREME COURT OF CANADA

After 1982, the courts soon became the necessary way to assert linguistic minorities' rights, including the right to instruction in their language, as guaranteed by section 23 of the charter. From 1985 to 2015, the Supreme Court heard 19 cases seeking to have reluctant provincial governments uphold these rights, and other Canadian courts heard a further 150 cases. The federal Court Challenges Program provided financial support for a number of these landmark lawsuits. Credit: © Supreme Court of Canada, Philippe Landreville, photographer

that the Constitution Act is a "living tree," as Lord Sankey described it, meaning a series of standards that constantly need to be adjusted as moral and social values change, the courts clearly must not rewrite the Constitution and must respect the will of Parliament and the legislatures when it comes to statutory rights. Nevertheless, the symbolic value of the *Charter*, the indisputable importance of the fundamental principles of law, and the current culture of rights have permeated the practice of statutory interpretation. The courts are at the heart of the language regime.

In a country such as Canada, many have difficulty accepting that the underlying principles of the Constitution and the unwritten principles stemming from the preamble to the Constitution can be used to set limits, at the Supreme Court's discretion, because to them that means that the Court would have excessive discretionary authority. To some, that is akin to saying that there is a constitutional common law that the Court itself interprets. In practice, though, the situation in Canada is paradoxical, in that legal behaviour is often at odds with political discourse, or at least it was until quite recently. There is always a disconnect between formal legal equality and substantive equality. The recent language-related cases in British Columbia, the Northwest Territories, and the Yukon clearly illustrate the formal approach some governments take in response to minority communities' desire for substantive equality.[40] However, given that language rights have existed for forty-five years now, one wonders why we continue to have to go to court to ensure that they are implemented.

What is significant is that the Supreme Court decision on the secession of Quebec gave new support to the protection of linguistic minorities.[41] In this constitutional opinion, the Supreme Court maintains that the protection of minorities is an unwritten constitutional principle, as assertion that has the potential to change mindsets and promote a new political culture. We are in a unique situation. In spite of this historic decision and the new laws, in spite of the courts' liberal interpretations, minorities still have a sense of insecurity. They are afraid that linguistic groups' expectations and attitudes have not changed significantly and that the gains are only temporary. In its discourse, the federal government tries to stress linguistic minorities' cultural security and social integration. It says that the problem of insufficient use of French is not the result of prohibitions on the use of the minority language, but social conditions that often make equality of opportunity illusory. That is not enough to reassure minorities, especially since the federal government is still refusing to update the regulations on access to federal services guaranteed by section 20 of the Canadian Charter of Rights and Freedoms.

After Senator Maria Chaput failed in her attempt to correct this problem in 2015, the Société franco-manitobaine (SFM) filed a lawsuit in Federal Court criticizing in particular the formula used to determine the numbers that were sufficient to warrant the right to federal services in the minority official language in the province. The SFM argued that the federal regulations prescribed by the Treasury Board contain an unduly restrictive definition of the word "francophone." This definition excludes individuals who are able to ask for service in French, individuals who self-identify as francophone, individuals recognized by the minority community as members of that community, and individuals who are likely to use a service in French if there is an active offer.

The federal regulations, which were adopted without consultation with the francophone minority, have not undergone any significant review or consultation since they came into force in 1992. According to the SFM, the thresholds are doubly inconsistent with section 20. First, the thresholds vary in a clearly arbitrary way, as the regulations themselves reveal. Second, the government has not presented any evidence to justify the rationality or proportionality of the thresholds that were set. In addition, the definition of "demand," which is based on Method 1 developed by Statistics Canada, violates section 20 because it is at odds with the freedom of choice that the framers of the Constitution intended to establish with section 20 on offer of service in the minority language.

To summarize, Method 1 – on which the regulations are based – divides the population of Canada into watertight compartments made up of "francophones" and "anglophones." Only the so-called "minority" category in a province is counted for the purposes of estimating "demand," even if much of the "majority" category speaks the minority language. Thus, under the regulations, only individuals who, according to Statistics Canada, demonstrate an overwhelming attachment to French warrant the status of "francophones" and are used to establish the right to services in that language.

There is another major problem, however, and that is demographic trends. Canada's linguistic fabric will change considerably by 2036, according to the experts at Statistics Canada. In fact, 30 per cent of Canadians will not be born in Canada, and new Canadians will make up 49 per cent of the population. Moreover, 30 per cent of Canadians will report neither English nor French as their mother tongue, and just 1.8 per cent of Canadians outside Quebec will speak French most often at home. Fortunately, it seems that the use of French at home will be determined on the basis of frequent rather than predominant use, which is much more realistic. However, the profound changes in society, which will be much more diverse, will still have an impact. In this context, we have to ask ourselves about the foundations of bilingualism. If it is a fundamental standard, then clearly bilingualism must not be justified on the basis of a numerical criterion or practical necessity. Instead, it will be a question of values, of recognition of an objective, of Confederation, and of dignity for people who want to maintain their culture and their language and participate fully in the life of society without having to assimilate. Canada's efforts to expand individual bilingualism must be increased, not reduced. This is not just a matter of national unity, but also of social justice. There is also the fear that the predominance of English on social media and the increased use of the Internet are new factors in assimilation. This fear is no doubt justified, but the Internet can also be better used as a tool to expand the use of French and access to many cultural resources in French. This is another space where creativity can be demonstrated in planning government and private actions to promote bilingualism.

Already, changes in the recognition of language rights are evident. Initially, the equality of languages was recognized regardless of the speakers. This reductive

DEMONSTRATION IN SUPPORT OF HÔPITAL MONTFORT, 22 MARCH 1997

Every time linguistic minorities are threatened with losing their right to services in their language, people rally together and the media pay attention. When Ottawa's suburban Hôpital Montfort, the only French-language teaching hospital in Ontario, was threatened with closure in February 1997 after hospital services were reorganized, numerous demonstrations in support of the hospital were held and a lawsuit was launched, eventually making its way to the Ontario Court of Appeal. Premier Mike Harris's government reversed its decision on 1 February 2002. The battle had lasted five years! Today, Hôpital Montfort is a leading-edge teaching hospital. Credit: Hôpital Montfort

position led to the decision that the right to use French or English in court applied not only to litigants, but all participants in the judicial process. It led to the conclusion that the right to use a language did not include the right to be understood.[42] This view was rejected and the equality of speakers was recognized, including the right to choose either language without being disadvantaged. More recently, in *Beaulac*, the Supreme Court recognized that the right to a trial in the language of one's choice is a collective right that includes the obligation for the government to provide an institutional structure for speakers of both languages and not just an accommodation. This marks a transition from the obligation to do no harm to the obligation to act.

Gradually, people seem to be coming around to the idea that language rights are about cultural security and respect for human dignity, the right to self-expression.

In that sense, the goal now is integration. The problem is that some governments either entertain the notion that assimilation is inevitable in the medium or long term and there is no point in supporting minority language communities or have a persistent fear that demand for services can only lead to demands for a degree of autonomy, which is currently reflected in the right to schools, media, hospitals, and so on. Autonomy could mean the right to decentralize or reorganize some public services. The Supreme Court decision in *Desrochers* may be exacerbating governments' fears.[43] But the situation is evolving in a positive way.

As I mentioned, the federal government accepts the duty to make an active offer of service. All departments and agencies are responsible for implementing the Official Languages Act, under the watchful eye of the Treasury Board, which regulates activities and ensures that federal employees' rights are respected. Canadian Heritage coordinates activities to promote the official languages. The department responsible for international co-operation is also responsible for Canada's involvement in the international Francophonie. In fact, since 1970 Canada has been very active in the Organisation internationale de la Francophonie, of which it is a founding member. This eighty-four-member organization is currently headed by a Canadian.

In addition to these departmental responsibilities, two standing committees of the Senate and the House of Commons ensure that the government remains accountable to Canadians regarding its obligations. I would also like to mention the work of the Commissioner of Official Languages, who reports to Parliament and represents the first level of redress in cases of alleged violations of language rights. Complainants can also request support from the Language Rights Support Program to fund their cases.

In conclusion, it is clear that the language issue, which is so important, will continue to command attention, if only because of the strong pressure on the French language as a result of globalization and demographic trends that are reducing the relative number of French speakers. However, the heightened awareness in recent years and the willingness to take real steps to achieve national bilingualism objectives do give us some hope.

### NOTES

1 Michael D. Behiels, "Contested Ground: The State and Language Rights in Canada, 1760–2000," in Joseph Eliot Magnet, ed., *Official Languages of Canada: New Essays* (Canada: LexisNexis, 2008), 24–89.

2 *Quebec Act, 1774* (U.K), 14 Geo. III, c. 83.

3  Behiels, 28.

4  *Act of Union* (U.K.), 3 & 4 Vict., c. 35.

5  Lord Durham, *Report on the Affairs of British North America* (London, 1839), cited in Jacques Monet, *The Last Cannon Shot: A Study of French-Canadian Nationalism 1837–1850* (Toronto: University of Toronto Press, 1969), 24.

6  *British North America Act, 1867* (U.K.), 30 & 31 Vict., c.3, reprinted in R.S.C. 1985, App. II, No. 5.

7  Behiels, 34.

8  Behiels, 38.

9  Behiels, 36.

10  *Manitoba Act, 1870*, S.C. 1870, c. 3.

11  *Pellant v. Hébert*, St. Boniface Co. Ct., 9 March 1892, reported in (1981), 12 R.G.D. 242; *Bertrand v. Dussault and Lavoie*, St. Boniface Co. Ct. 30 January 1909, reported in *Forest v. Manitoba (Registrar of Court of Appeal)*, [1997] 77 D.L.R. (3d), 445–8 (Man. C.A.).

12  *Re Manitoba Language Rights*, [1985] 1 S.C.R. 721.

13  Behiels, 35.

14  *Common Schools Act, 1871*, 34 Vict., c. 21.

15  Behiels, 37–8.

16  *An Act Respecting Public Schools*, S.M. 1890, c. 38; *Winnipeg v. Barrett*, [1892] A.C. 445 (P.C.).

17  *The North-West Territories Act*, R.S.C. 1886, c. 50, s. 110, repealed and replaced by 1891, 54–5 Vict. c. 22, s. 18.

18  *R. v. Mercure*, [1988] 1 S.C.R. 234.

19  *Languages Act*, RSA 2000, c. L-6; Chapter L-6.1 of the Statutes of Saskatchewan, 1988–89 (effective 26 April 1988) as amended by the Statutes of Saskatchewan, 2001, c. 9.

20  *R. v. Caron*, [2011] 1 S.C.R. 78.

21  Behiels, 47.

22  Behiels, 48.

23  Behiels, 49.

24  *Official Languages Act*, R.S.N.B. 1973, c. O-1.

25  *Official Languages Act*, R.S.C. 1970, c. O-2.

26  Canadian Charter of Rights and Freedoms, Part I, *Canada Act 1982* (U.K.), 1982, c. 11.

27  Behiels, 58–9.

28  *Att. Gen. of Quebec v. Blaikie*, [1979] 2 S.C.R. 1016 [*Blaikie* 1979]. The decision extended the constitutional obligation of bilingualism to delegated legislation passed or submitted for the approval of the Quebec government and to rules of practice enacted by Quebec courts: *Attorney General of Quebec v. Blaikie*, [1981] 1 S.C.R. 312. In 1984, the main provisions of the chapter on language of instruction were invalidated: *Attorney General of*

*Quebec v. Quebec Protestant School Boards*, [1984] 2 S.C.R. 66 [QPSB]. In 1988, the Court dealt with the language of public signs and commercial advertising and the use of firm names: *Ford, supra* note 39; *Devine v. Quebec (Attorney General)*, [1988] 2 S.C.R. 790. In 1990 and 1992, Quebec's legislative bilingualism obligation was again broadened: *Quebec (Attorney General) v. Brunet*, [1990] 1 S.C.R. 260; *Sinclair v. Quebec (Attorney General)*, [1992] 1 S.C.R. 579. In 2005, the criterion for determining the right to English-language instruction was softened: *Solski, supra* note 37. Subsequently, in 2009, the Court invalidated the provisions that put an end to transfers of children of francophone and allophone parents to the publicly funded English-language school system: *Nguyen v. Quebec (Education, Recreation and Sports)*, 2009 SCC 47 [*Nguyen*].

29  *Mahe v. Alberta*, [1990] 1 S.C.R. 342.

30  *Re Manitoba Language Rights*, [1985] 1 S.C.R. 721.

31  *R. v. Beaulac*, [1999] 1 S.C.R. 768.

32  *An Act Recognizing the Equality of the Two Official Linguistic Communities in New Brunswick*, R.S.N.B., c. O-11.

33  Canadian Charter of Rights and Freedoms, sections 16.1(1) and (2).

34  *Société des Acadiens du Nouveau-Brunswick Inc. v. Association of Parents for Fairness in Education, Grand Falls District 50 Branch*, [1986] 1 S.C.R. 549.

35  *French Language Services Act*, R.S.O. 1990, c. F.32.

36  *Lalonde v. Ontario (Commission de restructuration des services de santé)*, [2001] 56 O.R.(3d) 505.

37  *Reference re Education Act of Ontario and Minority Language Education Rights*, [1984] 47 O.R.(2d) 1 (ON CA).

38  *Arsenault-Cameron v. Prince Edward Island*, [2000] 1 S.C.R. 3.

39  *An Act to amend the Official Languages Act (promotion of English and French)*, S.C. 2005, c. 41.

40  *Yukon Francophone School Board, Education Area #23 v. Yukon (Attorney General)*, 2015 SCC 25, [2015] 2 S.C.R. 282; *Fédération franco-ténoise v. Attorney General of Canada*, 2006 NWTSC 20.

41  *Reference re Secession of Quebec*, [1998] 2 S.C.R. 217.

42  *Société des Acadiens du Nouveau-Brunswick v. Association of Parents for Fairness in Education, Grand Falls District 50 Branch*, [1986] 1 S.C.R. 549.

43  *DesRochers v. Canada (Industry)*, [2009] 1 S.C.R. 194.

# 4

# Citizens Empowered by the *Canadian Charter of Rights and Freedoms:* A More Fundamental Turning Point than Was Anticipated[1]

The Hon. Serge Joyal, Senator

*I*n 1967, federal legislation was subject to the Canadian Bill of Rights *adopted in 1960 by the government of John G. Diefenbaker. However, the courts were reluctant to invalidate legislation that conflicted with the* Bill of Rights *unless there was a specific mention in the text of that legislation. This compliance strategy was relatively ineffective. The courts were reluctant to call into question the principle of parliamentary supremacy, inherited from the Westminster model and confirmed in the introductory clause of the* Constitution Act, 1967.

*In that centennial year, only four provinces had provincial human rights legislation on their books: Ontario (1962), Nova Scotia (1963), Alberta (1966), and New Brunswick (1967).*[2] *As part of its 1968 campaign platform, the Liberal Party of Canada, under Pierre E. Trudeau, pledged to adopt a charter of rights to protect all Canadians.*[3]

*In the years that followed, Prince Edward Island (1968), British Columbia and Newfoundland and Labrador (1969), Manitoba (1970), Quebec (1975), and Saskatchewan (1979) each in turn followed the nationwide legislative trend toward a better understanding and enhanced protection of human rights.*[4]

*In 1971, the federal government and the provinces agreed to include in the draft* Victoria Charter *(a proposed amendment to the* Constitution Act, 1867*) a human rights charter with common provisions that would be binding on the Parliament of Canada and all of the provincial legislatures. Although the draft* Victoria Charter *died on the vine, both levels of government recognized that a patriated constitution should include a charter of rights.*[5]

*In 1977, the Parliament of Canada passed legislation to establish the Canadian Human Rights Commission and create a tribunal to receive citizens' complaints and order remedial measures as required.*

*In 1978, the federal government tabled Bill C-60, An Act amending the Constitution.[6] This bill contained a charter "des droits et libertés à l'intérieur de la Fédération canadienne"[7] and provided for remedies before "une cour compétente au Canada" to guarantee recognition and enforcement of those rights and freedoms (clause 24). Bill C-60 died on the* Order Paper,[8] *but not because of that particular proposal.*

*The federal government tabled a draft constitutional resolution in 1980 to patriate the Constitution. It contained a proposed charter of rights and freedoms that took up the elements contained in previous proposals and added several other elements. Ontario and New Brunswick supported the draft resolution from the outset. They also came out in favour of a charter of rights. The proposal was referred to a Special Joint Committee of the Senate and House of Commons for study.[9]*

*The sessions of this joint committee were televised, a first for the Parliament of Canada. From the comfort of their own homes, Canadians had the opportunity to watch parliamentarians carry out their legislative role. Committee members listened carefully to and questioned hundreds of witnesses who wanted their rights to be recognized in the future Constitution. The Special Joint Committee held 106 meetings over fifty-six days. In all, the sessions lasted more than 267 hours.*

*It was also inundated with submissions: the committee received 962 written briefs, including 639 from individuals and 322 from groups requesting to appear before the committee.[10]*

*Nothing like it had been seen before in the annals of Canadian parliamentary history. No issue had ever generated so much public interest or had such a high turnout. It was the purest form of participatory democracy at work, a brand-new way of approaching public discourse – truly a historic moment. Everyone felt personally affected because the debate was about the rights of individuals in a society where everyone wanted to be respected for who they were. The public was truly engaged, and interest did not wane. Canadians understood that they would have to speak up in order to be heard by politicians and governments. The rights revolution grew out of this nationwide public interest movement, driven by the shared conviction that it was possible to live in a fairer, more equal society.[11] The history of democracy teaches us that a law gains legitimacy when it has been debated extensively by the population as a whole.[12]*

*Every day, citizens' groups appeared before the committee. They represented a broad cross-section of Canadian society, from persons with disabilities to women calling for equality, and Indigenous people telling Parliament for the first time ever about the conditions in which they lived and pressing their claims for explicit recognition of their right to self-government. On some sitting days, the committee heard union representatives who argued to have their freedom of association enshrined in the constitution, thus protecting it from suspension by a parliamentary majority. The committee also heard representatives of linguistic minorities, Acadians, and Canadians of Japanese descent, whose relatives in Canada were forced into internment camps during the World War II. In all, more than ninety-five groups expressed their belief that they would be better protected if their rights and freedoms were enshrined in a charter that would preserve them from removal or suspension by governments or parliaments responding to particular circumstances or at the whim of the majority.*

*This was the first milestone.*

*The Special Joint Committee made numerous amendments (a total of fifty-seven) to the initial proposal.[13] Those amendments acknowledged the changing nature of the rights enumerated in the Charter and, in particular, recognized the role of the courts, whose responsibility it would be to interpret the Charter. This issue was of great concern to the committee because it was central to the effectiveness of the Charter.[14]*

*Before the text of the Charter was finalized, numerous often tense negotiations took place between first ministers, and a number of court rulings were made.[15] Ultimately, it became necessary to determine whether the final word rested with Parliament or the judiciary. The compromise solution took the form of a so-called "notwithstanding" clause added to section 33 of the Charter. Prime Minister Trudeau was hesitant to accept the compromise because he thought it would dilute the Charter, but he eventually relented because he felt that the heightened interest aroused by the Charter debate could re-emerge and mobilize Canadians if politicians ever sought to suspend their rights.*

*When the proposed* Charter of Rights and Freedoms *was finally approved by the federal government and nine of the ten provinces,[16] in accordance with the Supreme Court opinion on the legality of patriation, Canada began a new chapter. It became a constitutional democracy in which the legislative activities of all parliaments and legislatures, whether federal or provincial, must be measured against the rights and freedoms of individuals. The principle of parliamentary supremacy applicable to institutions under the Westminster model now became specifically subject to the control of the courts,[17] which were expressly invested with this responsibility under section 24 of the* Charter of Rights and Freedoms.[18] *Judges did not ask for this responsibility. It was thrust upon them by the political leaders of the day, who took it upon themselves to amend this fundamental constitutional principle. As the Supreme Court pointed out: "With the adoption of the [Charter], the Canadian system of government was transformed to a significant extent from a system of Parliamentary supremacy to one of constitutional supremacy."[19] Anyone today who calls into question the authority of the judiciary in this area should be reminded of that fact.*

JUSTITIA IN FRONT OF THE SUPREME COURT OF CANADA

Bronze, 1920 by Walter Seymour Allward. The certainty that one is able to obtain justice when a right or freedom guaranteed by the Charter is at stake is a key part of Canadian citizenship. The Charter is more than just a statement of principles. It reflects values that underpin our sense of what it is to be Canadian and guarantee everyone the same degree of equality and dignity. The Charter is the national symbol Canadians value most, even more than hockey! Credit: Aram Adjemian, photographer

*This new system would transform the foundation of the "social contract" in Canada, not to mention the very substance of what it means to be Canadian. Canada had become, on paper at least, a society based on rights.*

*As early as 1983, Canadians began taking advantage of this new recognition of their rights, as guaranteed by the courts. Canadians quickly understood and were conscious of the fact that, in order to be legal and valid, legislation adopted in compliance with the legislative and procedural provisions of the Constitution also had to fully respect their rights and freedoms.*

*In other words, a parliamentary majority was not enough to ensure the validity of legislation. A freely voting majority within the framework of parliamentary institutions can be considered "dictatorial" if it infringes upon the rights of a minority or an individual for any number of reasons.*

*Canadians accepted this protection at face value. Each section of the Charter recognizing a specific right formed the subject of numerous court decisions over the years. In fact, the courts progressively defined the scope of these rights and freedoms and developed analysis methods and rationales that improved over time, adding to the credibility of the decision-making process used by the courts.[20]*

*From the very beginning, the courts took very seriously the role conferred upon them by the Charter as the interpreters of its provisions. As American historian Howard Zinn put it: "A Bill of Rights on paper comforts people. You don't have to take it seriously."[21] In short, as long as rights remain merely on paper, they may reassure people, but they have not withstood challenges or been tested in the courts, and that is the key step. The Charter became more than just a paper tiger because the courts immediately seized the opportunity they had been given to define how, and how "seriously," they would address the resolution of conflicts pitting a citizen or individual against a law allegedly infringing upon his or her rights. The courts had a firm grasp of the concept. "Patriation of the Constitution was accompanied by the adoption of the* Charter of Rights and Freedoms, *which gave the courts the responsibility for interpreting and remedying breaches of the Charter."[22]*

*The courts were venturing into new territory. No one could anticipate that the Canadian public would become so highly conscious of its rights and so keen on protecting them and ensuring that they are respected. Because the courts took their responsibility so literally and because they were able to extract the spirit of the Charter and its underlying values, and identify its nature, it was their interpretation that it served "a remedial purpose," and therefore sought to correct a deficiency or repair harm.[23] Canadians quickly realized that they could have confidence in this "impartial [independent] and authoritative judicial arbiter."[24]*

*Not only did the courts declare government decisions or laws to be at odds with the rights of Canadian citizens, they even awarded financial compensation for flagrant violations.[25] The large settlements paid to Maher Arar and Omar Khadr, whose rights had been trampled by the government, are still fresh in our minds.*

*Canadians became convinced that the courts fully recognized their rights, often in contrast with long years of discrimination by governments that were reluctant to change practices or brave public opinion, essentially living in fear of criticism and public reactions. In fact, governments often prefer to let the courts "fire the first shot." They like to be able to blame the judges if something goes wrong.*

*The courts realized that they had a fundamental role to play in making the constitutional supremacy that would now characterize Canada a reality, and in giving tangible effect to the power given to citizens to defend their rights, often against politicians, doctrines, dogmas, or beliefs that stultify evolution or hamper the will of the people to decide for themselves.*

*The numbers are surprising. From the first decision in 1983 until 2017, Canadian courts of all levels rendered 23,939 Charter-related decisions.[26]*

*This was the second milestone.*

*Another step forward was taken after 1982. The federal government decided to expand the financial support provided under the Court Challenges Program[27] after the equality rights recognized in the Charter (section 15) came into force. This was a major advancement for a society with a rights culture permeating all social strata, without regard to wealth, income, origin, class, or level of education.[28] The Court Challenges Program had previously been extended to language rights cases in 1982.*

*The ability to assert one's rights was no longer restricted to those who had the financial means to pay for a lawyer. If an independent government authority determined that a case was judicially valid, the state would provide funding to support a court challenge by an individual and help that individual obtain the desired legal redress.*

*No other Western democracy offered its citizens the opportunity to obtain public funds to mount court challenges against any legislation or decisions made by the government of the day that infringed upon their rights. This was unheard of and quite remarkable. Canada was truly governed by the rule of law, and it was up to individual citizens to determine what measure of justice they were entitled to obtain.*

*These funded challenges led to more than 371 court decisions from 1994 to 2006. They included:*

- *fifty-four cases concerning issues of colour, race, nationality, or ethnicity;*
- *seventeen cases dealing with age;*
- *forty-four cases based on sexual orientation;*
- *forty-one cases based on gender equality;*
- *twenty-eight cases involving poverty; and*
- *ninety-six cases dealing with Indigenous rights.[29]*

*The Court Challenges Program had a rather rocky existence.*

*It was cancelled in 1993, restored in 1994, abolished again in 2006 and re-established again in February 2017. In its most recent incarnation, the program was expanded to encompass the Charter sections on fundamental freedoms (section 2), democratic rights (section 3), the rights to life, liberty, and security of the person (section 7), equality rights (section 15), multicultural heritage (section 27), and equality of the sexes (section 28).[30]*

*The Court Challenges Program put the power into the hands of individuals. The fact that this program was abolished in 1992 and again in 2006 was no coincidence. Cancelling this program took the power out of the hands of Canadians and handed it to parliamentary majorities that did not actually represent the majority of Canadians, based on the popular vote.[31]*

*The social dynamic triggered by open access to this program was unprecedented in the history of Canada. Canadians from all walks of life assumed control of their rights and broadened the horizons of tolerance, inclusion, and respect for diversity. Through force of will and the conviction that they were within their rights, Canadians helped to redefine the fundamentals of a new society beyond the confines of dogma, doctrines, and prejudice. Set in stone, dogma, doctrines and prejudice cannot take into account adjustments, changes in thinking, scientific discoveries, and new outlooks on the world. Such pre-set beliefs have an ossifying effect on now obsolete social structures, render-ing them devoid of all meaning. A simple comparison of the evolution of American and Canadian society paints a clear picture of the dynamic at work in Canada.[32] The Charter is a living document that evolves in tandem with Canadian society.*

*A number of court decisions became milestones for Canada as it continued to evolve with the greatest respect for the rights of all Canadians. As Pierre E. Trudeau pointed out in 1968: "A good Constitution is one that leaves citizens free to orient their destinies as they see fit."[33] Such profound transformations are initiated and driven by ordinary citizens, not politicians. Given the nature of their profession, politicians are often overly cautious or too vulnerable to pressures from lobby groups representing any number of interests. They may also be at the mercy of their electors or held hostage by their own beliefs.[34]*

"IT'S THE CHARTER, STUPID!"

Plasticized buttons, 2005. This was the slogan for a campaign launched in early 2005 in favour of the Civil Marriage Act. Inspired by James Carville's 1992 slogan "It's the Economy, Stupid!," which was used in Bill Clinton's presidential campaign against George H.W. Bush, the slogan was criticized as condescending by opponents of the redefinition of marriage. By focusing on the *Charter*, a fact of life that applies to everyone regardless of personal convictions, the campaign organizers were making the point that it is rather inevitable. Credit: CHSJ

*Issues legitimately interpreted by the courts include women's right to control their own bodies (Morgentaler, 1988), the right to live according to one's sexual orientation and have access to civil marriage (M v. H, 1999), the right to physician-assisted dying (Carter, 2015), and the prohibition of the death penalty (Burns and Rafay, 2001). These court decisions, all stemming from challenges filed by Canadian citizens themselves, progressively redefined the values that are now at the core of our freedoms.[35]*

*Since 1982 the* Charter of Rights and Freedoms *has been the subject of countless analyses and comments. It spawned a rights theory unlike any other in parliamentary democracy, whether in Europe or the United States.[36] It gave ordinary Canadians the conviction that they were protected from the vagaries of elected majorities and that the courts could ensure that citizens' rights were respected by invalidating law provisions or even by setting deadlines for Parliament (or legislatures) to provide alternatives meeting specific court-defined criteria.[37]*

*Such a fundamental reform could not help but arouse criticism directed at the courts, including accusations that they were engaging in "judicial activism" (i.e., overstepping their bounds and assuming the role properly reserved for legislators) or that they had given the Charter a scope and heft far exceeding the protection it was originally intended to provide.*[38]

*These criticisms fail to recognize the unique nature of the Charter, which adds a dynamic element to the interpretation of rights by allowing for them to evolve in tandem with the prevailing facts and conditions in any given era. In other words, rights are not static concepts encased in rigid definitions. They are not frozen in time like an inspired dogma that can never evolve to take into account new circumstances.*

*So there is no "literalism" or strict interpretation doctrine with respect to the terms of the Charter, nor is there any "originalism" (an American school of thought that seeks to limit the scope of rights on the basis of the intent expressed by the framers of the constitution at the time of adoption).*[39] *As early as 1985, the Supreme Court of Canada stated that it gave minimal weight to the debates surrounding the advent of the Charter, since it did not consider those debates binding upon it. The Court then noted that "[t]he truly novel features of the* Constitution Act, 1982 *are that it has sanctioned the process of constitutional adjudication and has extended its scope so as to encompass a broader range of values."*[40] *The rights set out in the Charter and their underlying values are by their very nature dynamic, and the courts must take into account any new conditions that may arise. This principle applies to several other provisions of the* Constitution, *which have been interpreted according to the "Living Tree" theory.*[41] *The priority given to this type of interpretation allowed women to become senators in 1929. The interpretation principles applied by the courts to the* Constitution Act, 1867 *and the* Constitution Act, 1982 *are marked by continuity and rationality.*

*This rights and freedoms dynamic gave rise to a society whose people believe they are not at the mercy of untimely majorities or the overwhelming power of big money. Canada is evolving into a particular type of humanistic society: after enshrining major principles and their underlying values in the* Charter of Rights and Freedoms, *Canada resolutely undertook to integrate them into the reality of everyday society. The most sensitive issues were referred to the courts as Canadians proceeded to exercise their rights.*[42] *The Supreme Court established a clear distinction between the right of persons to decide for themselves, under certain conditions, and any doctrines or precepts that individuals are free to adopt or follow in their personal conduct. Albeit protected by the freedom of thought or religion recognized in the Charter, such precepts or doctrines cannot be imposed on society.*[43]

*This innovative model instilled in Canadian society a dynamic of ongoing rational adaptation, subject to the rule of law as interpreted by the courts. Canadian citizens are the driving force behind this continuing evolution. Under this model, citizenship took on special meaning within a context of dynamic integration. Citizens consider the Charter to be our most important national symbol, more so than hockey or the Canadian flag.[44] The respect they have for court decisions is a determining factor in the stability and cohesion of Canadian society. The judiciary has become "the guardian of the constitution."[45] By and large, the Canadian public respects court decisions. Hence, debates over matters decided by the courts are not perpetuated, revived, or revisited during each election or by each new generation, as is often the case in other countries. The kind of social tensions we see in the United States over the abortion issue or in France on the subject of civil marriage, for example, would not occur in Canada.[46] Canadian society adapts to Canadian court rulings and weaves them into everyday life, thereby strengthening the humanistic foundations of the country and its secular nature as a society.*

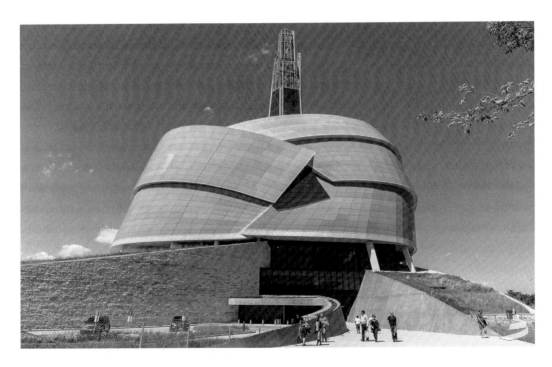

CANADIAN MUSEUM FOR HUMAN RIGHTS IN WINNIPEG

Designed by American architect Antoine Predock and opened in 2014, the Canadian Museum for Human Rights is the result of a public-private partnership and was built on the initiative of Gail Asper, at a total cost of $351 million. The only national museum of its kind in the world, it traces the evolution of human rights around the world and particularly in Canada. The museum has an important educational mission and aims to make visitors aware that human rights can never be taken for granted and that vigilance is crucial. Credit: Aaron Cohen/CMHR-MCDP

*The* Canadian Human Rights Act *(CHRA) should be amended to ensure permanent access to public funds under the Court Challenges Program and thus shelter such funding from the political vagaries of successive governments (as occurred in 1992 and 2006, for example). Since the CHRA has been deemed quasi-constitutional by the courts, guaranteed access to this financial support within the CHRA would make tangible support for the respect of rights and freedoms a responsibility for which governments remain accountable.*

*In the years to come, the growing diversification of the Canadian population could give rise to clashes between different world views, rooted in the religious or philosophical beliefs of groups of varying origins. The responsibility for striking a balance among different mindsets and opposing views on various rights, such as the right to freedom of religion and the right to equality,[47] or the right to information and the right to privacy, will be left to the courts. It will be up to the judiciary to interpret the values contained in the Charter. To resolve such rights conflicts, the Supreme Court, in various judgements, developed an analysis process that allows it to arbitrate and reconcile differing views.[48] To beat back the rise of fanaticism, intolerance, and the kind of nationalism exacerbated by cheap populism, all of which feed mostly on ignorance and fear of whatever is different, the Canadian public knows it can rely on an impartial and independent judiciary that remains sensitive to the views and experiences of individuals.[49] The cohesion of Canadian society will be strengthened by the capacity of individuals to have their rights recognized and respected, even in opposition to governments.*

*The new Canadian Museum for Human Rights in Winnipeg, established by Parliament through amendments to the* Museums Act *in 2008 and opened in 2014, is an institutional testament to this novel approach focusing on the fundamental importance of rights and freedoms in Canada. This new museum clearly demonstrates our public commitment to the continued existence and recognition of rights and freedoms in this country.*

*This institution should be the focal point for a permanent national public awareness program on the importance of respecting, recognizing, and understanding the nature and presence of human rights in every aspect of our daily lives – within our families, at school, at work, in society and across the full spectrum of our public interactions.*

*The National Capital Commission's* Plan for Canada's Capital: 2017–2067 *calls for the addition of a monument to commemorate the* Canadian Charter of Rights and Freedoms, *"providing a physical manifestation of this hallowed document that underpins Canada's just and diverse society."[50] This monument would also acknowledge all those who, by "daring" to stand up for their rights, played a key role in ensuring that the equality and dignity of all minorities in this country would be recognized and guaranteed.*

NOTES

1  The author is indebted to the Library of Parliament of Canada for its meticulous work in checking the accuracy of the figures and historical facts contained in this text.

2  The Canadian Human Rights Commission published a "Time Portal" summarizing the history of human rights in Canada since 1900. The four provincial laws mentioned are consolidations rather than new legislation without legislative historical precedent. See: http://www.chrc-ccdp.gc.ca/historical-perspective/en/timePortals/1900.asp, consulted on 26 October 2017.

3  Campaign platform of the Liberal Party of Canada – Trudeau – William Vander Zalm (*Liberal – Surrey*), June 1968: "We propose a Charter of Human Rights. In this Charter, rights of four different categories will be constitutionally respected: political rights […]; legal rights […]; egalitarian rights […]; and finally, linguistic rights." Author's private collection – pledged for donation to the Canadian Museum of History.

4  Saskatchewan adopted a *Bill of Rights* in 1947.

5  The then Quebec government of Premier Robert Bourassa reserved its endorsement at the close of the conference and ultimately expressed its opposition at the end of June 1971, primarily because Quebec wanted recognition of its legislative primacy in the areas of health care and social services.

6  Bill C-60, *An Act to amend the Constitution of Canada with respect to matters coming within the legislative authority of the Parliament of Canada, and to approve and authorize the taking of measures necessary for the amendment of the Constitution with respect to certain matters.*

7  Bill C-60, first reading, 20 June 1978, clauses 5–29.

8  *Re: Authority of Parliament in relation to the Upper House*, [1980] 1 s.c.r. 54. The opinion rendered by the Supreme Court of Canada at the request of the federal government declared the provisions of Bill C-60 pertaining to Senate reform to be unconstitutional.

9  The Special Joint Committee on the Constitution of Canada.

10  *Statistical Account of Written Submissions,* (https://historyofrights.ca/wp-content/uploads/SJC/statistics.pdf), Library of Parliament, Research Branch, 26 January 1981.

11  Adam Dodek, ed., *The Charter Debates: The Special Joint Committee on the Constitution, 1980–81 and the Making of the Canadian Charter of Rights and Freedoms* (Toronto: University of Toronto Press, 2018), 30–4, 69, 79.

12  Guillaume Rousseau, "L'outrage de 1982 et la Charte québécoise," *Le Devoir*, 28 April 2017, A8.

13  The author co-chaired the Special Joint Committee on the Constitution of Canada when he was a member of Parliament.

14 "It is hard to imagine any subject that was clearer (in the minds of the Special Joint Committee) than that of judicial review." Adam Dodek, "The Supreme Battle: How Antonin Scalia's brash ideas influenced Canadian Courts," *The Walrus*, 22 February 2016.

15 *Re: Resolution to amend the Constitution* [1981], 1 SCR 753, p. 905.

16 The Quebec government, under René Lévesque, refused to sign off on the Charter. However, the Quebec Court of Appeal and the Supreme Court of Canada had both ruled that Quebec did not have a constitutional right of veto. See: *Re: Objection by Quebec to a Resolution to amend the Constitution*, [1982] 2 SCR 793.

17 The "notwithstanding" clause championed by Premier Blakeney of Saskatchewan would have been valid for five years, half-reassuring the proponents of the principle of parliamentary supremacy. See: Canadian Intergovernmental Conference Secretariat, *Federal-Provincial Conference of First Ministers on the Constitution: verbatim transcript*, 2–5 November 1981.

18 Section 24(1) of the *Canadian Charter of Rights and Freedoms*: "Anyone whose rights or freedoms, as guaranteed by this Charter, have been infringed or denied may apply to a court of competent jurisdiction to obtain such remedy as the court considers appropriate and just in the circumstances."

19 *Re: Supreme Court Act, ss.5 and 6*, 2014 SCC 21 [2014], 1 SCR 433, para. 89.

20 Justice Richard Wagner, "Early approaches to how judges analyzed discrimination did not stand up to the task, Charter interpretation is a 'work in progress,'" speech given to the Faculty of Law of the University of Ottawa, 9 March 2017; Tonda MacCharles, "Canadian legal system supports refugee welcome – Supreme Court judge says Canada is strong enough to accept migrants," *Toronto Star*, 10 March 2017, p. A7.

21 Howard Zinn, *The Zinn Reader – Writings on Disobedience and Democracy – The Bill of Rights* (New York: Seven Stories Press, 1997), 413.

22 *Re: Supreme Court Act, ss.5 and 6*, 2014 SCC 21 [2014], 1 SCR 433, para. 89.

23 *R. v. Ferguson*, [2008] 1 SCR 96, 2008 SCC 6; *Wilson v. Alharayeri*, 2017 SCC 39, [2017] 1 SCR 1037.

24 *Re: Supreme Court Act, ss.5 and 6*, 2014 SCC 21 [2014], 1 SCR 433, para. 89.

25 *Vancouver (City) v. Ward*, 2010 SCC 27, [2010] 2 S.C.R. 28; Laureen Heuser, "Why Charter lawsuits won't stop," *National Post*, 5 September 2017, p. A11.

26 *WestlawNext. Canada,* consulted on 7 September 2017 by the Library of Parliament. This database does not include all court decisions, and its coverage of decisions before the early nineties is limited.

27 The program had existed in a limited form since 1978, but its scope was broadened in 1982 and 1985 upon the initiative of the author, who was then the secretary of state for Canada. See: Government of Canada, *Backgrounder – Court Challenges Program* (https://www.canada.ca/en/canadian-heritage/services/funding/court-challenges-program/backgrounder.html),

August 2017; Standing Committee on Justice and Human Rights, *Report 4 – Access to Justice – Part 1: Court Challenges Program*, September 2016.

28  From 1985 to 1992, the Court Challenges Program received 951 requests for financial assistance in equality rights cases. The majority of cases (125) were brought before a trial court, 26 went to a court of appeal and 24 were heard by the Supreme Court of Canada. During that same period, the Court Challenges Program subsidized 77 linguistic rights cases, 35 of which were heard by a trial court, 23 by a court of appeal, and 19 by the Supreme Court [research carried out by the Library of Parliament, 22 September 2017]. For more information, visit the Court Challenges Program website at https://www.canada.ca/en/canadian-heritage/services/funding/court-challenges-program/program-administration.html.

29  Debates of the Senate, 10 December 2015, 1st Session, 42nd Parliament, vol. 150, no. 5, p. 86. Figures cited by Senator Maria Chaput (retired). The *Court Challenges Program of Canada Annual Report 2006–2007* indicated that 416 cases were funded from 24 October 1994 to 25 September 2006. See: http://www.ccppcj.ca/docs/CCPC-AR2007(eng).pdf.

30  Government of Canada, *Backgrounder – Court Challenges Program*, last amended on 22 November 2017. See also: Government of Canada, *A Guide to the Court Challenges Program of Canada,* http://www.ccppcj.ca/docs/InfoKit_EN.pdf.

31  The government of Justin Trudeau was elected with 39 per cent of the popular vote. See: "Results of the Canadian federal election, 2015," at https://en.wikipedia.org/wiki/Results_of_the_Canadian_federal_election,_2015.

32  Sam Harris, *The End of Faith*, (New York: W.W. Norton & Co, 2005), 229–31.

33  Campaign platform of the Liberal Party of Canada – Trudeau – William Vander Zalm (*Liberal – Surrey*), June 1968. Author's private collection – pledged for donation to the Canadian Museum of History.

34  Prime Minister Jean Chrétien expressed his own reservations about recognizing civil marriage: "I was caught by surprise, at the time I was 69 years old, you know, and this way of living was not very [much] a part of my culture […] It was when they used the word marriage, that got [to] rubbing people on the wrong side, including me." See: "Gay rulings stunned Chrétien." *The Star.com*, 15 April 2007. In June 2005, the Hon. Irwin Cotler, minister of justice, told the author, who was sponsoring a bill on civil marriage in the Senate, that he was not very enthusiastic about the bill because his spouse was personally opposed to it due to her personal convictions. Similarly, when formal apologies were issued in the House of Commons on 30 November 2017 to the members of the LGBTQ2 community, several opposition MPs voiced their uneasiness. See: Marie Vastel, "Excuses aux LGBTQ2 : des conservateurs avouent leur malaise," *Le Devoir*, 30 November 2017, A2.

35 Andrew Coyne, "Judges rule to hold Parliament to its word, not to usurp its power," *National Post*, 16 July 2014.

36 Trudel, Pierre, "Liberté d'expression – l'Europe diffère du Canada," *Le Devoir*, 18 July 2017, A7; Howard Zinn, *The Zinn Reader*, 412–19.

37 In *Carter v. Canada* (Attorney General) in 2014, the Supreme Court gave Parliament a deadline of one year and identified four specific criteria for access to physician-assisted dying. See: *Carter v. Canada* (Attorney General), 2015 SCC 5, [2015] 1 SCR 331.

38 Jackson Doughart, "The case against judicial supremacy," *National Post*, 25 July 2014, A10; Benjamin Perrin, "There's a rift on the Supreme Court over 'judicial activism,'" *iPolitics*, 22 December 2016; Andrew Petter, "The politics of the Charter. (Canada)," *Supreme Court Law Review, Annual*, 1986, vol. 8, pp. 473–505.

39 A school of thought defended in particular by the US Supreme Court concerning the original text of the American Constitution. See: Fuchs, Erin, "Alan Dershowitz told us Scalia's 'most fundamental' contribution to the Supreme Court," *Business Insider*, 13 February 2016; Adam Dodek, "The Supreme Battle, how Antonin Scalia's brash ideas influenced Canadian Courts," *The Walrus*, 22 February 2016.

40 *Re: B.C. Motor Vehicle Act*, [1985] 2 SCR 486.

41 *Edwards v. Canada* [1930] A.C. 128 60 (I.C.R.C.); The Honourable Justice Robert J. Sharpe, "The Persons case and the Living Tree Theory of Constitutional Interpretation," (2013) 64 U.N.B.L.N. 1.

42 The right to an abortion, the right to civil marriage, the right to physician-assisted dying, the death penalty.

43 Serge Joyal, "Leadership de la très honorable Beverly McLachlin et l'émergence des valeurs canadiennes," article to be published in 2018.

44 According to a 2015 Statistics Canada survey, 70 per cent of Canadians consider the *Charter* to be the most important national symbol – well ahead of the Canadian flag.

45 *Hunter et al. v. Southam Inc.,* [1984] 2 SCR 145, p. 155 (quoting the judgement delivered by Justice Dickson).

46 Civil marriage was accepted at the 2016 convention of the Conservative Party of Canada.

47 *Law Society of British Columbia v. Trinity Western University*, 2018 SCC 32; *Trinity Western University v. Law Society of Upper Canada*, 2018 SCC 33.

48 Jena McGill, "'Now It's My Rights Versus Yours': Equality in Tension with Religious Freedoms," *Alberta Law Review*, vol. 53, no. 3, March 2016, pp. 583–608.

49 "But identity is not about labels; it is a shorthand for how people see themselves, how others see them, and how those two things interact in peoples' lives." Justice Richard Wagner, *Constitution 150 Conference*, address delivered to the Faculty of Law of the University of Ottawa, 9 March 2017, p. 6, para. 13; and speech given during a benefit

evening for the Fondation Lafontaine-Cormier, Montreal, 23 October 2017 (https://www.fondationlafontainecormier.org).

50 National Capital Commission, *The Plan for Canada's Capital: 2017–2067*, p. 34 and Appendix 2 (Milestone Projects), p. 79 (available for consultation at http://capital2067.ca/wp-content/uploads/2017/05/PFCC-English-complete-optimized.pdf ).

# Celebrating the Charter: Respecting the Rights of Individuals and Protecting the Rights of Minorities

The Rt. Hon. Beverley McLachlin, P.C., Chief Justice of Canada (2000–17)

I am delighted to be here in the Senate of Canada to reflect on the enactment of the Canadian Charter of Rights and Freedoms, the culture of rights it has fostered in Canada, and the broader impact it has had on our society.

On a rainy morning thirty-five years ago, Queen Elizabeth II, by one stroke of the pen, signed the official proclamation that ushered in two significant changes to Canada's constitutional life. The first was to move the Canadian Constitution from Britain to Canada, allowing Canadians – and only Canadians – to determine their constitutional future. The second change was to adopt the Canadian Charter of Rights and Freedoms.

In my brief remarks today, I offer two simple yet important ideas – first, that the enactment of the Charter did not occur in a vacuum but was part of a natural evolution based on our nation's most cherished values; and second, that expressing our values in a constitutional document like the Charter has in no insignificant part helped shape the diverse, accommodating, and just society that we live in today.

Today, I will offer reflections on two matters – first, the story of how we came to have the Charter; and second, how the Charter has been interpreted and how it has impacted Canadian society.

## 1. THE ROAD TO THE CHARTER

Let me start with the evolution of the Charter. The story begins soon after World War II. In response to the atrocities of the Holocaust and the harm caused by totalitarian regimes, Canada, like many other countries, followed in the footsteps of the United Nations' Universal Declaration of Human Rights. One by one, the Canadian provinces began adopting bills of rights or human rights codes.

In 1960, the Canadian Parliament followed suit, passing the Canadian Bill of Rights.[1] On paper, the Canadian Bill of Rights' reach was large. In elegant prose, it offered protection for a host of fundamental freedoms – freedom of religion, freedom of speech, freedom of assembly and association – and legal rights, including protections against arbitrary detention and imprisonment, the right to counsel, and equality "before the law."

Sadly, the promise of the Canadian Bill of Rights was belied by the reality that followed. There were three reasons for this. First, the bill applied only to the federal government, not to the provinces. Second, it was not constitutionally entrenched; as a mere statute, it was unable to trump legislation that might offend its terms. Finally, perhaps because of these two features, the courts interpreted the Bill of Rights narrowly, as generally not creating new rights.

From the disappointment of the Canadian Bill of Rights sprang a new idea – the idea that Canada needed a constitutionally entrenched bill of rights. Within eight years of the Bill of Rights' enactment, the federal justice minister of the time – Pierre Elliott Trudeau – proposed a draft charter of human rights that would apply to all governments and would provide constitutionally enshrined protections. When he became prime minister in 1968, he added this idea to what has been called the "Quest for Patriation,"[2] the search for a made-in-Canada process for amending the Constitution without the need to seek the British Parliament's approval. In 1971, in Victoria, British Columbia, the prime minister and the provincial premiers reached an agreement – the "Victoria Charter," as it came to be known – which provided for both a bill of rights and a domestic amending formula. The agreement unravelled quickly, but the desire for an effective constitutional human rights charter remained strong.

After the Quebec Referendum on sovereignty-association and the victory of the "No" side in 1980, an intense period of constitutional negotiations led to proposals for reform around three aspects: (1) the patriation of the Canadian Constitution; (2) the adoption of a domestic amending formula; and (3) a charter of rights and freedoms. A joint committee of the House of Commons and the Senate was struck to study those matters. Significantly, the hearings were televised, and many different groups, from all segments of Canadian society, appeared before the committee and thus became important participants in the constitutional conversation.

The "People's Package," as the Charter became known, captured the hearts and minds of the public. In November 1981, after protracted debate that involved individuals and groups from every part of the country, and a Supreme Court of Canada decision on the legality of the Patriation process itself, the federal government and nine provinces – sadly, Quebec did not, in the end, sign on – agreed to send the constitutional reform package to the British Parliament. The British Parliament passed one final act,[3] the Canada Act 1982, liberating the Canadian Constitution from the United Kingdom. On 17 April 1982, the Queen came to Ottawa to sign the official proclamation that gave effect to the new Constitution Act, 1982. Canada finally had its own constitutionally entrenched bill of rights.

The Charter protects many of the same rights as did the Canadian Bill of Rights. It protects freedom of religion, speech, association, and assembly, as well as legal rights. It guarantees life, liberty, and security of the person (s. 7), and protects against unreasonable searches and seizures (s. 8) and arbitrary detention (ss. 9–10). It guarantees everyone the right to a fair trial (ss. 11–13). But it adds new protections. For the first time in Canada's history, it constitutionalizes the right to vote. And beyond this, the 1982 Constitution Act recognizes the diversity inherent in Canada's multicultural society by guaranteeing minority language and religious rights, and by broadening the guarantee of equality for everyone – not merely equality "before the law," as the old Bill of Rights said, but also "under the law," regardless of race, religion, or other improper ground. In addition, the Constitution Act, 1982, proclaimed Canada's commitment to multiculturalism and gender equality, and provided for a constitutional guarantee for the rights of Canada's Aboriginal peoples.

In an important sense, the Constitution Act, 1982, is a document of inclusion and accommodation suited to the diverse makeup of Canadian society. The Charter does not merely recognize and guarantee rights. It provides for a powerful unifying symbol – a statement about what Canada stands for, and what kind of society Canadians wish to build for themselves and for generations to come.

## 2. THE IMPACT OF THE CHARTER

Let me turn now to the impact the Charter has had on Canada's constitutional life. From the moment it was adopted, the Constitution Act, 1982, introduced a fundamental change to the Canadian constitutional order. Section 52 of the Constitution Act, 1982, provides explicitly that the Constitution is "the supreme law of Canada" and that any law inconsistent with it is "of no force or effect." This signalled that Canada had moved from a system of parliamentary supremacy derived from the Westminster model to a system of constitutional democracy. From that moment on, Parliament's supremacy would be limited by the Constitution itself. Moreover, the activity of all legislatures and governments, both federally and provincially, would now be subject to the rights and freedoms set out in the Charter.

THE HANGING OF STANISLAUS LACROIX IN HULL, 21 MARCH 1902

The debate on abolishing the death penalty has always divided public opinion. In 1976, Parliament passed a law that did away with the death penalty for civil offences. In 1998, Parliament abolished the penalty for some crimes committed by military personnel. In 2001, the Supreme Court ruled in an extradition case (Burns and Rafay) that the death penalty was contrary to section 7 of the charter, which recognizes the right to life, liberty, and security of the person. Credit: Napoleon Belanger/Library and Archives Canada/ c-014078

This change in the political order brought with it a change to the constitutional role of the judiciary. Henceforth, courts would be responsible for reviewing challenged government action and legislation for compliance with the Charter and with the Constitution, and for fashioning remedies for Charter breaches that were "appropriate and just in the circumstances."[4] The courts became the guardians of the Constitution and the arbiters of the rights and freedoms guaranteed by the Charter.

Let me be clear: it is not just the courts that are responsible for ensuring that laws and government action conform to the Constitution and the Charter. This is the fundamental obligation of every branch of government – legislative, executive, and judicial. In a constitutional democracy, all three branches share the profound responsibility of ensuring that the exercise of government power conforms to the Charter.

The Charter does not guarantee absolute rights, however. It adopts instead a twentieth-century European approach to rights, where laws can limit rights, provided the government can show that this is reasonable and justifiable. This approach is reflected in the very first section of the Charter, which provides that the rights it contains are subject to "such reasonable limits prescribed by law as can be demonstrably justified in a free and democratic society."[5]

Under the approach to rights prescribed by the Charter, the burden of justifying the limits on rights falls to the government. The state must establish an important societal objective capable of justifying the limit in question. It must show that a rational connection exists between the limit on rights and the legislative objective. Most importantly, it must demonstrate that the limits are proportionate to the objective – rights can be limited, but no more than necessary to achieve the government objective, and in a way that maintains a proportionate balance between the negative effects on the right and the salutary effect of the infringing law. It is through this exercise of justification that the Charter permits a balancing of individual rights and societal needs.

The requirement of justification in the Canadian Charter aligns it with European human rights documents, such as the European Convention on Human Rights[6] and the International Covenant on Civil and Political Rights.[7] The proportionality principle, originally developed in Germany, has in turn influenced the constitutional jurisprudence of countries as diverse as Ireland,[8] Israel,[9] and South Africa[10] – even some whose constitutions do not contain a rights-limiting clause similar to section 1 of the Charter.

What has emerged from this constitutional arrangement and from this approach to rights is a relationship between the legislative and judicial branches that has been described as a dialogue. The elected representatives of the people enact laws in furtherance of important societal objectives, and the courts ensure that these laws comply with the Constitution. When courts find a law to be unconstitutional, the legislature may respond by passing new legislation that pursues the original objective in a way that is consistent with the Charter. Through this approach, the law develops in harmony with the Constitution.

That is the system that was adopted by our elected representatives thirty-five years ago. How has it fared? My answer is "Quite well." In the early years of the Charter, the Supreme Court of Canada plotted a course for the rights and freedoms contained in the Charter. Pundits who predicted that the Court would adopt a narrow view similar to the one prevailing under the Canadian Bill of Rights were proved wrong. Case after case, with clarity of vision, the Court proclaimed that Charter rights should be interpreted purposively and generously, with a view to promoting human dignity, equality, and respectful accommodation.

Bertha Wilson, the first woman to be appointed to the Supreme Court, set the tone in an early case on abortion rights. She said:

> The idea of human dignity finds expression in almost every right and freedom guaranteed by the Charter. Individuals are afforded the right to choose their

own religion and their own philosophy of life, the right to choose with whom they will associate and how they will express themselves, the right to choose where they will live and what occupation they will pursue.[11]

The Supreme Court took the same generous approach to the equality guarantee in section 15 of the Charter. In *Andrews v. Law Society of British Columbia*,[12] the court rejected the formalism of equal opportunity and articulated a model of substantive equality that looks at the on-the-ground impact of a law on members of a claimant group. At the heart of the substantive guarantee of equality in section 15 is the goal of promoting a "society in which all are secure in the knowledge that they are recognized at law as human beings, equally deserving of concern, respect and consideration."[13]

MICHAEL STARK AND MICHAEL LESHNER AT THE END OF THEIR WEDDING CEREMONY, 2003
The legislative recognition of civil marriage in 2005 came after a long legal battle. Over the years, the courts in all ten provinces and finally the Supreme Court ruled on the scope of the principle of equality guaranteed in section 15 of the charter. At the time, public opinion was divided more or less equally. Today, a large majority (around 70 per cent) supports the definition of marriage as the union of two persons. Credit: The Canadian Press/Frank Gunn

And this guarantee of substantive equality has led to a search in the past three decades for a country where the human dignity of every person is respected.

The Charter and the jurisprudence that has interpreted it have enunciated two fundamental values that define the Canadian approach to rights. The first is respect for the rights of the individual. The second is respect for minorities and accommodation of difference. Often these two values find themselves in tension. But it is a healthy tension. Let me offer examples.

- Gay people in Canada have gone from being treated as criminals under the law until 1969 to being allowed to marry whomever they love, in 2005. Breaking down the legal barriers to equality has helped recognize the human dignity not only of gay people, but also of many other sexual minorities.

- In an effort to accommodate individuals and groups within our diverse society, religious rights like the right to wear a niqab in court,[14] the right to place a succah on a person's balcony,[15] and the right to wear a kirpan in school[16] have been vetted and defined.

- Two years ago, the Supreme Court held that the liberty guarantee in section 7 of the Charter protected the right to obtain assistance in dying in some circumstances[17] – a result that could not have been contemplated early in the life of the Charter, but that was now required in light of changes in the law and in the social landscape.

- Indigenous rights and the process of reconciliation have been enhanced. The Supreme Court in decision after decision has stressed the importance of adopting a fulsome and generous approach to Aboriginal rights – not all-or-nothing solutions, but reconciliation. But it has also said that those rights can be limited if the state can justify doing so in the broader public interest.[18] As former Chief Justice Antonio Lamer stated at the end of his landmark judgment on land rights in *Delgamuukw*, "Let us face it, we are all here to stay."[19]

These are but some of the examples of the changes the Charter has helped bring about in our country.

I conclude. When I first embarked on my journey as a judge thirty-five years ago, the air was filled with high expectations, but also apprehension. The new constitutionally

### THE RIGHT TO MEDICAL ASSISTANCE IN DYING

In a decision handed down in 2001 (in the Latimer case), the Supreme Court had refused to recognize mercy killing. However, in 2015, in *Carter*, the court held that section 7 of the charter guaranteed access to medical assistance in dying for every mentally competent adult with an irremediable medical condition that causes intolerable suffering. Parliament passed legislation in June 2016 (Bill C-14), adding the criterion that the death must be "reasonably foreseeable." Currently, the courts are again faced with a challenge, this time to this added condition, which reduces access to this now-recognized right. Case law is evolving with factors such as the social conditions in place when an action is brought before the court to recognize a right. Credit: Kuzma (Getty Images)

entrenched Charter promised broad guarantees of fundamental freedoms to cleanse the disappointing record of the old Canadian Bill of Rights. But just how far would these guarantees reach? How would the courts, which had been entrusted to define these rights – and their limits – exercise their new-found powers? And how would citizens react?

Thirty-five years later, as Canada celebrates 150 years as a country, the answers to these questions are clear, at least to me. The Canadian Charter has had a lasting and positive impact on our country. Not only has its enactment proved to be one of the defining moments of the last 150 years, the Charter has, quite simply, become part of the Canadian identity. The Charter has given expression to our citizens' most fundamental values. It has enriched Canada and made it a better country. And it is no small matter of pride that in the years since the Charter's adoption, other countries have taken note of what we have built in Canada, and have emulated us.

The Charter has not fulfilled the expectations of either its harshest critics or its most ardent defenders. It has neither led to chaos nor produced a rights utopia. Its great achievement, in my view, is both more modest and more important than either of these extremes – it has provided a mechanism for balancing conflicting interests and goals in Canadian society.

In doing so, it has improved Canadians' lives, and brought Canadian society closer to the ideal of the "just society" that Prime Minister Pierre Elliott Trudeau articulated more than thirty-five years ago.

## NOTES

1   S.C. 1960, c. 44.

2   Adam Dodek, *The Canadian Constitution*, 2nd ed. (Toronto: Dundurn 2016), at p. 25.

3   *Canada Act 1982, 1982*, c. 11 (U.K.).

4   *Canadian Charter of Rights and Freedoms*, s. 24(1).

5   *Canadian Charter of Rights and Freedoms*, s. 1.

6   *Convention for the Protection of Human Rights and Fundamental Freedoms*, 4 November 1950, 213 U.N.T.S. 221–3, Eur. T.S. 5.

7   *International Covenant on Civil and Political Rights*, G.A. res. 2200A (XXI), 21 U.N. GAOR Supp. (No. 16) at 52, U.N. Doc. A/6316 (1966), 999 U.N.T.S. 171.

8   *Heaney v. Ireland*, [1994] 3 I.R. 593 (adopting the proportionality test in *R. v. Oakes* despite the absence of a constitutional clause like s. 1 of the Charter).

9   HCJ 721/94 *El-Al Israel Airlines Ltd. v. Jonathan Danielowitz* et al (relying on Canadian precedents on rights for same-sex couples, like *Vriend v. Alberta*, [1998] 1 S.C.R. 493).

10  *S. v. Williams and others*, (CCT 20/94), [1995] (3) S.A. 632 (S. Afr. Const. Ct.) (referring to *R. v. Oakes*).

11  *R. v. Morgentaler*, [1988] 1 S.C.R. 30, at 166.

12  [1989] 1 S.C.R. 143.

13  Ibid., at p. 171.

14  *R. v. N.S.*, 2012 SCC 72, [2012] 3 S.C.R. 726.

15  *Syndicat Northcrest v. Amselem*, 2004 SCC 47, [2004] 2 S.C.R. 551.

16  *Multani v. Commission scolaire Marguerite-Bourgeoys*, 2006 SCC 6, [2006] 1 S.C.R. 256.

17  *Carter v. Canada (Attorney General)*, 2015 SCC 5, [2015] 1 S.C.R. 331.

18  *R. v. Sparrow*, [1990] 1 S.C.R. 1075.

19  *Delgamuukw v. British Columbia*, [1997] 3 S.C.R. 1010, at para. 186.

# The Charter and the Idea of Canada

Mark D. Walters, F.R. Scott professor of Public and Constitutional Law at McGill University

I

The Canadian Charter of Rights and Freedoms has had a profound impact on Canada. One of its principal champions went so far as to say that "the *Canadian Charter* was a new beginning for the Canadian nation."[1] As Canada marks 150 years of Confederation, now is a good time to reflect upon this claim. How has the commitment to protect human rights through the adoption of the Charter in 1982 affected the idea of Canada that was initiated by Confederation in 1867? Is the Charter a new beginning for a nation, or a new way of understanding a nation that began long ago? The constitutional scholar and poet F.R. Scott once wrote: "If human rights and harmonious relations between cultures are forms of the beautiful, then the state is a work of art that is never finished."[2] Perhaps Canada can be seen as a work of art in this sense – perhaps as a sort of dramatic narrative about rights and cultures. Like any good narrative, however, Canada must be constantly interpreted and re-interpreted if it is to be meaningful today. What part should the Charter play in our interpretation of the dramatic narrative that is Canada?

I have put this question in a very broad way that could elicit broad answers shaped by insights drawn from political science, sociology, or history. It is worth remembering, however, that the Charter is law and law affects actual people in their daily lives. In thinking about the meaning of the Charter for Canada, it may be helpful to start on the ground level by asking how it has affected individual Canadians. The Charter meant that Delwin Vriend could make a claim of discrimination when he was fired because of his sexual orientation;[3] that young Gurbaj Multani could wear his kirpan to school as his Sikh religion requires;[4] that Shelly Tomic and others addicted to drugs could access a life-saving safe-injection site in downtown eastside Vancouver;[5] that

Sharon McIvor could ensure that her grandchildren would have status within her Aboriginal community despite rules that would have barred them because of her gender;[6] and that Tom Dunmore and his fellow farm workers could demand protection for their right to associate to improve working conditions.[7] The number of examples could be multiplied into the hundreds. Each of these individuals could do things important to their sense of human dignity and equal worth that they could not have done without the Charter.

The Charter is thus felt at a "profoundly personal level."[8] Of course, as a society we cannot remember each personal story. Charter cases accumulate over time and meld into our public consciousness; the details of particular cases fade in the process, but over time a general sense of what the Charter is and why it is important comes into ever sharper focus. The resulting impression upon the public imagination seems to have been powerful: it has been said that the Charter has "captured Canadians' understanding of themselves,"[9] that it is the expression of their "moral identity as a people."[10] A study commissioned by Statistics Canada recently found that 93 per cent of Canadians agree that the Charter is important to Canadian identity and that nothing else (not even hockey) ranks higher.[11]

This is not to say that Canadians always agree about how Charter cases should be resolved; indeed, they often disagree about what human rights mean. What Canadians do appear to agree upon, however, is that there are such things as human rights, and that the Charter allows us to work through our disagreements about these rights in a just and fair way, one that gives a voice to individuals and minorities who would have difficulty being heard otherwise. It is not just that people accept the increased role that the Charter gives judges in resolving hard issues confronting the country – though they do accept it.[12] It is that they appear to value the way in which the Charter structures and disciplines public discourse generally. Although judges may have played a part in resolving the issue of same-sex marriage, for example, the real importance of the Charter for this issue, as with many others, may have been its influence on the broader societal debate that unfolded, a debate about equality and dignity that was ultimately resolved through an act of Parliament rather than a judicial ruling.[13]

II

The Charter has affected the character of legal and political discourse about shared values in Canada. But how has this affected the *idea* of Canada? Is there *one* idea of Canada? Turning back to the suggestion that Canada is a work of art, we might be tempted to say that it is one of those iconic Group of Seven paintings of a northern vista of river, rock, and forest. Even then, however, we would still contest its meaning. Is the river to be dammed, the rock drilled, and the forest levelled? Is the scene a metaphor for freedom and imagination or for responsibility and duty? How do the peoples of Canada fit into the landscape? "If the mind stretches from the western bounds of civilization through those great north-western regions," stated George Brown during the Confederation debates in 1865, "what vast sources of wealth … lie there ready to be developed" and what an "industrial spectacle British America will present after the union has been accomplished."[14] On this account, our painting records the memory of a country that was to be remade. In the treaties that would soon be signed to open the western parts of the country to development, however, Aboriginal peoples would articulate a different vision for the land, and treaty promises would be made to protect their right to pursue traditional "avocations" within their territories, excepting only such places "taken up" for "settlement, mining, lumbering or other purposes."[15] Aboriginal peoples would see these treaties as compacts establishing equal partnerships between peoples in which land was to be shared, not surrendered.[16] Our painting, on this view, is not a memory of something that would disappear but a reminder of commitments made for the future.

Different peoples have interpreted the picture or narrative of Canada differently over time. When considering the impact of the Charter on the idea of Canada, we therefore do well to remember that it represents one strand within a complex constitutional narrative that has other, older strands of text, principle, vision, and value. Indeed, critics of the Charter argue that its imposition in 1982 conflicts with venerable traditions that used to define the idea of Canada – that the ethic animating the Constitution Act, 1982,[17] conflicts with the ethic animating the Constitution Act, 1867,[18] thus producing a state of normative discordance between our two principal constitutional texts.[19]

This claim deserves attention. An analysis of Canada since 1867 is impossible here. However, if we pick up the Canadian narrative at its centenary, we may see just how complex the story had become and why the introduction of a charter of rights would indeed present certain challenges. To this end, I turn to the final report of the Royal Commission on Bilingualism and Biculturalism as a sort of mirror that reveals the idea of Canada as it was fifty years ago.[20]

Co-chaired by André Laurendeau and Davidson Dunton, the commission was established in 1963 to report upon "the existing state of bilingualism and biculturalism in Canada" and to recommend how "to develop the Canadian Confederation on the basis of an equal partnership between the two founding races [*les deux peuples fonda-teurs* in the French text], taking into account the contribution made by the other ethnic groups to the cultural enrichment of Canada."[21] The Laurendeau-Dunton Commission concluded that the two founding peoples of Canada, French Canadians and English Canadians, constituted two "distinct societies" and that there must be an "equal partnership not only of these two peoples … but also … of their languages and cultures."[22] The commission made influential recommendations on bilingualism, including the recognition of French and English as official languages and educational rights for official language minorities in the provinces. The commission advanced a significant but underdeveloped vision of Quebec. The existence of a French-Canadian majority in Quebec, itself a "distinct society," gave the idea of an "equal partnership" of peoples "some reality" in Canada, and it would be necessary to recognize in more concrete ways that Quebec was "not 'a province like the others.'"[23] The commission observed that immigration had introduced other cultures, but that unlike the American "melting pot," Canada had become a "cultural mosaic."[24] Although newcomers were to accept the "fundamental duality of Canada" as a country with French and English societies, they were to be free to integrate into either without giving up their own languages or cultures, for "integration" is not "assimilation."[25]

The Commission acknowledged, in passing or indirectly, challenges presented by other Canadian realities – in particular that Canada was a federation of ten provinces (not two societies),[26] and that its political culture was based upon the Westminster parliamentary system or the "framework of institutions shaped by the British tradition."[27] It acknowledged the unique position of Canada's "native populations" and "indigenous cultures," and although it concluded that Aboriginal peoples formed neither part of the "two founding races" nor "other ethnic groups," and so their concerns fell outside the commission's mandate, it did insist that "the traditions and customs of native society" needed to be preserved as "an essential part of the patrimony of all Canadians."[28] Finally, the commission stated that the equal partnership between two societies and the cultural mosaic produced by newcomers were limited by the "more basic" rights enjoyed by "all human beings."[29] Citing the 1948 United Nations Universal Declaration of Human Rights, the commission concluded: "These individual human rights are unquestionable, and hold for all Canadians without exception."[30]

From this overview of the Royal Commission on Bilingualism and Biculturalism, *seven* themes central to the idea of Canada may be identified, namely, dualism, bilingualism, multiculturalism, individualism, Aboriginalism, federalism, and parliamentarism, and also two organizing theories, liberalism and communitarianism. The report did not use most of these terms, and nor did it try to resolve how they might all fit together. However, the image of Canada of fifty years ago suggested by the report is that of a country trying to juggle these different ideas in a way respectful of both the liberty of the individual and the good of communities.

The juggling act was all the more difficult given that each idea Canada was juggling was contested and changing in the sixties. The constitutional text from 1867 does not speak explicitly about a compact between two founding peoples, though its drafters spoke of two peoples, one "French and Catholic" the other "British and Protestant."[31] French Canadians were concentrated in Lower Canada/Quebec and English Canadians elsewhere, but the two identities cut across provincial boundaries. With the Quiet Revolution a century later, however, a distinct Québécois national identity would emerge.[32] As for English Canada, the assumption of the Laurendeau-Dunton Commission that its identity was characterized by a "fundamental unity" that was basically "British" was already outdated.[33] Canadians outside of Quebec came to see themselves not as "English" or "British" Canadians but simply as "Canadians" with diverse cultural backgrounds.[34] Newer ideas about the two founding peoples thus obscured older notions of compact and dualism. At the same time, the national identities of Aboriginal peoples began to re-emerge within the larger public consciousness – though the memory of a partnership evidenced by treaties in certain parts of the country, and of the bitter sense of exclusion felt where no treaties had been made, had never disappeared from the Aboriginal consciousness. The Laurendeau-Dunton report alluded to native societies only briefly. However, the year before the Hawthorn report had examined parts of the question in detail, concluding that "Indians" enjoyed a "distinct status" with a "separate culture" and many of them perceived "treaties as basic items in self-identity," and that they therefore should be acknowledged as "citizens plus" possessing "certain additional rights as charter members of the Canadian community."[35] How would the realization that there were more than two founding nations affect the idea of Canada? Finally, the quiet and not-so-quiet social revolutions of the sixties challenged orthodoxy everywhere, and talk of individual liberties and the need for a bill of rights intensified.[36] How would a commitment to human rights fit within the shifting conceptions of federalism, nation, and identity?

The government of Pierre Elliott Trudeau responded to these various developments with a series of policy initiatives in the late sixties and early seventies. In 1968, Trudeau proposed a charter to restrict "parliamentary sovereignty" in favour of the "fundamental freedoms of the individual."[37] Responding to the Hawthorn report, a 1969 white paper proposed significant changes to Indian Affairs.[38] Responding to the Laurendeau-Dunton report, official bilingualism was secured with the Official Languages Act, 1969,[39] and a "multiculturalism" policy was introduced in 1971.[40] The classical liberal individualism that informed the Charter proposal also informed the other policy initiatives. There were to be two official languages in Canada, said Trudeau, but there could not be two official cultures for "no particular culture is more 'official' than another"; "a policy of multiculturalism within a bilingual framework is basically the conscious support of individual freedom of choice."[41] Aboriginal cultures were to be celebrated, the 1969 white paper stated, but not legally protected, for "Indians" were to be treated equally with others and special Aboriginal rights phased out – though after criticism by Aboriginal groups and judicial rulings on Aboriginal title this proposal was withdrawn, and by 1973 a modern land-claim settlement or treaty process had been introduced and a new approach to Aboriginal rights slowly began to emerge.[42]

Each of these ideas would find their way into the Canadian Charter of Rights and Freedoms a decade or so later. Of course, the Charter protects individual rights and freedoms to expression, religion, liberty, equality, and the like; however, it also constitutionalizes official bilingualism and minority language educational rights (ss. 16–23); it provides that the rights it protects must be interpreted consistently with the "Aboriginal, treaty or other rights or freedoms that pertain to the Aboriginal peoples of Canada" (s. 25) defined elsewhere in the Constitution Act, 1982, as including "the Indian, Inuit and Métis peoples of Canada" (s. 35(2)); and, it provides that it shall be interpreted consistently with "the preservation and enhancement of the multicultural heritage of Canadians" (s. 27). We may say, then, that the Charter clearly promotes *four* of the *seven* ideas of Canada that we drew from the report of the Bilingualism and Biculturalism Commission, namely, individualism (or individual rights), bilingualism, multiculturalism, and Aboriginalism. But what of the other three ideas? What of parliamentarism, federalism, and dualism?

III

Critics of the Charter insist that the principles of parliamentarism, federalism, and dualism, each central to Canada's identity prior to 1982, have been undermined or even destroyed by the Charter. It is said, first, that the Charter transfers decisions about public policy from sovereign legislatures and elected representatives to unelected judges – an exchange, in effect, of the Westminster parliamentary system for an American bill of rights system. The Charter thus represents a "flight from politics" and a "deepening disillusionment" with representative democracy,[43] and it encourages the "moral inflation of rights claiming" transforming "reasonable disagreement" about matters of public policy into "uncompromising rights talk."[44] Advocates of this position come from both the political left and right and tend to be cynical about rights and rights discourse.[45] Second, it is said that the Charter imposes a centralized standard that suppresses provincial differences thus undermining the principle of federalism. Although it binds both federal and provincial legislatures, the Charter is said to favour "Canadian values" over "provincial values" and thus federal over provincial authorities.[46] The Charter, on this account, is defined by Trudeau's project of building a "pan-Canadian nationalism" at the expense of provincial identities.[47] Third, finally, it is said that the Charter denies the dualistic conception of Canada as a union of two founding peoples. With the Charter, on this view, a single Canadian idea is advanced and Quebec's distinct national identity is denied – with the Charter "le Canada se trouvait define comme société multiculturelle, sans reconnaissance constitutionnelle du principe de la 'dualité canadienne' et de la spécificité du Québec."[48] Not only does the Charter restrict Quebec's ability to protect the French language, but it protects cultural minorities through a singular conception of individualism and multiculturalism that ignores the vulnerable position that Quebec itself occupies as a distinct national minority within Canada. As Gérard Bouchard and Charles Taylor wrote in the report of their inquiry into the "reasonable accommodation" debate triggered in part by Charter cases on religious freedoms in Quebec, "we … believe that Canadian multiculturalism, inasmuch as it emphasizes diversity at the expense of continuity, is not properly adapted to Québec's situation."[49]

There is arguably an element of truth in each of these claims. It cannot be denied that the Charter has shaped the developing story about what Canada is. But has the Charter been a cause or an effect of social and political change? And just how deep has that change been? The Charter remains only one part of the narrative of the Canadian idea. If we are to interpret that narrative as if it is – or could be – a story about rights and cultures that is compelling for us today, then we should attend to the ways in which the ethic of 1982 may be seen to complement rather than contradict the ethic of 1867. We have, for better or worse, inherited a certain set of constitutional arrangements and we have a responsibility to see whether we can picture those arrangements as holding together in a manner that is coherent and unified in light of the underlying principles that they presuppose and that we value. Once re-integrated into the larger constitutional narrative, the Charter is, as one of its expounders insisted, far "less radical" than is supposed.[50]

Far from adopting the American model of rights protection, where rights trump legislative decisions, the Canadian Charter affirms the power of legislatures to override most important rights and freedoms by explicit statutory language (s. 33). For this reason it has been characterized as a leading example of the "new Commonwealth" model of rights protection,[51] one that modifies without rejecting parliamentary sovereignty.[52]

THE SUPREME COURT IN SESSION

In 1982, the country's political leaders (the federal Parliament and the governments of nine provinces) gave the courts responsibility for interpreting the rights and freedoms set out in the charter, enforcing those rights and freedoms and imposing sanctions. The courts embraced this new constitutional responsibility, giving Canadians the confidence that they themselves were the guardians of their dignity because they could apply directly to independent, impartial courts, often challenging their own governments. Since it came into effect, the charter has been invoked more than 23,939 times, at all levels of the justice system. Credit: The Canadian Press/Pool – Blair Gable

But no doubt the most innovative part of the Charter (given that the override is so rarely used) is found in its opening provision, section 1, which states: "The *Canadian Charter of Rights and Freedoms* guarantees the rights and freedoms set out in it subject only to such reasonable limits prescribed by law as can be demonstrably justified in a free and democratic society." A rich jurisprudence has emerged around these words.[53] The proportionality analysis first articulated in the *Oakes* case provides that legislative limits on rights may be justified before the courts under section 1 if they are rationally connected to a pressing public purpose, impair rights minimally, and produce salutary benefits that outweigh deleterious effects.[54] This means that judges are increasingly involved in policy questions – not as *making* policy, however, but as *measuring* policy against legal standards that prevent arbitrariness or irrationality. This is not an entirely new role for judges within the parliamentary tradition. As the nineteenth-century constitutional scholar A.V. Dicey explained, the principle of parliamentary sovereignty is inseparable from the values associated with the rule of law, and the true meaning of any law will ultimately be understood by judges in light of the "spirit of legality" or the "spirit of the common law" with judges reading legislation, where possible, so that policy objectives are pursued in non-arbitrary ways respectful of rights.[55] Dicey's idea of rights as embedded within the ordinary or common law and integrated into legislation through interpretation contrasts with the assumption, sometimes associated with the American Bill of Rights, that rights emanate from an extra-ordinary or pre-legal source that imposes an external limit on legislative power. Rather than departing from the common law–parliamentary tradition, then, the Charter may be said to sharpen significantly the interpretive process that has always existed within that tradition of seeing law as something to be justified to the people it affects through the integration of legislative will and legal reason.

As for its impact on federalism, there is no doubt that the Charter advances a common set of rights across Canada. But this is hardly a novel idea. The celebration of the "general principles of British law and liberty" – the principles enshrined in, for example, the *Magna Carta*, Petition of Right, and writ of *habeas corpus* – as "the birthright of a free people"[56] was a familiar trope within legal and political discourse throughout British North America from the late eighteenth century on. The new "political nationality" that George-Étienne Cartier said in 1865 would be established among diverse peoples upon Confederation was understood to derive in part from a shared attachment to a vision of rights and liberties based on parliamentary democracy and the rule of law.[57] Even in Quebec, where civil law would govern private law matters, it was said that these general constitutional principles were so well known that they hardly needed to be discussed.[58] Long before 1982, a common commitment to rights was one thing that defined the country, and provinces knew that the principle of federalism did not mean that these rights could be ignored with impunity. Judges found ways to strike or read down provincial laws that invaded or could be used to invade the basic rights integral to the structure of Canadian constitutional arrangements.[59]

The degree of judicial scrutiny of provincial legislation has, of course, increased considerably under the Charter, but provincial differences have not been erased as a result. As Justice Louis LeBel observed in a 2001 Supreme Court of Canada decision, "[t]he law flows from our past experiences, in its failures and disappointments, trials and successes," and it is "grounded on a wealth of historical developments and human experience that the *Charter* does not command the courts to discard." Indeed, "the *Charter* is itself an expression of our traditions, of our debt to them as well as of the evolving values of our society," and it follows that "where the members of the federation differ in their cultural and historical experiences, the principle of federalism means that the application of the *Charter* in fields of provincial jurisdiction does not amount to a call for legislative uniformity," for the Charter "expresses shared values, which may be achieved differently, in different settings."[60] That provinces may select different ways to respect shared values is, LeBel wrote more recently, "a mark of Canadian legal pluralism."[61] There is little evidence that the Charter has smothered the diversity in policy development that Canadian federalism celebrates.[62]

These observations take on special meaning in relation to Quebec.[63] Of course, there is historical support for the view that the Charter's focus on individualism and multiculturalism denies dualism and Quebec's distinctiveness. In an implicit rejection of statements in the Laurendeau-Dunton report asserting the "fundamental duality of Canada" involving an "equal partnership" between English and French societies, Trudeau was blunt in 1971: "biculturalism does not properly describe our society; multiculturalism is more accurate."[64] The Charter's embrace of individualism and multiculturalism is often taken to be the constitutional affirmation of Trudeau's dismissal of dualism.[65] In his rejection of the proposed constitutional amendment in the 1987 Meech Lake Accord that would have provided textual acknowledgment of Quebec as a "distinct society," Trudeau was again blunt: the vision of "two Canadas" must be rejected in favour of the "dream" offered by the Charter of a "single Canada" of equal citizens holding commonly shared values.[66] These sentiments proved influential during the constitutional debates of the late eighties and early nineties, and it is easy to see why one might have concluded at that time that "the idea of a Canadian people with an identity based on the Charter is hardly compatible with the concept of Canadian duality."[67]

Yet the Charter could not have swept basic truths about Confederation away completely. As the Supreme Court of Canada has acknowledged, Canada adopted a federal structure in 1867 in part to allow Quebec to protect the "distinct" culture of its French-speaking majority, or, as John A. Macdonald had put it in 1865, federalism was necessary to respect the separate "nationality" of the "people of Lower Canada" as expressed through language, religion, and the civil law tradition.[68] This point has informed constitutional interpretation on occasion. It was at least partly to ensure the integrity of Quebec's distinctive civil law system that courts adopted a broad reading of the provincial power over property and civil rights in the nineteenth century.[69] Judicial acknowledgment of Quebec's legal traditions, social values, and culture has informed interpretation more recently.[70] In the Charter's early days, the court ruled that Charter rights had to be interpreted in light of Quebec's position as a linguistic and cultural minority within Canada.[71] The Charter does not force Quebec to "mimic" other provinces, Justice Rosalie Abella has written more recently, for it "not only has a separate system of private law from the rest of Canada, it also has unique historical and societal values which it has a right to express through its legislation."[72] It may even be said that the status of Quebec as a distinct society within Canada is an unwritten constitutional principle underlying and animating Canada's constitutional texts.

But what of the concept of dualism? The theory that Confederation is the result of a compact between two nations or peoples is problematic given the shifting senses in which nations and peoples identify in Canada.[73] Quebec itself argued before the Supreme Court of Canada in the 1982 Quebec Veto Reference that "the principle of duality" in its "Canadian" sense refers to the duality of French and English Canadians throughout Canada, but in its "Quebec" sense it embraces "all the circumstances that have contributed to making Quebec a distinct society."[74] The court in that case may have concluded that there was insufficient evidence that political actors had accepted a non-legal convention giving Quebec a veto over constitutional amendments, but it did not reject (or even address) the idea that dualism might be a legal principle relevant to constitutional interpretation in other contexts.[75] It remains possible to say, as one judge recently did, that "[l]e dualisme canadien" goes back to the Quebec Act 1774 and is now enriched by multiculturalism and that the Canadian Charter affirms "le caractère distinct du Québec en élément fondamental du Canada."[76]

In the end, dualism or biculturalism is best understood not as a compact made at a particular moment in time but as a normative ideal capturing the values of constitutional justice that ought to inform a legal order consisting of different nations or peoples.[77] Once the compact idea is untethered from the constitutive moment of 1867, however, its normative aspirations must be seen to extend to – using the Hawthorn report's expression – other "charter members" of Canada, meaning, of course, the Indigenous or Aboriginal peoples of Canada.[78] Indeed, it is now a principle of Canadian law that compacts must be negotiated with those Aboriginal nations that do not yet enjoy a treaty relationship with the Crown, for "[t]reaties serve to reconcile pre-existing Aboriginal sovereignty with assumed Crown sovereignty."[79] The terms "dualism" and "biculturalism" are thus misleading descriptors of an important aspect of the Canadian story, and as essential as it is for other parts of the story, "multiculturalism" does not capture this aspect either. It is fair to say that a constitutional principle of multinationalism has always formed an implicit part of the structure or architecture of the Constitution along with the other underlying or unwritten constitutional principles that give shape to that constitutional structure, including multiculturalism, parliamentarism, legality, and federalism.[80] Likewise, the principle of bilingualism, reoriented to accommodate Indigenous languages, may now be seen as a constitutional principle of multilingualism.[81]

We are still learning to juggle the various principles that define Canada. One thing we may have learned over the last fifty years – indeed, perhaps, the past 150 years – is that it is very difficult to articulate a grand vision in abstract terms that accommodates all of the principles of Canadian constitutionalism. Experience has shown that it is far too easy for protagonists in any constitutional debate to say that, at an abstract level, principles – whether liberty and equality or equality and nationalism or nationalism and federalism – conflict. Experience has also shown, however, that within the Canadian narrative as it has evolved bit by bit, or case by case, principles that compete at an abstract level *can* be reconciled at a human level, and a coherent and compelling story that includes diverse peoples and their ideas about constitutional justice *can* flourish. There may be a time when we are able to pause and rewrite the formal texts of the Constitution of Canada so that they better reflect the truths about Canada that may be inferred from the evolving narrative about the country.[82] But in the end, the Canadian story will always be, as F.R. Scott reminds us, a work in progress – one in which we learn the essence of our commitments to each other through the daily attempt to reach some kind of equilibrium between the concrete truths we accept and the larger values we share.[83]

IV

We may close by returning briefly to the theories of liberalism and communitarianism mentioned earlier. In understanding the Charter, it is always important to remember the people affected by it – like Delwin Vriend, Gurbaj Multani, and Sharon McIvor. If we are to live in a society governed by the rule of law, where power is not arbitrary but legal, then laws must be capable of reasoned justification. Indeed, the law must be justified to each person whose rights are affected by it, for each person must be treated with equal concern and respect in a liberal democracy. This is the liberal part of the Canadian story. The communitarian part comes with the answer given by the community in response: the community is always in a position to say that the challenged law is a *true* law because it was made for the public or common good and it affects rights only insofar as necessary and in ways that are proportionate to our commitment to living together peacefully in a free and democratic society. Perhaps this is the brilliance of the Charter and its importance to our interpretation of the Canadian narrative: the Charter enhances dramatically our ability to engage in a structured and principled discourse about individuals and communities and about the cherished values of legality and legitimacy that have formed the heart of the idea of Canada for the last 150 years at least.

NOTES

1   Pierre Elliott Trudeau, *Memoirs* (Toronto: McClelland & Stewart, 1993), 363.

2   Frank R. Scott, *Essays on the Constitution: Aspects of Canadian Law and Politics* (Toronto: University of Toronto Press, 1977), ix.

3   *Vriend v. Alberta*, [1998] 1 S.C.R. 493.

4   *Multani v. Commission scolaire Marguerite-Bourgeoys*, 2006 S.C.C. 6, [2006] 1 S.C.R. 256.

5   *Canada (Attorney General) v. PHS Community Services Society*, 2011 S.C.C. 44, [2011] 3 S.C.R. 134.

6   *McIvor v. Canada (Registrar, Indian and Northern Affairs)*, 2009 BCCA 153, 306 D.L.R. (4th) 193 (B.C.C.A.); leave to appeal refused, [2009] S.C.C.A. no. 234.

7   *Dunmore v. Ontario (Attorney General)*, 2001 S.C.C. 94, [2001] 3 S.C.R. 1016.

8   Rt. Hon. Beverley McLachlin, "Courts, Legislatures and Executives in the Post-Charter Era" in Paul Howe and Peter H. Russell (eds.), *Judicial Power and Canadian Democracy* (Montreal and Kingston: McGill-Queen's University Press, 2001), 63–72.

9   Rt. Hon. Beverley McLachlin, "The Canadian Charter of Rights and Freedoms' First 30 Years: A Good Beginning" (2013), 61 S.C.L.R. (2d) 25, 32.

10  Michael Ignatieff, *The Rights Revolution* (Toronto: House of Anansi Press, 2000), 2.

11  Maire Sinha, *Spotlight on Canadians: Results from the General Social Survey* (Ottawa: Statistics Canada, 2015), 3.

12  *The Charter: Dividing or Uniting Canadians?* (Centre for Research and Information on Canada, April 2002), 7.

13  Luke McNamara, *Human Rights Controversies: The Impact of Legal Form* (Abingdon: Routledge-Cavendish, 2007), 105–19.

14  *Parliamentary Debates on the Subject of the Confederation of the British North American Provinces* (Quebec: Hunter, Rose & Co., 1865), 98.

15  North West Angle Treaty, 3 October 1873, in Hon. Alexander Morris, *The Treaties of Canada with the Indians of Manitoba and the North-West Territories* (Toronto: Belford, Clarke & Co., 1880), 320–7.

16  See evidence and findings in the trial decision in *Keewatin v. Ontario (Minister of Natural Resources)*, 2011 ONSC 4801; 2013 ONCA 158; *Grassy Narrows First Nation v. Ontario (Natural Resources)*, 2014 S.C.C. 48, [2014] 2 S.C.R. 447.

17  The Canadian Charter of Rights and Freedoms is Part I of the Constitution Act, 1982, being Schedule B to the Canada Act 1982 (UK), 1982, c. 11.

18  Constitution Act, 1867, 30 and 31 Vict, c. 3 (UK).

19  E.g. *Rapport de la Commission sur l'avenir politique et constitutionnnel du Québec* [Commission Bélanger-Campeau] (March 1991), 34: "[l]oin de reviser la *Loi constitutionnelle de*

*1867*, la Loi de 1982 renferme une nouvelle définition constitutionnelle du Canada qui a modifié l'esprit de 1867 et le compromise alors établi."

20 *Report of the Royal Commission on Bilingualism and Biculturalism*, book I: *The Official Languages* (1967), book II: *Education* (1968), book III: *The Work World* (1969), book IV: *The Cultural Contribution of the Other Ethnic Groups* (1969), book V: *The Federal Capital* (1970), and book VI: *Voluntary Associations* (1970).

21 Ibid at I: xxi.

22 Ibid at I: xxii, xxxiii.

23 Ibid at I: xxxiii, xlvii.

24 Ibid at IV: 225.

25 Ibid at IV: 5.

26 E.g., ibid. at I: chap. V (addressing bilingualism in a federal setting).

27 Ibid at I: xxxiii.

28 Ibid at I: xxvi-xxvii.

29 Ibid at I: xxxix.

30 Ibid.

31 *Parliamentary Debates on Confederation*, 60 (George-Étienne Cartier); see also 27, 29, 31 (John A. Macdonald).

32 Michel Seymour, *La Nation en question* (Montreal: Hexagone, 1999); Louis Balthazar, *Nouveau bilan du nationalisme au Québec* (Montreal: VLB, 2013).

33 *Bilingualism and Biculturalism Commission*, I: xxxiii-xxxiv.

34 José E. Igartua, *The Other Quiet Revolution: National Identities in English Canada, 1945–71* (Vancouver: UBC Press, 2006); C.P. Champion, *The Strange Demise of British Canada: The Liberals and Canadian Nationalism, 1964–1968* (Montreal and Kingston: McGill-Queen's University Press, 2010); Philip Resnick, "English Canada: The Nation that Dares Not Speak Its Name" in Kenneth McRoberts (ed.), *Beyond Quebec: Taking Stock of Canada* (Montreal and Kingston: McGill-Queen's University Press, 1995), 81–92.

35 H.B. Hawthorn (ed.), *A Survey of the Contemporary Indians of Canada: A Report on Economic, Political, Educational Needs and Policies* (Ottawa: Indian Affairs Branch, 1966–67), 1:6, 10, 13, 248, 299.

36 Dominique Clément, *Canada's Rights Revolution: Social Movements and Social Change, 1937–82* (Vancouver: UBC Press, 2008).

37 Hon. P.E. Trudeau, *A Canadian Charter of Human Rights* (Ottawa: Queen's Printer, 1968).

38 Canada, *Statement of the Government of Canada on Indian Policy* (Minister of Indian Affairs and Northern Development, 1969).

39 *An Act Respecting the Status of Official Languages in Canada*, S.C. 1969, c. 54.

40 Rt. Hon. P.E. Trudeau, "Multiculturalism Policy Statement to the House of Commons,"

House of Commons, *Official Report of Debates*, 28th Parliament, 3rd Session, 8 October 1971, 8545–6 and Appendix.

41 Ibid.

42 For negative reaction, see Harold Cardinal, *The Unjust Society: The Tragedy of Canada's Indians* (Edmonton: MG Hurtig, 1969). Common law Aboriginal title to land was recognized in *Calder* v. *Attorney-General of B.C.*, [1973] s.c.r. 313. For the commencement of modern land-claim negotiations, see Department of Indian Affairs and Northern Development, "Statement Made by the Honourable Jean Chrétien, Minister of Indian Affairs and Northern Development on Claims of Indian and Inuit People" (8 August 1973).

43 Peter H. Russell, "The Effect of a Charter of Rights on the Policy-Making Role of Canadian Courts" *Canadian Public Administration* 25 (1982): 1, 32.

44 F.L. Morton and Rainer Knopff, *The Charter Revolution and the Court Party* (Peterborough: Broadview Press, 2000), 157.

45 Examples of the critique from the left: Allan C. Hutchinson and Andrew Petter, "Private Rights/Public Wrongs: The Liberal Lie of the Charter" *University of Toronto Law Journal* 38 (1988): 278; Andrew Petter, *The Politics of the Charter: The Illusive Promise of Constitutional Rights* (Toronto: University of Toronto Press, 2010); Michael Mandel, *The Charter of Rights and the Legalization of Politics in Canada* (Toronto: Wall & Thompson, 1989). Examples of the critique from the right: Morton and Knopff, *The Charter Revolution*; Christopher P. Manfredi, *Judicial Power and the Charter: Canada and the Paradox of Liberal Constitutionalism*, 2nd ed. (Don Mills: Oxford University Press, 2001); Patrick James, Donald E. Abelson, and Michael Lusztig (eds.), *The Myth of the Sacred: The Charter, the Courts, and the Politics of the Constitution of Canada* (Montreal: McGill-Queen's University Press, 2002).

46 Alan C. Cairns, *Charter versus Federalism: The Dilemmas of Constitutional Reform* (Montreal and Kingston: McGill-Queen's University Press, 1992), 76–7.

47 F.L. Morton, "The Effect of the Charter of Rights on Canadian Federalism," *Publius* 25 (1995): 173, 178. Also Peter H. Russell, "The Political Purposes of the Canadian Charter of Rights and Freedoms," *Canadian Bar Review* 61 (1983): 30.

48 Bélanger-Campeau Commission, 33.

49 Consultation Commission on Accommodation Practices Related to Cultural Differences, *Building the Future: A Time for Reconciliation*, Gérard Bouchard and Charles Taylor, commissioners (Quebec, 2008), 121.

50 Rt. Hon. Brian Dickson, "The Canadian Charter of Rights and Freedoms: Context and Evolution" (2013) 61 s.c.l.r. (2d) 3, 15.

51 Stephen Gardbaum, *The New Commonwealth Model of Constitutionalism: Theory and Practice* (Cambridge: Cambridge University Press, 2013).

52 Jeffrey Goldsworthy, *Parliamentary Sovereignty: Contemporary Debates* (Cambridge: Cambridge University Press, 2010), 202–24.

53 Grégoire Webber and Luc Tremblay (eds.), *The Limitation of Charter Rights: Critical Essays on R. v. Oakes = La limitation des droits de la Charte: Essais critiques sur l'arrêt R. c. Oakes* (Montreal: Thémis, 2009).

54 *R. v. Oakes*, [1986] 1 S.C.R. 103.

55 A.V. Dicey, *Introduction to the Study of the Law of the Constitution*, 7th ed. (London: Macmillan, 1908), 402–9.

56 Beamish Murdoch, *Epitome of the Laws of Nova-Scotia* (Halifax: Joseph Howe, 1832), 1, 30, 35.

57 *Parliamentary Debates on Confederation*, 60. See in general Janet Ajzenstat, *The Canadian Founding: John Locke and Parliament* (Montreal and Kingston: McGill-Queen's University Press, 2007).

58 Edmond Lareau, *Histoire du droit canadien depuis les origines de la colonie jusqu'a nos jours* (Montreal: A. Périard, 1889), 54.

59 *Union Colliery Company of British Columbia v. Bryden*, [1899] A.C. 580; *Reference re Alberta Statutes* [1939] A.C. 117; *Saumur v. Quebec (City of)* [1953] 2 S.C.R. 299; *Switzman v. Elbling* [1957] S.C.R. 285; *Roncarelli v. Duplessis*, [1959] SCR 121.

60 *R. v.* Advance Cutting & Coring Ltd., [2001] S.C.J. 68, [2001] 3 S.C.R. 209, paras. 259, 275.

61 *Quebec (Attorney General) v. A*, 2013 S.C.C. 5, [2013] 1 S.C.R. 61, para. 279.

62 James B. Kelly, "Reconciling Rights and Federalism during Review of the Charter of Rights and Freedoms: The Supreme Court of Canada and the Centralization Thesis, 1982 to 1999," *Canadian Journal of Political Science* 34 (2001): 321; Jean-François Gaudreault-DesBiens, "La *Charte canadienne des droits et libertés* et le fédéralisme: quelques remarques sur les vingt premières années d'une relation ambiguë," *Revue du Barreau,* special edition (2003): 271.

63 Sébastien Grammond, "Louis LeBel et la société distincte" *Cahiers de droit* 57 (2016): 251.

64 Trudeau, "Multiculturalism Policy Statement to the House of Commons."

65 E.g., Guy Laforest, *Trudeau and the End of a Canadian Dream* (Montreal and Kingston: McGill-Queen's University Press, 1995).

66 Pierre Elliott Trudeau, "Say Goodbye to the Dream of One Canada," [27 May 1987] in Donald Johnston (ed.), *With a Bang, Not a Whimper: Pierre Trudeau Speaks Out* (Toronto: Stoddart Publishing, 1996), 18–22.

67 Pierre Coulombe, "The End of Canadian Dualism?," *Parliamentary Review* 7 (Winter 1992–93): 7–8. See also Charles Taylor, "Can Canada Survive the *Charter*?," *Alberta Law Review* 30 (1992): 427.

68 *Reference re Secession of Quebec* [1998] 2 S.C.R. 217, para. 59; *Debates on Confederation*, 27.

69 *Citizens Ins Co v. Parsons* (1881) 7 App Cas 96 (PC), 113.

70 *Reference re Supreme Court Act, ss. 5 and 6*, S.C.C. 21, [2014] 1 S.C.R. 433, paras. 18, 93.

71 *Ford v. Quebec (A.G.)*, [1988] 2 S.C.R. 712.

72 *Quebec (Attorney General) v. A*, 2013 S.C.C. 5, [2013] 1 S.C.R. 61, para. 371.

73 Ramsay Cook, *Provincial Autonomy, Minority Rights and the Compact Theory, 1867–1921* (Ottawa: Queen's Printer for Canada, 1969); Paul Romney, "Equality, Special Status and the Compact Theory of Canadian," *Canadian Journal of Political Science* 32 (1999): 21.

74 *Reference Re Amendment to the Canadian Constitution*) [1982] 2 S.C.R. 793, 812–13.

75 The Court had earlier stated that the theory of Confederation as a compact of *provinces* (not peoples or nations) operated mainly in the political realm, though it might have some relevance for constitutional interpretation: *Reference re Resolution to amend the Constitution*, [1981] 1 S.C.R. 753, 803.

76 *Gosselin (Tutor of) v. Quebec (Attorney General)*, [2000] R.J.Q. 2973, [2000] Q.J. No. 4688 (Maurice Laramée J. at paras. 54–5, 156, 162); aff'd [2002] R.J.Q. 1298, [2002] Q.J. No. 1126, aff'd [2005] 1 S.C.R. 238, 2005 S.C.C. 15.

77 Sébastien Grammond, "Compact Is Back: The Supreme Court of Canada's Revival of the Compact Theory of Confederation," *Osgoode Hall Law Journal* 53 (2016): 799.

78 See also Royal Commission on Aboriginal Peoples, *Partners in Confederation: Aboriginal Peoples, Self-Government, and the Constitution* (August 1993).

79 *Haida Nation v. British Columbia (Minister of Forests)*, [2004] 3 S.C.R. 511, para. 20 (McLachlin C.J.).

80 On the idea of multinational federations, see in general Alain-G. Gagnon, *The Case for Multinational Federalism: Beyond the All-Encompassing Nation* (London: Routledge, 2010).

81 Hugo Choquette, *The Constitutional Status of Aboriginal Languages in Canada* (Ph.D. thesis, Queen's University, Faculty of Law, 2016).

82 Now is such a time according to the Quebec government: *Quebecers: Our Way of Being Canadian – Policy on Québec Affirmation and Canadian Relations* (Government of Quebec, 2017).

83 On this approach, see in general Donald G. Lenihan, Gordon Robertson, and Roger Tassé, *Canada: Reclaiming the Middle Ground* (Ottawa: Institute for Research on Public Policy, 1994). For a slightly different way of celebrating day-to-day accommodation, see Jeremy Webber, *The Constitution of Canada: A Contextual Analysis* (London: Bloomsbury, 2015), 259–66.

# 5

# National Unity:
# High-Risk Tensions That Lead to Progress[1]

The Hon. Serge Joyal, Senator

*F*ollowing *its centennial in 1967, Canada took the necessary steps to gain full con-*
*trol of its constitutional destiny. The patriation of the Constitution in 1982 was*
*an achievement that for fifty years had eluded several previous governments,*
*despite good faith and commendable efforts on their part.*

*At the same time, Canada adopted the* Charter of Rights and Freedoms *(the*
*Charter), which gave added significance to citizenship and strengthened Canadians'*
*confidence in the humanist nature of its society. By protecting minority rights from the*
*whims of the majority, this fundamental change served to enhance citizens' faith in*
*Canada and their belief in what it represents.*

*In 1996, Canada also adopted regional veto legislation (the* Act respecting constitutional amendments*) clarifying the level of agreement that is required from the prov-*
*inces before any constitutional amendment resolution may be tabled in Parliament. In*
*2000, pursuant to an advisory opinion from the Supreme Court of Canada, the federal*
*government passed legislation on the legal process that must be followed if a province*
*wishes to hold a secession referendum (the* Clarity Act*) or obtain a fundamental consti-*
*tutional amendment.*

*It should be borne in mind that all these initiatives, which profoundly altered the*
*exercise of democracy in Canada, took place as a result of serious political tensions,*
*originating mainly in Quebec. There were also demands from Western Canada –*
*primarily Alberta – which heightened the climate of dissatisfaction in the country and*
*helped create a widespread feeling of political unrest. Canada was forced to confront*
*numerous crises and challenges that at times severely tested its resilience and, twice*
*during that period, even threatened its very survival.*

*The October Crisis of 1970, which included a public call for armed insurrection from*
*the Front de libération du Québec (*FLQ*), the kidnapping of British diplomat James*

Richard Cross and the assassination of Quebec minister Pierre Laporte, led the government to invoke the War Measures Act, *previously used only in response to global conflict. The turmoil followed numerous acts of sabotage and urban guerilla warfare that had left innocent victims in their wake. Homemade bombs placed in mailboxes bearing the insignia of the Crown or in locations frequented by the public, such as the La Grenade shoe factory, created a climate of constant social upheaval.*

*The decision of Pierre E. Trudeau's government to resort to the War Measures Act, at the request of the Quebec government, left a lasting impression. In a democracy, change – no matter how radical – cannot be the result of blackmail, public mischief or the assassination of defenceless individuals. While the ensuing 450 arrests were carried out indiscriminately, with no charges being laid, the application of the War Measures Act did have a somewhat salutary effect: the use of violence to bring about regime change was vanquished from Canadian politics. If Quebec were to separate, it would be the result of a democratic process, and that was the path the Parti Québécois promoted from the outset.*

*In 1976, for the first time in the country's history, a secessionist government was democratically elected in Quebec. The province was the focal point of all the tension, and Canada's survival as a country was now in question. The referendum on separation that was held in Quebec on 20 May 1980 had some unexpected consequences. First, one can assume that, had it not been for the impending referendum in Quebec, Pierre E. Trudeau would not have returned as leader of the Liberal Party of Canada and formed a government. Second, particularly in view of its failed attempts in 1970 (Victoria Charter) and 1978 (Bill C-60), his government would not have committed to a new round of constitutional talks had he not promised to reopen the Constitution during the referendum campaign.*

*The political dynamic brought about profound changes, both in defining the foundations of Canadian society (through the adoption of the Charter) and in establishing new rules to maintain national unity in the event of secessionist initiatives. These changes resulted first from a referendum campaign in Quebec and second from what the federal government considered fair and appropriate responses. When political power relationships arise in which the parties' fundamental interests are viscerally opposed, a two-track process is set in motion: there is always a certain amount of unpredictability that can produce unexpected results, from which both parties may emerge quite different.*

*Quebec refused to give its political consent to the constitutional proposal to patriate the Constitution and adopt the Charter in 1982.[2] This self-exclusion of Quebec created an unprecedented situation. For the first time in the political history of Canada, Quebec was not a determining stakeholder in the definition of the constitutional regime of the*

"YES – OUI"

1980 referendum button, Basilières Inc. Montreal. In the 20 May 1980 referendum, the Quebec government asked the people to give it a mandate to negotiate a new agreement with Canada, nation to nation, and promised to submit the results of the negotiations to a second referendum for ratification. The "No" side garnered 59.56 per cent of the vote (compared to 40.44 per cent for the "Yes" side). During the campaign, the prime minister of Canada promised to overhaul the constitution. Credit: Canadian Museum of History (CHSJ), IMG2012-0259-0011-DM (artifact 2011.21.300)

*country. This challenged the so-called theory of the two founding nations, whereby Canada would not alter the constitutional regime without the agreement or concurrence of Quebec. Prime Minister Trudeau, himself a Quebecker, and the sixty-eight Liberal MPs from Quebec,[3] claimed that they were equally legitimate as representatives of Quebec's interests. By boycotting any constitutional negotiations that were not devoted to solve its claim, Quebec was stalling any future changes to the constitutional acts of 1867 and 1982. However, the provisions of the new constitutional legislation took full effect immediately, and the protection provided by the Charter was quickly invoked by a Quebec union.[4] In 1997, the government of Lucien Bouchard availed itself of the provisions of the amending formula in the* Constitution Act, 1982, *to request a change to the denominational school structures guaranteed in section 93 of the* Constitution Act, 1867.[5]

*In the six years during which Brian Mulroney's government negotiated the Meech Lake Accord (1987) and then the Charlottetown Accord (1992), Canadians were subjected to prolonged reconciliation efforts aimed at meeting Quebec's five prior conditions for consenting to the* Constitution Act, 1982. *Yet despite the best efforts of all the signatory political representatives, the entire Canadian population, including that of Quebec, rejected the outcome of those negotiations in a national referendum held on 26 October 1992.*

*All this work was ultimately set aside following the 1993 general election, for a variety of reasons: the length of the debate, which the public felt had dragged on for more than six years; voter fatigue at seeing the same issues, some of them trivial and of no interest to Canadians, resurface again and again; the clearly unfair perception that all this chaos of compromise was more fascinating for politicians than for "ordinary people"; the impression that Canadians themselves were more or less ignored in this never-ending cycle; and the intervention of former prime minister Pierre E. Trudeau, who evoked a vision of a simpler and more accessible Canada, one he championed while brandishing the Charter, which was widely supported by the public.*

*But the re-election of a secessionist Quebec government on 12 September 1994 plunged the country into another referendum process the following year. Canada barely emerged intact, with a majority of just 54,288 votes.[6] Had it not been for the sovereignists' near-victory in that 1995 Quebec referendum, Jean Chrétien's government would never have given priority to passing legislation on regional vetoes and adopting a motion recognizing Quebec as a distinct society in 1996, and it would not have considered it essential to seek an advisory opinion from the Supreme Court on provinces' right of secession under the Canadian Constitution. Finally, it would not have passed the* Clarity Act *following the court's response to the three questions put by the government.[7]*

*The Supreme Court responded that the provinces did not have a right to unilateral secession, under either Canadian or international law, as they were not subject to a colonial power. The court also stated that a question put during a referendum must be clear and that a clear majority of votes must be earned in order to oblige the parties to negotiate in good faith.*

*Adoption of the* Clarity Act *in 2000 led Lucien Bouchard's government to respond with the* Act respecting the exercise of the fundamental rights and prerogatives of the Québec people and the Québec state. *That Act, also passed in 2000, stated that the province does indeed have the right to unilateral secession, if that is the will of the Quebec people (section 1). It was adopted for future purposes, again against the backdrop of a fairly indifferent public.*

*By 2001, the Act was the subject of a legal challenge by a Quebec citizen, Keith Owen Henderson. After multiple delays, a hearing was finally held in the spring of 2017, 16 years after the fact! The decision was rendered the following spring. The*

*Superior Court took a somewhat unorthodox approach to its analysis of sections 1 to 5 and 13 of the Act. It failed to define the true nature of these sections – namely, their purpose, their legal and practical effects and their link to the powers attributed to the province of Quebec in the* Constitution Act, 1867, *and the* Constitution Act, 1982 *(section 45). The court found that these sections simply reiterated existing principles and that the Act could not be described as twisted, covert, harmful or illegal.[8] It remains to be seen what the Court of Appeal of Quebec will conclude.*

*In any case, there is little doubt the public debate will eventually recommence, but no one can predict under what circumstances. Through the years, successive Quebec governments of federalist allegiance have reaffirmed their desire to sign the* Constitution Act, 1982, *and to reclaim their status as a full participant in future constitutional discussions, provided that specific conditions to protect its cultural character can be met. However, since there is no immediate need at the national level to initiate any negotiations, the Quebec question could remain pending for a very long time.*

*In 2006, the newly elected government of Stephen Harper promised to stay away from the constitutional file, viewing it as a pitfall of Canadian disunity. It strove to respect provincial jurisdictions to avoid creating conflict and instability. Constitutional peace was the prime minister's stated objective.[9] But an opening quickly appeared that would be seized upon and used to continue the debate on Quebec's status and, unexpectedly, some years later, the debate on the political status of Indigenous peoples.*

*The initiative took the form of a simple motion tabled on 22 November 2006 by Prime Minister Harper himself: "That this House recognize that the Québécois form a nation within a united Canada." The motion was passed on 27 November by a vote of 265 to 16. All parties in the House voted in favour of it.[10] The motion was the government's response to an earlier Bloc Québécois motion that simply stated that Quebec was a nation. It was not linked to any request from the Quebec government to endorse the* Constitution Act, 1982.

*The prime minister maintained that his initiative was intended as an affirmation of national unity and reconciliation with Quebec.*

*The only discordant note came when intergovernmental affairs minister Michael Chong[11] resigned from Cabinet on the spot, stating, "I believe in one nation, undivided, called Canada."[12]*

*The choice of the word "nation" may appear to be purely semantics, but it reflects a fundamental political reality. Its deep significance cannot be ignored, particularly when the topic is independence, a profoundly emotional identity issue. Prime Minister Harper had unintentionally resurrected an argument that secessionists would immediately seize upon. For proponents of independence, "nation" includes the concept of* state sovereignty; for the Harper government, it implied "sociological" recognition (Mr Harper's own words), in the sense of a group of people living in a given area who wish to live together.

According to Prime Minister Harper, all Quebecers, regardless of their first language, race or date of arrival in Quebec – anglophones, francophones or allophones – form a "nation within Canada." It could therefore be said that New Brunswickers, with the Acadians, people of British descent, loyalists and more recent immigrants, also form a "nation"! Thus defined, the scope of the term "nation" does not extend to statehood.

Under that definition, the term clearly has little actual political meaning.[13] But that is not how the secessionists saw it. They immediately identified it as the basis for a claim to the right of self-determination, focusing on the political dimension of the term "nation," which is much more significant than that of "distinct society," the expression used up to that point to describe Quebec. Truth be told, "nation" is clearly related to statehood, whereas "distinct society" does not have that connotation and is essentially much more sociological. Proponents of separation fully understood this, and as former Quebec premier Bernard Landry said, "... once that recognition [of nation] is achieved, you must know, in all honesty, that you will then be faced with the question: why should the nation of Quebec be satisfied with the status of province of another nation and forego equality with yours and every other nation?"[14] The secessionists' plan was very clear, as was their goal.

The current government of Quebec also seized the opportunity in June 2017, when it outlined its position in the document Quebecers, Our Way of Being Canadian, with a view to initiating constitutional negotiations.[15] It states in that document: "To summarize, recognition of the Québec nation is now primarily political."[16] It goes on to argue that recognizing Quebec as a "political" nation would ensure that "Quebecers no longer feel like exiles in their own country." The table is once again being set to claim a right to unilateral secession irrespective of Canadian and international law, which must govern any secession initiative, as the Supreme Court recognized in 1998. The inviolability of Canada's borders is guaranteed by the rule of law.[17] The rule of law, when it applies to an issue so critical to the survival of the country, cannot be ignored if the country is to avoid descending into a political imbroglio that could lead to anarchy.

Furthermore, in claiming the status of a "political nation," Quebec is definitively severing the historical ties that bound it to Canada's other francophone communities, many of them born of its own migrant population. Their leaving Quebec would therefore be equivalent to having politically renounced their historical identity. Having settled elsewhere in the country, often for economic reasons, when agricultural land in Quebec became too

"ON A RAISON DE DIRE NON – LA SÉPARATION?" [WE'RE RIGHT TO SAY NO – SEPARATION?]
Coroplast sign, Unicom Sérigraphie Ltée, Saint-Laurent, 1995.
After Brian Mulroney's government failed in its reconciliation efforts, Quebecers were once again faced with a referendum on separation, on 30 October 1995. Early in the campaign, voters favoured the "No" side, but a coalition between the Parti Québécois, the Bloc Québécois and Action Démocratique swung public opinion over to the "Yes" side. The result of the vote was very close. Credit: Canadian Museum of History (CHSJ), IMG2014-0128-0060-DM (artifact 2011.21.690)

*cramped in the nineteenth century, these people must bear alone the burden of having broken with their homeland, just like the Franco-Americans of New England.*

*The divide that has been created between Quebecers and French Canadians else-where in the country is so great[18] that Quebec has even challenged recognition of bilingualism for these minority communities before the courts in order to protect the status of French as the official language of Quebec.[19] Is it really necessary to deny the rights of some so as to recognize those of others? True protection from assimilation lies in the minority official-language education rights recognized in section 23 of the Charter in 1982 and supported by the federal government's Court Challenges Program, the only program that promotes an approach placing linguistic minorities at the heart of Canadian values and identity.[20] As a way of shirking responsibility, in 2008 Quebec created the Centre de la francophonie des Amériques, theoretically merging Canadian francophone minorities with other francophones scattered across the American continent, without any specific rights or language recognition.*

*But who in Quebec truly cares about protecting the rights and survival of Canada's francophone minorities? Did René Levesque not refer to them as "lame ducks," and writer Yves Beauchemin as "still-warm corpses"?[21] In fact, their presence is regarded in some circles as an obstacle to independence, the only goal being the growth of French in Quebec alone. Their historical fate is thus removed from the so-called "national" conscience of Quebec.*

*Playing with such highly political concepts fuels the confusion that traps people in word games and leads them straight to disillusionment.*

*Prime Minister Justin Trudeau has clearly defined what could compel him to engage in constitutional negotiations: "If we were at a stage where we could point to something in the Constitution and say: because of this or that, the country is not working, everything is about to break down, I would say: 'Maybe we should discuss that.' But if it is only for political ends, for symbolic reasons or for other good, but not clear and urgent, reasons, I prefer to avoid them."[22] [Translation]*

*In short, only under exceptional circumstances, where the very survival of the country is at stake, should the two levels of government enter into constitutional negotiations.*

*However, the word "nation" was used in Prime Minister Justin Trudeau's own statement, made recently when he committed to placing the relationship between Canada and Indigenous peoples on a "nation-to-nation"[23] and "government to government" footing.[24] Perhaps without realizing it, the prime minister risks shifting the fundamental framework of the constitution that his father has always stood for.*

*The term is still confusing in that Indigenous peoples clearly constitute "ethnic" nations; i.e., groups of people who share a common origin, such as the Mohawks, the Inuit, the Cree and all other Indigenous peoples. Canadians also form a nation in that they have a political "nationality" that is clearly identified on their passports and recognized abroad. All Canadians have a "sociological" and "state" nationality. What the government of Justin Trudeau is actually seeking to achieve is recognition of a form of state nationality for "ethnic" Indigenous nations to help them exercise government powers (currently undefined) on behalf of their members – in short, the exercise of a form of legislative sovereignty.*

*Clearly, in a debate over the "sovereignty" to be recognized for an "ethnic" nation, the ground is not the same as for the recognition of a nation in a "sociological" context, where the group's political sovereignty is not at issue.*

*The ambiguity of the discussion illustrates the semantic pitfalls: in seeking to play subtle games with political concepts, people can find themselves caught in a web that does nothing to advance the debate and can even plunge it into confusion.*

*Political concepts must be used consistently; the constitutional debate is not a game of Scrabble, where players form words at random. Indeed, words used for the purpose of political appeasement can reappear in another, completely different, context.*

*What may seem surprising is the use of "nation-to-nation" in Prime Minister Trudeau's public statements given that, on other occasions, he argued that Canada was the "first postnational state."[25] He supported this claim by stating that, in his opinion, "There is no core identity, no mainstream in Canada." However, he added that "there are shared values" and that those are the "qualities" that make Canada "the first post-national state."*

*So, to paraphrase Hamlet: to be a nation or not to be a nation? Some analysts see in the prime minister's statement an unbridled celebration of Canadian multiculturalism,[26] or even "extreme multiculturalism."[27] But while Indigenous peoples should now see their relationship as being one of "nations" on an equal footing with "the other" nation, this must be understood as referring to the Canadian nation in its entirety, as a political and sociological entity. There are certainly various ways of belonging to the Canadian nation, and although they are different from those that gave rise to European nation-states in the 19th century, Canadians nevertheless feel a very strong attachment to Canada. Unlike in some older states, this attachment is not based on shared racial or ethnic characteristics, a common traditional religion, or even a typical character or a dominant mentality.*

*As is commonly known, since 1763 two major cultures of European origin have lived in Canada alongside Indigenous cultures (which have experienced numerous setbacks but are now recognized and being invited to retake their place in the public domain). For more than 100 years, large-scale immigration has brought its share of new ways of "reading" the world. The fact that Canada was built over centuries on diverse foundations and with very different inputs does not inevitably lead to the conclusion that it is a "postnational state" that has no strong identity or shared culture based on a genuine desire to live together. French historian Ernest Renan wrote in 1882 that a nation "is a daily plebiscite." That is indeed what Canadians experience on a regular basis in welcoming immigrants from all over the world, without diluting the Canadian identity. This contradicts the views of some European political leaders, who see mass immigration as a threat to European civilization.[28] According to those leaders, national identity is fragile and soluble, hence their idea of sealing borders and imposing a nativist vision of the nation that strongly opposes "the ethnic, religious or racial dilution of their country."[29] This concept of the nation-state asserts the primacy of the national aspect of the state over the principle of equality among all citizens, over minority rights and over the foundations of democracy. The emphasis is on the nation, and the threat of dilution is at the borders: the "other," that which is different, is feared and remains forever suspect.[30] This vision sustains the fear, and even anger, of the masses. It is in fact what feeds populism.*

*The entire public discourse surrounding shared Canadian values is somewhat evanescent and fraught with traps. Sociologist Joseph Heath warns of the pitfalls of the "myth of shared values," or the straitjacket of trying to understand the world through a single interpretative grid consisting of dominant patterns.[31] This negatively affects the freedom of individuals to choose what is best for themselves, for who they are and for who they want to become. Heath claims that these "common values" are deadly for individual freedom. Quebec, at one time predominantly Catholic, experienced this problem, as did Ontario, whose proud celebration of British imperialism excluded many.*

*For a long time in Canada, at least three distinct cultural traditions, each with its own language, coexisted and clashed with each other. Numerous others have been added over the years, and they will continue to diversify rapidly and expand in the future. It cannot be argued that there is now a "dominant culture," a single mentality, a single language, a single ethnic origin. Just because there is no single "dominant" culture does not, however, mean that there is no distinct Canadian identity or nationality.*

*Today's Canada is founded on a culture of the right to be different, which is equally apparent across the country and which ensures that everyone has the same measure of equality, dignity and freedom. Comparable access to education, health care, income support, a fair share of the country's prosperity and an equal opportunity to realize one's potential according to one's individual choices and values is certainly a catalyst for national cohesion, if only, more prosaically, because everyone can benefit without having to give up an Indigenous identity that has existed for thousands of years, or francophone pride dating back more than four hundred years, or 250 years of British ancestry, or 100 years of Italian ancestry, or Ukrainian, Vietnamese, North African, Haitian or Indian backgrounds, and so on, regardless of how long ago one's first ancestors arrived.*

*In certain enlightened decisions dealing with Charter rights, the Supreme Court has had occasion to refer to the existence of "Canadian values based on multiculturalism."[32] However, in another decision, the Court also stated that "[t]he right to have differences protected, however, does not mean that those differences are always hegemonic. Not all differences are compatible with Canada's fundamental values and, accordingly, not all barriers to their expression are arbitrary."[33] In other words, protection of multicultural differences is not absolute. There are limits, and these limits are contained in "fundamental Canadian values."*

*But what are these fundamental values that are supposedly held by everyone across the country? The Court wisely adds "the right to integrate into Canada's mainstream … has become a defining part of our national character."[34] If there is to be integration, there must be a "common unit," a nucleus that binds all these distinct parts. As the court further specified, "These shared values – equality, human rights and democracy – are values the state always has a legitimate interest in promoting and protecting. They enhance the conditions for integration and points of civic solidarity by helping connect us despite our differences."[35] These fundamental values identified by the Supreme Court have a vital impact on social cohesion and, it should be added, on national unity. The human rights cited by the court are principally those recognized by the Charter, and as the court points out, there are "values that underpin each [Charter] right and give it meaning."[36] This is also the case with the language rights in sections 16 to 23. The court had already stated as early as 1985 that "[l]anguage bridges the gap between isolation and community, allowing humans to delineate the rights and duties they hold in respect of one another, and thus to live in society,"[37] and that "[l]anguage … is part and parcel of the identity and culture of the people speaking it."[38] The values underlying the existence of two official languages in the country (and soon of Indigenous languages that will be formally recognized) are among the essential elements of civic solidarity: far from isolating the communities that speak them, they serve to bring them closer together and are "means by which a people may express its [distinct] cultural identity."[39] For example, Quebec is free to proudly promote its language and to expect the same from the federal government across the country. Likewise, New Brunswick[40] and Ontario have found their own ways of supporting those language rights.[41]*

*Therefore, this is the level at which a shared culture exists, and its values are essentially a common vision of the equality of human beings, respect for their rights and the practice of democratic life. That is the heart of Canada as a nation-state. The accelerated demographic diversity that marks the country's growth requires it to maintain conditions for living together that primarily serve to enable everyone to exercise their individual freedom, as well as to meet the need to facilitate integration into the country's civic life and provide the opportunity to participate in collective prosperity. In short, Canada must promote the progressive search for both equality and convergence among human beings. This is how true national solidarity is strengthened.*

*The catalyst for national unity resides within this robust nucleus of human rights and guaranteed access to all types of public services and benefits. It is what defines the national will, what cements our desire to live together. Everyone can choose to preserve the language, customs, beliefs and traditions of their country of origin, just as Quebec has always consistently supported its language and Canada has shared that objective.*

*But it is primarily because there is substance to the reality of guaranteed freedom that Canada constitutes a nation and is the envy of many foreigners, who would love to live their lives as they please. This is where Canadians feel their attachment to their country and the conviction that they have a strong identity and freedom, which they cherish. Canada is a nation-state with real responsibilities, which its democratic system has supported and enhanced over the years.*[42]

*The role of politicians is not to propose or celebrate a single allegedly dominant mentality, for which potential citizens should be screened, as suggested by some* MPs,[43] *nor to promote a "charter of values," such as that proposed by Pauline Marois's Parti Québécois (PQ) government in the 2014 election, which served to undermine the notion of a pluralist Quebec open to the world and to immigrants and led to the party's defeat at the polls.*[44] *Rather, politicians should guarantee that everyone can decide for themselves who they want to be and facilitate the exercise of everyone's right to integrate into Canadian society by upholding equality, human rights and democratic principles.*

*Canada is not the "first postnational state," but rather the first state founded on the recognition of a universal humanism that gives priority to the dignity of human beings, the equality of all and the right to integrate into a society founded on sharing and respecting such a culture of rights. This is certainly not "extreme multiculturalism" or the rejection of a common national identity. It is a model of belonging that is not based on ethnicity, shared religious belief or geographic origin (as in European nation-states). Canada is a state that was built in an attempt to accommodate numerous differences in order to create a more open, inclusive society based on the same measure of freedom, not to defend the virtues of a dominant character that would forever be threatened by the contributions of demographic diversity. This is the best lens through which to understand the future of Quebec within Canada.*

*Supporting Quebec's French-language cultural identity and civil law tradition will always be at the core of the government of Canada's obligations. The highest court in the land has clearly recognized Quebec's uniqueness in a number of rulings and has managed to do so in a very straightforward manner.*

*In the 1998* Reference re Secession of Quebec, *the Supreme Court clearly defined and recognized the special character of Quebec. This is worth noting, given that the court gave substance to the notion of "distinct society" and defined the constituent parts of what it recognizes as the undeniable constitutional basis of its approach to Quebec: "The principle of federalism facilitates the pursuit of collective goals by cultural and linguistic minorities which form the majority within a particular province. This is the case in* Quebec, where the majority of the population is French-speaking, and which possesses a distinct culture.... *The social and demographic reality of Quebec explains the existence of the province of Quebec as a* political unit *and indeed, was one of the essential reasons for establishing a federal structure for the Canadian union in 1867."* [45] *(Emphasis added.)*

*Indeed, the court encapsulated the essential elements of the notion of a "distinct society" found in the Meech Lake Accord: provisions 2.(1)(a) "the recognition that the existence of French-speaking Canadians, centered in Quebec but also present elsewhere in Canada… constitutes a fundamental characteristic of Canada;" and 2.(1)(b) "… Quebec constitutes within Canada a distinct society."* [46]

THE PATRIATION OF THE CONSTITUTION, 1982

Duncan Macpherson cartoon, *Toronto Star*. After debate on a draft charter and amending formula went on for over a year and a half, Canada and nine provinces reached an agreement on a proposal that saw at the end the Parliament of Westminster give up all legislative power to Canada. The Queen herself came to sign the law proclaiming the new Canadian constitution and its charter of rights and freedoms. In Quebec, René Lévesque's government was vehemently opposed to the new constitution. Credit: Torstar Syndication Services, *Toronto Star*, 16 April 1982, p. C1

*The Supreme Court clearly identified (1) the francophone majority living in Quebec, the fact that its nature gives rise to (2) a distinct political unit and, finally, that this fact underlies (3) a specific societal reality.*

*Twenty years later, in its response to the Nadon reference case in 2014,[47] the court had the opportunity to recognize another essential element of Quebec's uniqueness, which is the importance of the civil law tradition in defining Quebec society: "The purpose of s. 6 [of the* Supreme Court Act*] is to ensure not only civil law train-ing and experience on the Court, but also to ensure that* Quebec's distinct legal traditions and social values *are represented on the Court, thereby enhancing the confidence of the people of Quebec in the Supreme Court as the final arbiter of their rights."[48] (Emphasis added.)*

*It is worth mentioning that these two Supreme Court decisions recognize and define the constituent elements of the unique character of Quebec that are protected by the Canadian Constitution, and that circumscribe the exercise of executive and legislative powers that could result in their being undermined.*

*More than a simple statement recognizing Quebec as a distinct society (as found in the Meech Lake Accord), these Supreme Court decisions provide a substantive legal guarantee that goes beyond a simple general interpretive standard, as proposed in the Meech Lake Accord. Unless there is a desire to relaunch the debate on the unilateral right of secession based on the definition of Quebec as a sovereign "nation," it must be recognized that the highest court in Canada has clearly identified the legal nature of Quebec's specific linguistic, cultural and social reality. The judges of the highest court, tasked with interpreting the Constitution, have defined what Quebec uniquely represents in the Canadian federation and have given it substantive legal effect in their decisions.*

*Does this legal guarantee not provide the greatest certainty, far more than the grand speeches or statements of politicians, who in seeking to offer assurances often sow confusion?*

*The court is well aware that every Quebec government has always eagerly sought to maintain and revitalize the language, culture and institutions that characterize it as the main home of the French language in the country.*

*Further, Quebecers have no reason to feel inferior. They have always been full par-ticipants in building Canada. They have a dual attachment: to their homeland, now Quebec where they settled centuries ago; and to Canada as a whole, that they explored as trappers as far as its western frontiers, pushing their vision for its future ever further. They have never abandoned their historical right as stakeholders in the development of the entire country.*

*How can one ignore the fact that, for almost forty of the last fifty years, the prime minister of Canada has been a native Quebecer? And that is yet again the case. Quebecers themselves know that very well. To his credit, Prime Minister Harper always began his public speeches in French, a sign of his respect for the country's historical linguistic duality.*

*Our constitutional reality, which, taken together, includes everything related to political life in Canada, the relationships between the provinces and the federal government, and those between citizens and their various governments, is not fixed in the 1867 text, or in that of 1982. Far from it. This reality is constantly evolving, and it reflects primarily the political dynamic and the objectives expressed by Quebec and its government when its specific interests or powers are at stake.[49] Quebec itself is a dynamic force in the country's evolution, and it has effective constitutional guarantees of its distinct character, which ensure that being part of this great country enables it to pursue its goals in complete freedom and that each citizen has the same social rights and can work to protect and enhance them.*

*Of course, future governments of Quebec will continue to demand guarantees in the form of constitutional amendments: that is the nature of political relationship dynamics that have always existed. But the developments experienced since 1967 and adaptations to a completely different socio-economic context have significantly reduced the urgency of doing so. The response is different today, while remaining sensitive to what it means to have a society whose cultural character must always be affirmed in order to remain vibrant and grow in a constantly changing environment.*

*As long as a majority in Quebec strongly believes that its cultural identity is not threatened and its influence in Canada's progress is real, the legitimate ambition to participate in the adventure of building a society founded on humanist values will continue to mobilize Quebecers, as it has done since the arrival of the first French settlers in the 16th century. In fact, Quebeckers' presence in the federation gives them the opportunity to affirm and develop their distinct character and afford them the occasions to share its dynamic creativity with other communities in the country.*

*But Quebec's was not the only voice heard during all those years of constitutional tension. Repeated demands from the West for more direct participation in determining Canada's political direction were also heard across the country, put forward first by the Reform Party of Canada, and then by the Canadian Alliance. These political parties were very popular in Western Canada.*

*The Pierre E. Trudeau government's adoption of the National Energy Program in 1980 crystallized Western opposition to the federal government, which was seen to be cannibalizing Western resources on behalf of Eastern Canada (meaning Ontario and Quebec). The impression that they were being stripped of their oil revenues became entrenched in the discourse of politicians and in public opinion in Western Canada, and served as a rallying cry for demanding a stronger and more effective voice in the country's central institutions.*

*The economic wealth of Western Canada provided a solid basis for its demands and the confidence of its political leaders. But unlike the tensions with Quebec, those created by Western Canada did not jeopardize the country's survival. The main goal was the sharing of "central" power, followed by Senate reform to make it an elected body and the adoption of legislation and policies favourable to energy resource extraction and development.*

*The slogan "The West wants in," used by political parties with strong regional roots, said it all. The slogan was realized in 2006 with the election of the Harper government, which for nearly 10 years reassured Western Canadians that they could also govern the country and advance their vision and values.*

*Since the creation of the Canadian federation, reaching a compromise to reconcile competing interests has been an ongoing challenge for the country's political leaders. Quebec is home to specific interests, of language and cultural identity, issues that remain sensitive and often emotional for many Quebecers. On another level, in Western Canada, people feel they are undervalued and always overshadowed by Ontario, which brings its share of frustrations, given that the development of natural resources, oil and gas, is the cornerstone of Canada's current wealth and its high standard of living. Recent tensions have surfaced on the argument that confederation does not function in the best interests of the West and that there is a "case of Western independence."[50]*

*Those intense years of constitutional conferences, discussions and negotiations, which sometimes seemed like a national psychodrama, did generate some useful insights for the future.*

*First, the Constitution of Canada (which extends far beyond the 1867 and 1982 documents) is based on federalism, democracy, and respect for minority rights, but is not, as one might think, so rigid as to leave the country paralyzed. Quite the contrary. Canada has come a long way since 1867. And for the better, despite the many compromises necessary to ensure that each province could continue to develop at its own pace and make its own choices.*

*Over the years, Canada reached agreement with various provinces (Newfoundland and Labrador, and Quebec, in 1997) on amendments to constitutional education provisions that specifically concerned them. It also signed multiple administrative agreements to set policy objectives in areas of mutual interest: natural resource revenue-sharing (Alberta); management of immigration conditions (Quebec); changes to health care cost-sharing and different arrangements for Quebec; recognition of parental leave for*

*workers; redistribution of equalization payments; setting of post-secondary educa-*
*tion and research support payments; representation for Quebec at the United Nations*
*Educational, Scientific and Cultural Organization (UNESCO); funding for minority*
*official-language education, etc. All these agreements, several of which include specific*
*terms for Quebec, reflect the social and political dynamic faced by successive govern-*
*ments. The flexibility and practicality needed to address the needs of citizens first and*
*foremost require all parties to find an honourable compromise.*

*These negotiated and ratified agreements enable the two levels of government to*
*pursue complementary objectives, giving each the necessary latitude to make the deci-*
*sions it deems appropriate based on its own priorities while protecting the interests of*
*the country as a whole.*

*Quebecers maintain and develop a multitude of economic, social, cultural and*
*scientific relationships with the rest of the country and with the federal institutions*
*representing them, such as Radio-Canada, the Canadian Radio-television and*
*Telecommunications Commission, the National Film Board of Canada, the Canada*
*Council for the Arts, the national museums and Library and Archives Canada, to men-*
*tion but a few cultural institutions. That is what the government of Quebec document*
*was referring to with its title* Quebecers, Our Way of Being Canadian. *Perhaps this*
*reality of belonging to a greater whole and these legal guarantees help explain the hesi-*
*tation, even the fatigue, felt by some Quebecers at the thought of embarking on another*
*constitutional "saga."[51]*

*In an essay published in 2008, philosopher Daniel D. Jacques, who favours inde-*
*pendence, made the same observation.[52] He went so far as to argue that sovereignist*
*Quebecers should perhaps learn to become French Canadians again and focus more on*
*preserving and fostering their cultural identity and economic interests, as painful as that*
*is for those who fervently believed in Quebec independence.[53] Philosopher Serge Cantin*
*reached the same conclusion and called on sovereignists to work on securing the future*
*by fighting for survival in order to protect their distinct character in America.[54] For*
*Quebecers, it becomes now possible to discuss federalism during an election campaign*
*without the cleavage of separation.[55] On average, about 70–71 per cent of Quebecers say*
*they are attached to Canada, with highs of 79 per cent (2017 and 2001) and lows of 60 per*
*cent (2009). About 90 per cent of English speakers say they are attached to Canada.[56]*

*In fact, if Quebecers fully invested the best of their talent, energy and political intel-*
*ligence (which they demonstrated during the struggle for independence) in Canadian*
*politics, they would have significant and lasting influence on the country's choices in*
*this era of globalization. The history of their role since 1840[57] in making Canadian*
*society such an enviable example to the rest of the world has yet to be written and*

*explained.[58] Quebecers would be surprised to learn, for example, how influential they were in shaping the contemporary principle of peaceful coexistence of groups whose past had pitted them against each other, or the principle of distributive justice adopted by the state, or the strategy of supporting peace rather than using force. These are all values held by a large number of Quebecers.*

*History teaches us, however, that a single incident perceived by a majority of Quebecers as an affront to their linguistic identity can sometimes be enough to resurrect an emotional mobilization.[59]*

*It would be helpful to learn to manage current aspirations and needs in forums other than formal constitutional negotiations, whose inherent dynamics often lead to a power struggle that usually boils down to which government will ultimately either give in or lose. It is certainly far more profitable to focus on improving relationships between the two linguistic communities by getting them to work together on joint projects in areas such as education, culture, health care, business or community support in order to break down the walls of suspicion and the distance that has traditionally isolated communities.*

*The world and the paradigms of Canadian society have changed significantly over the past fifty years. National attributes alone no longer determine citizens' living conditions. Their aspirations relate more to their personal situation and increasing autonomy, to the importance of well-being and to their detachment from spontaneous enthralments with idealized visions of social or political reforms. The "flower-power" generation, which once carried the torch of independence, is now retired; the current generation's social aspirations focus on a horizontal society in which hierarchical institutions are less accepted than they once were: family, corporations, political parties, unions, and state agencies.*

*The social changes and instability visible in some of Canada's most stable traditional partners, such as the United States, the United Kingdom, and France, are challenging what has long been taken for granted in those countries. The profound and unexpected tensions among these traditional partners and neighbours are changing Canadians' perspectives and aspirations. For example, effectively fighting inequality and tax evasion in a twenty-first-century global economy requires working with key players in international forums.*

*In such a context, priorities have shifted more toward securing what is already available than attempting to challenge the status quo when there is no guarantee or certainty of a better outcome. Whether it be for its standard of living, prosperity, social solidarity or individual freedoms,* in the eyes of the world's young workers, Canada remains the second choice, *right behind the US and ahead of the UK and Germany, according to an international survey conducted by the World Economic Forum in August 2017.[60] The fact that so many people around the world would like their passport to bear the maple leaf must mean that Canada is doing something right. Canadian "nationality" must have some unique and special "value" to be so appreciated across the planet.*

*Resolving the major issues of the day – the environment, climate change, and the economic and financial consequences of digital globalization – requires concerted action by political partners, whether here at home or abroad, rather than the fragmentation and crumbling of political power. Canada is respected around the world, and it plays a useful role in ensuring peace, security, and humanitarian aid wherever they are needed. Quebecers realize this as much as other Canadians and make an important contribution to it.*

*While Canada does not have the economic heft of the US or the wisdom accrued over centuries of France or the UK, there is such a thing as the Canadian "experience" – a shared history – that consistently ranks this country among the leaders in terms of quality of life, social solidarity, protection of citizens, and opportunities for personal fulfillment.*

*Because Canada is so widely admired in the world, there must be something in the "national" psyche that gives rise to this belief in freedom, respect for individuals, valuing people and a respectful "live and let live" attitude toward the ethnic and cultural diversity of its inhabitants. The reason Canadians can prosper and support each other to this extent, through a social safety net that ensures no one is pushed beyond the margins of a decent life, is that the political character of this country possesses a humanism that is not entirely subject to the tyrannical law of financial markets or the absolute power of money in politics. Canadians are well aware that a modicum of social justice underpins their society and distinguishes them from their southern neighbours.*

*Canadians know this intuitively, they perceive it, and that is what binds them intimately, even instinctively, to their country. They know that they must now restore the right to self-governance to Indigenous peoples while respecting their identity and their ancestral rights, and that this long-overdue process to redress a historic wrong will require as yet undefined and novel solutions. Integrating Indigenous participation into governance of the federal government is the most demanding challenge facing Canadians at the national level today.[61]*

*Canada was born in 1867 more of pragmatism and necessity than of ideology. It has been able to gradually build a society that embraces diversity and tolerance, but not without its share of hurdles, struggles, and failures. The imperialist levelling forces of the nineteenth century and religious prejudices also weighed heavily for a long time, maintaining a pernicious divide, but common sense and more thoughtful self-interest eventually prevailed. The desire to keep the country united resulted in compromises that over time proved to be the most reasonable choices. Strengthened by this history,*

*Canadians are deeply convinced that their country embodies a human experience founded on values that are different from those of its partners and that are more respectful of individuals. Canada continues to represent real hope for all those in the world who seek peace, freedom, equality, and human dignity.*

NOTES

1  The author is indebted to the Library of Parliament for its careful work in verifying the accuracy of the historical facts and figures in the text.

2  However, in 1981 the Court of Appeal of Quebec and the Supreme Court of Canada confirmed that Quebec did not have a constitutional veto.

3  On December 1981, out of seventy-four Quebec Liberal MPs, sixty-eight voted for patriation, four abstained, two voted against it, as did the Progressive Conservative MP for Quebec.

4  *Alliance des professeurs de Montréal v. Procureur général du Québec*, [1985] C.S. 1272.

5  *Constitution Act, 1982*, Part V (s. 43).

6  The author represented the government party on the No Committee during the 1995 referendum campaign.

7  *Reference re Secession of Quebec*, [1998] 2 SCR 217.

8  *Henderson v. Québec (Procureur général)*, 2018 QCCS 1586, para. 579. The Attorney General of Canada is a respondent and an intervenor.

9  Chantal Hébert, "Harper's hands-off approach to Quebec," *Toronto Star*, 7 September 2017, p. A6.

10  Under parliamentary custom, this motion stood only for the duration of the Parliament in which it was adopted. It does not bind subsequent Parliaments. Nevertheless, politicians continue to cite it to support their positions.

11  Member of Parliament for Wellington-Halton Hills (Ont.).

12  Tonda MacCharles, "Tory minister quits over Quebec vote," *Toronto Star*, 28 November 2006.

13  Ibid.

14  *House of Commons Debates*, 22 November 2006, The Right Honourable Stephen Harper, quoting former Quebec premier Bernard Landry.

15  Marco Bélair-Cirino, "Couillard enfourche le cheval identitaire," *Le Devoir*, 14 and 15 October 2017, p. A3.

16  *Quebecers, Our Way of Being Canadian* (Quebec City: June 2017), p. 47.

17  *Reference re Secession of Quebec*, [1998] 2 SCR 217, para. 222.

18  *Quebecers, Our Way of Being Canadian* (Quebec City: June 2017), pp. 25-9.

19  Ibid., p. 86.

20  Ibid., p. 139.

21  Louis Bélanger, "Le Québec aux Québécois / Daniel Poliquin, *Le roman colonial*," *Spirale*, September-October 2001, p. 27.

22  Marco Bélair-Cirino, "Mieux vaut laisser la Constitution en son état, dit Justin Trudeau," *Le Devoir*, 19 January 2018, p. A3.

23  Speech from the Throne, "Making Real Change Happen," 2015.

24  News release, "The Prime Minister of Canada and President of the Métis National Council Welcome the Signing of the Canada-Métis Nation Accord," https://pm.gc.ca/eng/news/2017/04/13/prime-minister-canada-and-president-metis-national-council-welcome-signing-canada, 13 April 2017.

25  Guy Lawson, "North Star," *The New York Times*, Sunday Magazine, 13 December 2015, p. MM88.

26  Francine Pelletier, "Sur le multiculturalisme," *Le Devoir*, 22 August 2018, p. A7.

27  Teresa Wright, "Maxime Bernier dénonce le 'multiculturalisme extrême' de Trudeau," *La Presse.ca*, 13 August 2018. http://www.lapresse.ca/actualites/politique/politique-canadienne/201808/13/01-5192877-maxime-bernier-denonce-le-multiculturalisme-extreme-de-trudeau.php.

28  *Agence France-Presse*, "L'immigration de masse," une "menace pour la civilisation européenne," Statement by Laurent Wauquiez, president of the Les Républicains (LR) party, before 1,500 people in Haute-Loire, France, on 22 August 2018, p. B2; Olivier Baube, "Les penchants nationalistes de Salvini inquiètent les pro-Europe," *Le Devoir*, 28 August 2018, p. B5; François Brousseau, "Les batailles de l'Europe," *Le Devoir*, 4 September 2018, p. B1.

29  Eva Illouz, "Israël contre les juifs," *Le Monde*, 9 August 2018, p. 20.

30  Claire Bastier, "La nouvelle loi fondamentale fracture Israël," *Le Monde*, 9 August 2018, p. 2

31  Joseph Heath, "The myth of shared values in Canada," John L. Manion lecture given at the Canadian Centre for Management Development, Ottawa, 15 May 2003.

32  *Multani v. Commission scolaire Marguerite-Bourgeoys*, [2006] SCC 6, [2006] 1 SCR 256 (SCC), para. 71.

33  *Bruker v. Marcovitz*, [2007] SCC 54, [2007] 3 SCR 607 (SCC), para 2.

34  *Bruker v. Marcovitz*, [2007] SCC 54, [2007] 3 SCR 607 (SCC), para. 1.

35  *Loyola High School v. Quebec (Attorney General)*, [2015] SCC 12, [2015] 1 SCR 613 (SCC), para. 47, cited in *Law Society of British Columbia v. Trinity Western University*, 2018 SCC 32, para. 41.

36  *Loyala High School v. Quebec (Attorney General)*, [2015] SCC 12, [2015] 1 SCR 613 (SCC), para. 36.

37  *Reference: Manitoba Language Rights*, [1985] SCC 36, [1985] 1 SCR 721, p. 744.

38  *Mahé v. Alberta*, [1990] 1 SCR 342, 68 DLR (4th) 69, p. 362.

39  *Ford v. Québec*, (AG) [1988] 2 SCR 712, 54 DLR (4th) 577, pp. 748-49.

40  Sections 16(2), 16.1(2), 17(2), 18(2), 19(2) and 20(2) of the *Canadian Charter of Rights and Freedoms*.

41  *French Language Services Act*, R.S.O. 1990, c. F.32.

42  Charles Foran, "The Canada experiment: Is this the world's first 'postnational' country?" *The Guardian*, 4 January 2017.

43  Janice Dickson, "Leitch releases her list of 'Canadian values' test questions for immigrants," *IPolitics*, 6 March 2017. Kellie Leitch, MP for Simcoe-Grey, Ontario, candidate for the leadership of the Conservative Party, received 7 per cent of the votes on the first ballot, finishing fifth at the party's convention on 27 May 2017; Guillaume Bourgault-Côté, "Legault joue la carte de l'identité - les immigrants ne parlant pas français constituent une menace potentielle dit le chef de la CAQ," *Le Devoir*, 7 September 2018, p. A1.

44  Francine Pelletier, "Le mystère des jeunes," *Le Devoir*, 5 September 2018, p. A7.

45  *Reference re Secession of Quebec*, [1998] 2 SCR 217.

46  *1987 Constitutional Accord,* (Meech Lake Accord), Complete text of 3 June 1987, Schedule – Constitutional Amendment, 1987, *Constitution Act, 1867,* 2.(1)(a) and (b).

47  The Honourable Marc Nadon, a supernumerary judge of the Federal Court of Appeal, whose appointment to the Supreme Court was challenged.

48  *Reference re Supreme Court Act, ss. 5 and 6*, [2014] 1 SCR 433, para. 49.

49  *Reference re Senate Reform*, 2014 SCC 32; *Reference re Securities Act*, 2011 SCC 66.

50  Title in the *Calgary Herald* of an article signed by former federal Tory MP and ex chief whip Jay Hill, quoted by Yakabuski, Konrad, "Les séparatistes de l'Ouest," *Le Devoir*, Idées, 28 July 2018, p. B9.

51  The Parti Québécois committed to not holding a referendum if it formed the next government.

52  Daniel D. Jacques, *La fatigue politique du Québec français*, Boréal, 2008.

53  Louis Cornellier, "Déchirements souverainistes," *Le Devoir*, Culture section, Lire-Essai, p. 33.

54  Serge Cantin, *La souveraineté dans l'impasse* (Presses de l'Université Laval, 2018).

55  Patrice Ryan, "Parler de fédéralisme, c'est enfin possible – campagne électorale au Québec," *La Presse+*, débats 7, 7 August 2018.

56  René Bruemmer, "Poll shows language divide in Quebecers' attachment to Canada," *Montreal Gazette*, 30 June 2018, p. A5.

57  Éric Bédard, *Les Réformistes* (Montreal: Boréal, 2012).

58  Serge Joyal, *90 ans de relations diplomatiques: les rapports de deux États (France/Canada) engagés à développer une vision humaniste du monde*, Forthcoming, 2018.

59 Andrew Caddell, "Quebec separatism isn't dead: Public opinion in La Belle Province can turn on a dime," *The Hill Times*, 13 September 2017.

60 Kar Rettino-Parazelli, "Le Canada prisé par les jeunes travailleurs de la planète – Le pays arrive deuxième parmi les états ciblés par les 'milléniaux'," *Le Devoir*, 29 August 2017, p. B1.

61 Jean Leclair, "Penser la Constitution et le fédéralisme avec les peuples autochtones," *Le Devoir*, 29 June 2017, p. 7.

# The Unfinished Canadian Dream: Building on its Promise and Challenges

The Hon. Bob Rae, former premier of Ontario (1990–95)

I will, in a sense, comment a bit on much of what Professor Walters had to say, which was extremely stimulating, as well as the remarks of the chief justice.

Occasionally, I will speak about events in the first person because, without borrowing from the famous phrase of Dean Acheson about being present at the creation, I was actually here in the other chamber during a couple of notable moments, and then I was premier during a time of particular interest in terms of discussions around unity, so I want to refer to those a couple of times.

I think you have had a good description of how the Charter arose and the origins of the debate in the country around patriation. I think the thing that I want to stress to this group is that, borrowing from Peter Russell's use of the word "odyssey," and he has written another brilliant book on the history of the country, we really have to see ourselves as part of a process.

I don't mean this to be in any way discourteous to Pierre Trudeau, with whom I had a vigorous relationship over a long period of time, but it didn't all start with Mr Trudeau. The idea that, somehow, patriation and the Charter was simply a personal project of his is just not the case. It had much deeper origins in the history of the country. We can trace the Charter back, in addition to what the chief justice and Professor Walters had to say, even to some of the decisions of the Supreme Court of Canada itself, particularly of Mr Justice Rand. He made it very clear that the notion of rights was firmly embedded in our own Constitution and our own principles of democracy and process, and that these are not foreign imports simply based on a document.

Involved as I was, I had the opportunity as a young member of Parliament in the late seventies and early eighties to be part of the parliamentary debate and part of the parliamentary process, and I had the opportunity at what I thought would be my final vote as a member of Parliament to vote in favour of the patriation package that was in front of us in 1982. It was my last vote before I went off to become leader of the New Democratic Party in Ontario. Of course, other things have happened since then; you never know when your last speech or your last vote will be. It can come at any time.

I was one of those who voted for the package and voted for the Charter with a sense that the work was still unfinished; that it wasn't, in fact, the final word; that we needed to continue to engage in dialogue as a country about a number of issues that were not put to rest with the passage of the Charter. I didn't see the Charter as a threat to the unity of the country. I didn't see it, in the way in which it came about, particularly with the addition of the notwithstanding clause, as a threat to parliamentary democracy or to the work of Parliament. I didn't see it as a threat to our federation, and I still don't.

However, we did have to take into account, as a country, the fact that Quebec was absent from full support and adoption of the Constitution, which I think remains a serious issue for the country. I felt at the time that, while section 35 was a significant addition to the Constitution and I was proud to be part of a caucus that had something to do with its existence in 1982, the Constitution still did not adequately express the nature of the relationship between settlers and the original inhabitants of the land. That's a reconciliation that has still not fully taken place in a way that I feel would be fully adequate.

So the work continued. I was a provincial leader at the time that Meech was negotiated. I was a strong supporter of the Meech Lake package. It was not fully endorsed by all the members of my own party, but I got used to that. As well, it was not fully endorsed by members of the Liberal Party, and in that sense it was not an easy package.

Despite the extensive work we did in repatriating the Constitution and creating the Charter, as well as entrenching human rights in our Constitution, we must acknowledge that it was not ratified by Quebec. The partnership between francophones and all other Canadians is a fundamental aspect of our country. I also agree with those who say that Canada would not exist without the creation of a federation in 1867. To my mind, it is clear that the constitutional path would have been completely different.

I raise the principle of the protection of francophone rights and of the existence of Quebec as a distinct society that protects the rights of francophones in Canada. These are remarks from the Supreme Court and, as Professor Walters mentioned, from the Royal Commission on Bilingualism and Biculturalism. Finally, there was the attempt to reform the Constitution through the Meech Lake Accord, but the negotiations failed.

Here, I return to a little bit of personal history. My friends Jean Charest and Gary Doer were reminiscing before the meeting here. The three of us were present on the sidelines during the last week of the crazy days in June 1990. Gary was reminding me

"here..." – the queen presents the new constitution
Aislin cartoon, *The Gazette* 15 April 1982. Many Quebecers were uncomfortable that Quebec had to refuse to express its political agreement with the new constitution. They felt it was incomplete. Cartoonist Aislin with *The Gazette* in Montreal shared that sentiment. Here he shows Her Majesty holding out the patched-together document, but there is no sign of celebration. The debate would continue in the years that followed. Credit: Aislin, *The Gazette*, 15 April 1982, McCord Museum, m2012.42.43

my final words to him were that I had to get on a plane – I think I might have used a couple of other additional adjectives in there – because I was convinced that Mr Peterson was going to call an election, and that he was going to win a huge majority anyway because he had emerged from that meeting a great hero.

A funny thing happened to me on the way to the election, which was indeed called, and I was elected in the fall of 1990, as some of you will recall. It was an extraordinary time. Not only had the bottom fallen out of the Ontario economy, an event for which

I have been given almost total responsibility by my critics, but I think more objective observers would say there was this thing called a recession and we went from 5 or 6 per cent unemployment to 12 per cent unemployment in nine months. Not even I could have done that in my wildest, craziest notions of what might be the appropriate public policy to apply.

Support for separation was at 60 per cent in the province of Quebec, and the Conservative Party had been completely divided in Quebec by virtue of Mr Bouchard's departure. There was the Oka Crisis in Quebec, and Mr Bourassa was diagnosed with a serious form of cancer. The country was in deep trouble. I feel a bit like Talleyrand, who was asked, "What did you do in the French Revolution?" and he said, "J'ai vecu." I was asked, "What did you do during the constitutional crisis of the 1990's, Premier?" I survived. The country survived. We came through it.

Charlottetown was really an effort to broaden the conversation to include Quebec, although Mr Bourassa was not present for the discussions, which I think was regrettable. Nevertheless, eventually it became a package that he could support, and we included a deeper attempt to deal with the issue of self-government and with the nationality, if you like, of the Aboriginal people in the country. It included an effort to strengthen the social and economic union and to reform the Senate, dare I say it in this place. We agreed to it. Not only did the premiers agree to it, but there were territorial leaders who were there for the first time. We failed to convince the public that it was the appropriate thing to do.

At that point, having come through a variety of other crises, the government changed. Mr Chrétien became prime minister, and there was the sense that we shouldn't try big things anymore, because we had tried the big things twice. We ratified the Constitution, we negotiated constitutional change twice and failed to ratify it twice, and so where did we go at that point? How did we go forward?

I don't have to recall all the steps that have been taken to improve things, to deal with the crises as they've arisen, to find the right formulas in words and parliamentary resolutions and the ways in which Parliament has tried to respond to the failure to complete the constitutional journey for this moment. I just want to make a couple of observations before allowing my colleagues to tell me the points that I've missed. I'm sure there are many.

The first one is that in understanding the concept of unity in the country – and Professor Walters pointed this out very well – we have to look at all of the elements. We used to say, in debating Charlottetown, that if we see the Constitution as a mirror, it's important for everyone to somehow see themselves in that mirror. Up to that point, we had not been able to do it, and we still have not been able to do it.

But that doesn't mean that the Constitution is a failure. The critics of Canada would say we don't live in a real country. We do live in a real country. We live in a real place with real laws and a real federation.

What it means is that we have, in a sense, invented and found other ways to express who we are as a country, not only in the form of Supreme Court decisions, but also in the efforts that are now being made to find the basis for not only truth but also reconciliation, as I'm sure Mr Justice Sinclair has even said in this chamber. He certainly said to me on a couple of occasions, "Remember, the truth will set you free, but first of all, it will really piss you off." That, unfortunately, is true.

We are finally coming to terms, as a country, with the nature of the colonial project and the damage that it has done over centuries to the original inhabitants of the land. And we have been struggling to find the ways of making amends for what has happened, and it's a long, difficult, and sometimes painful journey.

It is interesting that section 35, which might not have gotten into the Constitution, has actually been interpreted by the court in such a way that it has forced governments to take other steps. One other major decision of the court before section 35, which was the *Calder* case, dramatically transformed the entire legal landscape of Canada by forcing governments across the country, including particularly the province of Quebec, initially, to recognize that they can't actually do big projects in the resource field without full participation of Aboriginal people. That's what the James Bay treaties were all about. They would not have happened without the *Calder* case and the impact that it has had across the country.

There are still those who say that our work is done, that we've succeeded in introducing the Charter, that the issue of the exclusion of others is one that's never going to be solved and that we're never going to be able to deal with it, so we should just forget about thinking about the possibilities of constitutional change in the years ahead. Then there are, on the other side, those who say, "Let's try it again. Let's go for it one more time."

I must confess, on the basis of all my experience, I'm not really comfortable in either camp. That, perhaps, defines my political status at the moment. That is to say, we should never be so complacent as to think that our work is done, or to believe that people's quest for recognition and inclusion in the Constitution is somehow illegitimate or wrong or doesn't need to happen, or doesn't need to be done.

But we should learn from our experience. As I've said, we've had two intense rounds of discussion and negotiation. In fact, if you go back to the process that began in the mid-sixties, we had twenty-five years of constitutional discussion, which, in the end, produced the Charter and patriation, but no truly effective way to amend the

RALLY AT PLACE DU CANADA, MONTREAL, 27 OCTOBER 1995
Colour photograph with the autographs of the members of the "No" committee. To regain lost public support, a huge rally was held in Montreal, three days before the vote, to show Canadians' affection for Quebec as an essential part of Canada. Some 100,000 people from across the country gathered at Place du Canada. The "No" side narrowly won the referendum by 54,288 votes (No: 50.58 per cent; Yes: 49.49 per cent). Credit: Canadian Museum of History (CHSJ), IMG2012-0313-0021-DM (Artifact 2011.21.598)

Constitution; two really tough failures; and two referenda, one of which came very close to causing a unity crisis such as we've never experienced. So we need to recognize that we can't enter into this discussion lightly or without acknowledging that, in many respects, the real life of the federation goes on.

Here I want to just make two further points. The first is that I think it's important for us to recognize that, from an economic standpoint, we are an intensely decentralized federation. I say this as a former premier.

The provinces have real powers, real authority, and real sovereignty in our federation. We don't use this latter word because it creates all kinds of other anxieties, but the fact is the whole purpose of the federation was to recognize that it wasn't simply going to be run by the central government. Sir John A. Macdonald might have had a different vision, but it's not the vision that actually held sway as we went forward.

So we still have to, then, look at how we create better institutions that help the economy to integrate and to change, and how we make sure that our internal economy is operating as effectively as it can, despite the existence of all the governments that have a stake in their own self-interest.

The second is that we should not underestimate at all the significance of one other major change that Mr Pearson introduced, which is not often discussed as being at the core of the social change that we've seen in our country, and that was – we did this in parallel with the Americans – to introduce a point system in our immigration system and to get rid of the notion that we would have quotas by countries, and to replace it with the view that we would take in people from all over the world. We are, and we became, a deeply multicultural, multiracial, and multinational society. We've become that way over the last quarter or half century – thirty, forty, fifty years – in a time frame that I don't think anybody could have anticipated when that law was introduced in 1967.

This brings me to my final point: there is one law that we should all be aware of and that should slightly humble all of our efforts, and that is the law of unintended consequences.

If we'd had a debate on immigration in 1967 in which we went to the doors of Canadian people and said, "We want to fundamentally change the makeup of this country over the next fifty years," it wouldn't have happened. But the consequence was simply in the event and the evolution of our reaffirming the immigrant nature of a good part of our identity. At the same time, if we'd said in Parliament that in bringing in the Charter, we were going to be endorsing the marriage of same-sex couples, it wouldn't have passed.

We have to allow for the great strength of the federation and the great strength of our country, which is that we have strong institutions. I say now in a moment of post-partisan generosity that we've had great leadership, and we've had a commitment to public service and to public values that have allowed us to evolve and to keep on building, even though, like the cathedrals that we look at, some destroyed and some now rebuilt, we still have building to do. That shouldn't be a cause for a sense of failure. It should rather be a cause for a sense of confidence that we're going to keep on doing what we can in the hope for a better future.

# Canadian Federalism: A Dynamic Partnership of Contested Rights and Responsibilities

The Hon. Jean Charest, former premier of Quebec (2003–12)

## INTRODUCTION

In my remarks, I want to talk about the last fifty years, with a particular emphasis on the role of Quebec. But I want to start with remarks about our federal system that I believe we need to remind ourselves of to better understand our country.

First, Canada is one of the most decentralized federations in the world. Our federal government is – I say this respectfully – like a holding company. If you look at the budget of the federal government, 60 per cent of the money is transferred to individuals or to the provinces for health care, social services, education, or old age pensions. The governments that run this country on a day-to-day basis are the provinces. Look at the budgets in terms of salaries. Close to 60 or 70 per cent of the budgets of provinces are for salaries. Here in Ottawa, this figure is probably around 15 to 18 per cent.

The point I want to make here is about the reality of governance. I regret that sometimes the national press misses the story of what is happening in Canada. Most of the decisions by governments affecting people in their day-to-day lives are made at the provincial level.

I want to respond to a comment made by Bob Rae and others on how to approach this debate. In the political universe, we would all like to believe that everything starts and ends with oneself.

I was pleased to hear Chief Justice McLachlin mention former prime minister John Diefenbaker. The latter, who had populist leanings, believed deeply in the recognition of human rights, was the first to promote Aboriginal rights, and relied on his life experience coming from Saskatchewan. All of this contributed to the eventual adoption of the Charter of Rights and Freedoms. This did not happen by spontaneous combustion! There are many before us who believed in it. The experience of public life teaches us, with humility, that many have come before us, and others will follow.

Another thing that stays with me is the importance of exercising caution when judging the past. Those who preceded us may not have had a very open perspective on same-sex marriages. Mr Justice Bastarache, you impressed me greatly with your description of the evolution of our language rights. And elsewhere in the world, in the eighteenth and nineteenth centuries, are there many societies that did as much as we would have liked Canada to do on the issue of minority protection? Probably not. That said, past mistakes should not be glossed over. One has to be lucid enough to say, "We take note of what we could and should have done and we will correct the injustices of the past."

Like Bob Rae, I believe we have been blessed with a period of strong leadership in Canada. One of the things to evoke is continuity in governance. A country is stronger when its government, once elected, does not instinctively undo what had been done previously. Having enough wisdom to maintain the policies of a previous government, even when past decisions are imperfect, is a strength.

Jean Chrétien was elected in 1993. I liked him, but on the issue of the goods and services tax (GST) and with the support of the Senate, he took a position that was contrary to the common interest. His choice of words was inelegant, but the message was, "We're going to scrap the GST." Fortunately, he changed his mind. Good governments break bad promises: remember that. And the best do so with skill and get re-elected. We have been fortunate to have consistent leadership at both the federal and provincial levels.

## REMARKS

Now, about the last fifty years, I want to warn you that in 1967 I was nine years old. I grew up with the Quiet Revolution unfolding in front of me, literally, and it was a very exciting period of change. It seems that everything in our lives back then was questioned, everything about the economy, society, and our relationships. Even a young boy who was nine years old could feel it. You could see it around you. Everything seemed to be changing.

For the people of Quebec and Francophones in particular, including Acadians, it was an extraordinary period of affirmation that would drive a lot of change throughout the country.

Affirmation of the French language and culture, affirmation over the control of our economy, and affirmation of the leadership and role of the state in protecting and promoting the common good – that was a big part of the story behind the Quiet Revolution.

This period of affirmation would open a new chapter in the history of our country. It was encapsulated in two questions that were formerly asked by the Laurendeau-Dunton Commission. They asked two very fundamental questions, the first being, "How do we integrate the new Quebec into present-day Canada without curbing Quebec's forward drive and, at the same time, without risking the breakup of the country?"

When you think about it, even in the sixties, in formulating that question, they were already contemplating the possible breakup of Canada.

The other very compelling question was, "Is there a common will for Francophones and Anglophones to live together?"

Why this question? Because a country, in the spirit of the French philosopher Ernest Renan, is about common will. Do we want to live together? They tried to answer that question. A more pointed way of asking the question, as we moved on, was, "What does Quebec want?" It seemed to be the overriding question for most Canadians living outside of Quebec.

Now, before I revisit the last fifty years, I do want to return to things that I believe are fundamental about our history and who we are. I happen to believe that the [Quebec] Act of 1774 is part of the hard drive and the DNA of Canadians. Why? Because in 1774, after the Conquest, the British realized that their only hope of holding on to British North America was to strike a deal with the French who inhabited the territory. They were trying to recruit people to come to North America but without success. These sixty thousand French-speaking people were not going away. They had been abandoned by the French elite, who had returned home.

What did the British do? They did something quite extraordinary for that period. They recognized the Catholic religion of the French community, which was synonymous to recognizing the French language. They recognized their system of civil law. Bear in mind, a codification of a system of law is first and foremost a codification of values. And they exempted them from the oath test, what they called the "*serment du test*." From my perspective, I think that is one of the most important, if not the most important, decision that was made in regard to how we as a country would organize ourselves.

At this very early point in our history, it was decided that our country would be founded on the principle of duality and diversity. It may have been an accident of history, a gesture born out of self-interest. But self-interest in itself does not exclude self-enlightenment. This recognition of the dual and diverse nature of our country, which we would forever be recognizing from that time on, has since become one of the common and defining threads of our existence.

Justice Bastarache spoke clearly, as we move to 1867, when he said that the application of those rights was very uneven and unfair, and we'll get to that. But the adoption of the Quebec Act in 1774 by the British authorities was, in my point of view, very significant.

The notion of partnership recurs constantly in Canadian history: in 1791, with the creation of Upper and Lower Canada, and later, with the heroic leadership of Robert Baldwin and Louis-Hippolyte Lafontaine, pioneers within the Commonwealth who fought for the principle of responsible government. Despite all of our imperfections, it is we Canadians who have created this concept of responsible government. Fighting for it in Ontario and Quebec, we gave birth to a principle of governance that helped advance and evolve democracy.

This partnership principle is symbolized in the relationship between George-Étienne Cartier and John A. Macdonald. As Bob Rae so aptly put it, this country would never have seen Confederation in 1867 had it not been for the federal compromise. Never would the Quebecers of the day – who were referred to as "Canadiens," by the way – have accepted such an agreement, had it not been for the ability to preserve our language and our culture. Looking back over the past 150 years, we see that this is a common thread that explains who we are.

Now, let me return to 1967, when I am still nine years old, by the way. I did not attend the Montmorency thinkers' conference organized by the Progressive Conservatives of Robert Stanfield, but I did read about it. This conference is significant in that, after much heated debate and soul searching, the PC Party decided that Canada should embrace the concept of a country that was founded by two nations. *Deux Nations*. This would be one of the intense subjects of debate that would occupy our public discourse for the next fifty years.

The election of Pierre Elliott Trudeau in 1968 was, in my view, a part of that affirmation of the Quiet Revolution. The Official Languages Act that he brought forward formally embraced and formalized this concept of duality and this period of affirmation. It was also a period in which we saw the creation of a more radical separatist movement in Quebec. The battle for the hearts and minds of Quebecers would become the dominant political theme for the next fifty years. This single issue has been the common thread of my own political life.

The terrorist actions of the Front de libération du Québec (FLQ) in the late sixties and early seventies left a profound mark on the country. There was the failed 1971 Victoria conference on the constitution. There was the election of the Parti Québécois in 1976 that gave political legitimacy to the separatist movement, and the country sighed in relief in 1980 when the referendum was won by the federalist side. The patriation of our Constitution in 1982, with the inclusion of the Charter of Rights, was obviously a very significant milestone in the history of our country.

But this fundamental change was made without the active support of the National Assembly of Quebec, thus leaving open the question of Quebec's future. That is a very important point. It is the National Assembly, the elected people in the legislative body of Quebec, including a fair number of Liberals, that did not support the 1982 constitutional change. It wasn't just the government of Quebec, the government of the day; and that is a very important point to keep in mind.

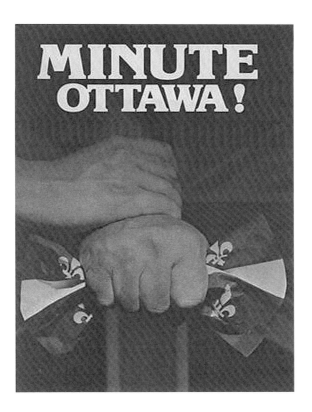

"MINUTE OTTAWA!" [NOT SO FAST, OTTAWA!]

Sign, 1982. The Government of Quebec launched a campaign to form the broadest possible consensus to oppose patriation, seeing it as a heavy-handed tactic by the federal government. Large billboards and brochures showed a hand preventing another hand from crumpling the Quebec flag, the strongest image of the campaign. In the end, the vote in the National Assembly of Quebec on 2 June 1982 on Bill 62, which proposed to override all the provisions of the *Charter*, was 63 yeas to 37 nays. Credit: Government of Quebec, 1981; Canadian Museum of History, MCH/CMH BIBLIO: RARE COLL FC 633 C6 M56 1981

There are those who would have argued back then that the polls said that Quebecers in general supported patriation and the Charter. We live within the federal system of government, and some in the federal government would argue they had the legitimacy to go ahead. But in this federal system of government, it is the elected members of the National Assembly of Quebec who speak on behalf of Quebecers in the areas of jurisdiction for which they are responsible. That is why their lack of support remained a very important issue of contention.

This fundamental change is something that we sought to address. In 1984, the Progressive Conservative government of Brian Mulroney was elected with a strong contingent of members of Parliament from Quebec, including myself. The new government had run on a platform of national reconciliation.

In 1987, the government convened a first ministers' meeting to address the issues of Aboriginal people's self-government. This meeting was a commitment that had been made to Canada's Aboriginal people in 1982, because their issues had not been sufficiently addressed at the time. The anticipated recognition did not materialize. There was no consensus and the conference failed.

This was a very important event in our modern history, because from that day on, from what I interpreted – Ms. Gabriel and Phil Fontaine would be much better and more competent interpreting that than I would – a marker was set down. The leaders of Aboriginal communities in this country came to the conclusion that they needed to draw a line, that this would not happen again, and that if there were any future negotiations their issues would be addressed. But for many Canadians, all of this clearly went under the radar.

Senator Peter Harder said something to us a moment ago, as we were chatting about the things we have done and the things we tried to do and did not succeed at doing, and which are a very important part of this story. This is one of them, the Victoria conference, the *rendez-vous manqué*, we would say in French, that would also have a significant impact on what happened afterward.

In 1987, the government delivered the Meech Lake Accord on the promise of reconciliation. It essentially reshaped previous attempts to change our constitution with a view of bringing Quebec into the fold. We all thought this would allow us to go ahead, and yet the Aboriginal people were excluded from it. As we looked ahead, little did we know that time would be our worst enemy. The three-year delay used to adopt the amendments, and the prolonged and often painful debate left the country politically divided. The delay was devastating as the political debate soured and went off the rails.

At that point, there was a very deep misunderstanding of what this accord was about. For French-speaking Quebecers, it was about recognition and respect, what some would describe as the mirror effect of constitutions. In constitutions, we should be able to look into that mirror and see a reflection of ourselves. That was very much the story of the distinct society clause for Quebecers.

I chaired a special committee of the House of Commons to study a companion resolution to the Meech Lake Accord, and one of the most compelling testimonies we heard was from Charles Taylor, one of Canada's greatest philosophers. He came before us and made a statement that had a great impact on us, saying that the distinct society clause for Quebecers was the bridge between their identity of being a Quebecer and a Canadian, and that failure to recognize it would destroy that bridge.

For Quebecers, that was the story of Meech Lake. For other Canadians, it was a legal document, a constitutional document in which there was too much uncertainty. For yet other Canadians, it was all about Quebec and it wasn't about Western Canada, and it wasn't about First Nations, and it wasn't about women's issues. It was about them and it wasn't about us, and that wasn't good enough, and so the debate became acrimonious and the accord failed.

"OUI" [YES]

Pin, 1995. The campaign leading up to the 30 October 1995 referendum in Quebec was a trying and unexpected experience for supporters of both the "Yes" and "No" camps. The leader of the Parti Québécois, Jacques Parizeau, declared on the evening of the vote that the defeat was due to "money and the ethnic vote," words that led him to resign as premier the following day. On the other hand, Jean Charest, a federal MP at the time, had spoken passionately in favour of remaining in Canada, showing that he had what it took to be a leader; he became premier of Quebec in April 2003.

Credit: Canadian Museum of History (CHSJ), IMG2012-0002-0039-DM (artifact 2011.21.543)

After that, well, we all tried to put – let me phrase it simply – the toothpaste back in the tube. Constitutional committees, the Spicer commission report – you remember that happy moment in the history of our country – constitutional committees again, and finally, the negotiations of Charlottetown.

The Charlottetown Accord was substantial. This time, Aboriginal issues were addressed; Western Canadians' issues were addressed. Bob Rae played a very important role; Joe Clark played a very important role. In the referendum of 1992, Canadians said "No." At that point, Canadians were politically exhausted and tired, and frankly, they had stopped listening.

Subsequently, the Progressive Conservative government of Kim Campbell experienced the worst political debacle in Canadian politics and was reduced from government to two seats. In the House of Commons, I was the only member of that government to be re-elected. And for the Liberals, it was their turn to govern. The Parti Québécois returned to government in 1994, and in 1995, the second referendum came very close to breaking up the country. Then followed the Clarity Act of 2000.

For me, the next chapter of this story was the most important election I ever fought, but lost, in 1998, as the new leader of the Liberal Party of Quebec. In 1998, Lucien Bouchard was a formidable adversary. He laid down his plan: a majority government and another referendum. I was new and unprepared for the particular codes of Quebec politics. It was one of the worse campaigns of my life. And believe me, I have been part of bad campaigns. In the final twelve days, we changed the campaign to a single message: no referendum.

On the night of the election, Mr Bouchard's Parti Québécois won a majority of seats, but we won a plurality of the votes. There would be no referendum. The country would be allowed to breathe, let the dust settle, catch our breath, progress, and start a new era of rebuilding our relationship. That is what I sought to do in opposition from 1998 to 2003, and I did it with an extraordinary colleague named Benoît Pelletier, my critic for intergovernmental affairs and a professor of constitutional law at the University of Ottawa.

Between 1998 and 2003, he and I set out across the country to prepare a new plan and a different approach to defending the interests of Quebec within Canada, and to reconcile the agenda of Quebec with the rest of Canada.

We were successful in winning a majority government in 2003. We believed in the opportunity of administrative agreements that would be substantive and ground-breaking, without forcing the country into an existential debate about its future. Nobody would be excluded, and yet we would regain the ability to address specific issues, and more importantly, to be successful in addressing them.

Here are some of the things that we were able to accomplish: In 2003, we proposed the creation of the Council of the Federation, which would emphasize interprovincial co-operation. In 2004, the Health Accord, in which Gary Doer participated, would be the first successful project of the Council of the Federation. For the first time in history, and to the benefit of Quebec and the country, we recognized the principle of asymmetrical federalism, to which every single premier signed on.

In 2005, Quebec secured a particular agreement with the federal government on a parental leave program, which became one of the foundations of a very progressive family policy in Quebec.

Again in 2005, both the government of Quebec and the federal government worked successfully in international forums for the adoption of the treaty protecting cultural diversity. Because we live in a federal system of government and these were mostly our areas of provincial jurisdiction, my government was the first in the world, out of 144, to adopt the treaty.

In 2006, Quebec signed an agreement with the Government of Canada, based again on the principle of asymmetrical federalism, which provided a permanent place and role for Quebec within the Canadian delegation at the United Nations Educational, Scientific and Cultural Organisation (UNESCO). The person who played a key role in making that agreement happen is the leader of the Senate today, Peter Harder. By the way, the implementation of this agreement has been, for all concerned, a success.

Also in 2006, the House of Commons, by resolution, recognized Quebec as a nation within Canada. Who would have thought that the "distinct society" clause, which was too much for many, would one day migrate to the concept of "nation"?

In fact, there is a story behind that. I will share this anecdote with you.

Prime Minister Stephen Harper, elected in 2006, decided he was going to come to Québec City on Saint-Jean-Baptiste Day in 2006, hold a cabinet meeting, and meet Quebecers directly. The leader of the Opposition in Quebec at the time is André Boisclair, who challenged the prime minister: "Mr Harper, if you are sincere about federalism, why don't you recognize Quebec as a nation?" Of course, it was rather awkward for the new prime minister to say either yes or no.

That evening I met with Prime Minister Harper, and I brought with me the text of the letter that Sir John A. Macdonald had written to a journalist of the *Montreal Gazette* – I think it was in 1864 – explaining why Canada was a federation. In that text he says essentially this, in talking about Quebecers: "Treat them as a nation, and they will act as a free people generally do – generously. Call them a faction and they become factious."

I said to Prime Minister Harper on that evening, "If the first of all the prime ministers of Canada could describe Quebec as being a nation, why would you want to contradict him today?" It is one of the few times he may actually have taken my advice – excuse me, the only time. The next year, in 2007, the government of Stephen Harper moved substantially in resolving the outstanding fiscal imbalance within our federal system.

In 2007, it was Quebec that proposed to the European Commission the negotiation of a trade agreement between Canada and the European Union. This would form the basis of the Comprehensive Economic Trade Agreement (CETA) negotiations. For the first time ever, the provinces sat at the table, participated directly, and made the success of this agreement a possibility. The leadership role played by the Quebec negotiator, former Premier Pierre-Marc Johnson, was pivotal in the success of the negotiations.

This new era of successful administrative agreements has allowed Quebec and all of Canada to evolve and progress. It was made possible because we can use the flexibility of the federal system, outside of constitutional amendments, to make very substantive changes. This approach has also allowed us to lay the groundwork for any subsequent constitutional changes our country may seek to make, whenever that day will come. In the meantime, Canada continues to evolve and to assume its place in the world.

I believe in a federal system of government that allows us to recognize and respect our differences while building on shared values, and I believe it has made us a much better country, admired throughout the world. If citizenship were a lottery, you and I and our children know that we have won first prize.

Now, did I tell you that in 1967 I was nine years old? I think I did mention that. I just turned fifty-nine years old. Over the past fifty years, I have had the great privilege of serving my country and fighting for its future, serving with people like Bob Rae, Gary Doer, Serge Joyal, and the senators who are here. I want to close by saying how privileged I feel and how proud I am to be a Quebecer and a Canadian.

# Enhancing Canadian Values

Verbatim transcript of symposium speech

Gary Doer, former premier of Manitoba (1999–2009)
and former ambassador to the United States (2009–16)

Pleased to join my colleagues, Jean and Bob, in our presentations. The last time we were together in Ottawa was during the discussions on the Meech Lake Accord.

I want to mention my experience at the premiers' meeting in Ottawa with the Meech Lake Accord. As Jean Charest described it, we were in the bleachers, but we had a lot of time together for four or five days, sharing rumours. What is happening upstairs and downstairs, and who is meeting with whom? What is the latest move? When will they come downstairs into the media centre for the press conference? Then I remember finding out that the premier of Ontario had generously contributed – administratively – senators from Ontario to other provinces that had only six senators. I mentioned to Bob Rae this potential development, and he was very dramatic in his words – I won't repeat them – but he basically said, "I am going to go back to Toronto." He was going to be Captain Canada. He said, "I am going to lose the election. I am going to lose my seat. I will be out of politics in four weeks." And fourteen weeks later, he was premier of Ontario. So it goes to show you what can happen in the conference centre of Ottawa and at events subsequent to that.

Something else that got my attention during that meeting of Meech Lake was my opportunity to meet a couple of times with Robert Bourassa. You certainly learn, as a public or elected figure, that probably one of the toughest jobs, if not the toughest job, in elected politics in Canada is to represent the people of Quebec as premier. I certainly understood that in partnership with Jean Charest, later on when we were both elected as premiers.

We had proposed the solution to the 1987 constitutional resolution with Aboriginal people, recognizing the distinct society in something called the "Canada clause" (mentioning Aboriginal people first, then the distinct society, et cetera.) We proposed that, and I remember Robert Bourassa looking at me and stroking his hair a couple of times and if I had to do that, I'd go back to Quebec as a tourist. I gathered that was "No," and we learned that week, that month didn't turn out too well for Canada, and it didn't turn out too well for getting an ultimate agreement at that time.

As leader of the opposition, I supported the Charlottetown Accord, and there was a lesson to be learned. It was a perfect document, developed with a perfect consensus, with Aboriginal people, with the territories, with the provinces, and with all political parties. It was a much more comprehensive document, but, regrettably, the proposal to ratify it was for every province to approve it separately, and that is a tough threshold, particularly, I would say, in terms of referenda. If you have five or six proposals in a referendum, people will come out and vote against only one of them and register a "No" vote.

The federal government told me, when I supported then-premier Gary Filmon for the Charlottetown Accord, that the rolling polls predicted the document's ratification. My rolling nose really worried me after that because I kept hearing about this issue, which was only one out of five or four items or proposals. And, regrettably, Manitoba didn't carry it, and I was very disappointed about that. Again, I thought we had most of the members of the legislature supporting it, with all the members of the Conservative and New Democratic parties at that time.

Fast-forward to the referendum in 1995. I had a political science class in our caucus room. We had participated in a large rally at the Forks. Many other people had participated in other similar national unity rallies. We were told forty-eight hours before by Lloyd Axworthy and Gary Filmon that it was tight and could go either way. We read the public polls. I was concerned when I saw one of the leading Quebec business people say on television, "We don't want to just win the referendum; we want to humiliate the opposition." A good lesson for all of us is that elected or not elected, you are always one vote behind. You are in it to win because you have the right cause, but you are never in it to humiliate your opponent.

I remember sitting at home and saying, "Oh my God. I thought we were still ahead in the polls, but it sure got tight." I think all Canadians were very nervous and worried.

Later on when I became Premier I kept in close contact with Jean Charest when he was leader of the opposition to let him know what I saw was going on in the premiers' meeting so he would be informed.

The proposal in the 2003 Quebec provincial election from Jean Charest of an alternative to separatism was the Council of the Federation. It talked about the participation, involvement, and inclusion of provinces in international trade. It talked about the inclusion of provinces in health reform. It spoke of the issue of energy and the environment, and, again, the inclusion of provinces with the federal government. It talked about the need for future reform with Aboriginal people.

When Jean Charest was elected premier in 2003, immediately at the first premiers' meeting we had, we had a discussion. In fact, we met separately, one on one, on that proposal. If you looked at the western premiers' proposals to the federal government, it had international trade, energy and the environment, Aboriginal people, land use. It had many of the same items that were proposed in the Council of the Federation document in that Quebec election.

So we prepared a grid to present to the premiers to show which resolutions we had passed. We could support, immediately, the Council of the Federation proposal that was being made by the premier of Quebec on behalf of the Quebec people.

I thought at one point, right before we had an agreement, that Jean Charest almost blew it at that meeting. Ralph Klein flew in on his King Air all the way from Fort McMurray, and he poured coffee all over his tie. Just as we were going out to the press conference to support the Council of the Federation, Ralph asked Jean – both of them former environment ministers – for a tie. Just as Ralph was heading out, Jean gave him a fleur-de-lis and told him to wear it at the press conference. I thought that was it, but thankfully Ralph didn't wear a tie, and we had unanimous consent from all the provinces and premiers to proceed with that proposal.

It has had tangible benefits. Premiers' meetings are always perceived to be, and portrayed as, an exercise in being Oliver Twist – "Please, sir, we want some more" – or as a conflict between different regions, or different provinces, or whatever. But there were some real results coming out of the Council of the Federation that didn't get a lot of media coverage.

The inclusion of provinces at the front end of international trade was both an offensive proposal with the European Union, in my view, and a defensive proposal when we were dealing with the Buy American provision, when the Recovery Act was passed by the Obama administration in 2009. It allowed all of us to be present.

Quebec had proposed a partnership with the European Union, but to deal with the European countries, we had to put procurement of all the provinces on the table. In fact, I think Jean Charest and I went to Brussels for a few days, maybe a week, to show that this was a real proposal, and it wasn't just flowery language without any ability to back it up. It had every premier's support. And of course, it was important

THE WEST WANTS IN — "I WANT IN..."
Cartoon, tabtoons@telus.net. This political slogan, which became a mantra for the western provinces' desire to be heard and participate fully in governing the country, galvanized all the western political representatives in Ottawa. The West had the perception that central Canada had always governed the country for its own benefit, at the expense of the west and its needs, which had been expressed countless times through history. The Reform Party had been formed on that basis in 1987 and was calling for sweeping changes to federal institutions. The Reform Party would go on to become the Canadian Alliance in 2000 and later merged with the Progressive Conservative Party in 2003 to form the Conservative Party of Canada. Credit: Cagle Cartoons

for the federal government to re-engage in the European discussions. Again, this was a Quebec initiative supported by all provinces. Some of the proposals on procurement were eventually part of the original agreement and the final agreement that, as the leader indicated, was approved here in the Senate.

On the United States' proposal on Buy American, because the North American Free Trade Agreement didn't cover sub-national governments, we again, as premiers, proposed that we would put provincial procurement on the table with reciprocity for state procurement as a way of offering something tangible, not just saying we'd like to get rid of the Buy American provision. The Americans couldn't get their act together on procurement with the States, but we ultimately got a waiver for all of the nine areas that were affected. It was a year later than when they brought it in, but again, I think having the Council of the Federation was very useful. It produced results.

The Kelowna Accord was also something we worked on as a Council of the Federation. I was very disappointed that we weren't able to implement land use and education policies that were agreed to by the federal and provincial governments and Aboriginal leaders; again, this was an effort that came out of that formal process.

We weren't always able to agree on all items on our agenda. For example, climate change. Because of that, Manitoba, Ontario, Quebec, and British Columbia proceeded with the Western Climate Initiative, but beyond that, all provinces committed to producing 25,000 megawatts of renewable energy by the year 2020, a number I think will be exceeded times two, and which, again, came out of a meeting of the Council of the Federation.

The Health Accord, as Jean has described it, was one of two health accords I was part of to reinstate some of the money that had been cut out of the budget in 1995. The document that Jean described, the asymmetrical federalism with the Health Accord, is one I recall directly. We all supported it. A special arrangement for Quebec was included on the document, but we did not need or want to have a one-size-fits-all approach. The Quebec minister of health at that time is now the premier of La Belle Province; it was a very positive proposal in Quebec and very positive with all premiers. It was unanimous, as Premier Charest has said.

Those were four or five items that came out of the Council of the Federation. When our Premiers met recently you did not hear anything come out of the meeting except media coverage of conflict. You did not hear of the the ninety per cent consensus based on the agenda of the Council of the Federation. But there is certainly some good work coming out, based on the 2003 proposal from the premier of Quebec.

I also would just like to say that we've talked a lot about law, constitution, constitutional amendments, constitutional proposals, and ideas that have been very important for our country.

I just have another view of the values of Canada, as a citizen, as a Canadian politician, and as a former Canadian representative in Washington. There is no reason for

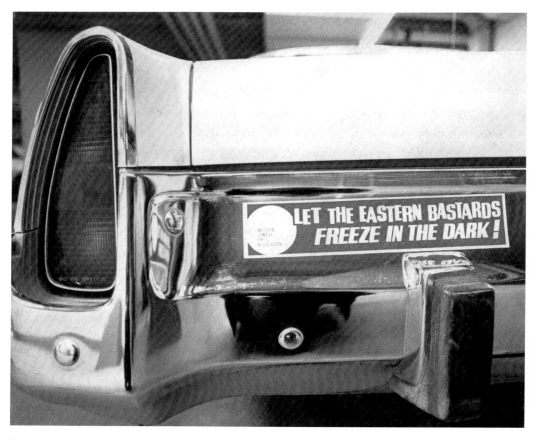

"LET THE EASTERN BASTARDS FREEZE IN THE DARK"
Bumper sticker. The virulence of this slogan, which appeared on bumper stickers on cars in the west, speaks eloquently to the frustration westerners felt after the creation of the National Energy Program (NEP) in 1980, which set a lower price for oil sold in Canada. The perception that the west was subsidizing eastern Canada (everything east of Manitoba) gave rise to lasting bitterness that resurfaced in October 2017, when Enbridge abandoned its proposal to build a pipeline to carry western oil to a port in New Brunswick. Credit: Postmedia STARCANWEST, *Calgary Herald*

Canada to be smug when it comes to the United States. There are many things that they do better. Senator Joyal talked about the fact that they use former leaders in a much more effective way, whether it's in Haiti, after a tsunami, or something else. Former presidents work together much more effectively. I think we should be doing more of that with former prime ministers. We have a lot of horsepower, knowledge, and gravitas in our country, and a lot of great leaders who could be used more effectively.

When I was in Washington, I would see President Carter, President Bush 41, President Bush 43, President Clinton, and, of course, President Obama, all together on a common cause. I think that's a wonderful message to your country. They fight very vigorously and ferociously in election campaigns, but after that's over, they work together as Americans.

Having said that, I saw many programs in Canada during the time I was representing Canada that made me very proud that our country, however it did it, with all of the people in this country and all the different leaderships, had reached a consensus on certain values to be implemented in programs that would make a real difference for the people of Canada. I was often very proud to go to the Hill or the White House and have people raise questions about some of these things. "How did you do it? Is it still a controversy?" Nothing is ever obviously perfect, but I just want to mention five areas that I think should make us very proud as Canadians and continue to work to make it even better into the future for our children and our grandchildren.

The first is education and training. We have much higher per-capita graduation from post-secondary education than many countries, including the United States. We have a much more affordable post-secondary system than the United States. We have a much more accessible way of getting to post-secondary education. We have a great community-college system that is tied to our university system, again with much better results than our American friends. Now, we're not as good as Germany or some other countries, but we have a huge competitive and social advantage with this value in Canada.

Second, as Bob Rae mentioned, is the turmoil and the chaos in the immigration system of our friends to the south of us, and of some other countries as well, relative to what we have in Canada, where there is consensus on immigration, I believe. We have a system now that is two-thirds skilled and one-third family, with a strong recognition of supporting refugees where they need support. The Americans try, from time to time, to amend their immigration policy to allow for students who have visa recognition to stay in the country after graduation.

I point out that in Manitoba we used to go to Stanford to get graduating students, some of whose educations were paid for partially by American taxpayers, to come up and support our knowledge economy. I think every province in Canada was doing it; it makes a lot of sense. I just think it has credibility with the public, and where I come from, in Manitoba, we went from two thousand immigrants a year to seventeen thousand. For our province, it has made a huge difference in the quality of life of our citizens.

Third, health care. You know all the issues: the disparity between health care costs in the United States and Canada (18 per cent of GDP in the United States versus 11 per cent in Canada), the fact that our system covers everyone, that life expectancy is longer and that infant mortality rates are lower. You know all those numbers. Now we're seeing another conflict and partisan disagreement on health care go on in the United States, and it's gone on year after year.

There are lots of people who will campaign against you to improve the health care system. There are lots of people who say they can do it better than you. A lot of people will campaign against you and say, "It's time for a change," but nobody will say, "This isn't a value that's worth keeping and improving in Canada."

Fourth, financial institutions. David Dodge is here. How can you get an old NDP premier supporting banks and financial institutions? Go figure. But when I look through the history of the House of Commons and provinces that have partial jurisdiction or total jurisdiction on some of the regulatory bodies, and what we've done over the years – sometimes through a minority report against going too far on derivatives, sometimes on housing policy and through not having a tax deduction – the banking and financial system in Canada makes me very proud.

In the United States, people are more vulnerable to economic downturn. When your house value goes down 40 per cent in one year, which happened in 2008–09, and your taxes then go to Wall Street to bail out the banks, every day I would get a question about, "What did you do, and how did you do it?" In Canada, we have no idea of the anger in the United States following the 2009 housing crisis. We value the entrepreneurship and the risk associated with it but we also have a minimum protection for everyone.

Finally, I want to say that getting money out of politics is a very positive value in Canada. I dealt with projects like the Windsor-Detroit bridge, where many stakeholders had received donations from individuals who did not want to see the bridge built. In Canada, we have banned union and corporate donations, and I was proud to have Manitoba be the second province after Quebec to do that.

The fact that we have taken the influence of money out of politics and political fundraising is extremely important, I think. It's important not only in terms of the competitiveness of political parties and individuals, but also to public perception; when you're making a decision, you're doing it in the public interest and you're perceived to be doing it in the public interest. If you're passing a law on workplace safety and health, you want to do it to make sure a miner goes home to their family, not to get yourself a cheque from a union or from a corporation.

The Canadian government decided, with the support of the Supreme Court, to limit financial contributions in politics, whereas in the United States, the opposite is true. Their system is closer to the "Wild West," even though the West has never been wild! It has always been fun, but it has never been wild. Ours is certainly a different system. As ambassador, I was proud of the values and programs we have in our country.

Through the past years we have spent a lot of time on the Constitution with little progress, but we moved on, concluding policy arrangements among governments to better serve Canadians. We should never forget our Canadian values, which have a tremendous degree of consensus and support around the country.

If we can just use all our energy and means over the next fifty years to deal with each of the challenges facing Aboriginal people, I think our two hundredth anniversary will be an even greater time to celebrate the values of being Canadian.

# 6

# Gender Equality: Power, Money, and Sex[1]

The Hon. Serge Joyal, Senator

*I*n the last fifty years, tangible progress has been achieved toward making the principle and practice of gender equality a reality.

Gender equality is a fundamental tenet upon which social relations in a free and democratic society must be built. It is rooted in the civil principle that all human beings are born free and equal in dignity and rights, and that women are not lesser beings subject to male dominance.[2] The patriarchal model of society, a relic of a bygone era, clearly runs counter to the basic values underlying the Canadian Charter of Rights and Freedoms *(the Charter).*[3]

Following the 1970 publication of the report of the Royal Commission on the Status of Women (the Bird Commission), which contained 167 recommendations, the government of Canada undertook a review of its legislation and practices with a view to enshrining the principle of gender equality. Canada comes from far back: from 1920 to 1955, a Privy Council Office policy forbid married women "from holding fulltime federal government jobs unless their husbands were unable to work."[4]

In 1980, Canada became a signatory of the United Nations Convention on the Elimination of All Forms of Discrimination Against Women. *The principles recognized therein helped to galvanize women's groups as they pressured the government to take their views into account in constitutional talks and lobbied actively for specific recognition of gender equality in the text of the proposed Charter.*[5]

In 1982, the principle of gender equality was affirmed in section 28 of the Charter (and in section 35(4) with respect to Indigenous women).[6] Since then, it has been interpreted in numerous decisions by the highest courts of the land, progressively knocking down the barriers restricting the independence of women and the right of women to make their own decisions. Many of these court challenges received financial support from the federal government's Court Challenges Program. Moreover, the principle of *gender equality inspired legislation and specific programs to make it easier for women to exercise their equality rights.[7]*

*This principle has been embraced by civil society to varying degrees (notwithstanding any religious doctrines, convictions or beliefs), serving the cause of women's liberation in many ways. For instance, it was a major contributing factor in improved access to contraception, divorce by mutual consent and a more equitable alimony system, women's accession to full legal capacity (in Quebec),[8] the decriminalization of abortion (the* Morgentaler *case in 1988),[9] the redefinition of crimes of sexual violence and criminal harassment (the* Janzen *case in 1989),[10] and the decriminalization of prostitution (the* Bedford *case in 2013)[11] – not to mention the massive public outcry, conveyed by social media, against assaults on women following the high-profile condemnation of film producer Harvey Weinstein in the United States, which triggered one of the fastest shifts in Western culture since the 1960s.[12] The ability of women to decide for themselves invalidated the argument that women were incapable of acting responsibly and autonomously when making decisions that affect them.*

*Legal recognition of women's ability to decide for themselves is the foundation of the women's liberation movement and the quest for gender equality that is political (i.e., sharing equally in the power to govern), economic (i.e., sharing in the power to hold any job or assume any responsibility at any level in the workplace for equitable pay, as in the phrase "equal pay for equal work") and sexual (i.e., having physical closeness between men and women without any form of domination). This last type of equality must be predicated on the understanding that the apparent vulnerability of women can no longer be a pretext for tolerating physical abuse of women by men in positions of authority and power.*

*In the political arena, a vital step toward gender equality was the recognition of equality in employment. The regulations governing the public service, which are part of the* Canada Labour Code, *were all amended, and the traditional barriers that had stopped women from holding certain jobs were eliminated. In the Royal Canadian Mounted Police and the Canadian Armed Forces, on the bench in Canada's courts, at the helm of political parties (both federal and provincial), at the head of federal and provincial governments, in the Speaker's chair in the Senate and the House of Commons, and even in occupations representing the Queen in Canada, glass ceilings were shattered, trails blazed and precedents set that would serve as examples to the private sector.*

*Despite the exemplary conduct of governments and their role in helping women hold decision-making positions (e.g., Clerk of the Privy Council, deputy minister, CEO of a major Crown corporation), the fact remains that a good example can only go so far in some traditional fields that have a long history of atavism, such as engineering, mathematics, science and technology.[13] According to Statistics Canada, in 2011, only 14 per cent of women students graduated in science, mathematics, computer science and engineering, while men accounted for 35 per cent.[14] In 2017, the government issued an ultimatum to universities to ensure the fair representation of women as Canada Research Chairs (CRC), with the sanction that if the targets are not achieved in 2019, a portion of the federal funding would not be renewed. The Canadian average of women as chairs in June 2018 was 30.24 per cent. Without clear targets enforced by penalties, the progress would be minimal or even nonexistent.[15]*

*Major hurdles were overcome when equal representation of women on boards of directors of Quebec Crown corporations became law in 2011, and when Quebec Premier Jean Charest appointed a gender-equal Cabinet in 2007.[16] This last precedent was emulated at the federal level in 2015, when Prime Minister Justin Trudeau announced his slate of Cabinet appointments.[17] The prime minister's commitment to the principle of gender parity in more than 1,500 appointments to positions in federal institutions, agencies, offices and Crown corporations will be remembered as a milestone and should have a ripple effect at the provincial and municipal levels. Another 1,167 judicial positions under federal jurisdiction will also be filled equally. As a result, gender parity in employment is on the verge of becoming a reality and setting an irreversible precedent.*

*That said, gender parity in the Parliament of Canada and the provincial legislatures is a long way off. The proportion of women Members of the House of Commons has hovered around 20 per cent to 26 per cent for decades, even though several political parties have been striving to recruit an equal number of women candidates, and working hard to elect them in ridings where they have a real chance of winning. Imposing quotas for women candidates in federal and provincial general elections remains a topic of debate, and experience shows that, without restrictive measures (in the form of quotas or penalties) or strong incentives (such as public funding), there is little hope of shattering the glass ceiling that has been blocking gender parity in Canada's various parliaments and legislative assemblies for 50 years.[18] It would be a delusion to think otherwise, given the distortions inherent in our first-past-the-post voting system.*

*In a poll, more than 8 out of 10 Canadians (89 per cent) agreed with the statement that women are just as qualified as men to lead the country, and 62 per cent of respondents totally agreed with this statement.[19] In Western Europe, 77 per cent of respondents felt that women are just as qualified. Canadian public opinion toward women's participation in government is generally favourable: until recently, two of Canada's provincial premiers were women (in Alberta and in Ontario until 2018)[20]; British Columbia had a woman premier until the election of 9 May 2017; and Quebec has also been led by a woman.*

*Prime Minister Trudeau committed to achieving gender parity in the Senate, where 46.6 per cent of the members are currently women.*[21] *Since taking office, Mr Trudeau has appointed 49 senators, 29 of them women (59.2 per cent). At this rate, however, the Senate will not be gender-equal before the next general election in the fall of 2019. To reach this goal, the prime minister will have to appoint more women to the Senate before then. As an example to others, gender parity in the Senate would demonstrate in new and practical ways the irrefutable value of the principle set out in section 28 of the Charter.*

*The* Beijing Declaration and Platform for Action, *sponsored by the* UN *and signed by Canada in 1995, gave further impetus to the principle of gender equality by making Canada accountable internationally for its initiatives to achieve this objective. In Buenos Aires, in December 2017, "Canada supported the* Joint Declaration on Trade and Women's Economic Empowerment *made at the World Trade Organization's (*WTO*) ministerial Conference."*[22] *Prior to the 2018* G7 *Summit (8-9 June 2018 in La Malbaie, Quebec), a Canada-US advisory committee was established to promote equality. During the summit itself, Canada and its* G7 *partners pledged C$3.8 billion over three years to support the education of girls in conflict zones, as well as investments in projects that will primarily benefit women.*[23]

*The government has also adopted the practice of requiring a comparative gender analysis for Cabinet memoranda and Treasury Board submissions. Although this initiative was a step toward a systemic remedy, its effectiveness remains problematic and unfortunately cannot be meaningfully reviewed.*[24] *Since such comparative analyses are not released to the public because of Cabinet secrecy, evaluating their usefulness in fostering the amendments or changes necessary to achieve equality is impossible. Such analyses are certainly useful in the early stages of a process, but their findings must be assessed in order to weigh the efficacy of any corrective measures implemented. The systemic change being sought is a profound one, so there is a vital need to identify any flaws at the very root of the decision-making process.*

*That said, the federal government is unfortunately under no obligation to review all of its policies through the lens of comparative gender analysis. Its regulations, practices and policies should also be subject to a thorough review of their possible impact on various groups of men and women.*

*Barriers and (it goes without saying) long-standing prejudices continue to exist, and without clear and binding obligations, prevailing habits and ways of doing things, together with their attendant inertia, will weigh heavily. In a report tabled in the House of Commons in June 2016, the Special Committee on Pay Equity recommended that the government review all of its practices and give account of those practices to Parliament.*[25] *It also recommended that the government require in legislation that the*

Monument on Parliament Hill, Ottawa. When the high court in London ruled in 1929 that the word "persons" in section 24 of the Constitution Act, 1867, should be interpreted to include women so that they too could be recommended for appointment to the Senate, Canadian women began a long march toward equality that has not yet reached its goal. This victory was due to five women from Alberta, none of whom was ever appointed to the Senate, as it turned out! The government of Mackenzie King suffered a bitter defeat. Edmonton sculptor Barbara Paterson imagined the scene represented by this monument, which was erected on Parliament Hill in Ottawa in 2002. It is the only monument depicting women, other than the statues of Queen Victoria (1900) and Elizabeth II (1992). Credit: Aram Adjemian, photographer

*proposed federal Pay Equity Commission report annually to Parliament.[26] Without such an obligation, public servants acting under a veil of confidentiality will have the last word on how a fundamental Charter principle is applied in the federal public service, and the government will not be accountable to Parliament in this regard.*

*In order to sketch an accurate overall portrait of the progress of gender equality in Canada, the initiatives taken in this area by the various provincial and territorial governments must be considered. Indeed, without federal-provincial-territorial coordination of the various action plans developed by individual governments, the goal of gender equality will remain out of reach, as it consists in a true cultural shift that will eventually make gender stereotypes vanish.*

*The province of Quebec, to name but one example, released a strategy paper in late June 2017 entitled* Together for Equality: Government Strategy for Gender Equality – Toward 2021, *which reaffirmed and updated the six guidelines set out in its 2007 gender equality policy and proposed new measures, such as the creation of a "Québec gender equality index," the passage of "a framework bill aimed at gender equality in fact," and the use of a gender-based approach in interventions.[27] However, the last comprehensive review in this area dates back to 2015, and no useful summary report has been produced since that time.[28]*

*Clearly, Canada must review its approach to gender equality and reassess what has been done to date in order to identify priorities that can be shared by the various levels of the federal government and thus reorient Canada toward measurable targets. This is what political leadership that truly wants to achieve gender equality should offer, more than occasional speeches implying that the country is making progress when real change has been too slow in everyday life. The annual federal-provincial-territorial conference of ministers responsible for the status of women rarely ends with the adoption of a package of common reforms, the specific progress of which can be tracked at each level of government.*

*In the private sector, gender equality has made considerable strides in the last 50 years. In many respects, however, a great deal remains to be done.*

*The past trend for women to be underrepresented in certain professions, such as medicine and law, has now reversed itself. In fields such as management, accounting and administration, the representation of women has improved considerably.[29] Successful women in those fields include Sheila Fraser, an exemplary auditor general who is without question one of the leading lights of her profession. In engineering-related fields, progress has been slower, although there have been some notable successes, such as astronauts Roberta Bondar and Julie Payette, and astrophysicist Victoria Kaspi, the first woman ever to receive the Gerhard Herzberg Canada Gold Medal for Science and Engineering from the Natural Sciences and Engineering Research Council of Canada.[30]*

*It is important to look beyond these success stories, however; while they are reassuring, they do not tell the whole story. For example, women lawyers are underrepresented among partners in law firms, and earn only half as much as male lawyers, even though women actually outnumber men in this profession.[31]*

*In many business sectors where women have been historically underrepresented, such as banking, financial services, insurance and investment, women are still in the minority on boards of directors and among senior management. In fact, women are often entirely absent from boards and senior management in these sectors, even though they make up the majority of university graduates in most of the fields from which such board members are drawn.[32] Women remain well-represented in the ranks of middle management, but genuine progress at the executive level is far too slow.[33] In fact, the last data show that they "have gone backwards."[34] Male conservatism remains strong in these professional circles.*

*Indeed, Canada is lagging behind: according to the World Economic Forum's latest report on gender equality, Canada ranks thirty-fifth among the 144 countries surveyed for the gap that needs to be closed in order to achieve equality between men and women, despite women's comparable education levels. At its current rate of progress, Canada will need 158 years to achieve parity! Moreover, as international news service* France 24 *highlighted, the report found that gender inequality actually increased for the first time in 2017, after 10 years of progress.[35] So let there be no illusions: gender parity will not just happen spontaneously.*

*In Ontario in 2011, for instance, there was still a wage gap of 31.5 per cent between men and women. At the national level, women earn only 73.5 per cent of what men do in comparable jobs.[36] In the last ten years, this gap has narrowed by only two percentage points.[37] Furthermore, there are more women than men in lower-paying jobs.*

*The existence of a female "proletariat" is therefore undeniable. The gender wage gap is one of the factors keeping many women in a state of poverty, insecurity and dependency – vulnerable and systemically exploited. Furthermore, the status of women varies widely from one area of the country to another. For example, access to abortion is particularly limited in some of the Maritime provinces, such as Prince Edward Island, where the first clinic to offer this service opened only in February 2017.*

*The Conference Board of Canada gave Canada a "C" for its efforts to narrow the gender wage gap, with Canada ranking thirteenth among sixteen countries of comparable economic status.[38] More effective initiatives, in the form of tax incentives or even penalties, for example, should be considered if the goal of wage parity is to be achieved in the foreseeable future.*

*Wage parity would also help prevent bullying in the workplace. Money would no longer support the prejudice that women are inferior or vulnerable, but would instead serve to buttress their social and psychological position.[39]*

*Leadership at the executive level is seriously falling short of the mark, and there is now an urgent need to consider legislative measures that might lead to the desired changes. Access to private financing for women entrepreneur remains often difficult, if not problematic. Business women are not trusted at par with men, are seen with less decision-making ability and not as daring as their male counterpart. The federal government intervened to facilitate women-led businesses access to federal lending and financing agencies.[40]*

*Progress on increasing the number of women in the boardrooms of major companies has been too slow – in some there are still no women at all. Moreover, when they are named executive officers they earn 64 cents for every dollar paid to their average male counterpart in a similar position.[41] The federal and provincial governments should pass legislation setting specific targets and timeframes. The government rejected a Senate amendment to Bill C-25, which concerned Canadian corporations, that would have obliged companies to set specific gender targets and deadlines. The government preferred to maintain the status quo, namely, its "comply or explain" policy, which provides absolutely no guarantee of progress.[42] To the contrary, there is now a lower number of women at the higher level of large companies active on the stock market: in 2018, none of them is CEO of Canada's TSX 60 companies.[43] Meanwhile, provincial governments are currently adopting legislated incentives, but these measures are limited and do not guarantee that this barrier will be overcome in the foreseeable future. In the short run, specific deadlines for achieving true equality must be imposed. Only in this way will paternalistic attitudes and bias against the capabilities of women in the workplace be relegated to the past.*

*In 2015, 82 per cent of Canadian women were in the labour market. There are economic and social costs to inequality and marginalization, and more support measures and initiatives are needed to close the gap between men and women.[44]*

*By and large, women continue to perform double duty, with more than 73 per cent assuming the entire burden of household work.[45] This unequal sharing of family responsibilities weighs heavily on the careers of women and on the effort required to be considered for promotion on an equal footing with men. Achieving a balance between family and work must still be an objective and must be incorporated into everyday practices if the desired equilibrium and equity are to be restored.*

*In this respect, the province of Quebec's analyses and experience clearly show that a public daycare system is a vital investment that all governments should make to support women at work and their families.[46] Without federal leadership in this area, Canadian women will continue to struggle in a society where dominant male interests take precedence over equality and the advent of equal opportunities for men and women.*

*In addition to these changes in the political and economic arenas over the last fifty years, society has sought to correct the cultural and sociopolitical conditions that prevailed for centuries and that always subjugated women, who were forever viewed through a prism of male dominance.[47] Besides the religious freedom issues involved, which must be respected, the wearing of garments that completely hide women's bodies is considered by some to erase their identities from social or community relations that foster empathy and bring human beings closer together.[48] This issue has been hotly debated and has already been the subject of a Supreme Court decision in 2012,[49] which has maintained the woman's freedom to choose.*

ANTI-ABORTION DEMONSTRATION IN FRONT OF THE MORGENTALER CLINIC, 4 JANUARY 1985

No issue is more controversial than abortion, because of the serious moral implications and obvious religious connotations for many people. After the Supreme Court struck down the Criminal Code provisions that prohibited abortion in 1988, Brian Mulroney's government introduced a bill to regulate access to abortion. Passed in the House of Commons, the bill was unexpectedly defeated by a tie vote in the Senate in 1992. Since then, women have had full control over their own lives. Cases are regularly brought before the courts in an attempt to have the fetus declared a "human being," and similar private members' bills are introduced in the Commons, but they eventually die on the order paper. Women's freedom to choose is a right that continues to generate controversy in some circles.

Credit: *The Globe and Mail*, Thomas Szlukovenyi

*The sexual exploitation of women and the various forms of violence against women have been the subject of numerous criminal court decisions over the years. Amendments have been made to eliminate the sexism in the law. In many cases, however, these initiatives were of limited use because they did not fundamentally call into question or address the systemic causes of the relative ineffectiveness of such corrective measures.[50]*

*Even today, one in four women in Canada is a victim of sexual violence,[51] yet only 18 per cent of sexual assault complaints brought to police are pursued by the Crown.[52] Furthermore, the majority of victims fear being stigmatized and being unable to obtain justice through the courts.[53] According to Statistics Canada, only 5 per cent of sexual assaults were reported to police in 2014.[54] The victims of these crimes are often women with mental illnesses, immigrants with a poor command of Canada's official languages, Indigenous women, transgender persons, women living in poverty or sex workers.[55] Many are subjected to three types of discrimination: based on their gender, origin and social standing.[56] This situation is a challenge for the entire justice system, because it clearly represents a systemic failure that cannot be remedied by merely increasing penalties or improving the effectiveness of investigation services.[57]*

*The problems with the terms of reference of the National Inquiry into Missing and Murdered Indigenous Women and Girls shed light on yet another aspect of the lives of especially vulnerable women.[58] The broader societal problem behind this situation should be addressed comprehensively and directly by the government; indeed, the government should indicate in no uncertain terms that the principle of gender equality calls for radical solutions to a discrimination problem perpetuated by the current system as a whole (from the police to the judiciary to Crown prosecutors), and for a support program for victims and their loved ones.*

*The wave of public condemnation that arose in the fall of 2017 following the Weinstein scandal and the #MeToo movement shows the scope of a problem that had remained hidden behind positions of power, authority and dominance. Clearly, the approach taken to date falls considerably short of the systemic changes needed to combat this scourge, the extent of which defies comprehension. Philosopher Valérie Cayouette-Guilloteau, recalling the conclusion reached by American theorist Gayle Rubin in her 1975 work* The Traffic in Women: Notes on the "Political Economy" of Sex, *to the effect that sex is always political, recently pointed out that women's bodies always have been and continue to be used by those in positions of power.[59]*

*What changes must society make to its laws, labour standards and professional standards and ethics to ensure that rules governing behaviour are clear? And what institutions must be established to ensure that harassment complaints are dealt with effectively, while protecting the rights of the parties involved in accordance with the Charter?*

*The Parliament of Canada passed Bill C-65,* An Act to amend the Canada Labour Code (harassment and violence), the Parliamentary Employment and Staff Relations Act and the Budget Implementation Act, 2017, No. 1, *but the required changes in overall behaviour are so profound that this legislation alone will not suffice. The federal and provincial governments should work together to develop a coordinated plan for action at all levels in order to effect the radical transformation the #MeToo movement demands.*

*In a report tabled in the House of Commons in March 2017, the Standing Committee on the Status of Women proposed forty-five potential solutions.[60] However, the Committee failed to recommend a national action plan with a stable, long-term budget, whose effectiveness could be measured on a regular basis. This is the only path to eliminating this systemic discrimination, which cannot be tolerated in a society that enjoys the protections set out in the Charter.*

*The Canadian government recently announced a strategy and a budget of $77.5 million to prevent and address gender-based violence, which is commendable.[61] However, such violence against women stems from a systemic condition that requires a complete reassessment of the social parameters of our lives in order for the strategy to be truly effective and reach all the way to the underlying causes. According to a report produced by Human Rights Watch (based in New York), sixty-four cases of mistreatment of Indigenous women by police in Saskatchewan show that this intolerable behaviour affects all levels of society.[62]*

*In addition, cultural patterns and social structures continue to perpetuate gender stereotypes in advertising, movies, television and magazines. The available data indicate that stereotypes take hold very early in life, starting in primary school and solidifying at university and in the working world.[63] It should be acknowledged that many of the cultural products available to the general public come from abroad, particularly our neighbour to the south, where awareness and understanding of women's equality remains a secondary consideration, often far removed from the priorities of top executives, up to and including the actual president. North American culture is filled with millions of examples of women being portrayed in supporting roles that emphasize their traditional and even objectified status, without the least critical nod to gender equality.*

*While some awareness is beginning to emerge and a number of companies are working together to implement better advertising standards to eliminate sexist stereotypes, this is a task that must necessarily involve consumer society as a whole, primarily in the Western world and soon in China as well.*

*What remedy can our education system offer to counter this negative messaging among younger generations, whose primary source of information is the Internet and social networks? This would appear to be a near-Sisyphean task: it is difficult to see how governments could put an end to such gender stereotyping in the near future other than by adopting an international convention to promote better advertising practices. However, the world of advertising is wildly diverse and essentially driven by market-driven financial considerations and a place where the law of competition reigns supreme. The United Nations Entity for Gender Equality and the Empowerment of Women (UN Women) has joined with major multinationals such as Unilever, Johnson & Johnson, Procter &*

"KIM"

Plasticized button, 1993. On 25 June 1993, Kim Campbell, minister of national defence and veterans affairs, was elected leader of the Progressive Conservative Party, succeeding Brian Mulroney. It was the first time in history that a woman had become the head of the Government of Canada (June to November 1993). Her party was defeated in the general election of 25 October 1993. A true pioneer who had held a number of ministerial portfolios (including justice), Kim Campbell opened the door to equality in Canadian politics and still campaigns actively for greater access to political life. Credit: CHSJ

*Gamble, Facebook and Google to set up an "Unstereotype Alliance" committed to the elimination of sexist clichés in advertising.[64] While this is a good first step at the international level, it is not sufficient to eliminate gender bias in advertising because "ads" are merely a symptom and reflection of society's ills.[65]*

*At the international level, Canada and its partners in a number of multilateral organizations should be far more proactive in this area. Recently, the Canadian government confidently announced the establishment of a "feminist" international assistance policy under which it would invest $650 million "to close persistent gaps in sexual and reproductive health and rights for women and girls" in emerging countries.[66] However, all of these women are struggling in the broader context of fundamentally sexist societies where the inertia of the system against which they are pitted has not been challenged. No matter how great the effort or how good the intentions, it is the systemic causes, and not just their effects, that must be targeted first. A collective effort is needed* *to change mindsets and continue educational efforts, without underestimating the potential impact of social networks. While these networks can convey the worst aspects of gender bias, they can also provide a counterweight by showing the advantages of a society in which gender equality governs all human relations.*

*Fighting gender stereotypes in advertising, movies and social networks also serves the cause of human rights.[67] Society evolves as a single, unitary whole. There is no segregation in the cultural imaginations of peoples: the contradictory perceptions to which individuals or consumers are beholden impede the emergence of norms likely to help shape behaviour that spontaneously upholds the principle of gender equality.[68]*

*Society's paradigms have always been established and maintained by men in order to preserve their exclusive grip on power, and they themselves set the limits of what was acceptable – to them.*

*People must be realistic. What is being attempted is a radical change of the very roots of Western culture....[69]*

### NOTES

1  The author is indebted to the Library of Parliament for its careful work in verifying the accuracy of the historical facts and figures in the text.

2  United Nations, *Universal Declaration of Human Rights*, Article 1.

3  Michael Adams, "Trump, Trudeau and the patriarchy," *The Globe and Mail*, 27 May 2017, p. F7. According to a survey conducted by the Environics Institute, 23 per cent of Canadians agree with the statement that "the father is the head of the household," compared with 50 per cent of Americans. Since 1992, this figure has been increasing in the US and declining in Canada.

4  Taylor Blewett, "Museum exposes barriers to early women scientists," *Ottawa Citizen*, 27 July 2018, p. A2.

5  Adam Dodek, *The Charter Debates: The Special Joint Committee on the Constitution 1980–81 and the Making of the Canadian Charter of Rights and Freedoms* (Toronto: University of Toronto Press, 2018), 49-57.

6  Justice Canada, Justice Laws Website, *Constitution Act, 1982*, http://laws-lois.justice.gc.ca/eng/Const/page-15.html, consulted 2 November 2017.

7  From 1982 to 1984, the author was the federal minister responsible for the administration of status of women programs.

8  With the coming into force of the *Act respecting the legal capacity of married women* (Bill 16), which amended sections 174 to 177 of the *Civil Code of Quebec*.

9  *R. v. Morgentaler*, [1988] 1 SCR 30.

10  *Janzen v. Platy Enterprises Ltd.*, [1989] 1 SCR 1252.

11  *Canada (Attorney General) v. Bedford*, [2013] 3 SCR 1101, 2013 SCC 72.

12  Chan, Melissa, "The story behind the woman you don't see on TIME's person of the year cover," http://time.com/5052362/time-person-of-the-year-2017-arm-cover/, *TIME*, 6 December 2017, consulted 16 January 2018.

13  *Status of Women Canada Ministerial Transition Book*, https://www.swc-cfc.gc.ca/transition/tab_2-en.html?wbdisable=true, consulted 2 November 2017.

14  Paul Journet, "Science, on est en retard," *La Presse+*, Débats 2, 5 August 2018.

15  Thomas Dufour, "Des cibles – Chaires de Recherche," *La Presse+*, 21 August 2018, Actualités 2.

16  See section 43(2) of *An Act respecting the governance of state-owned enterprises and amending various legislative provisions*: "that the boards of directors of the enterprises as a group include an equal number of women and men as of 14 December 2011."

17  Appointed on 4 November 2015, Prime Minister Justin Trudeau's Cabinet of fifteen men and 15 women was a first at the federal level.

18  Manon Cornellier, "Représentation des femmes – Viser la Parité," *Le Devoir*, 9 March 2017, p. A6.

19  In the United States, the level of agreement is only 48 per cent. See Terry Glavin, Environics Institute, for the *National Post*, "Women in politics? Poll surprises," *The Gazette*, 1 March 2017, p. A2. See also "Global attitudes about women as national leaders," Report prepared by the Environics Institute, p. 3.

20  Sylvia Bashevkin, "Empowered or imperiled? Women as Canadian political party leaders," *Toronto Star*, 22 August 2017, p. A11.

21  There are 49 women in the Senate out of a total of 105 senators, accounting for 46.6 per cent of current Senate seats.

22  Oonagh Fitzgerald, "No. It was obligated to defend women's rights," *Toronto Star*, 14 August 2018, p. A11.

23  Laura-Julie Perreault, "Coup de circuit pour les femmes au G7," *LaPresse.ca*, 9 June 2018.

24  Joanna Smith, and Blatchford, Andy, "Gender analysis kept under wraps – cabinet secrecy," *National Post*, 20 March 2017, p. A4; Chapter 5 of the 2016–17 Budget, entitled "Equal Opportunity: Budget 2017's Gender Statement," contained charts and tables detailing the gender wage gap, which "remains significant." It made reference to poverty and violence against women and to "investments to support gender equality."

25  Canada, House of Commons, *It's Time to Act: Report of the Special Committee on Pay Equity,* June 2016, 42nd Parliament, 1st Session, Recommendation 4.

26  Ibid., Recommendation 9.

27  Isabelle Porter, "La lutte pour l'égalité piétine au Québec," *Le Devoir*, 30 June 2017, p. A3.

See also the news release from the Quebec status of women secretariat, http://scf.gouv.qc.ca/index.php?id=998, 29 June 2017.

28  Robert Dutrisac, "Égalité entre les hommes et les femmes, une nouvelle stratégie à l'aveugle," *Le Devoir*, 7 July 2017, p. A8.

29  Statistics Canada reports, "Women are underrepresented in leadership positions in the private sector, although not in the public sector." *Women and Paid Work*, https://www150.statcan.gc.ca/n1/pub/89-503-x/2015001/article/14694-eng.htm, 9 March 2017.

30  Statistics Canada, *Women and Paid Work*, https://www150.statcan.gc.ca/n1/pub/89-503-x/2015001/article/14694-eng.htm, 9 March 2017.

31  Marie-Hélène Alarie, "La lente marche vers l'égalité," *Le Devoir*, 6 May 2017, p. A9; Brière, Sophie, "La progression des femmes dans des professions et métiers historiquement occupés par des hommes," Presentation to the Association Francophone pour le savoir (ACFAS), 10-11 May 2017.

32  Catalyst, 2013 Catalyst Census: Financial Post 500 Women Board Directors, http://www.catalyst.org/knowledge/2013-catalyst-census-financial-post-500-women-board-directors, Research project, 3 March 2014.

33  Catalyst, Statistical Overview of Women in the Workforce, http://www.catalyst.org/knowledge/statistical-overview-women-workforce, consulted 29 October 2017.

34  Armina Ligaya and Tara Deschamps, "Stalled progress for top female executives – among TSX 60 index companies, none listed a woman as its CEO," *Toronto Star*, 1 August 2018, p. A2.

35  World Economic Forum, *The Global Gender Gap Report 2017*, 2 November 2017; see also "L'année 2017 marque un 'coup d'arrêt' pour l'égalité femmes-hommes," http://www.france24.com/fr/20171102-annee-2017-marque-coup-arret-egalite-femmes-hommes-parite-wef, *France 24*, consulted 17 January 2018.

36  Statistics Canada, *Women and Paid Work*, https://www150.statcan.gc.ca/n1/pub/89-503-x/2015001/article/14694-eng.htm, 9 March 2017. According to Statistics Canada, "Women earn $0.87 for every dollar earned by men, largely as a result of wage inequality between women and men within occupations."

37  Lia Lévesque, "Rémunération – les femmes n'ont gagné que deux points en 10 ans sur les hommes," *Le Devoir*, 7 March 2017, p. B1.

38  The Conference Board of Canada, *Gender Wage Gap*, https://www.conferenceboard.ca/hcp/provincial/society/gender-gap.aspx, consulted 29 October 2017.

39  John R. MacArthur, "Le sommeil des hommes," *Le Devoir*, 5 February 2018, p. A7; Howard Levitt, "Motherhood – Main reason that a wage gap exists," *Ottawa Citizen*, 18 August 2018, p. C-15.

40  Armina Ligaya, "Quashed without question – Female entrepreneur's barriers to scaling up part of a wider problem," *National Post*, 20 August 2018, p. FP1.

41  Armina Ligaya and Tara Deschamps, "Stalled progress."

42  *Debates of the Senate*, 1ˢᵗ Session, 42ⁿᵈ Parliament, Volume 150, Issue 161, 23 November 2017, Speech to the Senate by the Hon. Senator Serge Joyal on second reading of Bill C-25; *Debates of the Senate*, 1ˢᵗ session, 42ⁿᵈ Parliament, Volume 150, Issue 181, 14 February 2018, Speech to the Senate by the Hon. Senator Serge Joyal on third reading of Bill C-25.

43  Armina Ligaya and Tara Deschamps, "Stalled progress."

44  Statistics Canada, *Women and Paid Work*.

45  Statistics Canada, *Families, Living Arrangements and Unpaid Work*, https://www150.statcan.gc.ca/n1/pub/89-503-x/2010001/article/11546-eng.htm#a1, consulted 29 October 2017.

46  Allison Hanes, "Math shows Quebec gets daycare right," *The Montreal Gazette*, 8 August 2017, p. A1.

47  Suzanne Zaccour, "Le féminisme : un combat dépassé?" *La Presse+*, 19 September 2017.

48  Angus Reid Institute, *Religious Trends: Led by Quebec, number of Canadians holding favourable views of various religions increases*, http://angusreid.org/religious-trends-2017, 4 April 2017.

49  *R. v. N.S.*, [2012] 3 SCR 726, 2012 SCC 72.

50  Linda Silver Dranoff, "Would a lawyer in 2017 advise a woman to report a rape?" *Toronto Star*, 13 September 2017, p. A15.

51  "Une femme sur quatre victime de violence sexuelle au Canada," *Journal de Montréal*, 21 March 2017, p. 20.

52  Samuel Perreault, *Criminal victimization in Canada, 2014*, https://www150.statcan.gc.ca/n1/pub/85-002-x/2015001/article/14241-eng.htm, Statistics Canada, consulted 16 January 2018.

53  Sarah R. Champagne, "L'agression sexuelle se vit encore en silence," *Le Devoir*, 12 July 2017, p. A3.

54  Statistics Canada, *Criminal Victimization in Canada, 2014*, https://www150.statcan.gc.ca/n1/pub/85-002-x/2015001/article/14241-eng.htm#a10, consulted 29 October 2017.

55  Status of Women Canada, *Issue Brief: Sexual Violence Against Women in Canada*, https://www.swc-cfc.gc.ca/svawc-vcsfc/index-en.html, consulted 29 October 2017.

56  "Femmes immigrantes et autochtones : doublement discriminées en emploi," *La Presse.ca*, 27 February 2017.

57  Miriam Katazawi, "New Trial ordered in sexual assault case," *The Globe and Mail*, 21 July 2017, p. A3; Robyn Doolittle, "Unfounded," *The Globe and Mail*, 15 September 2017, p. A1.

58  Commissioner Marilyn Poitras, a Métis woman from Saskatchewan, resigned from the commission of inquiry precisely for this reason. http://ici.radiocanada.ca/nouvelle

/1044622/nouvelle-demission-commission-enquete-femmes-autochtones-disparues-assassinees-marilyn-poitras.

59 Valérie Cayouette-Guilloteau, "Le corps des femmes soumis à des rapports de domination," *Le Devoir*, 26 and 27 May 2018, p. B10.

60 House of Commons, *Taking Action to End Violence Against Young Women and Girls in Canada: Report of the Standing Committee on the Status of Women*, http://www.ourcommons.ca/Content/Committee/421/FEWO/Reports/RP8823562/feworp07/feworp07-e.pdf, March 2017.

61 Among other things, this budget will be used to establish a Knowledge Centre on Gender-Based Violence to collect sorely lacking data on the scope of violence against women and to conduct research, particularly on visible minorities, the LGBT community and Indigenous peoples. "A Wise investment – Gender-based violence," *Toronto Star*, 25 June 2017, p. A12; Status of Women Canada, *Strategy to Prevent and Address Gender-Based Violence*, https://www.swc-cfc.gc.ca/violence/strategy-strategie/index-en.html, consulted 29 October 2017.

62 Human Rights Watch, "Canada: Police Fail Indigenous Women in Saskatchewan," https://www.hrw.org/news/2017/06/19/canada-police-fail-indigenous-women-saskatchewan, consulted 29 October 2017.

63 Marie-Hélène Alarie, "La lente marche vers l'égalité," *Le Devoir*, 6 May 2017, p. A9.

64 *#WomenNotObjects*, http://womennotobjects.com/, consulted 4 June 2017; Julie Rambal, "La pub s'attaque aux clichés sexistes… qu'elle a fabriqué," *Le Temps* (online), 27 June 2017, reprinted in *Le Devoir*, 1–2 July 2017, p. A6.

65 UN Women, "Press Release: In Cannes, UN Women Executive Director calls on members of global industry to eliminate gender stereotypes in advertising," http://www.unwomen.org/en/news/stories/2017/6/press-release-in-cannes-un-women-ed-calls-to-eliminate-gender-stereotypes-in-advertising, consulted 29 October 2017.

66 Global Affairs Canada, *Canada's Feminist International Assistance Policy*, http://international.gc.ca/world-monde/issues_development-enjeux_developpement/priorities-priorites/policy-politique.aspx?lang=eng, consulted 29 October 2017. The government added "$150 million over five years to respond to the needs of local women's organizations in developing countries that are working to advance the rights of women and girls and promote gender equality." See Global Affairs Canada, "Canada launches new Feminist International Assistance Policy," https://www.canada.ca/en/global-affairs/news/2017/06/canada_launches_newfeministinternationalassistancepolicy.html, News release, 9 June 2017; and Global Affairs Canada, *Canada's Feminist International*

*Assistance Policy*, http://www.international.gc.ca/gac-amc/campaign-campagne/iap-pai/index.aspx?lang=eng.

67  Nancy Houston, "Le marché a démocratisé le droit de cuissage," *Le Monde*, 31 October 2017, p. 20.

68  Marc-Olivier Bherer, [remarks reported by] Olivia Gazalé, "Il faut ouvrir les yeux sur la réalité du malaise masculin," *Le Monde*, 31 October 2017, p. 21.

69  Simon Langlois, *Le Québec change: chroniques sociologiques*, (Montreal: Del Busso, 2017).

# A Personal Reflection on Gender Equality in Canada

The Rt. Hon. A. Kim Campbell, nineteenth prime minister of Canada

As we celebrate Canada's 150th anniversary, I think back on the last fifty years since our centennial celebration in 1967, a period coinciding with my own adult lifetime. As such, I reflect on the changes that have occurred in Canadian society over that time with respect to the status of Canadian women and the opportunities available to them.

At the Senate symposium honouring the anniversary, we have a situation unimaginable in 1967 – the presence of three female Right Honourables representing the three offices that carry that title in Canada – governor general, prime minister, and chief justice of the Supreme Court of Canada. While Madame Jean is the third woman to be governor general, Madam Justice McLachlan and I are the only women to have held our "Right Honourable" conferring positions, and so it was historical that we were all three together in the Senate, and a powerful indicator of change for Canadian women.

I remember when I was ten years old telling my family doctor that I thought I might like to be a doctor. He said, "Oh, girls can't be doctors." I had an aunt who was a doctor, so I knew he was entirely wrong, but I have often wondered how his negative reaction to my youthful ambition might have affected it, had I not had an aunt who was a doctor, and how many more men there were who thought just like him.

The doctor's response was more common than not for postwar baby boomers like me, who started life in an era of the phrase "girls can't do that." This period went on for some time. I had a good American friend who had wanted to study physics and was told that women were not allowed to do so at her midwestern university. So she wound up going to MIT, where she could study physics but, as a woman, could not receive the scholarship she had been awarded – the ambiguity of her first name had led the university to believe she was a man.

At sixteen, I was the first girl elected as student council president of my high school. Years later, when I was a school trustee in Vancouver in the early eighties and I told this story to students, they looked at me like I had said I went to school in high-button boots, because by that time many girls were student council presidents. But in the spring of 1963, when I was elected student council president of Prince of Wales Secondary School in Vancouver, the *Vancouver Sun* sent a reporter to interview me; I was "news." I had my picture in the paper, it was so unusual. The reporter asked, "What are you going to do with all those boys on the council?" I said, "There are a lot of big boys on the council, but I'll have a big gavel." I hope my political rhetoric improved over the years. That was not my finest moment. Then again, I always maintained a sense of humour.

I went to UBC in 1964, and while I continued to achieve other firsts in student government, my time at university was when I began to see a difference in opportunities for men and women. For example, Rhodes Scholarships were not open to women. It would be another eight or nine years before a woman could be eligible. Many other recognitions and memberships that have provided very important paths to advancement in networking for young men were not available to women. I did not get involved in a political-party club, because the men in those groups got to go to Ottawa and be executive assistants to cabinet ministers, but the women never did. A woman was very welcome to make the coffee and knock on doors in an election campaign, but being a Tiny Tory or a Young Liberal or what have you was not a path for an ambitious woman. I took a different route because it became clear to me that certain paths were available only to men. It is interesting to think of Bill and Hillary Clinton, who are of the same generation. Bill Clinton was a Rhodes Scholar. Hillary should have been but was not because she was not eligible. Women couldn't be. Many of the things that have anointed young men and given them the opportunity to become figures of importance and to build on their skills and networks simply were not available to women.

In the sixties, there were not a lot of women in Canadian politics. Since the first female member of Parliament, Agnes McPhail, was elected in 1920, there have been one or two women in each session of the House of Commons, with the exception of 1949, when no women were elected. In 1968, the first election of Canada's second century, only one woman MP was elected. Ellen Fairclough was the first woman to be appointed to cabinet in 1957. I remember a wonderful story of Pauline Jewett, who was a member of the Liberal caucus in the early sixties. She talked to her mother about the fact that she was enjoying being an MP but felt she was ready for more challenges. Her mother said, "Why don't you talk to Mr Pearson?" That is not really how you do it when you want to go into cabinet, but, anyway, she spoke to Prime Minister

Pearson. He said, "Ah, but Pauline, we already have a woman in the cabinet." It is important to remember what the mentality was. Places of power were men's places, and when women wanted to participate, they were interlopers. So, for much of my life, I was part of a group that was seen as interloping into domains belonging to men. I think that is no longer the case. I think I and other women now take our places in seats of power where we are not necessarily seen as interlopers, but how we got there and where we continue to go from there is a very important question.

Who then, are the female role models in Canadian history? Most of us have heard of Laura Secord, if only because her face appears on boxes of chocolates. She was a remarkable woman, a true heroine who was not officially recognized until almost the end of her life when she finally got a small pension from the governor general. She was a courageous and resourceful woman who, during the War of 1812, walked for twenty miles to warn of an American attack. When I think of the origins of Canada, I think of the role of First Nations women in that development. I had a friend at the London School of Economics whose wife was doing her PhD on the subject of the role of First Nations women in opening up the West. The Hudson's Bay Company archives are in London, and they tell the story of the Hudson's Bay Company factors who came from Britain to run the company and who often took "Indian wives," as they would call them. These First Nations women, as wives, served as liaisons between Indigenous communities and the Hudson's Bay Company. They played an incredibly valuable role. Often, when the Hudson's Bay factors were ready to go back to England, they simply abandoned these wives and their children. These women were essential in many ways and were very smart and able.

I was recently in Italy, where I saw a poster from 1913 encouraging people to come to Canada for wonderful futures. Nowhere, even in the fine print, did it say how cold it was. When you think of all of the people from Eastern Europe, for example, who were encouraged to come in the late nineteenth century, you understand the reason why Ukrainians feel that they constitute another founding group in Canada. Many of them – including Ruthenians, Bukovenians, et cetera, whose countries of origin were not called Ukraine at the time – came out to the Canadian prairies, where they were given land grants. The winters were bitterly cold and they endured them in sod houses while they farmed the prairie. Many of the women had to bear their children without any support or services. Some of them went mad from loneliness.

I think of the early Chinese families. I saw a documentary on the CBC about Chinese families who came to the prairies after the men were allowed to bring wives to Canada. A family would go to a small town, just one family, and open a Chinese restaurant. They would be very successful, and they had to work very hard. Everybody loved to eat their inexpensive and tasty food. (It was the Chinese who taught us in Canada how to stir-fry our veggies and eat them al dente.) The program included an interview with a woman whose children were off to university. They did not want to stay in a small town. The woman broke down remembering the loneliness of being the only Chinese family in town, and of everybody being happy to go to their restaurant but never including them socially. It is heartbreaking to imagine the life of this woman without a single woman friend.

So we are a country built on many sacrifices and a lot of women's loneliness, and as in the case of those First Nations wives, abandonment. When we ask, "Why should women be included?" the answer is that we have paid our dues as much as anyone. We are as integrally woven into the fabric of this country as anyone. When I think of the barriers I have broken down, yes, gender was a challenge for me – I was a woman who wanted to do things that women did not do – but I was otherwise very privileged. I was a white, middle-class, British-origin person growing up in Vancouver, where many of the barriers that others faced did not confront me. So the gender barrier was significant, but I had many other resources to support me. Many women have endured struggles without having those privileges that I could count on. So this sometimes bothers me: Why are we even asking this question of gender equality? Why was the exclusion of women something that we had to struggle against?

Many of the places of power in Canada were seen by men as belonging to them. Winston Churchill once said that, when Lady Astor came to the British Parliament as its first female MP, he felt like he had been "found in his bath without a sponge to cover himself." She famously assured him that he had nothing to fear from her. While their acrimonious exchanges are the stuff of humorous anecdote, Churchill's sense of Parliament as a man's place was not unique to him or to Britain.

If I had gone to law school right after my BA, I would have been in the seventies generation of students. In that decade, women started out as a small minority but grew considerably as a percentage of graduates by the end. I was recently talking to a woman who studied law at UBC in the early seventies, and she said to me, "I was part of the class that liberated the coffee room at the UBC law school." There was a student coffee room in the building that was off limits to women. Think about that. Imagine anybody believing, at a publicly funded university, where the women are paying the same fees and are the same students, that they had the right to exclude women from the coffee room. So I want people to remember what people took for granted in their right to exclude women, that we were the interlopers. We were spoiling things. It was so nice before we came and brought all of our femaleness into these wonderful male institutions. A few women were okay, but more than that were a problem.

In 1972, around the same time that the UBC law school coffee room was being liberated, there was an interesting legislative development in the United States. The American Congress passed legislation called Title IX, which required universities that received federal funding for athletic programs to give equal contributions to women's sports as to men's. Now, if I had been in the American Congress in 1972, I might not have voted for that, because I might have been like a lot of people and thought, "Well, women aren't as interested in sports as men are. After all, don't we give men sports so that they won't kill each other?" What was interesting is that, when Title IX came into force, there was a huge explosion of interest among women in playing sports. All this repressed desire emerged. It taught a very important lesson and one that I have borne in mind not just with respect to women but with every group in society. You cannot tell what people *can* do by what they *do* do because what they *do* do is a reflection of what they are allowed to do, of their competences that are not suppressed. When you open up the opportunities for women, for people of colour, for Indigenous people, for all the people who have been told, "You can't do this," or "People like you don't do this," you get a big surprise. You discover, "Oh, they really like to do this, and they can do it."

THE BIRD COMMISSION

Chaired by noted journalist Florence Bird (1908–88), the Royal Commission on the Status of Women, which was established in 1967, helped to lay the groundwork for the principle of gender equality and gradually led Canada out of patriarchy. It marked a cultural shift that would span many years to come and be reflected in section 28 of the Canadian Charter of Rights and Freedoms in 1982. The commission's report would challenge and redefine all the social paradigms around the status of women, the perception of women, and the stereotypes that had been perpetuated for millennia. Florence Bird sat in the Senate from 1978 to 1983. Credit: *Le Soleil* Photo Archives, 11 June 1968, p. 7

So we have learned a lot in the last fifty years. There was an explosion of women in sport. It actually, I think, changed our ideas of what we think is a beautiful female body. We no longer see female beauty as necessarily being powerless, wan, ready for the fainting couch. Rather, we now admire a strong, athletic, buff female body.

So there were gradual changes in government. Ellen Fairclough was the first woman to be named to cabinet by John Diefenbaker, but there was a humorous twist. Diefenbaker ran in the election of 1957, promising he would appoint a woman to the cabinet. The only woman who got elected in his caucus was Ellen Fairclough, and he did not like her very much because she had not supported him in the leadership; she had supported Davie Fulton. So Diefenbaker kept her "cooling her heels in the anteroom" as long as he could before naming her to cabinet, but sure enough, he eventually did.

Then the Pearson government, as I said, had at least one. Prime Minister Trudeau had a few more women and was dragged, kicking and screaming, to appoint the first woman to the Supreme Court of Canada. He really did not think there was a woman capable, and Bertha Wilson proved him wrong. (Ronald Reagan had appointed a woman to the US Supreme Court, so we figured that we had better do that here.)

Jeanne Sauvé served with distinction as our first female speaker of the House of Commons and then our first female governor general. It was she who swore me into my first cabinet portfolio in 1989.

We gradually began to create some new role models. If we look at Parliament today, first of all, having a gender-balanced cabinet is a great thing. Canada was the fifth country to do it, and now France has done the same thing. I lived in Spain in 2004, when José Luis Rodríguez Zapatero was elected. He had promised to have a fifty-fifty, gender-balanced cabinet. He did not think he was going to get elected, but he did, and he did deliver on his promise.

This has become a much more common idea, and it is great and important, but look at the portfolios – we still have some women-free zones. In Canada, we have had one female prime minister in 150 years. I may have been the "Hail Mary" pass for the Progressive Conservative Party, since the Bloc Québécois had taken our Quebec vote, and we had nothing to beat off the Reform Party with in the West. But still, becoming the leader of a governing party is harder than it looks.

There has never been a female finance minister. I am the only woman who has been defence minister. Three have been justice minister. Three women have been foreign minister. Two have been trade minister. There are still a number of significant portfolios with the kinds of responsibilities that engender respect and would enhance the power of women in Cabinet, where as yet no woman has served.

When I was minister of justice and attorney general, I felt it was important to acknowledge that I was the first woman. There were expectations of me because of my breakthrough. So I convened the first-ever National Symposium on Women, Law, and the Administration of Justice in Vancouver in 1991. It was remarkable, and again, it showed why tokenism does not work. I cannot represent all women. I reached out to stakeholders across the country and had agenda items suggested that I would not have identified.

A number of judges came to the conference. The good thing about being the minister of justice is that the judges know that you will respect their independence, so they feel comfortable coming to the conference to see what is being said. At the conclusion, a number of judges said to me individually, "Before I came, I thought I was pretty liberal on these issues. I realize I didn't know anything." They had never heard directly from women about the ways in which the justice system did not work for them, or was letting them down. We are inclined to think the law is this wonderful crystalline, pristine thing that comes down from on high – some kind of Olympian neutrality. It is not. It is a social construct.

Having these conversations, which I continued to do when I was undertaking a complete revision of the law on sexual assault, enabled a much broader scope of consultation than had been conducted before. This opened up new avenues of understanding. We went out and talked to women in the sex trade, and we talked to organizations representing women of colour. We learned about a lot of different things going on in society, which helped us to draft a sexual assault law that was much more realistic and respectful of the lived experiences of Canadians. The Hon. Anne McLellan, who was the second woman to serve as justice minister, talks about being briefed on the "Campbell mode of consultation."

That was also part of my lesson: namely, how important it is to have many voices, why it matters to have these diverse voices around the table, and why it matters who is asking the questions. It is not that a group of all men is not going to do a good job. They will do the best they can, but they can only do what they are capable of doing. They can only ask the questions that it occurs to them to ask. It is only when we reach out and draw on all the people who will be affected by what we do that we can get the best kind of legislation.

I had many experiences as prime minister that were perplexing – basic things such as people putting words in my mouth, and my never being able to get the benefit of the doubt. I wondered, "What is going on here? Does this happen as regularly to men as it does to me?"

When I had political retirement thrust upon me by the Canadian electorate, it gave me the leisure to explore an interesting and growing body of behavioural-science

ASTRONAUT ROBERTA L. BONDAR (1945–    )
The first Canadian woman to become an astronaut (1983), Roberta Bondar served on the crew of the Discovery mission in 1992. She is a leader in the aerospace field, which was the preserve of men for the first several decades. The biased view was that women did not have the physical stamina for this kind of job. A physician herself, she oversaw the study on the effect of space on the human body for ten years. Men had always dominated the realms of engineering, physics, and astrophysics. Some professions had always been gendered, and men had reserved the discovery and exploration of the universe for themselves. Credit: NASA Image and Video Library, s91–51633 (November 1991) – Astronaut Roberta L. Bondar, Canadian payload specialist

research that focuses on cognitive biases, implicit attitudes, and the ways in which we try to reconcile things that make us uncomfortable. For example, there is some interesting research on prototypical and nonprototypical leaders. If you are proto-typical, you will be assumed to belong; if you are non-prototypical, people will try to reconcile their discomfort with your presence.

While doing a fellowship at the Shorenstein Center at Harvard, I wrote a paper on the press coverage of the 1993 election. The theme of the paper was how unfair the coverage was. A reporter would write, "Kim Campbell said such and such and we jumped all over her; Jean Chrétien said the same thing and we left him alone. Gee, that Jean Chrétien sure can manipulate the media." No, he couldn't. He just belonged. His mistakes were forgiven. I did not belong. I made a mistake – Aha!

All these things boil down to one question: "What can we do about it?"

First of all, we have to change the landscape from which people get their sense of how the world works. That means doing whatever we can to bring women into positions of decision-making.

I was a founding member of an organization called the Council of Women World Leaders, which is an organization of current and former female presidents and prime ministers. You would be surprised at how many there are – over fifty now – because when leaders are non-prototypical, when they are seen as anomalies, they fall off the radar screen afterward. Women are doing these leadership jobs and we wanted to create an organization that made this fact visible.

When the prime minister creates a cabinet that is half men and half women, he is putting in the window women, female faces, and a physiognomy that are not normally seen there. From that, people gradually broaden their sense of who gets to do that job. It takes time. This was demonstrated by a delightful response that Prime Minister Justin Trudeau gave to a foreign leader who asked him why he had created a gender-balanced cabinet – why he did not appoint on merit. "If I had appointed on merit," the prime minister replied, "I would have appointed more women!" This exchange reflects the degree to which men are considered the "default" category of leaders. They are the expected, prototypical leaders. Women are by definition the exceptions.

There are some human sacrifices on the road to enlightenment, but every step you take and every woman who girds her loins and "goes for it" contributes to changing that set of expectations.

How do we get there? There are a lot of suggestions to be made. I want to make a couple of observations. First of all, I signed a letter to Prime Minister Justin Trudeau when he took office and received that absolute windfall of twenty-two Senate seats (Who gets twenty-two empty Senate seats as a new prime minister? You open up this "gift," and you go, "Oh, my God. There are twenty-two Senate seats in here." I would have had to govern for years to get that many). I thought he should name women to all of them. Why? Because the number was just right to give instant gender parity in the Senate. What a gesture that would have been! Go for it. Then, as the vacancies came he could alternate genders. He did not take my advice, but still I thought it was a good idea.

Secondly, since 1967, law and policy have been very important, and since 1983, the Charter of Rights and Freedoms has given us a tool to challenge legislation and to change policy. That is really excellent.

Finally, I would also like to share my modest proposal for achieving gender parity in the House of Commons. We need to take the next step and say, "Gender equality in legislative bodies is a fundamental principle." It is becoming much more accepted around the world – not just in cabinets. In France, President Emmanuel Macron has named a gender-balanced set of candidates. It is no longer something that only radical feminists are arguing for. Many mainstream men and women are saying, "Let's get on with it." Why? Because it matters. The outcomes matter. We need to have that kind of representation – and beyond those gender groups, much further representation and diversity.

My recommendation used to be that we could take our constituencies and go back to a very old Canadian tradition of two-member constituencies. When I was elected to the legislature in British Columbia in 1986, I was elected from a two-member constituency. All the constituencies in the major cities of Vancouver and Victoria elected two members. The province ended the practice a few years later because there was no longer an underlying rationale for it, but it had worked quite well.

But I discovered that this practice had also occurred in the Maritime provinces; they used to have two-member constituencies at the provincial level, right up until the end of the nineties, to balance Catholics and Protestants. So in every riding each party would nominate a Catholic and a Protestant, and voters got one of each. Balancing religious representation was considered extremely important for political stability.

Why couldn't we do the same for men and women? Each party would nominate a man and a woman for each constituency, and voters would cast two ballots – one for each list of candidates. I am not suggesting doubling the size of the House of Commons, which has grown enormously since I was there, incidentally. It used to have 285 seats, and it has 338 now. We could use that great Canadian institution, the royal commission – and maybe a Senate committee – to sit down and figure out how to redraw the ridings so that they are manageable. Each riding would elect a man and a woman. The men and women would not be competing with one another for nominations; you would still have grassroots input. You would not have the annoyance of the prime minister or the party leader coming along and saying, "We want more women so, sorry guy, you're out; she's in." That really annoys people and puts women on the defensive by casting them as somehow unfairly preferred. Then we would have automatic parity in the House of Commons. I think that would be a statement about what it means to be a truly representative democracy.

Although the issue of gender balance in the business and financial world will be dealt with in another presentation, I would like to comment on this issue. There is research that establishes that companies with women in senior management and on boards of directors perform better and give a better financial return than those

CANADA'S MOST POWERFUL WOMEN – TOP 100

Barriers are falling one by one, but some circles remain stubbornly hostile to the presence and full participation of women. Examples include professions in finance, stock exchange, banking, and the management of large industrial groups. Parity on corporate boards of directors, the last bastion of male power, has not yet been achieved. Without specific targets to be met within a reasonable time frame that is clearly set out in a law, pockets of resistance will remain, stonewalls of the male rearguard and a holdover from the old boys' club of years past. Credit: PhaseNyne Inc.

without. So now, rather than justify the absence of women in senior corporate positions by a need to tend to the bottom line, companies should explain an absence of women to their shareholders when the research says that they would be more profitable if they included women. That's an issue that, like the number of women in the science, technology, engineering, and mathematics fields, may take some time to resolve, because doing so requires input, pipelines, and other changes.

But gender parity in Parliament? That we could do immediately. Imagine what it would say to the rest of the world. Actually, the rest of the world is saying this already: "We need to find ways to create gender parity in our legislative bodies." That is, the people who are making the rules for our society need to reflect the gender balance of our society.

There is a lot of research now that supports the aspiration to empower women. One source is in the Pew research. Their research shows that the status of women is the most important indicator of a country's level of social and political development. Women are the canary in the mine. When women are losing status, when women are not respected, when women are not protected, that is a danger sign. I also believe that when we look to empower women – and with the same reasoning and commitment, *mutatis mutandis*, when we ask whose voices are not being heard – we create and solidify a process that opens up to all people the chance to no longer be invisible, to be first-rate citizens, and to lead us to the future that we hope to have in the next fifty years.

Since this Senate symposium, the prime minister has announced the new governor general, who took office in the autumn of 2017. She is Julie Payette, one of two Canadian women astronauts. In an interview, Ms. Payette recalled how when she first expressed an ambition to be an astronaut, she was told, "Well you certainly cannot do that!" I am so excited to contemplate how the new governor general will be able to use her "non-prototypical" life to inspire other young women to feel that they belong as engineers and scientists and space travellers. She and Roberta Bondar are important role models for Canadian boys and girls in showing what women can do. I remember how, when I became prime minister, many of my men friends celebrated their ability to tell their daughters that nothing was beyond their reach – not even being prime minister. It is time to replace the "girls can't do that" culture with a society whose women leaders at all levels encourage Canadian girls to reach for the stars.

# The Need for Inclusive Leadership
# and Canada's Influence

Monique F. Leroux, Chair of the Board of Investissement Québec, Vice-Chairman
of Fiera Holdings Inc., former President and CEO of Desjardins Group, and former
president of the International Co-operative Alliance

It is an honour and a privilege to take part in this Senate symposium marking the 150th anniversary of Confederation. I commend the Upper Chamber on this initiative, which honours its institutional mission by adding to the celebration of a special occasion with reflections on how the country has evolved.

This approach reflects a reality: any country, even one that is among the most admired in the world, is inevitably and essentially a work in progress and can always be improved.

I speak from experience, because I have the privilege of seeing Canada as my fellow Canadians see it, but also as others see it.

As chair of the board of Investissement Québec, I see our businesses and our institutions making use of our expertise. I see Quebec and Canada through the lens of strengths and challenges. At the International Co-operative Alliance and the B20, I see how Canada is perceived by other countries. People in many parts of the world see Canada as a sort of ideal.

As the world turns inward, tensions rise and political rhetoric heats up, Canada is seen more than ever as a land of opportunity and freedom. In a world that has darkened, Canada shines with the light of openness and generosity.

With this perception comes a responsibility: we have to set an example here at home and promote hope and reconciliation internationally.

In speaking today on gender equality, I will naturally talk about inclusive leadership. I will look at the progress we have made, the road that lies ahead and the influence we have in the world.

## 1. AN INSPIRING STORY

With an intuitive concept of time comes the general perception that as society has evolved, women have naturally occupied a growing place in our country's economic and political life.

The reality is not so linear. History is a dance through time, with steps forward and steps backward, as we move in the general direction of progress, optimists will say, and I am an optimist.

Few people know that one of the greatest success stories in the economic history of Quebec and Canada was made possible by dozens of women working in obscurity.

This morning I would like to take you back in time, because it all started right here in Ottawa, in the House of Commons. It is Tuesday, April 6, 1897. The member of Parliament for Montréal-Ste-Anne, Michael Quinn, has the floor. He is arguing strenuously in favour of a law against usury. I am quoting from the *Official Report of the Debates*: "We have had cases throughout the country, particularly in the city of Montreal, in which a rate of interest equal almost to 3,000 per cent per annum has been collected. There was one notable case in Montreal within the last few days, in which a man obtained a loan of $150, and was sued for, and was compelled to pay, in interest, the sum of $5,000 for the loan of $150."[1]

On the floor of the House, a man is stunned. It is the francophone reporter, a man named Alphonse Desjardins. He turns his indignation into a mission: to offer people affordable credit and give their communities a democratic tool for economic development. For three years, he corresponds diligently with the promoters of the European co-operative and mutualist movement. On December 6, 1900, in Lévis, he founds the first caisse d'épargne populaire in North America. From that original caisse populaire in Lévis sprang Mouvement Desjardins (Desjardins Group), which today is the largest co-operative movement in Canada, with over $260 billion in assets, and is ranked by Bloomberg as the second-strongest financial institution in the world.

This story also played out in part here in this room. Alphonse Desjardins' proposal had the support of then prime minister Wilfrid Laurier and the governor general at the time, Lord Albert Grey. However, the federal bill providing for the creation of caisses d'épargne died here, defeated in the Senate by a single vote.

So it was that the government of Quebec Premier Lomer Gouin enabled the creation of caisses populaires. This explains why the co-operative financial movement was mainly overseen by the provinces, and it also explains the extremely modest beginnings of Desjardins Group. Alphonse Desjardins may have had the vision, the connections and the knowledge, but he had neither the time nor the means to pursue his dream. His initiative would certainly have foundered had it not been for his wife, Dorimène.

Marie-Clara Dorimène Roy-Desjardins was born in Sorel in 1858. Because her family was poor, she was sent to Lévis to live with her mother's sister, who raised her as her own daughter. She was fortunate enough to be educated at the Notre-Dame-de-Toutes-Grâces convent. When she was just twenty, she met Alphonse Desjardins, who lived nearby. He was working at the time as a journalist with *Le Canadien*, a newspaper in Quebec City.

Although some prominent residents of Lévis were appointed as officers of the caisse populaire after it was created, volunteer work was neither prestigious nor exciting. With neither title nor salary, Dorimène Desjardins took charge of managing the caisse during her husband's long absences, essentially running the business from the family home.

She was authorized to sign all receipts and cheques in amounts up to $500 on behalf of the manager, her husband; she deposited available funds and extended temporary advances to caisse members.

She contributed to the development of the caisses by taking an active role in correspondence and information sharing. When her husband fell ill in 1915, she became involved in the work to form a federation uniting the caisses in an authentic "Desjardins Group." In 1920, on Alphonse Desjardins' death, she became the conscience of the Group, in a way, and was regularly consulted for advice.

Listen to the authority with which this woman spoke in 1924. She was addressing a Mr Laflamme, the president of the Union des caisses Desjardins de Québec: "You talk about the many obstacles you are encountering in your work to continue and consolidate the caisses; I hope that they will not stop you and that, on the contrary, you will march firm and confident toward your goal."[2]

So spoke Dorimène Desjardins. On her death in 1932, *L'Action catholique* stated, "Without her, there probably would be no Desjardins Group."

Dorimène Desjardins was recognized as the "co-founder" of the Mouvement des caisses Desjardins (Desjardins Group) in the mid-1970s. The Government of Canada also designated her as a "person of national historic significance" in 2012, forty years after her husband.

But she was not the only one. Rosario Tremblay, who was the head of inspection of the Fédération des caisses populaires Desjardins from 1924 to 1966, wrote, "In 75 per cent of cases, the caisses were founded by women."

We need to recognize the work done by these outstanding women who, like many other unsung heroines, contributed to our country's economic and social success. They are deserving of our deepest gratitude.

## II. MY COMMITMENT TO INCLUSIVE LEADERSHIP
### BASED ON GENDER EQUALITY

I was born in Montreal into a family of modest means. My parents ran a small shoe store. I benefited fully from everything Canadian society had to offer young people during those years of change known in Quebec as the "Quiet Revolution." I studied music and public accounting, passions that are not mutually exclusive. They are two ways of achieving harmony and working together.

When I studied accounting, I was part of a visible minority, because no more than 10 per cent of the students were women. I made my way in the world among men; some of them were great Canadians who acted as mentors to me, opening up their networks to me and helping me build my confidence. I am very grateful to them for that.

Like so many other women, I saw before me the ladder of career advancement … and the glass ceiling, which lets many of us see the highest rung, but too often prevents us from reaching it, even today. The glass ceiling is such that in many organizations, the feminine form of "president" is "vice-president."

Over time, I saw the often unconscious cultural biases in our organizations that make it difficult for women to rise to decision-making positions. But I also witnessed the progress that could be made and the power of the movement for change when teams and leaders believed in equity in decision-making. And that was a great source of inspiration to me.

During my professional life, I had the privilege of being elected CEO of Desjardins Group for two four-year terms between 2008 and 2016, which allowed me to walk humbly in the steps of Dorimène Desjardins. I was the first woman to head a major financial institution in Canada, and I want to thank the 50,000 employees and the 5,000 elected officers of Desjardins who gave me the privilege of their trust.

During the period of great change that began with the financial crisis, Desjardins Group saw strong growth of its business in Canada and became very involved in international co-operative development.

As much by conviction as by nature, I exercised leadership based on four principles: inclusion, democracy, transparency and rigour. The implication was that Desjardins' success depended on making full use of all its talent, male and female. We reviewed our compensation practices and our processes for hiring, making appointments, training, and supporting our budding leaders to eliminate any unconscious bias that could prevent women and men from advancing equally.

I knew from experience that having women in leadership positions is not a given, not yet, and that it takes decisive action to move toward parity. We cannot wish for diversity and inclusion in the same way we wish for good weather. We cannot make progress by crossing our fingers. Because habit carries great weight. Because corporate culture conditions behaviours and attitudes without our realizing it. Progress takes strong actions, firm commitments.

In April 2013, at Desjardins Group's Congress, the delegates voted 92 per cent in favour of a commitment to make the proportion of women and men on the boards of directors of caisses reflect the proportion of women and men among the membership of each caisse. It was a bold move, because it did not set parity as an absolute target, but symbiosis between the administration of the caisses and their members. If more women are members, the board should be mainly female. I would remind you that one of the fundamental features of co-operatives is democratic governance. This commitment by the board members of Desjardins Group clearly shows that democratic governance is alive and well and remains an extremely modern value. This stand did not solve everything, but it sent a message that resonated throughout the financial sector.

The co-operative movement is a world leader in promoting gender equality. Moreover, there are a number of women among the senior managers of the Canadian co-operative movement.

The International Co-operative Alliance is fully committed to the UN's 50-50 initiative. And that is a strong voice. The co-operative and mutualist movement represents a force of one billion people in over 100 countries, and businesses with combined sales of more than $3,000 billion. If you doubt the weight of the co-operative and mutualist movement in the world, consider this: if co-operation were a country, it would be among the world's ten largest economic powers. That is the value of the co-operative economy.

To illustrate the co-operative movement's leadership on equality, I would like to quote a recent statistic from the International Cooperative and Mutual Insurance Federation. In 2015, 48 per cent of the world's co-operative and mutual insurers had at least three women directors on their boards, whereas the industry average was just 17 per cent.

### III. WOMEN ARE GROWING THE CO-OPERATIVE MOVEMENT

It is important to point out that performance is not suffering because of this significant presence of women in decision-making positions in co-operatives and mutuals. On the contrary, co-operatives are the business model showing the strongest growth in the world.

We have to send a message. Major corporations need to get on board. Publicly traded companies need to make commitments to their shareholders. Public institutions and governments need to set an example. Normality comes from precedents that are repeated, so we need to set precedents and repeat them.

One of the positions I hold is that of chair of the board of directors of Investissement Québec, which is the Quebec government's main economic development arm. Our board has equal gender representation, like the boards of Quebec's twenty-two government-owned enterprises. Paragraph 2 of section 43 of Quebec's Act respecting the governance of state-owned enterprises is very clear: "that the boards of directors of the enterprises as a group include an equal number of women and men as of 14 December 2011."[3]

In 2007, the Government of Quebec formed the first gender-balanced cabinet. Prime Minister Trudeau did the same thing at the federal level in 2015.

In Ontario, the government recently set targets, aiming to have women make up at least 40 per cent of all appointments to boards of government agencies by 2019. The province is also telling businesses that they have three to five years to appoint at least 30 per cent women to their boards.

These are actions that count. They are actions that exert leverage and have a ripple effect on businesses and institutions by recognizing new talent and having a positive influence on the social, economic, and political ecosystem.

## IV. AN ISSUE OF FAIRNESS, BUT ALSO PROSPERITY

We tend to look at gender parity as an issue of fairness, and that is true. Strictly from a democratic standpoint, it should be a matter of course that half the population exerts half the influence over the conduct of our businesses and institutions.

But we are not there yet. According to various studies, women hold roughly 37 per cent of middle management positions in companies in Canada at present and only 18 per cent of senior management positions. The figures are similar in politics. In Quebec City and Ottawa, women hold only about 30 per cent of seats in our parliaments in any election. The same is true at the municipal level in Quebec. Women make up 30 per cent of municipal officials, but only 17.3 per cent of mayors.[4]

Aren't you surprised that the business world and the various levels of government line up almost perfectly when it comes to women's representation? That should make us sit up and take notice. It reflects Canadian society's persistent inability to put large numbers of women in decision-making positions. Clearly, this is an issue of fairness.

But there is a whole other aspect of this issue that is rarely talked about, and that is the price of women's under-participation. A price women pay personally and a price we all pay as Canadians.

Today in Canada, a woman earns on average $81 for work that will pay her male colleague $100. That is two dollars less than the OECD average. Canada performs poorly relative to the average developed country. This difference of $19 for every $100 earned by a man represents a colossal amount. According to PricewaterhouseCoopers, closing the pay gap between women and men would add $92 billion to Canada's GDP.[5]

But there is more to the issue than all the billions of dollars that are not flowing into our economy: there is all the intelligence we are depriving ourselves of.

Catalyst showed that companies with women in management positions had better results. We read that "Fortune 500 companies with the highest percentages of female directors on their boards reported a 53 per cent higher return on equity than others."[6] This is not because women are better than men, but because they are as good, and when women sit at the decision-making table, an organization has access to all its intelligence.

Here again, I am speaking from experience. I can testify to the strength of gender-diverse teams. How many times have I seen bold men want to move quickly? How many times have I seen prudent women suggest acting over the longer term? The beauty of gender diversity lies in the variety of viewpoints. You will say that I am speaking in stereotypes, but they are not without some basis. A company is a human organization that seeks to meet human needs; it will make better decisions if both genders are involved in the decision-making process.

The equality we all aspire to is not a negation of the differences between women and men, but an appreciation of difference and views.

In a series of studies begun 10 years ago on the theme "Women Matter," the McKinsey Global Institute has also concluded that there is a link between business performance and women's presence at decision-making levels. However, the organization adds an interesting detail: women's presence pays off for a business once a certain critical mass is attained; it takes at least three women on a ten-person management team for a business to reap the benefits of gender diversity. Companies cannot get away with just looking good and having a woman in the executive team photo. Women need to have a real voice.

Here in Canada, as in most developed countries, women's presence at decision-making levels in organizations has not followed the same trajectory as women's presence on university faculties. Think about it for a moment: today women make up the majority in many faculties, and if their influence had increased accordingly, Canada and all the OECD countries would be led by women.

There is a social reason for the fact that women's influence in business has not kept step with their influence in academia: there are fewer women in fields of study that have a reputation for producing the most executives, such as MBA and engineering programs. But that is just a small part of the answer.

We have some extraordinary women with us here: Kim Campbell, the first woman to become prime minister of Canada; Huguette Labelle, the former deputy minister of transport and chancellor of the University of Ottawa; Senator Chantal Petitclerc, one of the greatest athletes in Canadian history; and Senator Joan Fraser, an icon of Canadian journalism.

So many women have put their mark on this country's recent history: Julie Payette, Céline Dion, Heather Munroe-Blum, Louise Arbour, Linda Hasenfratz, Beverley McLachlin . . .

I commend you on your outstanding leadership. You have left an indelible mark on the history of Canada!

In all fields of endeavour, women have cleared the way to the top, giving inspiration to younger generations in the process. But in spite of the many women we can look to as role models and the actions that have been taken – some symbolic, some legislative – the gap separating women and men when it comes to pay and economic and political influence has not yet been closed. How many female astronauts, how many female chief justices, how many women on the podium will it take to achieve full equality? The hard truth is that despite real progress, despite the amazing accomplishments made by countless Canadian women, women still have far less overall influence on our society than men.

Those who believe that doing nothing is the best option and that the movement toward full equality of opportunity will happen on its own should consider this: in a recent study, *Getting to Equal 2017*, Accenture concludes that if we do nothing and rely on people's goodwill, it will be 2168 before the gender pay gap in developed countries is closed.[7]

However, the same study concludes that if young women are encouraged to study math and science and gain skills in digital technology, which they gravitate toward less than young men do, and if they are also taught to manage their careers strategically, which young men do more intuitively, the gender gap could be closed in ten years.

### V. ACTING DECISIVELY

The great Montreal poet Leonard Cohen wrote, "There is a crack in everything, that's how the light gets in."

We are at a point where the model is cracking and we can see the way to full equality of opportunity. But we have to give history a push, because it is being written too slowly.

As legislators, you have a role to play. As influencers, you carry weight. All the business leaders in this country have the ability to effect change.

At the governmental and institutional level, you can act in a very practical way. You can see to it that Crown corporations and all federal government agencies have clear gender-parity targets.

You can also put pressure on securities regulators so that companies make a greater commitment to parity. In the fall of 2014, the securities regulatory authorities in Manitoba, New Brunswick, Nova Scotia, Nunavut, Ontario, Quebec, Saskatchewan, Newfoundland and Labrador, and the Northwest Territories adopted a rule requiring disclosure of the number of women on the boards of publicly traded companies.[8]

This is a small step, but it is a far cry from a firm commitment. Government institutions and regulatory bodies can exert leverage and need to do everything they can to that end. Don't fail in your duty to set a good example and exert influence.

In companies as well, executives have responsibilities. They need to realize that their company's long-term success depends in part on the presence of women in senior management.

Studies unanimously show that three specific conditions must be in place for change to happen.

First, there needs to be a firm commitment at the highest decision-making level; the head of a company and the board of directors need to take responsibility for increasing women's representation in senior management positions.

Second, there needs to be a clear plan, with numerical targets and time frames – three years, five years, ten years – a plan tailored to each company's reality, with a reporting process so that progress can be measured and adjustments made as needed.

Third, this priority needs to be incorporated into all of the company's human resources policies, whether they have to do with hiring, making appointments to senior management positions, channelling talent, or supporting up-and-coming leaders.

In this march toward full equality of opportunity, toward equality in decision-making circles, women too have responsibilities. They need to step up. They need to take ownership of their career and build the self-confidence that men possess more naturally. We talk a great deal about entrepreneurship, and rightly so, but we also need to talk about intrapreneurship, the ability to make one's own way, to set oneself apart.

We all need to get involved. Women and men. We need to make parity a common cause. Political leaders at all levels, business people, educators, social and community organizations: everyone needs to work to the same end.

We need to tell ourselves that we all stand to gain and that we have everything to gain. It is a question of fairness, certainly. We need to realize that it is also an economic issue with extremely important repercussions. It is also a necessity in light of the major challenges we face.

## VI. CHALLENGES OF UNPRECEDENTED COMPLEXITY

We are at a turning point in history. The complexity of the challenges we face is unprecedented.

Think of the huge issue of climate change and the economic, social, and environmental revolution it implies. "Revolution" is not too strong a word. Quebec, for example, has made a commitment to reduce its greenhouse gas emissions by 37.5 per cent compared to 1990 levels by 2030. To that end, it has set five targets, including a 40 per cent reduction in the use of petroleum products. This means reorganizing our cities, changing people's travel habits and rolling out new economic policies in less than 15 years. Faced with this global threat and the imperative of sustainable development, former UN secretary-general Ban Ki-moon made this powerful statement: "There is no plan B, because we do not have a planet B."

Think also about the revolution in mobile digital technology, which is transforming public space and expanding with the promise of artificial intelligence. Montreal and Toronto are among the cities that are emerging as hubs in this futuristic field. Montreal is attracting leading experts and investments from all over the world in the niche known as "deep learning," which has to do with computers that learn almost like humans.

The potential is limitless, from self-driving cars to telemedicine to speech recognition. We stand on the brink of a new world. But at what price? At the World Economic Forum in Davos in January 2016, a study was unveiled that concluded that the robot economy would destroy five million jobs in developed countries by 2020.[9] The spectacular potential progress will come with a social challenge: protecting and reskilling thousands of workers who face the threat of being thrown out of the labour market by technological change.

Lastly, think about the aging population. This is first and foremost a sign of progress, something we too often neglect to say. More women and men are remaining active and healthy as they age because we have done things right. We have improved our living conditions. We have learned to take care of ourselves and others. That is good. Of course, there is the flip side of the coin. In Quebec, since 2013, we have been at a tipping point. Since that year, the number of experienced workers who are retiring each year has exceeded the number of young people who are entering the labour market. This erosion of our labour force is having serious repercussions: increased health care costs, weaker economic growth potential, growing pressure on the public purse with fewer workers to provide the tax revenue to fund services that more people need.

These three fundamental issues – climate change, the technological revolution and the aging population – bring us right back to full participation of women and inclusive leadership.

First, because we need all the available intelligence to make the right decisions so that men and women across the country can move forward and make progress together at this key point in our history.

UNITED STATES-CANADA COUNCIL FOR THE ADVANCEMENT OF WOMEN ENTREPRENEURS AND BUSINESS LEADERS, 13 FEBRUARY 2017, THE WHITE HOUSE

Created in February 2017, at the behest of Prime Minister Justin Trudeau and President Donald J. Trump to promote the recognition of the vital role and potential influence of women in the business community, the Council is composed of ten women business leaders from the United States and Canada. Its role is to provide advice to encourage women's economic engagement, as well as to share inspiring achievements and success stories of women entrepreneurs, with the goal of motivating other women to follow in their footsteps. The Council's goal is to remove the barriers preventing women from providing equal contributions to business development and to prosperity in both countries.
Crédit: Adam Scotti/Prime Minister's Office

Second, because we need everyone to play a part in the success of our society. Achieving full equality of opportunity between women and men should be seen not as an end in itself, but as the decisive and determined step toward truly inclusive leadership. Canada is a generous country that opens its arms to tens of thousands of people every year, that offers unlimited possibilities, but that must keep its promises. I am talking about women and men, side by side, in mutual respect; I am talking about women and men of all backgrounds; I am talking about women and men from all Indigenous nations.

Our challenge is to give newcomers not only a roof over their heads, but an opportunity to contribute to our common future. In Quebec, where the French language is a specific condition of integration, our job is to better integrate newcomers into the labour force. In Quebec and elsewhere in Canada, we will have to find a way to better recognize skills acquired abroad and counter the corporatism that forces many immigrants to take jobs for which they are overqualified or to jump through too many hoops to bring their credentials in line with our rules.

Our Indigenous brothers and sisters are in a different situation that also means they are excluded, which costs Canada dearly. There were the mistakes of the past. There is the unparalleled clash between tradition and modernity. The desire to improve the living conditions of this country's First Peoples should motivate us and lead to avenues of co-operation whereby Indigenous people can play a role in Canada's success, in keeping with their unique identity. We cannot rewrite the past, but we can write our common future every day.

## VII. A MISSION FOR CANADA

Is there a better common cause to embrace than full equality of men and women of all backgrounds? Is there a better example to set for the world than truly inclusive leadership? Is there a better way to honour our international reputation than becoming a beacon of parity and participation?

And why not promote this cause on the world stage? The impact could be transformative.

If, in every country of the world, women held the same place as women in the top countries in their region, $12 trillion would be added to global GDP by 2025. Even better, if women's role were identical to men's, then $28 trillion would be added to the global economy, as much as the GDP of China and the United States combined.[10]

Imagine the economic boom that would result, but also the social impact. Because there is a direct link between women's economic insecurity and all forms of vulnerability: systemic injustice, violence, child poverty. Economic instability is the root of the most serious social problems.

Canada has always been a country of influence in the world. We have fought tyranny in major international conflicts. We have separated combatants, worked for peace, soothed tensions. We have promoted justice, condemned atrocities, eased suffering.

Canada has a long tradition of diplomacy that far outstrips its demographic or economic importance. Canada is practically the world's conscience. And this world, which today is becoming more black and white and is in the throes of ideological entrenchment and disengagement, needs a strong voice for progress, like Canada's.

In the current context, our openness and generosity set us apart. But we can do more than stand for justice and openness. We can do more than open our arms. We can actively promote human dignity and the universal nature of gender equality and inclusive leadership.

No country is in a better position than Canada to promote greater equality globally and make it the key to a more peaceful, more prosperous world.

No issue can better symbolize human progress and faith in the future than the full, generous and engaged participation of women and men of all backgrounds in the operation of a country's institutions and businesses.

That is what an admired country like Canada could advocate for.

That is the mission Canada could take on as we celebrate the 150th anniversary of Confederation: being the staunch promoter of gender equality and inclusive leadership, in order to build a better world together!

### NOTES

1  *Official Report of the Debates, House of Commons of the Dominion of Canada*, Vol. XLIV (Ottawa: S.E. Dawson 1897), 550.

2  Archives of Desjardins Group.

3  Government of Quebec, *Act respecting the governance of state-owned enterprises*, Chapter 1, s. 43, paragraph 2.

4  Government of Quebec, Municipal Affairs and Land Occupancy, 2013 municipal election results.

5  PricewaterhouseCoopers Canada, *PwC Women in Work Index 2016*.

6  Catalyst's Bottom Line Reports, 2007.

7  Accenture, *Getting to Equal 2017*, 3 April 2017.

8  Ontario Securities Commission press release, 15 October 2014.

9  World Economic Forum, *The Future of Jobs*, January 2016.

10  McKinsey Global Institute, "How advancing women's equality can add $12 trillion to global growth," September 2015.

Writing assistance, Patrice Servant.

# 7

# The Environment and the Arctic

# The Environment:
# Denial Is No Longer an Option[1]

The Hon. Serge Joyal, Senator

T he condition of the planet has caught up with the entire world and revealed its moral cowardice.

Over the past fifty years, Canada's perennial illusions about its relationship with the bounty of nature within its borders, the virtually infinite extent of its natural resources and its respect for the environment have been repeatedly shattered. Canada has been living in denial, deluding itself that it values its 31,752 freshwater lakes[2] and with the fact that 10.5 per cent of its land mass and 0.96 per cent of its waters have been protected by being designated national parks, wildlife preserves, marine protected areas or sanctuaries for rare animal species.[3] But the fact is that Canada's apparently clean conscience disguises its predatory side as an unfettered despoiler of natural resources. And this has been true since Jacques Cartier first explored this country in 1534, when he thought he had stumbled on a source of diamonds that would make him rich and allow him to repay the cost of his voyage to France's King François I.

By essentially focusing on the development of its many natural resources, from its earliest occupation and colonization, first in the fur trade and fishing, then in logging and mining of all kinds, and finally in the extraction of fossil fuels (the oil and gas industry), water and strategic materials (uranium), Canadians led themselves to believe that the tapping of Canada's exceptional wealth of natural resources had no impact and did not generate toxic waste that would find its way into the air, water, or soil, and that nature was capable of regenerating itself. The fundamental myth is that one just has to go a little farther north to find more resources and continue to reap their benefits, as the reserve of resources is essentially infinite.[4]

Is Canada not home to nearly one quarter of the world's pristine forests, one quarter of its wetlands, one fifth of its freshwater resources, and nearly one third of its *coastlines?[5] This overabundance of riches creates the myth that these resources are inexhaustible and can be exploited forever.*

*This Janus-like Canadian persona – smiling on one side as it holds nature and its wide-open spaces to be sacred; grim on the other side as a thirsty profiteer exploiting natural resources – is a fair representation of the inherent contradictions of this country since it was settled by the first Europeans. However, the gap between perception and reality certainly widened with the advent of the modern consumer society in the post-war era. The way of life of Canadians leaves some of the worst ecological footprints of the planet. According to Global Footprint Network, Canada ranks fifth behind the United States.[6]*

*The Department of the Environment was created in 1971 to generally protect the biosphere. This was before the concept of sustainable development appeared, in 1980,[7] and before it was popularized by the Bruntland Commission, in 1987.[8] It was also before people realized that the planet is a delicately balanced ecosystem that cannot be disturbed without consequences that can quickly become seriously harmful to human life and health.*

*In July 2017, a huge iceberg (A68) calved from the Larsen C section of the Larsen Ice Shelf in Antarctica, potentially weakening the ice shelf. The iceberg's surface area was 5,800 square kilometres, as large as Prince Edward Island and eleven times the size of the Island of Montreal, and its thickness varied between 250 metres and 700 metres. Similar calving events occurred in 1995 (Larsen A) and 2002 (Larsen B). The ice shelf has been holding back Antarctic glaciers that, if they were to melt, would raise sea levels significantly, with all the consequences that would entail.*

*In Yukon, accelerated melting of the terminus of the Kaskawulsh Glacier caused the Slims River to the southwest to dry up. The small lake at its source drained into another watercourse! As journalist Marie Tison noted, receding glaciers could have repercussions for other watercourses and mountain lakes in northwestern North America.[9] If global warming continues at this pace, all of the ski resorts along the British Columbia coast will close their doors well before the end of this century.*

*The boreal forest, a treasure of Canadian nature, is also seriously endangered, according to the magazine* Nature Communications: *it will be witness to an accelerated growth of the tress, followed by a rapid decline.[10]*

*Global warming is definitely being felt all over the world, and Canada is one of those adding to the problem. A recent United Nations Environment Programme report is chilling.[11] Unless countries ramp up their efforts considerably, the target of reducing greenhouse gas (GHG) emissions enough to keep global warming below two degrees Celsius will be unattainable, and this will have dire consequences for life on Earth.*

MOUNT SIR DONALD AND THE ILLECILLEWAET GLACIER
Postcard, The Valentine & Sons Publishing Co. Ltd., Montreal and Toronto
Climate change has dramatically changed Canada's ecosystem by causing the large glaciers that cover the highest peaks in the Rockies to melt more quickly. The ecology as a whole is disrupted. This photograph taken in the early 20th century clearly shows the Illecillewaet Glacier. Today this glacier has retreated by several hundred metres. Credit: CHSJ

*According to the latest available data, the last three years were the warmest on record: the planet is warming even faster than expected.[12]*

*In the 1960s, scientists were already aware of the devastating effects pollution was having on certain animal species and in the atmospheric condition of the planet, and they began measuring the impact of unbridled natural resource development. Thirty years ago, immediate action could have been taken that would have prevented the accelerated deterioration of the ozone layer, but the Americans' lack of political leadership, the inability of scientists to agree on an action plan, and the effective lobbying of major oil companies stalled the interventions that would have prevented the ecological disaster now facing us.[13]*

*A succession of ecological disasters here and abroad, however, regularly shook public opinion and clearly revealed Canada's ambivalent position on the environment. Canada cleans up damage when it occurs, often at the last minute, but its everyday resource exploitation activities are allowed to continue essentially unabated. Canada would rather clean up the messes after the fact, using taxpayer dollars, of course.*

*Accordingly, waterfront cities released wastewater containing phosphates from domestic cleaning products into the Great Lakes. The resulting proliferation of algae led to the realization, in 1968, that the entire St. Lawrence corridor was contaminated. In the 1970s, the toxicity of nuclear waste reared its ugly head in Port Hope, Ontario, forcing the entire town to undergo decontamination. The policy governing the disposal of nuclear waste is still today much criticized by the public.[14]*

*Yet a dire warning signal had already been received in 1952, when the NRX nuclear reactor in Chalk River had a partial-core meltdown. Less than 20 years later, a somewhat naive proposal was put forward to bury radioactive waste 1.2 kilometres from the shores of Lake Huron, in the municipality of Kincardine, Ontario (the site of the Bruce Power nuclear plant). Bitter protests were mounted, and it was decided instead to bury this waste as far away as possible, in the Far North, thereby contaminating that entire region for generations to come.*

*Uranium mining operations near Great Bear Lake in the Northwest Territories ultimately resulted in the contamination of that lake, thus harming the Indigenous peoples residing along its shores.*

*Underground testing of nuclear weapons by the United States Army on Amchitka, a volcanic island in southwestern Alaska, spawned protests in Vancouver in 1971 that ultimately gave birth to the Greenpeace movement. Today, this NGO has 2.9 million members and is active in more than forty countries. The full extent of the environmental destruction caused by nuclear testing subsequently became known.*

*When oil spilled in Vancouver harbour in 1973 and created a slick that washed ashore on Ambleside Beach (in West Vancouver) and in some areas of Stanley Park, local residents came face to face with the environmental damage and harm such accidents can do to wildlife and human health.*

*The Mackenzie Valley Pipeline Inquiry, headed by Justice Thomas R. Berger from 1974 to 1977, produced 204 volumes of studies and seventy-seven volumes of hearing transcripts. Hearings were held for the first time in the Far North, where Indigenous communities could easily participate. The results of this inquiry changed public opinion about the supposed safety of transporting oil by pipeline. The inquiry's findings effectively put an end to the project. From 2010 to 2015, the Transportation Safety Board of Canada recorded 8,144 "accidents" and "incidents" involving rail transportation of petroleum products, and 875 such events involving pipeline transportation of those products. While obviously fewer in number, the latter caused far more extensive damage than the former. The Lac-Mégantic rail accident in July 2013, which killed forty-seven people and destroyed the Quebec town's entire downtown core, is still fresh in the memories of many. Moreover, the town has yet to rebuild.*

*It took the devastation of forests and farm fields by acid rain that was caused by air pollution from industrial activities, often located thousands of kilometres away from the damage, for people to suddenly realize that pollution is a problem for every country. In the 1970s, INCO built a "superstack" in Sudbury, Ontario, to filter out and capture residues. However, it had the perverse effect of dispersing industrial mine waste well beyond the Sudbury area, causing damage over an even wider area and complicating the task of capturing the pollutants that cause acid rain.*

*Pollutants travel much farther than one might think. DDT and PCBs have been found in blood and tissue samples from Indigenous peoples in the Arctic. This revelation forced people to stop pretending that dispersing pollutants into the atmosphere was equivalent to magically making them disappear or sending them into some sort of "Neverland" out of reach.*

*The hydroelectric megaprojects of the 1970s also had a considerable impact, creating huge reservoirs that put millions of hectares of forest land under water. This resulted in the release of GHGs – primarily methane – just as toxic as any produced by heavy industry. While the 1973 James Bay Hydroelectric Development was a marvel of engineering, the cost of its atmospheric environmental footprint must be taken into account.*

*Farming is also contributing to the problem. Neonicotinoid pesticides and other similar substances like glyphosate, used in farming, are now found in the food chain and in substantial concentrations in watercourses, posing a threat to all farming operations. The Pest Management Regulatory Agency (PMRA) has known their potentially harmful nature for a long time but has given them a conditional authorization for fifteen years, which expired in 2016, and does not propose to ban them before three to five years.[15] The agency is not concerned about the precautionary principle.*

*Groundwater and stream contamination caused by swine manure, first noted in 1978, has become a problem of critical proportions. A hog produces 10 times more fecal matter than a human being. In 2016, Canada slaughtered nearly 21.3 million hogs for commercial purposes.[16]*

*Major agricultural or industrial projects always have consequences. They leave a deep environmental footprint in the soil, the water or the air.*

*The cement plant in Port-Daniel–Gascons, Quebec, which opened on 25 September 2017, will generate 1.76 million tonnes of GHGs annually once it is operating at full capacity. These emissions will certainly need to be offset elsewhere, if only to keep overall GHG emissions at their current level. Yet this issue was never considered before the operating permits required by the authorities were issued.[17]*

*Storing waste in landfills, warehouses or remote areas creates the illusion that sub-urbanites need not worry about it. However, in 1988 a fire in a makeshift PCB storage facility in Saint-Basile-le-Grand, near Montreal, revealed just how dangerous this waste can be.*

*Abandoned mines and industrial sites are genuine disasters. In the Far North, for example, cleaning up the 21 abandoned sites of the Distant Early Warning (DEW) Line, a relic of the Cold War era now threatening the health of Indigenous people, will cost approximately $575 million.[18] Private dumps filled with hazardous waste, such as the Recyclage Aluminium Québec facility containing 360,000 tonnes of residue from aluminum production, which the now-defunct company abandoned in 2003, are equally problematic. This is one of too many examples of the risks and costs that the government and, as usual, taxpayers, must bear, invariably at the expense of other public priorities. In this particular case, the estimated cleanup cost is between $40 million and $80 million. It has become urgent to request financial guarantees based on the risk*

LAC-MÉGANTIC DISASTER, JULY 2013

The derailment of 72 tanker cars in downtown Lac-Mégantic on 6 July 2013 caused the deaths of 47 people when 63 of the cars exploded and a huge fire destroyed the town. Transporting oil by rail poses the risk of much greater damage than moving it by pipeline, because accidents often result in enormous conflagrations. These rail lines criss-cross the country, spreading the risk everywhere. Every year, 875 accidents and incidents are reported to the Transportation Safety Board.
Credit: The Canadian Press/Paul Chiasson

*assessment of companies whose activities may cause serious environmental damage that would have to be paid by taxpayers.[19]*

*Often, the drinking water supply takes the hit. That was the case in 2000 in the town of Walkerton, Ontario, whose drinking water was contaminated with* E. coli *bacteria, causing an outbreak of illness. Likewise, in the Ontario community of Grassy Narrows, Indigenous families have been dealing with the terrible effects of mercury poisoning for more than 50 years.*

*Canada's fish and wildlife resources are not inexhaustible. This realization has come back to haunt us time and time again. More than a century ago in Western Canada, from 1880 to 1890, bison were hunted to near-extinction. But the lesson learned there was long forgotten by the time of the 1981 salmon crisis in Restigouche, Quebec, and the 1992 cod crisis, when the entire commercial cod fishery was placed under moratorium, devastating the economy of the Maritime provinces. In 2000, a moratorium had to be imposed on all commercial salmon fisheries in Eastern Canada.[20]*

*Threatened species, such as orcas of the Salish Sea off the coast of British Columbia, or belugas and right whales in the Gulf of St. Lawrence (which are down to only 525 individuals), are dying from collisions with ship hulls, from becoming entrapped in fishing nets, or from ingesting the toxic waste that has found its way into the St. Lawrence. Such were the results of the necropsies performed on about 10 of the 17 right whales found dead in the summer of 2017.*

*Faced with ongoing public pressure and the Marine Stewardship Council's threat to close the US market to Canadian fish products, the federal government finally agreed, in the spring of 2018, to establish vessel speed limits and close fishing areas when right whales enter the waters of the gulf.[21] This was not a popular decision among lobster and crab fishers.[22] The government also imposed approach-distance limits for threatened or endangered marine mammals throughout the St. Lawrence estuary.[23] It should also intervene to save the orcas of the West Coast seriously at risk of extinction.[24]*

*The amount of waste produced by consumer society is reaching staggering proportions. Worldwide, 8.3 billion tonnes of plastics were produced between 1950 and 2015; of that amount, 6.3 billion tonnes are not meaningfully biodegradable. According to a study by* Nature Communications *published last year, the rivers of the world spill in the oceans between 1.15 and 2.41 million tons of plastic every year, a rate of about 50 kilos per second.[25] All this plastic is also a major source of greenhouse gases (GHGs) through the effect of solar radiation.[26]*

*The microplastics in cosmetics, toothpastes, and several other seemingly innocuous products are just as harmful, if not more so, because they create the impression that they will disappear more easily, when in fact they are more insidiously absorbed by aquatic or animal wildlife.*[27] *According to a recent US study, more than 10,000 tonnes of plastics are dumped into the Great Lakes each year, and this waste subsequently spreads throughout the St Lawrence water system.*[28] *These billions of tonnes of discarded plastics wind up floating around in the oceans until they reach other continents. While plastic may be inexpensive to produce, its cost to the environment is enormous. Canada wants to convince its G7 partners to sign a pledge to stop plastics from entering the oceans.*[29] *While this aim is commendable, it is plastic itself that must be reduced or even eliminated if the goal is truly lasting change.*[30] *At the same time, electronic waste is accumulating at breakneck speed: the cellular telephones, computers, and other electronic devices that people regularly discard can end up in landfills and be harmful to human health in the*

## HI. I'M THAT MARGARINE TUB YOU THREW OUT IN 1989

MARGARINE TUB – "SLOGANS FOR THE TWENTY-FIRST CENTURY"

Douglas Coupland, *Margarine, Slogans for the Twenty-First Century*, Digital proof mounted on diabond, 2011-16. Every year, 10,000 tonnes of plastic enters the Great Lakes and flows down the St Lawrence corridor to the ocean, where it pollutes the rest of the planet and creates greenhouse gases under the heat of sun rays. Microplastics are the most insidious because they are used in cosmetics and even toothpastes. They are easily absorbed by fish and marine birds, contaminating the food chain.

Credit: By kind permission of the artist and the Daniel Faria Gallery, Toronto

*long run. In 2016, 44.7 million metric tonnes of electric and electronic equipment were discarded, an 8 per cent increase over 2014 according to a report from the International Telecommunication Union. The scrap value of all the metals in this equipment was $55 billion. The industry should be recovering these old devices to mitigate all sorts of contamination, but it is not required to do so.[31] According to the Conference Board of Canada, this country produces 25 million tonnes of garbage each year – more per capita than any other country.[32] Indeed, figures from the Organisation for Economic Co-operation and Development (OECD) indicate that the amount of domestic waste produced by Canadian households increased by 30 per cent between 2002 and 2014!*

*The media regularly report on major disasters elsewhere in the world: the Three Mile Island nuclear accident (1979, Pennsylvania, US), the Bhopal disaster (1984, Madhya Pradesh, India), the thinning of the ozone layer (confirmed in 1985), the Chernobyl nuclear disaster (1986, Pripyat, Ukraine), the Exxon Valdez oil spill (1989, Alaska, US), the Fukushima nuclear accident (2011, Japan),[33] lead contamination of the city of Flint's entire drinking water supply (the Flint water crisis, 2014-2016, Michigan, US)[34] and the recent sinking of the Iranian-owned tanker* Sanchi *(14 January 2018, in the China Sea). All these disasters are damaging to the planet, and their impact is ultimately felt here in Canada.*

*On 19 October 2017, a major study published in the prestigious British medical journal* The Lancet *generated headlines to the effect that pollution kills more people than wars and famines. The study found that "[o]ne out of every six premature deaths in the world in 2015 – about 9 million – could be attributed to disease from toxic exposure."[35] It also found that the percentage of premature deaths caused by pollution was 24.5 per cent in India, 19.5 per cent in China, 5.7 per cent in the US and 5.3 per cent in Canada.*

*These pollution-related deaths and their effects on the physical and mental health of surviving individuals could one day serve as grounds for legal action against governments pursuant to section 7 of the* Canadian Charter of Rights and Freedoms, *which protects the right to life, liberty and security of the person.[36] Such a challenge was successfully launched in the Netherlands and resulted in the first-ever condemnation of a government for inaction on climate change.[37] In January 2018, a Norwegian court found that article 112 of the Norwegian constitution, which states that "[e]very person has a right to an environment that is conducive to health and to a natural environment whose productivity and diversity are maintained," is legally binding. The court held that this is a genuine right, not merely a nice principle.[38] Canada's courts should draw on these precedents. In a decision of 22 June 2018 in the Canadian Federal Court,[39] protecting an endangered species, Judge René Leblanc reminded us that biodiversity is a common concern for humanity, and the protection of the environment a fundamental value. He wrote that today there is "a universal legal concept whereby wildlife species and ecosystems are part of the world's heritage."[40] This judicial recognition should constitute a precedent that can pave the way for decisions much more sensitive to the protection of the human condition endangered by environmental degradation.[41]*

*For both humans and the economy, the truth is a hard pill to swallow: according to the World Bank, Canada ranked 152nd in terms of terrestrial and marine protected areas as a percentage of total land area in 2014, and 82nd in terms of protected forest area in 2015.[42] Canada has a terrible record compared with its G7 partners, with only 10.6 per cent of its total land area protected as of late 2016. Under the plan produced pursuant to the United Nations Convention on Biological Diversity, the target is 17 per cent of land and inland waters by 2020.[43] Canada protects only 1 per cent of its oceans. This is certainly not the exemplary leadership portrayed in Canada's lofty, heartfelt rhetoric! Canadians like to believe that Canada is a "green" country. This illusion is dangerous because it implies that the country simply needs to stay the course: maximizing resource exploitation and trumpeting mini-measures as though they were heroic decisions.*

*For instance, Canada's largest national park, Wood Buffalo National Park (a UNESCO World Heritage Site straddling the border between northern Alberta and the southern Northwest Territories), is facing threats to its ecology and wildlife because of the Site C dam hydroelectric project in British Columbia. In 2017, a group of scientists commissioned by UNESCO warned Canada that the park would lose its World Heritage Site status unless the group's seventeen recommendations were implemented.[44]*

*On four different occasions since 1991, Canada has made an international commitment to reduce its GHG emissions: at the Rio Summit in 1992, at the Kyoto Summit in 2005, in Copenhagen in 2012 and, finally, in Paris in 2015. Yet it has never come close to reaching its targets. According to the federal environment commissioner, Canada is currently emitting approximately 230 million tonnes too much, taking into account the continuing increases in GHG emissions in the natural resource sectors.[45] Canada has adopted only two regulations to reach its GHG emission targets, and its oversight of polluting industries (oil and gas) has been a failure. Canada produces more emissions than any OECD country, besides the US and Australia.*

*According to the report Canada submitted in December 2017 in compliance with the* United Nations Framework Convention on Climate Change *(UNFCCC), the country's GHG emissions have increased so much that it is now farther away from its 2030 target of 523 megatonnes. The gap went from 44 megatonnes to 66 megatonnes. The minister responsible indicated that this increase was due to economic growth projections in the oil and gas sector and population growth.[46] The report confirmed that oil production would continue to increase between now and 2030, reaching nearly six million barrels a day, including 4.2 million barrels from the oil sands. What this means is that Canada is continuing to drift away from its commitments under the Paris Agreement.*

*Canada continues to ease its conscience by boasting about its continuing leadership in both economic growth and environmental policy. But to be truly serious, Canada would have to go back to the drawing board. Otherwise, it is pretending to have the situation well in hand while in fact continuing to behave in a manner that undermines sustainable development.*

*Canada has signed numerous international treaties and agreements over the years: the* Great Lakes Water Quality Agreement *(1972), the* Convention on International Trade in Endangered Species of Wild Fauna and Flora *(1973), the* Convention on Long-range Transboundary Air Pollution *(1979), the important* United Nations Convention on the Law of the Sea *(1982), the* Montreal Protocol on Substances that Deplete the Ozone Layer *(1987), the* Canada-US Arctic Cooperation Agreement *(1988), the* Protocol on Environmental Protection to the Antarctic Treaty *(1991), the three Rio conventions (namely, the* Convention on Biological Diversity, *the* United Nations Framework Convention on Climate Change *and the* United Nations Convention to Combat Desertification, *1992-1994), the* Kyoto Protocol *(1997) and the* Paris Agreement *(COP 21) (2015). The newly elected US government, however, decided to withdraw from this last agreement in June 2017, much as the previous Canadian government pulled out of the Kyoto Accord in 2011 and the Convention to Combat Desertification in 2013. So nothing is ever set in stone. To its credit, the current Canadian government decided to restore Canada's signature to the Convention to Combat Desertification in 2017.*

*In 2001, the Canadian government published* The Millennium Ecosystem Assessment, *which sought to determine what effects ecosystem changes will have on human well-being. While the desired intent was certainly broad in scope, it was subjected to pressures from the oil and gas industry and the forest industry, which are still among the cornerstones of Canada's economic wealth, and whose appetite for profit limits Canadian commitments to reducing environmental impacts. In addition, governments and their agencies are often complicit with these resource industries. In July 2017, the government announced an action plan to protect the boreal caribou (a species found in seven provinces and two territories that has been listed as threatened since 2003) after legal action was undertaken against the environment minister.*[47] *In August of that same year, the National Energy Board approved a pipeline extension through threatened caribou habitat because the pipeline was considered in Canada's interest.*[48]

BOREAL CARIBOU

Associated with the image of a Canada that, to a large segment of the public, is an immense zoo where the animals roam free, boreal caribou are the magical symbol of Christmas, supposedly waiting quietly in the Far North to pull Santa's sleigh and land on people's rooftops. However, the truth is that this species has been threatened since 2003 and its habitat is being disrupted by the extension of federally approved gas pipelines and mining exploration, which, according to governments, serve Canada's interests.
Credit: milehightraveler (Getty Images)

*In October, a government report concluded that more had to be done because the species was continuing to decline owing to the growing disturbances to its habitat.[49]*

*Furthermore, the government acknowledged in Federal Court that the department of the environment simply does not have enough staff or resources to enforce the* Species at Risk Act (SARA) *and thus protect woodland caribou and other threatened species in Canada.[50]*

*Likewise, in June 2018 the federal government approved the Akasaba West Copper-Gold Mine Project near Val d'Or, Quebec, at the very heart of the natural habitat of a herd of threatened caribou. It did so despite an unfavourable report from the province's environmental consultations office, the Bureau d'audiences publiques sur l'environnement (BAPE), and the project's substantial cumulative effects on the ability of Indigenous peoples to engage in their traditional hunting and gathering activities in the area.[51]*

*Meanwhile, in November 2017 Quebec established a protected area for woodland caribou in the Manicouagan area, but at the same time authorized mining operations for another decade.*

*Sometimes the provinces are unable to enforce their own legislation: although widely recognized, the massive dumping of contaminated soil into the natural environment in Quebec could not be prosecuted because, according to the Crown, it was an insurmountable task in the current context.[52]*

*It sometimes seems that progress is being made, but without reducing the impact on the environment at all![53]*

*There is no more disappointing and, unfortunately, convincing example of the political contortions the Canadian government does every day when it comes to the environment. On the one hand, it takes action when forced to by the courts; on the other, it undoes the virtuous cloth with which it cloaks itself. Only the government has the power to take the steps necessary to create a green economy, which must be the way of the future for an industrialized country whose standard of living depends on its ability to adapt and to make the most of all that new green technologies have to offer.*

*What is needed is the kind of leadership that can recognize how much of an effort is required and establish tangible goals. Examples have been set by countries such as France and the United Kingdom, which partnered with Canada in the new European free trade agreement. Both these countries have decided to ban the sale of diesel- and gasoline-powered engines within their borders as of 2040. Industry will have to adapt by then. Germany has set 2030 as its target, while the Netherlands has opted for 2035, and Norway, 2025. China's fifth-largest automobile manufacturer, BAIC, will stop selling combustion engines in Beijing by 2019 and in the rest of the country by 2025. The decline of the combustion engine is already in progress.[54] Comparable legislation is expected from the European Union.[55] Furthermore, EU parliamentarians have adopted a goal of "carbon neutrality" by 2050.[56] The Netherlands recently decided to ban the use of coal, which accounts for 40 per cent of worldwide carbon dioxide emissions, and to transition to renewable energy sources. Sweden passed an ambitious piece of climate legislation that commits it to achieving carbon neutrality by 2045.[57] This legislation came into effect on 1 January 2018.*

*These examples of leadership from countries as industrialized as Canada clearly demonstrate that governments truly motivated by the fight against GHGs can take strong actions that send clear signals and show the way to the future. The problem with Canadian leadership is that it often straddles the middle and rarely risks losing political capital. It prefers to be pulled along by others who champ at the bit. This is distressing and, to some degree, threatens the health of Canadians and the future of the country. Justin Trudeau's government, which was expected to change the targets set by its predecessor (30 per cent below the 2005 level by 2030), instead adopted them, even though the prime minister boasted during COP21 that "Canada is back" in the environmental protection fight.*[58] *The office of French President Emmanuel Macron had good reason to declare in December 2017 that it was expecting more of an effort from Canada.*[59]

*To everyone's surprise, in May 2018 the Trudeau government decided to purchase the Trans Mountain Pipeline from the Canadian division of the US-based company Kinder Morgan for C$4.5 billion.*[60] *It plans to proceed on its own with the pipeline expansion project, at a projected cost of $9.3 billion,*[61] *even though the project may not turn a profit.*[62]

*When the* UN *General Assembly adjourned on 24 December 2017, 140 member states approved the opening of negotiations toward an international treaty to protect biodiversity on the high seas. This proposed treaty would be appended to the Law of the Sea Convention that was adopted in 1982.*[63] *Canada should take the lead in these negotiations, just as it should ramp up its efforts alongside the forty countries that pledged in late 2017 to stop using coal.*

*About 100 major companies that extract and use fossil fuels are responsible for more than 70 per cent of all* GHG *emissions caused by human activity, according to a report prepared by the UK-based Carbon Disclosure Project. Over a period of twenty-eight years (from 1988 to 2015), the activities of those companies produced as many* GHG *emissions as were produced in the previous 231 years combined (from 1757 to 1988).*

*At this rate, the planet could be as much as four degrees Celsius warmer in another twenty-eight years. According to the International Energy Agency, global energy demand is expected to increase by 23 per cent by the year 2040, at a rate of approximately 1 per cent per year.*

*Last summer, newspaper headlines called 2016 another dark year for the Earth's climate.*[64] *Rising sea levels and* GHG *emissions reached new highs last year. On 13 November 2017, more than 15,000 scientists from 184 countries signed a joint manifesto warning that "a great change in our stewardship of the Earth and the life on it is required, if vast human misery is to be avoided."*[65]

*Canada therefore faces an enormous challenge. It blows hot with environmental protection measures while blowing cold with approvals to build oil and gas pipelines – three permits issued in recent years: Enbridge expansion projects (2014–15), Trans Mountain (2016) and Keystone XL (2007–10) – as well as oil and gas exploration licences in marine protected areas. In fact, in June 2017 the government granted an exploration licence for an area at the mouth of the Gulf of St. Lawrence, south of Newfoundland, contrary to a federal scientific study advising against it because of the foreseeable ecological and biological impacts of such a project. As the fisheries minister genially pointed out, "the effect of oil exploration and production on fish, marine mammals and sea turtles is considered reversible due to the species' behaviour." In other words, fish can be pushed to swim elsewhere, but they will come back when the time is right – it's all water!*

*The previous government's fisheries minister decided to scuttle a proposal for a marine protected area in a large section of the St Lawrence estuary (the only one in Quebec among six areas of interest across the country) in order to ease the way for an oil terminal project.[66] Yet in Nagoya, Japan, Canada made a commitment to protect 10 per cent of its marine areas by the year 2020. Canada currently protects 1.3 per cent of those areas, which is less than countries such as China and Russia.[67]*

*In June 2018, the governments of Canada and Quebec agreed to designate the American Bank, which covers 1,000 square kilometres east of the Gaspé Peninsula, a marine protected area. However, it is the entire St. Lawrence ecosystem that needs to be protected, while allowing for fisheries and marine transportation.[68] In so doing, the Canadian government could honour the commitments it made in Nagoya.*

*Lastly, in October 2017 the Caisse de dépôt et placement du Québec, the public pension fund that manages a global portfolio worth $286.5 billion funded by all Quebeckers, decided to limit its investments in fossil fuels, including coal.[69] Until then, the government's left hand was content to ignore the environmental goals touted at every opportunity by its right hand, namely, the environment minister. It is not unheard of for public agencies to be complicit in undermining their own government's objectives in the fight against climate change. Hence, the federal government sent out feelers to the Canada Pension Plan Investment Board (CPPIB) about the possibility of contributing to the acquisition of the Trans Mountain Pipeline. The chair of the CPPIB expressed some interest, provided a decent rate of return could be assured.[70] Clearly, oil money is as good as any other kind! CPPIB already owns an important share in* Enhance Energy *pipeline. For instance, OMERS, the pension funds of the Ontario municipal employees, one of the largest in Canada, has recently bought an important stake in* Bridge Tex, *a Texas pipeline.[71]*

*In December 2017 in Paris, the World Bank decided to stop financing oil and gas projects.[72]*

*Only a few of the five hundred biggest portfolio managers on the planet are currently taking tangible steps to mitigate climate change risk within their portfolios. This "portfolio decarbonization" process was undertaken in the fall of 2017 by the FTQ's Solidarity Fund,[73] and some thirty institutional investors have followed suit.[74] In Canada, however, 40 per cent of institutional investors are either averting their eyes or sitting on their hands.[75]*

*There is no moratorium on extractive industry growth, other than the five-year ban on new Arctic exploration licences ordered by the federal government in 2016.[76] The US, meanwhile, at the insistence of President Obama, adopted a policy not to grant future offshore oil and gas concessions in most US Arctic waters for an indefinite period. The current US administration, however, sees things rather differently.*

*European countries have also made major decisions on the use of nuclear power. France plans to shut down one third of its nuclear reactors by 2025 as it begins transitioning to other energy sources. Canada, which created and started marketing the CANDU reactor some fifty-five years ago, is by no means ready to get out of the nuclear industry, even though it is a staunch defender of nuclear non-proliferation.*

*While the federal government supports energy conversion and transition and claims to champion a green economy, it also greenlights all sorts of exploration and extraction projects, making any contemplated transition that much more difficult. At best, when it is not acquiring pipelines, the government relies on the private sector and, sometimes blindly, hopes private business will shift toward real sustainable development. Yet a major spike in oil prices, similar to what occurred twice in the 1970s, would be sufficient to roll back any progress to date and give new impetus to oil sands development.[77] Current projections indicate that oil sands production will continue to rise. In 2030, it is expected that 475 million more barrels will be extracted annually for export to foreign markets.[78]*

*The federal government is proposing to revamp its environmental assessment process by combining its three agencies into a single assessment authority that would be wholly independent from regulated sectors and would take into account upstream and downstream impacts of projects on human health and the economy, as well as their social repercussions.[79]*

*In fact, a better strategy would be to first determine what overall changes Canada's energy industry needs to make in order to reach the country's carbon reduction targets, and then to measure the effect of proposed projects on Canada's carbon footprint. Any project that would significantly increase that footprint would necessarily have to include offsetting measures elsewhere in the overall planning scheme so as to maintain or even significantly reduce Canada's carbon emissions.*

*The federal government's national carbon pricing policy is certainly, in principle, a step in the right direction. However, as the OECD notes, its practical implementation will be a colossal challenge, and Canada will have no choice but to do more.[80] The proposed pricing, however, favours large emitters of GHGs, who also receive subsidies. Hence the impact of the legislation will remain far less than it should be.[81] The upward revision of the acceptable thresholds, announced in August 2018, is not the only adjustment to come.[82] The carbon tax of $20 per tonne, which is to apply on January 1, 2019, until it reaches $ 50 in 2022, is now challenged.*

*Ontario's withdrawal from the carbon emission trading system, officially announced in July 2018 by the Ford government, its decision to challenge the federal carbon tax in a reference to its Court, its joining of Saskatchewan's April 2018 legal action challenging the federal jurisdiction to impose the tax,[83] are already hampering the effectiveness of the national plan.[84] In August 2018, the government of Alberta announced its decision to pull out of the national carbon plan after the federal Court of Appeal quashed the approval of* Trans Mountain *pipeline following its challenge by West Coast aboriginal nations.[85] Two other provinces, Newfoundland and Labrador, and Prince Edward Island, have also expressed opposition to the federal carbon tax.*

*The government should be much more proactive in informing the public of the positive impact of its plan; but its credibility flounders since its purchase of the* Trans Mountain *pipeline.[86] The agreement signed between Canada, the United Kingdom, and four other countries to create the first common carbon market, following the Paris Agreement on climate change, is an important step in the right direction that deserves to be better explained to the public, to demonstrate that solutions must be shared by the responsible countries to deal with a global problem,[87] even if the United States has decided to withdraw. Canada must stay the course with its international partners[88] and counter the setbacks that the Trump administration[89] would like to impose on it by revising the emissions of vehicles that had previously been agreed upon for 2022–25[90] by the previous American president.*

*Canada has always kept Indigenous peoples out of environmental policy-making and implementation, even when it comes to designating national parks. This was true as far back as 1885, when Banff National Park was created. Indeed, several Indigenous nations even had their lands taken from them during the development of the national parks system and are now seeking to recover their ancestral rights. In 1974, the Ojibway occupied Anicinabe Park, near Kenora, Ontario. In 1995, the Ipperwash crisis resulted in the death of Ojibway protester Dudley George, an event that remains fresh in Canadians' memories. Indigenous peoples are always forced to go to court (e.g.,* R. v. Sundown, *1999) or to hold public demonstrations to prevent the government from unilaterally creating or enlarging parks, including those of Pukaskwa, Point Pelee, Wager Bay and Great Slave Lake.[91]*

*Yet the Indigenous peoples are closest to the land. Their civilizations, languages, and mythologies are rooted in their on-the-ground experience. It would thus be highly appropriate to involve Indigenous peoples and guarantee them a role in environmental assessments and in the management of natural resources. Their understanding is essential to the process of making the sorely needed changes to the current approach – an approach that puts resource extraction ahead of respect for ecosystems and their renewal.[92]*

*Without such changes, Canada will be trapped in a sort of schizophrenic situation, implementing one policy and acting contrary simultaneously. Governments are imposing a carbon tax to promote the use of clean energy while issuing new fossil fuel extraction licences and approving the construction of new oil and gas pipelines that will add to the global carbon footprint. This is not a political zero-sum game! Canada cannot continue to increase its carbon emissions indefinitely and propose only partial offsetting measures while believing it will reach its emissions reduction targets. It is rather magical thinking!*

*Canada's environmental policy is not just horizontal. The 10 provincial governments and three territorial governments also sometimes pursue contradictory environmental objectives within their own legislative and regulatory contexts. For these governments, natural resource development contributes substantially to economic development objectives. No forum or institution exists to make legislation and policies more coherent across both levels of government. Federal leadership certainly needs to be reoriented in order to guarantee consistency across environmental initiatives. The approaches taken by the provinces have the same failings as the federal government's approach: contradictory objectives that do not reduce the overall negative impact on the environment, despite all the professed best intentions.[93] Article 92A of the Constitution recognizes the provinces' fundamental control over natural resources. Indeed, provincial governments earn $27 billion in revenue from natural resources annually.[94] They are not prepared to part with this prize, no matter how much green rhetoric they may spout.*

*No one should kid themselves: without more-serious efforts and the kind of clear-eyed leadership needed to actually reach the objectives Canada has agreed to on the international stage, the country's environmental policy will always be lame and even misleading. The transition to other sources of energy is a huge challenge. In order to make that transition by 2050, Canada must halve its overall oil, natural gas, and coal consumption, even as its population grows substantially.*

*First, Canada must decide to put an end to all use of fossil fuels in the Arctic. Second, the granting of all new fossil fuel development and transportation permits must be tied to offsetting GHG emission reductions elsewhere in the economy. Lastly, effective carbon dioxide capturing measures must be implemented, like its transformation into a product with "market value," thus preventing it release in the atmosphere.[95] Can Canada foster enough political will and leadership to really protect its future? Or will it continue waiting to make meaningful decisions that would alter its approach to unbridled resource exploitation and thus transform it from a centuries-old eco-predator into an environmentally responsible state?*

*The Canadian Constitution does not recognize a formal right to a healthy environment. As of this writing, Canada's courts have not interpreted section 7 of the Charter (the right to life, liberty, and security of the person) to include an environmental aspect.*

*Is there a hope that the courts will one day recognize that the damage to the health and lives of individuals caused by deficient environmental policies makes the government constitutionally liable?*

*In too many situations, the government is simply reactive. Without constant pressure and vigilance from environmental groups, public opinion, and the courts, it is usually satisfied to take half-measures that do not make waves and leave it with a clean conscience.*

*Canada is therefore faced with making a profound change in its culture of consumerism and natural resources development. It can no longer maintain its age-old delusions about its seemingly endless oniric natural landscapes. Canada must now justify its choices and use the financial and political means necessary to remain credible in protecting the health and well-being of its inhabitants and, especially, in safeguarding the portion of the planet under its stewardship.*

NOTES

1  The author is indebted to the Library of Parliament for its careful work in verifying the accuracy of the historical facts and figures in the text.

2  Lakes larger than three square kilometres. See Worldatlas, *The Largest Lakes in Canada*, http://www.worldatlas.com/articles/which-are-the-largest-lakes-in-canada.html, consulted 29 September 2017.

3  Environment and Climate Change Canada, *Protected Areas*, https://www.canada.ca/en/services/environment/conservation/protected-areas.html, consulted 29 September 2017.

4  Lev Bratishenko and Mirko Zardini (eds.), *It's All Happening So Fast: A Counter-History of the Modern Canadian Environment,* Canadian Centre for Architecture (Montreal: Jap Sam Books, 2016).

5  Peter Christie, "Trump's attack on wilderness is our wakeup call," *The Globe and Mail*, Opinion, 9 December 2017, p. 7.

6  Guillaume Lepage, "Le Canada parmi les mauvais joueurs – Pourquoi notre mode de vie laisse-t-il une des pires empreintes écologiques sur la planète," *Le Devoir*, 4–5 August 2018, p. B1.

7  Defined in the *World Conservation Strategy*, published in 1980 by the International Union for Conservation of Nature (IUCN).

8  Ms Gro Harlem Brundtland of Norway chaired the World Commission on Environment and Development established by the United Nations General Assembly in 1984. The commission's report, entitled *Our Common Future*, was published in 1987 and launched the henceforth indispensable concept of "sustainable development."

9   Marie Tison, "Ces rivières qui disparaissent dans l'indifférence," *La Presse+*, 27 June 2018.

10  Alexis Riopel, "La forêt boréale va croitre, puis décliner," *Le Devoir*, 20 August 2018, p. A2.

11  Alexandre Shields, "Un rapport de l'ONU sur le réchauffement climatique donne froid dans le dos," *Le Devoir*, 1 November 2017, p. A3.

12  According to a report by the Word Meteorological Organization , a specialized agency of the United Nations Organization, cited by Agnès Pedrero in "Le réchauffement de la Terre s'accélère," *Le Devoir*, 19 January 2018, p. A4.

13  Nathaniel Rich, "Losing Earth: the decade we almost stopped climate change. A tragedy in two acts," *The New York Times Magazine*, 5 August 2018.

14  Mia Rabson, "Critics say handling of nuclear waste is 'pathetic,'" *Ottawa Citizen*, 22 August 2018, p. A4; Crête, Mylène, "Le démentèlement de Gentilly-I crée des craintes," *Le Devoir*, 22 August 2018, p. A2.

15  Éric Atkino, "Canada to restrict use of two pesticides. Ottawa says it will phase out most outdoor applications of pair of chemicals shown to be harmful to bees and other wild-life," *The Globe and Mail*, 16 August 2018, p. A3; Gravel, Pauline, "Des néonics seront interdits… dans cinq ans," *Le Devoir*, 16 August 218, p. A3.

16  A total of 21,263,560, according to Canada Pork International.

17  Karl Rettino-Parazelli, "Le Québec aurait besoin d'une 'révolution énergétique,'" *Le Devoir*, 14 December 2017, p. A5.

18  According to the Department of National Defence and the Canadian Armed Forces.

19  François Desjardins, "Les minières doivent-elles payer en cas de catastrophe? Des chercheurs proposent aux décideurs de tarifer les sociétés canadiennes afin de réduire les risques environnementaux," *Le Devoir*, 11 July 2018, p. B5.

20  "… moratoria on commercial salmon fisheries [were imposed] in 1992 for insular Newfoundland, 1998 for Labrador and 2000 for all commercial fisheries in eastern Canada." See Fisheries and Oceans Canada, *Canada's Policy for Conservation of Wild Atlantic Salmon*, http://www.dfo-mpo.gc.ca/fm-gp/policies-politiques/wasp-pss/wasp-psas-2009-eng.htm, consulted 20 September 2017.

21  Sara Champagne, "Protection de la baleine noire – Des règles plus strictes pour les pêcheurs de crabe des neiges," *La Presse+*, 29 March 2018.

22  Alexandre Shields, "Pêcheurs en colère," *Le Devoir*, 16-17 June 2018, p. B2.

23  Andréanne Chevalier, "Une 'très bonne nouvelle' pour les bélugas du fleuve," *Le Devoir*, 13 July 2018, p. A5.

24  Cameron Jefferies and Nicolas Rehberg-Besler, "Sympathy for whale mom Tahlequah not enough to save the orcas," *The Globe and Mail*, 18 August 2018, p. 08.

25  Alexandre Shields, "Lutte contre le plastique dans les océans: on s'attend à des engagements symboliques," *Le Devoir*, 2-3 June 2018, p. B3.

26  Helen Moka, "Le plastique des océans produit des GES," *Le Devoir*, 6 August 2018, p. A3.

27  J. Boucher and D. Friot, *Primary Microplastics in the Oceans: A Global Evaluation of Sources*. (Gland, Switzerland: IUCN, 2017).

28  Alexander Shields, "La pollution plastique dans nos assiettes," *Le Devoir*, 10 August 2017, p. A5.

29  Alexandre Shields, "Lutte contre le plastique dans les océans: on s'attend à des engagements symboliques," *Le Devoir*, 2-3 June 2018, p. B3.

30  Mia Rabson, "Canada will push G7 partners to sign no plastic pledge to save the oceans," *Ipolitics*, 25 January 2018.

31  Pauline Gravel, "Les déchets électroniques s'amoncellent à la vitesse grand V," *Le Devoir*, 13 December 2017, p. A5.

32  Stephen Hazell, "Why the world needs a little less Canada in 2018," *Hill Times*, 17 January 2018.

33  William T. Vollmann, *No Immediate Danger – Volume One of Carbon Ideologies*, (New York: Viking, 2018; John Schwartz, "Many, Many Words of Warning ," *The New York Times* Book Review, 12 August 2018, p. 10.

34  Anna Clark, *The Poisoned City – Flint's Water and the American Urban tragedy* (New York: Metropolitan Books, 2018); Jeff Goodell, "Troubled waters – What went wrong in Flint," *The New York Times* Book Review, 15 August 2018, p. 12.

35  Katy Daigle, "Pollution killing more people every year than wars, disasters and hunger, study says," *Chicago Tribune,* 20 October 2017.

36  Clémentine Thiberge, "Le réchauffement climatique affecte notre santé mentale," *Le Monde – Cahier du Monde*, No. 22656, 15 November 2017, p. 2.

37  "900 recours judiciaires dans le monde," *Le Monde – Cahier du Monde*, No. 22656, 15 November 2017, p. 6.

38  Olivier Truc, "Climat: les ONG perdent leur procès contre la 'pétromonarchie' norvégienne," *Le Monde*, 6 January 2018, p. 6.

39  *Groupe Maison Candiac Inc. v. Canada (Attorney General)*, 2018 FC 643.

40  *Groupe Maison Candiac Inc. v. Canada (Attorney General)*, 2018 FC 643. para. 117 : Federal Court judge Leblanc citing Justice Martineau, in *Centre québécois du droit de l'environnement*, para. 6.

41  Robert Dutrisac, "Ottawa à la rescousse," *Le Devoir*, 11 July 2018, p. A6.

42  World Bank, *Terrestrial and marine protected areas (% of total territorial area)*, https://data.worldbank.org/indicator/ER.PTD.TOTL.ZS?view=chart&year_high_desc=true, consulted 29 September 2017.

43  Canadian Parks and Wilderness Society, *From Laggard to Leader,* July 2017, p. 4.

44  Bob Weber, "Canada's biggest national park under threat, scientists say," *Toronto Star*, 16 November 2017, p. A2.

45  The Canadian Press, "Le Canada n'est pas prêt, dit la Commissaire à l'environnement," *Le Devoir*, 4 October 2017, p. A3.

46  Alexandre Shields, "GES : le retard du Canada s'accentue," *Le Devoir*, 24–5 February 2018, p. A1.

47  The Canadian Press, "Ottawa annonce un plan d'action pour protéger le caribou boréal," *La Presse.ca*, 28 July 2017.

48  Alexandre Shields, "Un gazoduc passera à travers l'habitat de caribous menacés," *Le Devoir*, 22 August 2017, p. A5.

49  Shawn McCarthy and Ivan Semeniuk, "Boreal Caribou continues to decline five years after recovery plan's introduction," *The Globe and Mail*, 1 November 2017, pp. A8 and A9; "Caribou forestier : aucun plan de protection déplore Ottawa," *Le Devoir*, 1 November 2017, p. A5.

50  Éric-Pierre Champagne, "Ottawa dit manquer de ressources pour protéger les espèces en péril," *La Presse+*, 8 April 2018.

51  Marie-Lise Rousseau, "Le projet de mine Akasaba Ouest est approuvé," *Le Devoir*, 28 June 2018.

52  Vincent Larouche, "Pas d'accusations contre les pollueurs – déversements massifs de sols contaminés," *La Presse+*, 27 June 2018.

53  Alexandre Shields, "Une aire protégée pour le caribou forestier," *Le Devoir*, 28 November 2017, p. 1.

54  Jean-Michel Normand, "Le crépuscule du moteur," *Le Monde*, 9 January 2018, pp. 4-5.

55  Alain Mckenna, "Vers la fin annoncée du moteur thermique," *Le Devoir*, 31 July 2017, p. 8.

56  Simon Roger, "L'Europe en pleine contradiction sur le climat," *Le Monde*, 23 January 2018, p. 7.

57  Olivier Truc, "La Suède se dote d'une loi climatique extrêmement ambitieuse," *Le Monde.fr*, 22 January 2018.

58  Joël-Denis Bellavance, "GES : Trudeau s'en tient aux cibles de Harper," *La Presse+*, 12 September 2016.

59  Alexandre Shields, "La France appelle le Canada à renoncer à exploiter ses énergies fossiles," *Le Devoir*, 15 December 2017, p. I.

60  John Geddes, "Who will build the Trans Mountain pipeline – and at what cost?" *Maclean's*, 29 May 2018.

61  "Le coût d'acquisition de Trans Mountain grimpe," *Le Devoir*, 8 August 2018, p. B4.

62  Agence Science-Presse, "Cinq choses qui restent à prouver au sujet de Trans Mountain," *Le Devoir*, 2 and 3 June 2018, p. B5.

63  Martine Valo, "L'ONU ouvre la voie à un futur traité sur la haute mer," *Le Monde*, 28 December 2017, p. 5.

64 Jean-Louis Santini, "2016, une autre année noire pour le climat," *Le Devoir*, 11 August 2017, p. A2.

65 William J. Ripple et al., "World scientists' warning to humanity: a second notice," *BioScience*, Vol. 67, No. 12, 1 December 2017, pp. 1026-1028 (published 13 November 2017).

66 In September 2017, Quebec and Ottawa reached an agreement to create three marine protected areas in Quebec; Alexandre Shields, "Entente entre Québec et Ottawa en vue de la création d'aires marines protégées," *Le Devoir*, 28 September 2017.

67 Alexandre Shields, "Ottawa élimine un projet de protection marine," *Le Devoir*, 25 July 2014, p. A1.

68 Alexandre Shields, "Le Banc-des-Américains devient une zone marine protégée," *Le Devoir*, 27 June 2018, pp. A1-A2.

69 Gérard Bérubé, "La Caisse de dépôt fait écho," *Le Devoir*, 26 October 2017, p. B1.

70 Manon Cornellier, "Trans Mountain : le baron du pétrole," *Le Devoir*, 24 July 2018, p. A6.

71 Jeffrey Jones, "OMERS buys pipeline stake for $1.4 billion," *The Globe and Mail*, 22 August 2018, p. B2.

72 Alexandre Shields, "Énergies fossiles : la Banque mondiale ferme le robinet," *Le Devoir*, 13 December 2017, p. A5.

73 FTQ: Fédération des travailleurs et travailleuses du Québec [formerly called the Quebec Federation of Labour]. See Gérard Bérubé, "Le Fonds de solidarité fait ses adieux au charbon," *Le Devoir*, 30 September and 1 October 2017, p. C1.

74 Gérard Bérubé, "La Caisse de dépôt fait écho," *Le Devoir*, 26 October 2017, p. B1.

75 Bérubé, Gérard, "Déni climatique," *Le Devoir*, 31 August 2017, p. B1.

76 Alexandre Shields, "Pas de nouveaux permis d'exploitation pour au moins 5 ans," *Le Devoir*, 21 December 2016.

77 Gary Mason, "The brewing political battle of environment vs. the economy," *The Globe and Mail*, 16 August 2017, p. A11.

78 Alexandre Shields, "Pipeline Énergie Est : la logique d'affaires l'emporte," *Le Devoir*, 6 October 2017, p. A1.

79 The Enbridge company had planned to build a pipeline to carry oil extracted from the oil sands from Alberta to New Brunswick, at a cost of $15.7 billion. However, on 5 October 2017 it announced the cancellation of the project, citing as one of the reasons for its decision the restrictions imposed by environmental assessments.

80 François Desjardins, "Le marché du carbone canadien est à peaufiner, dit l'OCDE," *Le Devoir*, 20 December 2017, p. B1; Editorial, "Right direction, little ambition," *Toronto Star*, 17 January 2018, p. A12.

81 Manon Cornellier, "Il faut serrer la vis," *Le Devoir*, 19 January 2018, p. A8.

82 Hélène Buzzetti, "D'autres changements sont à venir, prévient le fédéral," *Le Devoir*, 3 August 2018.

83 Keith Doucette, "La Saskatchewan et l'Ontario s'unissent contre le fédéral – tarification du carbone," *Le Soleil*, 20 July 2018, p. 12.

84 Shawn McCarthy, "Poll suggests majority of Canadians oppose provinces taking Ottawa to Court over carbon tax," *The Globe and Mail*, 13 August 2018, p. A5.

85 Shawn McCarthy, Kelly Cryderman, and Wendy Stueck, "Alberta ditches Ottawa's carbon plan after court blocks pipeline," *The Globe and Mail*, 31 August 2018, p. A1.

86 "The need to sell carbon pricing," *The Globe and Mail*, 13 August 2018, p. A8.

87 Mathew Carr, "Canada, U.K. plan the first Paris Climate Deal Carbon Trades," *National Post*, 17 August 2018, p. FP 10.

88 Brenda Byd and Barry Rabe, "Le Canada doit prendre ses distances des États-Unis," *La Presse+*, Débats, screen 6.

89 Alexandre Shields, "Normes antipollution: Ottawa tiendra compte des positions de Trump," *Le Devoir*, 21 August 2018, p. A4; Shawn McCarthy, "Ottawa reviews fuel standards as US retreats from tighter rules," *The Globe and Mail*, 21 August 2018, p. B1.

90 Anna Desmarais, "Canada launches review auto emission," *IPolitics*, 20 August 2018; Mia Rabson, "Les règles canadiennes sur les émissions seront revues," *Le Devoir*, 7 August 2018, p. B4.

91 Robert Jago, "Canada's national parks are colonial crime scenes," *The Walrus.ca*, 30 June 2017.

92 Jamie Munson, "Carr points to Indigenous power to monitor Trans Mountain," *IPolitics*, 15 August 2017; Shawn McCarthy, "Ottawa eyes efficiency in overhaul of environmental review process," *The Globe and Mail*, 16 August 2017, p. B2.

93 Alexandre Shields, "Les plans d'eau du Québec ouverts aux pétrolières," *Le Devoir*, 21 September 2017, p. A1 and A8.

94 Wendy Stueck, "First Nation to battle mine plan in court," *The Globe and Mail*, 31 July 2017, p. S1.

95 Mathieu Perreault, "Du $CO_2$ qui vaut son pesant d'or," *La Presse+*, Actualités 9-2, 29 July 2018.

# Canada at a Crossroad: Setting the Bottom Line

David Suzuki, geneticist, journalist, and co-founder of the David Suzuki Foundation

First, I would like to acknowledge that we are meeting on the unceded, traditional sovereign territory of the Algonquin First Nations. All across Canada today, formal meetings are opened with this acknowldgment. It's a remarkable change from only a few years ago. We are one of the wealthiest nations in the world, and yet the first people whose territory we acknowledge are the poorest. How can we hold our heads up with pride as a nation if this isn't redressed?

But it's more than an economic or social justice issue; we need Indigenous guidance because, currently, we are on a suicidal collision course with the life support systems of the planet and we must learn from Indigenous people, who are the only people with a track record of living sustainably in balance with nature for thousands of years.

Scientists today call this period in geological time the Anthropocene, when human beings have become the dominant factor shaping the physical, chemical, and biological properties of the planet.[1] This has come about as the result of sudden and massive change in a number of areas. From just another animal on the plains of Africa, we have exploded in numbers after reaching a billion in population in the early decades of the nineteenth century. When I was born, in 1936, there were just over two billion people. In my lifetime, the population of the world has more than tripled, and each new addition must be fed, clothed, and sheltered, so that just to stay alive, our species makes an enormous collective ecological footprint;[2] that is, it takes a lot of air, water, and land to support us.

But unlike rabbits or rats or mice, we develop science and technology that amplifies our ecological footprint. As well, most of the application of our knowledge has happened in little more than a century. To illustrate the enormity and speed of change, consider that when I was a boy, I wasn't allowed to go to movies or public swimming pools in the summer because my parents feared I might catch polio, a disease most children today have no knowledge of, thanks to Jonas Salk and his vaccine. In my childhood, my parents didn't worry that I was on my cell phone, or watching too much television, or playing video games, because none of that had yet been invented. Each year, millions of people contracted the deadly virus causing smallpox, a disease that has been extinct for more than thirty years. When I was a child, no one knew what DNA was, how many chromosomes humans have, or what determined sex. Back then, there were no jet planes, oral contraceptives, organ transplants, satellites, xerography, or computers. Each innovation has changed the way we live and often the very definition of what it is to be human, and much of it has increased our ability to exploit raw materials from the planet and to spread our waste and toxic materials worldwide.

Ever since the end of World War II, which had pulled America out of the Great Depression, North American economies have increasingly used consumption as the means of growing economies. And everything we buy and consume comes ultimately from the earth and goes back to it when we are finished with it, so our consumptive habits now greatly elevate our ecological footprint.

Today, most countries have become enthusiastic members of the global economy, which is based on exploiting the planet's resources as rapidly as possible to serve the wants of people worldwide. And when we combine the effects of population growth, technology, consumption, and the global economy, we can see why scientists believe we are the major factor shaping the properties of the planet.

Not long ago, we called mega-fires, hurricanes, floods, droughts, tornadoes, and earthquakes "natural disasters" or "acts of God," but not anymore. Remember the fires in Kelowna and Fort McMurray, drought in southern Alberta, and floods in Calgary, the Okanagan, Toronto, and Quebec? The human hand is now part of these disasters – they are not natural.

But we have taken the place of gods without the knowledge to apply our powers wisely, and so we are on a path that is destroying a future for our children. You know the consequences:

- Our industrial use of fossil fuels has altered the chemistry of the atmosphere, carbon levels are higher than they have been in millions of years, and the planet is warming.

- The oceans are a mess with dead zones in every ocean, as eutrophication from agricultural runoff snuffs out life; global fishing fleets, armed with refrigeration, stronger nets, bigger ships, GPS, radar, and so on, are effective killing machines that empty the waters of fish; increased atmospheric carbon is dissolving into oceans as carbonic acid, acidifying the water and rendering it more difficult for shellfish to form their shells; and much of our waste discarded on land ends up in great oceanic gyres, where it is centrifuged into enormous islands of plastic.

- More than 80 per cent of the world's forests have been attacked and decimated, and large pristine areas will be gone by the middle of this century.

- Human activity is altering the biological makeup of the planet, spreading alien species in new areas, introducing large-scale monocultures of plants (such as wheat, corn, rice, eucalyptus, and pine) and animals (including chickens, cows, and pigs) while driving wild species to extinction in a catastrophic loss of biodiversity often referred to as the sixth great extinction.[3]

- In June 2017, the medical profession announced that half of all Canadians will develop cancer over their lifetimes, thereby replacing heart disease as the number-one killer.[4] But what else can be expected when air, water, and land are used as a waste dump for toxic chemicals so that every one of us now carries dozens of toxic compounds dissolved in our bodies?

How did we arrive at this moment in history? Every society has its creation and origin stories, and today science adds insights that go far back beyond human memory, indeed before human existence. As a geneticist, I have been intrigued by the way DNA, the genetic material, can be used to infer the movement of people across the planet, and all trails lead back to Africa 150,000 years ago. We are all Africans in origin.

If we were transported back to Africa at the time of our species' birth, we would witness herds of animals in abundance and diversity beyond anything we could encounter on the Serengeti today. Seen in the context of all those other animals on the plains, we were not very impressive. There weren't many of us; we weren't very big, fast, or strong; and we didn't have special acute senses of vision, hearing, or smell. I am sure no other animals, on seeing a human, pulled their children close and whispered, "Don't piss them off. They're going to take over the planet." Yet in a mere blink in evolutionary time, we have become the dominant species on the planet. So what made us special?

The answer is the 1.4-kilogram organ buried in our skulls – the human brain more than compensated for our lack of physical or sensory ability. It had an enormous memory capacity and we learned and remembered a lot. We were observant and inquisitive, we learned through trial and error, and we were impressively inventive – a stone could be fashioned into a point, a stick into a spear, a large frond into a shelter.

The French Nobel laureate Francois Jacob suggested our huge and complex brain has an inbuilt need for order. We don't like it when things happen that don't make sense or that we don't understand, so to replace the chaos, we create world views in which nothing exists separately or in isolation, where instead everything is connected and interdependent. Thus, the birth of a severely deformed child or observation of an albino animal was not viewed as some kind of isolated freak event. In a world view where everything including time is part of an interconnected whole, people pondered these unusual events – could they be punishment for something done in the past, or a portent of something yet to come? They lived in a world where every human action was seen to have consequences and, therefore, responsibilities.

WHALE SLAUGHTER

An endangered species, with no more than 525 left in the world, the right whale is frequently found in the Gulf of St Lawrence, where a dozen perished in the summer of 2017 as a result of human activity, as was readily apparent from the necropsies performed on the carcasses that were recovered. The whales had died after becoming entangled in fishing nets, sustaining injuries from boat hulls or being poisoned. At this rate, right whales will soon disappear from the world's oceans. Credit: Andyqwe (Getty Images)

And the human brain invented a concept called the future, which enabled us to recognize that we could affect that future by what we do now – by looking ahead, recognizing dangers and opportunities, and then deliberately choosing to act in a way that would reduce the risk of dangers or increase our chances to exploit opportunities.

Foresight gave us a huge advantage, and its importance can be seen in some of our most profound myths. The Bible recounts the story of Joseph, whose jealous siblings sold him to the Egyptians, among whom Joseph became renowned for his ability to read dreams. He gained the trust of the pharaoh, to whom he indicated that Egypt was headed for a massive famine that could be averted by saving grain. Thanks to that foresight, Egypt survived seven consecutive years of drought. In the same way, the biblical story of the carpenter Noah tells us how Noah received a message from his lord to build an arc and fill it with biodiversity. Despite his concerns about becoming the laughingstock of his neighbours, Noah complied with the orders and built his ark; foresight thus enabled him and his passengers to survive catastrophic floods.

Today, scientists armed with supercomputers can look ahead with greater precision by extrapolating curves of our past and present trajectory, and for decades, leading scientists of the world have warned that we are on a dangerous path and have urged all humanity to act on their warnings by taking a different route (see Addendum). But now, in pursuit of political and economic agendas, we are ignoring the very survival trait that enabled us to survive and flourish to the present.

While the great plains of Africa were our birthplace and our home, over time, people began to move to new territories. Perhaps they were in search of new opportunities – slow-moving giant sloths, edible fruits, delicious flightless birds, et cetera. Perhaps it was necessary because of depletion of resources, population pressures, or even rambunctious teenagers seeking excitement or new sexual possibilities (DNA evidence shows that our distant ancestors did mate with Neanderthal people). Whatever the reasons, in these new lands we were an invasive species; we didn't have experience there to guide us. Even with simple tools like spears, digging implements, and stone axes, we were an effective predator. In fact, there is a strong correlation between the movement of humans and an ensuing wave of extinction of animals.

As we moved, we continued a cycle of occupation and over-exploitation over thousands of years, while those who remained behind had to learn to live differently. So the mistakes, successes, and failures of ancestors were remembered and passed on through generations, a priceless legacy that was the origin of Indigenous knowledge and critical to survival for each generation. That knowledge, much of it embedded in language, gave people a profound rootedness in place. Indigenous knowledge encompassed lessons that will never be duplicated by science, and right up to the present, the utility of that knowledge has been attested by the survival of those that hold it. The only groups with track records of living sustainably for millennia are Indigenous peoples all across the globe. As the Brundtland Report stated:

> Their very survival has depended upon their ecological awareness and adaptation … These communities are the repositories of vast accumulations of traditional knowledge and experience that links humanity with its ancient origins. Their disappearance is a loss for the larger society, which could learn a great deal from their traditional skills in sustainably managing very complex ecological systems. It is a terrible irony that as formal development reaches more deeply into rainforests, deserts, and other isolated environments, it tends to destroy the only cultures that have proved able to thrive in these environments.[5]

Canada is a very young nation, and science provides an origin story that extends back ten thousand years ago, when it was emerging from beneath a sheet of ice more than two kilometres thick. As the ice retreated, plants and animals took advantage of newly exposed land, and following them were the ancestors of Indigenous peoples who had moved across the planet from Africa.

Indigenous knowledge can never be duplicated by science. Most science is carried out by focusing on a part of the world – a seed, a cell, an atom – and trying to separate or isolate it from everything else, measuring and controlling factors impinging on that fragment, thereby acquiring insights into the behaviour and properties of those bits and pieces. And in science, it's better to look at the world as objectively and free of emotion as possible. This is in stark contrast with Indigenous ways of knowing, in which the observer would never try to view nature dispassionately from a distance because he or she is deeply embedded in nature and revels in that relationship. Indigenous knowledge is imbued with a strong sense of wonder, awe, and gratitude.

Ever since Isaac Newton suggested that the universe can be viewed as a giant clock-like mechanism, scientists have assumed that by analyzing parts of it, eventually, like an immense puzzle, the pieces can be fitted together to create the whole. This approach is called reductionism and has been very powerful in providing insights into the structure of matter, the genetic blueprint, and the energy of stars. But as Nobel Prize–winning scientist Roger Sperry has pointed out, reductionism doesn't work, because at each higher level of order, properties emerge that cannot be predicted on the basis of the properties of the parts.[6]

Physicists may describe all of the physical properties of atomic hydrogen and atomic oxygen, but those properties have little value in anticipating the combination of two atoms of hydrogen with one of oxygen because of the emergent properties expressed by a molecule of water. The whole is greater than the sum of its parts. Furthermore, in isolating and focusing on parts, scientists lose sight of the context within which those parts function and have meaning.

Over and over, scientists rush to apply their powerful but fragmentary insights, only to discover phenomena they did not know about. When Paul Hermann Müller found that dichlorodiphenyltrichloroethane (DDT) selectively kills insects, he was awarded a Nobel Prize in 1948. But after widespread use of DDT, bird watchers began to report a decline in bird populations, especially raptors like American bald eagles. Biologists eventually found the reason – biomagnification, the increased concentration of the insecticide up the food chain. Thus, while initially sprayed in concentrations of parts per million, the DDT is ingested and absorbed without killing its microbial hosts, which are consumed by progressively larger organisms at each level of the food chain, concentrating the DDT. So when we get to the fatty tissue in shell glands of birds or in the breasts of women, the pesticide is concentrated hundreds of thousands of times. Because biomagnification was only discovered as a biological phenomenon when bird numbers began to decline and biologists traced its cause to biomagnified DDT that interfered with proper formation of egg shells, the pesticide was not properly managed.

When atomic bombs were dropped on Japan in 1945, scientists did not know about radioactive fallout, electromagnetic pulses of gamma rays, or the possibility of nuclear winter. When chlorofluorocarbons (CFCs) were used as agents in spray cans because they were chemically inert and therefore wouldn't react with the molecules of perfume or whatever other main ingredient was in the cans, no one knew that in the upper atmosphere, ultraviolet light from the sun would break off chlorine free radicals, which scavenge ozone.

So over and over, we use our discoveries for their immediate benefits only to find that we don't know enough to anticipate their consequences. As we pursue the promise of genetically modified organisms, artificial intelligence, nanotechnology, and geo-engineering, we must always be aware of our ignorance and temper our rush to apply new technologies immediately with much more forethought.

Five centuries ago, European explorers travelled to distant lands in search of treasures and opportunity. Thus, they "discovered" lands (the Americas, Africa, Australia, New Zealand) already occupied by people with rich, vibrant cultures, who were written off as "savages" because they looked and behaved differently from the newcomers. In a quest for riches, colonizers often saw Indigenous people as impediments to their access to the land and so tried to extirpate the people, their languages, and their cultures by policies of genocide, confinement within reserves, or assimilation. We have heard all about that in Canada from Phil Fontaine and Ellen Gabriel.

My grandparents were part of a continuing wave of settlers when they came to Canada from Japan in the first decade of the twentieth century. Uneducated and driven by poverty, they came for the promise of opportunity. To them, the Indigenous plants and animals were alien but useful as resources, while they knew nothing of the Indigenous peoples and, consequently, learned nothing from them. They just wanted money and security.

My parents were born and raised in Canada, and like all of the other Japanese Canadian kids born around that time, they grew up without grandparents or elders, who were still back in Japan. In other words, they were rootless. My grandparents learned only rudimentary English, so I never had a serious conversation with them because I couldn't speak Japanese.

My values were formed by my parents, who were married in 1934, when the world was still enduring the Great Depression, which shaped their priorities and values. So they constantly instilled their values with homilies repeated again and again: live within your means; save some for tomorrow; share, don't be greedy; help you neighbours because someday you may need their help; work hard to earn money to buy the necessities in life, but don't run after money as if it makes you a better or more important person. Those hard-won life lessons from my parents seem so quaint in today's high-consumption world, in which the economy no longer functions to fulfill our needs and instead serves our limitless wants.

World War II pulled America (and Canada) out of the Depression, but as the war was drawing to a close, the Council of Economic Advisors to the President were asked how to transform a wartime economy into a peacetime economy. Their solution: consumption. Retailing analyst Victor Lebow illustrated the vision of this path:

> Our enormously productive economy … demands that we make consumption
> our way of life, that we convert the buying and use of goods into rituals, that
> we seek our spiritual satisfaction, our ego satisfaction, in consumption …
> We need things consumed, burned up, worn out, replaced and discarded
> at an ever-increasing rate.[7]

But if goods are well made and durable, the market eventually becomes saturated. In a time when expensive pants already have built-in tears and rips or rubbed-in dirt, durability and reuse are hardly a boast. And what better than disposability – use something once, then throw it away – for an endless market for a product. Today,

SUPERSTACK CHIMNEY, INCO, SUDBURY

When it was built by Inco in the 1970s, the Superstack chimney was supposed to spare the Sudbury area from the effects of mining-related pollution because of its height. What no one realized was that winds dispersed the particles that cause acid rain elsewhere in the country, spreading them over a larger area and making the remnants of this pollution more difficult to recover. Surely, in this day and age, nobody believes that such pollution disappears in a faraway place where it is no longer harmful. Credit: Wikimedia Commons, P199 (talk | contribs)

consumption is more than 70 per cent of the American economy. This is in stark contrast with the long history of the human condition having accounted for 95 per cent of our existence when we were nomadic hunter-gatherers carrying everything we owned as we followed animals and plants through the seasons. We knew we were deeply embedded in and utterly dependent on nature for our survival and well-being.

The agricultural revolution that took place ten thousand years ago transformed humanity from nomadic hunter-gatherers to farmers who settled down. And farmers know very well that they are deeply reliant on nature – they know weather and climate are critical elements of their livelihood, that winter snow is related to summer moisture in the soil, that pollination by insects is critical for many crops, that some plants fix nitrogen from the air as fertilizer in the soil. In other words, farmers know they are deeply immersed in and dependent on nature.

In the twentieth century, our species underwent another astonishing transition. In 1900 there were 1.5 billion people in the world, but only fourteen cities with more than a million. London was the largest, with 6.5 million, while Tokyo was seventh, with 1.5 million. At the beginning of the twentieth century, most people still lived in rural villages because agriculture was the dominant activity of our species. But in a mere century, by 2000, the population had grown fourfold to 6 billion, while the number of cities exploded to four hundred. Tokyo became the largest city with 26 million, while the ten largest cities all had more than 11 million, and more than half of the world – as well as 85 per cent of Canadians – lived in big cities. Human beings moved from farming to urban living in only a century.

But a city is a human-created environment where we live primarily in the company of other people as we lose our contact with nature. Today, the average Canadian child spends less than eight minutes a day outside and more than six hours a day in front of a television, computer, or cell phone screen. In cities, our highest priority becomes a job, which we need to earn money to buy the things we want (not need), and so the economy becomes our primary focus.

This shift changes our priorities and emphases while diminishing our sense of place and belonging. It runs counter to what our biology dictates, as the eminent Harvard biologist E.O. Wilson informs us that we have an innate need to be in the company of other species.[8] He calls it biophilia, and numerous studies indicate that this need is real in physical, psychological, and spiritual terms.[9] In an urban setting where sanitation has become an obsession, we often demonize nature, demonstrating our attitude to our children if they bring in an insect, a spider, or a slug with exclamations of "Don't touch!", "It might bite or sting!", "Oh, that's disgusting!" Thus, we instill a sense of biophobia, which is contrary to what may be a genetic need.

And we pay a price for our alienation from nature. Writer Richard Louv suggests that in distancing ourselves from nature, our children express a suite of behavioural traits from bullying to hyperactivity, attention deficit disorder, and depression.[10] Louv says they suffer from "nature deficit disorder."[11] And, increasingly, we are finding that in our obsessive attempts at sanitation, we fail to maintain a microbial diversity in our microbiome that turns out to be crucial to our digestive and immune systems. In Japan, an ancient Shinto practice called *shinrin-yoku* or "forest bathing" has become widely practised, as walking among trees has been shown to lower heart rate and blood pressure, reduce stress hormones, boost the immune system, and improve over-all feelings of well-being. "Tree-hugger" was once a pejorative to denigrate environmentalists, but not anymore as we recognize the real health and economic benefits of being among trees.

From an ecological perspective, the current economic model is fundamentally flawed and destructive. For one thing, nature performs services that keep the planet habitable for animals like us – pollination, water filtration, soil creation, exchange of oxygen with carbon dioxide, the nitrogen cycle, and so on – yet they are dismissed as externalities, irrelevant to the economy. That is madness. When ecological econo-mist Bob Constanza asked what it would cost us to replace the "ecosystem services" provided by nature (if that were possible) – for example, filtering water instead of letting nature's wetlands, plant roots, and soil fungi and microorganisms do the job; storing carbon and generating oxygen; controlling pests; et cetera – he concluded that it would add up to $33 trillion, which was almost twice the collective annual gross domestic product (GDP) of all the countries in the world, yet these services provided by nature have no value in the economy![12]

And second, economists believe endless growth is possible, though in reality it is not. Growth is simply a description of the state of a system not of use by itself. Growth is the creed of cancer cells, and if unchecked, it always results in death. But our blind obsession with growth prevents us from asking the important questions like "What is an economy for?", "Are there no limits?", "Are we happier with all this stuff?", "How much is enough?" These are the critical questions all societies should be asking. But we define progress as economic growth. Just ask a corporate executive or politician how well they have done and they will immediately point to growth in the economy, GDP, or profit. The biosphere – the zone of air, land, and water where all life exists – is our home. It is fixed and finite and nothing within it can grow indefinitely.

Let me show you why endless growth is impossible. Any steady increase over time – of population, size of cities, amount of garbage, et cetera – is called exponen-tial growth. And anything growing exponentially has a predictable doubling time. Something growing at 1 per cent a year will double in seventy years; at 2 per cent, in thirty-five years; at 3 per cent, in twenty-three years; at 4 per cent, in seventeen and a half years; and so on.

Now let us take a test tube full of food for bacteria, where the test tube and food represent the planet and the bacteria are us. Suppose the bacteria divide every min-ute, so at time zero, there's one bacterium; at one minute, two; two minutes, four; three minutes, eight – that's exponential growth. And at sixty minutes the test tube is full of bacteria and all the food is gone. When is the test tube half full? At fifty-nine minutes, of course. So at fifty-eight minutes, it's 25 per cent full; at fifty-seven min-utes, 12.5 per cent full; at fifty-five minutes, is 3 per cent full. Suppose one bacterium pipes up at fifty-five minutes and says, "I think we have a population problem." The other bacteria would scoff: "What have you been smoking? Ninety-seven per cent of the test tube is empty and we've been around for fifty-five minutes." But they'd be five minutes away from a full world. At fifty-nine minutes, all hell breaks loose – there is only one minute left before all the food is gone.

Suppose that in desperation the bacteria give their scientists huge grants and miraculously, in less than a minute, they come up with three more test tubes full of food. That would be like our finding three more close-by planets perfectly suited for us. So they are saved, right? Well, at sixty minutes, the first test tube is full, at sixty-one minutes, the second test tube is full, and after sixty-two minutes, all four are full. By quadrupling the amount of food and space, the scientists buy two extra minutes! And every scientist I've spoken with agrees that there is no other planet nearby to occupy and we are past the fifty-ninth minute. So all the talk about growing the economy means we accelerate along our destructive path.

Business people and politicians become livid when I say this, citing stores full of goods and people living longer, but I make no apology. We create the illusion of well-being by using up the rightful legacy of future generations. Ask any elder in a community what the world was like when they were children. Inevitably, the answer is laced with the phrase "There used to be …" when referring to birds, forests, fish or mammals, clean rivers and lakes.

But somehow, the economy and its steady growth have become our highest priority above anything else. Donald Trump and the Wall Street and corporate executives he has installed to run the American government are the ultimate expression of the devotion to economic growth – to hell with ethics, climate, or the health of all the people; just make more money, the faster the better.

As prime minister, Stephen Harper did all he could to prevent discussion of climate change and claimed (incorrectly) that to try to reduce our impact on climate would "destroy the economy." Thus, he elevated the economy above the very atmosphere that keeps us alive and creates weather and climate.

Yet, of all the industrialized nations, Canada is most vulnerable to the impact of climate change. We are a northern country, and the Arctic is warming far faster than areas farther south, and for decades, Inuit have been telling us climate and ice are changing. Canada has the longest marine coastline of any nation and when water warms, it expands. Sea level rise due simply to warmer oceans will impact Canada most, and when the great ice sheets of Greenland and Antarctica slide into the oceans, waters will rise by several metres.

And then think of the climate-sensitive parts of our economy – agriculture, forestry, fisheries, tourism, and winter sports. Politicians who ignore or deny the reality of climate change are being willfully blind and already have put this country at great risk by failing to act strongly enough. Many of my fellow environmentalists are saying that massive deposits in the earth of frozen methane, which is a much more potent greenhouse gas than carbon dioxide, are being released and could trigger warming that would threaten our survival as a species before the end of this century.

As battles rage over fracking, tar sands, pipelines, and mega-dams, we first have to decide as a society what we all agree are our highest real priorities, and then we can ask how to work our way out of this mess and into the future. Let me suggest a starting point: we live in a world that is shaped and constrained by laws of nature and there's nothing we can do but live within them.

Physics informs us that we cannot build a rocket that will travel faster than the speed of light; gravity dictates that if we trip over a rock, we will fall flat on our face; and we cannot build a perpetual motion machine. That's physics and we live with it.

FRACTURE IN ANTARCTICA

As a result of global warming, an iceberg the size of Prince Edward Island – 5,800 km² and 250 to 700 metres thick – broke away from Antarctica during the summer of 2017, further weakening the Larsen ice shelf, which has held in the glaciers until now. If these glaciers should enter the water, ocean levels would rise by 10 centimetres. Millions of people would be forced to move, causing population migrations never before seen in the history of humankind! Credit: John Sonntag/NASA/AFP

Chemistry tells us the atomic properties of the elements determine their boiling and melting points, while reaction rates and diffusion constants thus dictate the kinds of reactions that can be carried out and the molecules that can be synthesized. We can't change that.

Biology sets the maximum number of any species of plant or animal that can be maintained indefinitely by the "carrying capacity" of ecosystems or habitats. Exceed that number and populations will crash. Humans are not confined to ecosystems or habitats, because we're smart and can adapt to many different habitats. But the biosphere – the zone of air, water, and land where all life exists – is finite and fixed and sets limits on how many of us can be sustained. The late astronomer Carl Sagan told us if Earth was reduced to the size of a basketball, the biosphere would be thinner than a layer of sandwich wrap. And that thin layer sustains all life forms.

Of course, the number of humans indefinitely sustainable is determined by both numbers and per capita consumption, and every expert I've talked to agrees that we are far past the carrying capacity of the biosphere for our species. But we maintain an illusion that all is well by undermining the posterity of succeeding generations.

Biology tells us we are animals, most closely related to the great apes. As biological organisms, our highest need is clean air (without air for three minutes, we die), clean water (we are 70 per cent water, and without water for four to seven days, we die), clean soil to give us food (we can last four to six weeks but eventually die without food, and most grows in soil), clean energy (every bit of the energy in our bodies is sunlight captured by photosynthesis, and all the fuel we burn – coal, oil, gas, wood, peat, dung – was produced by photosynthesis).

Biology reveals that these elements – earth, air, fire, and water – are created, cleansed, and replenished by the web of life, which science will never duplicate. Plants on land and sea create the oxygen-rich atmosphere we depend on; plant roots, soil fungi, bacteria, and other microorganisms filter water as it percolates through soil so we can drink it; plants capture and store all the sun's energy through photosynthesis. Every bit of food that we consume to create our bodies was once alive, and the soil on which food grows is created by the decayed carcasses of plants and animals. It is our kin, related through a shared evolutionary history, who maintain a planet habitable for us.

Today, human activity has set us on a suicidal course, undermining the very life-support systems of the planet to maintain our high-consumption economic growth strategy. We are not even willing to pay to pollute those elements. We use air, water, and soil to spray and spread toxic chemicals, often justifying the ecological and health consequences as the "price of doing business."

These are the critical factors that keep us alive and healthy, and in our own self-interest, every human being on Earth should hold their protection as our highest priority if we are to live and thrive sustainably. They should be sacred, beyond economic valuation. We can't change this fundamental biological truth. But other things – borders around property, cities, provinces, and countries; capitalism; the economy; markets; corporations – these are not forces of nature. We created them, and they are the only things we can change so we don't compromise our basic needs. That is the foundation of sustainability.

How can we change direction? Here, the remarkable fact is that we still have among us the remnants of Indigenous cultures that have survived the last 150 years despite Canada's efforts to expunge them from our midst. Through the values and perspectives of Indigenous people, we have an opportunity to fundamentally change directions by recognizing that Earth is our mother and gives us everything we need to be happy and healthy if we care for her.

In decades of working with Indigenous people, I have been impressed with the key role of elders, especially in communities coping with enormous problems of poverty, alcoholism, diabetes, obesity, violence, and so on. Elders occupy the highest position of respect in the community, serving as links to the past and repositories of values and lessons learned through experience. And, overwhelmingly, their rituals, songs, and dances constantly give thanks to their Creator for nature's abundance and generosity, and in recognizing and expressing gratitude, they accept a reciprocal responsibility to ensure nature's health and well-being. That is what is missing today from modern, economics-dominated society. In this, the 150th anniversary of the creation of Canada, we acknowledge the rights of the first peoples and give thanks that they and their cultures have survived more than a century-and-a-half of oppression. Their persistence provides a moment of great opportunity if we recognize what we are doing to the planet, and give the respect to Indigenous perspectives that have enabled them to flourish for thousands of years and could help guide us in a different direction.

It has been clear to me in the battles I've had with politicians and corporate leaders that most are well-meaning, good people. But they are locked into playing games with rules set by the economy (which is flawed and inevitably destructive) and time frames that simply don't allow them to tackle big issues like climate change. Corporations are driven by the quarterly report while politicians' highest priority is to get re-elected, so whatever they do must pay off before the next election. There is no place in political agendas for children who don't vote or future generations that don't exist.

That's why my wife, Dr Tara Cullis, suggested that the Senate could be the place to raise questions on behalf of seven generations to come. Senators are not elected, so they needn't worry about voter reprisals. Depending on the terms under which they are appointed, they could be the one group without vested interests in the status quo or specific corporate or political agendas. They can consider the best scientific evidence and ponder what lies ahead on behalf of all Canadians, including those yet to come. And senators can speak out without worrying about getting fired or losing a promotion.

I remember Senator Herbert O. Sparrow's groundbreaking report on the state of Canada's soil,[13] which remains a very important document for all Canadians concerned about the future of agriculture. That's what senators can do. And a Senate that embraces the perspective and guidance of Indigenous people would be a truly unique body that would have the potential to genuinely address the challenge of sustainability. Now that would be a path to follow for the next 150 years.

ADDENDUM

*Science Matters – by David Suzuki*

The longer we delay addressing environmental problems, the more difficult it will be to resolve them. Although we've known about climate change and its potential impacts for a long time, and we're seeing those impacts worsen daily, our political representatives are still approving and promoting fossil fuel infrastructure as if we had all the time in the world to slow global warming.

We can't say we weren't warned. In 1992, a majority of living Nobel Prize–winners and more than 1,700 leading scientists worldwide signed a remarkable document called "World Scientists' Warning to Humanity."

It begins:

Human beings and the natural world are on a collision course. Human activities inflict harsh and often irreversible damage on the environment and on critical resources. If not checked, many of our current practices put at serious risk the future that we wish for human society and the plant and animal kingdoms, and may so alter the living world that we will be unable to sustain life in the manner that we know. Fundamental changes are urgent if we are to avoid the collision our present course will bring about.

It then outlines critical areas where the collision was and is still occurring – the atmosphere, water resources, oceans, soil, forests, species extinction, and overpopulation. In the twenty-five years since the letter was published, these problems have worsened. The document then grows bleak:

> No more than one or a few decades remain before the chance to avert the threats we now confront will be lost and the prospects for humanity immeasurably diminished. We the undersigned, senior members of the world's scientific community, hereby warn all humanity of what lies ahead. A great change in our stewardship of the earth and life on it is required, if vast human misery is to be avoided and our global home on this planet is not to be irretrievably mutilated.

Now, as monthly and annual records for rising global average temperatures continue to break, as extreme weather events become more frequent and severe, as refugees overwhelm the capacity of nations, and as tipping points for climatic feedback loops and other phenomena are breached, the need to act is more urgent than ever.

The warning suggests five steps needed immediately. That was a generation ago. These actions can still help prevent the worst impacts.

"We must bring environmentally damaging activities under control to restore and protect the integrity of the earth's systems we depend on."

The letter specifically mentions reducing greenhouse gas emissions and air and water pollution. It also highlights the need to address deforestation, degradation, and loss of agricultural soils and extinction of plant and animal species.

"We must manage resources crucial to human welfare more effectively."

This one is obvious. Finite resources must be exploited much more efficiently or we'll run out.

"We must stabilize population. This will be possible only if all nations recognize that it requires improved social and economic conditions, and the adoption of effective, voluntary family planning."

"We must reduce and eventually eliminate poverty."

"We must ensure sexual equality, and guarantee women control over their own reproductive decisions."

The warning recognizes that we in the developed world are responsible for most global pollution and therefore must greatly reduce overconsumption while providing technical and financial aid to developing countries. This is not altruism but self-interest, because all of us share the same biosphere. Developing nations must realize environmental degradation is the greatest threat to their future, while rich nations must help them follow a different development path. The most urgent suggestion is to develop a new ethic that encompasses our responsibility to ourselves and nature and that recognizes our dependence on the earth and its natural systems for all we need.

The document ends with a call for support from scientists, business and industrial leaders, religious heads, and all the world's peoples. Like Pope Francis's groundbreaking 2015 encyclical "Laudato Si," the "World Scientists' Warning to Humanity" was an attempt to galvanize the world to recognize the dangerous implications of humanity's path and the urgent need for change.

Forewarned is forearmed. We can't let the lure of the almighty buck blind us. We must come together, speak up, and act for the good of all humanity.

NOTES

1 P.T. Crutzen and E.F. Stoermer, "The Anthropocene," *IGBP Global Change News* 41 (2000): 17–18.

2 M. Wackernagel and W. Rees, "Our Ecological Footprint" (Toronto: New Society Publishers, 1996).

3 E. Kolbert, *The Sixth Extinction*, (New York: Henry Holt & Co, 2014).

4 Canadian Cancer Society, "Nearly 1 in 2 Canadians Expected to Get Cancer," June 2017.

5 G.H. Brundtland, *Our Common Future* (Oxford: Oxford University Press, 1987).

6 R. Sperry, *Science and Moral Priority* (New York: Columbia University Press, 1983).

7 V. Lebow quoted in V. Packard, *The Wastemakers* (New York: Van Rees Press, 1960).

8 E.O. Wilson, *Biophilia* (Cambridge, MA: Harvard University Press, 1986).

9 S. Kellert and E.O. Wilson, *The Biophilia Hypothesis* (Washington, DC: Island Press, 1995).

10 R. Louv, *Last Child in the Woods* (Chapel Hill, NC: Algonquin Books, 2005).

11 R. Louv, *The Nature Principle* (Chapel Hill, NC: Algonquin Books, 2011).

12 R. Costanza *et al.*, "The Value of the World's Ecological Services and Natural Capital," *Nature* 387: 253–60.

13 H.O. Sparrow, "Soil at Risk," report of Canadian Senate, 1984.

# The Arctic, or the Risk of Making the Calamities of the South Worse in the North[1]

The Hon. Serge Joyal, Senator

*There is no region in Canada where the effects of global warming are more apparent than the Arctic. At the same time, the Arctic is the most vulnerable, the most untapped, the richest in virgin resources and, above all, the most exposed to any kind of excess in the absence of a clear and assertive approach to the country's environmental and geopolitical interests and full recognition of Inuit Aboriginal rights.*

*Canada needs to adopt an inspired vision and not simply export to the North the same flaws of consumer society entrenched in the South. Fifty years ago, Canada's main objective in this vast region was to harness its strategic potential for the defence of North America. NORAD established itself there in 1957, during the Cold War era. As a human presence in the High Arctic region was necessary to assert sovereignty over these archipelagos, in 1953 Inuit populations from Inukjuak, in northern Quebec, were simply moved to Resolute, 2,000 km to the north. In 1955, another group of Inuit, from Pond Inlet, Nunavut, was transplanted to Grise Fiord, on the southern tip of Ellesmere Island. They were left in a hostile environment, with almost no equipment and a promise to be returned to their place of origin in two years. Seen as useful "subjects" for Canada's sovereignty claims, these Inuit were in fact kept in their new locations until the 1980s. Political pressure and the possibility of legal action forced the government to repatriate those who wished to return to their home communities. After repeated refusals and prevarications in the 1990s to avoid taking responsibility, the government ended up officially apologizing on 18 August 2010 and compensating the families. The Inuit living at Lake Ennadal, who were removed by force in 1949 by the Canadian army to allow the construction of a radio station, finally got a settlement of their legal proceedings – initiated in 2008 – only on August 20th 2018.[2] This tragic chapter in contemporary Arctic history shows how the government perceived the usefulness of Inuit in this part of Canada and utilized them, as objects, to further its policies in the South. This instrumentalization of human beings was shameful.*

"ESQUIMAUX/ESKIMOS" – "TRAINE ET BARQUE DE PEAU/ESKIMO SLED WITH SKIN BOAT"
Postcard. Pôle et Tropiques, Lyon, circa 1960. "Eskimo" is an old expression to describe all the inhabitants of the Far North. In addition to damaging the environment, the disruptions caused since the 1950s by the presence of non-Indigenous people in the Arctic are also affecting the Inuit populations. Previously nomadic, the Inuit now live in twenty-five villages in Nunavut, where a lack of work and deplorable housing conditions are exacerbating the social problems seen in the South – a high youth suicide rate, a resurgence of tuberculosis, widespread addiction, family violence – leaving them with little in the way of resources to help them live a normal, decent life. Credit: CHSJ

*The Arctic is the ultimate frontier that Canada shares with a number of countries: the United States, Russia, Norway, Denmark, Sweden, Finland and Iceland. Canada's territorial claims to the Arctic extended continental shelf and its statements that the Northwest Passage is within Canadian territory are contrary to US claims that the passage lies in international waters.*

*The Russians also made claims in 2007, following a submarine expedition that successfully planted a flag on the bottom of the Arctic Ocean. That was how the Russians asserted their sovereignty over that ocean, as would have been done in the time of Christopher Columbus or Jacques Cartier, the era of the Renaissance explorers!*

*In the summer of 2017, a Russian ship, the* Christophe de Margerie, *transported liquefied natural gas across the Arctic with no icebreaker escort, from Norway to South Korea, in 30 per cent less time than is required by the conventional Suez Canal route.³ A Chinese ship, the* Snow Dragon, *also traversed the Northwest Passage in the summer of 2017, this time with Canadian permission, for the alleged purpose of conducting scientific research. But everyone knows that what really interests China is the potential to ship goods by this route, which would save time and money.[4]*

*Arbitration under the* United Nations Convention on the Law of the Sea (UNCLOS) *will eventually decide among all these claims. Since Canada announced in May 2016 that it supports "without qualification" the* United Nations Declaration on the Rights of Indigenous Peoples, *along with the US, this conflict will be resolved under the aegis of the UN. The UN should give priority to the Inuit – who have occupied this region since time immemorial – and to their recognized right to the area (land and water) and its resources.[5]*

*During his tenure, Prime Minister Harper worked to educate Canadians about the importance of the Arctic and the need for Canada to develop an approach that respects the Inuit.*

\* \* \*

CAMBRIDGE BAY RADAR STATION - DEW LINE

"A completed DEW Line radome, circa 1956," colour photograph. The stations of the DEW (Distant Early Warning) Line, which later became NORAD in 1957, were set up across the Far North as far as Greenland to prevent a possible Soviet missile attack. They left in their wake tonnes of toxic waste that contaminated the local food chain. It cost $575 million and took decades (until 2014) to complete the cleanup, under pressure from environmental groups and Inuit populations. Credit: The Porticus Centre, Ollie Ekstedt

*Canada has already undertaken initiatives to assert its sovereignty, including mapping of the seabed of its continental shelf. After a decade of equivocation, Canada has just inaugurated the Canadian High Arctic Research Station, managed by Polar Knowledge Canada, with the goal of developing "a long-term, systematic, multidisciplinary view of this part of the world, which is really understudied." The research station is also intended to be "part of the community" in order to benefit from the Inuit's in-depth knowledge of the Arctic. The station will also join the network that includes all the foreign science stations active in this part of the world. Even South Korea has asked to be affiliated.[6]*

*Yet funding for ArcticNet, a consortium of climatology researchers,[7] and the Polar Environment Atmospheric Research Laboratory (PEARL) on Ellesmere Island, is not assured over the medium term, as Budget 2017 did not renew it.[8] However, $73.5 million was set aside to create a Canadian Centre for Climate Services. Funds are still being sought from the Natural Sciences and Engineering Research Council to maintain it.[9] In addition, the Climate Change and Atmospheric Research program, created five years ago, has been discontinued.[10]*

*Last summer, Canada finally decided to order a new fleet of six patrol ships and six supply ships specifically designed for Arctic deployment from the French company Thales at a cost of $5.2 billion. If Canada wants to assert its sovereignty, it must have a presence and enforce its maritime laws and regulations.[11]*

*In 2014, Canada authorized underwater seismic blasting in coastal areas of Nunavut. These detonations have direct impacts on marine habitats and traditional Inuit fishing activities. In July 2017, a Supreme Court decision overturned this authorization and recognized the National Energy Board's duty to consult and accommodate the Clyde River Aboriginal community, and to respect its Aboriginal hunting and fishing rights that ensure its "economic, cultural, and spiritual well-being." Once again, it was the courts that dictated to the government the approach acceptable in the circumstances – namely, genuine consultation and accommodation measures for the benefit of these populations, whose Aboriginal rights must be upheld.*

*This vast part of Canada is particularly sensitive given melting ice, permafrost subsidence, the fact that sea ice is melting more quickly than initially believed and the potential opening of the Northwest Passage.[12] A 2016 report by two renowned international agencies, the US National Oceanic and Atmospheric Administration (NOAA) and the American Meteorological Society (AMS), to which 500 scientists in more than 10 countries contributed, pointed out that, in the Arctic – the area most sensitive to global warming – the average surface temperature in 2015 was two degrees above the 1981–2010 average. This was a record high. The report added that at winter's end, in March, the maximum extent of Arctic ice was the lowest it had been in twenty-seven years of satellite observation.[13]*

*Canada must take the lead with its allies to regulate entry into the Northwest Passage in order to keep control over its internal waters and protect the rights of the Inuit.[14] The Crown has a special responsibility to these populations, and its honour is at stake, as the Supreme Court has already found in judgments that have defined the nature of Canada's unique relationship with Aboriginal peoples. It is important to note that Inuit do not live on reserves and are not subject to the infamous* Indian Act. *Yet the Canadian government, when it needed strategic settlements or defence facilities, never hesitated to utilize Inuit communities or move them far from their lands, uprooting them and then often abandoning them in villages, with all the problems of sedentary, "urban" living, which is alien to their way of life.*

BESTIARY

Kuppapik Ragee, Stonecut, 17/50, dated 1963. The Inuit have developed an outstanding form of cultural expression, profoundly influenced by the animal world around them and their day-to-day reality in a seemingly hostile environment. Their connection with nature nurtures their almost surrealistic vision of beings and people. Their unique language, Inuktitut, is alive and well. Their ancestral way of life should be recognized in the record of humankind's intangible heritage. Credit: Senate of Canada (CHSJ)

*Canada has enacted legislation to govern this vast area. In 1970, Canada passed the* Arctic Waters Pollution Prevention Act *after the 1969 crossing of the American icebreaker-tanker* Manhattan *through the Northwest Passage without Canada's prior authorization. Twenty years later, in 1988, Canada and the US signed the* Agreement on Arctic Cooperation. *In 1991, Canada signed the* Protocol on Environmental Protection to the Antarctic Treaty. *Five years later, in 1996, the Arctic Council was created. Its mandate is to ensure shared governance by member states, in part to promote the social and economic aspects of sustainable development in the Arctic. On Canada's behalf, an Inuk woman, Mary Simon, led the negotiations that established the council. Canada chaired the council twice, first in 1996–98 and again in 2013–15. However, Inuit are not full members of the Arctic Council: they have observer status. This status should be changed in order to comply with the provisions of the* United Nations Declaration on the Rights of Indigenous Peoples.

*The Inuit Circumpolar Council, an international non-governmental organization established in 1977, represents Inuit and Yupik. The Circumpolar Council should permanently co-chair the Arctic Council so that Inuit are always part of the various working groups and remain involved in any negotiations of agreements concerning the Arctic and the development of its resources.*

*In 2000, the federal government published* The Northern Dimension of Canada's Foreign Policy, *and in 2009, it implemented* Canada's Northern Strategy. *The following year, Canada established the Northern Canada Vessel Traffic Services Zone. Finally, in 2012 the International Polar Year Conference was held in Montreal.*

*To maintain a presence in this immense region, Canada must ensure that its navigation regulations are always adapted to the region's particular and changing conditions. It must put in place the necessary infrastructure, set out a resource development policy that makes its greenhouse gas reduction objectives a priority and, finally, implement fishing regulations that also aim to protect species, and regulations banning the dumping of waste water from cruise ships.*[15]

*In late 2017, the European Union and four other countries with commercial interests in the Arctic, including China and Japan, joined Canada and the other four countries whose borders extend into the northern Arctic Ocean in agreeing to a sixteen-year moratorium on all fisheries in the region until scientific studies have determined how to protect biodiversity and species renewal.*[16]

*The issues surrounding the future of the Arctic are tremendously significant. A quarter of the world's oil resources – up to 10 billion tonnes of hydrocarbons – and vast gas and diamond reserves are buried north of the Arctic Circle. The lure of huge profits arouses all kinds of desires. The US and the EU are challenging Canadian jurisdiction over these waters. Canada will have to establish environmental policies that are extremely faithful to all of its national and international objectives to prevent the degradation and indiscriminate exploitation of this enormous part of the country, which accounts for more than 40 per cent of its landmass.*

*The current radar detection system operated by* NORAD *has reached the end of its useful life, and replacing it will soon become an urgent priority. The new system should be operational by 2030, as work has already begun. But changes in the physical environment of the Arctic, combined with increasingly frequent access to these locations, pose new challenges to regional security, law enforcement, sovereignty protection, and national defence and strategic stability requirements.[17]*

*Canada must remain at the forefront of the international stage in advocating bold measures to protect the Arctic environment. It must show much stronger leadership on the Arctic in all forums. It must present itself as an environmentally responsible steward of this vast area. And its approach to Arctic issues must be irreproachable in every respect and constitute clear proof of its ability to be a role model for other nations in conserving these resources.*

*In December 2016, Canada and the United States jointly declared a five-year moratorium on all new oil and gas exploration in Arctic waters.[18] In March 2016, the two countries issued a joint statement promising to rely on scientists to better understand the issues involved. In so doing, Canada is taking the only logical path to preventing immeasurable damage. Any development plan must be developed in close consultation with the Inuit.*

*On August 19, 2017, the Canadian government announced the creation of the Lancaster Sound National Marine Conservation Area, strategically located at the eastern entrance to the Northwest Passage, with its western end in Barrow Strait. This area is twice the size of Nova Scotia. This decision ensures there will never be drilling in the Northwest Passage, a victory for the Inuit.[19]*

*Canada must now agree with the Inuit populations who have lived on these lands since time immemorial on a common approach that is consistent with a "nation-to-nation" and "government-to-government" relationship. For example, it must accommodate the Inuit's exercise of their sovereignty over this area. Note that the Inuit are claiming sovereignty over the internal waters of Nunavut, an issue that Canada did not expect, as demonstrated by the Inuit's claim to the wrecks of the two ships from Sir John Franklin's historic 1845 expedition,* Erebus *and* Terror, *that were found in their waters in 2014 and 2016 – right where the Inuit had always said they were!*

*In April 2018, the United Kingdom formally agreed to transfer ownership of the two wrecks to Canada. The Canadian government then committed to share ownership and management of the artifacts with the Inuit Heritage Trust, which represents Inuit interests in making the most of the historic discoveries.[20]*

*On another subject, according to the latest Statistics Canada report (2013), the social condition of Inuit in the Far North has seriously deteriorated. The infant mortality rate in Nunavut (20 per cent for girls and 16.5 per cent for boys) is three to four times higher than the national rate (4.6 per cent for girls and 5.2 per cent for boys). The youth suicide rate is ten times higher than the national average. The report notes that these data are "an important indicator of both maternal health … and of the availability and effectiveness of health care services." Food insecurity persists, and the assistance provided by the Canadian government is not enough to make everyday products available to families at an affordable cost.*

*The government has announced a plan to eliminate the extraordinarily high rate of tuberculosis among Inuit, which is 270 times that of the Canadian population. It also proposes to compensate Inuit who were relocated and poorly treated during the tuberculosis epidemics of the 1940s, 1950s and 1960s.[21]*

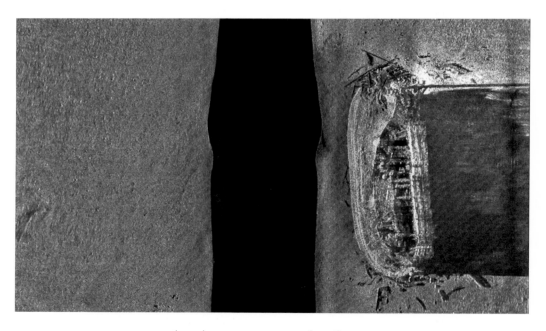

THE WRECKS OF THE *EREBUS* (2014) AND THE *TERROR* (2016)

The celebrated Sir John Franklin expedition to find the Northwest Passage was lost in the ice in 1845, and many attempts have since been made to find the two mythical ships and explain their mysterious disappearance. The wrecks of the two ships were found in 2014 and 2016 lying in the inland waters of Nunavut. The Inuit claim sovereignty over these waters and, consequently, ownership of the historic wrecks. An agreement was signed with the Canadian government to share the responsibility of their upkeep.
Credit: Parks Canada

*Domestic violence,[22] overcrowded housing, unsatisfactory academic performance and poor physical health are common problems. Many of the social problems that exist in the South are worse in the Far North. But the Inuit have no resources to fight these scourges from the South.*

*Canada will remain a trustee of the interests of Inuit people for generations to come, as the Supreme Court has stated in numerous judgments. The Government of Canada's recognition of the Inuit nation, which plans to assume all the prerogatives stemming from its Aboriginal rights, will require these two partners to negotiate in good faith and develop joint and harmonious policies that respect its lands, which the Inuit have held since time immemorial. There can be no doubt: without the cooperation and voluntary support of the Inuit, it will be difficult for Canada to maintain its international sovereignty in the Arctic. Canada will have to abandon its archaic colonial approach toward this people and develop a nation-to-nation relationship that respects the right of the Inuit to decide for themselves how they will exercise their sovereignty in order to develop their ancestral lands.*

*With the valued and sought-after contribution of the Inuit people, Canada will be able to ensure the sustainable development of this immense region, which climate change threatens with upheaval or, worse, a social and natural disaster never before seen in human history.*

NOTES

1  The author is indebted to the Library of Parliament for its careful work in verifying the accuracy of the historical facts and figures in the text.

2  "Entente entre Ottawa et les Inuits – Déplacements forcés dans les années 50," *La Presse+*, Actualités 13-4, 28 August 2018.

3  "The rush to exploit the Arctic," *The New York Times*, 27 August 2017, p. 8.

4  Robert Fife and Steven Chase, "Chinese ship sails Northwest Passage," *The Globe and Mail*, 1 August 2017, p. A3.

5  Oral testimony of Dalee Sambo Dorough, former chairperson of the United Nations Permanent Forum on Indigenous Issues, at a joint Senate caucus meeting, 28 September 2017.

6  Bob Weber, "Canada's High Arctic Research Station gives scientists a new window to the North," *The Globe and Mail*, 31 July 2017, p. A5.

7  "Canada's commitment to Arctic research in doubt, says prominent scientist," *IPolitics*, 10 November 2017.

8   The laboratory is located 15 km from the village of Eureka, in Nunavut.

9   Judith Lavoie, "Key Arctic research station set to close because of Liberal Government's funding cuts," *De Smog Canada*, http://www.desmog.ca, consulted 20 September 2017.

10  Alexandre Shields, "Ottawa abandonne un programme scientifique sur l'Arctique," *Le Devoir*, 23 January 2018, p. A1.

11  "Thales Canada gets $5.2 million contract," *The Globe and Mail*, 16 August 2017, p. B3.

12  Miriane Demers-Lemay, "L'amincissement de la banquise sous-estimé," *Le Devoir*, 26 October 2017, p. A4.

13  Jean-Louis Santini, "2016, année noire pour le climat," *La Presse.ca*, Agence France-Presse, Washington, 10 August 2017. http://www.lapresse.ca/environnement/dossiers/changements-climatiques/201708/10/01-5123474-2016-annee-noire-pour-le-climat.php.

14  Daphné Cameron, "Arctique: un ex-premier ministre française appuie le Canada," *Le Devoir*, 9 August 2011, p. A10.

15  *La Presse canadienne*, "Les rejets d'eaux usées dans l'Arctique inquiètent," *Le Devoir*, 27 August 2018, p. A8.

16  Gloria Galloway, "International deal reached on Arctic fishing," *The Globe and Mail*, 1 December 2017, p. A4.

17  Ernie Regehr, OC, Senior Fellow in Arctic Security and Defence, "Replacing the North Warning System: Strategic competition or Arctic confidence building?" Arctic Security Briefing Paper, *The Simons Foundation*, 1 March 2018.

18  Alexandre Shields, "Pas de nouveaux permis d'exploration pour au moins cinq ans," *Le Devoir.com*, 21 December 2016. https://www.ledevoir.com/societe/environnement/487529/moratoire-canadien-sur-l-exploration-petroliere-dans-l-arctique.

19  Margaret Wente, "A protected place and a long-awaited victory for the Inuit," *The Globe and Mail*, 19 August 2017, p. F1.

20  Kathleen Harris, "Canada, Britain formalize agreement on Franklin expedition wrecks," CBC *News*, 26 April 2018. https://www.cbc.ca/news/politics/franklin-expedition-hms-erebus-terror-1.4636222.

21  Kristy Kirkup, "Federal-Inuit task force formed to tackle sky-high tuberculosis rates," *National Post*, 6 October 2017, p. A7.

22  Anna Desmarais, "Indigenous mothers more susceptible to post-partum depression, study finds," *IPolitics*, 15 August 2018.

# An Inuit Nunangat, "First Canadians, Canadians First" (Jose Kusugak)

Natan Obed, president of the Inuit Tapiriit Kanatami (ITK)

*Nakummek*[1] for that warm introduction. *Ullaakkut*,[2] everyone. As introduced, my name is Natan Obed, president of Inuit Tapiriit Kanatami. It is an honour to be here to talk to you about Inuit Nunangat. What you may call the Arctic is what we Inuit call Inuit Nunangat.[3] It is our homeland. I want to talk to you first about symbolism in history and the weight of those things on us as a people, and on the imagination that Canadians have about our homeland and the Arctic.

I am struck when I come to Centre Block of the imagery displayed throughout it: the portraits of former prime ministers, the ever-present pictures of the Queen at various years of her life, the lions, and the other regal images that associate this parliamentary process and the Senate. There are also Indigenous people that are part of this building, outside this very chamber. In other democracies, even in Europe, Arctic images were a part of European seals, especially a narwhal or a polar bear. These images don't just run 150 years of Canadian mythology. They span Europe as well.

It makes me think of me, as an Indigenous person, and how I fit. Indigenous people are not a part of the row of former prime ministers that you see hallowing these halls. Are we more like the animals or the cherubs or the imagination of Canada and what it is versus an actual part of Canada, an actual part of this governance? It saddens me to think that these images, these pieces of our identity and our culture, were here during the time of the residential schools. They were here during the time when policies and legislation were put in place, which was specifically thought through to marginalize us, to take away our rights, to imagine us as less than human.

We're on this long path back, and reconciliation is only a part of what is happening across Canada, across the world, when it comes to Indigenous issues. And for Inuit, we play a very clear and specific role within the Aboriginal context in Canada, if you're using constitutional language; within the Indigenous discussion, if

A map illustrating the four Indigenous land-claims regions.
Sourced from Inuit Tapiriit Kanatami

you're using contemporary language, which this government has swapped out from "Aboriginal"; and, if you look through Supreme Court cases and at the growing and mounting evidence of our rights and the explicit role that we play, within Canada. We have the weight of the United Nations, the weight of human rights, the weight of the higher sense of the honour of the Crown that is with us as we assert our role for self-determination within this country of Canada.

Inuit have long said that we are proud Canadians, and it isn't necessarily a view that is held among all Indigenous peoples across Canada. The late Jose Kusugak,[4] who is someone very dear to me and who was the president of Inuit Tapiriit Kanatami, coined the phrase "first Canadians, Canadians first." And that is the way that most of us, most Inuit, describe ourselves to Canada and to the world. We are proud Indigenous people, we are proud Inuit. But we don't feel like we have to give up or somehow not be at peace with being Canadian as well.

We cheer for team Canada and we accept that we are part of this great democracy. But the time has come now to think critically about where we are going. And if we truly want a reconciliation moment, we have to imagine a future that isn't built upon the dysfunction of the past.

I'll start with a conversation in this country, and within Arctic studies, and broadly within North America, within Indigenous studies. In the late 1800s, it was imagined that Indigenous people would disappear, and that it was only a matter of time before our cultures, our societies, our languages, and we as people would just die out. This was based on a number of very unsound principles, but also on an explicit government-focused genocidal program for Indigenous people, taking our lands, resettling our people, not providing the same services for Indigenous people that you do for the rest of your society, not imagining Indigenous people within legislative policy or with programs or services that you deem appropriate for all other people in your society.

So we have been forcibly removed from a lot of these policy debates for the entire history of this country. And don't think of it as a historical footnote that I'm bringing to you today just to say that it happened. It is still happening to Inuit. And this is the imagination that I believe we all have to have about where we are today and where we want to go moving forward.

Jose Kusugak (1950–2011), former president of Inuit Tapiriit Kanatami. Sourced from Inuit Tapiriit Kanatami

I really appreciate having the wisdom of David Suzuki precede my presentation. I feel a little bit guilty about being a politician at this moment, but I recognize the truth in the words you say about the system. I am an optimist at heart. I believe that good people, even good politicians, can actually make a tremendous difference in the way that the country thinks about itself and the way that legislation, policy, and programs are changed to affect the common good of our people. And I'm thinking about different points in our history, in Inuit Nunangat, that we know as people who have lived through them, which then underpin the reality we have today.

If you think about why it was that it was imagined that we were to die out, you think of 1918 and Spanish Flu, which was a global pandemic. But in the region that I come from, Nunatsiavut, one of our communities, Okak, was completely wiped out.[5] There is actually a National Film Board video called *The Last Days of Okak*,[6] made in 1985, that I recommend people watch. But the destruction that colonizers brought to us, and then the lack of interest in guarding against that destruction, is a part of our history.

Think of the tuberculosis epidemic that happened in the fifties in Inuit Nunangat and across the Canadian Arctic, and the fact that the Canadian government mobilized ships to bring infected patients to sanatoriums in the South for sometimes one, two, or three years, and they didn't bother to tell families whether or not the people who had died actually had died or when they were coming home. Especially among young children who were sick when they left, their families were never told where they were going, when they might be back, or, if their child had died, that they had died at all. This is a part of our history. It's a part of today, because those connections for health service delivery, which were established in the fifties, still are alive today.

So the North-South links that we have between our homeland and our service provision for most of our health services follow those same lines, the historical lines, and also follow the same principles, that they cannot serve our people in our homeland. They cannot serve our people in our language. They don't necessarily even have to tell us why they are doing the things the way they are doing them. We should be satisfied just for the very fact that they acknowledge that there is a problem, and that they are able to give this to us today.

Today, our tuberculosis rates are 330 times the average of all other Canadians born in Canada. Tuberculosis, as a disease, is one that is thought of in relation to developing countries. The idea that today this country is not able to mobilize against it is inconceivable, especially for a population of sixty thousand people. We know where Inuit live. We know where the tuberculosis is happening, yet there is no political will to actually solve the problem.

The medical model for the solution has been around for, I would say, fifty to seventy-five years. The understanding we have now through modern science about how to treat it, how to cut down the time to identify active tuberculosis, the contact tracing, all those different public health mechanisms, have been proven to be effective across the world, but somehow, Inuit are not Canadian enough for the federal government or provinces and territories in which Inuit live to provide a solution. It's pretty profound. I can go through a number of different social indicators that all point to a profound lack of interest in having the Inuit population imagined as a part of the Canadian population.

# SOCIAL AND ECONOMIC INEQUITY IN INUIT NUNANGAT

Many Inuit face social and economic inequities that impact our health and wellbeing

## Inuit Nunangat

**52%** of Inuit in Inuit Nunangat live in crowded homes *[1]

**34%** of Inuit aged 25 to 64 in Inuit Nunangat have earned a high school diploma [1]

**70%** of Inuit households in Nunavut are food insecure [2]

**$23,485** The median before tax individual income for Inuit in Inuit Nunangat [1]

**30** The number of physicians per 100,000 population in Nunavut [4]

**47.5%** of Inuit in Inuit Nunangat are employed [1]

**72.4 years** The projected life expectancy for Inuit in Canada† [5]

**12.3** The infant mortality rate per 1,000 for Inuit infants in Canada. [6]

## All Canadians

**9%** of all Canadians live in crowded homes *[1]

**86%** of all Canadians aged 25 to 64 have earned a high school diploma [1]

**8%** of all households in Canada are food insecure [3]

**$92,011** The median before tax individual income for non-Indigenous people in Inuit Nunangat [1]

**119** The number of physicians per 100,000 population in Urban Health Authorities [4]

**60.2%** of all Canadians are employed [1]

**82.9 years** The projected life expectancy for non-Indigenous people in Canada [5]

**4.4** The non-indigenous infant mortality rate per 1,000 for Canada. [6]

Infographic courtesy of ITK which demonstrates the inequities Inuit face compared to non-Inuit counterparts on multiple social outcomes. For more information and data sources, please visit https://www.itk.ca/social-and-economic-inequity-in-inuit-nunangat/

Looking at our housing overcrowding rates, which stand at 40 per cent, and considering that we were coerced into communities in the fifties, it's clear that we have only known severe overcrowding in our communities. We have only known a lack of basic infrastructure and a lack of access to education services. This is the only reality that Canadian Inuit understand about the way in which the Canadian government and provinces and territories deliver services to Inuit, and yet we still call ourselves proud Canadians.

I think it speaks to our resilience. We are resilient people. If you fly to the Canadian Arctic and you have never been there before, I guarantee that you will wonder how people lived in the Arctic. Juxtapose that with the way we see the world. We fly over the Arctic and we see places to camp in the spring or in the fall, or the lakes where the Arctic char are in the winter, the places where our caribou have calving grounds, the inlets that there are plenty of, where we know that even on the coldest day in winter there will be open water and the chance to catch a beluga or a seal.

I think that is part of the difference in this country, when people and governments look past other people's realities, knowledge, and political place in the world. Here we are today, talking about the future of the Arctic and talking about sustainable development. When we as Inuit often look to these discussions and look to the myriad Arctic university chairs, and the global interest in us to be researched or for sovereignty, or all these conversations about animal rights and our specific Arctic populations, we are confused why it matters to you at all. Then we follow that up with, "Why aren't we the ones telling our stories and giving our positions? Why does the rest of the world somehow feel as though it's their space?"

Our democracy is founded on modern land-claim agreements, modern treaties. There are four land-claim settlement regions across Inuit Nunangat[7] that range from Nunatsiavut in northern Labrador: Makivik Corporation's[8] Nunavik James Bay and Northern Quebec Agreement in northern Quebec; the Nunavut Agreement,[9] which created the Government of Nunavut, changing the political face of Canada; Nunavut Tunngavik,[10] which is still the Inuit organization that represents the rights of the Inuit in Nunavut; and in the Northwest Territories, the Inuvialuit Regional Corporation.[11]

So from 1975 to 2005, we did our own nation-building. We did our own Inuit governance exercise. We were already owners of Inuit Nunangat. Even though we don't imagine ourselves with a simple, capitalistic understanding of the word "owners," we have had to really come to terms with the fact that we have to speak in that language, and our elders, especially in the land-claims period, had to be convinced that this was something we could even say to the Government of Canada, that we somehow own this land.

I think back again, because of being from Nunatsiavut, about the Moravian missionaries[12] who settled there in 1771. They had orders in council from the British government to set up mission stations because Inuit in northern Labrador were a hindrance to the whaling and fishing interests of Britain at the time, and the British were concerned that Inuit were getting in the way of the work, so they provided the opportunity for Moravian missionaries to come and basically colonize the Inuit. There are logs that exist. They were German missionaries who were orderly and took lots of detailed notes, so the record survives about these first contacts.

It is kind of an amazing look into life during one particular colonial moment, where you have a benevolent person, in their mind, coming and saying, "We want to buy this land from you," and Inuit on the other side saying, "There is lots of land and we don't own it, so why would you buy this from us?" And then the conversation continues: "Well, we need to do something, otherwise we won't have the ability to build here." So it's that certainty from the very second of the colonial discussion that is demanded of Indigenous people by an incoming power.

In the end, Inuit just weren't interested in mobilizing the way that this representative of the Crown wanted them to, so the missionaries basically made contracts with all the families in the surrounding region. It's not necessarily detailed what was given to them, but that was the land transfer. That was the beginning. That was the genesis of 250 years of Moravian occupation in northern Labrador.

In 1971, the first president Tagak Curley (centre) speaks with the first members of the Inuit Tapirisat of Canada (Inuit will be united in Canada), now named Inuit Tapiriit Kanatami (Inuit are united in Canada). Sourced from Inuit Tapiriit Kanatami

This is an important story because it gets to the heart of what we're trying to undo now. What this country is founded on – the rules, policies, and programs – they have never, ever considered the interests of Inuit within the development of them. Yes, we may have been consulted. Yes, we may have had the ability to be part of a standing committee or be part of your political process, but we need to go beyond that. We need to recognize that we do now have land-claim agreements, and the implementation of those land-claim agreements implicates the honour of the Crown and the very basic nature of the relationship between Inuit and Canada.

We also need to recognize that Inuit are Canadians, and what we want for ourselves and our families we would also like for other Canadians. That is a very Canadian thing to feel like you're a part of, that we have universal healthcare, that we are a friendly, giving people, but we have huge holes in that tapestry we weave. I'm here not to judge you all on that. I'm here to say that we're still here and we want to partner with you to create a better Canada, to lift up populations that need help, to not only accept that there are Indigenous people in this country but respect our rights and respect Inuit governance.

I am the president of Inuit Tapiriit Kanatami. I am the national Inuit leader. It is not a position that I take lightly, and it is at its base an Inuit democracy that comes from every single Inuk that is registered within a land-claim agreement who votes for their presidents, and those presidents sit on my board and vote for the national Inuit leader. They elect me.

Canadians don't necessarily know or care about this. I'm saying you should, and not because I have some sort of ego. It is because there is an Inuit democracy that sits alongside the Canadian democracy, and we have chosen to try to work with you, to work with Canada to make it all integrated.

The UN Declaration on the Rights of Indigenous People is very instructive. Our land claims are instructive. Supreme Court cases are instructive, but then it comes down to actually doing it, so the creation of an Inuit Nunangat policy space where we could reimagine what we do in federal budgets, allocations, programs, or services and imagine that we get out of the boxes that we have created for ourselves in this country.

This country is divided into very specific policy spaces. With an Indigenous policy space, it usually just starts and ends with the Indian Act. Inuit are not a part of the Indian Act. We aren't governed by the Indian Act. We pay taxes. We are another thing all together, yet there is no policy space ever that is considered for us as one of the three recognized Indigenous peoples in this country.

So there are very easy things to start with. Social equity is a difficult thing and can happen over time, and we're patient and resilient and we can make it happen. We're not expecting the world today, but we are expecting the world to change incrementally,

ᐃᓄᐃᑦ ᑕᐱᕇᑦ ᑲᓇᑕᒥ
## INUIT TAPIRIIT KANATAMI

Inuit Tapiriit Kanatami's current logo represents the four land-claims regions through the four Inuit. The maple leaf located in the negative space portrays the Inuit connection to Canada, and the ulu, traditionally an Inuit woman's knife, located in the negative space is a part of Inuit culture. Sourced from Inuit Tapiriit Kanatami

and we're expecting in this time when we talk about reconciliation and about how much Indigenous peoples mean to Canada that it goes beyond words and that your life actually changes because of it.

It's not to say that we're asking Canadians to give up their wealth and their own identity and replace it with something that was taken away three or four hundred years ago. It is to say that we can still do something today, that we can respect each other, we can respect Indigenous human rights, and we all have a role to play in building a better Canada. For Inuit, we don't just see these as our own issues only. In many cases, when we hear about floods or other natural disasters all over the world, Inuit are some of the first to donate, some of the first to be compassionate about other people who are going through difficult times, and so I think that also speaks to the fact that we understand what it's like.

I'll just close on one thing, and it's in relation to language. This government has pledged an Indigenous languages protection act. Inuktitut, our language, is still viable. Sixty per cent of Canadian Inuit still use Inuktitut as our mother tongue, yet there's nowhere in this country that you can go to school beyond grade 4 with Inuktitut as the language of instruction, even in Inuit Nunangat.[13]

We are in the process of unifying our written language, and to my knowledge it's one of the first times this has happened in North America, where we are taking back our language. It was missionaries, governments, and individuals who created the written language that we now use, and there are many dialects and many ways of writing it. We are saying this is our language; we are going to repatriate it; we are bringing it back.

It's with that sort of process that is already started by us that I think other Canadians can help us, that you can make space for meaningful change in the way Indigenous languages and our language, Inuktitut, are uplifted into a space where, for us, there should be no difference between English, French, and Inuktitut in the way that we access funding for promotion and services in our language, in our communities, and in the way that our education system is run. The media that we consume doesn't have to be English all the time. We can do that, and we have the wealth and the imagination and also, I believe, the initiative to work through this together.

### NOTES

1 "Nakummek" translates from Inuttut to English as "thank you." "English-Inuttut Dictionary," Labrador Virtual Museum, http://www.labradorvirtualmuseum.ca/english-inuttut.htm. Accessed 16 June 2017.

2 "Ullaakkut" translates from Inuktitut to English as "good morning." "Alphabetical List of Vocabulary," Inuktitut Tusaalanga, http://www.tusaalanga.ca/glossary/inuktitut?pager=U. Accessed 16 June 2017.

3 Inuit Nunangat Map, 21 January 2016, http://www.aadnc-aandc.gc.ca/Map/irs/mp/index-en.html. Accessed 16 June 2017.

4 "Inuit Leader Jose Kusugak Dies," CBC News, 19 January 2011, http://www.cbc.ca/news/canada/north/inuit-leader-jose-kusugak-dies-1.1028807. Accessed June 16, 2017.

5 "Labrador Inuit," Nunatsiavut Government, http://www.nunatsiavut.com/visitors/labrador-inuit/. Accessed 16 June 2017.

6 *The Last Days of Okak*, National Film Board of Canada, https://www.nfb.ca/film/last_days_of_okak/. Accessed 16 June 2017.

7 "Inuit Nunangat Canada," Inuit Tapiriit Kanatami, https://www.itk.ca/portfolio/inuit-nunangat-canada/. Accessed June 16 2017.

8 "JBNQA," Makivik Corporation, http://www.makivik.org/history/jbnqa/. Accessed 16 June 2017.

9 Nunavut Agreement, http://nlca.tunngavik.com/?lang=en. Accessed 16 June 2017.

10 Nunavut Tunngavik Inc, http://www.tunngavik.com/. Accessed 16 June 2017.

11 Inuvialuit Regional Corporation, http://www.irc.inuvialuit.com/. Accessed 16 June 2017.

12 "The Moravian Church," Newfoundland and Labrador Heritage, http://www.heritage.nf.ca/articles/society/moravian-church.php. Accessed 16 June 2017.

13 Inuit Nunangat Map, 21 January 2016, http://www.aadnc-aandc.gc.ca/Map/irs/mp/index-en.html. Accessed 16 June 2017.

# 8

# Science and Culture

# Science: Is Canada in Danger of Missing the Fourth Industrial Revolution?[1]

The Hon. Serge Joyal, Senator

*D*oes Canada want to be a leading player in the fourth industrial revolution that will be sparked by artificial intelligence, robotics, and the digital universe? And what ethical standards will it set to ensure that humans keep control of this metamorphic process?

In the last fifty years, science policy has not always been a top priority for the Canadian government. In fact, for the past fifteen years science has been a secondary consideration of no immediate relevance to the government's main priorities: free trade, commerce, resource development, and the security of Canadians. Science has been flying below the public radar.

Although Canada has been a G7 member since 1976 and is proud to be among the world's most developed economies, its spending in support of science has been shrinking steadily. Canada has fallen to the back of the pack in this area, far behind its competitors.

According to the Naylor Report on Canadian science policy, released in April 2017,[2] the proportion of GDP devoted to research and development in Canada declined from 1.86 per cent in 2000-2001 to 1.61 per cent in 2014-2015. Among all other G7 countries and many G20 countries, this figure increased during the same period.[3] Canada is no longer one of the world's top thirty countries in terms of research support. The 2.38 per cent of GDP that Canada spends on research places it well below the average for OECD countries.[4]

Canada's public research spending as a percentage of GDP was frozen at 0.55 per cent in 2000-2001 and increased only slightly to 0.56 per cent in 2014–15, before levelling off again in the 2017 budget.[5]

Canada is constantly falling farther behind its peers. Canada's research spending (total gross expenditures) is the lowest among 18 countries with advanced economies. Its 1.61 per cent spending level places it atop the trailing group of countries, followed by Italy at

*1.29 per cent. A small country like Sweden spends almost three times as much as Canada, devoting 3.16 per cent of its GDP to research. Even China, which has a per capita GDP five times lower than Canada's, invests 2.05 per cent in research – well ahead of Canada. South Korea, the dragon of the Asian economy, leads the way at 4.29 per cent.[6] It has even signed a preliminary partnership agreement with the Canadian Network of Northern Research Operators, which is active in the High Arctic. Therefore, it would not be surprising if the fourth industrial revolution were to benefit those countries that understand that the prosperity and future of leading economies is tied to artificial intelligence.*

*Evidence of Canada's lagging behind in research support can be seen on several levels.[7] The number of Canadian researchers engaged in fundamental research has declined in recent years. This is almost the equivalent of a "brain drain." Talented individuals are in great demand, and countries compete ferociously to attract these individuals. As a result, in highly specialized fields, today's world has no real national borders.*

*Many laboratories are prepared to make highly lucrative offers to researchers whose work is published regularly in* Nature *or* Science, *the world's leading scientific journals. Indeed, a country's reputation depends on how many of its researchers publish articles on their work or discoveries in scientific journals. Canada has accounted for only about 3.5 per cent of the articles published in such journals since 1980. Last year, its share was only 2.86 per cent.[8]*

*This stagnation affects the next generation of researchers. The number and value of grants and scholarships available to science students have remained the same for 10 years, despite an increase in the number of students. Science students therefore have little choice but to study abroad. For example, American recruitment companies such as Riviera Partners in San Francisco have identified the University of Waterloo as their second-best source of talent (behind Berkeley) for high-tech employers in the San Francisco Bay area.[9]*

*The indifference shown by successive governments will fritter away one of Canada's greatest assets in the competitive field of science.*

*Yet Canada has a history of remarkable successes which, in their day, revolutionized the economy and improved the health and quality of life of Canadians, if not the country's overall prosperity.*

*The construction of the world's first nuclear reactor for peaceful purposes, the CANDU (Canada Deuterium Uranium) reactor in 1962, and the opening of the first multi-unit power station in 1971, ushered Canada into the inner circle of leading post-World War II economies. Canada had been lucky enough to welcome highly skilled French research scientists when they fled France ahead of the Nazi occupation in 1942. Those scientists were able to continue their research on nuclear fission in Canada.*

*The proposed Avro Arrow MRI supersonic jet, which was to be armed with nuclear missiles, was a revolutionary breakthrough at the height of the Cold War in 1957. The total cost of the project would have been $1.1 billion. However, the project was cancelled by the government of the day, and 15,000 aerospace workers were laid off in the process. Canada's future in aviation's next generation thus came to an abrupt end.[10] However, the design team's chief engineer, Jim Chamberlain, and thirty of his most promising colleagues were immediately recruited by NASA to work in the Mercury, Gemini, and Apollo space programs. They were members of the NASA teams that enabled the United States to send its first man (John Glenn) into space in 1962 and made Neil Armstrong the first man to set foot on the moon in 1969. As he put it, "That's one small step for man, one giant leap for mankind."*

*In 1967, Canada benefitted from the unique contributions of the Senate Special Committee on Science Policy, also known as the Lamontagne Committee, after its chair, Senator Maurice Lamontagne.[11] When the Lamontagne Committee published the first of its three reports in 1970 (others followed in 1972 and 1973), the Pierre E. Trudeau government immediately appointed a minister responsible for science policy.[12] With those reports in hand, the Canadian government had an unrivaled overall action plan that was recognized abroad as one of the most comprehensive in the world.[13] The report recommended grouping the basic research conducted by the government's various departmental organizations. It also proposed a support program for research conducted by major universities and private institutions, and advocated that these organizations work in networks. Finally, it put forward an ambitious support program for private sector research and development (R&D) and innovation.*

*The path was therefore staked out. Equipped with this plan, Canada joined a select group of countries that supported science, the dynamics of discovery, and the successes of innovation. The tangible results of this national science policy grew over the years.*

*In 1972, Telesat Canada launched its first communications satellite, ANIK A-1. It launched thirty-two more in the years that followed.*

*Five scientists who had worked and made their discoveries in Canada were awarded the Nobel Prize in their disciplines.[14] And many more researchers received prestigious awards or international recognition for their fine work.*

*The development of the Canadarm, a robotic remote manipulator system originally built for the US space shuttle* Columbia *in 1974, remains the most publicized of Canada's high-tech achievements in the aerospace sector. The Canadian Space Agency was established in 1989 to bring together Canada's expertise in this sector, and it has since made key contributions to space programs in the US and the European Union.*

"THAT'S ONE SMALL STEP FOR A MAN – ONE GIANT LEAP FOR MANKIND"
Commemorative plate, plastic, Texas Ware, by PMC, AP PHOTO/NASA #6907200304, 20 July 1969.
The 1960s ended with an incredible event that would leave its mark for years to come. American astronaut Neil Armstrong became the first man to walk on the moon on 20 July 1969. This was a major victory for the US aerospace industry in the Cold War era. Canada's technological research led to the launch of its first communications satellite, ANIK A-1, in 1972. It would be followed by 32 others over the years. Credit: CHSJ

*Last fall, Canada provided a laser altimeter to enable NASA's Osiris-Rex space probe to sweep the surface of asteroid Bennu, a remnant of the birth of the solar system. Aethera Technologies of Halifax is currently working with the Houston company Ad Astra on a new type of engine for use in space travel that will propel rockets up to 10 times faster with only a fraction of the fuel.[15]*

*Since 1967, there have been 23,658 patents registered at the Canadian Patent Office. However, according to a report from the Centre for International Governance*

*Innovation, Canadian companies register three times more patents in the US than in Canada. Because the American market is ten times larger, it offers that much more potential for profit. What is more, US firms hold nearly four times more Canadian patents than do Canadian firms.[16]*

*While Canada can contribute on a macro scale, it can also contribute at the micro level. As part of the international Human Genome Project led by the United Kingdom, Genome Canada contributed to the complete mapping of all the genes of human beings in 2003. This achievement opened the door to countless promising treatments for human maladies. The cloning of Dolly the sheep, which made headlines in 1996, heralded a new wave of research in the revolutionary field of genetics, which could one day make it possible to replace damaged organs.*

*In agriculture, biochemistry research led to the development of canola oil, a Canadian invention developed in 1970 by crossing various varieties of rapeseed. The domestic cooking oil produced from those seeds is now exported throughout the world.*

IMAX — THE ULTIMATE FILM EXPERIENCE

The IMAX film system was designed in the late 1960s and early 1970s by four Canadians (Graeme Ferguson, Roman Kroitor, Robert Kerr, and William C. Shaw). During Expo 67, they developed the idea of using several projectors simultaneously to display the same image on a giant screen. This technology has since been improved and is now used worldwide. Crédit: © Justin Smith / Wikimedia Commons, CC-BY-SA-3.0

*China is one of the biggest buyers of canola oil. Producers in Western Canada are finding it difficult to keep up with the demand from growth markets in India, Pakistan, and other Asian countries. This is a powerful example of how fundamental laboratory research can have tremendous economic benefits.*

*Research and discoveries in biomedicine have saved thousands of lives. In May 1968, a team led by Dr. Grondin at the Montreal Heart Institute carried out Canada's first successful heart transplant surgery.*

*A logistics expert working for Doctors Without Borders and his brother successfully developed a solar-powered pump capable of supplying running water to a hospital in the Democratic Republic of the Congo.*

*In June 2017, Dr D. Shepard's team at the McGill University Health Centre successfully pierced the armour of certain types of bacteria, thereby reducing the need to use ever-more-powerful antibiotics. The second phase of this clinical research will be supported by the US defense department, which is particularly interested in hospital-acquired infections. In the October 2017 issue of the journal* Nature Communications, *McGill University researchers published their findings on the role of ribonucleic acid (RNA) in the development of Alzheimer's disease. This was a key step in the fight against this debilitating illness, which affects 564,000 Canadians, 65 per cent of them women.[17]*

*The first network of university centres of excellence was established in 1983–84 by the then-secretary of state. This network helped realign and strategically maximize existing research capabilities and resources in Canadian universities.[18] Canada has remarkable achievements to its credit. Furthermore, it has the potential, given the formal education level of its population, to carve out an even greater role for itself in the top discoveries and achievements of human ingenuity.*

*What is clearly disappointing, in light of the inventiveness, intellectual resources, and personal commitment of all these researchers, is the lack of vision in government in a country whose future economic vitality is directly tied to its ability to make discoveries such as new green technologies, which offer the most promising path to escape global warming. Unless Canada provides tremendous support for the various fundamental and applied research projects conducted in its government research centres, the private sector, and academia, it will lag further behind and be quickly overtaken by its US, European and, now, Asian competitors, all of whom have decided to make the most of the current shift toward artificial intelligence (AI).*

*Consider the example of drones – programmed equipment guided remotely from long distances – which are revolutionizing military strategy. The use of AI has transformed drones into fearsome weapons of war. From 2004 to 2008, the number of robots used in combat zones in Iraq increased from 150 to 12,000, and nearly two dozen types are deployed in that country.[19] In 2017, the 123 signatories to the Convention on Certain Conventional Weapons commissioned a group of experts to revise its provisions to take into account lethal autonomous weapons systems.*

*Military strategy has completely changed in only a few years, and technological change is outstripping strategic decision makers' ability to keep up with it. AI is causing a genuine "military revolution," with an impact comparable to that of gunpowder and the atomic bomb in their respective eras. Investing robotic weapons with AI to create autonomous weapons essentially transforms them into "algorithms of war." At least six countries are currently trying to incorporate AI into their military technologies: Israel, South Korea, the US, the UK, China, and Russia.*

*The ethics of technological research will have to be reviewed in light of these profound changes, which challenge humanity to retain control over the use of such weapons. The philosophical reflection that must accompany these unprecedented developments has only barely begun. These technological advances deprive life and its complexity of meaning. Franco-Argentinian philosopher Miguel Benasayag has noted that unbridled machines hoard information, while flesh and blood individuals have limits yet find meaning in that information.[20] What restrictions should be placed on such superintelligence, and who will control it?[21]*

*The founder of eBay (Pierre Omidyar) and the founder of LinkedIn (Reid Hoffman) quickly recognized this conundrum and decided to create a $27-million fund for the ethics and governance of AI. One of the fund's purposes is to establish pathways between computer science and the social sciences to ensure that innovations from these new systems continue to serve the general interest – in short, to make sure that AI benefits society and that any potential damage to humanity can be mitigated. Social science experts, ethics watchdogs, philosophers, religious leaders, economists, lawyers, and policy makers will all have a part to play.*

*Elsewhere, parliamentarians have already understood this. On 15 March 2017, the French Senate and National Assembly published a major report on these issues entitled* Pour une intelligence artificielle maîtrisée, utile et démystifiée *[Toward a controlled, useful, and demystified AI].[22] The EU has produced two reports on the subject, as have the House of Commons in the UK and the White House in the US.*

*Canada can no longer put off public debate on this subject. The implications for the future of the society Canadians want to build and for the preservation of their values throughout this upheaval – which strikes at the essence of humanity – are simply too broad. The Senate of Canada should not hesitate to tackle this public and legislative debate.*

*Forward-looking decisions will be required in the areas of quantum technology and AI, and in the management and analysis of so-called big data, which will generate a wide range of undreamed-of advances. These advances will change people's lives so deeply that today's world will seem just as outdated as the early twentieth century, when rotary telephones were the norm.*

*Canada can discuss this coming revolution in every possible forum, but to avoid being on the sidelines of the changes that are already happening, it must quickly revise its budget priorities. Canadian society must focus on fundamental science research, funding for universities – which support most Canadian research – and assistance to private-sector R&D and innovation. In short, Canada must strengthen the full range of human and scientific infrastructure.*

*The modern world has moved on to another level in the use of artificial intelligence. The more widespread use of AI in industry has completely changed the game. The New York Times reported on 19 July 2018 that, if America wants to keep control of advanced technologies in the future, and prevent China from gaining a leg up in the revolutionary developments to be derived from AI, the US government has no choice but to develop a plan for massive investments in AI research and implementation.[23]*

*It is estimated that nearly half of all repetitive in-plant tasks will be performed by machines within twenty to fifty years. This will lead to the loss of 1.5 million to 1.7 million jobs, and 42 per cent of all jobs will be directly affected by robotization.[24] The automobile industry alone is on the verge of radical changes. Canada ranks fifth among the countries engaged in this field of research, which will have a decisive effect on the future prosperity of this country.*

*Canada has no choice but to embark on this revolution. On the other side of this revolution, new job opportunities, markets, and capital will arise. Annual sales in the industrial robotics market are expected to reach $37 billion in 2018.*

*If Canada fails to make its research policy a permanent priority, strengthen its infrastructure, and substantially increase the budgets of its four granting councils (the National Research Council of Canada (NRC), established in 1916; the Social Sciences and Humanities Research Council (SSHRC), established in 1977; the Natural Sciences and Engineering Research Council (NSERC), established in 1978; and the Canadian Institutes of Health Research (CIHR), established in 2000), it will be left behind. Its economy will lose momentum and its standard of living will remain stagnant at best and might even decline. Current global competition to attract the best talent is greater than ever before, particularly now that the Asian countries have fully entered the race.*

*Scientific research does not have direct economic effects just on employment. It influences the development of medical science and, consequently, the health of Canadians.*

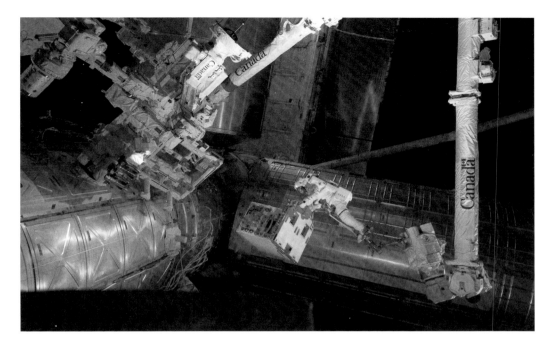

THE CANADARM — A SYMBOLIC SUCCESS

Developed in 1974, the Canadarm was a remote-controlled mechanical arm developed for the space shuttle Columbia (STS-2). A high-tech success story, the Canadarm proved its usefulness by performing more than eighteen intricate procedures in space. Canada has entertained an ongoing interest in space and focuses on developing technical elements vital to the success of these exploration missions. In 1989, it consolidated its activities within the Canadian Space Agency; Canadian astronauts have since established a solid reputation, among them the Rt. Hon. Julie Payette, governor general of Canada.

Credit: Rex Feature

*Remote medicine and online consultations are becoming more common and more effective.[25] Patients can use a smartphone to submit their symptoms and medical history to a health care practitioner, and they no longer have to wait months for an answer. Telemedicine is progressing quickly, and the practice of medicine will become less and less cloistered. A digital revolution is coming in health care, and the potential for improvement is considerable.[26] In October 2017, a Senate committee tabled a report dealing with exactly this issue. It was entitled* Challenge Ahead: Integrating Robotics, Artificial Intelligence, and 3D Printing Technologies into Canada's Healthcare Systems.[27]

*Scientific research also has a critical influence on social cohesion. It can help eliminate long-standing prejudices that are sources of social tension.*

*For millennia, the chromosomal difference between men and women was not known, and women were considered inferior to men. Religious beliefs and doctrines were developed on the basis of flawed premises that gave rise to the worst kind of discriminatory practices.*

*The same could be said of sexual orientation until the American Psychiatric Association, after years of research and clinical studies, removed homosexuality from the* Diagnostic and Statistical Manual of Mental Disorders *(DSM) in 1973. In fact, homosexuality was made a crime under the* Criminal Code *in the nineteenth century. Later, the government kept gay people out of positions of responsibility and authority, considering them a disruptive influence on the social, political, military, and judicial order.[28] Parliament enacted legislation in June 2018 to substantiate the government's official apologies to the gay community and enable some of the victims of repression to have their criminal records expunged.[29]*

*Science identified the biological evidence behind the principles of gender equality and respect for sexual orientation.*

*Data produced by scientific research are essential to the advancement of humanity. A society that does not value science is condemned to regress back toward the dark ages. Alexis de Tocqueville, a shrewd observer of North American society in the first half of the nineteenth century, wisely urged leaders of nations to embrace a long-term approach that supports higher education and fosters a greater passion for science in order to counterbalance the tendency to prefer quick and easy solutions to practical problems.[30]*

*Since scientific research results are peer-reviewed, scientific findings – no matter where they are made – are universal in value and constitute a source of progress the world over. Science is legitimately independent, and it evolves outside the framework of dogmas or beliefs.[31]*

*Science creates upheaval and calls into question people's views of the world, as well as the place human beings occupy in the universe.*

*After making numerous mathematical calculations and scholarly observations in the seventeenth century, Galileo logically concluded that the Earth was not immobile, but was in fact orbiting around the sun. He was excommunicated for his work and was not formally welcomed back into the Catholic Church until 1992, when Pope John Paul II accepted the recommendation of a special panel that had studied Galileo's case for ten years! So it took more than 350 years to "morally" validate the obvious cosmology of the universe.*

*The most recent Nobel Prize in Physics was awarded to three American scientists who successfully proved the existence of gravitational waves created by black holes – an idea previously proposed by Einstein in 1916. This "revolutionary thinking" extended human knowledge of the universe into the heart of the Big Bang.[32] This discovery effectively demonstrates that basic research cannot be ignored in favour of applied research, which is what Canada focused on over the past decade. Both are deserving of equal support.*

*In a world where social media convey everyone's prejudices, emotions, and "fake news," science is ever more important. The populism that can lead an autocrat to power feeds on disinformation and anti-science. Scientific awareness is an antidote to this modern virus that contaminates democratic discourse. Research scientists must assume their proper role in public debate in order to prevent the kind of obscurantist abuses worthy of Arthur Miller's depiction of the Salem witch trials in* The Crucible.

*Today, the people opposing science are mostly climate sceptics and creationists. Not surprisingly, regressive government regimes often cut spending on research or let it wither on the vine until it becomes insignificant. Such regimes sometimes prohibit government researchers from sharing their findings with the media. They may even go so far as to simply abolish the gathering of objective data to support policy-making based on evidence rather than unfounded beliefs.[33] The free flow of scientific research results is still the best guarantee of their veracity. Those with doubts can make them known publicly and present the data supporting their own conclusions.*

*According to the dean of the Harvard School of Medicine, the new US government's decisions to cut $7 billion in budget spending on science, reduce funding for the National Institutes of Health by 18 per cent and cut the Environmental Protection Agency's funding, not to mention its cuts to basic research spending, will have "catastrophic" economic repercussions for US citizens and for the entire world. A study published in* Nature *found that the entire global research ecosystem will be affected by Brexit and the current US administration's decisions.[34] In light of this information, the Canadian government should be campaigning to recruit highly-skilled foreign researchers.[35]*

*In response to an appeal from their American colleagues, scientists in several hundred cities worldwide took to the streets in April 2017 to defend the importance of science and to condemn regressive populism that denies evidence and embraces myths and beliefs without regard for proven facts and rigorous analyses. This mobilization of opinion is a unique opportunity for Canada to clearly state its priorities and reassert its leadership, giving hope to the free world that science is inextricably linked to democracy and the progress of civilization. Scientists should be put on the same kind of pedestal as sports heroes and entertainment figures. Changes in social paradigms can be traced back to the work of scientists and their discoveries. They deserve public recognition and should be a source of tremendous public pride. It is surprising and unfortunate that a country such as Canada, which boasts about promoting a knowledge economy, does not shower more acclaim on the people who devote their full intelligence to improving our knowledge of the world*

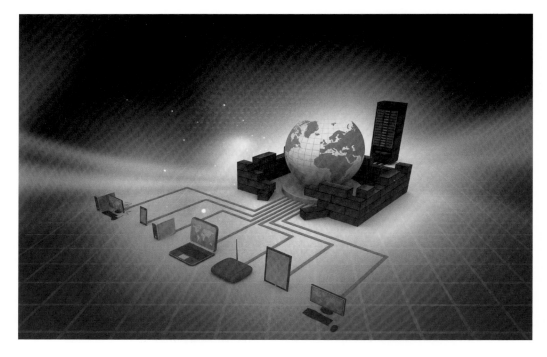

THE COMPUTER REVOLUTIONIZES HUMAN EFFECTIVENESS

The search for the key to the complexity of the human brain has fascinated scientists since the "computer" created by British mathematician Alan Turing cracked Germany's Enigma code during World War II. Computer technology has skyrocketed over the past thirty years. The mass marketing and increased accessibility of computers have led to massive change. Computers exponentially increase the potential for thought, research, and creativity. Users communicate instantly using words and images, and can broadcast their lives around the world. But technological advances threaten privacy and democratic debate, both of which are now controlled by the four American giants of the Web that have access to the algorithms. Credit: bluebay2014 (Getty Images)

*around us and, ultimately, of the human condition. Ready-made ideologies and doctrines that are set in stone do not drive human progress, permanently improve living conditions, or increase prosperity. It is scientific research that increases human freedom, quite apart from any political or dogmatic frameworks or beliefs.*

*Last year, the government announced the creation of a chief science advisor position.[36] The goal was to enable the government (i.e., the prime minister and Cabinet) to make informed policy decisions based on sound scientific evidence compiled by scientists of all stripes.[37] Dr Mona Nemer, vice-president of research at the University of Ottawa,[38] was appointed to the post in the fall of 2017.[39] The Naylor Report (April 2017), which examined federal support for science, stated "that the Government of Canada, by an Act of Parliament, should create a new National Advisory Council on Research and Innovation (NACRI) ... to provide advice to the prime minister and Cabinet on federal spending as well as broad goals and priorities for research and innovation" and to engage in "public reporting and outreach on matters" pertaining to research and innovation (Recommendation 4.1).*

*The government should give effect to these important recommendations without delay. The report did have one flaw in that it disregarded direct involvement by parliamentarians in following up on government decisions, advice from the chief science advisor, and the annual reports produced by each of the government's four granting agencies, as well as the Canada Foundation for Innovation.*

*The report failed to recommend that parliamentarians be supported by an agent of Parliament, such as the chief science advisor, to provide day-to-day oversight and assume on behalf of parliamentarians responsibility for reviewing and analyzing policies and decisions. For example, the very useful role played by the parliamentary budget officer (PBO) should serve as a model for this specific function. The PBO's studies and findings have helped make parliamentary debates on financial issues more on-point, informed and effective, which has greatly improved the government's accountability to Parliament. The same should be true of the new chief science advisor, who should be recognized as an agent of Parliament and report primarily to Parliament, instead of to the government of the day.*

*The accountability of the chief science advisor must be institutionalized in legislation if Parliament is to rigorously monitor and correct all of Canada's science policy decisions, given its strategic importance to the immediate future of the country. As a public institution with a non-partisan science advisor, the necessary support services and a committee of senators and MPs appointed for this purpose, Parliament could be a vital link that continually holds Cabinet accountable for any decisions made in support of Canada's science policy objectives.*

*Otherwise, a future government could abolish the position, as was done in 2008, and Canada's overall capability in this area would be weakened accordingly. The Naylor Report, one of the most comprehensive reports of its type produced in the last forty years, recommended that the government increase the annual budgets of Canada's research granting agencies by $1.3 billion. The government must make this strategic move, as the tendency is to underestimate the size of the coming technological wave and the scope of future needs. Canada cannot afford to miss the fourth industrial revolution.[40]*

*In the budget tabled in the House of Commons in February 2018, the government announced that it was injecting more than $3.8 billion into Canada's research system. This plan included the reinvention of the NRC. In his budget speech, the finance minister stated that "Budget 2018 represents the single largest investment in investigator-led* *fundamental research in Canadian history."[41] Of the total amount, $1.2 billion will be allocated to Canada's granting councils over five years; $763 million will go to the Canada Foundation for Innovation; $572 million will be set aside to exploit big data and digital research; and $210 million will be used to create nearly 250 additional research chairs by 2023. Budget 2018 also includes $627 million to be spent on federal science resources, including $540 million to strengthen and redefine the role of the NRC, and $87 million to update federal laboratories.*

*Overall, the government is increasing the annual budgets of its granting councils by 25 per cent over three years, in part to help researchers in the early stages of their careers, women and under-represented groups. It would of course be premature to assess the impact that this injection of funds will have on the research system as a whole. Will it lead the provinces to pull back? Will it stimulate complementary investment by the private sector? What might happen if a new government focuses on deficit reduction, given that these investments are spread over five years? Will Canadians then have to take up the torch again and return to pressing their case in public forums? These are all real challenges that will require firm leadership from the minister responsible for science and the Group of Canadian Research Universities.[42]*

*Human ingenuity is an endless reserve of inventiveness, and public policies on research support cannot be restricted primarily to applied research, as has been the case for the past decade. During that time, the development of industrial or commercial products was emphasized over fundamental research conducted by public agencies, universities, or private institutions. Basic research may seem costly, but in the long run its results lead to numerous applications that are surprisingly practical and liable to generate substantial revenue. Indeed, basic research and applied research are complementary. Both have vital roles to play in improving Canadians' health and standard of living and in protecting their rights and freedoms.*

*By supporting and valuing its scientific culture, Canada can boost public confidence in the future. That confidence is built on faith in progress and the emancipating effect of scientific discoveries and inventions.*

## NOTES

1 The author is indebted to the Library of Parliament for its careful work in verifying the accuracy of the historical facts and figures in the text.

2 Advisory Panel on Federal Support for Fundamental Science, *Investing in Canada's*

*Future: Strengthening the Foundations of Canadian Research,* Final Report, C. David Naylor (Chair), University of Toronto, 10 April 2017.

3 Total gross public and private expenditures.

4 William D. Fraser, "Le Canada doit rattraper son retard en financement de la recherche en santé," (citing the report by C. David Naylor), *Le Devoir,* 7 September 2017, p. A7.

5 Intramural government spending remained frozen, but in real terms only. Spending increased at the same rate as inflation. Source: OECD, Stat.

6 Country size is taken into account in the comparison because it determines GDP, which is closely linked to the population of each country.

7 Data compiled and provided to the author by Professor Yves Gingras, 21 September 2017.

8 Hugo Pilon-Larose, "Des scientifiques pressent Ottawa d'éviter un 'exode des cerveaux' – Financement en recherche fondamentale," *La Presse+,* 24 September 2017.

9 Riviera Partners, *Engineering Candidate Marketplace Review,* 2014.

10 Colin Perkel, "Secret Avro Arrow test model found in Lake Ontario," *National Post,* 9 September 2017, p. A11.

11 Senator from 1967 to 1983. Senate Special Committee on Science Policy, *A Science Policy for Canada,* Vol. 1, Ottawa, 1970.

12 The Hon. Alastair W. Gillespie, 12 August 1971.

13 G. Bruce Doern, "The Senate Report on Science Policy: a political assessment," *Journal of Canadian Studies,* 6 May 1971, p. 42.

14 Nobel Prize in Physics: Bertram N. Brockhouse in 1994, Arthur B. McDonald in 2015; Nobel Prize in Chemistry: Gerhard Herzberg in 1971, John C. Polanyi in 1986; Nobel Prize in Medicine: Frederick G. Banting in 1923. Other Canadian scientists have won Nobel prizes for research work conducted in the United States.

15 Philippe Mercure, "L'Agence spatiale canadienne investit dans un nouveau moteur spatial," *La Presse+,* 1 July 2018.

16 Matt Jeneroux, "Liberals must prioritize growing research and development sector – Canadian innovators' apparent preference for filing patents in the United States over Canada shows a disconnect between labs and the marketplace in this country," *Hill Times,* 20 September 2017.

17 Miriane Demers-Lemay, "Maladie d'Alzheimer : le rôle de l'ARN découvert à McGill," *Le Devoir,* 14-15 December 2017, p. A6.

18 The author was secretary of state from 1982 to 1984.

19 Agnes Barr-Klouman, "Robotics and Artificial Intelligence, Part 2: Military Applications," Research paper distributed at a Senate of Canada open caucus on robotics and artificial intelligence, 3 May 2017.

20  Marie-Claude Goulet, "Les menaces technicistes de l'intelligence artificielle," *Le Devoir*, 26 November 2017, p. B12.

21  Morgane Tual, "Intelligence artificielle – Promesses et périls," *Le Monde*, Cahier du Monde, No. 22696, December 2017-January 2018.

22  Government of France, No. 4594 and No. 464, French National Assembly – Senate, 14th Legislature, 2016–17 Ordinary Session, registered at the Office of the President of the National Assembly on 15 March 2017.

23  Farhad Manjoo, "How to slow China in race to the future: spend big on tech (lay off the tariffs)," *The New York Times*, 19 July 2018, p. B1.

24  Agnes Barr-Klouman, "Robotics and Artificial Intelligence, Part 1: Advantages and Challenges," Research paper distributed at a Senate of Canada open caucus on robotics and artificial intelligence, 29 March 2017.

25  François Béguin, "Bientôt remboursée, la télémédecine devient réalité," *Le Monde*, 19 January 2018, p. 10.

26  Miriane Demers-Lemay, "Comment mener la révolution numérique en santé," *Le Devoir*, 18 October 2017, p. A5.

27  Standing Senate Committee on Social Affairs, Science and Technology, 31 October 2017, https://sencanada.ca/en/Committees/report/46292/42-1.

28  John Ibbitson, "Ottawa set to announce council for apology to LGBT Canadians," *The Globe and Mail*, 15 September 2017, p. A9.

29  Bill C-66, the *Expungement of Historically Unjust Convictions Act*, given royal assent on 21 June 2018.

30  Yves Gingras, "Tocqueville, la science et la démocratie," *Le Devoir*, 9 and 19 June 2018, p. B14.

31  Anne Muxel et al., *Croire et faire croire, usages politiques de la croyance*, Les presses de Science Po, 2017. See in particular the article by sociologist Myriam Revault d'Allonnes.

32  Agence France-Presse, "Le Nobel de physique remis à trois Américains," *Le Devoir*, 4 October 2017, p. A5.

33  The federal government abolished the compulsory long-form census questionnaire in 2010, arguing that it infringed on the right to privacy. It was restored in 2015.

34  Philippe Mercure, "Trump et le Brexit nuiront à la science mondiale, selon une étude," *La Presse+*, 6 October 2017.

35  Annabelle Caillou, "Des chaires réservées aux chercheurs à l'étranger," *Le Devoir*, 2 August 2017, p. A1.

36  The previous Conservative government had abolished it in 2008.

37  "Le fédéral se dote d'un conseiller scientifique," *Le Devoir*, 6 December 2016.

38 Director of the University of Ottawa's Molecular Genetics and Cardiac Regeneration Laboratory.

39 Isabelle Paré, "Mona Nemer nommée conseillère scientifique en chef du Canada," *Le Devoir*, 27 September 2017, p. A4.

40 Hugo Pilon-Larose, "Des scientifiques pressent Ottawa d'éviter un 'exode des cerveaux.'"

41 Guillaume Bourgault-Côté, "Près de 4 milliards pour la recherche scientifique," *LeDevoir.com*, 28 February 2018, https://www.ledevoir.com/societe/science/521442/science-pres-de-4-milliards-pour-la-recherche.

42 Group of Canadian Research Universities, "Significant investments in budget 2018 will revitalize Canadian scientific research," News release, 27 February 2018, http://u15.ca/what-we-are-saying/significant-investments-budget-2018-will-revitalize-canadian-scientific-research.

# Scientific Success Stories and Modern-Day Threats

Hubert Reeves, astrophysicist

Canada holds an enviable place in the field of scientific research in the world today. Obviously, I will not be able to mention all the important contributions that Canadian scientists have made in the past 150 years, but I would like talk about a few that I feel are particularly important.

I will start with astrophysics, my own field, and I will touch briefly on other disciplines, including nuclear physics, chemistry, geophysics and botany.

Geology and geophysics were revolutionized a few decades ago by the discovery of what is called plate tectonics. This theory holds that the earth's surface is made up of a dozen independent plates that move more or less freely. John Tuzo Wilson, a geologist at the University of Toronto, made a major contribution to this theory. He understood and clarified the role that volcanoes and fractures play in the dynamics of these plates, which have a huge impact on the behaviour of our entire planet.

For decades, Canadian astronomical observatories and telescopes have been major centres of scientific research. In particular, the Canada-France-Hawaii Telescope in the Hawaiian islands was long one of the most important telescopes on the planet because of its exceptional site. The Dominion Astrophysical Observatory on Vancouver Island was a pioneer in measuring the velocities of stars. I was lucky enough to spend a summer there when I was attending university. I worked with Andrew McKellar, who was the first person to observe fossil radiation, the light from the beginning of the universe. I would also mention the contributions made by the David Dunlap Observatory in Toronto and the telescope in Mont-Mégantic, Quebec, where scientists are very involved in research on exoplanets and very active in popularizing science.

In the nineteenth century, philosopher Auguste Comte said, "We will never know what the surface of the sun is made of," yet astronomy has answered that question. Today, we know not only what the sun's surface is made of, but what the inside of

THE LABORATORY – UNIVERSITY OF TORONTO, CIRCA 1932

Oil on wood panel, 25 cm x 34.5 cm. By Sir Frederick G. Banting (1891–1941)

Sir Frederick G. Banting was the first Canadian to receive the Nobel Prize in Medicine in 1923, along with John James Rickard Macleod, for discovering insulin to treat diabetes. Banting was also a painter. This painting shows the Toronto laboratory where he worked. Scientific research is the key to improving health, fighting infections that could cause pandemics, and combatting degenerative diseases. Major pharmaceutical companies focus on developing drugs that can be sold widely. University research concentrates more on identifying symptomatic elements leading to biochemical developments and medical treatments. Credit: Power Corporation of Canada Collection

the sun is made of, right to its core. Here, it is important to mention the role played by Georges Michaud of the Université de Montréal and his colleagues, who studied atomic physics and research by numerous observatories, and succeeded in describing in detail the chemical composition of stellar structures and understanding how these atoms migrate throughout the life of stars.

The geometric shapes of molecules play a major role in the chemical reactions that take place within these stellar phenomena. Gerhard Herzberg of Carleton University in Ottawa made a significant contribution to this field of research. Using atomic and molecular spectroscopes, he successfully represented the structures of diatomic and polyatomic molecules by mapping the free radicals that were particularly difficult to study. This work earned him a Nobel Prize in chemistry in 1971.

A number of Canadian institutions have contributed to the development of nuclear physics in Canada, particularly the Triumf laboratory in Vancouver, under the direction of Erich Vogt. Moreover, some luminaries in the field of nuclear physics have done important work in Canadian laboratories, including James Chadwick, the discoverer of neutrons, at the University of Ottawa; and Ernest Rutherford, who discovered the structure of atomic nuclei, at McGill University. Another Canadian researcher, Alastair Cameron, profoundly influenced the development of nuclear astrophysics and the theory of the origin of chemical elements, nucleosynthesis.

The first half of the 20th century was a period of great activity in botany in Quebec. The leading researcher, Brother Marie-Victorin, and his many colleagues took this field to a high level of excellence on the international stage.

In the field of health, I must mention Hans Selye of the Université de Montréal for his world-renowned work on the effect of stress on living organisms subjected to various stressors and the physiology of the adrenal glands.

These are a few of the researchers and laboratories that came to mind as I thought about some highlights of Canadian science. I apologize to all the others who are also deserving of recognition and whom I neglected to name or failed to mention for lack of time.

Now, I would like to talk about some serious problems that threaten the future of scientific research in Canada and around the world. These problems are related in particular to the fierce competition between the pursuit of immediate profit and human health and welfare at a time when the very future of humanity is at stake.

When Canada as a confederation was born 150 years ago, science had relatively little impact on people's lives. The massive influx of science into our daily lives, with all the benefits to our comfort and health, completely transformed that situation. Today, science affects practically every aspect of our lives. It is neither good nor bad in and of itself; everything depends on how we use it.

I want to talk in particular about four serious problems that threaten scientific research today in connection with human health and welfare and could get even worse if we are not careful.

First, there is government censorship. In the past few decades, we have witnessed the emergence of a global phenomenon: political censorship of scientific research. Publicly funded laboratories are specifically targeted. In the United States, the Bush administration subjected the publication of environmental research to government control and approval at a time when the future of the planet had become critical. The United Nations conference in Paris in November 2015 clearly showed how serious things are. At that forum, 194 countries recognized the urgent need to stop climate change or else risk being faced with unmanageable situations.

COMPUTERIZED BRAILLE

Computers can compensate for our impairments or expand our abilities in many ways. Take the case of braille, a writing system created in France in 1829. In 1972, Canadian Roland Galarneau (1922–2011) developed a computer program to produce braille, making it a faster and easier tool for visually impaired people to communicate. Credit: zlikovec (Getty Images)

The Harper government in Ottawa imposed similar censorship on the Bush administration in Washington. Fortunately, it was cancelled by Justin Trudeau's government.

Clearly, the future of humanity requires top-quality scientific research conducted under the best possible conditions, with no outside influence. Researchers need complete freedom to publish their findings without being subjected to political, ideological, economic or financial pressure. Our children's and grandchildren's future is at stake. We can expect this problem to grow in the combined context of globalization and the environmental crisis. It will require constant vigilance.

A second threat comes from the advent of what is known as "junk science." It relates particularly to the tobacco, asbestos, and sugar industries.

Scientists, sometimes renowned individuals, agree, for a fee, to provide laboratory analysis results that are sometimes fabricated, in order to downplay the dangers these substances pose to our health. These fraudulent papers are then used in Parliament by lobbyists who are opposed to bills put forward by various humanitarian associations to protect nature.

A third problem has to do with the relationship between health and drug marketing. The research pharmaceutical laboratories conduct to develop new drugs can be extremely costly. Specialized instruments are needed to obtain credible, useable results. In addition, pharmaceutical companies make choices to ensure that they reap benefits commensurate with the money they spend on research. This is how government granting bodies often find themselves in difficult situations.

Health is something that affects everyone, rich or poor, which is why medical laboratories are often criticized for focusing their research on developing drugs that have more to do with marketing than health. This attitude is reflected in the drug market's reluctance to tackle rare diseases, especially if they affect lower-income populations. Today this is a major problem, not only in Africa, but also in disadvantaged urban areas, including in Canada.

The fourth problem has to do with science as a career. In the past few decades there has been a disturbing decline in young people's interest in studying sciences, especially what are known as the hard disciplines: physics, chemistry, and mathematics.

One of the main causes of this problem is no doubt the fact that it is very difficult to find jobs in these fields.

Added to the job shortage is the growing discredit scientists face in our society. In the not-too-distant past, people often referred to the "scholarly vocation." There was an aura of respectability around scientific researchers. Scientists' loss of prestige is not unrelated to certain developments that have marked human history over the past two centuries: nuclear terror and the environmental crisis. The fact that humanity is capable of wiping itself out with a nuclear bomb or by destroying the environment with floods of pesticides has profoundly damaged the image people have of scientists. Added to these seismic shifts is widespread chemical pollution of the air, water, and soil.

Even worse, there are rumours of agreements between international health organizations and nuclear energy organizations that people would like to know more about. Educators are also faced with the uphill task of restoring the image of scientific researchers if we do not want our young people to turn away from this profession and our country's scientific reputation to be tarnished.

Clearly, these problems are due not to the quality of the researchers, but to the use of science for immediate profit. Canada has to be a model citizen in this respect or else it could lose the trust of Canadians.

In conclusion, the tough economic battles today between various global powers lead us to believe that such situations could get worse.

# Milestones in the Development of Science in Canada

Yves Gingras, Canada Research Chair in the History and Sociology of Science
at the Université du Québec à Montréal and Scientific Director of the
Observatoire des sciences et des technologies

Major historical commemorations tend to lose sight of (or take for granted) the importance of science in the history of a nation. It is significant that at this symposium, science is placed with culture and before the session on the economy. On the one hand, science is part of culture; on the other hand, it affects the economy. When we talk about the "new economy," the "knowledge economy," we think of biotechnology in the 1980s and 1990s and informatics and artificial intelligence today, areas that come under science and generate innovations and various applications with important economic impacts.

As a complement to the presentation by my colleague Hubert Reeves, who spoke to us about some twentieth-century science luminaries in Canada, and since we are celebrating Canada's 150th anniversary, I think we should look at science from an institutional standpoint.

What can Canada as a federal entity do for science, which itself is a social institution? Certainly, it is individuals who conduct research and make scientific discoveries, but science in the more general sense is a social institution with rules and standards to ensure that discoveries are objective. From that standpoint, science is neither optimistic nor pessimistic, but simply realistic. Science seeks to describe and explain natural phenomena. In his presentation, my colleague David Suzuki gave a good description of how the laws of different sciences are teaching us important facts about climate change and forcing societies to make important decisions to secure their future. Sometimes we have a hard time understanding that we cannot change the laws of nature and that we are the ones who have to change, adapting our behaviour to minimize the undesirable but predictable effects of some of our collective actions. If apples fall from trees, we may wish they didn't and want them to stay on the trees, but the fact is that apples fall. We have to learn from what is happening around us, not try to deny reality. As Hubert Reeves said, science strives to be as objective as possible and steer clear of ideologies and commercial interests so that scientists can think independently. This cultural aspect of science gives us an understanding of our universe. Hubert Reeves worked in the field of astrophysics and helped humankind better understand the origins of the universe. Knowing that the universe has existed for about 14 billion years may not help drive up stock prices, but it does help us understand the world we live in and where we come from.

However, in order that scientists can focus on their research and potentially make important discoveries, society has to put in place institutions that make scientific research possible. I would like to look briefly at the history of the main institutions created by Canada's Parliament since the nineteenth century.

### CANADIAN SCIENTIFIC INSTITUTIONS

The first Canadian institution put in place by the Government of Canada was the Geological Survey of Canada, created in 1842. The purpose of this institution was to look for coal, as the industrial revolution was in full swing. At that time, geology was the queen of the sciences, so to speak, because it made it possible to find natural resources to exploit in the service of economic growth. Although popular rhetoric would have it that Canada is a knowledge society, economists are well aware that we still depend heavily on mineral, oil, and forest resources. The Canadian economy therefore still depends heavily on Canadian geology.

When I see how little governments invest in science, I tell myself that our elected officials often confuse the fact that we are in a knowledge economy with economizing on knowledge – that is, doing without knowledge. This is what happens, for example, when people are not happy to learn that humans are animals, as Charles Darwin's work showed in the mid-nineteenth century. Scientific discoveries often disillusion people and break down prejudices.

The year 1842 is very important, because it marks a first milestone in the development of Canada's scientific institutions. This year, in 2017, the Geological Survey of Canada is celebrating its 175th anniversary as Canada is celebrating its 150th anniversary.

The second important milestone in the development of Canadian scientific institutions is 1882. That year, the fourth governor general of Canada, the Marquess of Lorne, founded the Royal Society of Canada. As governor general, he believed that a modern self-respecting nation should have a learned society. England had had the Royal Society of London since 1660. Drawing inspiration from this prestigious model, the Marquess of Lorne created the Royal Society of Canada, an institution that is still active today.

Science's usefulness to the country's economic development also led to the creation of experimental farms in Canada in 1886. Why did the government think to create experimental farms? Because elected officials realized that a modern nation needed to have the means to control its environment for health and safety reasons. Canada needed to control agricultural production, which was often threatened by adverse weather, diseases, and infestations of harmful insects that affected the plants. Researchers on experimental farms developed the Marquis variety of wheat early in the twentieth century. Genetically modified organisms, the GMOs people talk so much about nowadays, are actually very old and form the basis of crop genetics. Think also about the wheat rust that devastated Canada's production in 1916, 1927, and 1935. Wheat is a very important commodity in the development of western Canada, and researchers and geneticists developed wheat varieties that could resist drought, cold, and various diseases. Science also serves countries, and those that are not science-centred today likely will not be celebrating their next centennial.

Another important milestone in the history of science in Canada was the creation in 1916 of the National Research Council of Canada (NRC), which was responsible for coordinating scientific and industrial research during the First World War. In 1929, the NRC set up its own research laboratories in Ottawa. In time, new National Research Council laboratories would be created in fields such as agriculture, materials, biotechnology, aviation, astronomy, and photonics to meet new needs, and today there are labs in every province in the country. These labs are extremely important, because thanks to them and the various advisory committees set up by the NRC, many of the scientific and technical problems encountered by Canadian industry in relation to health, the environment and the economy have been solved.

The NRC also played a pivotal role in the development of academic research, because early on it put in place a system of research grants for professors and scholarships for graduate students. Previously, researchers could rely only on universities' meagre internal resources or the patronage of a few wealthy donors who took an interest in science. William Macdonald, who at the time was the "tobacco king," gave a great deal of money to McGill University, and it was in part thanks to him that Ernest Rutherford was able to acquire the expensive radium and cutting-edge instruments to conduct his research on the atom, which won him the Nobel Prize in chemistry in 1908, a year after his return to England.

With academic research spurred on by NRC grants, the number of scientific publications grew rapidly in the 1920s. To facilitate the dissemination of Canadian research findings, the NRC also created the *Canadian Journal of Research* in 1929. As the president of the NRC, H.M. Tory, noted when the decision was announced, "Canada shall never get recognition scientifically until we have some science journals of our own." Like the Marquess of Lorne a half-century before him, H.M. Tory understood that science can also help shape a national identity and that an independent country cannot be content to publish its research findings in foreign journals, which were mainly British and American at the time. In the early 1950s, the growth and diversification of research would lead to the creation of specialized journals, including the *Canadian Journal of Chemistry*, the *Canadian Journal of Biology*, the *Canadian Journal of Physics*, and a dozen others covering the spectrum of scientific research.

In the mid-1970s, the awarding of academic research grants, which the NRC had looked after until then, was taken over by independent organizations: the Natural Sciences and Engineering Research Council and the Medical Research Council, which became the Institutes of Health Research in 2000. That reform also led to the creation in 1977 of the Social Sciences and Humanities Research Council. Once again, the federal government created these institutions to promote the development of the sciences across the country, in all fields. We must not forget that in an advanced society, scientific research cannot exist socially without the institutions that are research universities, government research laboratories, and public investments in higher education. In other words, these institutions must exist and be appropriately funded so that researchers can make discoveries and train the next generation of researchers. Science is a product not of nature, but of culture. Just as civilizations are mortal, scientific research too is fragile and must be nurtured constantly in a climate of freedom of thought and action, without which it cannot flourish.

Just as the circumstances of the First World War led to the creation of the NRC, the consequences of the Second World War transformed the relationship between the government and scientific research, not just in Canada, but around the world. With the increased need for funding, patronage, which was rather random, was not enough of a funding base. Research had more and more technological applications and, consequently, a growing impact on the economy. This change ushered in a new age that I call the age of science policy, which dominated from 1965 to about 1980 and gave way in the decades that followed to technology and innovation policy.

### FROM SCIENCE POLICY TO INNOVATION STRATEGIES

In the early 1960s, the Organisation for Economic Co-operation and Development (OECD) began a series of studies on member states' national science policies. In 1969, the OECD released its report on Canada's science policy, or rather its lack of policy. In November 1967, Canada's Senate, which understood that science was becoming an important issue, struck a committee on science policy chaired by Senator Maurice Lamontagne. The committee's report, which was published in four volumes between

CANOLA OIL — A TOP EXPORT TO CHINA

Canola oil, the result obtained in laboratories following the breeding of colza seeds (made from pressed canola seeds), is a vegetable oil used for cooking that was developed in Canada in 1970. The oil is produced mainly in western Canada and is a leading export, finding markets in such countries as China, India and Pakistan. In fact, Canada cannot produce enough to meet the demand. Credit: ImagineGolf (Getty Images)

1971 and 1977 under the title *A Science Policy for Canada* and is better known as the Lamontagne Report, is a seminal document in the history of science policy in Canada. In the wake of the Senate study, the federal government created the position of minister of state for science and technology (MSST) in June 1971. Interestingly, the minister of state did not have a portfolio; science and technology were not considered important enough to warrant an actual department, but it was a start.

A few years earlier, in 1966, the government had created the Science Council of Canada, an independent body responsible for preparing discussion papers and analyses on topics considered important to the country's future. A survey of the titles of the many reports published by the Science Council shows that many issues that are still topical today were addressed in the 1970s. I will mention just the reports on Canada's space program (1967), science and technology in urban planning (1971), the problems of innovation in Canada's manufacturing industry (1971), Canada's energy options (1975), academic research at risk (1979), and biotechnology and the primary sector (1985), but there were many more on various sciences (physics, psychology, chemistry, agriculture, and so on). In 1993, Brian Mulroney's Conservative government abolished this think-tank and other similar organizations, like the Economic Council of Canada, which had also been created in the mid-1960s, thereby putting an end to more than 25 years of expertise in science and technology policy.

In the early 1980s, the economy began to feel the effects of the oil crisis, and public decision-makers placed greater emphasis on technological development. This change was also evident in the titles of policy statements, where "technology" was added to "science." For example, in 1985, the MSST issued a working paper entitled *Science, Technology and Economic Development*, followed two years later by the InnovAction policy. The 1990s marked the shift to a third stage: innovation policy. The 2014 federal policy was entitled *Moving Forward in Science, Technology, and Innovation*. Science was no longer an end in itself, but a way of serving innovation. Significantly, the website of the department formerly known as Industry Canada even places innovation before science – Innovation, Science, and Economic Development Canada – reversing the logic of research, as though it were possible to actually *innovate* before *researching*.

The more the focus is on the economy, the less important science seems. The goal is to quickly find the applications of scientific research. The problem, though, is that

ARTHUR B. MCDONALD (1943–   )
Through his work, Queen's University physicist Arthur B. McDonald successfully demonstrated that neutrinos have mass. McDonald began his career as a researcher with Atomic Energy of Canada (AECL – Chalk River), eventually teaching at Princeton and later Queen's University. He received the Nobel Prize in Physics in 2015. Credit: european pressphoto agency (epa)/JONAS EKSTROMER

science does not have a predictable rhythm or timing; it does not work like the economy, for a very simple reason: research means venturing into the unknown! Researchers are not sure that they will find anything. Some say, "We don't want researchers, we want finders," as though it were easy or a given that research will lead to discovery. What is more, sometimes researchers do not find what they were looking for, but something even more interesting! There is a term for these surprise discoveries: serendipity. This concept can be defined as the fact of making an unexpected scientific discovery or technical invention as a result of a fortuitous set of circumstances, and very often while searching into another area.

In addition to being unpredictable, research usually takes years to produce results and does not fit neatly into a plan requiring quarterly financial reports. All historical and sociological studies show that twenty to twenty-five years can pass between a major scientific discovery and technological applications. Those who talk only about technological innovation often have short memories. The biotechnology industry grew dramatically in the 1980s because in 1953, in a small laboratory at the University of Cambridge in England, two researchers, James Watson and Francis Crick, looked into the problem of how DNA was structured. They found that the DNA molecule was made up of two strands that wound around each other: the double helix. This discovery was of no benefit whatsoever to the economy! All it did was help in understanding the mechanism for coding genetic information. It would take two more decades before another discovery was made in the early 1970s: restriction enzymes, which can be used to cut the genome in various places and perform genetic manipulations that can give rise to technological applications.

Between 1954 and 1970, knowing the structure of DNA was a little like knowing the age of the universe: it was nice and it was interesting, but there was no profit (or market speculation) in it. Thirty years later, this discovery transformed the economy. Today, biotechnology is a fact of life and people get more excited about algorithms and artificial intelligence. But here again, that is because for decades, in many universities, away from the media spotlight, researchers came up with new math, new types of digital and statistical calculations, and faster computers, which now enable businesses to make a lot of money, and that is good. However, people who speculate today on the future of these businesses too often forget that their profits were made possible by researchers in years past who had ideas that seemed at the time to be useless, but eventually proved to be very useful indeed.

The story goes that English mathematician George Boole, who was interested in the "laws of thought," as evidenced by the title of one of his books, which was published in 1851, boasted that what we now call "Boolean algebra" would never be useful for anything. However, Boolean algebra is the basis for the computational logic of electrical circuits, a use Boole himself never imagined! It would be easy to come up with many more examples.

Clearly, not only are scientific discoveries unpredictable, but even their applications are often unexpected. It can be said that science is first part of culture before leading to economic applications and that its main mission is to understand the world, not serve the economy.

## CANADA'S SCIENTIFIC DECLINE

While it is generally accepted that we live in a knowledge society and economy, Canada has actually lagged behind other OECD countries in investments in research and development for a dozen years, as figure 8.1 illustrates. In fact, according to OECD data,[1] general investment in research and development in Canada, which tended to catch up with the OECD average in the 1990s, has steadily declined since about 2005. After reaching roughly 2 per cent of gross domestic product (GDP), it declined to 1.6 per cent of GDP in 2014, while average investment by OECD countries continued to rise, reaching 2.4 per cent.

The trend in industrial research is the same (figure 8.2), with Canada investing half of what OECD countries invest on average.

The picture is no better when it comes to government research, as figure 8.3 shows. However, government research is very important to people's health and safety. Government laboratories have a specific function: regulatory science, which means research on which regulations are based. Regulatory science is not pure science or science applied to the economy, but science that supports regulations in such areas as air quality. In 2000 in Walkerton, Ontario, seven people died and more than 2,500 others became ill because officials put an end to water quality testing, which had previously been conducted using chemical techniques to detect germs.

In fact, Canada ranks ahead of other OECD countries only in academic research (figure 8.4).

What effect do these investments have on scientific publications?[2] As figure 8.5 shows, Canada's share of world scientific publications rose in the late 1990s, but has been declining since 2005 despite increased investments, as shown in figure 8.4.

In short, all the data indicate that Canada has been declining on the scientific front for 15 years. Justin Trudeau's Liberal government, which was elected in October 2015, wanted to set itself apart from the previous government by focusing on the importance of science and independent research. The government also appointed a new chief science advisor: Mona Nemer, a renowned Canadian scientist. That is good news, because with her appointment, science once again became a national priority.

The position of chief science advisor to the prime minister was actually created in 2004 by Prime Minister Paul Martin. The Harper government, which was elected in 2006, did not see fit to maintain the position and, in 2008, let go the first and only person to hold it, Arthur Carty. The Harper government did not have much interest in science, not because it was against science, but because it believed only in technological innovation. It did not seem to understand that innovation requires research. However, as the figures show, the decline in the indicators is visible across the board starting in the mid-2000s, when Stephen Harper's Conservative government came to power, except for government research, which has declined steadily since the 1980s.

## CONCLUSION: A NEW SENATE COMMITTEE ON SCIENCE POLICY?

I would like to conclude with a quote from a great Quebec researcher, Jacques Rousseau: "In 1930 we sowed, in 1960 we reaped."

Jacques Rousseau was one of the greatest disciples of Brother Marie-Victorin, the botany professor at the Université de Montréal and founder of the Montreal Botanical Garden whom my colleague Hubert Reeves mentioned. Like Marie-Victorin, Jacques Rousseau was a great researcher in botany and ethnology and a pioneer of research on northern Quebec. This quote referred to important developments in Quebec during the Quiet Revolution in the 1960s. Rousseau, who had worked hard with his colleagues through the 1930s to build viable, dynamic scientific institutions such as such as ACFAS (French-Canadian Association for the Advancement of Science, founded in 1923), of which he was general secretary from 1930 to 1946, used this image to explain the Quiet Revolution. Interestingly, there was no Canadian Association for the Advancement of Science, which could have promoted science as did (and still do) the BAAS, the AAAS and AFCAS.[3]

If sowing is conducting scientific research and reaping is deriving applications and innovations from that research, then Canada needs to start sowing today if it wants to reap technological innovations in the decades to come. But what should Canada sow? Science and curiosity.

Since the Senate Committee on Science Policy was created in 1967, exactly 50 years ago, maybe this is the right time for the Senate to add an item to its to-do list. The Lamontagne Report was a landmark document in the history of science policy in Canada. With the huge transformations brought about by the sciences in the past 50 years in all areas of society, perhaps the time has come to resume this analytical work and see what policies could best promote the development of the sciences and their applications to benefit people for the next 50 years.

Perhaps the time has come to look at how to sow in order to reap again in fifty years.

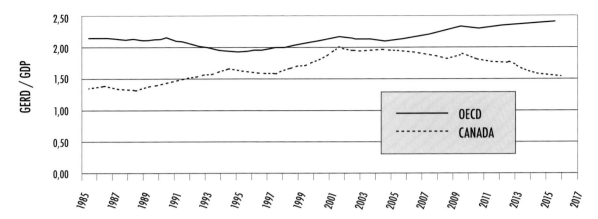

Figure 8.1: Gross domestic expenditure on research and development (GERD) as a percentage of gross domestic product (GDP), Canada and OECD.

Figure 8.2: Business enterprise expenditure on research and development (BERD) as a percentage of gross domestic product (GDP), Canada and OECD.

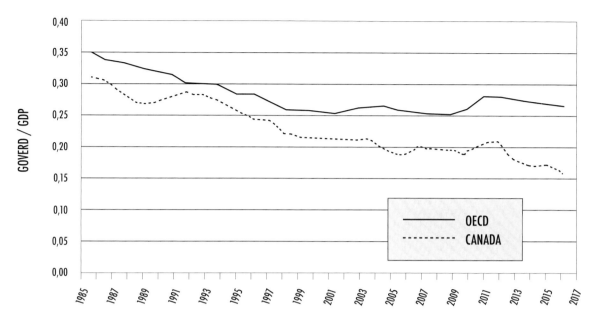

Figure 8.3: Government expenditure on research and development (GOVERD) as a percentage of gross domestic product (GDP), Canada and OECD.

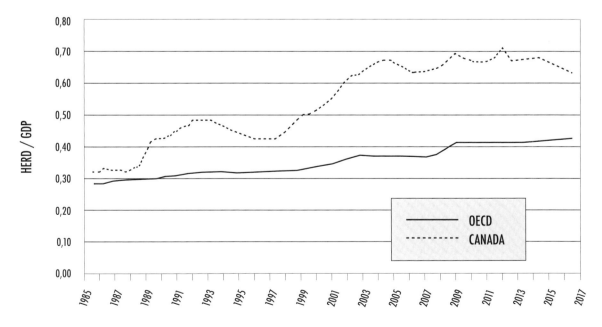

Figure 8.4: Higher education expenditure on research and development (HERD) as a percentage of gross domestic product (GDP), Canada and OECD.

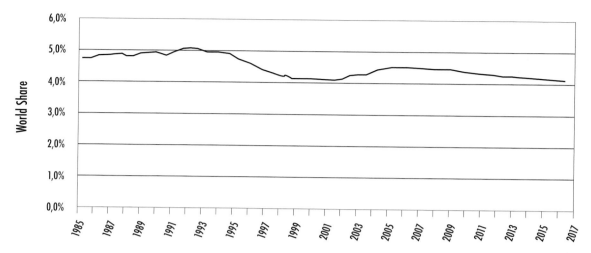

Figure 8.5: World share of Canadian scientific publications (all disciplines).

NOTES

1 Figures 8.1 to 8.4 are based on statistical data compiled by the OECD. See "Main Science and Technology Indicators": http://stats.oecd.org/Index.aspx?DataSetCode=MSTI_PUB.

2 The data on publications were compiled by the Observatoire des sciences et des technologies from the Web of Science database of Clarivate Analytics.

3 Yves Gingras, "Why Canada Never Had a National Association for the Advancement of Science," *Physics in Canada*, November/December 2006, p. 355–9.

# Culture: How Much of Canada's Cultural Visibility Will Remain in the Digital World?[1]

The Hon. Serge Joyal, Senator

*The Canadian cultural life, in English and French, has flourished over the past fifty years. During this period, a truly Canadian cultural identity has emerged, thanks largely to the talents of individual Canadians, but also to the support provided by dynamic national institutions such as CBC/Radio-Canada, the Canada Council for the Arts, Telefilm Canada and the National Film Board of Canada (NFB); the availability of support programs such as the Canada Media Fund; and the existence of key pieces of legislation and regulations such as the Copyright Act and the Canadian Radio-television and Telecommunications Commission Act. Without numerous government interventions over the past half-century, Canadian culture would never have achieved its current level of excellence and international recognition.*

*Masterpieces have been created and talents of unimagined depth, diversity, and quality have emerged. Yet all of this growth could wither away in the ongoing digital revolution, which is dominated almost entirely by four massive American corporations: Google, Apple, Facebook, and Amazon (GAFA).[2] These four players set the conditions and access requirements for media content and are free to determine the space and visibility accorded to other cultures. As a result, nothing can be taken for granted now. The viability of Canadian culture is threatened by the new conditions imposed by these titans, who control the lion's share of the digital world. This is particularly true of Canadian French-language cultural expression, which has been relegated to the margins of digital platforms.[3]*

*Is Canada condemned to put up with this situation, as the government's approach would seem to indicate? In a September 2016 consultation paper, the department of Canadian heritage dismissed out of hand the idea of "attempting to regulate content on the Internet" and focused instead "on how to best support Canada's creators and cultural entrepreneurs in creating great content and in competing globally for both*

*Canadian and international audiences."[4] In other words, if Canadian culture is even better, more inventive, and more original, the global digital market will recognize that and come back for more.*

*This approach, which depends on the principle that healthy competition exists, is somewhat naive. All the major American network operators that control access to content, using algorithms that establish a profile for each user, have the ability to tailor their offerings to users and, by the same token, to filter out content, preventing users from seeing or reading material.[5] In short, users are manipulated and lose control over their lives, fates, and futures.[6] Indeed, the very freedom of humanity is being called into question.*

*The original cultural vitality that Canada managed to foster in the last fifty years is under threat of being choked off. Today, 90 per cent of young adults between the ages of eighteen and thirty-four own a smart phone.[7] If Canada does not meet this revolution head on, it runs the risk of being marginalized in the new era, which is already well underway, and of losing control of its identity as a society.*

*In traditional and popular forms of expression, the cultural dynamic supported by successive governments has transformed Canadian society from a consumer of imported cultural products into a creative society whose artists have carved out a niche for themselves among the many voices made available by modern technology.*

*This is where the real challenge lies: not in the quality of Canada's varied talent, but in the ability of that talent to make its presence known on almost exclusively American digital networks – in forms of expression essentially determined by the four US titans. The issue is not fear of competing against other creative talents, but rather equal access to broadcasting networks, stages, screens, and distribution platforms. In a now-globalized cultural marketplace, those who control access to the digital networks and the big data they generate have the power to decide which talents will become international stars and which will have to be satisfied with performing for a necessarily smaller domestic audience.*

*Canadian filmmakers have demonstrated their ability to reach the highest levels of excellence. Norman McLaren, David Cronenberg, Atom Egoyan, Denys Arcand, Guy Maddin, Denis Villeneuve, Jean-Marc Vallée, and Xavier Dolan have shown their films at the most prestigious festivals and received some of the most coveted awards. Canadian cinema has truly come into its own and become world-class. The NFB, established in 1939, long served as an incubator of unique talent, and it is still considered a school of cinema unlike any other. In the early days of broadcasting, the cultural productions of CBC/Radio-Canada set the standard for the field.*

*Actors working in English and French have had impressive careers abroad – people such as Donald Sutherland, William Shatner, Michael J. Fox, Jim Carrey, Ryan Gosling,*

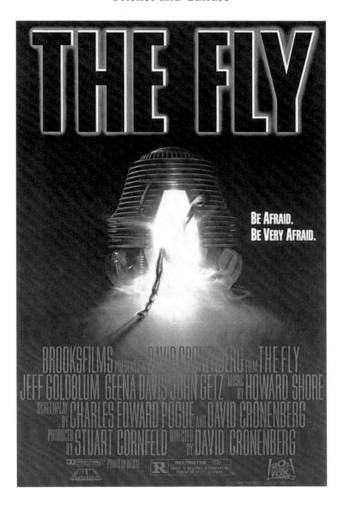

*THE FLY*

Poster for 1986 film by David Cronenberg. The success of David Cronenberg's 1986 movie *The Fly*, a science-fiction masterpiece, brought rapid recognition of his talent and won him an Oscar in 1987 for Best Makeup. Credit: Wikipedia, Melesse

*Marie-Josée Croze, and Karine Vanasse, to name but a few. Canadian musicians have become famous through sheer virtuosity: think of Glen Gould; young classical pianist Charles Richard-Hamelin, who won a silver medal at the 17th International Chopin Piano Competition, held in Warsaw in 2015; or the spellbinding voice and poetic songs of Leonard Cohen. In the last ten years, the meteoric career of young maestro Yannick Nézet-Séguin, recently named music director of the New York Metropolitan Opera, has commanded the admiration of the most demanding critics. Robert Lepage and Wajdi Mouawad are known for their stunning stage productions, whether in Avignon or New York City.*

*The protean works of painter Jean-Paul Riopelle, Peter Doig's astonishing paintings, the disturbing works of young sculptor David Altmedj, and the dreamlike pictures of photographer Jeff Wall have been exhibited and sold in galleries throughout the US, France, and England. Many younger Canadian artists are already following in their tracks.*

*Canadians in the entertainment industry have reached unparalleled levels of success. The shows of Cirque du Soleil have delighted millions, even in China and the Middle East. Céline Dion has become a global phenomenon. Justin Bieber and Drake have become astoundingly popular. Never before have so many Canadians found so much success, serving as role models for thousands of other artists, who can now dare to dream, take their first steps, and reveal the full diversity of their talents.*

*Many Canadian writers are extremely well-regarded and widely read internationally. These include Jacques Godbout (Prix Georges-Dupau awarded by the Académie française, 1973); Anne Hébert (Prix Femina, 1982); Marie-Claire Blais (Prix de l'Académie française, 1983); Margaret Atwood (Arthur C. Clarke Award, 1987; Franz Kafka Prize, 2017); Michael Ondaatje (Golden Man Booker Prize, 2018); Eleanor Catton (Man Booker Prize, 2013); Yann Martel (Man Booker Prize, 2002); Nancy Huston (Prix Femina, 2006); Joseph Boyden (Amazon.ca First Novel Award, 2006); Dany Laferrière (Prix Médicis, 2009), who is the first Canadian elected to the Académie française (established in 1635); and Alice Munro (Nobel Prize in Literature, 2013; Man Booker International Prize, 2009). Such recognition for Canadian literature was almost unheard of prior to 1967.*

*Canada's museums of national importance now develop exhibitions that are shown widely abroad, and our symphony orchestras and prestigious dance companies now appear in major world capitals, giving performances every bit the equal of their more illustrious counterparts.*

*Clearly, Canada has matured as a country and can speak with an original voice and have its identity recognized throughout the world. Canadians have finally rid themselves of an endemic complex that made them feel inferior to Americans, less original than the French, and less surprising than the British.*

*These examples plainly illustrate that, when avenues are kept open and talent is nurtured and given freedom of expression, our creative artists, performers, and writers can hold their own with the very best in every forum imaginable. Canadian culture exists. It is seen as unique, and it is appreciated throughout the world for its originality and boldness.*

*This confidence and the need to be creative exist all across Canada. To a certain degree, Quebec laid the groundwork for what followed nationally. An importer of talent from France until 1960, Quebec became an incubator of singer-songwriters, with Félix Leclerc, Robert Charlebois, and Gilles Vigneault leading the way. Dozens more Quebeckers, Acadians, and francophones from the rest of Canada followed in their footsteps and launched careers with equal confidence and stunning panache.*

*These many talented faces, which now emerge generation after generation, are shaping Canadians' confidence in their identity, in the stories they have to tell, and in the unique vision of the world they write about, present on stage, project on screen, or share in every other forum.*

*All of these works strengthen the social fabric of a country, bring communities closer together, and eventually become part of its collective memory and subconscious. As one writer put it, a people that does not create has no soul.[8]*

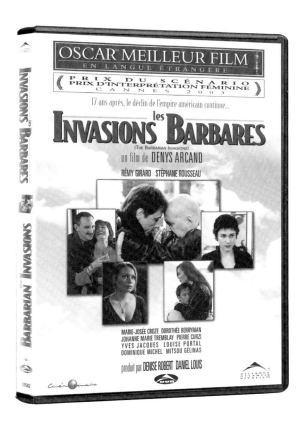

THE BARBARIAN INVASIONS

DVD case for 2003 film by Denys Arcand. Denys Arcand's 2003 social critique was a hit with US film reviewers for its caustic look at the filmmaker's generation and its obsession with individualism. In 2004, the movie won the César Award for Best Film and the Academy Award for Best Foreign Language Film. Credit: Alliance Vivafilm

*The ability of human beings to reshape their existence, to reinvent themselves, is their most precious characteristic.[9] Discovering this common human trait through artistic works brings people even closer to what it means to be human. Access to creative diversity is an essential part of life.*

*Cultural identity is primarily a matter of self-confidence; confidence in who one is and what one expresses; and confidence in what is understood by others and appreciated for its originality, meaning, and ability to reveal new forms of human expression.*

*The sports world and the world of culture have one thing in common: those who are the best of their time make their mark on that era and become representative of it.*

*On the global cultural scene, Canada has entered the race and is leaving its mark. All those who are working hard to push the envelope of creativity, who dare to explore every facet of their personal universe, and who have their own unique interpretation of the profound changes stirring the modern world deserve recognition.*

*Canada has stopped looking inward and has overcome a paralyzing lack of confidence. It has taken a vital step. But in this digital age, is Canada ready to continue along a path where the market is controlled by an oligopoly?*

*Talent alone, however exceptional it may be, is not enough. Canada cannot allow the digital marketplace controlled by American capital to determine the position and visibility of its artists in that marketplace. Canada is a small market of 36 million people. It is impossible for all these talents to express themselves fully within or mainly within its borders. The international scene is a vital outlet. It would be naive to think or argue that Canada has sufficient resources and budgets to withstand the unrestrained dumping of American cultural products onto today's globalized digital networks. The reality is that the American digital giants control most platforms. They have the power to choke things off or breathe life into them, depending on what they decide is in their interest.*

*Google, Amazon, Facebook, and Netflix all share the same fundamental interest: selling American products and raking in as much profit as possible while paying no, or a minimum of fees to the countries they are flooding with content.*

*Moreover, quite apart from freedom of access to platforms, the exercise of democratic freedom is at issue. At age thirty-three, the founder of Facebook presides over a company that arbitrates the world's democratic processes without any measure of accountability.[10] The Cambridge Analytica scandal, which revealed that the personal data of 87 million Facebook users had been utilized without their knowledge to influence the outcome of the US election and the Brexit referendum, and the 50,000 fake Facebook accounts Russia created to manipulate the 2016 presidential election in the US, are evidence of the perverse and appalling effects of an economic model that provides no-cost access to social networks in order to monetize personal data and indiscriminately manipulate users,[11] without their knowledge.*

*In addition, according to 3,000 of its own employees, Google has entered into a partnership with the Pentagon to help develop combat technologies.[12]*

*Amazon has been denounced by some of its employees, shareholders, and by American civil rights groups for the sale of its facial-recognition technology (Rekognition) to police services, considering its negative impact on the protection of privacy and its open door to social profiling of immigrants, people of colour, and protesters.[13]*

*The age of innocence when people believed in the miracle of Silicon Valley, where any and all problems could be solved by connecting everyone, has drawn to a close.[14] The initial phase of the digital revolution, which was left completely alone to regulate itself, is well and truly over.*

*In the US, this monopoly has been roundly criticized because it imposes restrictions on democratic debate, which should always remain free and critical.[15] Many have called on the government to launch antitrust investigations against this "tech monopoly."[16] American professor Jonathan Taplin described the issue perfectly in his book* Move Fast and Break Things: How Facebook, Google, and Amazon Cornered Culture and Undermined Democracy.[17] *All Canadian culture ministers should consider the real aims of these potentates, which hold in their hands the future of culture and the very existence of free, open, and democratic debate.*

*Canada previously got an inkling of what a monopoly in this sector could do when, not that long ago, American film distributors gained control of a majority of the country's movie theaters and filled screens with the best and worst of their films, thereby minimizing the visibility of Canadian movies and leaving them nothing but crumbs. It is impossible to grow Canada's film industry without enabling Canadians to see Canadian movies. This is in a way, but on a gigantic scale, precisely the situation Canada is facing with the giant digital networks that are exclusively owned by Americans.*

*The argument that if our movies were better and more original than American movies they would be shown on Netflix is irresponsibly short-sighted and misleads the public. In an open letter, Quebec's minister of culture and communications urged the federal government to reconsider its position on the digital giants.[18] A Canada-wide coalition of some forty organizations called for the American behemoths to pay the same taxes as Canadian broadcasters.[19] Instead of taxing Netflix at the same rate as Canadian broadcasters and enforcing regulations that require them to broadcast a certain percentage of Canadian-produced programs and to contribute to the Canada Media Fund, as all Canadian undertakings are required to do, Canada's heritage minister threw in the towel. She chose to secretly negotiate with Netflix a five-year*

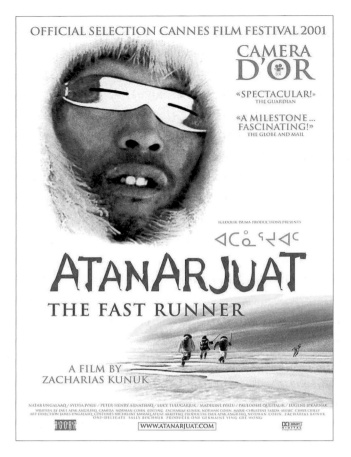

ᐊᑕᓈᕐᔪᐊᑦ– *ATANARJUAT* (THE FAST RUNNER)
Poster for 2001 film by Zacharias Kunuk. The first feature film by Zacharias Kunuk won critical acclaim for its authenticity, spectacular northern scenery, and integrity of its lead character. *Atanarjuat* was the first film written and produced entirely in Inuktitut, and it won the Camera d'Or at the Cannes Film Festival in 2001. Credit: Wikipedia, Andrzej Banas

*$500-million agreement to fund Canadian productions over which it would retain control. What portion of that amount would go to French-language productions was not revealed. The total freedom given to this oligopoly has a direct impact on the very survival of print media in this country and of Canada's public broadcaster, CBC/ Radio-Canada.*

*Canadian media have lost as much as 80 per cent of their advertising revenue, mostly to the digital giants. The minister responsible decided to postpone any decision that might immediately staunch the bleeding and ensure the survival of media outlets. Meanwhile, the print media are dying. Some very limited measures, mostly to help community newspapers, were announced in the February 2018 budget. Until more is done, the downward financial spiral threatening the existence of the press will continue.[20] The authenticity and vigour of democratic debate is at stake. Since 2010, 225 weekly newspapers and twenty-seven dailies have either merged or stopped publishing altogether.[21] This selling-out of Canada's cultural and democratic sovereignty has been met with widespread condemnation.[22]*

*Is Canada defenceless against the relentless onslaught of these giants? Do they really dictate the law? Do consumers and users truly have no choice but to take them or leave them? Must governments stand by while the privacy rights of citizens are effectively being trampled, the survival of democratic discourse is being threatened,[23] and the electoral process is being rigged? Noted scholars and senior analysts have intervened publicly to press the government to act, but it does not seem to realize the importance of the risk that threatens democracy in Canada.[24] Are there no weapons to put a stop to this oligopoly, which is setting the rules of the game and squeezing the life out of Canadian society?[25]*

*According to the Organisation for Economic Co-operation and Development (OECD), forcing companies such as Netflix to collect and pay the goods and services tax (GST) or provincial sales taxes is strictly a matter of political will.[26] Executives at Google acknowledged as much. They said that it is not up to their company to act and that it will comply if the Canadian government changes the law.[27] In a June 2016 briefing note to the minister, Canadian Heritage deputy minister Graham Flack warned that not applying sales taxes to foreign-based digital platforms creates an uneven playing field that puts Canadian suppliers at a disadvantage.[28] Canada is governed by the rule of law. It considers fairness and respect for diversity to be essential values of the civilization and democracy it represents.*

*In June 2017, the Supreme Court of Canada surprised everyone who thought that Google was beyond the reach of Canadian law, existing in a sort of lawless zone not subject to Canadian values. In so doing, the court stiffened the backbones of governments that had already abdicated to oligopolies founded on the mastery and control of powerful algorithms and supported by the financial omnipotence of the owners of this system, who in a few short years became some of the richest men in the world. The owners of the five largest personal fortunes on the planet include Jeffrey P. Bezos, who owns Amazon ($94.1 billion), Bill Gates of Microsoft ($88 billion), and Mark Zuckerberg of Facebook ($76.3 billion).[29] In the summer of 2018, Apple became the first private company to be worth more than $1000 billion![30] When big money reaches that kind of scale, it no longer seems real. The combined value of the four leading high-tech companies exceeds $3.4 trillion.*

*Given the size of the giants of the new economy, many think it is crazy to believe the government of Canada could carry out its responsibility to make them respect the values on which our democracy is based and recognize our cultural identity. Some people still believe in the complete freedom of the Internet – as a dreamt-of Eden. However, some rules are needed, if only to prevent messages that promote violence or hatred toward specific groups.[31]*

*Sixteen countries have already imposed their tax laws on these titans, the most recent being Australia with a tax of 10 per cent.[32] On 18 July 2018, the European Union's Commissioner for Competition, who is responsible for fighting monopolies, levied a record fine of $4.3 billion (US$5 billion) against Google for abusing its market power.[33] In 2016, the commissioner ordered Apple to repay Ireland $13 billion in improper tax benefits. Apple and Dublin worked out an agreement on 24 April 2018 to have the money paid into a blocked separate account. Meanwhile, Netflix publicly acknowledged that its investment in Canada was in no way contingent on any kind of tax break.[34]*

*In two decisions, the Supreme Court of Canada noted the foundations of the rule of law and drew a line in the sand.[35] The court clearly recognized that "there was gross inequality of bargaining power between the parties," and that there is a responsibility to uphold "these rights [that] play an essential role in a free and democratic society and embody key Canadian values." In other words, Canada must assume all the responsibilities inherent in its role as custodian of the public interest, and democratic states have a duty to defend themselves, regardless of how big a fortune or how powerful an oligopoly is involved. Cowards never get any respect. As Churchill said about the retreat from Dunkirk during the Second World War, "Wars are not won by evacuations."*

*Since the challenge exists on a global scale, the action to be taken should be determined at that level. As the Supreme Court rightly pointed out, "The problem in this case is occurring online and globally. The Internet has no borders – its natural habitat is global."[36]*

*Canada has privileged access to the EU and to the United Nations Educational, Scientific, and Cultural Organization (UNESCO). In 2017, it signed a trade agreement with the twenty-eight EU countries, all of which are extremely well informed about the implications of the digital marketplace.*

*On 15 June 2017, the European Parliament adopted a lengthy 78-paragraph resolution in which it clearly set out a fundamental framework of rules governing online platforms.[37] Among other things, this framework provides a high level of protection for intellectual property rights and the digital single market. The resolution called on the European Commission and the member states "to examine the potential for error and bias in the use of algorithms in order to prevent any kind of discrimination, unfair practice, or breach of privacy." It noted that specific action should be taken to address the fact that, although "more creative content is being consumed today than ever before [...], the creative sectors have not seen a comparable increase in revenue from this increase in consumption," and stressed that there should be more "clarity regarding the status of these online services under copyright and e-commerce law." The resolution also stated "that an unfair market has been created, threatening the development of [...] cultural and creative industries."[38] One could not put it more eloquently.*

*The resolution makes it clear that digital platforms now constitute a preferred means of broadening access to cultural and creative works. However, European creative works must be among the products presented to users.*

*The European Parliament took action accordingly. On 23 May 2017, following a decision by the EU Council of Ministers, it issued a directive that increased the quotas for European content in Netflix product offerings to 30 per cent.[39] The Greek minister effectively summed up the argument: European audiovisual works cannot be left unprotected on an uneven playing field that favours international productions. The European*

NETFLIX

Internet giants Netflix, Google, Facebook, and Amazon have a hand in controlling everything that consumers see, buy, and even think. This dictatorial power has so far gone unchecked by Canadian laws and regulations, enabling these companies to impose their conditions on society as a whole and on producers, creators, performers, authors, journalists and writers without any fiscal or legal responsibility to support Canadian production, pay royalties, or foster the vitality of the Canadian media. The debate is open on the government's responsibility to legislate on that oligopoly as other countries, like Japan, Australia, and countries of the European Union, have done already. Credit: Coolcaesar, Wikipedia *ministers thus decided to ensure an adequate level of visibility for European works and to demand a share of revenue and profits to support European audiovisual production. Paris and Berlin, for their part, agreed to impose taxes proportional to* GAFA *revenues in their respective countries and to overcome the financial arrangements used to reduce taxes to insignificant proportions of the profits actually earned.[40]*

*This firm stance, based on the decisions of the 28-member-state Parliament and supported by the subsequent ministerial directive, lays the groundwork for an initiative that Canada should implement, initially at home. Canada must ensure that its artists are paid properly and their copyrights are protected, and make certain that these giant corporations pay their fair share of taxes and, like other Canadian broadcasters, support Canadian productions by contributing to the Canada Media Fund.*

*The Canadian government's stated intention to negotiate bilateral compensation agreements with the members of this oligopoly weakens public authority.[41] The government must defend the principle of fairness for all taxpayers, which is fundamental to a democratic system of government. Canada must begin by asserting its duty as a government to charge income taxes and other taxes and fees, and then negotiate if necessary. It must not create the impression that it is too weak to legislate or proclaim its jurisdiction.*

*There is now an urgent need to adapt Canadian privacy laws and policies to modern technological realities. The powers of the privacy commissioner must be reviewed and strengthened to counter the abuses that have become evident and are undermining Canada's democracy.[42] In early June 2018, the government finally announced the cr'eation of an expert panel to advise it (by the end of 2019) on the future mandate of* CBC/Radio-Canada *and communications legislation, further to a report from the* CRTC.[43] *The government apparently plans to require new media such as Netflix and Spotify to contribute to the funding and distribution of Canadian content.[44] But this is a long way from a complete answer to the radical revolution currently underway.*

*As one of the original states party to the 2005* Convention on the Protection and Promotion of the Diversity of Cultural Expressions, *Canada must turn to* UNESCO. *In the context of the digital marketplace, Canada must invite all* UNESCO *member states to give effect to article 5.2 of the convention, which specifically states that a country may take and implement "measures to protect and promote the diversity of cultural expressions within its territory." This initiative should take the form of a supplementary protocol to the 2005 convention and be based on the 2017 European Parliament resolution on online platforms and the digital single market. The protocol would set conditions for adopting policies to manage digital distribution according to the principles set out in the convention.[45]*

THE HANDMAID'S TALE

*The Handmaid's Tale*, a novel by Margaret Atwood (1939–    ), was published in 1985 and became a best-seller in Canada, Great Britain, and the United States. It won the Arthur C. Clarke Award in 1987 and inspired a movie (1990), an opera (2000), and a 10-episode series produced by Hulu in 2017. Audiences were hooked by its fascinating plot, and the series received thirteen nominations and eight Emmy awards in 2017, and two Golden Globes in January 2018. Netflix, in cooperation with the CBC, produced and broadcast Alias Grace in 2017, based on Atwood's successful 1996 novel.

    *In its decisions, the Supreme Court of Canada found that Canadian law applies to the Internet giants, just as French and Belgian courts recognized that the American oligopoly was abusing its dominant position. On that basis, Canada must bring in new legislation and standards and ensure the digital titans comply with those rules and pay their fair share of taxes in the country where they earn a corresponding share of their revenue. According to a study by the C.D. Howe Institute, "Canada hasn't kept pace in adapting tax policy to the digital economy in comparison to its peers."[46] The time has come to "normalize" the situation in Canada. The government needs to show leadership, following the examples set by Australia, Japan, and the EU: first, to restore an equitable playing field; second, to provide fair compensation to the creative artists and journalists whose works are pirated; and third, to require these giants to responsibly contribute to the funding of Canadian productions and pay their rightful share of tax in this country.[47]*

    *The digital beast is hungry. In the ongoing negotiations to revamp NAFTA, the Americans proposed raising the threshold above which goods purchased online in the*

*US would be taxed to $800. This would eliminate taxes on the bulk of online sales. Not satisfied to be the lion in the fable,* GAFA *is grasping for more. Google and Facebook together carry as much as 80 per cent of all online advertising without paying a penny for all the articles they reproduce, cutting into the revenue of Canada's print media in the process.[48] Those who think it is possible to obtain a reasonable amount of space for Canadian cultural products in the online marketplace without establishing specific legislative requirements that will ultimately have to be enforced by the Supreme Court are only fooling themselves. There is no room for delay. That approach will only undermine the efforts of Canadian creative artists, allow Canada's cultural presence on the Web to become marginalized, and permit one of the democratic pillars upon which this country is built, namely the existence of a vigorous free press, to erode into dust.*

*It is unfortunate that the Canadian government does not appear to grasp the importance of the issues at stake and remains so insensitive to the need for leadership to restore the freedom the* GAFA *oligarchs have taken away from Canadians and secure the future of democracy in this country against Machiavellian machinations.*

*That is the essential debate that must be held in the open. It is an unprecedented strategic challenge not only for Canada, but also for all other cultures grappling with the same levelling forces and total US dominance.*

### NOTES

1 The author is indebted to the Library of Parliament for its careful work in verifying the accuracy of the historical facts and figures in the text.

2 This acronym is more common in Europe.

3 Jean-Benoît Nadeau, "La découvrabilité," *Le Devoir*, 28 August 2017, p. A7.

4 Government of Canada, *Canadian Content in a Digital World: Focusing the Conversation*, Consultation paper, September 2016, p. 7.

5 Pascale St-Onge, "L'avenir de l'information : la 'patate chaude' des nouvelles politiques culturelles à l'ère du numérique," *Le Devoir*, 11 September 2017, p. A6.

6 Milad Doueihi, "Le numérique comme nouveau processus civilisateur," *Le Monde*, 23 January 2018, Cahier du Monde, p. 4.

7 Agnes Barr-Klouman, "Robotics and Artificial Intelligence, Part 1: Advantages and Challenges," Research paper distributed at a Senate of Canada open caucus on robotics and artificial intelligence, 29 March 2017.

8 Émile Gaudreault, "Sauvez mon âme," *La Presse+*, 22 September 2017.

9 Francine Pelletier, "L'art n'est pas la politique," *Le Devoir*, 18 July 2018, p. A7.

10   Corine Lesner, "L'humiliation de Mark Zuckerberg convoqué au Congrès," *Le Monde*, 11 April 2018, p. 23.

11   Malcolm Nance, *The Plot to Destroy Democracy* (Hachette, 2018).

12   Jean-Michel Bezat, "La deuxième vie des géants du Net," *Le Monde*, 10 April 2018, p. 24.

13   *USA Today*, "Amazon's facial tool misidentified 28 members of congress in ACLU test," 30 July 2018; *Le Journal de Montréal*, "L'intelligence artificielle: enjeux et défis pour le Québec," 25 August 2018, p. 58.

14   Corine Lesner, "De la Réforme à la Silicon Valley," *Le Monde*, Économies et Entreprise, 11 April 2018, p. 1.

15   Kenneth P. Vogel, "Google-funded think-tank ousts its own Google critic," *The New York Times*, 31 August 2017, p. A1.

16   Jonathan Taplin, "Google's disturbing influence," *The New York Times*, 31 August 2017, p. A23; Julie Charpentrat, "Google visé par une enquête aux États-Unis," *Le Devoir*, 16 November 2017, p. B3.

17   Published by Little, Brown and Company, 2017.

18   Luc Fortin (Quebec's minister of culture and communications), "Ottawa doit revoir sa position sur les géants du numérique," *Le Devoir*, 6 September 2017, p. B5; Tommy Chouinard, "Québec taxera Netflix avec ou sans le fédéral," *La Presse+*, 8 November 2017.

19   "Netflix et Spotify : une grande coalition culturelle demande plus de fermeté," *Journal de Montréal*, 14 September 2017

20   Benoit Chartier et al., "Un retour déplorable à la case 'conversation' pour les éditeurs de presse," *La Presse*, 30 September 2017, p. A19.

21   Senate of Canada, Open Caucus. Threats to Traditional Journalism in Canada, 28 February 2018.

22   Guillaume Bourgault-Côté, "L'entente Netflix doit être dévoilée," *Le Devoir*, 3 October 2017, p. B8; Bryan Myles, "En finir avec l'iniquité," *Le Devoir*, 5 October 2017; Robert Everett-Green, "A stunning fall from grace for Melanie Joly," *The Globe and Mail*, 5 October 2017, p. A7; Graeme Hamilton, "French free Netflix deal trips up Joly in Quebec," *Ottawa Citizen*, 5 October 2017, p. NP3.

23   Fanny Lévesque, "Le Québec et le Canada ne sont pas à l'abri", *La Presse+*, Actualités 2, 1 August 2018.

24   Edward Greenspon and Taylor Owen, "We can save democracy from destructive digital threats," *The Globe and Mail*, 24 August 2018, p. A11; Trudel, Pierre, "Internet : le retour sur terre," *Le Devoir*, 21 August 2018, p. A7.

25   Guillaume Bourgault-Côté, "Politique culturelle : front commun pour forcer Ottawa et Québec à agir," *Le Devoir*, 14 September 2017, p. B8; Guillaume Bourgault-Côté, "Les appels à la réglementation se multiplient," *Le Devoir*, 27 September 2017, p. B8.

26 Guillaume Bourgault-Côté, "OCDE : taxer Netflix fonctionne," *Le Devoir*, 24 October 2017, p. B8.

27 Philippe Orfali, "Géants du Web et impôts : à Ottawa d'agir, dit Google," *Le Journal de Montréal*, 17 January 2018, p. 29.

28 Guillaume Bourgault-Côté, "La ministre Joly a favorisé Netflix en dépit d'une mise en garde de son ministre," *Le Devoir*, 14 October 2017, p. A1.

29 *Bloomberg Billionaires Index*, https://www.bloomberg.com/billionaires/, consulted 1 November 2017.

30 Juliette Michel, "Apple, première entreprise privée à valoir plus de 1 000 milliards", *Le Devoir*, 3 August 2018, p. B7.

31 Thomas Urbain, "Facebook pris dans une nouvelle polémique – Zuckerberg refuse de bannir les négationnistes," *Le Soleil*, Agence France-Presse, 20 July 2018, p. 20.

32 Quebec is considering imposing its provincial sales tax (TVQ) on Netflix. See Guillaume Bourgault-Côté, "TVQ : Netflix collaborera avec Québec," *Le Devoir*, 4 October 2017, p. B8; Alain Dubuc, "Les demi-vérités de Mélanie Joly," *La Presse*, 30 September 2017, p. A19.

33 Adam Satariano and Jack Nicas, "E.U. slaps Google with record fine in software case – penalty of 5.1 billion," *The New York Times*, 19 July 2018, p. 1.

34 Daniel Leblanc, "Netflix moves to set record straight on 500 million pledge," *The Globe and Mail*, 10 October 2017, p. A7.

35 *Douez v. Facebook, Inc.*, 2017 SCC 33 (23 June); *Google Inc. v. Equustek Solutions Inc.*, 2017 SCC 34 (28 June).

36 *Google Inc. v. Equustek Solutions Inc.*, 2017 SCC 34, [2017] 1 SCR 824, p. 827.

37 P8_TA-PROV(2017)0272. Online platforms and the Digital Single Market: European Parliament resolution of 15 June 2017 on online platforms and the digital single market (2016/2276 [INI]).

38 Paragraph 30 of the resolution.

39 Directive 2010/13 EV.

40 Agence France-Presse, "Taxation des GAFA : Paris et Berlin feront une nouvelle proposition," *Le Devoir*, 28 August 2017, p. B7.

41 Guillaume Bourgault-Côté, "Taxe Netflix. Ottawa négociera des ententes bilatérales," *Le Devoir*, 21 September 2017, p. A3

42 Art Eggleton and Raymonde Saint-Germain, "Privacy laws must catch up with technology," *Toronto Star*, 18 July 2018.

43 Canadian Radio-television and Telecommunications Commission.

44 Vincent Brousseau-Pouliot, "Nouveaux médias : Ottawa veut mettre fin au régime à deux vitesses," *La Presse.ca*, 5 June 2018, http://www.lapresse.ca/affaires/economie/

medias-et-telecoms/201806/04/01-5184478-nouveaux-medias-ottawa-veut-mettre-fin-au-regime-a-deux-vitesses.php.

45 UNESCO, Diversity of Cultural Expressions. "Diversity of Cultural Expressions in the Digital Age," Debates on the implementation of the 2005 Convention on the Protection and Promotion of the Diversity of Cultural Expressions, 9 June 2015.

46 Alain Dubuc, "Une nouvelle taxe près de chez vous? Netflix et les services numériques," *La Presse Plus*, 24 August 2017.

47 Pierre Trudel, "La 'taxe' de la désinformation," *Le Devoir*, 19 September 2017, p. A7

48 Bob Cox, Jerry Dias, and Edward Greenspon, "Journalism matters more than ever: we need to help save it," *The Globe and Mail*, 14 September 2017, p. A15.

# Culture Lies at the Heart of What Makes Us Human

Pierre Lassonde, philanthropist, Chair of the Board of Directors
of the Canada Council for the Arts

I grew up in a house that was full of art, thanks mainly to my mother, who was a collector. It was a time when you took courses with names like "methodology," "literature," "rhetoric," and "philosophy." It was a little before Jean Charest, who is sitting here right now. I was a bit older than nine in 1967. In our house, we listened to everything from Bach to the Beatles to jazz. That was the environment I was raised in and I recreated it in my adult life. It is also something I want to pass on to my children and grandchildren.

When I reflect on all that, I believe the key to any passion lies in a very simple question: what drives us as individuals and as a society?

Yesterday, Gary Doer, the former premier of Manitoba, spoke about the values Canadians held thirty or forty years ago. When we used to talk about our values as Canadians, we would say that we were not American. But that's not enough. We are much more than that. I would like to share a pivotal moment in my life, an event that really gave me food for thought when I first became involved in philanthrophy.

Before her untimely death, my first wife had promised the mother superior of a convent, who was trying to build a new girls' school, that she would contribute to the project. Unfortunately, she died before that could happen and it was up to me to honour her pledge. So, six, seven, eight or nine months after she passed away, I heard a call from beyond telling me to go to the school to talk numbers.

I arrived at the school on the agreed-upon day and was led into a large room. I don't know how to describe it, but I sort of felt like I was in a courtroom. There was a long and imposing table. All the nuns were seated on one side and dressed in their full habit: coif, robe, the whole works. I sat opposite them in a low, short-legged student's chair.

The mother superior said, "Mr. Lassonde, we are sorry for your loss and we are praying for you." She went on for two or three minutes explaining how the community was praying especially for me. Then she stopped and looked at me. It was my turn to speak.

I had given this meeting a lot of thought. I thanked them and said that their prayers helped me. Then I got down to brass tacks and said, "I would be happy to contribute half a million dollars to your new project." I was met with total silence.

The mother superior turned to her left and spoke to the nun in charge of finance. Then she turned to her right and spoke to another nun. Finally, she turned to me and said, "Mr. Lassonde, that is a very generous offer, but it is not what God wants."

She continued, "We urge you to pray to the Holy Spirit and come back in a month. Perhaps by then the Holy Spirit will have enlightened you." It's amazing sometimes how the Holy Spirit works. He must have a cell phone or something. Anyway, the project cost me a million dollars.

I like to tell that story because, I have to admit, I was not really prepared to donate so much at the time. I later realized that when you invest in something, you have to go

*ICEBERG NO 1*

Jean-Paul Riopelle (1923–2002). 1977, oil on canvas, private collection, Montreal, © Estate of Jean-Paul Riopelle / SODRAC (2018), Photo MBAM, Christine Guest.

*Iceberg No. 1* is the first in a series of close to thirty paintings by Canadian artist Jean-Paul Riopelle, painted almost exclusively in black and white following his trip to Baffin Island in 1977. In great demand internationally, Riopelle's works fetch high prices and are found in the collections of major museums. Riopelle consistently described himself not as an abstractionist but as a landscape painter inspired by Canada's rugged beauty. Credit: SODRAC (2018) all in. It's funny because, since then, whenever our family is considering a project and discussing how much to invest, we ask ourselves, "So, how much would God want?" It has become a benchmark.

Our family's philanthropic work focuses mainly on three areas. Number one is education, number two is the arts and number three is the community where we live.

In terms of the first area, it is vital that we support institutions that contribute to our education. Educating our young people is the most important issue for our country and has the closest correlation with the GDP.

I have worked in the natural resources sector and I was often asked, "What is our greatest resource? Oil? Mining? Our forests and lakes?" The answer is none of the above. In my view, our greatest resource is our millions of young people, our educated population. They are our natural resources.

However, Canada's natural resources sector has one advantage. This country will always be involved in natural resources because of one incredible fact: we have the second-largest land mass in the world. We will always have an advantage over every other country except one. We also have one of the best-educated populations in the world, which gives us an advantage over other countries.

We must also support institutions. Museums are not businesses. Universities are not businesses. They need support, not just from government but from philanthropists.

Philanthropy is critical to maintaining our institutions, not just arts institutions but educational institutions and all those not involved in business.

About a year ago, I spoke to the members of the Quebec City chamber of commerce about how beauty inspires goodness. When you are surrounded by beauty, it makes you want to do good. The two go together.

I talked about the importance of investing in arts and culture to foster creative cities. Creative cities support an ecosystem in which the arts become an integral part of life. Think about cultural tourism, where all the businesses are self-sufficient. That's beauty.

At the Musée des beaux-arts in Quebec City, we have just finished building a new pavilion that is an absolutely incredible piece of architecture. My vision was very simple: create a building that is the equivalent of a Fabergé egg; as you know, the Fabergé eggs were designed to hold treasure. When you look at this building from far off, you want to visit it. How will you react to it? You will definitely want to see the treasures inside. Thanks to the new pavilion in Quebec City, attendance has doubled and own-source revenues have tripled because business people now want to hold events there. The public is getting to know the gallery and feel a sense of ownership. In addition, two million people visit Quebec City by boat; if we attract 5 per cent to 10 per cent of cultural tourism, that's 100,000 or 200,000 people. That's huge for a city of one million. That is primarily the kind of project that we support.

The other project that I mentioned to the chamber of commerce was Zita Cobb's initiative on Fogo Island.

Fogo Island was a dying community off the coast of Newfoundland. When I say "dying," I mean it. A community that once had a population of more than 15,000 was down to only a few thousand residents.

The government actually wanted to wipe it off the map. It didn't want the island to have a post office, so it closed it. It didn't want the island to have a hospital, so it closed it. It did everything it could to get rid of the community, but the people wouldn't leave the island.

One woman said, "You know what? Our community has been here for more than 200 years. We should know how things work here. If your family has been here for 200 years, what do you know that the rest of the world doesn't?"

To make a long story short, she established Fogo Island Inn with support from the arts and the community, and it is now one of the top tourist destinations in the world. It is a five-star hotel. If you have never been there, I strongly encourage you to go. The artists-in-residence program has four studios. Artists must live in the community on Fogo Island and they have access to the studios during the day. The only requirement is that they must exhibit their work or create works if they are poets or artists. The arts are now a core part of the island. They have created an incredible community. Now the fact that they are Irish and can tell stories is really beneficial.

Charles Landry is a respected expert on urban change who invented the concept of creative cities. He said that ordinary people can make the extraordinary happen if given the chance and the resources to step outside the ordinary framework of everyday life. That's a very powerful statement because it is art that makes this possible. If you are walking down the street in Ottawa or Toronto, for example, and you see a work of art that really resonates with you, then you step outside the ordinary.

This is exactly what we are trying to do in Canada. Why are Canadians different? Maybe part of the answer is because arts and culture are an integral part of who we are.

I touched on a few cities, but whether we are talking about the Art Gallery of Ontario in Toronto, the Royal Ontario Museum, the Musée des beaux-arts in Montréal or the Musée national in Québec City, all of these institutions create ecosystems that are vitally important for artists and communities.

When artists move into a neighbourhood, you often see that neighbourhood become gentrified, because everyone wants to live there. It gets too expensive and people have to move elsewhere, but that is what makes our cities so diverse and what makes people want to live there. You can go for a walk in the evening and you feel comfortable.

How many places in the world can you go for a stroll at midnight and not worry about being hit by a car or killed? That's how most, if not all, Canadian cities are. We have neighbourhoods in which we feel completely safe. Why? Partly because our eco-system, which I mentioned earlier, is so significant.

The concept of beauty that I discussed in Quebec City has also been explored in a book by Pierre Thibault and François Cardinal entitled *Et si la beauté rendait heureux*. It is essentially about the idea that I just mentioned. The authors talk about well-designed spaces that make life more enjoyable and change our relationship with the space, with other people and even with the weather. In their view, schools should be designed like neighbourhood places where we feel comfortable and not like we are in prison, which is the way most children feel. Imagine how happy children from disadvantaged neighbourhoods would be if they could go to that kind of school. The authors tested their theory and it had an enormous impact on children's learning.

To create spaces like that, we have to tap into our creativity and integrate the arts into our lives, but we must do more as well. I don't like to say that the only sure things in life are death and taxes. If we do not contribute to the greater good, to progress and to creativity, we are not living life to its fullest and we will fear death.

There is a project that is very close to my heart as a philanthropist. When we talk about the greater good of the country, there is one project that encompasses the arts, history, culture, philanthropy and just about everything else: a national portrait collection. This is not a new idea; it has been around for more than 20 years, but has not come to fruition. There is currently space opposite Parliament Hill and it has been available for about 20 years.

If we look back over 150 years of Canadian history, Library and Archives Canada has collected, stored and preserved more than 20,000 drawings and paintings, including portraits of the *Four Indian Kings*, an extremely rare collection of four oil-on-canvas portraits. Library and Archives Canada also has four million photos, including the complete works of Yousuf Karsh, the outstanding photographer who was so well known in the 1960s. He left his entire collection to Library and Archives Canada. His photos have never been exhibited. They are national treasures that are hidden away at Library and Archives Canada.

I haven't even touched on the portraits belonging to the Art Gallery of Ontario in Toronto or the Musée des beaux-arts de Montréal. I haven't gotten to the magnificent portraits and images in the Hudson's Bay Company private collections, which date

CIRQUE DU SOLEIL

Originally called The Waders, Cirque du Soleil was founded in 1984 by Guy Laliberté and Gilles Ste-Croix, and began as a small group of performers in Baie-St-Paul. It has grown to become a multinational company based in the United States, the Middle East and now China. Cirque du Soleil continues to thrill audiences with its acrobatics, spectacular set design, magical performances and increasingly innovative stage machinery. Credit: CirqueduSoleil©2017

back 400 years. Or the Canadian Imperial Bank of Commerce's Klondike gold rush collection and the private collections of the Bank of Montreal and donors.

These gems deserve to be exhibited so that Canadians can look directly at the people who shaped the country's history and paved the way for the future. Whether the images are of Indigenous peoples, early settlers, inventors, athletes, activists, artists, scientists, capitalists, feminist pioneers or political leaders, a portrait collection offers a panoramic view of the past and highlights the incredible diversity that shapes our identity as a country.

The old saying that "a picture is worth a thousand words" is still true today, especially in the world of Instagram, Snapchat and selfies. Why? Because the images represent our collective interest in sharing our common experiences.

The portrait gallery in London, which receives two million visitors each year, and the galleries in Washington, DC, and Canberra, Australia, are huge draws. Nowadays, galleries are even more cutting-edge and use interactive technology to engage visitors, historians and students in discovering history, society, previous generations, key figures and achievements. I sincerely believe that a Canadian portrait gallery would be an ideal way to mark Canada's 150th anniversary.

Throughout my life in business, I have had the good fortune to work with inspiring people and institutions. They don't call me "Lucky Pierre" for nothing. I have had a lot of luck. I have also been lucky in the world of art. Not only have I been chairman of the board of the Musée national des beaux-arts du Québec, but as you know, I have been chair of the Canada Council for the Arts for close to two years. This year, the Council is celebrating its 60th birthday. I am a little older, of course, but the Council is in much better shape than I am.

The Council has changed a lot in the past 60 years. To come back to the subject of philanthropy, the Council was a recommendation of the Massey Report. Vincent Massey chaired the Royal Commission on National Development in the Arts, Letters and Sciences. It was known as the Massey Commission, after Vincent Massey.

The Massey Report is the most comprehensive analysis of cultural life ever conducted in Canada. The cultural landscape it described was bleak. Professional theatres were dying, musical performances were confined mainly to church basements, and professional art exhibits were practically unheard of outside major centres.

To create a cultural and intellectual life in Canada, the Massey Report recommended that the federal government create a Canada Council for the Encouragement of the Arts, Letters, Humanities and Social Sciences, but it took two philanthropists to make that recommendation a reality. Together, Walton Killam and Sir James Dunn contributed $50 million in 1957. To give you an idea of what $50 million was worth in 1957, an ounce of gold was worth $20. That same ounce is now worth $1,200. Their contribution would be worth $3 billion today. That was a very generous gift in 1957, when you think of it. That council was the forerunner of the Canada Council for the Arts.

When he proposed the creation of the Canada Council to Parliament, then-prime minister Louis St-Laurent stated, "Our main object in recommending the establishment of the Canada Council is to provide some assistance to universities, to the arts, humanities and social sciences as well as to students in those fields without attempting in any way to control their activities or to tamper with their freedom."

That was a pretty visionary statement.

In my opinion, the government should support the country's cultural development without trying to control it. As a result, the Council is, in St-Laurent's words, "as free from state control as it is prudent for any body entrusted with public funds to be."

The Canada Council for the Arts operates at arm's length from government and has an eleven-member board. It reports to the minister of Canadian Heritage. When

CÉLINE DION (1968– ), AN INTERNATIONAL STAR
Céline Dion is, without question, one of the greatest entertainers in the world, with international record sales of 220 million and an almost unbroken string of Las Vegas shows, where she has been a top performer since 2003. This Canadian superstar has beaten all entertainment records.
Credit: The Canadian Press/Graham Hughes

the Council was established in 1957, it received a total budget of $1.5 million, divided between the humanities and social sciences. In 1964, it became clear that this amount was not enough.

As the Massey Report stated in 1951, it was incredible that English Canada produced only 14 works of fiction in an entire year. Hard to believe, isn't it?

Today, the Council has a budget of $257 million and we fund more than 2,300 Canadian agencies and institutions, as well as more than 17,000 writers and thousands of artists. We have come a long way.

Given that the Council's budget will double over the next five years to reach $360 million – at least that is what we have been told – the Council now has more resources than ever to meet its commitments to the arts in Canada.

It is important to remember that the Council's investment goes far beyond the projects that we fund. For example, a grant to publish a book could lead to a film version. The best example of this is *Life of Pi*. We supported Yann Martel and, guess what? An excellent film was made.

I could give you hundreds of examples of tiny seeds planted by the Canada Council for the Arts – whether it was Margaret Atwood close to fifty years ago, Leonard Cohen thirty years ago or Yann Martel more recently – that grew to shape Canadian culture.

The Canada Council for the Arts is not the only organization at work in this field. Our role complements that of other government agencies supporting the arts, but we play an essential part in the ecosystem that gave rise to the Creative City Network, an ecosystem that fosters cultural tourism.

The Council's plan for the coming years has the full support of artists and stakeholders in the arts community. The board of directors, which I chair, will explore what I think is a promising future, given the efforts to make the arts central to our lives and to discussions about where we are headed.

The law that established the Council says that it was created to foster and promote the study and production of works in the arts for the enjoyment of all Canadians. When I chair board meetings, I assure you that I constantly ask Council staff how we can reach out to all 36 million Canadians. I want to make sure that every citizen can benefit from the arts as much as you and I do.

Earlier, I said that art reflects our society and culture and, in particular, the many cultures that make up our society. The arts sector, and especially that supported by the Canada Council for the Arts, is a key driver of our cultural industries and the broader cultural sector because that is where most of the talent, knowledge, innovation and content is developed, without which the cultural economy would falter.

When the arts are an integral part of the life of a community, of its professional, personal and even parental life, of its activities, we see the effects on that community in terms of creativity, inclusiveness and values. This brings me back to the original question: what drives us as individuals and as a society? I think the answer is the same for everyone: the desire to build a better Canada and discover the value inherent in every person.

# 9

# The Invention of a New Economy: Can the Future Be Predicted?[1]

# The Hon. Serge Joyal, Senator

*T*he Canadian economy of 1967 had a conventional manufacturing base and limited exports, was focused on the development of natural resources with relatively stable prices, and supported a rather slowly developing financial market, given that the value of the Canadian dollar was based on the US greenback. In contrast, the Canadian economy of 2017 appears to be worlds apart, having been revolutionized in such a short span of time.

Are Canadians better off than they were fifty years ago? Do they have more money in their pockets after taxes and fees? Has there been a decline in the number of low-income Canadians? In short, is Canada wealthier overall? In 2007, its gross foreign debt was US$920 billion, or 66.8 per cent of GDP; in 2016, this figure had doubled to US$1.8 trillion. In 2015, the debt amounted to 91.5 per cent of GDP, and it is expected to grow to 127 per cent by 2022.[2] The federal debt[3] totalled $390.7 billion in 2007–08, ballooning to $688.2 billion by 2015-2016. The foreign-held share of the debt grew from 13 per cent in 2007-2008 to 28.9 per cent in 2015-2016. There is an obvious trend: the net debt[4] was 22.1 per cent of GDP in 2007, growing to 26.7 per cent in 2015.[5] In 1967, the size of the federal government was 225,342 employees; in 2016, this number grew by almost 15 per cent to 258,979.[6]

Although Canada is widely seen as a wealthy, prosperous country with virtually limitless resources, could it be that instead it is a not-so-unshakeable giant that is actually not one of the most robust or most secure economies? Could it aim for the top so as to avoid being ranked among the lacklustre (neither outstanding nor poor) economies and end up providing Canadians with a better quality of life? Are we dreaming when we hope for better or more? The last fifty years has been instructive, showing us what it takes to make strides and finally emerge from the middle of the pack, where Canada is currently stuck.

Since 1967, a series of disruptions occurred so rapidly that no economist could have predicted them, shaking Canada's economic and financial foundations. The country *has a fairly limited domestic consumer market; access to venture capital continues to be restricted, and the tax revenues able to support a large social safety net need to be stable, or else the deficit would soar. The country has gone through several crises that have seriously called into question the quiet certainties of its not-so-distant past.*

*Around Canada's centennial, Keynesian-inspired expansionary monetary policies, followed by the oil crisis of 1973, caused an initial inflationary spike, leading the government to initially pass legislation to limit profits, wages, and prices, and then establish an anti-inflation board, whose vice-chair was the authoritarian Beryl Plumptre. The second oil crisis of 1979 and a second inflationary spike led the Bank of Canada to tighten credit and drive up interest rates, which peaked at an unprecedented 22.75 per cent in 1982. The consumer price index grew at a rate of 10 per cent to 11 per cent each year. These policies resulted in a recession and an unemployment rate of 13.1 per cent (December 1982), never seen before in Canada since the Great Depression of 1929. In 1983–84, the government of Pierre E. Trudeau had to once again intervene by bringing in voluntary price and wage limits[7] of 6 per cent and 5 per cent, respectively.*

*The traditional clothing, textile, and footwear manufacturing industries, which dated back to the mid-nineteenth century and employed a large, low-skilled workforce, quickly crumbled during this period. Thousands of workers were laid off, and they had difficulty returning to the labour market.*

*However, in 1976, Canada became a member of the G7, the most industrialized group of countries in the free market, giving it a seat at the table with the most important economic decision-makers. The membership of Canada in this group helps the country to raise its international profile and promote its participation in the major world economic institutions and forums. Canada greatly benefited from that activity: through the years its credibility as an influential player has increased. When Paul Martin, the finance minister, succeeded in establishing the G20, grouping the finance ministers of the most developed economies in the North and South on the five continents, it was the recognition that Canada could act as a go-between among various countries to open and maintain an economic dialogue in order to secure financial stability for the world over.*

*Since 2008 the G20 has seen their respective heads of state and governments hold regular summits to give effect to the conclusion reached by the ministers of finance to prevent economic crisis and manage a fairer distribution of development between the North and the South, as was achieved in the Toronto Summit in 2010.*

*In 1982, the Trudeau government created the Macdonald Commission[8] on Canada's economic future to explore solutions and options for maintaining the country's prosperity. Its voluminous 1985 report concluded that it was important for the country to negotiate a genuine free trade agreement with the United States in order to gain better access to the large, vibrant, and promising U.S. market and to seek to conclude other trade agreements with other partners to widen the export potential of Canada. Brian Mulroney's new government immediately adopted this recommendation, and a new free trade agreement (FTA) with the United States came into force in 1989. Building on this momentum, a few years later the FTA was expanded to include Mexico in 1994 (NAFTA) so as to create "the largest free trade zone in the world." While these development opportunities certainly helped integrate the North American automobile industries, it also resulted in a number of relocations to Mexico – with its much cheaper labour and much lower labour standards – and the rapid disappearance of jobs in a manufacturing sector that was no longer competitive.[9] In 2017, NAFTA was opened up at the insistence of the US, who the Trump administration felt was the big loser in the agreement. The Accord was renegotiated but it is impossible to predict its outcome. New tariffs on aluminum and steel, printing paper, and lumber, along with threatened tariffs on vehicle imports into the US, have created a toxic environment where none of the previously made gains are guaranteed in the future. Even the very foundations of the World Trade Organization (WTO) are being challenged by Washington. Whether it is a simple negotiating tactic to increase pressure and extract greater concessions or an ill-advised policy position, is difficult to figure out from President Trump's tweets.*

*In order to raise revenue, the Mulroney government abolished the former manufacturers' sales tax and replaced it with the 7 per cent goods and services tax (GST), which turned out to be highly lucrative. The fall of the Berlin Wall in 1989 and the collapse of the USSR in 1991 marked the end of an economic model that had become completely exhausted. The free world believed that it was entering an era of development based on an expanded global market economy, with only China going on its own.*

*In the meantime, federal spending was spinning almost out of control. In 1992–93, the annual deficit reached $39 billion, or 5.3 per cent of Canada's GDP. Canada's financial situation had devolved into something comparable to that of a developing country. The warning signs of a catastrophic increase in the cost of money were looming, given that more than 28 per cent of Canada's overall debt in 1992–93 was held by foreign creditors. The Jean Chrétien government had no other choice but to take drastic action by making painful cuts that also had an impact on provincial revenues.*

*Canada's domestic market was still hampered by interprovincial barriers. In 1995, an Agreement on Internal Trade (AIT) had become urgently needed to facilitate trade within the country. However, this agreement did not have much of an impact. Two decades on, the situation remains virtually unchanged, as noted in the Supreme Court's April 2018*

Comeau *decision on the limited quantities of beer and spirits that an individual may acquire and transport from another province.[10] This maintains a certain contradiction in place: it is easier for goods and services to cross Canada's borders than it is for them to move from one province or territory to another. One textbook case involves the market for spirits, almost 100 years since the end of prohibition![11] In July 2018, at their annual meeting, the premiers agreed in principle to reduce commercial barriers for the transport of beer and spirits between the provinces and territories, but neither the quantity nor the date of implementation of the measures were included in the agreement.*

*In an increasingly finance-centred economy, where cash moves instantly around the globe, four of Canada's biggest banks were tantalized by the potential of massive profits. In 1997, they brought forward a proposal to merge into two "super-banks," in order to become what they referred to as "world-class institutions" among the globe's major players. For the Canadian market, such a restructuring of major financial institutions would mean a hyper-concentration of banking power and a commensurate maximization of public risk in the event of bankruptcy. "Too big to fail," as the saying goes. However, even titans can collapse (which is precisely what happened ten years later south of the border).*

*After consulting Parliament in 1998,[12] the Chrétien government wisely rejected the merger proposal, despite intense lobbying by much of the financial community and official opposition support for the plan. This decision would be proven correct when the banking crisis struck a few years later.*

*However, the year 2000, albeit without the dreaded Y2K bug, saw the dot-com bubble burst. The NASDAQ plummeted 77.4 per cent between March 2000 and October 2002,[13] causing widespread bankruptcies and spectacular financial losses. The unforeseen weakening of a new industrial sector, which had had such a promising future, was surprising in its magnitude. Nortel, an industry leader, was forced into liquidation in 2009 and vanished, and with it the boundless hopes it had had at the beginning.*

*The collapse of the World Trade Center's twin towers on 11 September 2001 set off a completely unforeseen upheaval in the financial markets: the world was changed forever. Currency flows, which until then had developed unimpeded, were now subject to a new regulatory system in order to prevent the financing of terrorism. Security became the dominant public concern. Governments also turned their attention to international drug trafficking, and currency controls were tightened. The fight against (or "the war on") terrorism shifted the priorities of Western governments and had an impact on the overall economy. The war in Afghanistan (2001), which Canada participated in, and then in Iraq (the second Gulf war in 2003), which the Chrétien government refused to enter, resulted in a realignment of powers. Religious fundamentalism destabilized*

FINANCIALIZATION OF THE ECONOMY

One of the most profound economic changes since the end of the twentieth century has been the financialization of the economy and the dematerialization of currency, which has almost become a novelty. Forget about the local bank with its classic stone exterior; now everything is done by card or smart phone and payment is instantaneous, no matter where you are. Capital exists but is anonymous, supported by algorithms that predict what consumers want to buy and influence their choices. Money flows between countries just as quickly, and financial turmoil and crises reverberate throughout the entire system in a fraction of a second! This situation weakens a State's political power somewhat by diminishing its ability to intervene, and technology further erodes its national independence.
Credit: AUDINDesign (Getty Images)

*the free world. A new wave of uncertainty did nothing to solidify the confidence that investors craved. With the arrival of President Putin to power in 2000, Russia revived a certain degree of post-war political isolation and brought about economic conditions that once again fractured the market between an Eastern bloc seeking to restore itself, and a West engaged in market liberalization.*

*Meanwhile, Canada had managed to reduce its public debt-to-GDP ratio to one of the lowest in the G7; the federal government even managed to achieve budget surpluses for eleven consecutive years, from 1997–98 to 2007–08. This achievement drew the attention of a certain number of European countries on the Canadian public management model, particularly the countries that wrestle with chronic budget deficits. The future looked promising, that is until the financial crisis of 2007–08, which caused a devastating fall in the value of commercial paper and the bursting of a mortgage market inflated by artificial financing. The collapse of an entire sector of financial products based on speculation and artificial guarantees led to the unexpected bankruptcy of Lehman Brothers, a US giant unable to weather the storm. The financial troubles of so many banks in both the United States and Europe, even some of the oldest institutions, showed that the financial community desperately needed more stringent rules and that these institutions could no longer be left to look after themselves, as the very health and stability of the entire global economy was at stake. Nowhere was the fallout of the 2008 crisis more negative than in United States, according to acute observers of American society. This crisis acted as a catalyst for many social forces that were around and that progressively came together: "stagnant wages, widening inequality, anger about immigration and, above all, a deep distrust of elites and government"*[14] *for their failure to prevent the crisis and how they managed it to their benefit.*

*The net effect of all these accumulated frustrations gave rise to a "wave of nationalism, protectionism, and populism" that now impacts totally the public discourse. The election of President Trump, who is inclined "to scrap the basic architecture of the system that America has painstakingly built since 1945,"*[15] *is the unexpected outcome.*

*Canada suffers directly from the aftershock, having chosen since 1989 (FTA) to build a closer economic integration with the United States, becoming almost hostage of capricious decisions by an unpredictable president. Its autonomy to decide is now limited in an economic framework that it does not control anymore.*

*However, the crisis had little impact on Canada's banking industry, which remained stable, enabling Canada to be the first G7 country to emerge from the 2007–08 recession. The ambitious bank mergers proposed in 1998 would have created giants with feet of clay. The financial crisis was however exacerbated by the spectacular bankruptcies of major US automakers such as Chrysler, forcing governments, including the Harper government, to put together costly taxpayer-funded bailouts to prevent thousands of job losses, which would certainly have caused a sudden return of ballooning budget deficits. But Canada succeeded in managing the shock, although federal budget deficits have since reappeared.*

*The drop in crude oil prices from US$106 per barrel in June 2014 to US$29 per barrel in February 2016 undermined the prosperity of a sector that seemed secure, and investment evaporated for a number of projects that had to be postponed indefinitely. However, the needs to be met by a green economy, still in the earliest stages of its* *development, provide opportunities that should encourage a significant share of these investments to be redirected toward this future-focussed industry. Earlier this year, the federal government announced that it was providing businesses with $700 million over five years in the form of commercial loans and venture capital for green technology projects,[16] and that it planned to invest $2.3 billion across the country over this period.*

*Large-scale economic globalization rapidly shifted employment abroad, where productivity was rather high and wages were rather low. The digitization of the economy caused the manufacturing sector to shrink as a result of technological innovation, without really creating a wave of new jobs.*

*Today, multinational corporations, taking full advantage of shelters provided by tax havens, avoid paying taxes in the countries where they make much of their revenue. This feeds public discontent, which will not abate anytime soon, given all the revelations about tax havens in the 2013 "Offshores Leaks," and the "Paradise Papers" in 2017. Shell companies, nominees, complex arrangements – the names and identities of those who use tax havens to hide financial assets and facilitate fraud, money laundering, and corruption have now been brought into the open. Offshore finance has emerged as a "veritable highway of crime"[17] and a way to divert taxes that should be paid into the public coffers, cheating regular taxpayers who have no choice but to pay their share.*

*Finally, in response to repeated calls from Senator Percy Downe and public pressure, the Canada Revenue Agency (CRA) released a 72-page report on 28 June 2018 revealing for the first time that the government loses up to $3 billion in unpaid taxes each year because of Canadians hiding income in tax havens. The study shows that the government loses a total of "$17 billion each year through tax evasion and avoidance," which "undermines Canadians' confidence in the tax system." But, in fact, "the biggest piece is yet to come. Next year, Ottawa is due to release an estimate of the taxes hidden by small and large companies. Only then will it have the complete picture."[18]*

*In 2016, Canadian assets stashed away in tax havens totalled $231 billion, representing lost tax revenue estimated at between $12 and over $20 billion.[19]*

*There has been an outcry over the unbridled accumulation of wealth by a tiny group with such immense revenues that does not meaningfully contribute to the public treasury. The sense of injustice regarding the 1 per cent who hold the vast majority of resources and profits from the new economy is causing governments to rethink the conditions of the social contract that ensure a prosperous and stable middle class. Governments must now restore a fair balance between the needs of overburdened taxpayers and the obligation of all these businesses and fortunes to pay their fair share in the jurisdictions where they make their earnings.[20] Governments must prevent capital flight to tax havens, where billions in unpaid taxes go uncollected. As Gabriel Zuckman wrote: "It is not possible to continue to sign free trade agreements and at the same time ignore their impact on tax evasion."*[21] *They must also review their legislation to combat tax avoidance strategies developed by large accounting and tax law firms.*

*The European Union, Japan, Norway, and Australia have already taken such steps. Fighting against the globalization of inequalities is now on the agenda of all* OECD *member countries and the European Union. However, too little action has let Canada fall behind more effective countries: "Canada has signed over 115 tax treaties and conventions, a world record."*[22] *Of these, about twenty tax agreements and conventions were signed with tax havens that allow subsidiaries of Canadian companies located in these countries to transfer profits to Canada entirely tax-free: "From 2012 to 2016, Canadian investment in the Cayman Islands increased by 166.7 per cent, in the Bahamas by 288 per cent and in the British Virgin Islands by 456.9 per cent."*[23]

*Canada has become beholden to this lobby and is not taking the leadership that would make it credible to Canadian taxpayers. It refuses to take steps to target or identify the ultimate beneficiaries of anonymous foreign corporations with subsidiaries in Canada that take advantage of tax havens without facing any consequences. What is more, many federal, provincial, and municipal pension funds (even the Caisse de dépôt et placement du Québec) use tax havens to grow their portfolios. That idea that governments are supposedly "fighting" tax havens appears more like smoke and mirrors on a massive scale.*[24]

*However, moving beyond these major economic considerations, how are the incomes of average Canadians doing? Has their financial situation improved over the past fifty years? All things considered, the fundamental objective of all these fiscal policies, financial activities, and development initiatives continues to be to improve the financial health of Canadian workers and households. After all, workers and households are the ones who really matter in a profits-based free-market economy.*

*The first observation, in terms of overall employment, is that the Canadian economy is resilient.*[25] *The 2007–08 financial crisis and subsequent drop in oil and commodity prices in 2014–16 showed that the interventionist policies of the Harper government, pressured by the opposition, allowed the social safety net, which remained effective, to cushion any resulting social shocks. Beyond the drop in commodity prices, the domestic consumer market remained dynamic overall, real estate development continued to grow, and the overall employment rate remained relatively stable. There was no subsidence that would have caused major social upheavals.*

*The second observation is not as positive: A few decades ago, Canada had one of the highest standards of living in the world. This is no longer the case.*[26] *According to the*

*OECD, in 2016, per capita GDP was US$42,376 in Canada, while it was $59,746 in Norway, $52,232 in the US, $43,076 in Germany, $38,450 in the UK, and $35,014 in South Korea.[27]*

*This places Canada in the lower median, $17,370 less than the top country. This slow erosion of per-capita GDP, seen in several advanced economies, is a genuine cause for concern. According to the OECD, the average annual growth in living standards in Canada between 1981 and 2016 was 1.75 per cent, while it was 2.66 per cent in the United Kingdom and 2.37 per cent in the United States. Among the G7 countries, Canada is almost at the bottom; Italy ranks last at 1.33 per cent. The risk that a child who has grown up at the bottom of the ladder will remain there once in the labour market is now one in three.[28]*

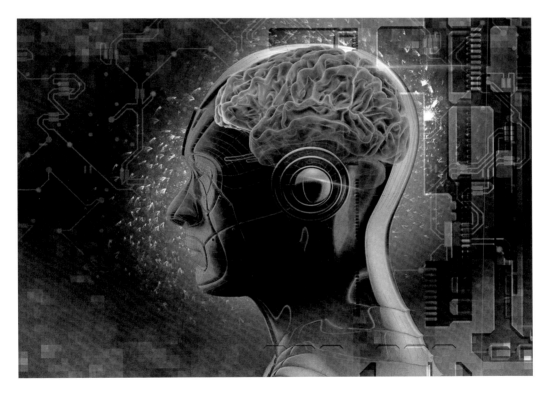

ARTIFICIAL INTELLIGENCE

It is essential for Canada to be a leader in the fourth industrial revolution. As the resource-based sector increases the country's revenues, Canada must now focus on incorporating robotization and artificial intelligence into the economy if it wants to remain prosperous. More than 80 per cent of Canadians live in large cities, where this type of research is based and expanding, close to universities and knowledge institutions. Massive investment in this emerging field is the answer, but thought must be given to the segment of the population that will feel its impact yet might not benefit directly from it.

Credit: Just_Super (Getty Images)

*Manufacturing output in Ontario, in constant dollars, was lower in 2016 than it was a decade ago.*[29] *The volume of Canadian exports in 2015, excluding energy products, is virtually the same as it was in 2000.*[30] *In other words, there has been almost no real growth in fifteen years!*[31] *Without the wealth generated by energy-resource development, Canada's economy would fall behind. This is what is keeping governments from pursuing ambitious greenhouse gas emission targets and an effective policy to reduce reliance on the development of fossil fuels.*

*The expected annual growth rate of the economy from 2016 to 2020 is 1.8 per cent, up from 2.3 per cent in real terms from 2000 to 2008.*[32] *At this rate, it will take forty years to double the size of the economy (GDP), while at 2.3 per cent it would take twenty-nine years.*[33]

*The main cause of this erosion of living standards in Canada is its low productivity. Throughout this period, the country recorded the lowest productivity growth of all wealthy countries (except Switzerland). This is an inescapable conclusion, and governments can no longer be satisfied with traditional formulas or solutions. Real action is needed.*

*The third observation concerns the aging population,*[34] *resulting in slower growth of the available labour pool.*[35] *While its growth rate was 1 per cent from 1985 to 2015, this rate is expected to drop to 0.2 per cent for the period from 2015 to 2025, which does not bode well. Natural economic growth will therefore be lower in the coming decades, if workers have the skills that the digital economy will require, and that is without counting an increase in automation, which will also result in significant job losses. Labour policy will need to be quickly rethought if Canada is to overcome this inevitable transformation and be able to retrain laid-off or unemployable workers and direct them to other productive sectors.*

*Other aspects are also worth noting: the gap in income distribution, the poverty level, and the economic status of the middle class that all politicians claim to care about. First, the proportion of low-income Canadians has been in decline*[36] *since 1992. However, Canada is not an example to follow: in 2014, this rate was 12.6 per cent, while the lowest rates were in Denmark (less than 5.5 per cent), France (less than 8.2 per cent), Germany (less than 9.5 per cent), and the United Kingdom (10.5 per cent). The highest rates were in Turkey (17.3 per cent) and the United States (17.5 per cent).*[37] *This means that Canada was average, neither one of the best nor the worst.*

*There is also no contraction of the middle class in the country: unemployment is rather low, incomes are increasing very modestly, and poverty is not growing. According to Statistics Canada, "the low-income rate was relatively stable over the last decade, rising marginally from 14.0 per cent in 2005 to 14.2 per cent in 2015."*[38] *At best, it has not increased, but it has not decreased either. About 12.1 per cent of Canadians live in poverty.*[39]

*There continues to be real pressure on household budgets from the rising cost of housing and of accessing home ownership. In reality, the middle class is hardly improving at all. The benefits of prosperity have actually gone to the wealthiest. The gap between the wealthiest and the middle class has widened significantly.[40] While it is certainly less blatant than in the United States, it does pose a real risk to social cohesion.[41]*

*Accelerated income growth in the new economy, finance, energy, and business services sectors has driven up incomes earned by taxpayers in these various sectors, while others are growing very slowly, often just keeping pace with inflation. In other words, for the majority, incomes are stagnating. The tax system has not adapted to this new situation, such as by raising income tax rates above a reasonable level. As a result, taxation is generally less progressive, and tax shelters continue to benefit the better-off. Governments can no longer use the tax system as an effective income-redistribution tool. Another reality that has not escaped public attention is the skyrocketing increases in executive compensation. "Since 2009, the salaries of the CEOs of [France's top forty corporations] have grown at about twice the rate of their companies' average salaries … they currently earn 119 times what the average employee makes."[42] This example of outsized compensation has repercussions elsewhere in large companies and a negative effect on corporate morale.*

*Lastly, income inequality in various regions of the country, already an issue 150 years ago at the birth of Confederation, still exists, albeit distributed differently. The establishment of the Department of Regional Economic Expansion (DREE) in 1969 was the answer to the need for a balanced regional economic opportunity, wherever Canadians live, so that everyone has equal access to the prosperity of the country. Many regional development programs have been implemented through the years, but their results have not been as beneficial as it was expected. Regional inequalities continue to exist through the country, although real efforts should continue to be made, particularly in regions where unemployment remains higher than the national average.[43]*

*The shift in the economic weight toward resource-producing (namely, oil-producing) provinces benefits those Canadians who live there: as of 1 July 2015, Alberta's GDP per capita was $76,161; it was $53,777 in Ontario, $45,386 in Quebec, $42,169 in Nova Scotia, and $40,697 in Prince Edward Island.[44] These are massive disparities, and they have far-reaching consequences in a number of areas.*

*The perception that Canada is a rich and prosperous country is more commonly held in the West. Elsewhere in the country, it is rather an "illusion" of prosperity. The consequence of this misperception is that the Canadian government continues to pursue policies that do not address the root of the problem of low productivity, which erodes personal incomes in other parts of the country. Equalization alone cannot compensate for this disparity. The country's industrial base is weakening, rapidly aging, and may have to turn to automation, like it or not. According to the C.D. Howe Institute, 45.1 per cent of jobs in Canada are exposed to automation, and 33.5 per cent are at risk.[45] Moreover, the country's monetary policy is affected by fluctuations in commodity prices, which are often set far from where these commodities are extracted.*

*Canada is facing some real challenges in 2018: renew and diversify its economic base by focussing on productivity, something it has so far failed to adequately improve; capitalize on new opportunities from a renegotiated NAFTA, whatever form that could take; and open up new markets made possible by the Comprehensive Economic and Trade Agreement (CETA), signed by the twenty-eight countries of the European Union, and the Trans-Pacific Partnership (TPP), signed by eleven Asian countries, not least of which is Japan.[46]*

*It is essential for Canada to negotiate additional free trade agreements with partners' countries to open new markets for the sale of its products and services in order to loosen the American prevalence. It should succeed to negotiate an agreement with the ten Asian countries of ASEAN, representing a market of 650 million people.[47] Since the year 1980, Canada has concluded no fewer than fifty-eight free trade agreements with countries on the five continents; twenty-four others are being negotiated. Those agreements pave the way for the future, considering the economic transformations that are underway and the need to diversify export markets.*

*However, Canada should be bold and take the lead in negotiating a major free trade agreement that would bring together the twenty-eight countries of the European Union and the eleven countries that have joined the Comprehensive and Progressive Agreement for Trans-Pacific Partnership (CPTPP). Canada, like Japan, now has access to both of these major markets, and they should work toward forming a broad Atlantic/Pacific free trade area. They should not wait for the United States, which has decided to withdraw from these two future agreements.[48] In addition, Canada should engage with the African Union to explore opportunities for a comprehensive free trade agreement with that continent. Africa has enormous demographic potential, and Canada should leverage its reputation and achievements to advance the common interests of both parties. Canada would signal confidence in the future by taking the first steps toward such a negotiation.[49]*

*Without making its industrial sector more competitive, Canada will not be able to take advantage of these new opportunities. It is absolutely critical for Canada to do what it can to boost competitiveness. It will have to continue talks with China on reaching a favourable trade agreement that does not strip the country of control over its natural resources, but this remains an issue. It will also have to ramp up the shift toward a green economy, which is still well below its potential. It will have to massively develop the resources of artificial intelligence, robotics, and the digital market to become a leading player by concentrating on sectors that are emerging from the transformative*

Photo of images by Andy Warhol, 1972. China has experienced two revolutions over the past fifty years: a cultural revolution (1966–76) under Mao Zedong, and an economic revolution under Deng Xiaoping (1978–92). Mao became an icon of Western culture thanks to the worldwide dissemination of his *Little Red Book*, an equal to the major works of popular political thought at the time. The Cultural Revolution that he launched, backed by his wife, Jiang Qing, and the Red Guards, and which claimed several million victims, nonetheless influenced an entire generation that had adapted Mao's image and made it familiar for everybody, notably through the portraits made of him by American painter Andy Warhol, following President Nixon's official visit to Beijing in February 1972. Credit: AP Photo/Jens Meyer

*technological changes already appearing elsewhere in the world. It will have to make fundamental and applied scientific research a priority, which means providing greater funding in this area, and take effective measures to encourage innovation and investment in both the workforce and production such as by making full use of tax policy tools and facilitating access to venture capital. All these objectives must be pursued concurrently and remain a constant focus of the country's policymakers.*

*Canada's economy will always be vulnerable to the risks of international conflicts, terrorist sabotage, and the winds of protectionism blowing through even long-time allies whose governments are being taken hostage by boisterous populism, claiming to protect themselves and restore their former economic activity by re-establishing artificial national borders. The election of Donald Trump led the United States to leave negotiations on a new Trans-Pacific Partnership agreement and suspend negotiations on an agreement with the European Union. After criticizing NAFTA, Washington adopted protectionist measures and imposed tariffs that are profoundly disrupting trade, whereas previously the US was believed to be a reliable and stable partner that had long been committed to a mutually beneficial trading relationship. The threat of tariffs on automobile exports, given that this industry is deeply integrated and balanced on both sides of the border, makes absolutely no sense and is completely unwarranted. But once the vicious circle of tariffs and counter-tariffs is set in motion, there is no telling what the impact of this free trade distortion will be.*

*Canada's future prosperity is not guaranteed. Canada will need to draw on extraordinary reserves of leadership, initiative and creativity if it is to seek not only to improve prosperity and employment, but also to ensure the health of its public finances, maintain the quality of its social services, and support growth in the incomes of the middle class.*

*The ups and downs of the past fifty years have taught Canada that its economy is vulnerable to unforeseeable external events and crises, many of them beyond its control. Its only true insurance policy is the continued responsible regulation of its financial sector, a progressive tax system that supports the principle of equity between taxpayers and generations, an educated workforce that can adapt effectively to a rapidly changing economy through an excellent university system, a vigorous policy of support for basic and applied research, and support for innovation and creation. This will help Canada address faltering and obsolete production methods and products that are being radically transformed at a pace never before seen in human history.*

## NOTES

1  The author would like to thank the Library of Parliament for checking the figures and historical facts in this document.

2  David Crane, "IMF warns Canada to rebalance, diversify economy," *Hill Times*, 14 August 2017.

3  According to the Department of Finance Canada, the gross debt includes amounts owed by all Canadian governments to foreign investors and Canadians.

4  The net debt excludes government assets.

5 The G7 average was 52.1 per cent in 2007 and 83 per cent in 2015.

6 Library of Parliament, Parliamentary Information and Research Service, 2 November 2017.

7 A cabinet committee co-chaired by Senator Keith Davey and the author, a minister at the time, was tasked with leading the commitments that big business and labour were encouraged to meet in order to achieve wage and price growth targets.

8 *Royal Commission on Economic Union and Development Prospects for Canada.*

9 Gabriel Bruneau and Kevin Moran, *Exchange Rate Fluctuations and Labour Market Adjustments in Canadian Manufacturing Industries*, staff working paper 2015-45, Bank of Canada, December 2015.

10 *R. v. Comeau*, 2018 SCC 15.

11 On 20 July 2018, the provincial premiers reached an agreement in principle to reduce trade barriers on the movement of alcohol between provinces and territories, but neither the quantities nor the effective date of the agreement were agreed upon.

12 National Liberal Caucus Task Force on the Future of the Financial Services Sector, *A Balance of Interests: Access and Fairness for Canadians in the 21st Century*, 1998; Standing Senate Committee on Banking, Trade and Commerce, *Response to the Report of the Task Force on the Future of the Canadian Financial Services Sector*, 1998.

13 Source: NASDAQ

14 Adam Tooze, *Crashed: How a Decade of Financial Crises Changed the World* (Viking, 2018), cited in Fareed Zakaria, ,"The aftershocks," *The New York Times*, Book Review, 12 August 2018, p.1.

15 Ibid., p.18.

16 Vincent Brousseau-Pouliot, "700 millions d'Ottawa pour les entreprises," *La Presse+*, 18 January 2018.

17 Jeremie Baruchand Maxime Vandano, "Paradies fiscaux – ce qu'ont changé dix ans de révélations," *Le Monde*, Économie et Entreprise, p. 2.

18 Guillaume St-Pierre, "Les Canadiens cachent des milliards dans les paradis fiscaux," *Journal de Montréal*, 28 June 2018, p. 8. https://www.journaldemontreal.com/2018/06/28/les-canadiens-cachent-des-milliards-dans-les-paradis-fiscaux; Deneault, Alain, "Les revenus de l'État, une priorité," *Le Devoir*, 2 August 2018, p. A7.

19 Nicolas Bourcier, "Le Canada, l'autre pays de l'offshore," *Le Monde*, 7 November 2017, p. 11; Alain Deneault, *Paradis fiscaux : la filière canadienne – Barbade, Caïmans, Bahamas, Nouvelle-Écosse, Ontario…*, Ecosociété, 2014, pp. 175 and ss.

20 Rosalie Wyonch, *It's Time for the Taxman to Join the Digital Age*, C.D. Howe Institute, https://www.cdhowe.org/intelligence-memos/rosalie-wyonch-it%E2%80%99s-time-taxman-join-digital-age, accessed 28 August 2017.

21  Gabriel Zuckman, *La richesse cachée des nations – Enquête sur les paradis fiscaux*, Seuil, 2017, p. 104, *La richesse cachée des nations : enquête sur les paradis fiscaux – Les leçons des Panama Papers*, Seuil, Paris, 2017, pp. 95-104.

22  Nicolas Bourcier, "Le Canada, l'autre pays de l'offshore," *Le Monde*, 7 November 2017, p. 11; Gabriel Zucman, *La richesse cachée des nations : enquête sur les paradis fiscaux – Les leçons des Panama Papers*.

23  "Lutte contre les paradis fiscaux, un bilan mi-figue mi-raisin," Collectif Échec aux paradis fiscaux (list of members on the digital platforms of *Le Devoir*), *Le Devoir*, 13 July 2018, p. A8.

24  Michel Girard, "Le coup 'fumant' des paradis fiscaux," *Le Journal de Montréal*, 23 January 2018, p. 34.

25  The author would like to thank Alain Dubuc, a columnist with *La Presse +*, for his insights on this topic.

26  Centre sur la productivité et la prospérité des Hautes Études Commerciales (HEC – Montréal) – purchasing power parity standard of living in 2015 – per capita GDP.

27  Source: OECD.Stat, national accounts, GDP per head (US$), constant prices.

28  Ariane Krol, "Où va l'Ascenseur social," *LaPresse.ca*, 18 September 2017.

29  This was a decrease of 14.3 per cent. Source: Statistics Canada, CANSIM Table 379-0030.

30  Crane, David, "IMF warns Canada to rebalance, diversify economy," *Hill Times*, 14 August 2017.

31  Specifically, an increase of 3 per cent in fifteen years for an average real annual growth of just 0.2 per cent. Source: Statistics Canada, CANSIM Table 228-0061.

32  Statistics Canada, CANSIM Table 380-0106.

33  David Crane, "IMF warns Canada to rebalance, diversify economy," *Hill Times*, 14 August 2017.

34  Statistics Canada, *The impact of aging on labour market participation rates*, 14 June 2017.https://www150.statcan.gc.ca/n1/pub/75-006-x/2017001/article/14826-eng.htm, accessed 6 October 2017.

35  The population between fifteen and sixty-four years of age.

36  Statistics Canada, *A backgrounder on poverty in Canada*, 2016. https://www.canada.ca/en/employment-social-development/programs/poverty-reduction/backgrounder.html, the proportion of population with incomes after taxes and government transfers below 50 per cent of the median Canadian income, accessed 6 October 2017.

37  Source: OECD Statistics, *Poverty rate after taxes and transfers, Poverty line 50 per cent*.

38  https://www150.statcan.gc.ca/n1/daily-quotidien/170913/dq170913a-eng.htm, accessed 6 October 2017.

39  David Crane, "Liberals' anti-poverty strategy a good start but we're a long way from world leadership," *Hill Times*, 27 August 2018.

40 Éric Desrosiers, "Mauvaises nouvelles sur le front de la bataille contre les inégalités," *Le Devoir*, 15 December 2017, p. B6.

41 David A. Green, W. Craig Riddell, and France St-Hilaire (ed.), "Income Inequality, the Canadian Story," Institute for Research on Public Policy (IRPP), *The Art of the State* Series, Volume v, 2016.

42 Denis Cosnard, "CAC 40 : la priorité aux actionnaires de plus en plus contestée," *Le Monde*, Économie et Entreprise, 15 May 2018, p. 3.

43 In 1971-72, the author was special assistant to the Hon. Jean Marchand, the first to occupy the position of minister responsible for DREE.

44 Source: Statistics Canada.

45 Gerald Bérubé, "L'automatisation n'est pas une réponse à la pénurie de main-d'œuvre," *Le Devoir*, 23 January 2018, p. B3.

46 Andy Blatchford, "Canada optimistic a Trans-Pacific trade deal within reach Tuesday," *Ipolitics*, 23 January 2018.

47 *Agence France Presse*, "Le Canada veut un accord de libre-échange avec les pays de l'ASEAN," *Le Devoir*, 28 August 2018, p. B1.

48 John Ibbitson, "As America retreats, Canada can lead in forging an Atlantic-Pacific trade agreement," *The Globe and Mail*, 20 July 2018, p. A10.

49 Vincent Brousseau-Pouliot, "Comment diversifier ses exportations à l'ère Trump," *La Presse+*, Affaires, screen 7, 21 July 2018; *Agence France Presse*, "Le Royaume-Uni post-Brexit, un grand investisseur en Afrique," *Le Devoir*, 29 August 2018, p. B5.

# Economic Policy in Canada
## 1966–2016[1]

David A. Dodge, former governor of the Bank of Canada (2001–08)

The purpose of this paper is to trace the evolution of economic policy in Canada over five distinct periods covering the last fifty years or so. The focus is on the policies pursued by the federal government to achieve economic growth, low unemployment and stable prices, a fairer distribution of income, fiscal sustainability, and a stable financial system.

## 1. INTRODUCTION

The main economic objective of the federal government is to provide the expenditure, tax, and legislative framework that facilitates the continuing improvement of the economic and social welfare of Canadians. While there has always been vigorous debate about which policies to follow, and which instruments to use to achieve this objective, over the last fifty years the four key economic goals of all successive governments have been the same:

1.  jobs and growth: high growth of output (gross domestic product) and income (net national income);
2.  low unemployment combined with stable prices;
3.  income security: more secure individual incomes and fairer income distribution;
4.  fiscal sustainability and stability of the financial system.

---

1 This is a shortened version of a paper originally prepared by David A. Dodge for the Senate Symposium "150th Anniversary of Confederation." The author thanks Richard Dion for his most able research assistance.

Different governments have placed different emphasis on the achievement of each of these four objectives. They have made these trade-offs in part due to differing political priorities but often due to changing global (that is, external) economic forces. But almost every budget contains a statement or plan with respect to all four objectives. The purpose of this paper is to tell the story of how successive parliaments and governments have made the trade-offs between the objectives, what policy instruments they have used, and how well they have succeeded. It is a story of both innovation and repeated application, a story of a few great successes and some disappointing results. It is also very much a story of how successive parliaments have responded to changing global economic conditions which both support and constrain federal government actions to achieve these four objectives.

## 2. 1966–74: FOCUS ON INCOME REDISTRIBUTION

### 2.1 Underlying Economic Conditions

The period of 1966 to 1974 was one of high growth in Canada as the economy benefitted from very favourable US demand conditions, from improved access to foreign markets, notably through the Autopact, and from strong growth in labour force and labour productivity. This high growth in demand and supply was accompanied by a relatively low and stable unemployment rate and federal budget deficits in relation to gross domestic product (GDP) (chart 9.1). From a relatively constant 1.4 per cent rate in the previous decade, consumer price index (CPI) inflation started rising in 1964 and was stable around 4 per cent from 1966 to 1971 before accelerating to a peak of 11 per cent by 1974 (chart 9.2). On the basis of prevailing economic doctrine, the government was willing to trade off a little higher inflation for lower unemployment. The actions of the government and the central bank indeed suggest that they were ready to tolerate inflation in the range of 3 to 4 per cent in the hope of creating sufficient demand to keep the unemployment rate below 6 per cent.

### 2.2 Policy Developments

This benign economic environment and the move from a fixed to a floating exchange rate for the Canadian dollar in 1970 (chart 9.3) gave the federal government much latitude to pursue stabilization policies as well as redistribution policies without compromising fiscal sustainability. Counter-cyclical fiscal and monetary policies in turn helped to keep inflation and unemployment relatively low and stable by the standards of the following two decades. Thus, fiscal policy moved to restraint in 1966, 1968, 1969, and 1973 to cool demand and ease inflationary pressures, and shifted to expansion in 1967, 1970, and 1971 to support demand and reduce unemployment. It was also felt in the late sixties that income policy might usefully supplement demand-management policies to rein in "cost-push inflation" and in so doing reduce the unemployment cost of disinflation. Thus, the Prices and Incomes Commission was established in May 1969 and provided guidelines and advice on appropriate rates of growth for prices and wages until 1971, but without any success in reaching agreements with unions on wages.

The period of 1966 to 1974 saw a number of redistribution policies put in place. In 1965, the Pearson Liberal government reconfigured the universal system of Old Age Security (OAS) and introduced a self-administered, income-tested Guaranteed Income Supplement (GIS) that became effective in 1966. Benefits were initially indexed to the cost of living at a maximum of 2 per cent a year. The government lowered the age of eligibility for OAS from seventy to sixty-five over a five-year period and exempted GIS from income tax effective in January 1971. Also in 1965, the Pearson government established a compulsory contributory Canada Pension Plan (CPP) program, which started in 1966. The program was intended to enhance income security at retirement, especially for below-average-income earners. Another policy measure that had important redistributive effects was the substantial increase in the generosity of Unemployment Insurance (UI) in June 1971. The program provided nearly universal coverage of wage- or salary-earning workers, eased eligibility, greatly extended the duration of benefits in some regions, and added a series of special benefits – sickness, maternity, and retirement.

The federal government also enhanced income redistribution indirectly by substantially boosting transfers to other governments under the categories of "fiscal arrangements," "insurance and medical care," "education support," and "Canada Assistance Plan," thereby allowing the provincial governments to finance expanded programs that had positive redistribution effects. The rapid increase in federal transfers to other governments was made possible by the sharp increase in fiscal revenues over the period, reflecting the rapid growth of the economy, significant inflation, and a high elasticity of income tax revenues to nominal GDP.

After long debate following the report of the Carter Commission, the federal government proposed a major tax reform in its June 1971 budget that aimed at redistributing the existing tax burden rather than increasing revenues. The effects of changes in statutory tax rates, exemptions, and deductions, and the introduction of indexing in 1974 materially enhanced the progressivity of the personal income tax, thereby contributing to the objective of fairer distribution of income.

Following the *Report of the Porter Commission* in 1964, the government took action to modernize the Canadian financial system in the 1967 Bank Act. With this legislation Canada led the United States and other countries in the Organisation for Economic Co-operation and Development (OECD) in the modernization of the financial system by extending to chartered banks the right to issue residential mortgages, and in strengthening the role played by deposit insurance (CDIC) and mortgage insurance (CMHC) in preserving the stability of the financial sector.

### 2.3 Conclusion

The period of 1966 to 1974 was one of high productivity gains and sustained economic growth in Canada. This growth resulted in sharply rising federal revenues, which allowed the federal government to actively pursue redistribution policies without compromising fiscal sustainability. By the end of the period, however, it was proving more difficult to contain inflationary pressures, and this was going to have major implications for government policies in the next two decades.

## 3. 1974–83: BATTLE AGAINST UNEMPLOYMENT AND INFLATION

### 3.1 Underlying Economic Conditions

Under the impact of the first oil price shock in 1974, growth in the United States and the rest of the OECD oil-consuming countries slowed in that year with the result that demand for Canadian-manufactured exports slowed. At the same time, upward pressure on prices increased, and more importantly, productivity growth started to fall.

The failure to appreciate that productivity growth was shifting downwards permanently – and hence potential output growth was slowing – meant that fiscal and monetary policies were too expansionary, with the result that inflation pressures continued through the second half of the seventies. Throughout this period, expectations of business, labour, and governments were not aligned with the economic realities that economists and policy-makers only later fully understood.

The Canadian labour force continued to grow very rapidly during this period as baby boomers flooded into the labour force, aggravating the youth unemployment problem, and as the participation rate of women rose sharply. Thus potential growth continued to increase through this period in spite of slowing productivity growth. These underlying demographic forces contributed to the rise in the unemployment rate from 5.4 per cent to 8.4 per cent between 1974 and 1980. But in 1981, the global recession and the sharp increase in oil prices created a severe recession in Canada, driving unemployment up to more than 11 per cent from 1982 to 1984. Throughout the whole period, inflation was unacceptably high. CPI inflation, which had risen to 11 per cent in 1974, declined at the start of the anti-inflation program to about 7 per cent in 1976, but then rose sharply to peak at over 12 per cent in 1981 (chart 9.2). Thus, during the whole period from 1974 to 1980, government policy had to battle high unemployment and very high rates of inflation at the same time.

Global economic conditions turned moderately favourable until 1979. In late 1979, however, the second oil price-shock hit and the price of oil (West Texas Intermediate, or WTI) more than doubled in real terms by 1980 relative to 1974 (chart 9.3). This shock further exacerbated Canadian inflation while at the same time dramatically reducing global growth and hence demand for Canadian exports. From 1981 to 1984, policy (especially monetary policy) was directed at inflation control. Mortgage rates hit 20 per cent. Unemployment rose to 11 per cent in 1982 and remained stubbornly above that level until 1985. The result was that CPI inflation fell dramatically to about 4 per cent by mid-1984.

### 3.2 Policy Developments

To try to counteract rising unemployment throughout the whole period, the government ran ever-larger deficits to provide fiscal stimulus. Deficits increased from 1.5 per cent of GDP in 1974–75 to over 5 per cent by 1978–79 (chart 9.1). The hope was that this application of pure Keynesian anticyclical policy would prompt a return to the high growth rate of the sixties. But policy failed to recognize that structural shifts were taking place that would reduce potential growth – a fact that was not apparent to analysts at the time. As it turned out, increased budgetary deficits further contributed to inflationary pressures over the period without having the hoped-for effect of reducing unemployment. In addition, the 1971 changes in the UI program raised the measured unemployment rate by incenting a larger share of the labour force to remain in seasonal employment and by reducing the incentives for rapid adjustment.

The structural shifts required became much more difficult to manage after the 1979 oil price-shock and the significantly altered Canadian and interprovincial terms of trade. With the 1980 budget and the National Energy Program (NEP), the government chose to manage the transition by suppressing the structural and income distribution impact of high oil prices through controlling the domestic price of oil and gas while providing incentives for exploration and development. To combat rising unemployment while managing this difficult transformation of the Canadian economy, the government chose

THE OIL SANDS (AND THE REFINERIES IN FORT MCKAY)

Revenues from the oil sands and gas reserves are the key to prosperity in Western Canada and Newfoundland-and-Labrador and also in Canada generally. However, the rapid drop in oil prices has threatened investments in this core sector of the Canadian economy and indefinitely delayed the construction of a pipeline to carry oil to an Atlantic terminal. If the price of these commodities remains low, the industry's entire future will have to be reconsidered, especially given that some of Europe's most prosperous countries, like Germany, France, and Great Britain have set deadlines to halt the production of fossil fuel-powered vehicles. Credit: dan_prat (Getty Images)

to further increase program spending from 17 per cent of GDP in 1979–80 to 21 per cent in 1982–83, and the deficit from 4.5 to about 7.5 per cent of GDP (charts 9.4 and 9.1).

From 1974 to 1983, the battle against inflation really proceeded in two phases: first from 1974 to the second oil price-shock in 1979, and second from 1980 to 1983. During the first phase, the Bank of Canada ran monetary policy by trying to manage the growth of M1, the narrow monetary aggregate. Notwithstanding the plan to reduce inflation, this approach was providing sufficient monetary accommodation to support a rapid increase in prices. During this phase, fiscal policy was generally expansionary, as it was primarily designed to deal with rising unemployment. Thus, in 1975 price and wage controls administered by the Anti-Inflation Board (AIB) were introduced as a third tool to battle inflation.

While the AIB did its job fairly well and did not provoke the social unrest that often accompanied controls programs in Europe and elsewhere, monetary policy was too accommodative and fiscal stimulus much too great to produce demand conditions consistent with 4 per cent inflation-control target in 1978 (chart 9.1). The result was that inflation went back up to 8 per cent when controls were removed and the government invoked a totally ineffective quasi-voluntary "6 and 5" program. In the presence of well-entrenched inflation expectations well above AIB inflation targets, Canada's experiment with controls failed, not because of bad design, but because both monetary and fiscal policies were too expansionary to bring aggregate demand to levels consistent with these inflation targets.

The 1979 oil price-shock produced a new impetus for rising prices (globally and in Canada) as well as generating a sharp rise in interpersonal and interprovincial inequalities. The government responded with the highly controversial NEP in the fall 1980 budget. The NEP involved four elements: (1) control of domestic prices of oil and gas for households and businesses; (2) tax and transfer provisions to redistribute the benefits to Canada from improved terms of trade; (3) a new Petroleum Incentive Program (PIP) of grants to encourage exploration and development; and (4) tax and expenditure changes that would allow the federal government to capture some of the expected additional revenues to reduce its own growing deficit. This attempt to override market forces dramatically altered the regional distribution of income relative to what it would have been otherwise, hampered economic adjustment, and created long-lasting political alienation of the West.

The NEP was based on the assumption that oil prices would continue to rise. In the event, that assumption turned out to be wrong. WTI oil price steadily dropped between 1980 and 1986, and by 1986 it was well below its 1978 level in real terms (chart 9.3). This decline was unhelpful for the growth in Canadian real incomes as terms of trade decreased from 1980 to 1986.

In 1980, following the second oil price-shock, a reacceleration of inflation, and growing worries of dynamic instability, it became clear that the classic remedy for inflation was needed. The Bank of Canada abandoned the targeting of monetary aggregates (M1) and drove up interest rates to choke demand and bring down inflation. Inflation did drop precipitously from over 12 per cent in 1981 to just over 4 per cent by 1984, but the price was a huge jump in the unemployment rate from 7.6 per cent to 12 per cent by 1983. Higher interest rates also greatly added to the debt service costs of governments, forcing the federal government to begin to retrench on program spending.

While the battle to control inflation was raging, the distribution of market income was stable until 1980, at which point it became more unequal as the recession deepened. But the efficacy of the redistributive transfer policies of the earlier period and of the 1974 indexing of the income tax meant that the distribution of disposable income was roughly stable through the whole period from 1976 to 1983.

Undoubtedly, the most significant change in distribution policy during this period was the change in policy of transfers to the provinces and territories. By the mid-seventies, it was becoming clear that the cost-sharing arrangements for Medicare and post-secondary education were becoming fiscally unsustainable for the federal government without a significant increase in federal taxes. Provincial expenditures were growing much faster than federal tax revenues (chart 9.4). In 1977, the government chose to address this problem after considerable and acrimonious debate by ending the cost-sharing for these provincial programs and replacing it with formula-driven cash transfers called Established Programs Financing. This change enabled the federal government to limit somewhat the relentless increase in its deficit and tax level by containing the growth of provincial transfers as a share of total expenditures.

The sharp rise in oil prices in 1979 implied a very sharp increase in equalization transfers to the provinces because of the massive increase in the fiscal capacity of the oil-producing provinces. Equalization transfers were effectively constrained by a change in the formula to exclude payments to any above-average province (i.e. Ontario) in terms of fiscal capacity and by including only part of resource revenues in the base to be equalized. These changes in transfers to provinces meant that on average provinces were having to cover a greater share of their expenditures through their own revenue sources, and hence that there would likely be a widening of inter-regional disparities in level of provincial services.

### 3.3 Conclusion

The years from 1974 to 1983 encompassed a period of extraordinarily complex change in the structure of the Canadian and global economies, change which Canadians generally failed to comprehend at the time. The result was that governments tried to override market forces with wage, price, and energy controls and overly expansionary fiscal policy, all of which slowed adaptation to the changed economic circumstances.

FREE TRADE — THE MAINSTAY OF THE ECONOMY

Mexican President Carlos Salinas, US President George H.W. Bush, and Canadian Prime Minister Brian Mulroney. The signing of a free trade agreement between Canada, the United States, and Mexico in 1992 created an effective tool for growing the country's economy. Since the 1980s, Canada has reached close to 58 similar agreements with other countries. It also concluded an ambitious trade agreement with the European Union, which came into force in September 2017, and signed the Trans-Pacific Partnership in 2018. Negotiations are under way on 24 other agreements with various countries. However, Canada must also be aware that these agreements can be destabilizing and lead to the elimination of some types of manufacturing, which hits some regions harder and causes layoffs and job cuts.

Credit: AP Photo/Marcy Nighswander

## 4. 1984–93: A NEW AGENDA FOR GROWTH

### *4.1 Underlying Economic Conditions*

While the very rapid growth in the Canadian labour-force-age population levelled off in the decade 1984–93, the government continued to face a continuing challenge of high unemployment and persistent inflationary pressure, especially in the latter half of the period (chart 9.2) as global economic conditions worsened. By 1986, the real price of oil had fallen back to levels not seen since 1973 (chart 9.3), and it remained low until

1999. In 1984–85, the federal deficit peaked at 8.1 per cent of GDP and despite continuing efforts to cut spending and raise taxes over the decade, the deficit remained stubbornly above 4.5 per cent of GDP over the whole period (chart 9.1).

The Canadian financial system came under pressure in the second half of the eighties, reflecting in part domestic problems in the mortgage market but also global instability, highlighted by the stock market crash of 1987 and the "savings and loan crisis" in the United States. Moreover, continuing inflation pressures in Canada prompted the Bank of Canada to maintain high real rates of interest at the end of the eighties and first years of the nineties, further aggravating the problems of trust and loan companies in Canada.

The government was unable to respond to the sharp economic recession in 1990–91 by further increasing already high deficits, with the result that Canadian unemployment peaked again at 11.5 per cent in 1993. Over the 1984 to 1993 decade as a whole, Canadian GDP growth lagged behind growth in the United States by about 0.75 percentage points. The Mulroney government gave priority to making structural changes to promote growth over the long term rather than providing additional fiscal stimulus to boost short-term demand. Likewise, at the end of the eighties the Bank of Canada focused on reducing inflation through high real interest rates regardless of rising unemployment.

### 4.2 Policy Developments

The new Progressive Conservative government tabled its first economic statement in November of 1984. The statement entitled "A New Direction for Canada: Agenda for Economic Renewal" represented a major shift in policy direction and reflected the new economic liberalism that had emerged in both the academic economic literature and in government policy statements in the United States and the United Kingdom. In essence, the new government promised to place emphasis on fostering medium- and long-term growth by structural (supply-side) policies that would improve the efficiency of market mechanisms to allocate capital and labour to their most productive uses rather than on promoting employment growth in the short run through fiscal policies providing support for aggregate demand.

#### 4.2.1 Policies for Growth

The new government moved quickly to remove controls on the oil and gas industry, to dismantle the NEP, and to allow domestic oil prices to be determined by global supply and demand conditions. The government also moved quickly to announce in July 1986 its intention to move forward with comprehensive tax reform. This included broadening the base and lowering the marginal rates of personal and corporate income taxes and replacing the outmoded manufacturers' sales tax with a federal value-added tax, the goods and services tax (GST). Income tax reform commenced in January 1988; the GST began in January 1991.

In May 1986, the government entered into trade negotiations with the United States, which eventually resulted in the signing of the Free Trade Agreement (FTA) with the United States following the 1988 election and in the ratification of the North American Free Trade Agreement (NAFTA) in 1993. These agreements represented a singularly important attempt at increasing the competitiveness and productivity of Canadian industry.

With the 1984 budget, the government began to reduce the rate of growth of program expenditures (chart 9.4). While those efforts continued until 1987, the rising level of debt service costs meant that the deficit as a share of GDP remained high (chart 9.1) and the debt to GDP ratio continued to rise. This situation was exacerbated by the economic recession in 1990–91 and the continued high level of interest rates after 1990 set by the Bank of Canada as it focused on achievement of the newly agreed inflation reduction targets.

By 1993, the government had sold forty public corporations including Air Canada, Petro Canada, and Telesat. Both federal and provincial governments greatly reduced the number of boards, commissions, and agencies engaged in commercial or semi-commercial activities between 1984 and 1993. The Conservative government made several attempts to reform Unemployment Insurance to enhance the efficiency of the labour market. The most important of these was the UI reform bill from the 1993 budget, which was left unpassed at the time of the election and was one of the first pieces of legislation passed by the new Liberal government in the fall of 1993.

As promised in the Agenda paper, from 1984 the Conservative government made a sustained effort to deregulate and promote competition in the transport and communications industries and to promote compliance with the Competition Act. It also moved to increase foreign investment by streamlining the application of the foreign investment review process in most industries, including oil and gas but excluding certain key areas such as culture. With the formation of the Committee of Ministers for Internal Trade in 1987, the federal government began to move, unfortunately with very limited success, to dismantle barriers to interprovincial trade.

*4.2.2 Policies for Fiscal Sustainability and Financial Stability*

A key goal of the Agenda paper, to achieve a sustainable level of federal debt, was not realized by the Conservative government. Indeed, the ratio of federal debt to GDP continued to rise from 1984 to 1993 despite almost continuous "program review" aimed at reducing federal expenditures. By 1993–94, the ratio of net federal debt to GDP reached 71 per cent, and 32 per cent of every dollar of revenue needed to be allocated to debt service. In part the Mulroney government failed to meet its fiscal goal because of adverse external circumstances, but more importantly because it placed greater priority on achieving the long-run goal of making the economy more flexible and competitive than on reducing the deficit. That flexibility would prove very valuable to the next government from 1994–97 as it moved directly to cut spending.

While the Conservative government failed to achieve fiscal sustainability, it made remarkable progress in building a much more stable Canadian financial system. Following the failure of two Canadian banks in 1985, the government moved expeditiously to totally overhaul the Canadian prudential regulatory regime for chartered banks and insurance companies. The Office of the Superintendent of Financial Institutions (OSFI) was created in 1987 with very much beefed-up staff and powers. New legislation reduced competitive barriers between financial institutions, allowed mergers between banks and securities dealers, strengthened the ability of OSFI and CDIC to intervene early to prevent bank failures, and facilitated the demutualization of insurance companies. In their entirety, these measures not only prevented a Canadian crisis similar to the collapse of the savings and loans companies in the United States during this period, but also strengthened Canadian financial institutions so that they were able to weather the 2008 great financial crisis better than their competitors in the United States and Europe.

*4.3 Conclusion*

Over the 1984 to 1993 period, the federal government made sustained efforts to improve the supply-side structure of the Canadian economy; i.e., the efficiency with which the Canadian economy allocated labour and capital, and hence to improve the prospects for long-term growth. In the short run, however, actual growth suffered from restrained federal program spending and the hoped-for improvement in labour productivity did not yet materialize.

## 5. 1994–2005: EMPHASIS ON FISCAL SUSTAINABILITY

### *5.1 Underlying Economic Conditions*

Globally, the period from 1993 to 2006, which has come to be known as the "great moderation," was one of generally favourable external economic conditions for Canada. The United States had recovered from the 1990 to 1992 recession and generally experienced more than a decade of robust growth of final domestic demand and industrial production. This was generally very favourable for Canadian exports, which surged as a share of GDP from about 26 per cent in 1992 to almost 45 per cent in 2000. Despite instability in global financial markets around the turn of the century (including the Asian crisis and the tech bust), and despite growing global trade and financial imbalances throughout the period, global economic conditions were favourable for Canada. Moreover, buoyed by developments in the information and communications technology (ICT) sector, US productivity growth surged to over 3 per cent in the decade to 2005. This spilled over into only a moderate improvement in Canadian productivity growth, which lagged further behind US productivity growth despite the very real improvement in Canadian structural policies in the previous decade.

The combination of very favourable conditions for Canadian exporters throughout most of this period, including an exceptionally favourable exchange rate (chart 9.3), and the recovery of domestic household demand due to the reduction in Canadian interest rates, created buoyant conditions for Canadian business. This higher demand was sufficient to both offset fully the withdrawal of federal and provincial government program spending amounting to over 7 per cent of GDP between 1994 and 2000 (chart 9.4) and to permit a fall in the unemployment rate from over 11.4 per cent in 1993 to 6.8 per cent in 2005 (chart 9.2).

### *5.2 Policy Developments: Fiscal Sustainability*

Despite an election campaign that focused on social issues, the first order of business for the new Liberal government was to initiate fiscal restraint to achieve their "red book" promise to reduce the deficit to no more than 3 per cent of GDP within three years. Not only did the government move to pass the previous government's unemployment insurance legislation in December 1993, but in Mr Martin's first budget in February 1994, broad expenditure reductions were proposed. The Expenditure Control Act was extended, defence spending cut, public service wages frozen, and further reductions in UI benefits proposed.

The market's reaction to the 1994 budget expenditure reductions was that they were insufficient; market interest rates initially rose and the Canadian dollar weakened. The government then initiated a new round of program reviews to cut spending further. Following the further depreciation of the Canadian dollar and rise in interest rates resulting from the Mexican peso crisis at the end of 1994, the minister of finance tabled a very restrictive budget in February of 1995. Operating expenditures, grants to business, and, in particular, transfers to the provinces, were substantially reduced. Only transfers to the elderly were left untouched, although review of elderly benefits was promised, and a further review of UI benefits was initiated. As markets found these reductions to be "credible," real interest rates fell, inducing increased household and investment demand, which spurred growth and employment. Fiscal consolidation continued in the 1996 budget, including a revamping of OAS. Further reductions in UI benefits were introduced in the summer of 1996, when the program was renamed Employment Insurance (EI). Very importantly, a federal-provincial overhaul of the CPP was initiated to move away from pay-as-you-go financing, to raise premiums, and to create a separate CPP investment board. These changes were agreed to in 1997 and came into effect in 1998.

With further declines in the exchange rate and interest rates, growth improved, and by 1997, it was clear that a balanced budget was in sight. Thus, the 1997 budget provided for some targeted tax relief, including a substantial enrichment of the Child Tax Benefit and a Working Income Supplement. The government also created the Canada Foundation for Innovation.

The realization of a budgetary surplus in 1997–98 marked the end of an extraordinary effort of fiscal consolidation on the part of the federal government, aided by similar actions by many provincial governments (chart 9.1). No major advanced country before or since has achieved such improvement over a period of less than five years – and none has done so while reducing unemployment at the same time. While Canada was lucky that strong foreign demand kept the economic cost of consolidation in terms of lost output low, it is also true that the actions of the previous government in strengthening the supply-side structure of the Canadian economy played an important role. Interestingly, it was the changed approach to fiscal consolidation set out in the Mulroney government's 1984 Agenda paper – and not pursued vigorously – that proved successful for the Chrétien government.

After 1997, the policy focus of the Chrétien and Martin governments shifted from fiscal consolidation to the "red book" priority of social and economic development. Strong revenue growth and falling debt service charges enabled the federal government to take initiatives to reduce income taxes (2000), boosting innovation and growth. At the same time, the government boosted social spending through major increases in transfer to the provinces for health care (2000, 2003, and 2004), increases in spending on First Nations and a sustainable environment (2005), easing of restrictions on EI benefits and reduction in EI premiums, and enrichment of both the Working Income Tax Benefit and the Child Tax Benefit.

### 5.3 Conclusion

By 2005, both federal and provincial public finances were once again sustainable (chart 9.1). Federal debt service costs had fallen to 15 cents for every dollar of revenue and were headed lower. The federal debt to GDP ratio was back to a more comfortable 35 per cent. The Canadian financial system was stable and resilient to global shocks after a decade of careful supervision by OSFI and strengthening of the Bank Act in two quinquennial reviews. Household debt relative to income had risen as mortgage rates declined, but it was well below the ratio in the United States. The Canadian government had resisted the pressure to weaken prudential rules for mortgages, as was taking place in the United States. And most importantly, by the end of the period both unemployment and inflation were low and stable (chart 9.2).

## 6. 2006–16: EMPHASIS ON SMALLER GOVERNMENT

### 6.1 Underlying Economic Conditions

The decade ending in 2016 encompassed a global financial crisis and severe recession in advanced economies in 2008–09, followed by a persistently sluggish recovery reflecting both inadequate demand growth and a decline in potential output growth. The global financial crisis left several advanced economies with a legacy of high public and private debts, severe housing correction, and financial fragility. This legacy in turn prompted a retrenchment in public and private spending, which contributed to a "new normal" regime of low growth in 2011 to 2016.

Following the G20 meeting in Pittsburg in November 2008, both monetary and fiscal policies in advanced economies became highly expansionary until 2010 to support aggregate demand. Monetary policy remained very accommodative through to 2016, with policy interest rates remaining near zero and major central banks sharply expanding their balance sheet through large bond purchases to reduce long-term interest rates even further. Discretionary fiscal policy which was highly expansionary in advanced economies in 2008 and 2009 with some further stimulus in 2010, tightened markedly from 2011 to 2015. Only in 2016 did this "austerity" fiscal policy start to ease. Throughout the post-recession period, core inflation remained subdued and interest rates low.

Although a resilient banking system and relatively buoyant housing market spared Canada from a domestic financial crisis in 2008–09, the Canadian economy nonetheless was hit hard by the severe recession and subsequent sluggish recovery experienced in the advanced economies, especially in the United States. The relatively weak growth rates over 2006 to 2016 also stemmed from a considerable loss of cost competitiveness in Canada as a result of a much stronger Canadian dollar exchange rate than in the previous three decades. Movements in the Canadian dollar relative to the US dollar largely reflected the rise and subsequent fall in US dollar commodity prices, especially oil prices (chart 9.3). The collateral movements in Canada's terms of trade boosted real income and final domestic spending up to 2014, at a time when the strong dollar was hampering net exports. Falling terms of trade depressed domestic spending in 2015 and 2016 at the same time as exchange-rate pressures on net exports started to ease.

### 6.2.1 Policy Developments: Stabilization

From 2009 onward, Canadian interest rates adjusted for inflation were exceptionally low, providing important support to final domestic demand, notably household spending. Discretionary fiscal policy by the federal and provincial governments also generated an important stimulus to the economy in 2008 to 2010, but afterward exerted a drag on growth until 2015 (chart 9.1).

The Harper government was very active both in modifying the structure of taxation and in reducing the level of federal taxation. While greatly reducing taxes overall, the Harper government decreased its relative reliance on broad-based consumption taxes. This structural shift, which reversed the thrust of the Mulroney government tax reform, failed to provide additional positive incentives for investment and growth through reducing marginal income tax rates.

In 2008, despite solid growth forecast for 2008 and 2009, the federal government relaxed its fiscal stance by 1 per cent of GDP, mostly through cuts in the GST rate and in personal and corporate income taxes. As it turned out, these cuts fortuitously helped stabilize the Canadian economy in 2008 as the US economy started experiencing a downturn early in the year and, contrary to expectations, the Canadian economy followed suit in the fourth quarter. It was only at the end of January 2009, with the Economic Action Plan, that substantive new measures to stimulate the economy were introduced, which along with the automatic stabilizers generated a total increase in net borrowing of nearly 3 per cent of GDP over 2009 and 2010, at a time of large excess supply in the economy (chart 9.1). One key action was to ramp up an ongoing infrastructure program, its core consisting of "shovel-ready" projects that had to be completed within two years or a little more to be eligible. Other important actions included the bailout of GM Canada and Chrysler Canada in 2009 (in collaboration with the Ontario government) and the introduction of the one-year Home Renovation Tax Credit.

The federal government and private forecasters repeatedly overestimated short-term growth rates in Canada during the recovery. The federal government steadily trimmed its net borrowing (deficit) in relation to GDP from 2011 to 2014 by the equivalent to 0.8 per cent of GDP per year. Federal fiscal stance inadvertently became mildly expansionary in 2015 as economic growth slowed to less than 1 per cent, but only because of the support of the automatic stabilizers. Over the 2011 to 2015 period as a whole, discretionary fiscal policy geared toward reducing the budget deficit through expenditure restraint. Consequently, fiscal policy did almost nothing to reduce slack and move the economy back to full employment.

With a new Liberal government elected in November 2015, discretionary fiscal policy appropriately turned moderately expansionary in 2016 partly through boosting child benefits, introducing a tax cut on middle-class income, and initiating an enhanced infrastructure program, measures which promoted income redistribution and aimed at facilitating long-term growth.

### 6.2.2 Policy Developments: Long-Term Growth

Over 2006 to 2015, the Harper government took policy action in a number of areas that could affect long-term growth, including taxation, measures affecting labour market behaviour and product competition, trade policy, industrial policy, and investment in infrastructure and research. Whatever net positive effects these initiatives might have had on labour productivity and the labour force over the period, these effects were unfortunately more than offset by factors over which the government had little or almost no control, including the lasting negative impact of the recession on business non-energy investment, a slower pace of innovation in advanced economies, and population aging.

The Harper government was very active both in modifying the structure of taxation and in reducing the level of federal taxation. While greatly reducing taxes overall, the Harper government decreased its relative reliance on broad-based consumption taxes in favour of income taxes. This structural shift, which reversed the thrust of the Mulroney government tax reform, over the longer term somewhat reduced the positive incentives for growth and investment provided by lower levels of federal taxes.

The Harper government introduced measures designed to improve labour market flexibility and enhance potential growth as a result. One was new EI rules in 2013 that aim at reducing repeat use of EI. Another was to prohibit federally regulated employers from setting mandatory retirement ages, starting in 2011. A third important one was to raise to sixty-seven the age of eligibility for OAS, although this labour-force-enhancing change was inappropriately reversed by the Trudeau government. A fourth one was the introduction in 2007 and enhancement in 2009 of the Working Income Tax Benefit, which aimed to help overcome work disincentives created by the high effective marginal income tax rates faced at low earnings levels.

In 2016, the new Trudeau government began to take some policy actions to support long-term growth, including a much-expanded infrastructure program and an agreement with provinces to expand the Canada Pension Plan.

### 6.2.3 Policy Developments: Distribution

The Harper government implemented several measures with potentially favourable distributive impact on lower-income groups. First, the federal government reduced the GST rate from 7 per cent to 6 per cent in July 2006 and 5 per cent in January 2008, while maintaining the GST credit level. It also introduced the Universal Child Care Benefit in 2006, a taxable universal benefit of uniform amount provided to parents of children ages zero to six. It launched in 2007 a new Child Tax Credit of uniform amount for each child under eighteen. Fourth, the Working Income Tax Benefit introduced in 2007 and enhanced in 2009 provided a wage subsidy to persons at low earnings levels who face high effective marginal tax rates at work. Finally, the progressivity of the federal income tax system was increased slightly during the Harper government years.

### 6.3 Conclusion

The key economic strategy of the Harper government was to reduce the level of taxation while maintaining the balanced budget they inherited. It achieved its objectives of balancing the budget, reducing taxes and, to some extent, improving the structure of the economy without sacrificing income redistribution. However, in so doing it failed to adequately support aggregate demand in 2011 to 2015 and thus prolonged the period of very slow growth. The policies of the new Trudeau government in 2016 put more emphasis on increasing short-term growth supported by an increase in the federal deficit. This policy shift toward expansion and enhanced redistribution was facilitated by the ample fiscal room that the Harper government had created during its second mandate.

## 7. CONCLUSION

Faced with changing and uncertain technological and geo-ecomonic conditions, federal governments over the last fifty years have actively pursued policies to stabilize the economy and the financial systems, to improve the distribution of disposable income, and to enhance economic growth. While policies promoting financial stability have generally been remarkably successful over the whole half-century, policies to achieve high and stable levels of employment with low inflation have had only a spotty record of success. Indeed, monetary and fiscal policies of the seventies and eighties failed spectacularly to achieve low unemployment and price stability.

Over the whole fifty-year period all governments placed great emphasis on achieving more equal distribution of household incomes; in some periods (particularly the decade following 1965) redistribution was the dominating economic policy objective. While distribution of market incomes widened significantly over fifty years, government policies to a great extent mitigated the impact of that widening on disposable income, even during periods when redistribution was not the primary focus of economic policy.

While economic growth with rising real average incomes has been the stated objective of all governments over the last fifty years, making the necessary policy changes to improve the structure of the Canadian economy proved to be neither easy nor politically popular. Looking back, it is clear that it was mainly in the decade following 1984 that the implementation of those growth-enhancing policies received the primary emphasis. However, despite improved structural policies, Canada did not achieve as strong a growth rate of GDP per worker as did many other OECD countries.

As we look forward to Canada's two hundredth birthday, there is much that can be learned from our policy successes and failures since our one hundredth birthday. The purpose of this essay has been to analyze the impact of past policies in the context of events of the time in a way that might provide insights helpful to those who will make economic policy over the next fifty years.

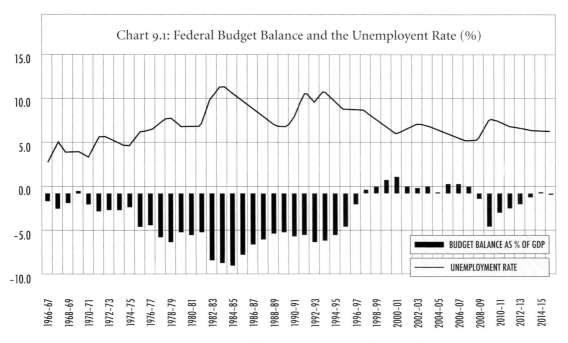

Source: Department of Finance Canada, Fiscal Reference Tables, 2016 and Statistics Canada

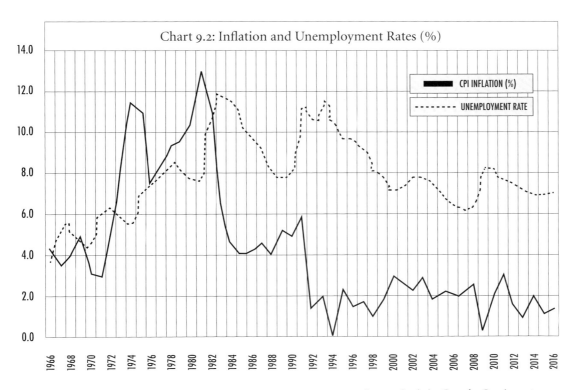

Source: Statistics Canada, Cansim 326-0020

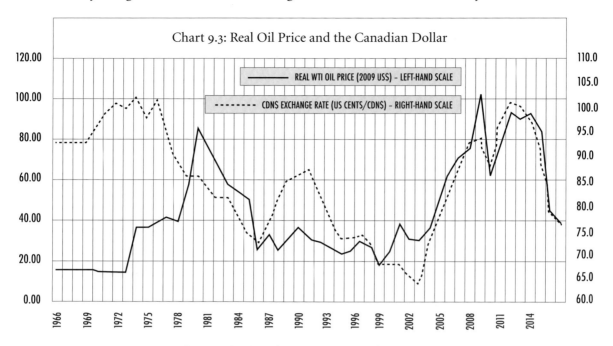

Sources: MacroTrends Data, U.S. Bureau of Economic Analysis and Statistics Canada

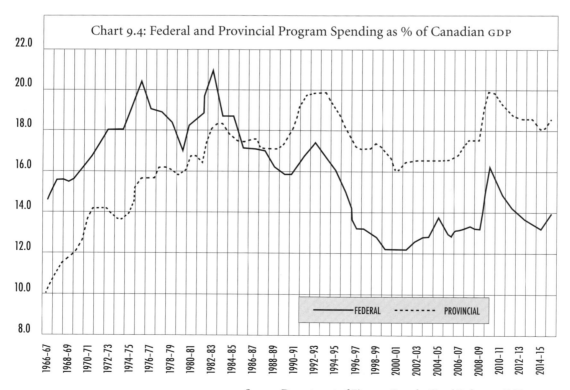

Source: Department of Finance Canada, Fiscal Reference Tables, 2016

# A "New Social Settlement" with the New Economy

Hassan Yussuff, president of the Canadian Labour Congress

I spend most of my days thinking about the "new economy." I devote a large amount of my time to criss-crossing this country, talking with workers about their experience in the new economy. Beginning in the eighties, Canada and other advanced industrialized countries invented a "new economy." But what I want to argue here today is that Canada's "old economy" problems and challenges continue into the present, in new forms.

Since the turn of the eighties, capitalism in Canada and the world has reinvented itself. In Canada and around the world, economic reforms over the last forty years have unleashed the productive powers and dynamism of global capitalism. Some refer to this as the period of "neoliberal globalization." Others call it "the New Gilded Age."

Out of the malaise and turbulence of the seventies, capitalism has transformed itself and recovered its dynamism, its restless change and creative destruction. Capitalism today means unleashed powers of competition, technological change, and innovation. This remarkable dynamism – from the physical transformation of cities before our eyes to the economic integration of billions of people and entire regions of the world once cut off to capitalism, to the dramatic technological changes in daily life – is often disorienting and breathtaking.

Life today features the wonders of innovation, new technologies, and constant change. In this sense, our economy is relentlessly vibrant and dynamic. The Canadian economy is far more productive today than fifty years ago, and wealth has grown significantly.

At the same time, "old economy" challenges remain with us in the present. Canada's historical role as a resource-dependent economy continues to cast a shadow over the present. Amidst global warming and a growing environmental consciousness, the ecological constraints on a development strategy built on resource extraction loom large.

Our economic integration with the United States, and our historical dependence on trade with the US, bedevils us still. And in particular, the enduring pressures that working people have always wrestled with – inequality, insecurity, and exploitation – continue in new forms.

To be sure, the working class today looks very different than it did in the sixties. Women play a vastly greater role in paid employment. The Canadian workforce is much more diverse ethnically and linguistically, with workers of colour participating in much greater numbers. And today, it is older than the workforce of fifty years ago.

Industries like e-commerce and occupations such as video-game programmer didn't exist fifty years ago. In other areas, such as financial services, media and graphic arts, even auto assembly, the nature of work has been transformed.

In other respects, changes wrought by the new economy have been more regressive than revolutionary.

Life for Canadian workers today also involves more economic insecurity, more inequality, more uncertainty and even foreboding about the future, and new existential threats such as climate change. Many workers have experienced the years since 1980 in terms of a growing struggle to get ahead and stave off decline.

## I. THE BREAK WITH THE POST–WORLD WAR II ECONOMIC ORDER

The critical moment in the creation of this new economy was the break with the Keynesian postwar order beginning in the late 1970s.[1] This was a global process, led by the United States Federal Reserve, and was not by any means restricted to Canada.

In Canada and around the world, governments responded to the crises of the seventies with a fundamental shift in economic policy. The basic objective was unleashing the dynamism of the market by reinforcing competitive forces. It was commonly argued that higher levels of economic efficiency and economic growth would result if governments better rewarded capital owners and removed restrictions on the movement and deployment of capital.

Since the early eighties, policy-making at home and abroad has increasingly aimed in the direction of unleashing the competitive forces of capitalism and reinforcing market discipline. Governments have sought to "restore business confidence" by bringing about low and stable inflation, even at the cost of high unemployment.[2]

Policy-makers have loosened regulations and reduced income taxes on corporations, top earners, and capital owners in order to stimulate investment. Political parties of virtually all stripes have accepted the essential principles of this economic model.

## II. THE EXPERIENCE OF WORKING PEOPLE IN THE "NEW ECONOMY"

How did working people experience the economic reforms of the eighties and onwards? These years were very different than the post–World War II decades. The features of the postwar order are relatively clear. They included:

- an official commitment to high and stable levels of employment;[3]

- strong trade unions, which ensured that rising wages kept pace with productivity growth, introduced a measure of economic and industrial democracy, and resulted in a period of falling inequality;

- an expectation of upward economic mobility, including for newcomers to Canada;

- the extension of non-market income and the expansion of public services in the sixties and seventies (including Medicare, the Canada Pension Plan, the Guaranteed Income Supplement, Employment Insurance, maternity/parental benefits, refundable child tax credits, et cetera);[4]

- expanding international trade and investment within a regulatory framework aspiring to balanced trade and permitting domestic economic development objectives (e.g., the 1965 Auto Pact, the Foreign Investment Review Act).[5]

The features of the postwar economic order underpinned expectations of economic security and rising prosperity for many Canadian workers.

In the neoliberal era, the experience of working people during this period has often been different.

Two important parts of the new-economy strategy for stabilizing inflation and reinforcing business confidence have been redistributing income upwards and undermining the bargaining power of working people.

The 1979 decision of the US Federal Reserve to sharply raise interest rates (preceded by related moves in Canada) in order to squeeze inflation out of the economy sparked a deep recession and generated high unemployment.

Beginning in the early eighties, full employment was abandoned as a policy goal, and high unemployment was accepted as a way to reduce wage expectations.[6]

In the eighties and nineties, the unemployment rate in each decade averaged above 9 per cent, before falling in the 2000s to an average of 7 per cent. Using the broadest measure of unemployment (one that includes discouraged searchers, workers waiting to begin a job, and involuntary part-timers), the rate hovers just below 10 per cent today.

Major economic changes included the following:

- Free trade and investment agreements strengthened the ability of industry to leave or threaten to leave.

  □ Global Affairs Canada reports that some fifty-four free trade and investment agreements have come into force since 1989, and Canada has concluded negotiations or signed another eleven agreements.[7]

  □ These agreements typically enshrine the rights and freedoms of companies and investors. Rarely do countries incur trade sanctions if they violate labour, environmental, or human rights.[8]

- Liberalized and globally integrated financial markets served to discipline Canadian policy-makers and reinforce spending cuts.

- Deregulation of telecommunications, airlines, truck and rail shipping, oil and gas, and other industries helped intensify competition, forcing employers to confront workers and unions to accept the new reality and punishing those who didn't.

- Labour law changes weakened unions over time, and employment standard laws were less and less effective at maintaining workplace standards, as new forms of employment spread (including temporary and contract employment, casual work, self-employment and independent contracting, et cetera). Between 1975 and 2014, the average minimum wage in Canada was unchanged in real terms.[9]

  □ At the federal and provincial levels, the seventies and eighties ushered in a period in which governments in Canada routinely violated trade union rights, tearing up contracts, legislating terms and conditions, and ordering striking workers back to work (sometime before the strike even began).[10]

□ The unionization rate in Canada fell from just under 38 per cent in 1981 to under 29 per cent in 2014.

• Changes to Employment Insurance (EI) and transfers for social assistance in the nineties made it harder for the unemployed to avoid taking low-wage, insecure jobs. As many as 84 per cent of unemployed Canadians had access to EI benefits in the early nineties; by 2016, this had fallen to fewer than 40 per cent.[11]

• A tripling in the number of migrant workers employed in Canada under the Temporary Foreign Worker Program between 2002 and 2012 also allowed employers to hold down wage growth.

Over time, disciplining labour has weakened the bargaining power of workers.

A consequence has been rising market inequality in Canada and a disproportionate share of income going to top earners, the top "1 per cent."[12]

Prior to 1978, wages and salaries increased alongside labour productivity. Since the late 1970s, labour productivity growth and the growth in hourly labour compensation have diverged.

Consider the following facts:

• The growth of earnings for typical workers has been very weak.[13]

• Between 1976 and 2014, labour productivity in Canada grew at 1.12 per cent per year. During this period, median real hourly earnings rose at just 0.09 per cent per year. The gap between labour productivity and median hourly earnings widened at 1.03 per cent per year. And as a share of gross domestic product, labour compensation fell between 1975 and 2005.

• Between 1981 and 2005, real median hourly wages in Canada rose by just 5 per cent.

□ While women's real median hourly wages rose significantly, men's real hourly wages were essentially unchanged during this period.

• For men employed full-time, real median wages for people aged thirty-five to forty-four fell.

### THE AUTOMOBILE INDUSTRY AND THE CHALLENGES OF ROBOTIZATION

In addition to developing its abundant natural resources in a sustainable manner, Canada must also focus on its human capital. The only way to meet the challenges of robotization and artificial intelligence is to have an educated populace equipped with the academic and technical training needed in a world of rapidly expanding knowledge and change. The past few decades have been a relatively peaceful social period for Canada. Responsible labour leadership, a social safety net that addresses marginalization and prevents increased poverty, and an education system that is open to everyone – these are the key elements to strengthening social cohesion in Canada.

In a world where there are numerous decision-making bodies, often based far from the regions where their policies are applied, the challenge lies in ensuring that purchasing power remains in the hands of workers and their representatives in labour bargaining. Credit: gerenme (Getty Images)

- Young workers in particular have gone backwards. Median real wages of men aged twenty-five to thirty-four fell by about 10 per cent between 1981 and the late nineties, returning to their 1981 level only by 2010.

- Among young men aged seventeen to twenty-four, the decline in median wages between 1981 and the late nineties was greater, at over 20 per cent, with only partial recovery by the end of the period.

- Real median hourly wages of full-time young women also dropped, while rising for older women.

These are among the conclusions of Statistics Canada and productivity researchers.[14]

For many Canadians, especially blue-collar male workers, the experience has been one of growing dislocation.

Manufacturing workers, and the manufacturing towns they grew up in, have been transformed through periodic restructuring, first in the deep recession of the early eighties, then in the "made-in-Canada" recession of the early nineties, and then in loss of manufacturing jobs accompanying the rise in the Canadian dollar after 2002.

As wages stagnated for many workers, single-earner households became dual-earner households. And households have taken on more debt to sustain living standards. The household debt-to-disposable-income ratio in Canada rose from about 85 per cent in 1990 to over 165 per cent today.

A growing segment of workers today, especially young workers and workers of colour, are experiencing declining job quality.

A 2013 study found that half of working adults in the Golden Horseshoe around Toronto have even moderately secure full-time jobs with benefits.[15] Temporary, part-time, casual, contract, and precarious work is diminishing the health and well-being of growing numbers of individual workers, their families, and their communities.

Technological disruption now threatens to add another layer of insecurity and economic anxiety to this already troubling picture. This is without even taking into account the eventual impact of robotics and automation.

### III. CONTRADICTORY RESULTS OF "NEW ECONOMY" ECONOMIC REFORMS

Even on their own terms, the structural reforms introduced since the Macdonald Commission (Royal Commission on the Economic Union and Development Prospects for Canada, 1985) have not produced the promised high rates of economic and productivity growth.[16]

In the late eighties, economists agreed what was needed to improve productivity growth: low and stable inflation; free trade, internally and externally; lower taxes on capital and a reduced regulatory "burden"; the removal of "disincentives to work" through the reduction of EI benefits; and so on.

By 2010, according to one estimate, Canadian governments had implemented some 70 per cent of this agenda.[17] Yet productivity growth worsened rather than improved.

In the postwar decades, Canada had the third-highest level of productivity among the original twenty-four Organisation for Economic Co-operation and Development (OECD) countries. Today it ranks fifteenth.[18] Since 1980, just three OECD countries have had a worse productivity growth rate than Canada.

Economic growth in the recent recovery was among the weakest it has been in any economic recovery in the last fifty years. Business investment remains sluggish, and

DENG XIAOPING (1904–97) AND US PRESIDENT JIMMY CARTER (1977–81)

Deng Xiaoping led the People's Republic of China from 1978 to 1992. His reforms helped transform China into the second-largest economy in the world and an exporting powerhouse. However, the country's domestic market is shielded by highly protectionist regulations and very hard to penetrate. Canada's challenge is to take advantage of the huge potential offered by China while maintaining control over its strategic resources. Any future free trade agreement would have a huge impact on the country's labour market, but the effects would be difficult to quantify as they would extend to the industrial, technological, and natural resources exploitation. Credit: Jimmy Carter Library, # nlc09217.11

Canadian employers continue to invest comparatively little in training and upskilling their workforce.

In the new economy, we confront many of the challenges that afflicted the old Canadian economy. The oil and gas boom of 2002 to 2014 generated enormous wealth not just in Alberta, but in Canada as a whole. But it also drove up the dollar and strangled central Canadian manufacturing, threatening to return Canada to its historical role of a resource and staple producer ("hewer of wood and drawer of water").[19]

Governments continue to face calls to invest in the refining and processing of resource products, in order to increase the added value of Canadian exports. As the world transitions to the new "green" economy, Canada risks remaining largely an exporter of mostly raw and semi-processed commodities. And our integration with and continued dependence on the United States represents a growing risk when the United States decides to change the rules.

## IV. CONCLUDING REMARKS

Beginning in the eighties, Canada and other advanced industrialized countries invented a new economy – but old-economy problems and challenges continue into the present, in new forms.

Let me conclude by arguing that in order to fully meet the demands and challenges of the new economy – an aging society in need of expanded immigration, an urgently needed ecological transition, an imbalanced economy needing a more equal and secure footing, rising economic insecurity against a backdrop of far-reaching technological changes – we need a new social settlement to accompany our new economy, one based on the principles of sustainability, inclusion, shared prosperity, economic democracy, and an equitable distribution of opportunities.

The working people of Canada and their organizations will be an important part of realizing this vision – or it will not materialize at all.

### NOTES

1   This is detailed in Leo Panitch and Sam Gindin, *The Making of Global Capitalism: The Political Economy of American Empire* (London: Verso, 2013).

2   Pierre Fortin and Lars Osberg (eds.), *Unnecessary Debts* (Toronto: James Lorimer Ltd, 1996).

3   Robert M. Campbell, *Grand Illusions: The Politics of the Keynesian Experience in Canada, 1945–1975* (Peterborough, ON: Broadview Press, 1987).

4  Keith Banting and John Myles (eds.), *Inequality and the Fading of Redistributive Politics* (Vancouver: University of British Columbia Press, 2013).

5  Dimitry Anastakis, *Auto Pact: Creating a Borderless North American Auto Industry, 1960–1971* (Toronto: University of Toronto Press, 2005).

6  Stephen McBride, *Not Working: State, Unemployment, and Neo-conservatism in Canada* (Toronto: University of Toronto Press, 1992).

7  Global Affairs Canada, http://www.international.gc.ca/international/. Accessed 14 May 2017.

8  Stephen McBride and John Shields, *Dismantling a Nation: The Transition to Corporate Rule in Canada*, 2nd edition (Halifax: Fernwood, 1997).

9  Eric Fecteau and Diane Galarneau, *The Ups and Downs of Minimum Wage*, Statistics Canada Catalogue, no. 75-006-X, July 2014.

10  Leo Panitch and Donald Swartz, *From Consent to Coercion: The Assault on Trade Union Freedoms*, 3rd edition (Aurora, ON: Garamond Press, 2003).

11  Georges Campeau, *From UI to EI: Waging War on the Welfare State* (Vancouver: University of British Columbia Press, 2005); David M. Gray and Colin Busby, *Unequal Access: Making Sense of EI Eligibility Rules and How to Improve Them*, C.D. Howe Institute Commentary no. 450, May 2016.

12  David A. Green, W. Craig Riddell, and France St-Hillaire, *Income Inequality: The Canadian Story* (Montreal: Institute for Research on Public Policy, 2016).

13  René Morissette, Garnett Picot, and Yuqian Lu, *The Evolution of Canadian Wages over the Last Three Decades*, Statistics Canada Catalogue no. 11F0019M347, 2013; Andrew Sharpe, "Canadian Productivity, Pay Increases, and Inclusive Growth: What Is Achievable?," address to the Ottawa Economics Association, 16 November 2016.

14  Ibid.

15  Poverty and Employment Precarity in Southern Ontario (PEPSO), *It's More than Poverty: Employment Precarity and Household Wellbeing* (Hamilton: PEPSO, 2013).

16  Don Drummond, "Confessions of a Serial Productivity Researcher," *International Productivity Monitor* 22 (Fall 2011).

17  Ibid.

18  Ibid.

19  Tony Clarke, Diana Gibson, Brendan Haley, and Jim Stanford, *The Bitumen Cliff: Lessons and Challenges of Bitumen Mega-Developments for Canada's Economy in an Age of Climate Change* (Ottawa: Canadian Centre for Policy Alternatives, 2013).

# 10

# The Senate – Better Protecting the Federal Principle[1]

## The Hon. Serge Joyal, Senator

We must reconcile ourselves to the fact that the Senate is here to stay. Over the last fifty years, there have been repeated calls to change it in every possible way, or simply to abolish it. It has been criticized repeatedly, but since the Supreme Court issued its advisory opinion on Senate reform in 2014,[2] the resurgent Senate is now stronger than ever, confounding its detractors. Since the Senate definitely has a future, we should get used to the idea and turn it into an effective counterbalance to a House of Commons increasingly dominated by an ever-powerful prime minister and Cabinet.[3] Indeed, the House has fallen prey to strong partisan politics that can only have a detrimental impact on the actual role of parliamentarians. The continued existence of the Senate can only benefit Canadian democracy and the Canadian public. Now that electoral reform has been shelved, the best way to improve the overall representativeness of Parliament will be to focus on the composition of the Senate and take advantage of the compensatory effect that can be achieved through appointments to fill vacancies in the Senate. Let us consider the Senate from another perspective.

In 1965, the composition of the Senate was made over in one key respect when a mandatory retirement age of seventy-five was imposed (from 1867 until then, senators had been appointed for life).[4] This reform revitalized the institution by lowering the average age of senators from seventy to sixty-four.

Senate representativeness also progressed over the years. The percentage of women in the Senate increased from as much as 35 per cent in 2003 to 46.6 per cent as of this writing. Visible and linguistic minorities, as well as Indigenous peoples, are better represented in the Senate than in the House of Commons.[5] Canadian prime ministers realized that the convention of recommending individuals for appointment to the Senate allowed them to compensate for the electoral system's failure to directly achieve proportional representation of genders and minority cultural groups.

*In 1971, within the context of a proposed constitutional charter (the* Victoria Charter*), the government of Pierre E. Trudeau formally recognized the role of the Senate in the constitutional amending formula (sections 49 to 52), as well as the number of senators representing each province and their residency requirements. This proposed charter also guaranteed the minimum number of MPs based on the number of senators allocated to each province (sections 55(5) and (6)). The proposal would thus have entrenched the federal principle by adjusting the relative weight of the provinces to that of the regions in the Senate. However, this reform project was eventually dropped.[6]*

*In 1978, the Trudeau government proposed a second significant reform of the Senate when it tabled Bill C-60. Clauses 62 to 70 of the bill redefined the Senate in depth. It would be called the "House of the Federation." Half the members would be appointed by the federal government and the other half by the provinces. The newly renamed Senate would lose its legislative veto, which would simply become suspensive, and it would have to yield in the majority of cases to the supremacy of the House of Commons, which would become the sole decision-making authority in the passage of bills before they received royal assent.*

*The provinces were opposed to this unilateral reform of the Senate, which was being pursued without their consent, and the matter was ultimately decided by the Supreme Court of Canada in 1979.[7] The Court found that the Senate is the embodiment of the original compromise that allowed the creation of the Canadian federation in 1867, and that the provinces must take part in any redefinition of its status, role, powers, and composition. Bill C-60 died on the order paper.*

*The Trudeau government revisited the issue in 1980 during the process leading up to the patriation of the Constitution. And those efforts were more on point. Concerning amendment by unanimous consent, it enshrined the role of the Senate in the very definition of the amendment formula (section 41(e)) as well as the federal principle of representation of the provinces in the Senate (section 41(b)) and the required participation of the Senate in any amendment under federal jurisdiction (section 44).[8] Prime Minister Trudeau and his advisors were fully aware that they were thus perpetuating the existence of the Senate,[9] which the Supreme Court later confirmed in its opinion of April 2014 when it determined that the Senate is an essential part of the "constitutional architecture of Canada."[10]*

*For amendments to the Constitution requiring the consent of the provinces, the House of Commons may bypass the will of the Senate after a period of six months by adopting a resolution again.[11] The logic here is that, since the consent of the provinces is required to adopt such reform proposals, the Senate must defer. Since the Senate must ultimately express the views of the regions, it is only fair for it to cede primacy to the provinces when their consent is explicitly required. In politics, however, a delay of six months can sometimes be an eternity.*

*In the years that followed, the government of Prime Minister Brian Mulroney tried again to amend the composition of the Senate. In 1987, the Meech Lake Accord gave the provinces the authority to identify candidates to be recommended by the prime minister to the governor general for appointment to the Senate.[12] This practice, granted to the provinces by the federal government pending a more-in-depth reform, lasted three years until the Accord became null and void when it failed to be ratified by all ten provinces within the time frame prescribed under the Constitution.[13]*

*Another attempt at reform occurred in 1992 with the Charlottetown Accord. This time, in response to demands from the western provinces, a "triple-E" approach to Senate transformation was used that would create an "effective, egalitarian, and elected" Senate in which senators would be either chosen by the provincial legislative assemblies or elected by the people they would represent. Each province would be assigned the same number of senators (six seats). The regional distribution of Senate seats would disappear, and the powers of the Senate would be redefined and limited.*

*This reform proposal collapsed when the Canadian electorate rejected it, together with the Accord as a whole, in a national referendum in October 1992 that put an end to the matter.*

*The government of Prime Minister Jean Chrétien shied away from tampering with the Senate. It limited itself to practising "revolving door" politics by recommending a large number of rather elderly (well beyond the age of seventy) appointees to the Senate. In fact, one woman was appointed to the Senate a scant six months before reaching the mandatory retirement age of seventy-five.[14] This practice had the effect of weakening the Senate's legislative capacity to debate bills thoroughly, since such senators did not have enough time to familiarize themselves with the complex workings of parliamentary procedure.*

*The government led by Prime Minister Stephen Harper showed itself to be firm in its resolve to reform the Senate as soon as it took office in 2006. The Prime Minister himself testified before the Special Committee on Senate Reform in September 2006 to present his objectives of first transforming the Senate into an elective body and then shortening the term of office for senators to eight years, while preserving the mandatory retirement age of seventy-five. The government tried several times to have this radical change in the Senate adopted. It tabled six bills for this purpose in less than five years: bills S-4 and C-43 in 2006, Bill C-19 in 2007, Bill S-7 in 2009, and bills C-10 and S-8 in 2010.*

*The government first ran into opposition from the Senate itself, which argued that this was a major constitutional reform proposal that should involve the provinces, since the federal Parliament alone cannot amend the fundamental nature of the Senate by transforming it from an appointed chamber to an elected body of members serving eight-year terms, without fundamentally calling into question the very nature of the Senate and its complementary relationship with the House of Commons.[15] The Committee on Legal and Constitutional Affairs studied the bill and recommended that it not proceed to third reading until the Supreme Court of Canada had ruled on its constitutionality.[16]*

*The federal government's reform proposal also ran up against opposition from the Quebec provincial government led by Jean Charest, which claimed that any effort to transform the Senate into an elected body required the participation of the provinces. According to Quebec, such a change would fundamentally alter Canada's electoral structure by creating a completely new order of elected officials who could claim to speak on behalf of their respective provinces.*

*The Quebec government felt it would be wise to refer the constitutionality of such a move to the Quebec Court of Appeal, in the form of three specific questions. The Court rendered its opinion on 24 October 2013,[17] ruling unanimously that the proposed federal reform exceeded the powers of the Canadian Parliament. In light of the constitutional arguments raised against its reform proposal, the federal government ultimately decided to refer the matter to the Supreme Court of Canada in February 2013. It put seven questions to the Court. These questions covered the full spectrum of issues under contention, from the constitutional impact of having an elected Senate to the duration of the term to be served by elected senators and the powers of the federal Parliament to make such changes. The federal government even asked the Court to rule on the level of consent required to simply abolish the Senate.*

*The Supreme Court issued a unanimous ruling on 25 October 2014 in which it provided clear and well-supported answers to all of the questions that had been put before it. This will be remembered as an important date in the history of Canadian parliamentary institutions. The Supreme Court expressly and emphatically confirmed the bicameral and egalitarian nature of Canada's Parliament, where both chambers have a role to play and specific duties in the legislative process. Each chamber must give its independent and autonomous consent before a bill can receive royal assent. The Senate is not subject to the House of Commons. Its views on bills are formulated from a different perspective, and thus its role is complementary in nature. In its extremely detailed and logical ruling, based on an interpretation of the "constitutional architecture" of the federal Parliament, the Supreme Court set out what amounted to a theory of federal bicameralism. According to the Court, "[t]he Senate is a core component of the Canadian federal structure of government."[18] It has a role to play in the legislative process, and that role is different from the role played by the House of Commons.*

*Not only is the Senate's participation in the parliamentary process essential to federal legislative activity, but the Supreme Court's ruling again clarified the bicameral nature of Parliament. The Senate is not a lesser chamber or second-tier body whose consent is subservient to the will of the Commons. Its status as a legislative chamber is in all points equal to that of the Commons.[19] This allows it to formulate views and provide consent in a wholly independent and separate manner in order to complete the study of bills adopted by the House of Commons.*

*According to the Court, debates in each of the two chambers must have different but complementary perspectives. One expresses the views of MPs elected to represent Canadian voters. The other expresses the findings of an independent and autonomous assessment of bills, viewed from the federal principle, taking into account regional interests and the rights of minorities, and sheltered from the imperatives of electoral cycles.*

*These two legislative perspectives are separate but complementary. Both are essential to formulating a well-rounded piece of legislation and ensuring its valid passage. It is up to the Senate to enhance the legislative process. The debates surrounding the passage of a bill must guarantee to Canadians that the legislation in question has been subjected to a dual legislative assessment. One cannot be given short shrift in favour of the other. Limiting or eliminating debate in one chamber would lead to a flawed piece of legislation with less credibility, since Parliament as a whole will not have had the opportunity to examine its full scope or its immediate and future implications.*

*The remarkable thing is that the Harper government, which was bent on effecting a radical transformation of the Senate, through no will of its own made the greatest contribution to entrenching the historic role of the Senate in the federal parliament, as originally envisioned and defined by the Fathers of Confederation. It advanced the debate on the Senate's place among parliamentary institutions by having the Supreme Court clarify the role and status of the Senate. The Court ruled that the Senate could only be abolished with the unanimous consent of the federal government and the ten provinces. There would be no more utopian pipedreams: the Senate was definitely here to stay. Therefore, it would be wise to ensure that it actually plays its proper role in the legislative process.*

*This reaffirmation by the Supreme Court of the Senate's key role in the parliamentary system raises a number of questions. What is the nature of the Senate's independence as an institution? Can the Senate stand in opposition to the views of the democratically elected chamber? Should it instead in practice exercise a suspensive veto, notwithstanding the apparent contradiction in these terms? Should it yield to the legislative will of the Commons, in cases where the House rejects its amendments? Ultimately, should it always refrain from voting against a bill referred to it by the Commons, whose members are elected? These questions are usually brought up to argue*

THE MACE AND THE CALENDAR — CELEBRATING THE DIAMOND JUBILEE OF QUEEN ELIZABETH II
The Senate is the House in which the three constituent parts of Parliament come together: the sovereign, symbolized by the thrones and the mace; the Commons, whose members stand at the bar at the entrance to the chamber; and the senators themselves. In 2012, to mark the Diamond Jubilee of Her Majesty Elizabeth II, Queen of Canada, the senators commissioned a commemorative calendar made of gilded bronze and copper to sit on the Clerk's Table, near the mace, in the centre of the chamber. Senate officials and all senators contributed financially to the calendar to show respect for and recognition of the sovereign's exemplary service to the country. Credit: Senate of Canada

*in favour of domesticating or enslaving the Senate and its members, without regard to the chamber's very nature or the implications of the legislative changes desired by the all-powerful Prime Minister's Office (PMO), which dominates the majority in the Commons and often tends to view Parliament as a unicameral institution. If only the Senate would comply with its wishes.*

*These questions took on new meaning with the swearing in of a large contingent of 49 new independent senators since 2016.[20]*

*Prime Minister Justin Trudeau wanted to differentiate himself from his predecessor by making a commitment to recommend to the governor general only individuals chosen from a list of candidates selected by an independent panel responsible for assessing their qualifications. Moreover, these future senators would be required to pledge that they have no particular political affiliation.*

*Prime Minister Trudeau's goal in making this move was to purge the Senate of partisan politics, which increased to unprecedented levels during the scandal surrounding alleged spending violations by some senators and an attempted cover-up by the Harper PMO. As the scandal continued to grow, the Senate was largely vilified in the media, and its reputation was damaged by a devastating report from the Auditor General. Ultimately, however, none of the charges alleging misuse of funds held up in criminal court, and the real scandal became the cost of the audit ordered by the government, which topped out at $23.6 million,[21] versus the total of about $185,918 recovered from a small number of senators after all of the expenses (even the tiniest ones) incurred over a two-year period by all serving senators were subjected to a rigorous forensic audit.[22]*

*The allegations against a number of senators stemmed from their partisan work on behalf of their political party and the direct link they entertained with the PMO. To put an end to this wayward behaviour, Prime Minister Justin Trudeau decided to eliminate political parties from the Senate entirely. Mr Trudeau felt that partisanship was at the root of much of the troubles in the Senate, so he resolved to make it more independent and less partisan. He immediately expelled all Liberal senators from the Liberal Party of Canada's national caucus in January 2014, and followed that up with a pledge to recommend for appointment to the Senate only candidates chosen from a list of qualified persons identified by an external evaluation committee. The selection criteria screened out all individuals who had previous parliamentary experience or who had recently worked for a political party.*

*When this momentous decision was announced in 2014, there had been no serious reflection or in-depth debate beforehand on the impact it would have on our parliamentary system. The decision was made in order to distance the prime minister and his party from an alleged scandal. The objective was commendable, but this kind of political reform entails unintended consequences that should be considered carefully by analysts who fully understand the nature of our political institutions and their internal workings. It is like flying blind, improvising solutions to situations without having given it much thought. The experiment of eliminating political parties from the Senate can certainly proceed for the stated purpose of increasing the credibility of the Senate, making it more independent and less partisan, but there is a certain logic to the exercise of legislative authority in our bicameral system that has its own requirements, which are tied to the very nature of the system. Hence, it makes sense to take a close look at our bicameral system and what is being eliminated from it when an element is removed that had given rise to conventions and practices that ensured its smooth operation and contributed to its vitality. As Michael Roth has written: "We may be rational beings capable of planning our future, but we also need customs and institutions to ground and sustain us over time."*[23]

*Although the British House of Lords contains a number of unaligned members, called "crossbenchers," who make up 23 per cent of sitting members, the burden of daily debate in the House of Lords is carried by the Lords who are members of Britain's political parties.*[24]

*What role do political parties play in our parliamentary system? Doesn't the decision to abolish party affiliations in the Senate undermine the very relevance of political parties in our democratic system by eliminating the effort at compromise upon which they are necessarily built? Isn't this decision related to the populist rhetoric that seeks to discredit traditional political parties by referring to them as "organizations belonging to the corrupt elites?"*[25] *The magazine* The Economist *in 2017 was refering to that fact in its review of the democratic index in the world and concluded that democracy was weakening even among the countires where it has been flourishing in the past.*[26] *And yet political parties are institutions that are supposed to mediate between citizens and help people live together in society. Doesn't this action validate the contemporary notion, nurtured by social media, now the fifth power,*[27] *that any individual can be just as right as the people who have been democratically elected or appointed specifically to carry forward a concept of common good by seeking compromise to sustain social cohesion? Political parties are, first and foremost, forums for the discussion of political choices. Their members are bound together by a common political vision of sorts. Institutions "are more easily destroyed than created"*[28] *and one cannot underestimate that political parties are at the heart of the democratic life as the Supreme Court has noticed it.*

*There are other tangible implications, of course. Doesn't expelling from the national Liberal caucus the senators who were the most experienced members of that caucus – the people who could express a more independent opinion to the prime minister or the party leader because they were no longer dependent upon that person for their career advancement, and who could thus perpetuate the party's values – have the effect of squelching the right to internal party dissidence and ultimately threaten the very stability of political parties? After all, dissident voices can provide a meaningful counterweight to the overwhelming power of the party leader, which is one of the most serious flaws in the party system. It is unlikely that caucus* MPs *will gain any more freedom of expression as a result of this move, or that the party leader's absolute control will in any way be diminished. How is the internal democratic life of a political party truly revitalized by such a move?*

\* \* \*

*There are also practical consequences for the very survival of political parties. After the 1993 general election, the Conservative Party was left with only two elected MPs in the House of Commons. The thirty-five senators who belonged to the Conservative Party's national caucus took up the torch to ensure the continued existence of the parliamentary life of a party that had governed Canada from 1984 to 1993. The forty-seven Liberal senators, not the least of them Allan J. MacEachen, played a similar role from 1984 to 1993 following the crushing defeat of the Liberal Party that left only thirty-four MPs. The survival of the Party was even in question. These recent situations are enlightening. It would be wrong to believe that the political scene is linear and that it would make sense to eliminate the safety nets that helped keep Canada's two main national parties alive when their very existence was threatened. History bears this out, and recalling those events is more than an exercise in nostalgia. There is a wise lesson to be learned here. By and large, party leaders do not think much about what comes after, or what will happen to their party when they leave. Most tell themselves that their successors will look after things. But that is not necessarily going to happen.*

*The proposed reform will also affect the role of caucuses. There is no longer a government caucus in the Senate, where senators sharing the values of the party in power would regularly go to express their understanding of the various bills or of the issues under debate, to discuss their sometimes-divergent views and apportion among themselves responsibilities to move debates and studies forward and, need we mention, to cultivate a strong sense of collegiality.*

*The fact that there is no longer a government caucus in the Senate does not mean that the needs met by such an institution in our system in order to keep our parliamentary machinery running smoothly no longer exist. On the contrary, the present government representative in the Senate cannot rely directly on the Independent Senators Group (ISG) to relay government initiatives, although in practice the vast majority of government bills are sponsored by independent senators. To remedy this necessity, ministers of the Crown whose bills are debated in the Senate have now made it a habit to engage in private discussions with the various senators concerned, expressing the government's views to them in the privacy of their office or by telephone. Hence, instead of occurring openly before the Senate as a whole in a national caucus forum, the "conversation" takes place away from prying eyes and without debate that would be open to the entire group. It should be pointed out that this type of exchange is not conducted on an equal footing. An "independent" senator is more vulnerable to individual pressure, whereas a group discussion has the merit or benefit of opening up debate and cushioning the unequal nature of the relationship. In practice, the group acts as a buffer. A new senator may be independent, but he or she is individualized in direct private contacts with a minister of the Crown who has the authority of his or her office and budget, and who is an elected official. The new senator is therefore more vulnerable to pressure, and the firmness of the senator's convictions is more likely to wilt.*

*In the pressure game that is politics, non-partisanship does not necessarily lead to independence of principle, which is supposed to be the purpose of eliminating political affiliations in the Senate. We have already seen this dynamic at work in the study of various bills. It is not theoretical. It is a more subtle way for government authority to maintain control, perhaps even more effectively, under the guise of freedom of thought and independence. The PMO no longer intervenes directly, but another more nebulous back channel has been opened to allow the government to exercise its political power.*

*The fact that independent senators are now on their own has another unintended consequence, it has reinforced the influence of lobbying. Nobody will be surprised to learn that the activities of registered lobbyists to communicate with senators have seen a resurgence since the appointment of independent senators. According to an analysis of January 2017 by the* Hill Times, *the meetings with lobbyists have tripled in the last three years. In 2016, communications had doubled (687) from 2015 and in 2017 they had again doubled to 1 443. As an experienced lobbyist stated: "lobbyist […] reach out to independent senators first"[29] to promote their interests or even propose amendments to Bills in the Senate. It is no more with the leadership of the parties that lobbyists concentrate their activities but rather with independent senators, individually, thus more influencable because isolated. The lobbyists saw the opening and they moved in. Is it a plus or an improvement of the democratic life of the country? Anyone[30] can draw its own conclusions.[31] But one thing, for sure, is that it is not the minorities, the poorer or the representatives of the middle class that are in the folders of the lobbyists and that are more often heard on the Parliamentary Hill.*

*That raises a serious question in relation to the fundamental role of the Senate which is to be the voice of the minorities and of those who don't have easy access to the decision making powers. Was that part of any reflexion on the increased influence that lobbyists would get before the decision was made to abolish political parties in the Senate?*

### 1. WHAT ABOUT THE INDEPENDENCE OF SENATORS?

*Liberal senators were expelled from the national Liberal caucus by Justin Trudeau nearly two years before he came to power. These senators form a group that is free of all ties to the governing party in the House of Commons. Any allegiance these senators have is primarily ideological, in terms of the values they espouse, and not merely political. They are not subject to party discipline and do not have to answer to a whip. They are entirely free to follow their conscience and their own conclusions whenever they vote. They are not required to toe a party line.*

*This "freedom" or independence has been the subject of two analyses. The first, made public by CBC in June 2017,[32] revealed that the group of senators voting most "freely" is the contingent of independent Liberal senators (78.5 per cent), whereas members of the Independent Senators Group (ISG), appointed by Prime Minister Trudeau, support the government 91.6 per cent of the time. The leaders of the Iindependent Senators Gourp (ISG), however, did not put a great deal of stock in the findings of this analysis.[33] A more recent study of Senate voting patterns, published on 25 July 2018, however, confirms that the government receives its greatest support for the passage of bills from Senate independents (84.2 per cent), whereas the rate of support for government bills among Liberal independents is 76 per cent.[34]*

*After expelling the Liberal senators from his caucus in 2014, Justin Trudeau explained that he wanted them to be "independent-minded."[35] Based on their subsequent voting patterns, this is precisely what happened. These senators demonstrated that it is possible to have a political allegiance, namely sharing the vision and values of a particular political party, while remaining entirely free to follow one's conscience in voting on government legislation and decisions.[36]*

*It is somewhat ironic to note that the senators who most embody Prime Minister Trudeau's stated objective of making the Senate an independent and less partisan chamber are, as of this writing, the Liberal independents. According to Mr Trudeau, "[i]f the Senate serves a purpose at all, it is to act as a check on the extraordinary power of the prime minister and his office, especially in a majority government."[37] According to the aforementioned most recent study, the independent senators recommended for appointment by the prime minister voted with the government more than 84.2 per cent of the time. The official opposition, meanwhile, continues to play its traditional role: opposing government initiatives as a matter of principle, and voting in favour of such measures only 22.2 per cent of the time.*

*Hence, allegiance to or identification with the values espoused by a recognized political party is not an insurmountable obstacle to the independence of the Senate or of senators themselves, insofar as there is no whip to impose a rigid party line or disciplinary measures when votes come up. The presence of wide-ranging views based on different schools of thought is good for democratic debate in a society such as ours, which is anything but monolithic in its thinking.*

*Is a majority of independent senators enough to guarantee Senate independence? Indeed, is anyone absolutely independent who professes no allegiance to a line of thinking identified with a given political party? The answer to this question is rather subtly shaded. Independent senators cannot claim to be as independent or objective as judges, who must be wholly impartial when conducting hearings or making decisions. Senators have a more qualified independence. A senator who does not have a stated allegiance to a recognized political party is presumed to adopt a position* de novo *on each new issue as it arises.*

*One very specific factor must be considered in trying to understand the independence of senators. Anyone who has had a full professional life (which is the case for the vast majority of Senate members) has developed over time and by dint of circumstances a scale of values and a personal vision of society and the world. With few exceptions, such individuals may not have shown it objectively in the form of writings or past structured public interventions, but they call upon a personal set of values and views acquired through experience when they are asked to express a considered opinion on, react to or adopt a stance on a particular social or economic issue. Unlike a judge, an independent senator does not weigh matters against a specific statute or well-defined evidence. Independent senators initially rely on their personal values, their vision of society, their professional experience, as well as any arguments made during the course of debate and, ultimately, their own personal assessment of a particular bill and any representations they may have received. This approach is quite different from the independence and objectivity that a judge must bring to the table when considering and resolving disputes. A senator will rely on experience and personal values as well as the particular circumstances surrounding a matter at issue; a judge will rely on objectively established laws and evidence supported by proven facts, both of which are entirely separate from any personal considerations.*

*Moreover, the interests developed by senators in their previous careers follow them into the Senate. In fact, the Senate constitutes a new platform where they can assert those interests. Someone who previously defended Indigenous issues, the cause of women caught up in the legal system or the integration problems facing immigrant groups, for instance, will continue to be an advocate for those issues once he or she becomes a member of the Senate. Is this senator more or less independent in this regard than a senator with a declared political affiliation acting as a spokesperson for the victims of crime, the Charter rights of minority groups or the working conditions of journalists? Such issues do not call for independence so much as a recognized and credible commitment to intervene within the Senate in support of the groups a senator is publicly known to have spent a lifetime supporting, often to the appreciation of his or her peers.*

*The independence of senators therefore has limits rooted in the notable experience they have acquired in supporting noble and even meritorious causes. When they intervene on such issues, there are no other interests at play and the Senate is better off because it has members whose background includes so much experience and commitment. The independence of each senator is therefore qualified by the nature of that individual's personal interests and professional experience. We all remember and regret the brand of narrow partisan politics of previous parliaments, characterized by strings being pulled from on high. Such loathsome behaviour must be avoided at all costs. But a recognized political party can inject healthy values into democratic discourse, insofar as senators with party affiliations remain independent-minded enough to reach conclusions in light of their own thoughts and reasoning. The presence in the Senate of members with a declared political allegiance does not hamper its ability to make meaningful and credible judgements through parliamentary debate in a system such as ours.*

*An analysis of the previous careers of the 49 "independent" senators appointed by the current prime minister places nearly all of them in the mainstream of moderate progressivism or centrist activism.[38] As independent Senator Frances Lankin put it, the first wave of senators recommended by Prime Minister Trudeau "had a centrist to centre-left perspective – not partisan, but general values."[39] In other words, they are rather sympathetic to or well disposed toward the present government's political ideology. While this is not a failing as such, it is clear that calling these new senators independent does not mean they are impartial, and saying so in no way impugns whatever contributions they have made or will continue to make.*

*We know from practical experience that any newly appointed senator will be somewhat hesitant to vote against the government or to argue strenuously for amendments to bills put forward by the government that recommended his or her appointment. When a new government assumes the reins of power, however, it becomes less embarrassing for such senators to express their independence.[40] There is nothing new under the sun in this respect. Past experience shows that it has always been this way. Even senators representing a political party exhibit more independence when there is a change in party leadership and they no longer owe allegiance to the former leader who appointed them.*

*With one notable exception,[41] none of the "independent" senators appointed by Prime Minister Justin Trudeau had ever served as an elected representative in a federal or provincial legislature. There was clearly no effort to give preference to people with parliamentary or government experience, probably out of fear of appearing to politicize or diminish the apparent "independent minded" nature of the senators who would now be "independent" and non-partisan. This is to some extent a weakness in the composition of the Senate: a command of parliamentary procedure and prior political experience would tend to prepare an individual for legislative debate involving truly complex public policy issues that cannot be mastered overnight. It is possible to learn the ins and outs of Senate practices in the long run, however, but if not enough senators manage to find their way through this procedural and legislative web, the efficiency and effectiveness of the chamber will be diminished, as well as its ability to study bills rigorously, carefully evaluate required amendments and hold the government to account for its decisions.*

*One fundamental question remains: will the country benefit from the elimination from the Senate, in the medium term, of the two major national political parties that shaped Canada into what it is today and contributed to the emergence of the values of freedom and equality that characterize Canadian society? Blindly partisan discourse is rightfully lambasted when it represses the free expression of divergent opinions and the casting of votes challenging the dominant consensus. But there is no denying that the country we are justifiably proud of grew out of debates fueled by the values and visions defended by these two important democratic groups. Who will champion these views in Senate debates once the two major political parties and their respective visions of Canadian society are eliminated from the red chamber? While we can wish for a more independent and less partisan Senate, which the current government is trying to achieve, we cannot help but wonder what is being lost in the process and consider the impact of that loss on the diversity and the very tenor of public discourse in the Senate.*

*The objectives of the Trudeau government's Senate reform, outside the framework of a formal constitutional amendment, in practice touch upon key elements of the workings of the parliamentary system. They are not aimed directly at increasing the powers of the prime minister. Rather, they seek to frame the prime minister's authority to select candidates for appointment to the Senate and to cut his influential ties with the senators representing his party. However, we are seeing unintended consequences on the day-to-day workings of the parliamentary system as time progresses.*

## 2. GREATER INDEPENDENCE IN SENATE DEBATES

*In the everyday practice of Senate debate, independence is becoming an increasingly complex and elusive criterion.*

*First of all, one must consider the vigour or robustness of debate. In order to emerge, real debate requires contrasting views. This is the very essence of the parliamentarianism upon which our democratic institutions are founded. As British politician and writer Edmund Burke once wrote, "our antagonist is our helper."[42] Hence, for debate to happen, there needs to be opposing views. This is the traditional principle of classroom debate, with one side arguing for the affirmative and the other for the negative. Without an adversary there can be no battle of wits or confrontation of ideas. Justice Lyman Duff of the Supreme Court of Canada put it clearly in a 1938 decision when he referred to the principles of our parliamentary system:*

> *The preamble of the [British North America Act (now called* The Constitution Act, 1867*)], moreover, shows plainly enough that the constitution of the Dominion is to be similar in principle to that of the United Kingdom. The statute contemplates a parliament working under the influence of public opinion and public discussion. There can be no controversy that such institutions derive their efficacy from <u>the free public discussion of affairs, from criticism and answer and counter-criticism, from attack upon policy and administration and defence and counter-attack; from the freest and fullest analysis and examination from every point of view of political proposals.</u>[43] [emphasis added]*

*According to Justice Duff, the important thing is the multiplicity of views contrasted against each other. This is the very essence of parliamentary debate: argument, counter-argument, criticism, defence, complete and open freedom, without fear of reprisals or personal consequences. The personal ambition of senators is not a factor, since a political party leader cannot dismiss them or promise them anything, and since they will hold their Senate seat until they retire. This is exactly the reverse of what MPs in the House of Commons have to deal with.*

*The "official" opposition in the Senate (the purpose of which is certainly not to constitute a shadow government) essentially assumes the role of opponent in principle on the debating floor, regardless of whatever bill or public issue is being discussed. Without a structured group or entity whose day-to-day responsibility is to disagree with the government position, will the independence of the Senate be reduced in practice? Will it be made to suffer by the disappearance of the group of senators whose primary responsibility is to hold the government to account every day and to force the government to justify each of its decisions and each of its bills, no matter who in the Senate sponsors them? If no senator has a duty in principle or an institutional responsibility to oppose a bill, namely to present and support a view that differs from the government's view, do we not run the risk of having a debate that is weak, flat or fails to examine all arguments in order to truly circumscribe an issue before bringing it to a vote? In so doing, in fact, aren't we weakening at its root the fundamental role of the Senate, which is to scrutinize all bills from different perspectives?*

*Until now, this opposing role was patterned after the one played by the official opposition in the House of Commons. Of course, the institutional structure of these two*

THE SENATE 150TH ANNIVERSARY MEDAL

Drawing by Lieutenant-Colonel Carl Gauthier, Director, Honours and Recognition, National Defense. The first sitting of the Senate of the new Dominion of Canada took place on 6 November 1867. To mark this anniversary, the Senate arranged for the Royal Canadian Mint to strike a commemorative medal, which has been awarded to Canadians who have volunteered with numerous community organizations and helped to improve the lives of others, relieve poverty, welcome newcomers, encourage tolerance, raise awareness of Canada's historical roots, and promote human dignity. More than 1,000 citizens from every province and territory have received a medal, each bearing the recipient's name on the back.
Credit: Senate of Canada

*chambers is not identical. In the House of Commons, the principle of responsible government requires that there always be a government in waiting to advise Her Majesty – whence the term "Her Majesty's loyal opposition." That being said, there is a vital opposition function to be assumed in the Senate in order to guarantee genuine parliamentary debate, which constitutes the very essence of democratic life. Without such vigorous discourse, there can be no institutional independence. Democracy is founded on the power to debate facts and their interpretation, to defend not an alleged truth but the common good defined by all citizens.[44] The role of political parties, in a system that supports a variety of party allegiances and media voices, is to ensure a plurality of opposing voices within a democratic society.*

*The traditional government versus opposition or majority versus minority structure is required in the House to guarantee this clash of ideas and values. Should the need arise to rely on 105 independent and unaligned senators (whom Sir John A. Macdonald called "loose fish"), however, a certain number of them would have to band together to present and articulate, on a daily basis, opposing views on all matters of public interest debated in the Senate. This dynamic is central to the parliamentary system under the Westminster model, confirmed in the preamble to the Constitution, as interpreted by the Supreme Court of Canada. The Canadian population would expect no less from the so-called "chamber of sober second thought," as it thoroughly examines each bill from all angles or political perspectives and prevents government excesses.*

### 3. TRUE INDEPENDENCE REQUIRES REAL LEGISLATIVE POWER

*Is it possible to want to strengthen the institutional independence of the Senate in order to ensure that bills are subjected to the highest possible level of sober second thought while also claiming, whatever the outcome of this fundamental exercise or the essential nature of any amendments the Senate feels it would be appropriate to make, that the Senate should under all circumstances yield to the elected House of Commons? This argument was put forward by the Government Representative in the Senate in a discussion paper entitled* Complementarity: The Constitutional Role of the Senate of Canada.[45]

*Let us set aside for a moment the underlying strategic objective of this government-issued document, namely how to ensure that independent senators, recommended for appointment at the prime minister's insistence, refrain from exercising their independence too often by amending bills, holding up the work of the Commons and ultimately defeating bills. In other words, faced with the reality and the letter of its discourse on Senate independence, the government is looking for a practical approach or interpretation to limit the manifestation or frame the exercise of such independence, even though it actually represents the very exercise of the Senate's constitutional legislative power. According to the underlying logic of this discussion paper, is this change in the makeup of the Senate really for the better? Is raising the spectre of the democratic nature of the Commons sufficient to keep the Senate in line? Is it really that simple? Upon further analysis, the constitutional considerations are far more complex, nuanced and especially incontrovertible.*

*In our bicameral parliamentary system, legislative power is not concentrated in a single chamber. Rather, it is shared equally between both chambers. This is spelled out clearly in section 91 of* The Constitution Act, 1867,[46] *and was reaffirmed by the Supreme Court of Canada in April 2014. In* The Spirit of Laws, *theorist Montesquieu said as much when he pointed out the need for the existence of counterbalances in a democratic system. Power should never be concentrated in one political place. It should be spread among various units that counterbalance each other to avoid dictatorship by a majority.*

*The Senate is the chamber that embodies the federal principle. The federal nature of the institution was well described by Professor David E. Smith: "The Senate expresses the sum of those other identities the constitutional architects believed essential to acknowledge at the creation of the Confederation."[47] In the legislative process, it is up to the Senate to express and safeguard the views of those "other identities" and the interests of minorities when it refines legislation.*

*The enactment of the* Charter of Rights and Freedoms *in 1982 fundamentally altered the Canadian parliamentary system. The principle of parliamentary supremacy became subject to the rights and freedoms recognized in the Charter, making our system of government one in which constitutional supremacy is predominant. The Supreme Court of Canada reaffirmed this in 2014.[48] In other words, rights and freedoms reign supreme, and the majority elected to the House of Commons no longer has the last word. Prevalence has shifted over to the rights and freedoms enshrined in the Charter. These limits on the legislative activities of the Commons are fundamental, and they must always be taken into account when bills are debated.*

*When studying bills, the Senate has a unique role to play in the expression of this constitutional perspective. Debate in the Senate takes on particular importance when it is viewed through the prism of the Charter and the protection of minority rights and regional interests. This is the very reason for the constitutional existence of the Senate at the core of Parliament's architecture. The Senate essentially speaks for the regions and minorities in this country, and the majority in the House of Commons cannot constitutionally do without it. The Senate's role is to express this perspective. Without the Senate's contribution, the legislative process would be incomplete and any laws stemming therefrom would be flawed in that they would not carry the full weight of the contributions that must be made by both chambers in the legislative process.*

*Seeking to restrict the exercise of legislative power by the Senate because the majority of its members are now independents, and making it, from then on, yield to the House of Commons in all cases, perverts the institution of the bicameral Parliament and threatens the constitutional protection of minority rights and regional interests. A Senate made up entirely of non-partisan independents would always have to yield to the Commons. Under this scenario, as proposed in the government's discussion paper, the legislative process would be diminished and both the spirit and letter of the Constitution would be perverted.*

*Let's look at this from a different perspective. If the Senate's legislative powers are equal to those of the Commons, for what purposes should it use those powers? Ultimately, under what circumstances should the Senate insist upon its amendments being accepted and, in fine, when should it exercise its veto over bills referred to it by the Commons? Because that is the crux of the matter: the Cabinet can always put up with the Senate "chatting," debating and holding "conversations"; but when the Senate opposes a piece of legislation in whole or in part, the Cabinet bristles and brandishes the electoral mandate of the Commons. Should we be surprised? Not in the least. The Senate is a counterweight that has been imposed on the Commons, and the Commons is dominated completely by the government, which has every conceivable weapon at its disposal: a majority in the House of Commons, the impetus of its legislative program and, finally, the ability to cut things off with a guillotine motion. When he was the leader of a second opposition party in 2014, current prime minister Justin Trudeau perceptively acknowledged that the PMO threw all of its weight behind its dominance of the Commons.*

*Since a majority contingent of so-called independent senators (all party or group origins combined) took up residence in the Senate, the red chamber adopted four times more amendments to bills than it did in the previous forty years.[49] The Commons accepted the majority of those amendments. This result is certainly a credit to the hard work of the senators as well as to the will of the government majority in the Commons. However, it is not the only test against which the independence of the Senate must be judged. Rather, the true independence of the Senate and of individual senators is tested when the Commons rejects an amendment.[50]*

*In our bicameral system, the legislative power of the two chambers is shared equally. The role of the House of Commons is to initiate bills and the role of the Senate is to refine them. Hence, the Senate completes the legislative process by ensuring that the views of other identities protected in our federal system and the minority interests it is called upon to represent are given due consideration in debates and incorporated into bills when the Senate deems it essential.*

*Justice Willard Estey of the Supreme Court of Canada, having reflected at length upon the legislative role of the Senate, explained it clearly when he appeared before a Senate committee in March 2000:*

> You [senators] have a duty. I thought pretty hard about this before coming here. The Senate has a senior duty to perform. It has to perfect the process of legislation. That duty must clearly entail, on occasion, an amendment or a refusal or an automatic approval. All three are within your power. Not only are they within your power, they are within your duty. You have to scrutinize this thing and see what is good and bad and purify it. That is why you are here. The second house invariably around the world is set up as a brake on the first level of legislation, but the executive branch tags along all the way up the ladder.[51]

*Justice Estey stressed the Senate's particular constitutional duty in the legislative process. The Senate may amend or even veto a bill. That is its duty, and that is why it has the power to exercise a veto if it so chooses. The Senate's inherent veto power can take different forms within the process of refining legislation. It allows the Senate to revise proposed legislation. It may also be used to negotiate amendments or written commitments from the government regarding the enforcement of a bill. It may also delay the passage of a bill – often to good effect. Ultimately, it can veto a bill, which it does under rare circumstances. We know from various precedents the circumstances in which the Senate's veto or rejection powers have been used in the past. They include instances when a bill:*

- *was seriously prejudicial to one or more regions of the country;*
- *violated the rights and freedoms guaranteed by the Constitution;*
- *compromised collective linguistic rights or minority rights;*
- *was so important to the future of Canada that the government had to request a mandate from the electorate; and*
- *generated so much hostility as to constitute a quasi-abuse of Parliament's legislative power.*[52]

*The current government has not presented any legal argument that would compel the Senate to give up its legislative veto.*

*In the past, the Senate has behaved responsibly. It has not abused its veto power or caused a crisis in the system, There is no valid reason today that might support an argument that it should abandon this power, since it now comprises a large number of independent senators who, in principle at least, are better suited to exercise the legislative powers of the Senate. The Senate's veto power is a constitutional safety valve that guarantees the supremacy of the rule of law in parliamentary process, the continued respect of the federal principle and the protection of rights and freedoms.*

*The fact that the Senate holds real constitutional power in the legislative process guarantees that it will be taken seriously by the Cabinet and the House of Commons, and that debate in the Senate will remain more than just a dilatory step with an always foreseeable outcome. The Senate is not a chamber with a mandate to provide advice and guidance to the Commons. It is not a consultative body placed at the disposal of the Commons. Rather, it is a chamber with real power that it must exercise for specific constitutional purposes. Its independence would be a mere facade if its sole purpose were to fuel a debate with foreseeable conclusions that are devoid of any practical effectiveness – the equivalent of the "suspensive veto" proposed by the leader of the government to assuage independent senators and circumscribe or limit the Senate's exercise of legislative power.*

*Because it has a constitutional duty and real power, the Senate can demand accountability and, if none is forthcoming, use its negotiating power. Through its actions, the Senate may inform the government of its positions of principle on an issue or problem of public interest and thereby lead the government to reconsider its positions. The Senate may also bring about the implementation by the government of corrective measures required with respect to incomplete or ill-considered initiatives. The Senate can also* a posteriori *supervise the establishment of a program to ensure that its recommendations are accepted or carried out.*

*The only particular instance in which the Senate could be persuaded to yield to the Commons, if at all, is when the government has a clear and precise mandate from the electorate to implement a specific measure. This is known as the Salisbury Doctrine,[53] which the Senate has lately embraced (e.g., following the election in which free trade was the central issue in 1988). Even in the context of an election promise, however, if the government's interpretation of the mandate it has received from the electorate leads it to violate any of the provisions of the Charter or the Constitution, the Senate would have ample grounds to protect the rights of an oppressed minority.[54] This actually occurred when a bill was brought before the Senate to cancel a construction contract at Toronto's Pearson International Airport (an election promise) in 1996. The bill in question deprived one of the parties to the contract of recourse before the courts – a clear violation of a right recognized in the Charter. More recently, in 2007, the Senate refused to vote for Bill S-4, a Senate reform bill crafted on the basis of an election promise made by the Conservative Party under Prime Minister Harper, because upon thorough consideration it was thought to be unconstitutional. In fact, the Standing Senate Committee on Legal and Constitutional Affairs recommended "[t]hat the bill, as amended, not be proceeded with at third reading until such time as the Supreme Court of Canada has ruled with respect to its constitutionality."[55] The Senate thus stood in opposition to an election promise because the government proposed to go ahead with it without respecting the provisions of* The Constitution Act, 1982. *Subsequent events confirmed that the Senate was correct in its assessment.*

*According to the Supreme Court of Canada's interpretation of the powers of the Senate,[56] the fundamental role of the Senate is to guarantee the expression of the federal principle and respect for the rights of minorities in the legislative process. The application of the Salisbury Doctrine does not override the principle of constitutional democracy that places the rights and freedoms recognized in the Charter above parliamentary supremacy, and even above the will of the electoral majority, which history teaches us can also be tyrannical. The mere fact that the electorate supports an election promise made by a political party does not allow the government of the day to subvert the constitutional order in order to deliver on that promise. Only by respecting both the letter and spirit of the Constitution can a bill be passed. The Senate has a duty to study a bill rigorously and determine its constitutionality by ascertaining whether it meets the provisions of the Charter and the Constitution. Any thoughts of transforming the powers of the Senate into a simple suspensive veto (similar to that of the British House of Lords) would pervert the federal constitutional order, as defined by the Supreme Court in April 2014. Indeed, the Senate of Canada differs fundamentally from the British House of Lords, which is not a federal chamber and is not subject to a charter of rights and freedoms imposing restrictions on parliamentary supremacy. The Senate has a specific contribution to make in order to validate the legislative process, and that contribution is integral to every bill that passes into law. That is its duty. Any contorted effort to dispense with it subverts the principle of constitutional supremacy that characterizes our federal bicameral system. A legislative conflict between the two chambers must necessarily be resolved through negotiation and, if necessary, by seeking to strike an honourable compromise that is acceptable to both sides, while respecting the rule of law. That is the very essence of our parliamentary system.*

*Any initiative calling into question the Senate's exercise of its constitutional legislative power by transforming it into a "suspensive veto," thereby reducing it to a mere delay before the passage of a bill, goes well beyond the framing of a convention. It would indirectly do what the Constitution prohibits without the expressed consent of the ten provinces, as the Supreme Court concluded in 2014. The Harper government put the question directly to the Supreme Court by asking whether the government could use the so-called 7/50 amendment formula, namely the support of seven provinces representing 50 per cent of the Canadian population, to abolish the legislative power of the Senate. The Court answered no. The unanimous consent of all ten provinces is required to abolish the legislative power of the Senate.[57]*

*In that particular instance, the government's proposal would have the Senate continue in ginving its advice, while eliminating the need for it to consent to legislation contrary to the letter of section 91 of the* Constitution Act, 1867. *Such a limitation of the powers of the Senate, as proposed by the government, is entirely unconstitutional. The Constitution specifically states that the Senate must give both <u>its advice and consent</u>, which are two separate elements, before a bill may receive royal assent.*

*In 1992, the Charlottetown Accord "converted" the Senate's legislative power into a "suspensive veto." Under the terms of that accord, a formal constitutional amendment would have been required to make this change. Today, the government representative in*

On Thursday, 25 May and Friday, 26 May 2017, the Senate held a symposium in the chamber to mark the 150th anniversary of Confederation. It invited twenty-one Canadians noted for their work and their community involvement to share their thoughts on Canada's development since its centenary in 1967 and on its opportunities for the future. In doing so, the Senate exercised its special role as a chamber of sober second thought that is inclusive and responsive to diverse interests of the Canadian population. The event was rebroadcast on the parliamentary channel.

Photo: Governor General David L. Johnston at the podium and, to his right, the Hon. George J. Furey, Q.C., Speaker of the Senate, and the Rt. Hon. Michaëlle Jean, former governor general; next row: the Hon. Serge Joyal, P.C., Senator and symposium coordinator, and the Hon. Judith Seidman, Senator and symposium advisor; next row: the Hon. Claudette Tardif and the Hon. René Cormier, Senators and session chairpersons. Credit: Senate of Canada

*the Senate would like to achieve a similar result in practice without the formal amendment procedure. This proposal is directly counter to the interests of the smaller regions of the country, whose voice is protected within the very structure of the Senate, lending strength and vigour to the federal principle. For these basic reasons, linked to the very nature of our system of government, this interpretation of the powers of the Senate cannot stand.*

*While the prime minister sought to subject his traditional power of recommendation of senators to an external evaluation in order that he might select only candidates without political affiliation and thus enhance the independence of the Senate while making it less partisan – a commendable objective – he cannot then seek to indirectly alter the Senate's constitutional legislative power without calling into question the federal principle at the very heart of its existence. The Supreme Court, which is the "guardian of the Constitution," has already clearly identified the principles that must be respected when it comes to redefining the legislative power of the Senate. The Constitution exists for specific reasons, and we have no alternative but to respect it. Our very freedom, as guaranteed by the rule of law, hangs in the balance.*

*Canada is a society in which the diversity of ethnic origins and religious antecedents is growing rapidly, and in which Indigenous representatives will be called upon to play an unprecedented role in guiding the ship of State. This diversity creates risks of tensions and even confrontations that are inevitable when people of many distinct cultures, languages, histories, religious beliefs and ways of life are asked to live together as minorities that continue to flourish. The Senate is the chamber of Parliament where all of these dynamic forces can be reconciled in their ongoing efforts to coexist harmoniously within the fabric of Canadian society in the years to come.*

*The Senate is here to stay, and it will benefit all Canadians by protecting the federal principle. Parliamentary bicameralism is not an easy system to live by. It must be understood in its essence and all of its nuances before we can consider tinkering with it, even with the best of intentions.*

### NOTES

1  The author is indebted to the Library of Parliament of Canada for its meticulous work in checking the accuracy of the figures and historical facts contained in this text.

2  *Reference re Senate Reform*, 2014 SCC 32.

3  Curry, Bill, "Party control on Parliament Hill is getting tighter, former MPs warn," *The Globe and Mail*, 12 June 2018, p. A6.

4  The amendment to section 29 of the *Constitution Act, 1867*, was passed in 1965.

5  Griffith, Andrew, "Diversity in the Senate," *Policy Options*, 14 February 2017; Joyal, Serge, ed., *Protecting Canadian Democracy – The Senate You Never Knew*, Appendix Part C – Social Diversity, McGill-Queen's University Press (MQUP), 2003.

6  Robert Bourassa's Quebec government ultimately refused to sign off on the *Victoria Charter* because it did not recognize the legislative primacy of the provinces in the area of social affairs.

7  *Re: Authority of Parliament in relation to the Upper House*, [1980] 1 SCR 54.

8  *Constitution Act, 1982*, ss. 41(e) and 44.

9  The author participated in these discussions at the time.

10  *Reference re Senate Reform,* 2014 SCC 32.

11  *The Constitution Act, 1982*, s. 47.

12  *1987 Constitutional Accord, Schedule – Constitution Amendment 1987*, s. 2(2), 3 June 1987.

13  Manitoba's legislature failed to adopt the resolution of assent, as per section 39(2) of the *Constitution Act, 1982*, and Newfoundland and Labrador did not put the resolution to a vote in its House of Assembly.

14  Senator Betty Kennedy was appointed in June 2000 and retired in January 2001.

15  The Liberal opposition held a majority in the Senate until January 2010.

16  Thirteenth Report of the Standing Senate Committee on Legal and Constitutional Affairs, 12 June 2007.

17  The author intervened before the Quebec Court of Appeal and the Supreme Court of Canada to present constitutional arguments based on his practical experience of the Senate.

18  *Reference re Senate Reform*, 2014 SCC 32, para. 77.

19  Except when it comes to appropriation and tax bills and other money votes. See: *The Constitution Act, 1867,* ss. 53 and 54.

20  As of 9 August 2018.

21  Jordan Press, "Auditor general Michael Ferguson breaks down $23M cost of Senate audit," 10 June, 2015, *CBC News,* article accessed online on 1 August 2017 (https://www.cbc.ca/news/politics/auditor-general-michael-ferguson-breaks-down-23m-cost-of-senate-audit-1.3108276).

22  An additional $508,243 was wiped off the Senate books, representing the total of seven claims involving already retired senators. Source: Pierre Lanctôt, CPA, CA, Chief Financial Officer, Finance and Procurement Directorate, Senate of Canada, 9 August 2018.

23  Michael S. Roth, "Against Progress," *The New York Times* Book Review, 12 August 2018.

24  *Senate Modernization: Moving Forward – Part II,* Interim Report of the Special Senate Committee on Senate Modernization, April 2018, p. 16.

25  Jan-Werner Müller, *Qu'est-ce que le populisme? – Définir enfin la menace* (Premier Parallèle, 2016), p. 57, 69, and 80.

26  Brian Myles, "Élections 2018 : retrouver le sens de l'action civique," *Le Devoir*, 23 August 2018.

27  Simon Langlois, "Le cinquième pouvoir et la liberté des créateurs," *Le Devoir*, 20 August 2018, p. A7.

28  Roger Scruton, *Conservatism – An Invitation to the Great Tradition* (New York: St-Martin's Press, 2018).

29  Samantha Wright Allen, "Lobbying spikes in 'wild card' Senate as groups target new independents", *Hill Times*, 24 January 2018.

30  Peter Mazereeuw, "Lobbyists get to 'much time' in the Senate committees says ISG deputy ahead of back-to-parliament meeting", *Hill Times*, 22 January 2018.

31  For reasons of transparency, the cited report shows that the author had no contact with lobbyists.

32  Éric Grenier, "Why the Senate is unpredictable – and its independents not so independent," *CBC News*, article accessed online on 19 June 2017.

33  "ISG leaders defend Senate Independents from 'fake news' voting stats," in Charelle, Evelyn, "ISG chief of staff named, membership charter to be developed in fall," *The Hill Times*, 27 June 2018. Article accessed online on 26 July 2018 (https://www.hilltimes.com/2018/06/27/isg-leaders-defend-role-voting-record-independent-faction-senate/149139).

34  Evelyn Charelle and Samantha Wright Allen, "Independent Senators still most likely to vote with government, but less and less," *The Hill Times*, 25 July 2018 (https://www.hilltimes.com/2018/07/25/independent-senator-voting-shifts-away-liberal-rep-isg-still-likely-allies-152033-152033/152033).

35  "'Mieux vaut laisser la Constitution en son état' dit Justin Trudeau," *Le Devoir*, 19 January 2018, p. A3.

36  According to the study conducted by *The Hill Times,* the author supported government bills 71.7 per cent of the time, and Senator Percy Downe did so 69.7 per cent of the time.

37  Joan Bryden, "Trudeau boots senators from Liberal caucus in bid to restore Senate independence," The Canadian Press, 29 January 2014.

38  Andrew Griffith, "Diversity in the Senate," *Policy Options*, 14 February 2017.

39  Evelyn Charelle and Samantha Wright Allen, "Independent Senators still most likely to vote with government, but less and less," *The Hill Times*, 25 July 2018 (https://www.hilltimes.com/2018/07/25/independent-senator-voting-shifts-away-liberal-rep-isg-still-likely-allies-152033-152033/152033).

40  Dale Smith, *The Unbroken Machine* (Toronto: Dundurn, 2017), p. 109.

41  Senator Francis Lankin was an Ontario Member of Provincial Parliament (MPP) and served as a Cabinet minister in Ontario's NDP government from 1990 to 1995. A former municipal government official was also appointed to the Senate: Senator Éric Forest was Mayor of Rimouski from 2005 to 2016.

42  David E. Smith, *The Constitution in a Hall of Mirrors – Canada at 150*, (Toronto: University of Toronto Press, 2017), p. 70.

43  *Reference re Alberta Statutes*, [1938] SCR 100, 133 (per Duff).

44  Natacha Polony, "Démocratie sous (bienveillant) contrôle," *Le Figaro*, 6–7 January 2018, p. 15.

45 Hon. Peter Harder, *Sober Second Thinking: How the Senate Deliberates and Decides*, Office of the Government Representative in the Senate, 31 March 2017, 21 p. Hon. Peter Harder, *Complementarity: The Constitutional Role of the Senate of Canada*, Office of the Government Representative in the Senate, 12 April, 51 p.

46 The opening clause of section 91 of *The Constitution Act, 1867*, establishes that it "shall be lawful for the Queen, by and with the Advice and Consent of the Senate and House of Commons, to make Laws for the Peace, Order, and good Government of Canada, [...]."

47 David E. Smith, *The Constitution in a Hall of Mirrors – Canada at 150* (Toronto: University of Toronto Press, 2017), p. 53.

48 *Reference re Supreme Court Act, ss. 5 and 6*, 2014 SCC 21, [2014] 1SCR 433, para. 89.

49 Elaine McCoy, (Senator), "Why a more Independent Senate is working better for Canadians," *Macleans.ca*, 21 August 2017.

50 In a crucial vote in June 2016 on the amendments to Bill C-14, the Senate independents voted against a motion to have the Senate insist that the Commons keep the amendments determining access to physician-assisted dying according to the criteria set out by the Supreme Court of Canada in *Carter*, and the motion was defeated. The only independent senator who voted in favour of the motion was Senator Meredith, a former Conservative senator.

51 *Proceedings of the Standing Senate Committee on Aboriginal Peoples*, Thursday, 23 March 2000, Bill C-9, An Act to give effect to the Nisga'a Final Agreement.

52 Serge Joyal, ed., *Protecting Canadian Democracy – The Senate You Never Knew*, MQUP, Montréal, 2003.

53 Named for the fifth Marquess of Salisbury, who was the Leader of the Conservative opposition in the British House of Lords while the Labour government of Clement Atlee was in power from 1945 to 1951. Under the Salisbury Doctrine, also known as the "Salisbury Convention," the House of Lords will not try to vote down at second or third reading a government bill mentioned in the election platform of the party in power. See: www.parliament.uk.

54 David E. Smith, , *The Canadian Senate in Bicameral Perspective*, 2003, p. 169, cited by the Supreme Court of Canada in *Reference re Senate Reform*, 2014 SCC 32, para. 59.

55 Thirteenth Report of the Standing Senate Committee on Legal and Constitutional Affairs, 12 June 2007.

56 *Reference re Senate Reform*, 2014 SCC 32, paras. 25 to 27 on the importance of federalism and protecting the rights of minorities in the constitutional order. See also: *Reference re Secession of Quebec*, [1998] 2 SCR, paras. 55 to 82.

57 *Reference re Senate Reform*, 2014 SCC 32, pp. 709–10.

# Whither the Senate at 150?

David E. Smith, distinguished visiting scholar at Ryerson University

In *Two Cheers for Democracy*, British author E.M. Forster advanced the proposition that "only what is seen sideways sinks in."[1] While it is unlikely that Forster had the Senate of Canada in mind when he made that observation, the comment offers a revealing perspective on an institution that is perennially criticized on grounds devoid of either constitutional substance or logic. In consequence, debate about the Senate has made little progress in effecting change or improving public understanding of the place of the upper house in the constitution. By contrast, it is of incontestable importance to the condition of the Senate today that the determining events at the present moment were, first, the decision of the current prime minister (Justin Trudeau) to establish an independent process to secure nominations of individuals to be recommended by him to the governor general for appointment and, second, the advisory opinion given by the Supreme Court of Canada in 2014 on the initiative of Trudeau's predecessor (Stephen Harper) to introduce consultative elections to nominate senators as well as establish terms to their appointment.[2] In other words, the consequential change that the Senate and Parliament, more generally, are at the present time experiencing has taken place as a result of actions outside the focus of everyday politics. Here in Canadian political terms, and as regards the Senate, may be an example of the type of oblique angle to which Forster's dictum speaks.

The Senate has never been perceived, by academics or the public, to be part of the mainstream of Canadian politics. It is important to understand why this is so if the change, which this paper argues has slowly emerged over the past fifty years and which is now accelerating, is to be appreciated. The heart of the explanation lies in the story of responsible government secured by colonial elected assemblies at the expense of appointed governors and legislative councils. (Parenthetically, it should be stressed, the prerogative power of the Crown has not contracted very much; it has been brought under the control of responsible ministers – a very different matter.) Before the victories of Robert Baldwin, Louis-Hippolyte Lafontaine, and Joseph Howe, appointed legislative bodies were viewed as restraints that distorted the public will expressed through the lower house; after the victories, they were viewed much the same way, except in United Canada, which with its territorially concentrated religious and linguistic populations distrusted the majoritarian premise that sustained the ideal of responsible government. To quote (or misquote) another English writer, this time William Wordsworth: if "the child is father of the man," politically, in British North America, the colony established in 1840 became father of the country after 1867, for its lineage remains on view in the federation to this day.

The orientation of Canadian politics after the mid-eighteen-forties was, one might say, "full-frontal" responsible government. Second chambers were deemed suspect and, even worse, dangerous for the latent threat they posed to parliamentary democracy. Only five provinces ever had second chambers, with Quebec's being the last to be abolished, in 1968. At Confederation, Ontario, then the most populous settler colony in the British Empire, and one highly British in its values, opted for a unicameral legislature. In sum, and outside the narrow lens of federalism, there has never been a popular attitude toward bicameralism in Canada, a disposition repeatedly demonstrated in debates over Senate reform of the past quarter century: the more the detail of bicameralism was revealed, the more, not less, remote the concept (and its institutional expression in Canada) seemed. It was for this reason that roles were invented for the upper house. Customarily over the last fifty years, these cited as their putative object remedying the problems of Canadian federalism. The Reform Party's advocacy of a "Triple-E" Senate (elected, equal, and effective) and studies promoting institutions reminiscent of Germany's Bundesrat to facilitate intrastate federalism, such as that written by Donald V. Smiley and Ronald L. Watts in *Intrastate Federalism in Canada*,[3] serve as illustrations. This is not the time or place to enter into an analysis of the intricacies of Triple-E, except to note that from its proponents' viewpoint the executive appeared as separate from the legislature, in an arrangement congressional in character. What might be said about this line of thinking is that it posited the relationship of legislature and executive as adversarial rather than parliamentary, where government sits in the legislature and is accountable to it. The relevance of that observation is that attitudes about the role and function of the House of Commons implicitly inform positions adopted toward the Senate. Thus, proposals for reform of the upper house have been based less on theories than on fractions of theories, often derived from political practices found in the constitutions of other countries. In consequence, much of the literature on the Senate of the last five decades has proved rich in rhetoric but poor in practice.

The same point might be advanced when a very different model is cited, that of the House of Lords. The preamble of Constitution Act, 1867, speaks of the desire of the colonies of British North America "to be federally united … with a Constitution similar in Principle to that of the United Kingdom." Therefore, it was perhaps to be expected that analogies would be drawn between the upper houses of the two countries, even though those countries were very different – one an historic island empire and the other a continent-wide country of settlement. Until well into the twentieth century, the House of Lords was a chamber comprised of hereditary members on whose numbers there was no upper limit. Canadian senators were fixed both in terms of total numbers and among divisions. Although senators initially were appointed for life, after 1965, retirement age was set at seventy-five. From the perspective of the present century, the notable contrast between the two parliamentary upper houses is that the powers of the Senate remain as they were set down in the Constitution Act, 1867, which is to say equal to those of the House of Commons except in the matter of appropriations, while those of the Lords have been constrained since the Parliament Act of 1911 (and further constrained by an amendment to that act in 1949) to a suspensive veto. In the mind of a scholar such as William Riker of the United States, the suspensive veto results in functional unicameralism, where Britain's "one-house legislature" is run by its "executive committee."[4]

One may argue the merits of a suspensive veto placed on a parliamentary upper chamber, and no doubt more will be heard on the subject in Canada, as witness a recent paper that advances this proposal, produced by former senators Michael Kirby and Hugh Segal for Canada's Public Policy Forum, "A House Undivided: Making the Senate Work."[5] In Britain, the serial expansion of the franchise after the Reform Act of 1832 and into the twentieth century created a House of Lords "problem": what was its purpose once political power became firmly lodged in the House of Commons?[6] I do not intend to be disrespectful to the history or present work of the House of Lords when I say that today the Lords is a vestigial chamber. In this respect, which is not to depreciate the substantial contribution it makes to the legislative process of the Parliament at Westminster – for it demonstrably does make such a contribution - the Lords is secondary to the Commons. Such cannot be said of the Senate – although, in fact, that is said rather frequently, but it is an incorrect evaluation. In its Reference Opinion in 2014, the Supreme Court of Canada clearly enunciated cardinal characteristics that inform the Senate's work and structure, among which are federalism, bicameralism, and independence. The history of the Westminster parliament over the last century underlines the inapplicability of using the same words to describe the activities of its upper house.

Unlike the borrowed governmental models that informed earlier discussions of upper chamber reform, the Supreme Court invoked no comparative exemplar in its analysis of the questions submitted to it. On the contrary, it spoke frequently of the Senate as "one of Canada's foundational political institutions" and the implications that the proposed changes in the term and selection of senators would have for the "Constitution's architecture." Critics of the court's language in these passages described it as "a delicate construct … conjured … out of the air."[7] The architectural metaphor was deemed inauthentic, when in fact the language the Court employed was not inauthentic but unfamiliar. It was not a metaphor in the sense of being like something else or about something. What the court offered was new imagery of Canada's constitution as it touched on two of the three parts of Parliament. It is not a common architectural façade that joins the two legislative chambers, but rather a common responsibility to produce good legislation for the people of Canada. Significantly, in light of the subject of this symposium, which is to mark the 150th anniversary of Confederation by assessing specific themes and how they have developed over the past half century, the crucial role the court ascribed for the Senate in its 2014 judgment had been signalled more than thirty years earlier (1980) in another opinion: *Reference Re: Legislative Authority of Parliament in Relation to the Upper House.*[8] At issue there was the Pierre Trudeau government's Constitutional Amendment Bill C-60 of 1978, which, among other objects, proposed a House of the Federation in place of the Senate. The members of the new house were to be selected by provincial legislative assemblies and the House of Commons. A position paper accompanying the bill suggested that the constitution could explicitly state that the government was "not formally obliged to command the second chamber's confidence," and Bill C-60 also provided for a suspensive veto of not more than 120 days over ordinary legislation. When doubt was expressed about whether Parliament possessed the power unilaterally to alter the composition of the upper chamber, the answer from the Supreme Court, whose opinion had been sought, was "No." Most significantly, the reason proffered by the court for its judgment was that "a primary purpose of the creation of the Senate, as part of the federal legislative process, was … to afford protection to the various sectional interests in Canada *in relation to the enactment of legislation.*"[9]

Once again, and adapting the language of William Riker, here is a striking contrast with Great Britain: rather than emulating the Lords' slow erosion of power into functional unicameralism, the Senate of Canada appears to be moving toward an enunciated, and perhaps in time robust, functional bicameralism. How to account for this contrasting development between the two countries and, indeed, if one compares past analyses of the Senate, such as the studies by Robert MacKay and F.A. Kunz, how to account for the sense of institutional metamorphosis apparent at the present time in Canada?[10]

One answer to that question may be stated negatively: it is not the result of a sudden reversal in popularity, for the reputation of the least reputable senator still goes far in determining the reputation of the chamber. It is a cardinal feature of the Senate, but not one the Supreme Court of Canada singled out for discussion, that, when compared to the Commons, it is isolated from the public. Unelected, senators have no constituents, as members of Parliament do, nor do they have constituencies smaller than the senatorial divisions provided for in section 22 of the Constitution

THE SENATE CHAMBER

This magnificent chamber creates an atmosphere of respect and decorum felt by everyone who enters it: at the north end, the thrones of the sovereign and consort stand on a majestic dais below the bust of Queen Victoria, who was Canada's sovereign in 1867. In front of the thrones and overlooking the Clerk's Table is the Senate Speaker's chair. On the table rests the mace, representing "the Queen in Parliament." Above the galleries on either side of the chamber are eight large paintings depicting major events during the First World War in which Canada for the first time played its part among the free and democratic nations of the world. Credit: Senate of Canada

Act, 1867. The exception to that statement is that there are twenty-four "electoral divisions" in Quebec, from each of which a senator is appointed. Here is but one example of the hold of United Canada's history on twenty-first-century Canada. Despite their generally longer tenure in office than MPs, senators are largely unknown to the public, an anonymity that until recently was accentuated by a process of partisan appointment. Add to that genesis the disparate length in office between an appointed senator and the prime minister who nominated him or her, and the senator may be viewed as unmoored from the contemporary political scene as he or she is from the public. Whatever else may be said of the newly instituted independent appointment procedure, it is the case that the sense of senatorial appointments as an afterlife of an earlier administration is disappearing.

Recent criticisms of the upper house – for example, the controversy over senatorial expenses – have deflected attention from claims the Senate may legitimately make for support. One of these criticisms, ironically, is a corrective to the exercise (albeit a less-than-pure exercise) of the principle of representation-by-population in the Commons. It is a well-known story that one of the major motivations promoting Confederation was to establish a constitutional system that would recognize Upper Canada's bourgeoning population but at the same time would protect those parts of the new arrangement (Lower Canada and any other colonies that joined) from being swamped in the democratic tide to follow. Here was the explanation for the Senate in the form it eventually took, in George-Étienne Cartier's words: "The count of heads must not always be permitted to outweigh every other consideration."[11] To argue, as former MP Patrick Boyer does in his recent book, *Our Scandalous Senate*, that the "appointed chamber [constitutes] an honourable creation story," and that it is no different from any of the other terms of the Quebec resolutions depreciates the central place of the Senate.[12] Nor does it acknowledge that the Senate's function as a counterweight to rep-by-pop did not end at the Quebec conference. In 1915, and in response to pressure from the Maritime provinces, an amendment to the Constitution Act, 1867, added section 51A, which said in effect that no province should have fewer members in the House of Commons than it had senators. Thus, a relationship was created between the two chambers of Parliament, one that continues today – indeed, the nexus established in 1915 became one of the five subjects for which the Constitution Act, 1982, requires unanimous consent to amend. Certainly, it helps explain the positions Canada's smaller provinces have adopted on the various schemes to reform the Senate over the years, and explains why, even if the Senate were abolished, it would not be possible to abolish the reasons why there is a Senate.

In the absence of constitutional intervention, the number of members small provinces have in the Senate is an assurance of a parliamentary voice for them, which each decennial redistribution of Commons seats lessens. Following the 2011 census, the total number of Commons seats increased by thirty, with fifteen going to Ontario, six each to British Columbia and Alberta, and three to Quebec. For the other six provinces, their comparative position in the lower chamber declined. Thus, from the perspective of arithmetic, the rationale for the Senate grows stronger and supports the Supreme Court's statement in 2014 that it provides a "distinct form of representation for the regions."[13] In the matter of numbers, it is worth noting that there is a very big difference in the size of the two chambers, 105 seats in the upper house versus 338 seats in the lower, and in their contrasting trajectories of growth. In 1917, the Commons had 235 seats; in 1974, the number was 264; and in 2015, 338. In other words, in the last century the House has increased roughly by the size of the Senate. In the same period, the Senate grew by just nine seats, with the inclusion of members from the northern territories and Newfoundland and Labrador. A variation on the theme of small provinces' voice in the upper house is the matter of the representation of minorities, be they ethnic, religious, or linguistic, in the Senate. Even when the subject concerns parliamentary representation of official languages, the Senate makes more audible at the centre the voice of French-speaking Canadians from those parts of the country where they do not comprise a majority of the population. In a 2007 study commissioned by the Office of the Commissioner of Official Languages, political scientist Louis Massicotte concluded that "official language minority communities have little to gain but much to lose if the selection process for senators is amended [that is, replacing appointment with election]." He noted that "official language minority communities are proportionately *better represented* [emphasis in original] in the Senate than in the House of Commons."[14] Two reasons explain the contrast between the chambers. First, senators are appointed on the recommendation of prime ministers, who, whether Liberal or Conservative, have treated the appointment of French-speaking senators (and not only from Quebec) as important. Second, MPs are elected, and in the absence of a territorial concentration of French-speaking voters – as occurs in New Brunswick and parts of Manitoba and Ontario – it is unlikely that French-speaking candidates will be elected.

The House of Commons might be expected to represent smallness because of the multitude and variety of its constituencies, but political party discipline obliterates localism – as it always has. The smaller, complementary, but free-of-constituency-accountability Senate is better positioned to articulate specific concerns whether or not rooted in geography. Again, the Commons is highly polarized in an era when the public is more pluralistic and volatile in party affiliation. According to Michael Adams in his 2014 Environics study *AmericasBarometer*, more than half the population had been active in the previous year signing petitions, sharing political information online, and participating in demonstrations and protest marches.[15] Political activity on the internet is growing rapidly, especially on social media, where it is most popular among younger Canadians. Those under the age of thirty are more than twice as likely (45 per cent) to use social media for political expression than those sixty years of age and over (19 per cent).

A number of reasons may be offered for this development. One relevant to the present discussion is a heightened belief in the need for real and perceived fairness and a resulting transformation in the sense of what rules should look like. Australian scholar Judith Brett has stated that people do not like the tone of parliamentary conflict: "For those experienced with the modern informal meeting and its consensual style of reaching a decision, parliamentary procedure is no longer seen as enabling but as precluding cooperative action."[16] There is a sharp contrast here between what might be termed a permissive view of organizing the public forum and the long, unchallenged authority of *Robert's Rules of Order* and the atmosphere required for its application. An example of the contrast is given by Sir George Ross, a former premier of Ontario and later a senator, in his autobiography: "[As a young man] I associated myself with a division of the 'Sons of Temperance' … The business of the division was conducted according to well-defined rules of procedure and debate, which gave it an air of dignity and self-restraint not unlike a parliament in miniature."[17] Parenthetically, it should be noted that Ross was the author of one of the earliest full-length studies of the upper house, *The Senate of Canada: Its Constitution, Powers and Duties, Historically Considered*,[18] and that he was an advocate of a suspensive veto of the House-of-Lords variant for Canada. In his opinion, the Canadian constitution had "more in harmony with the British constitution than that of any dependency beyond the sea."[19] The research of Michael Adams demonstrates that Brett's observation is not confined to Australia: "Half of Canadians (50 per cent) strongly agree with the statement: 'Political parties should allow MPs to vote in Parliament according to what they believe is right, even if it is not consistent with their party's position, with very few (six per cent) who strongly disagree.'"[20]

The dominion of the Senate derives from the chamber being accessible and scrupulous in the conduct of its legislative work (consider, and compare to the House of Commons, the breadth of its examination of the Fair Elections Act in 2014). Embracing these qualities, the Senate acts as a bridge to the public, whose concerns most often are not political so much as they are concerns about the workplace, family, religion, health, diversity, and citizenship. To that list of familiar topics may more recently be added civic issues that defy traditional jurisdictional compartments: science, the environment, and culture. These are not constituency or regional issues as those terms are generally understood. Still, they serve to thicken the network of Canadians interested in the activity of the upper chamber. There is another reason to see the Senate's contribution to bicameralism benignly: regional politics often tells us about ourselves more faithfully and more accurately than do the electoral returns from the constituencies or the nation. This is because region is more than a geographic expression. That is why the Senate is such a useful sounding board for cultural, professional, and social interests, among others, that are not territorially rooted: children, the elderly, the poor (rural and urban), the sick and dying are but examples of the demographic heterogeneity that constituency and even provincial profiles inadequately convey.

Like the country it serves, the Senate has demonstrated a capacity for adaptation. Over the past half century it is in such areas as these where the Senate has established a strong reputation for competence and responsiveness. Senate reports on the media (Davey), health care (Kirby, Nolin, and Carstairs), poverty (Croll), and agriculture and soil erosion (Sparrow) demonstrate the upper chamber's wide and deep capacity to review the social, cultural, economic, and international issues that reflect the concerns of a diversity of Canadian communities. On these and more general matters the Senate regularly invites experts to give evidence. Although the committee work of the Senate is invariably lauded by media, academics, and the public, the scope of that activity and the sense of access to its proceedings deserve close study. Indicative of its volume, for instance, are data in the annual Senate Report on Activities for the period between 2008–09 and 2012–13, which reveal over 2,300 committee meetings to have taken place with more than six thousand witnesses in attendance, and which produced roughly five hundred committee reports.[21]

Comparing the present moment to the first century of Confederation, it is clear that over the last half century a conjunction of concerns that play to the Senate's strength and capabilities has emerged. Nowhere is this more evident than in the acute sensitivity the Senate has displayed in its handling of issues that fall within the scope of the Canadian Charter of Rights and Freedoms. It has applied itself in rigorously measuring the impact of bills and government decisions on the rights and freedoms of Canadians – for example, on criminal justice for adolescents, the extradition of people to countries that have the death penalty, the need to control agencies responsible for the fight against terrorism, labour union freedoms, access to physician-assisted dying, and the legalization of cannabis. Debates in the Senate on such issues are more intense and probing than in the House of Commons, and thus allow senators to discern more acutely the long-term implications of policy for Canadian society.

Understanding the factors behind the broader issues that Canada is facing requires time, attention, and sustained interest. The duration of senators' mandates, which last far longer than the life of a single Parliament, encourages them to devote attention to the study of issues and thus assume responsibility to the public. It calls upon their judgment, wisdom, and life experience to help establish public policies that support the country's prosperity, improve the living conditions of Canadians, and ensure the country's ability to adapt to the challenges of a constantly changing world. The Senate is in a better position than the Commons to speak of the shared lived-experiences of the people of Canada no matter where they reside, because it has the potential and perspective to engage the interests of modern Canadians, who are less set than preceding generations in their partisan loyalties. John Stuart Mill argued that people are represented only if they think they are represented. Surveys repeatedly demonstrate that people believe the Commons is ineffective in representing them, particularly in holding government to account. Under a system of parliamentary government, the Senate must never replace the Commons and hold government responsible, but it may make government more responsive and, in that respect, help moderate public cynicism about politicians and the constitution.

There is no question but that senators possess qualities and the chamber itself resources to bring a perspective to public policy matters that is attractive to Canadians. In this encomium for the upper chamber, it is not my intent to disparage the Commons. Its claim to authority derives from the long – longer than Confederation – practice of enforcing responsible government. That achievement, warts and all, makes Canadian democracy the envy of many countries around the world. Still, there is also no question, in light of the Supreme Court's ruling in 2014 and following upon the change in senatorial nomination procedure now in effect, but that Canadian parliamentary government is entering a new era in which bicameralism must be viewed through other than the narrow lens of federalism. The maxims of Canadian politics are in the process of changing. The Senate is not just a second chamber but rather one equal part of a Parliament consisting of two chambers. The long-standing, and now clichéd, critique of the Senate as unelected and therefore lacking authority in its actions and opinions must change if Parliament is to function as a unity.

Andrew Coyne, by any measure an informed observer of Canadian politics, has recently written that "all that matters, as far as democratic government is concerned, is who has a democratic mandate, and who has not."[22] Yet recent events in Canada suggest that such a narrow interpretation of governmental practice tilts toward the antique. Opinion of this nature reminds one of Samuel Beckett's comment in his play *Endgame*: "The old questions, the old answers – there is nothing like them." But no longer. The Senate came about not, as Patrick Boyer implies, like the Intercolonial Railway, as a bargaining piece to secure agreement on the Quebec Resolutions, but as a body that provides continuing – sectional, regional, or divisional – compensation in a political system that acknowledges representation of population as a foundational principle of the constitution. Note, however, "a," not "sole," foundational principle. Otherwise, as noted at the outset, the disposition to look straight ahead, never to broaden one's perspective, induces a rigidity that is in conflict with Canada's adaptability verified each day in its economy, society, and plural culture.

I do not intend to trespass on Professor Docherty's lower-house terrain, except to note that the growth of party discipline in the House of Commons continues apace, and not only, as critics would have it, because of an insatiable thirst for power among leaders of all parties. In a new study of Canadian politics in an age of electronic communication, political scientist Alex Marland argues that "communication technology combined with institutional structures provides rulers – chiefly party leaders, senior cabinet ministers, and particularly the prime minister – with growing opportunities to have their way with parliamentarians."[23]

Much has changed in the three centuries since the rise of opposition as a component of Parliament's architecture. Indeed, one might say that much has changed in the last three decades. The iron discipline of party in the Commons and the entrenchment of the Prime Minister's Office (PMO) as guardians of government are predictable features of most accounts of Canadian politics today. Nor is Canada a solitary example of the phenomena, as British academics Andrew Blick and George Jones have demonstrated about the politics of the United Kingdom.[24] Yet, notwithstanding the familiarity of the argument, what might be called the interstices of control have received superficial examination. This neglect appears to be in the process of being remedied, however – and with ramifications for the Senate. "Branding," a variation on the more familiar tool of marketing in general, is as much a feature of politics today as it is of commerce and for many of the same reasons, especially in the field of communications: "Advocates of constituency representation underappreciate how forcefully communications technology shines the spotlight on party leaders and on any hint of group division."[25]

Unexpectedly, Marland asserts that "the Senate holds the most promise for the people's representatives to challenge the PMO's influence." More than that, he perceives "the public demand for that outdated institution to hold the political executive and permanent government to account [will] grow with the diffusion of communications technology."[26] In short, need and opportunity conspire to raise the Senate's visibility and legitimacy in modern Canada. The question that occasions the present commentary and which preoccupies Senate discussion today is how to operate the chamber in a situation where the consequences of the change in nomination practices for senators are no longer hypothetical but rather concrete. That this *is* the issue is indisputable, and the reason why it must be tackled is the one to which some senators have alluded: in light of oppressive party discipline in the Commons, the only real debate happens in the Senate. If the dialectic of parliamentary politics ultimately leads to a need to choose, and if party discipline suffocates meaningful choice in the lower chamber, then it rests with the complementary upper house to assure that real debate takes place on issues of national importance to the citizens of Canada. The imperative of the executive and the party discipline that makes that possible are detrimental to the House of Commons' fulfilling the functions that theories of parliamentary government assign it. By contrast, and stated most simply, the Senate of Canada is free of such constraints, as it is free of the gradations – backbench versus frontbench, for example – that characterize the Commons.

It is heartening to see recent assessments of the Senate's activities and membership adopt a more favourable tone than in the past, although it would be misleading to think revisionism is universal. Nor is it academics alone who speak less critically than they once did. It is not difficult to find statements from the public supportive of the work of senators during the debate on C-14 (Medical Assistance in Dying) in 2016. On that bill and on legislative participation generally, the public – and equally important, the media – have come to see and appreciate the crucial contribution the Senate can make to the passage of good legislation. All the more reason then, as the Senate traces its way along un-blazed organizational trails, to make haste cautiously. The most famous line in Giuseppe di Lampedusa's *The Leopard*,[27] a story of the Risorgimento in Italy, is the following: "If we want things to stay as they are, things will have to change." The conundrum articulated in that declaration is similar to the one that now faces senators: how to maintain the constitutional architecture intact (as regards the Senate) while at the same time incorporating structural alterations to accommodate change for which there is no blueprint?

Resorting to metaphors is a sure sign that a writer may be losing his way in the argument being advanced. And that is true when there is no right or, at the very least, obvious answer to the question posed. That question is how, in the new, non-binary world of independent, Liberal, and Conservative senators, is the chamber to organize its activities? My (to be personal) response is that the more immediate matter to study is not to answer to the query "How should the Senate organize it activities?" but rather to consider closely what it is senators think they should do in their capacity as members of

Parliament's upper chamber, and then develop mechanisms to enable them to accomplish that end. For instance, if as has been suggested, the Senate has a role as an organ of opposition at a time when the executive, and party discipline more generally, suffocate opposition in the Commons, how is that enterprise to be facilitated? Earlier the point was made that giving speeches is a central activity of Parliament in all its manifestations. But speech-making is about more than talking. It requires listeners and critics if it is to have an effect. That is a vital function of a caucus free of dictation. Caucus offers a forum where debate and analysis of proposed legislation may occur and be improved as a result of scrutiny. The result of caucus deliberations and informed debate, where arguments for and against whatever motion or subject is before the chamber are advanced, is a record of opinion which thereafter may be consulted, indeed cited, as in courts. The central question is how to organize the Senate's business so this function of the chamber – the free expression of informed opinion – is performed expeditiously and beneficially in the service of Canadian citizens.

It is at this point where analysis of the work of the Senate from E.M. Forster's "sideways" angle, rather than from the limited one that perceives it only as a challenge to the achievement of responsible government, enters the discussion. There is an essential need in the study of Canadian politics to abandon the assumption of a hierarchy of chambers and adjust to the sense of an emerging intercameral alliance. To that end, it is necessary to broaden both public and critical perspectives of the duties of the upper house of Canada's Parliament. This will be achieved not by depicting the Senate as a superlative legislative body but by recognizing it as a foundational partner in the conduct of good government.

## NOTES

1 The quotation is found in Alan Bennett, *Untold Stories* (London: Faber and Faber, 2005), 458. Forster's actual words were as follows: "The frontal full-dress presentation of an opinion often repels me. But if it be insidiously slipped in sidewise I may receive it." E.M. Forster, *Two Cheers for Democracy* (Harmondsworth, UK: Penguin Books, 1965), 225.

2 *Reference Re Senate Reform*, 2014 S.C.C. 32.

3 Donald V. Smiley and Ronald L. Watts, *Intrastate Federalism in Canada* (Toronto: University of Toronto Press in co-operation with the Royal Commission on the Economic Union and Development Prospects for Canada, 1985).

4 William H. Riker, "The Justification of Bicameralism," *International Political Science Review* 13, no. 1 (1992): 101–16 at 114–15.

5 Michael Kirby and Hugh Segal, "A House Undivided: Making the Senate Work" (Public Policy Forum, September 2016).

6 See John D. Fair, "House of Lords Reform, 1917–18," *British Interparty Conferences: A Study of the Procedure of Conciliation in British Politics, 1867–1921* (Oxford: Clarendon Press, 1980), 162–97.

7 Andrew Coyne, "Supreme Court Ensures Widely Reviled Patronage House (Senate) Will Stay Forever," *National Post*, 25 April 2014.

8 *Reference Re: Legislative Authority of Parliament in Relation to the Upper House*, 1980 1 s.c.r. 54.

9 Ibid, at page 67, emphasis added.

10 Robert A. MacKay, *The Unreformed Senate of Canada* (London: Humphrey Milford for Oxford University Press, 1926; rev. ed., Toronto: McClelland and Stewart, 1963); and F.A. Kunz, *The Modern Senate of Canada, 1926–1963: A Re-Appraisal* (Toronto: University of Toronto Press, 1965).

11 House of Commons, *Debates*, 3 April 1868, 455.

12 J. Patrick Boyer, *Our Scandalous Senate* (Toronto: Dundurn, 2014), 218.

13 *Reference Re Senate Reform*, 2014, para. 15.

14 Louis Massicotte, "Possible Repercussions of an Elected Senate on Official Language Minorities in Canada," Report for the Office of the Commissioner of Official Languages, March 2007.

15 Environics Institute and Institute on Governance, *AmericasBarometer: Citizens Across the Americas Speak on Democracy and Governance, Canada 2014: Final Report*, Ottawa, 2014. For more detail, see the special issue devoted to digital issues of *Canadian Parliamentary Review* 37, no.4 (Winter 2014).

16 "Parliament, Meetings and Civil Society," Senate Occasional Lecture Series, Australia, 27 July 2001, http://www.aph.gov.au/SENATE/pubs/pops/pop38/c08.pdf.

17 George W. Ross, *Getting into Parliament and After* (Toronto: W. Briggs, 1913), 7.

18 George W. Ross, *The Senate of Canada: Its Constitution, Powers and Duties, Historically Considered* (Toronto: Copp, Clark, 1914).

19 Senate, *Debates*, 22 January 1914, 31.

20 Environics, *AmericasBarometer,* 38.

21 Government of Canada, "The Senate – report on activities," 2013, http://publications.gc.ca/site/eng/9.506415/publication.html#.

22 Andrew Coyne, "Senate has no business toying with the budget," *National Post*, 19 January 2017, A8. See as well John Ivison, "Liberals tailor upcoming budget to pass through empowered Senate," *National Post*, 16 January 2017.

23 Alex Marland, *Brand Command: Canadian Politics in the Age of Message Control* (Vancouver: UBC Press, 2016), 46.

24 Andrew Blick and George Jones, *Premiership: The Development, Nature and Power of the Office of the British Prime Minister* (Exeter, UK: Imprint Academic, 2010).

25 Marland, *Brand Command*, 46.

26 Ibid, 375.

27 Giuseppe di Lampedusa, *The Leopard* (London: William Collins Sons & Co., 1961), 29.

# Reflections on the House of Commons

David C. Docherty, president of Mount Royal University

Our Westminster system of government has facilitated a standard of living in Canada that is the envy of many other nations. The laws, budgets, and debates that have taken place in Parliament have played an integral role in our national development. Since 1867, the fundamental functions of the House of Commons, to hold the government to account, to pass or defeat legislation, and to represent the local interests of voters, has remained constant. The role of the Senate, representing regional interests and acting as a check on the passions of the elected chamber, has been modified to include policy expertise and a willingness to listen to Canadians in a non-partisan fashion.

It is in Parliament that the best and worst of Canadian democracy are on display. We should be justifiably proud that the introduction of significant social and economic legislation that has fundamentally changed our society has taken place in Parliament. We can be less proud of the lower chamber, where visiting grade schools are often shocked at the childish behaviour of elected officials, particularly during question period. This paper examines Parliament but with a particular emphasis on the House of Commons.

Much has changed in the House of Commons since Confederation. The House has grown in fundamental ways. The demographics of both the electorate and the elected have expanded significantly. The size of the chamber has almost doubled since 1867, though the population of Canada has grown more than tenfold. And while the members of the 42nd Parliament of Canada are much more representative of the electorate, we still have a long way to go to achieve any semblance of mirror representation.

Political parties continue to dominate the House of Commons, so much so that in many ways, the important number in the lower house is not the number of members but the number of officially recognized parties. Though the names "Liberal" and "Conservative" dominate the benches, the parties themselves have changed over time. We have seen new parties form, parties merge, parties split, and parties disappear.

In 1957, Charles Gavin Power, one of Canada's most colourful and longest-serving members, observed that the ambition and profile of members of Parliament had changed dramatically in the ninety years since Confederation. The 1957 House was one of political careerists, where politics had then become profession and not a vocation.[1] Power was not incorrect in this assertion, though the ten years between 1957 and Canada's centennial saw just as dramatic changes. Canada had a new flag, new social policies and legislation, state supported health care, and by 1968 a prime minister who became the face of our modern county.[2] C.E.S. Franks has argued persuasively that a strong executive and caucuses that believed in partisan solidarity helped provide the conditions for the passages of such watershed policies.[3]

For those of us who are truly dedicated to Westminster parliaments, the present House of Commons can bring some joy. The House is more inclusive than it has ever been. The front benches of the government have gender parity, as Prime Minister Justin Trudeau noted, "because it is 2015."[4] There are more tools available to help members of Parliament perform their representative, legislative, and accountability functions. Opportunities to hold the government to account have never been greater, and occasional backbench revolts have allowed all members to flex their muscles and demonstrate some independence.

Yet fans of our parliament still feel like Charlie Brown hoping that Lucy (in this case, every new government) will hold the football that is true parliamentary reform, only to have it yanked away within months of the election. Every prime minister promising "a new era" of openness and transparency in government all too soon finds the power of party discipline, the introduction of omnibus legislation, and the reining in of opportunities to question the government are far more efficient than the promise of change. The reality is that there has never been a "Golden Age" of Parliament. Golden moments? Yes, but a golden age is more of a fond wish, not a memory.

This paper examines some of the fundamental changes in political life in Canada since Confederation. Politicians have a different relationship to their job and their party than they once did, a difference that finds some parallels to Canadians relationship to MPs and to political parties. The paper also examines the enduring strengths and weaknesses of the Commons. Parliament has a remarkable ability to facilitate the development of national laws and policies that positively impact citizens. Yet Parliament also has more recently developed a surprising capacity to avoid contentious issues. Since 1982, Parliament has gradually ceded ground to the courts when it comes to determining direction on fundamental social issues. Small wonder Canadians find more faith in judges than they do in politicians.

For the purposes of our analysis, we will be fluid in our approach to defining specific "eras" in Parliament. For example, we recognize that the "modern parliament" did not begin until after 1945 and coincided with the development of the modern welfare state. However, the House of Commons in 1967 was far different than it was even when Charles Power wrote about the modern house a decade earlier. Changes in the last fifty years have been even more dramatic, whether it is in the demographic makeup of our legislatures or the issues the House and Senate have been either dealing with or avoiding. As such, no hard eras in terms of years are used consistently in the following reflections.

## 1. THE CANADIAN POLITICAL FAMILY[5]

Drive through any small town in Canada and you are likely to see business signs that read "Johnson and sons, Electricians" or "J. James and daughters, photography."[6] Yet rarely will you see a sign that says "Trudeau and sons, politicians" or slogans like "The MacKays, keeping representation in the family for over forty years." But political families do exist in Canada, and politics as a family business may be more common than we think.

Two of our most recent three prime ministers come from political families. Paul Martin Jr rose higher, but for a briefer period, than his father, Paul Martin Sr. Justin Trudeau has equaled the electoral success of his father, though not yet in terms of political longevity. An outsider might look at these two cases and assume that politics as a "family business" is not uncommon in Canada in the twenty-first century. Actually, political families make up only a small part of the political class. Of the over 4,200 individuals who have been elected to the House of Commons, only about 2.5 per cent had sons or daughters decide to go into elected federal life. An additional number of members had further relations follow in their footsteps after seeing the family business skip a generation (and in many cases, there was more than one son, daughter, or grandchild to enter office). Adding those groups together, approximately 5.4 per cent of members of Parliament have historically had familial ties to office.[7] This is a not insignificant number. How best to describe these families?

First, there are historical trends. Most "fathers" came from earlier Canadian parliaments. Table 10.1 breaks the forty-one parliaments into four distinct temporal groups. While we would not expect to see many fathers in the most recent grouping of parliaments, it is instructive to see the linear decline of political families in Canada over time. Therefore, the largest share of family businesses began during the earliest stages of Canadian parliaments.

Table 10.1: Breakdown of Forty-One Parliaments into Four Distinct Temporal Groups

|  | *Fathers* | *Mothers* | *Sons* | *Daughters* |
|---|---|---|---|---|
| 1867–1919 | 52 |  | 35 |  |
| 1920–1962 | 24 |  | 33 | 1 |
| 1963–1992 | 12 | 2 | 11 | 2 |
| 1993–Present | 1 |  | 10 | 1 |

Source: Parliament of Canada Website – http://www.parl.gc.ca/parlinfo

The first period is marked by a parliament where political life was segregated into specific parts of the calendar year. The parliamentary calendar was in many ways built around the agricultural calendar. Post–World War I years to the early sixties was a period of greater independence from Canada's Commonwealth roots. It was only during the end of this era that elected politics began the transformation from a vocation, or part-time position, to that of a profession. During these formative years, local politics was run from a member's kitchen. There were no constituency offices or staff for members. Politics truly was a small business, typically run by a male elected official (the first female member of Parliament was elected in 1921, and the first female cabinet minister was appointed in 1957), whose spouse served as the constituency support staff. One could make the case that politics was literally closer to home and truly a family affair.

It is also worth noting that the low pay of the position meant that politicians had to rely on outside sources of income. Lawyers were over-represented in the national lower house during these two periods. Nearly one third of members of the 1941 House of Commons were lawyers, compared to only 0.2 per cent of the population. Just over 17 per cent of MPs in this chamber were farmers.[8] Careers in agriculture were well suited to part-time politicians, and the legal profession allowed MPs to retain the necessary income to serve their constituents as members. Passing on a political career to a son who ran the farm or inherited the legal practice would be easier than in some other occupations.

Like other Western democracies, Canada witnessed a rapid expansion of the state during the postwar era. As bureaucracy and administration grew so too did the need for oversight from the political branch. As stated earlier, Power argued that, starting in the fifties, politicians began the transformation from part-time practitioners to full-time legislators. In his view, this period witnessed men (and increasingly women) in politics move from being individuals who went to Ottawa to further their own interests to those who went to serve the public cause.[9] This period also saw increasing resources being devoted to MPs to serve constituency needs and a House of Commons that sat for longer periods that did not coincide with the seasons of an agricultural society.[10]

Did the professionalization of politics lead to the decline of politics as a family business? There is no statistical correlation for this hypothesis. Yet it is hard to deny that the professionalization of politics has caused the politician to be away from home more than ever. Representation is no longer practised at the kitchen table on a Saturday morning. MPs are now away from their families for longer periods of time.

THE HOUSE OF COMMONS IN SESSION

In 1967, the House of Commons consisted of 265 seats; the Senate, 102. By 2017, these numbers had grown to 338 and 105, respectively. Three political parties held seats in the Commons in 1967, and five were represented in 2017. The Cabinet dominates debates, and partisan interests are strongly voiced. Members must toe the party line, and free thinkers are fairly rare. Members are also anxious for promotion, and weekly caucus meetings are opportunities to build solidarity. Debates were first televised in 1977, and members began playing to the galleries rather than debating with the other members in the chamber. Social networks, the fifth power, give everyone a platform to share their views, putting them on the same level as their elected representatives. The result is that the exercise of democracy has been redefined and subjected to many external forces that are very difficult to harness in a globalized world. Credit: © The House of Commons

Even in their constituency, members are out of their homes more than ever. It is certainly possible that the sons and daughters of elected officials no longer personally witness the public good in serving as practised by their elected parents. Politics may be viewed by sons and daughters as an occupation, not a vocation.

## II. PARTY SWITCHING AND THE QUESTION OF POLITICAL LOYALTY[11]

The House of Commons is a legislature of political parties. The important number in the lower chamber is not the number of elected officials but the number of parties with official status.[12] Further, party loyalty and discipline are distinguishing features of the Canadian House of Commons. But a party is only as strong as the members who are elected under its banner. Further, as we witness a declining strength in party loyalty among voters, we might expect to see that mimicked in the House of Commons. The most dramatic and extreme statement of lack of loyalty is to leave the caucus you were elected with to sit across the floor with another party.

We know that party loyalty in the electorate is decreasing. Party membership is decreasing and party activism is also on the wane. Are such characteristics among the voting public shared by members of the modern Parliament? If so, we may be witnessing a very different dynamic in the Commons, one where members see themselves more as free agents than loyal party stalwarts.

It is important to distinguish floor crossing from moving from one party to another during election periods or leaving office to later run for another party. By "floor crossing" we refer to the act of switching parties during a Parliament. This act of switching may be done to satisfy personal political ambition, or can be due to a change in party leadership.

As it turns out, floor crossing has remained relatively constant in the Canadian House of Commons. There is evidence that at least temporary party switching is not in decline. Since Confederation, 257 members of Parliament have crossed the floor to sit with a party other than the one they represented during the general election. Although just a very small portion of all MPs ever crosses the floor, examining changes to floor crossing over time might tell us something about the culture of elected life in Canada.

If we collapse our 150-year history into three fifty-year periods, we find that the modern Parliament is just as likely to witness floor crossing as the other periods. In other words, there are at least as many "free agents" post-1990 than there were during the Macdonald "loose fish" era of the early years of confederation. In fact, the number of switchers is almost equal through the three fifty-year periods.

Over half of all party switchers leave to join another political party. Approximately 35 per cent of all switchers leave the party banner they first ran under to sit as independents, though some of these individuals eventually move to another party or return to their own party. The incidence of the latter was highest during two periods – the time of the Union Government of Robert Borden and its postwar aftermath, and the period leading up to and including the merger of the Progressive Conservative Party of Canada and the Canadian Alliance at the turn of the twenty-first century.[13]

Perhaps the most interesting finding of this analysis is the more recent success of many party crossers. Switching political parties was once the electoral kiss of death. This is no longer the case. Still, the public seems to have a better sense of why some members leave their original party banner than others. Simply put, those who leave the opposition to take a promotion (such as to a cabinet position) with the government are more likely to be shunned by voters than those who leave for presumably more altruistic reasons. Those who leave a party at the time of a merger are more likely to be forgiven by local voters.[14] That so few crossers leave to sit permanently as independents underscores that fact that political life in the House of Commons is based on party. The notion that people who cross the floor for reasons of ideology or leadership have been re-endorsed by local voters suggests that the decrease in partisan affiliation includes not just voters but the elected as well.

### III. SITTING DAYS

It is true that prime ministers can truly lead only when they know they have the confidence of the House. Yet this is only a matter of concern with minority governments. Why then do governments treat so many pieces of legislation as confidence and still worry about keeping all members in line? Perhaps nothing exemplifies the strength of party more than the reliance on party discipline. Canada adheres to one of strictest interpretations among Westminster parliaments of what constitutes party discipline. Despite some attempts during Paul Martin's brief stint as prime minister, there has been little desire from the government to allow members to vote against their party. With the exception of some private member's bills, all votes are party votes. However, the truth is that only a small number of votes (including the budget and the throne speech) necessarily would have to be treated as matters of confidence, as long as the prime minister indicated this at the introduction of legislation.

Party discipline can prevent members from properly representing their constituents. National governments have members from across the country, often with competing interests. Some legislation can make MPs choose between party loyalty and constituency loyalty. The British three-line whip system helps avoid this problem by clearly distinguishing which votes are seen as confidence and which are not. This opportunity is not present in Canada. There are other challenges to members' carrying out the functions of the House.

One axiom of accountable and transparent government is that the more a legislature meets, the more it can be held to account. No sittings means no question period, no member's statements, and no opportunity to debate the principles of legislation in second reading or in a committee of the hole.[15] Of all of these, question period remains the number-one method of public accountability. Every day, representatives of the Crown must answer for their actions or lack of action by government private members and opposition MPs. Canadian tradition (recently tested) holds that prime ministers should be regular attendees during question period. When the House does not meet, the opposition loses a huge opening to hold the government accountable and to ask them questions that may not be in their staff-prepared briefing books.

The data are clear. Governments are less inclined to face the opposition now than they were fifty years ago.[16] Between 1967 and 1976, the House of Commons met an average of 138 days a year. By 1997–2006, this figure was down to fewer than 100

Table 10.2: Legislative Sitting Days in the House of Commons 1967–2016

| *Decade* | *Average Sitting Days per year* |
|---|---|
| 1967–1976 | 138.6 |
| 1977–1986 | 151.1 |
| 1987–1996 | 131.1 |
| 1997–2006 | 99.9 |
| 2007–2016 | 112.0 |
| Minority government years | 114.5 |
| Majority governments years 1968–1992 | 155.8 |
| Majority governments years 1992–2017 | 115.1 |
| Election years | 104.8 |
| Non-election years | 136.1 |

Source: Parliament of Canada Website - http://www.parl.gc.ca/parlinfo

days per year. What is the cause of this decline? There are many factors determining the length of sitting days, and one of them is the reluctance of governments to face the opposition, instead governing outside the confines of the House they were elected to sit in.

There were far fewer sitting days in years when elections were held. This is not surprising; as the House dissolves, the writ is dropped, the election is held, and in the case of a change of government, a completely new cabinet is chosen and sworn in. There were an average of 104 sitting days in years when Canadians went to the polls compared to 136 days in years elections were not held.

The single biggest difference occurs in years that have experienced a minority government and those that have experienced only a majority government.[17] On average, minority government years have legislatures that sit for just over 114 days. By comparison. When the House is in a majority the average of sitting days is just under 130. It is apparent that minority governments are less inclined to sit longer, given that they face a greater risk of losing the confidence of the House.

What is more interesting is the decreasing number of sitting days in majority governments over time. Between 1968 and 1992, majority governments sat on average for 155 days. By contrast, post-1992 majority governments sat for 115 days, almost identical to all minority government years. The only truly significant variable is time. Our most modern governments are just as committed to high levels of party discipline. Sadly, they are just as afraid of the opposition as governments that do not have the luxury of governing with a majority of support in the House within their own caucus.

The tendency to not meet in times of minority governments was never more in evidence than during the aftermath of the 2008 general election when Prime Minister Harper sought to prorogue the House to avoid facing a vote of non-confidence.[18] Shortly after he won his minority government, the Liberal and New Democratic Party opposition agreed to form a coalition government with the support of the Bloc Québécois. To accomplish this, the three parties would first have to defeat the government. Then the leader of the coalition would meet with the governor general, the Rt Hon. Michaëlle Jean, to convince her that they could form a working government. There was never any question of the constitutionality of this plan, as the role of the governor general and the ability of a Westminster parliament to accommodate a new government without an election were both well established.

What was unprecedented in Canada was a prime minister seeking to shut down the House after barely sitting for the sole purpose of avoiding the opposition. It placed the governor general in a very awkward position. Whatever decision she made would be precedent setting. Never had a prime minister been refused prorogation, but neither had a governor general allowed a prime minister to avoid the will of the assembly. In the end, the strategy of the prime minister worked in his favour. Mr Harper received his prorogation and used the time to convince the public that the move by the Liberals and the NDP was not politically legitimate, despite its constitutional soundness.[19]

Despite the explanations of minority governments and elections, there is a clear trend. Governments do not meet the House that keeps them honest as much as they used to. This does not necessarily cause Canadians to believe the work of the House is less important, though it may well reinforce such views. Members themselves can be the most effective advocates of accountability when they have the opportunity to challenge the cabinet and meet them face to face.

## IV. THE IMPORTANCE OF POSITION

One of the biggest challenges for members when trying to undertake their roles is the problem of their own ambition. Politicians are by definition ambitious. Putting their name forth to be judged by thousands of citizens is done to further ambition, be it ambition to satisfy ego, to pursue particular policies, or to represent their constituents. Of these three ambitions, only the latter does not involve a seat at the cabinet table. All of them involve re-election.

Canadian elections are very competitive. Despite the conventional wisdom from the past twenty years that elections are won or lost in Southern Ontario or Southern British Columbia, that fact is that we have enjoyed robust turnover of both members and governments.

Between voluntary vacancy (retirement from elected office) and involuntary departures (the loss of a seat), the House of Commons enjoys a healthy turnover rate. Beyond ideology, there is little reason to support term limits in the Canadian House. We have very little trouble rewarding governments we like and punishing those we do not.

High turnover is assisted by the vagaries of our electoral system, where a change in vote is often far outweighed by a change in seats. In the 2015 election, the Conservative Party of Canada's vote share dropped by less than 8 per cent from the 2011 vote, yet their seat share was reduced by nearly 24 per cent. In 2004, a vote drop of 4 percent caused the Liberals to reduce their seat share by over 13 per cent and to go from a majority to a minority government.

There is also evidence to suggest that cabinet ministers enjoy much longer political careers than backbenchers, and that they are often shielded from the wrath of the public.[20] The irony here is somewhat rich. When governments are punished for being unpopular, the cabinet ministers who authored the unpopular policies are more

DEMONSTRATION IN FRONT OF PARLIAMENT, 29 NOVEMBER 2015

Canadian democracy is often expressed more forcefully outside Parliament than inside. A wide variety of groups regularly demonstrate on Parliament Hill just a few metres from the entrance, so close that members and senators can almost hear their voices. Demonstrators are free to speak, brandish placards, signs, or banners, play music, chant slogans, show their colours, get national media coverage, and make the news online, on social media, or on the all-news networks. It's an effective and unique form of direct participative democracy. Credit: The Canadian Press / Fred Chartrand

likely to be spared the ultimate punishment of losing their seat. The lesson learned by backbenchers is that job security is better attained by climbing the career ladder.

There are a number of important variables that are included in prime ministers' calculations about who makes it to cabinet. In an ideal world there would only be two factors, expertise and talent. For better or worse they are often the least significant variables in building a cabinet in Canada. Of course, talent and expertise are not mutually exclusive from the other considerations. Justin Trudeau's desire to have gender balance did not mean sacrificing talent (though it may have outweighed experience in the House).

Building a national cabinet first requires representing the nation in cabinet. Thus, where possible, every province has some cabinet representation. Gender, ethnicity, and loyalty to the leader are added to the equation. More populous provinces have greater representation, if only because regions within the provinces have to be represented. Smaller provinces have less representation. You may be the second-most talented MP in government caucus, but if you and the most talented MP are both from Prince Edward Island, chances are you will not serve as a member of Cabinet.

The real attraction of cabinet is obvious. Higher pay, a car and driver, and better pension implications may be important, but they pale in comparison to the influence and power that a cabinet minister holds. In the Canadian House, there is little attraction to a career as a parliamentarian. There is little glory in serving the bulk of your career on a committee, where the government still exercises great control (often including influencing the choice of chair). Nor is there much to boast about as a career parliamentary secretary. Aside from answering the occasional question in the House when a minister is absent, parliamentary secretaries do not enjoy the profile or influence of cabinet ministers. There is little evidence that parliamentary secretary positions are the stepping stone to cabinet that some would hope them to be. Few parliamentary secretaries make it to cabinet.[21]

Cabinet is thus the brass ring of Canadian politics, and members behave in a manner than increases their chances of being selected. They may not be able to control their demographic characteristics, but they can control their loyalty to their leader, both on the backbench and while in cabinet.

Despite the fact that cabinet is typically about 10 per cent of the House, the odds for government members are obviously better. In fact, the mathematical odds are better than the political realities. Since 1965, the ratio of government private members to ministers of the Crown is approximately 5 to 1. Paul Martin's larger cabinet and smaller caucus in 2004 gave him the smallest ratio at 3.5 to 1.[22] Brian Mulroney appointed the largest cabinet to date after his election in 1984, but given the size of his caucus, his ratio was still 5.4 to 1.

Despite the impediments, the lure of cabinet survives. Those serving as committee chairs or as a parliamentary secretaries see themselves as cabinet ministers in waiting, even if the reality is different. As a result, ambitious members engage in behaviour that should maximize their odds of being selected. The most critical behaviour is to stick to the party line, to endorse strong party discipline, and to not choose a career as a maverick.

## V. REFLECTIONS ON THE MODERN HOUSE OF COMMONS

The floor of the House of Commons has been home to some of the most important debates in Canadian history. From the national rail line to pipe lines, free trade to tariffs, the repatriation of our Constitution to the rights of women, marginalized

Canadians, new Canadians, and the land's original inhabitants, important debates and votes have all come via the lower house. One might argue that our recent debates have not had that flair. The free trade debates and the Clarity Act debates stand out as possible exceptions. We welcomed Nelson Mandela to address our Parliament before he had the right to speak in his own country's assembly, yet we have seen a diminution of the great oratory and debates in our nation's lower house. The days of the great orators seem to be over.

That is not to say that we have not witnessed historic moments in our Commons in the recent past. The speech from the throne lays out the government's intentions over the life of each session of Parliament. Every budget has to be first introduced, then debated, and finally supported by a majority of members of the chamber. On occasion this is more difficult than one might think. In 2005, Canadians witnessed the best "reality television" they could have imagined. A vote of non-confidence in the young Paul Martin government was going to a vote in the green chamber.

The government knew the vote was going to be tight. While the party votes were known, there were some unknowns. One member of Parliament, Chuck Cadman, won his seat as an independent after losing his nomination bid for the newly merged Conservative Party (he had been previously nominated and elected as a member of the Canadian Alliance). When Cadman stood in his place and indicated he would support the budget, the matter was then handed over to the Speaker to cast the tie-breaking vote. Speaker Peter Miliken made the proper procedural call in supporting the budget, but for the first time in Canada's history, the Speaker broke a tie on a budget vote.[23]

Three years later, the new prime minister, Stephen Harper, successfully avoided a vote of non-confidence with a precedent-setting prorogation of Parliament. The important point to note in both of these cases is that the government of the day faced a political crisis. At no time did the country face a constitutional crisis. Our Westminster system is built to stand these challenges.

But that is not to say there is not great room for improvement. In our last fifty years, we have seen many unsettling developments in the House of Commons.

First, the language of citizenship that characterized the Charter debates and repatriation of our constitution in the early eighties has been replaced by the language of the taxpayer. These two words have very different meanings. Telling someone that they are a taxpayer suggests the major responsibility of the state is low taxes, with the taxpayer having no obligation to the state. Telling someone that they are a citizen includes good stewardship of public monies, but also implies that citizens have a responsibility to the common good and to each other. One imagines this is exaggerated with Canadians under the age of twenty-five. Small wonder few youth vote, when politicians of all stripes call voters "taxpayers." They might just as well say, "Come back and talk to me once you have a job." Reclaiming the language of citizenship is one small start to renewing our faith in Parliament.

Second, in light of the arrival of the Charter we should not be surprised to see an expanded role for the courts in protecting rights and individual and group equality. Elected officials have often chosen a reactive role, hoping to avoid potential divisive (and non-partisan) debate on sensitive issues by implementing decisions made by the courts. This is unfortunate. Leadership on rights issues should be a hallmark of good government. Pierre Trudeau showed courage in declaring that the state had no place in the bedrooms of the nation. Decades later, the government was content to react to the Supreme Court in legalizing same-sex marriage. Further, avoiding debates on social issues reinforces the role of party discipline by highlighting government policy, and not the views of 338 representatives. This is an unfortunate trend.

Third, we have witnessed increasing moves to centralize authority within the Prime Minister's Office, at the direct expense of members of Parliament. Successive prime ministers have been elected promising democratic reform while lambasting the "dictatorial ways" of their predecessor. Sadly, this promise rarely comes to fruition.[24] Transparency and accountability under Prime Minister Harper and "Sunny Ways" under his successor soon turned to omnibus legislation, fewer attendances at question period, and an increasing reliance on party discipline to facilitate their policy and legislative plans. They are aided in this by the ambitions of members who understand that cabinet is the true seat of power. Until such time as members determine that a parliamentary career can be just as rewarding as a cabinet career, the balance of legislative power will lie with the prime minister and not other legislators.

There is little reason to see these trends changing. The desire to first gain and then hold on to power creates conditions where social issues are to be avoided and executive control becomes standard operating procedure. The House of Commons stands at a delicate point. It needs to reclaim the strength it once had and demonstrate to Canadians why members, all members, matter.

One possible remedy is to increase the incentive for backbenchers to enjoy parliamentary and not cabinet careers. In the much larger House of Commons in Great Britain, most members get elected knowing they have a very small chance of ever serving in cabinet. This, combined with a much less restrictive use of party discipline, allows members to better represent their constituents in legislative matters and have less fear of holding the government (in the case of government backbenchers) to account. Further, it puts more authority in the hands of the constituency and less in the whip's office.

It also encourages parliamentary careers, where individuals actively seek committee work that assists in their representative duties and develops policy expertise. Parliamentary careerists are more likely to see value in a House that meets more often, is not afraid of a looser understanding of confidence, and sees the importance of holding the government to account.

Such a move in Canada would require a relatively dramatic increase in the size of the chamber. Though that would not be inexpensive, we must recognize that democracy should not be governed by a bottom line. As indicated earlier, while our House has doubled since 1867, the Canadian population has expanded tenfold. An increase in the chamber is actually in order.

Such an increase must not be followed by a concomitant increase in the size of cabinet. It would also require some very sophisticated conversations with the public. In many Canadians' minds, more politicians equates to more spending. In a Westminster system, nothing could be further from the truth. In a Westminster system, members of Parliament do not spend money, cabinet spends money. It is the duty of all other members to hold cabinet accountable for how they spend tax dollars. Ironic, then, that as we celebrate our 150th anniversary of Confederation we should look to the mother of all Westminster parliaments for ideas on how to rejuvenate our own lower house.

NOTES

1  Charles Gavin Power, "The Rise of the Career Politician," *Queen's Quarterly* 1957.

2  Though a picture of members of Parliament in 1967 would look closer to a photo of the 1957 members than those in 2017.

3  C.E.S. Franks, *The Parliament of Canada*, (Toronto: University of Toronto Press, 1987).

4  It is interesting to note that in 1965, Judy LaMarsh was the sole woman in cabinet, a fact that irked talented MPs, such as Pauline Jewett, who were left off the frontbenches. See J. McKenzie, *Pauline Jewett: A Passion for Canada* (Montreal and Kingston: McGill-Queens University Press, 1999).

5  This section is a revision and synopsis from David Docherty, "Politics as a Family Business in the Canadian House of Commons," paper presented at the annual meeting of the Midwest Political Science Association, Chicago, 5 April 2014.

6  The latter is actually from my hometown of Owen Sound, Ontario.

7  All data found at https://lop.parl.ca/sites/ParlInfo/.

8  Docherty, *Legislatures* (Vancouver: UBC Press, 2005), 39.

9  Charles Gavin Power, "The rise of the career politician," *Queen's Quarterly* 1957, 49.

10  Jack Stillborn, "The Roles of the Members of Parliament in Canada: Are They Changing?" Library of Parliament Information and Research Service, 2002.

11  This section summarizes a longer analysis on floor crossing originally presented at the annual meeting of the Midwest Political Science Association: D. Docherty and D. Cloutier, "Look Both Ways before You Cross the Floor: Party Switching in Canada," Chicago, April 2016.

12  Official party status is a relatively new occurrence that coincided with more resources being made available to members based on the number of seats each party holds.

13  All data found at https://lop.parl.ca/sites/ParlInfo/.

14  For example, Scott Brison left the Conservative Party of Canada, indicating that the values of the newly merged party did not match his own. He won re-election as a Liberal four times and continues to sit as a member of cabinet under Justin Trudeau.

15  However, as far back as Dawson, many have questioned the real viability of a committee of the entire House of Commons.

16  All data found at https://lop.parl.ca/sites/ParlInfo/.

17  For purposes of this analysis, we use years and not legislative sessions.

18  For an excellent examination of this period, see Russell and Sossin, eds., *Parliamentary Democracy in Crisis* (Toronto: University of Toronto Press, 2009).

19  See A. Heard, "The Governor General's Decision to Prorogue Parliament: A Dangerous Precedent," https://www.sfu.ca/~aheard/elections/prorogation-2008.html.

20  David Docherty, *Mr. Smith Goes to Ottawa: Life in the House of Commons* (Vancouver: UBC Press, 1997); Docherty and White (with Graham White), "Throwing the Rascals Out: Backbench and Cabinet Defeats in the Canadian Provinces," paper presented at the Annual Meeting of the Midwest Political Science Association, Chicago, April 1999.

21  David Docherty, *Legislatures* (Vancouver: UBC Press, 2005).

22  These ratios were measured using the size of cabinet immediately after the election. Prime ministers often expand their cabinet as their term of office goes on. Thus, the opportunities for members do not end with the initial selection of the executive.

23  See S. Martin, "Chuck Cadman," *The Globe and Mail*, 11 July 2005, http://www.theglobeandmail.com/news/national/chuck-cadman/article1121860/; and O. Moore, "Speaker vote breaks first non-confidence tie," *The Globe and Mail*, 20 May 2005, http://www.theglobeandmail.com/news/national/speakers-vote-breaks-first-no-confidence-tie/article18227589/.

24  The author wishes to note that Paul Martin's short-lived government stands as a notable exception.

# List of Figures, Charts, and Tables

# Contributors

*Phil Fontaine*

Phil Fontaine served as national chief of the Assembly of First Nations for an unprecedented three terms, after being elected in 1997, 2003, and 2006. He was one of the first Aboriginal leaders in 1990 to denounce the inhumane condition of residential schools. In 2005, Mr Fontaine successfully negotiated the Indian Residential Schools Settlement Agreement for the benefit of survivors and the implementation of healing initiatives. The wealth of his experience makes him one of the most sought-after advisers in all matters related to Indigenous issues in Canada and the United States.

*Katsi'tsakwas Ellen Gabriel (Turtle Clan, Kanien'kehá:ka Nation [Mohawk])*
*from Kanehsatà:ke*

Ellen Gabriel began her public intervention during the 1990 Siege of Kanehsatà:ke (also known as the Oka Crisis) and was chosen by the People of the Longhouse and her community of Kanehsatà:ke to be their spokesperson in the defence of their ancestral territory. Ms. Gabriel was elected president of the Quebec Native Women's Association, a position she held from 2004 to 2010 with great honour. At the international level, she participated in the United Nations Permanent Forum on Indigenous Issues as well as the Expert Mechanism on the Rights of Indigenous Peoples.

*Paul Heinbecker*

With a long career in Canadian diplomacy, including posts as ambassador to Germany, permanent representative to the United Nations, and adviser to successive prime ministers, Paul Heinbecker has been a distinguished fellow with the Centre for International Governance Innovation in Waterloo since 2004. He was also the inaugural director of the Centre for Global Relations at Wilfrid Laurier University and is a fellow of the Balsillie School of International Affairs.

*Huguette Labelle*

Huguette Labelle is the first woman to serve as deputy minister in the federal public service, a position she held at such organizations as the Department of the Secretary of State and Transport Canada. Ms Labelle was also president of the Public Service Commission of Canada and the Canadian International Development Agency. A former chancellor of the University of Ottawa, Ms Labelle has held many senior positions in international organizations dedicated to promoting good governance, and fighting corruption and climate change.

*Her Excellency the Right Honourable Michaëlle Jean*

The Right Honourable Michaëlle Jean was elected secretary general of the Organisation internationale de la Francophonie on 30 November 2014, the first woman to serve in this capacity. A journalist by trade, Ms Jean was appointed Canada's 27th governor general in 2005. In 2010, she became UNESCO's special envoy for Haiti and was appointed chancellor of the University of Ottawa the following year. Well-respected internationally, Ms Jean is interested in French language and cultural issues in a world without borders.

*The Honourable Michel Bastarache*

Professor and dean of the Faculty of Law at the University of Moncton and later the University of Ottawa, the Honourable Michel Bastarache was appointed to the New Brunswick Court of Appeal in 1995 and to the Supreme Court of Canada in 1997. He served as a member of the Interim Constitutional Court of Kenya and is the president of the Administrative Tribunal of the Association of American States.

*The Right Honourable Beverley McLachlin*

Member of the Alberta Bar and British Columbia Bar, Chief Justice McLachlin taught for seven years in the law faculty at the University of British Columbia. In 1981, she was appointed to the Supreme Court of British Columbia. She was elevated to the British Columbia Court of Appeal in 1985 and was appointed chief justice of the Supreme Court of British Columbia in 1988. In 1989, she was sworn in as a justice of the Supreme Court of Canada. On 7 January 2000, she was appointed chief justice of Canada. She was the first woman in Canada to hold this position.

*Mark D. Walters*

Mark D. Walters holds the F.R. Scott Chair of Public and Constitutional Law at McGill University. He studied political science at the University of Western Ontario and law at Queen's University before completing a doctorate in law at Oxford. He taught law at Oxford for three years, and thereafter at Queen's for sixteen years. Professor Walters researches and publishes in the areas of public and constitutional law, legal history, and legal theory.

*The Honourable Bob Rae*

Bob Rae served as a New Democratic Party member of Parliament for Broadview, Ontario – he was one of the younger MPs in the House of Commons at the time – from 1978 to 1982. He then moved to provincial politics, serving as Ontario's twenty-first premier from 1990 to 1995, and participated in the negotiations following the Meech Lake Accord and the national referendum on the Charlottetown Accord. He was the interim leader of the Liberal Party of Canada from 2011 to 2013. Bob Rae teaches at the University of Toronto as a distinguished senior fellow at the School of Public Policy and Governance, and as distinguished professor at Victoria College.

*The Honourable Jean Charest*

Jean Charest was elected member of Parliament for Sherbrooke in 1984 and appointed deputy prime minister in 1993. He served as leader of the Progressive Conservative Party of Canada (1993–98) before becoming leader of the Quebec Liberal Party (1998–2012) and eventually premier of Quebec from 2003 to 2012. He was behind the creation of the Council of the Federation and was a proponent of the Canada–European Union Comprehensive Economic and Trade Agreement. His government launched the Plan Nord, an innovative sustainable development initiative for Northern Quebec.

*Gary Doer*

Gary Doer won three consecutive elections as premier of Manitoba at the head of the Manitoba New Democratic Party. As premier, he efficiently represented the burgeoning influence of the Canadian West as a powerful political force that was reshaping the Canadian landscape. He was recognized internationally as an influential leader on climate change, promoting hydroelectric power as a renewable source of energy in the United States. Mr Doer was appointed as Canada's ambassador to the United States in 2009. He is currently the co-chair of the Wilson Center's Canada Institute, based in Washington, DC.

*The Right Honourable Kim Campbell*

From the age of sixteen until thirty years later, when she served as Canada's nineteenth and first female prime minister in 1993, Kim Campbell has spent much of her life breaking barriers for women. She served at all three levels of Canadian government and was the first woman to become justice minister, and later, defence minister, as the first female minister of defence of a NATO country.

Ms. Campbell served as the Canadian consul general in Los Angeles until 2000. She has taught at the University of British Columbia as well as the Harvard Kennedy School. In 2014, she was appointed the founding principal of the University of Alberta's Peter Lougheed Leadership College.

*Monique F. Leroux*

The former president and chief executive officer of Desjardins Group from 2008 to 2016, Monique F. Leroux is currently chair of the board of Investissement Québec and chaired the Quebec Economic and Innovation Council. From 2015 to 2017, she was president of the International Co-operative Alliance. She is a member of the Canada-United States Council for Advancement of Women Entrepreneurs and Business Leaders and was co-chair of the B7 Summit in Canada in 2018. She serves on the boards of a number of major companies in Canada, France, and the United States. Ms. Leroux is a Member of the Order of Canada, an Officer of the Ordre national du Québec and a Chevalier of the Légion d'honneur (France) and holds honorary doctorates and awards from eight Canadian universities.

*David Suzuki*

David Suzuki is a scientist, a broadcaster, an author, and co-founder of the David Suzuki Foundation. Dr Suzuki is professor emeritus at the University of British Columbia. He is familiar to television audiences as host of the CBC television series *The Nature of Things*. Dr Suzuki's influence in the promotion and explanation of sustainable development has made him one of Canada's most well-known and appreciated personalities on the world stage.

*Natan Obed*

Natan Obed is the president of Inuit Tapiriit Kanatami, the national organization representing Canada's sixty thousand Inuit founded in 1971. Originally from Nain Nunatsiavut, he obtained his BA with honours in English with a concentration in native studies from Tufts University in Medford, Massachusetts. He has devoted his entire professional career to helping improve the well-being of Inuit; acknowledging

Inuit rights, culture, knowledge, and language; and the protection of the environment in the Arctic.

## Hubert Reeves

Hubert Reeves is an internationally renowned astrophysicist. A professor and scientific advisor to NASA, Dr Reeves serves as director of research at the Centre national de la recherche scientifique in Paris and has been a researcher with the Service d'Astrophysique de Saclay. He is currently president of the Humanité et Biodiversité association. Hubert Reeves has produced a number of films, presentations, talks, books, and publications that popularize science for young people and other audiences.

## Yves Gingras

Yves Gingras is a professor of history of science at UQAM and the Canada Research Chair in the History and Sociology of Science. He is also the Scientific Director of the Observatoire des sciences et des technologies, established 20 years ago to promote science and innovation. Dr Gingras has published numerous works on the transformations of the sciences in many languages (French, English, Portuguese, Russian and Chinese).

## Pierre Lassonde

Engineer, businessman, and philanthropist Pierre Lassonde co-founded Franco-Nevada Mining Corporation in 1982, the first publicly traded gold royalty company. It was later acquired by Newmont Mining Corporation. Mr Lassonde served as chairman of the World Gold Council from 2005 to 2009. A supporter of the arts, Pierre Lassonde chairs the Board of Directors of the Canada Council for the Arts. He applies his extensive experience in management and investment to foster excellence in post-secondary institutions and in all forms of Canadian cultural expression.

## David A. Dodge

David A. Dodge received his PhD in economics from Princeton and has taught economics at several universities. During a distinguished career in the federal public service, he held several senior positions in different departments and agencies, including eight years as deputy minister, first at Finance then at Health Canada at a critical moment for public choices and decisions. From 2001 to 2008, he was governor of the Bank of Canada. He also served as chancellor of Queen's University and on several corporate boards. Mr Dodge chairs the National Council of the C.D. Howe Institute.

Contributors

*Hassan Yussuff*
Hassan Yussuff was first elected president of the Canadian Labour Congress in May 2014, becoming the first person of colour to lead Canada's union movement, and was re-elected for a second term in 2017. Mr Yussuff has led Canada's unions in a major campaign to improve workplace rights for everyone and to transform the way Canadians view the labour movement. His advocacy has also earned him an international platform as president of the Trade Union Confederation of the Americas.

*David E. Smith*
David E. Smith is currently distinguished visiting professor at Ryerson University and professor emeritus at University of Saskatchewan. He taught for many years in the department of political science at the University of Saskatchewan and is a previous president of the Canadian Political Science Association. His publications include a trilogy of works on each of the parts of Parliament, as well as books on political parties, the Constitution, and federalism.

*David C. Docherty*
David C. Docherty holds a PhD from the University of Toronto. He is a recognized expert in parliamentary government in Canada. He is the author of a seminal work on politics, *Mr. Smith Goes to Ottawa: Life in the House of Commons*, and of numerous articles and chapters on Canadian legislatures. Professor Docherty served in a number of university postings and was appointed as the ninth president of Mount Royal University in 2011.

*The Honourable Serge Joyal*
A lawyer and legal expert, the Honourable Serge Joyal was appointed to the Senate of Canada in 1997. From 1974 to 1984, he was a member of Parliament in the House of Commons and held the positions of parliamentary secretary to the president of the Treasury Board (1980), minister of state (1981), and secretary of state of Canada (1982–84). In 1980 and 1981, Mr Joyal co-chaired the special joint committee that reviewed and recommended the adoption of the Canadian Charter of Rights and Freedoms. On a number of occasions, he has intervened before the highest courts in the country regarding issues related to parliamentary institutions, human rights, and language rights. Mr Joyal is also a patron of a number of Canadian museums, and has written and edited numerous articles and publications on parliamentary and constitutional law, Canadian history, and the fine arts.

*The Honourable Judith Seidman*

Judith Seidman is an epidemiologist, a health researcher, and a social services adviser who was appointed to the Senate of Canada in 2009. Prior to her appointment, she was an active health research professional in the McGill University Health Centre network in Montreal. As Deputy Chair of the Standing Senate Committee on Social Affairs, Science and Technology, she has devoted her time to advancing solutions for better health and seniors' care. Her professional experience as a member of a community health team has informed her work as a senator on key health policy issues, including artificial intelligence in health care, access to prescription medicine, and medical assistance in dying. As a proud Anglophone Montrealer, she is a tireless advocate for the vitality of Quebec's English-speaking communities.